MOON HANDBOOKS®
RHODE ISLAND

© ANDREW COLLINS

Southeast Light on Block Island

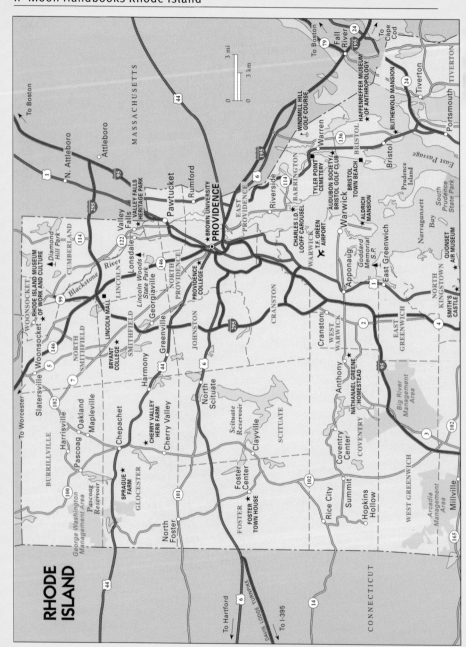

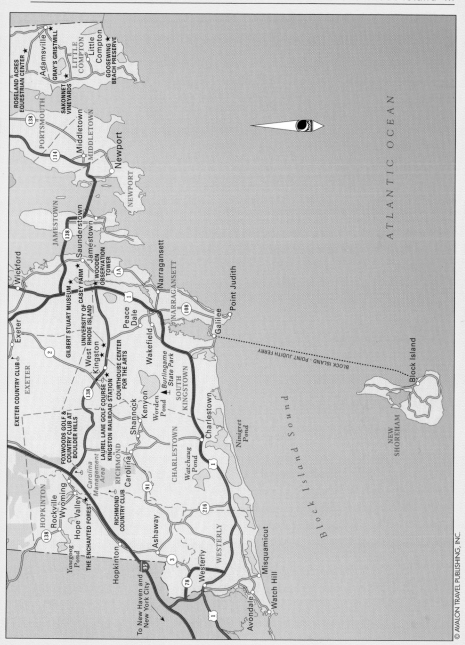

ROSELAND ACRES
EQUESTRIAN CENTER ★
Adamsville ★
GRAY'S GRISTMILL ★
LITTLE
COMPTON
Little
Compton ★
GOOSEWING
BEACH PRESERVE ★

PORTSMOUTH
138
SAKONNET
VINEYARDS
Middletown
114
MIDDLETOWN
Newport
NEWPORT
JAMESTOWN
138
Wickford
Jamestown
Saunderstown
Jamestown
1A
WOODEN
OBSERVATION
TOWER ★
Narragansett
Exeter
GILBERT STUART MUSEUM ★
UNIVERSITY OF CASEY FARM ★
RHODE ISLAND
Peace
Dale
108
NARRAGANSETT
Galilee
Point Judith
EXETER COUNTRY CLUB ★
EXETER
2
West
Kingston ★
Kingston
COURTHOUSE CENTER
FOR THE ARTS ★
Wakefield
1
138
HOPKINTON
Rockville
Wyoming
Hope Valley
THE ENCHANTED FOREST ★
Yawgoog
Pond
138
FOXWOODS GOLF &
COUNTRY CLUB AT
BOULDER HILLS ★
LAUREL LANE GOLF COURSE ★
KINGSTON RAILROAD STATION ★
Carolina
Management
Area
Shannock
Kenyon
Worden
Pond
Burlingame ▲
State Park
SOUTH
KINGSTOWN
Charlestown
Ninigret
Pond
RICHMOND
COUNTRY CLUB ★
Carolina
RICHMOND
91
CHARLESTOWN
Watchaug
Pond
1
216
Ashaway
WESTERLY
Hopkinton
3
Westerly
78
Misquamicut
Watch Hill
Avondale
1
To New Haven and
New York City
95
Block Island Sound
BLOCK ISLAND - POINT JUDITH FERRY
Block Island
NEW
SHOREHAM
ATLANTIC OCEAN

© AVALON TRAVEL PUBLISHING, INC.

view from the Southeast Light

MOON HANDBOOKS®
RHODE ISLAND

FIRST EDITION

ANDREW COLLINS

AVALON
TRAVEL

Moon Handbooks Rhode Island
First Edition

Andrew Collins

Text © 2003 by Andrew Collins.
Illustrations and maps
© Avalon Travel Publishing, Inc. 2003
All rights reserved.
Photos and some illustrations are used
by permission and are the property of their
original copyright owners.

Please send all comments, corrections,
additions, amendments, and critiques to:

Moon Handbooks Rhode Island
Avalon Travel Publishing
1400 65th Street, Suite 250
Emeryville, CA 94608, USA
atpfeedback@avalonpub.com
www.moon.com

ISBN: 1-56691-374-8
ISSN: 1542-3824

Printing History
1st edition—May 2003
5 4 3 2 1

Editors: Erin Van Rheenen, Kevin McLain
Series Manager: Kevin McLain
Copy Editor: Emily McManus
Graphics and Production Coordinator: Justin Marler
Cover Designer: Kari Gim
Interior Designers: Amber Pirker, Alvaro Villanueva, Kelly Pendragon
Map Editor: Olivia Solis
Cartographers: Mike Morgenfeld, Kat Kalamaras, Landis Bennett
Indexer: Vera Gross

Front cover photo: © Nik Wheeler

Distributed by Publishers Group West

Printed in the U.S.A. by Worzalla

ABOUT THE AUTHOR
Andrew Collins

Travel writer Andrew Collins spends most of his life on the road, driving back and forth across North America, logging about 40,000 miles annually. He's visited more than 1,600 of the nation's 3,145 counties, and has spent more than 2,000 nights residing in hotel rooms, slumming with friends, or crashing with various relatives— he is always most appreciative of his hosts' kind generosity. In recent years, he's lived in Manhattan, Brooklyn, and rural New Hampshire, and has spent extended periods in Atlanta, Boston, San Francisco, Connecticut, and Rhode Island, as well as overseas in London and Amsterdam. While presently based in Santa Fe, New Mexico, he still spends much of the year in New England.

Upon graduating from Connecticut's Wesleyan University in 1991, Andrew joined Fodor's Travel Publications, where he edited or co-edited more than a dozen travel guides. Since leaving Fodor's in 1993, he has contributed to more than 100 travel books as both writer and editor, authoring *Fodor's Gay Guide to the USA*, *Moon Handbooks Connecticut*, and now *Moon Handbooks Rhode Island*. His travel column "Out of Town" appears in gay and lesbian newspapers throughout North America; his work has also appeared in numerous magazines, including *Travel & Leisure* and *The Holland Herald*.

On those rare occasions when he's not on the road, Andrew can often be found browsing the goods at farmers markets and gourmet food stores, or putting them to use in his kitchen. He also enjoys a variety of outdoor activities, including jogging, kayaking, and golfing, and follows professional baseball with a disturbing degree of fanaticism. A confessed pop-culture junkie, he scans online newspapers and newswires every day in search of odd trivia and amusing gossip about has-been celebrities. After finishing one of his guidebooks, he's been known to watch Nick at Nite or the Game Show Network for hours on end, until fading blissfully into trance-like stupor. Such is the life of the professional traveler . . . .

Contents

SPECIAL TOPICS

SPECIAL TOPICS

NEWPORT 247

Keeping Current

A friend once astutely described the process of compiling a guidebook as "capturing a moving target." The very day this book is released to the public, no doubt at least one small—or possibly even major—piece of information contained within it shall change. Restaurants come and go, B&B owners sell and move on, new shops pop up every other day, and attractions constantly work to revamp and better serve their audiences. I've gone to great lengths to ensure that every detail is current as of this writing, and I'll continue to update the information in subsequent editions. Please address all correspondence to:

Moon Handbooks Rhode Island
Avalon Travel Publishing
1400 65th Street, Suite 250
Emeryville, CA 94608
atpfeedback@avalonpub.com

Maps

MAP SYMBOLS

═══	Divided Highway	◉	State Capital	⌢	Golf Course
══	Primary Road	○	City/Town	▲	State Park
──	Secondary Road	★	Point of Interest	✖	International Airport
··········	Ferry	•	Accommodation	✗	Airfield/Airstrip
- - - - -	Trail	▼	Restaurant/Bar	✚	Unique Natural Feature
— — —	Township Border	▪	Other Location		

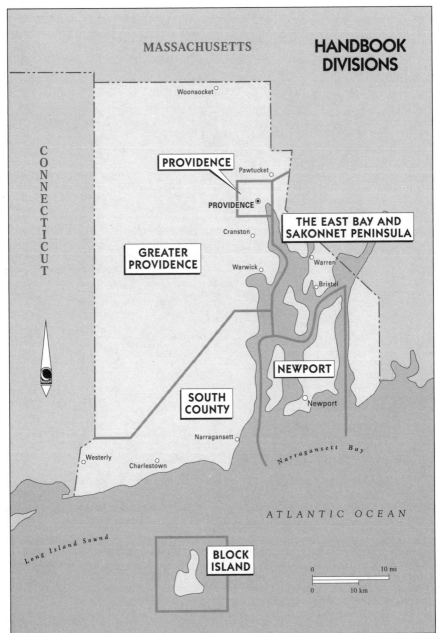

MASSACHUSETTS

HANDBOOK DIVISIONS

CONNECTICUT

Woonsocket

PROVIDENCE

Pawtucket

PROVIDENCE

**THE EAST BAY AND
SAKONNET PENINSULA**

Cranston

**GREATER
PROVIDENCE**

Warwick

Warren

Bristol

NEWPORT

**SOUTH
COUNTY**

Newport

Narragansett

Narragansett Bay

Westerly

Charlestown

ATLANTIC OCEAN

Long Island Sound

**BLOCK
ISLAND**

0   10 mi

0   10 km

Introduction

The nickname "Ocean State" may seem like a slight exaggeration for Rhode Island—it's just 42 miles, as the crow flies, from Napatree Point in the west to Little Compton's border with Massachusetts to the east; all but a handful of states with ocean frontage have longer shorelines. But in no other U.S. state has the ocean so dramatically shaped the economy, personality, and terrain.

Every resident of Rhode Island lives within a 30-minute car ride either of the Atlantic Ocean or the East Coast's second-largest estuary, Narragansett Bay. Roughly 70,000 of the state's 1,050,000 residents live on islands, and another 120,000 Rhode Islanders live in the East Bay area or on Sakonnet, which are connected to the rest of the state mostly by bridges. Trade, shipbuilding, fishing, and ocean-related tourism have each contributed mightily to the state's economy. And even textile production, which thrived from the 1790s until World War II, relied heavily on the power of several rivers that flow into Narragansett Bay and the Atlantic. It's the very rare art gallery or gift boutique in Rhode Island where you won't find works or products influenced by the ocean, from maritime paintings to sea shells to ships' clocks. And it's the even rarer restau-

rant that doesn't serve at least one dish containing scallops, lobsters, mussels, or the state's most treasured fruit of the sea, quahog clams. In terms of the relationship Rhode Island and its people have to the open water, no other state so deserves to be called the Ocean State.

But then there is this seeming contradiction: If you explore the entire state, you'll find that much of it looks and feels as though it could just as easily be hundreds of miles inland. The state's largest city, Providence, is defined as much by its hills and small rivers as it is by its location at the northern end of Narragansett Bay. It's a port city to some degree, but it doesn't especially feel like one if you walk around downtown or College Hill. The western and northern reaches of the state, while never more than 20 miles from the bay or ocean, are hilly, wooded, and lightly populated—the countryside is punctuated only by the occasional mill village or colonial crossroads. Were you blindfolded and driven to virtually any point in interior Providence, Kent, or Washington (aka "South") Counties, you'd never sense that you were in the nation's Ocean State. And Burlingame State Park in the coastal community of Charlestown lies just a couple of miles from the

Mohegan Bluffs and Southeast Lighthouse

ocean, but from standing on the edge of its wooded shoreline on Watchaug Pond, you could just as easily imagine yourself in upstate New York.

In Rhode Island, the coast is the coast—the interior is the interior. There aren't a lot of gray areas in between. This dichotomy keeps Rhode Island from feeling like one big seaside resort. There's something refreshingly down-to-earth about some of the state's old mill towns and interior highways—they remind you that Rhode Island is not simply a summertime playground of beachgoers and boaters. In fact, although Newport's Gilded Age of the early 1900s imbued the state with a reputation for privilege and excess, Rhode Island is mostly a place where middle-class, egalitarian values prevail, as they have since Roger Williams founded Providence Plantation as a haven for religious and political freedom in the early 1600s.

Rhode Island is sometimes described as the nation's only city-state, a tempting designation given its diminutive size and high population density. Here again, there are some contradictions at work. On the one hand, most of Rhode Island is served by one metro bus system and one main newspaper. You can commute to Providence from virtually anywhere in the state, and Providence's mayor until 2002, Buddy Cianci, probably wielded as much statewide clout as any of the men who served as Rhode Island's governor during his long mayoral tenure. In certain respects, the day-to-day events of Providence are the events of Rhode Island—and perhaps in no other state does a city wield so much influence.

On the other hand, only 174,000 Rhode Islanders actually live in Providence—that's barely more than 15 percent of the state. By comparison, about 25 percent of all Nevadans live in Las Vegas, and more than 20 percent of all Illinois residents live in Chicago. Rhode Island was founded as a collection of distinct communities, all headed by dissidents and freethinkers who had become unwelcome in Puritan Massachusetts. The towns of Rhode Island continue to function with very much their own autonomy and individual spirit. Newport sees itself as entirely distinct from and independent of Providence, and it always will. A Block Islander would laugh

aloud if accused of living in Greater Providence, even though the island lies just 40 miles from the state capital. Woonsocket is but 10 miles northwest of Providence, and yet these two cities have about as much to do with one another as Philadelphia and Pittsburgh, or so their residents would insist.

From the perspective of tourism, little Rhode Island is every bit a land of separate communities. You don't so much as vacation in Rhode Island as you do in Newport, Providence, South County, the East Bay, or Block Island. And yet, if you happen to spend time in any of these communities, you'll find it quite simple to venture over to virtually any other town in the state.

If it's a truly urban vacation you're seeking, Providence should be your base. One of the nation's metropolitan comeback kids of recent years, the city has a tremendous amount going for it, which is remarkable considering how bad off it was only 15 years ago. The presence of several colleges—Brown University, Rhode Island School of Design (RISD), Johnson & Wales, and Providence College—give the city a youthful, alternative edge and a thriving music, fine arts, and club scene. In particular, the hilly neighborhood fringing Brown and RISD is a must-see for lovers of collegiate life, but also for anybody interested in colonial architecture and art galleries. Providence also has a thriving Little Italy, a groovy warehouse district hopping with music clubs, and several good museums. Urbanites all over America love to brag about their great culinary scenes, but Providence can genuinely claim one of the best crops of restaurants of any city its size—and that's anywhere in North America, believe it or not.

Prior to the American Revolution, there were only a handful of major cities among the 13 colonies of the New World: Boston, New York, Philadelphia, Charleston, Newport. Well, we all know that the first three continued to grow and grow, and they remain among the most influential U.S. cities to this day. Poor old Charleston and Newport, however, endured a series of booms and busts and ultimately stayed small. Charleston, South Carolina, is now a city of just about 100,000. Newport, though technically a city, has barely more than 25,000 residents. Amazingly, its population has barely tripled since 1770 (Boston is about 40 times more populous).

Despite all this—or perhaps because of it—Newport is, from a tourism perspective, the jewel of Southern New England. Ironically, its position in the Northeast is rather similar to Charleston's vis-à-vis the rest of the South. It's a remarkably well-preserved, highly sophisticated, colonial seaport community with some of the best maritime art galleries, beaches, and sailing on the Eastern Seaboard. It's an adult-oriented city, with relatively few attractions and accommodations geared to kids, but this makes it an ideal getaway for a romantic weekend. Rates can be steep in summer, but in winter the city is considerably more moderate in temperature than the rest of New England, and hotel bargains are easy to come by.

Block Island, on the other hand, all but shuts down during the winter months—although if you can make it out here at that time and find one of the relatively few accommodations, you can have a wonderful time listening to the wind howl and hiking through the pristine paths that traverse much of the island. Throughout the summer, this tiny island bursts with vacationers, both families and adults traveling without kids, and it draws fairly steady crowds even in the spring and fall. Locals have done a commendable job staving off major development, having established a conservancy that preserves more than a quarter of the island's open spaces. Still, you'll find ample accommodations in the form of mostly historic B&Bs and inns, including several mammoth Victorian hotels, the likes of which are mostly extinct elsewhere along the Eastern Seaboard. Even if you're just in Rhode Island for a few days, do your best to take a trip out to Block Island (ferries run regularly year-round), even if just for the afternoon.

Two slightly quirky sections of the state, both of them appended to Massachusetts and otherwise connected to the rest of Rhode Island mostly by bridges, are the East Bay and Sakonnet, on the east side of Narragansett Bay. The former is partly a suburb of Providence but also a great weekend destination. Warren is an antiques hub, while stately Bristol has several charming inns

and good museums, and it hosts one of the country's most popular Fourth of July parades. Sakonnet makes a great day trip, as it's laced with country roads and contains a handful of fun shops and cafés, plus some roadside farm stands and a bit of beach access. Alas, there are hardly any accommodations in Sakonnet's two towns, Little Compton and Tiverton, but it's a short drive to this area from either Aquidneck Island (home to Newport) or Bristol.

These aforementioned areas are where the lion's share of Rhode Island vacationers end up, but don't overlook the rest of the state, which falls mostly inside a contiguous block of woodland that's south, west, and north of Providence (and therefore covered in the "Greater Providence" chapter of this book). Perhaps the most celebrated section, at least of late, is the Blackstone River Valley, which extends from Pawtucket northwest to Woonsocket (and then into Massachusetts clear up to Worcester). A renewed interest in Rhode Island's fascinating, mostly Victorian, industrial mill history, as well as a major cleaning up of the Blackstone River, has helped spur the popularity of this area that's easily visited from Providence and even South County. You'll find a handful of hotels in the area, and outstanding museums in Pawtucket and Woonsocket. This is not, however, an especially glamorous part of the state—its pleasures are simple and accessible, and the cost of staying and dining in the Blackstone River Valley is very low.

The far northwestern and western reaches of the state, which include some of Rhode Island's highest terrain, are sparsely populated and little visited. You'll find a few villages with distinctive shopping and dining, including North Scituate and Chepachet, as well as numerous opportunities for hiking, biking, and other outdoor pursuits. In northern South County, you'll also find excellent golf courses.

The last area of Greater Providence is the suburbs just west of the capital, Cranston, Warwick, and Johnston. While these three residential towns aren't major hubs of tourism, they do contain a vast number of chain hotels (plus a few inns), restaurants, shops and malls, and even a few museums. The collective population of these three communities is actually slightly greater than that of the city of Providence, and Warwick is notable as the setting of T. F. Green Airport, New England's third-largest such facility and Rhode Island's main air transportation hub.

The Ocean State—whether you experience it from the shores of Little Compton and Watch Hill, the isolation of Jamestown or Block Island, the bays of Bristol and Wickford, the urban landscapes of Providence and Woonsocket, or the hilly woodlands of Burrillville or Gloucester—packs a tremendous amount of variety into a tiny area. The first colony to declare its independence from Great Britain and the last to sign the U.S. constitution, Rhode Island today still marches to its own beat. It is not merely an appendage of neighboring Connecticut or Massachusetts, but a wonderfully dynamic and individualistic destination with a tremendous amount to recommend it.

The Land

A tiny state that's just about 1,500 square miles (about the size of greater Houston, Texas), Rhode Island contains some 400 miles of shoreline, including inlets, rivers, estuaries, and bays. Nearly every inch of the state lies within 20 miles of the ocean or Narragansett Bay, which begins at the northern end of the state first as the Seekonk River and then the Providence River, and a large chunk of the state is contained within the islands of Aquidneck, Conanicut, Block, Prudence, and a few others. And while Rhode Island has a very high population density, the state actually feels fairly rural and undeveloped in many places.

Despite the nearly constant proximity of water frontage, Rhode Island has a distinct inland region whose personality is much like the rest of interior southern New England. The southern end of the state, however, from Napatree Point in the extreme southwest to Point Judith to the east, is one long and scenic expanse of beautiful golden sand, punctuated only by the occasional inlet. Directly behind these beaches are long and deep salt ponds, created by occasional breaks in the beach that allowed saltwater to pour in and that have then been sealed by shifting sands. These salt ponds are sheltered havens for wildlife-watching, water sports, and fishing.

At Point Judith, the endless string of beaches gives way to the mouth of enormous Narragansett Bay. Beaches extend, off and on, up the western shore of the bay nearly to Providence. A little more than a mile across Narragansett Bay lies the long and narrow Conanicut Island and, another mile east of that, the considerably larger Aquidneck Island. About 10 miles due south of Point Judith, well away from the mainland, lies the summer resort community of Block Island. And another couple of miles east of Aquidneck is the final bit of Rhode Island's oceanfront, Sakonnet. Another five miles east and you're in Massachusetts.

The thin swath of land fringing the ocean from Napatree Point clear up around Narragansett Bay to Providence, is characterized by its low elevation and sandy soil. The East Bay and Sakonnet areas are slightly higher in elevation and are composed mostly of sandstone and other rock that hasn't eroded to nearly the degree that the low coastal plain has over the eons. Most of Rhode Island, however, is characterized by rolling terrain with peaks rising occasionally to 700 or 800 feet—not terribly high compared with northern New England or even the highest points in nearby northeastern Connecticut and central Massachusetts. But compared with other small states that fringe the Eastern Seaboard—New Jersey and Delaware, for example—Rhode Island is relatively hilly and offers a nice balance for anybody who loves to admire both the ocean and the hilly countryside. Especially in the western and northwestern sections of the state, the land has eroded much less than along the coast and in the East Bay and Sakonnet, and even Blackstone River Valley regions. Here the underlying geological composition is extremely old and hard crystalline rock.

Predictably, much of the terrain, and also the flora and fauna that thrives on it, is typical of what you'd find elsewhere along southern New England's coast. The state is a haven for bird watching, as towns all along the ocean and Narragansett Bay are a major migratory bird route. Several parks and preserves near the water have been established specifically for this purpose.

There's actually a misconception that the farther north you go in New England the more likely you are to see wildlife. In fact, in Vermont, New Hampshire, and Maine, so much of the land is undeveloped that many animals steer clear of roads, villages, and human life—they have the luxury of rarely having to leave their remote and pristine habitats in order to find food and shelter, and they maintain a healthy fear of mankind.

Rhode Island, however densely populated it may be, is actually an easy place to spot many animals. The state is heavily wooded, and there are quite a few parks and preserves, and yet it is also heavily developed. Wildlife and human life coexist, for better or for worse, in close proximity, and mammals in Rhode Island tend to be less afraid of people—and better able to feed themselves by scavenging through backyards, compost heaps, and garbage cans. This is nice, of course, for wildlife-watchers who get a kick out seeing deer racing across their lawns.

It's also unfortunate because wild animals have become increasingly dependent upon people and dangerously abundant in areas with heavy traffic and an environment that barely supports them. Where they are overpopulated, they are a nuisance in the eyes of many humans—blamed for spreading Lyme disease, ravaging gardens and yards, and causing traffic accidents. Rhode Island does have some sections that are sparsely settled by people, especially the western and northwestern sections of the state—you'll even find a few designated hunting grounds in some areas. But anybody who drives on a daily basis in Rhode Island is sure to have seen deer (sometimes several at a time) leaping across roads, usually at night—sadly, many drivers have struck them.

With all the talk these days of encroaching suburban sprawl—and it's true that this trend is one of the greatest threats facing the state in the 21st century—it's easy to forget that most of Rhode Island was already deforested by the early 1800s, when the state's economy was almost entirely agrarian.

Ironically, the region's woodlands were saved not so much by conservation efforts, which didn't develop in earnest until the 20th century, but by the coming of the industrial revolution. In places where the hilly, rocky terrain made fast and simple transportation routes difficult, or where a lack of rivers made hydropower impractical, the land was left largely to reheal itself. And some of it was reforested in order to increase the state's supply of lumber.

Now, Rhode Island's dense thickets of woodland can produce a sense of seclusion in even somewhat developed communities like Bristol and Westerly. Were you able to wander these tree-studded hillsides during the 19th century, however, you'd have observed an almost entirely deforested state of rolling meadows and pastures, land tilled to the hilt, much the way the Irish and Scottish countryside still appears today. You'd be quite able to see your neighbor's homestead a half-mile down the country road, whereas today residential architects are quite careful to ensure that neighbors living a mere 200 feet apart are obscured from one another.

The percentage of open and bare land has diminished at a rapid rate every decade since the late 19th century. In Rhode Island's countless river valleys, the fields of crops gave way to magnificent mills and manufactories. In a few towns throughout the state, both in the more rural western and northwestern sections and down along the coast, farms still thrive, but their number has decreased dramatically.

GEOGRAPHY

Rhode Island offers a classic view of how glaciers form the land. Virtually every square foot of the state owes its general appearance to the encroachment and then recession of a massive glacial formation that ended just a split second ago in geological terms, about 8,000 B.C.

Except for a narrow strip of coastal plain near

the ocean, the western two-thirds of Rhode Island sits atop very ancient igneous and metamorphic rock. The eastern third of the state (where you'll find Providence and the Blackstone River Valley, the islands of Narragansett Bay, the East Bay towns, and the Sakonnet Peninsula) lies on younger and softer sedimentary rock. Block Island and that little strip of coastal plain in South County, from Napatree Point to Point Judith, is made up of terminal moraine—rocks and debris deposited by a glacier.

A block of ice perhaps a mile high drifted as far south as the present tip of Rhode Island during the most recent Ice Age. This catastrophic action scarred the soil, lifting boulders, rocks, and sediment from northern New England and carrying them hundreds of miles south to the ocean, depositing a mound of debris at the glacier's leading edge. This mound is called terminal moraine, and it's the main ingredient of Block Island, which, geologically speaking, has almost nothing in common with the islands of Narragansett Bay (Aquidneck, Conanicut, Prudence, etc.) but is, rather, exactly like the other islands stuck out in the Atlantic, such as Long Island in New York, and Martha's Vineyard and Nantucket off Cape Cod.

As the earth's temperature rose, the glaciers began to melt or retreat north. Picture a large snowball filled with gravel, rocks, and debris and facing a heat source in one direction and a cold source in the other direction. The side of the snowball facing the heat source will melt as the side facing the cold source stays put, giving the appearance that the snowball is actually retreating toward the cold source. As the glacier on top of Rhode Island slowly melted, a stream of debris-laden water flowed downhill toward sea level, building up piles of rocks at the leading edge of the glacier—and forming the terminal moraine that underlies Block Island.

Back along the mainland, there's a narrow fringe of sandy coastal plain that lies along the shore, from Napatree Point east to Point Judith, and then along the southern tip of Aquidneck Island and Sakonnet. This swath was formed in part, and in some places, when there was a pause in the glacial recession. Let's say the giant snowball had melted for a time and then suddenly somebody turned off the heater. During this break, the snowball might even gain a little mass once again, before continuing its recession once the heat was turned back on. In glacier terms, there was likely a change in the earth's climate that stalled the warming process for a time, and so the glacier paused, perhaps even moved forward, and then continued its recession once the earth warmed again. This pause left another deposit of sand and debris farther north, called recessional moraine.

Of course, shifting currents have greatly affected the shape of Block Island and the shoreline of Rhode Island since the Ice Age—this accounts for features like Napatree Point and Point Judith. But the general layout of Block Island and the shoreline—a downward slope of hilly and rocky earth ending with a coastline of recessional moraine and then, farther out, islands formed by terminal moraine—is the result of glacial retreat and recession, as is the case all over coastal southeastern Massachusetts, Rhode Island, Connecticut, and New York. The major icecap that formed over what is now the northeastern United States only advanced as far south as about Long Island. It stopped there at the ocean, and across the lower Hudson River Valley in New York, the northern end of New Jersey, and then central Pennsylvania, but it never extended to the coastline of New Jersey, Delaware, Maryland, and points south, which are defined by a broad, low-elevation coastal plain.

Other than the extreme edge of coastline and Block Island, most of the land of Rhode Island was not deposited by glaciers, although every inch of it was shaped by glacial movement. Prior to the Ice Age, this land would have stood many, many yards higher in elevation and would have looked much different from the way it does today. The land that has now been displaced by Narragansett Bay would have been soft rock and soil that gave way easily to the tremendous weight and pressure exerted by the massive glaciers—this soil was pushed out into the ocean by the glacier's steady and freight engine–like push.

The islands of Aquidneck, Conanicut, and Prudence, along with the jagged peninsulas that poke into the bay from Bristol, Warwick, and other Narragansett towns, resisted the glacial erosion more effectively. The earth here is chiefly composed of ancient igneous and metamorphic rock—it's not as hard and erosion-resistant as the western and northwestern interior sections of the state, and so it's not nearly as hilly. But these islands and peninsulas provided a substantial enough resistance to survive the Ice Age above sea level, while the glaciers carved out what is now bay around them.

Throughout the state's interior, you'll see other evidence of glacial activity. Some of the state's many freshwater ponds and natural reservoirs were formed when a chunk of glacier broke off and glacial debris settled around it and over it. Eventually, the piece of ice melted, and the thin layer of land over it then collapsed and sunk. What remained was a pond of water, called a kettle pond. In other cases, freshwater bodies formed the glacier scooped up soil consisted of rather weak rock that was less able to resist glacial movement than adjacent areas of tougher rock. And even as far as Block Island, and no doubt along the ocean floor, you'll find boulders and rocks made up of granite, quartz, and other igneous and metamorphic materials that were carried out this far by glacial activity.

The igneous and metamorphic rock of western Rhode Island is mostly granite, much of it formed by molten lava that has, over many millions of millennia, pushed its way out from the earth's mantle but never actually reached the surface. Instead, it cooled and solidified into hard rock that's very resistant to erosion. Over time, the softer soil between it and the earth's surface eroded through wind and rain, and then gave way even more dramatically during the last glacial recession. The jagged, sharp rocky ridges you sometimes see rising out of the soil in Rhode Island formed this way. Many thousands of feet of soil once buried this layer of igneous rock.

The mostly sedimentary rock that forms the eastern third of the state is rather new by geological standards, perhaps a couple of million years old. This rock was formed by deposits of mud, gravel, and sand over a lower bedrock of igneous and metamorphic rock, which over eons of shifting and faulting earth were compressed and in some cases pushed up to the earth's surface. Some of this muck compressed into coal, of which small deposits have been found in Portsmouth, Cranston, and other parts of Rhode Island over the years; these are among the easternmost coal deposits found on the North American continent.

CLIMATE

Compared with some other regions of New England, Rhode Island enjoys a fairly moderate climate, especially the portions of the state that lie within 15 miles or so of the ocean and bay (which is most of it). The presence of the Atlantic Ocean and Narragansett Bay keep temperatures a bit warmer in winter than inland, meaning that big snowstorms in Massachusetts often take the form of rains here. Conversely, come summer, hot weather is often cooled by sea breezes, especially out on Block Island and the southern tips of Westerly and Newport.

Because Rhode Island catches a bit of the Gulf Stream and is so strongly affected by the water, it has a climate and therefore an ecosystem that's unique among New England's six states. Its position fringing the Gulf Stream ensures rather unpredictable weather, especially during hurricane season (midsummer through mid-fall), as ocean-driven winds often sweep across the entire state. The state has a long growing season by Northeastern standards, generally commencing in late April or early May and lasting through the better part of October (it's longer, obviously, along the coast).

Statewide, the average low temperature in January is about 29°, and the average high in July is a comfortable 73°. Annual rainfall is about 45 inches, and annual snowfall 35 inches (much lower than inland New England). Combined measurable precipitation (rain and snow) averages about 42 inches per year, ranging anywhere from 25 to nearly 70 inches. The state, at least in the northwestern hills, usually sees its first real snowfall in late November or early December, and its last one in April. Rain-

RHODE ISLAND CLIMATE STATISTICS

Average highs and lows (in °F)		Average precipitation		Average snowfall	
January:	36/19	January:	3.76 inches	January:	9.9 inches
February:	38/20	February:	3.29 inches	February:	9.8 inches
March:	46/28	March:	3.80 inches	March:	7.6 inches
April:	59/38	April:	3.71 inches	April:	0.7 inches
May:	68/48	May:	3.24 inches	May:	0.2 inches
June:	78/57	June:	3.06 inches	June:	0 inches
July:	83/64	July:	3.11 inches	July:	0 inches
August:	81/61	August:	3.67 inches	August:	0 inches
September:	74/53	September:	3.30 inches	September:	0 inches
October:	64/42	October:	3.15 inches	October:	0.1 inches
November:	52/33	November:	3.81 inches	November:	0.9 inches
December:	40/23	December:	3.89 inches	December:	7.0 inches

fall tends to be consistent throughout the year, with between 3 and 4 inches monthly (the lowest amounts are in summer, but passing and not infrequent late-afternoon and evening thunderstorms can dump significant amounts). Keep in mind that Rhode Island's coastal location can make it vulnerable to hurricanes and tropical storms late summer through mid-fall, and similarly havoc-wreaking nor'easters throughout the winter. Major damage–inducing storms rarely hit more than once every 5–10 years, however.

Flora and Fauna

TREES AND SHRUBS

There are about 50 species of tree common to New England, but only a fraction of these are present in Rhode Island. Broadly speaking, trees are either conifers (the softwood "evergreens" with needley leaves that maintain their look and shape year-round) or broadleafs (hardwood flowering trees that are, at least in the four-season climate of Rhode Island, deciduous—meaning they drop their leaves in the fall). Common conifers throughout the state include the conical eastern red cedars, towering reddish-brown tamarack trees, prickly blue spruce, white and red pine, hemlocks, and—right along the shore in some spots—gnarled pitch pine.

While you don't hear as much about leaf-peeping in Rhode Island as you do in other New England states, Rhode Island's broadleaf trees put on a spectacular show each fall, especially where you're able to find sugar, silver, and red maple trees—red maple is Rhode Island's state tree. The peak time for watching them burst with bright foliage is late October for most of the state, and mid-October in the northwesternmost and hilliest sections. Oaks, of which there are 11 species in New England, abound and can be quite brilliant in the fall—locally you're most likely to see white, scarlet, bear, swamp white, scrub, pin, post, chestnut, and black oak trees.

Some of the other tall Rhode Island broadleafs include beech, birch (the pretty white birch are more prevalent in the north), dogwoods (which flower beautifully all spring), elms (although many of these perished from disease during the middle of this century), holly, poplar, honey locust, hickory, and weeping willow. If you wonder why so many roads in the state bear the name

"Chestnut" but very few parts of the state actually bear the trees themselves, it's because they were once nearly as common in the state as oaks and maples. Unfortunately, disease has wiped them out except for in northern New England.

Smaller broadleaf trees and shrubs that dot the landscape, many of which bloom with a riot of colors, include speckled alder, dogwood, sumac, pink azalea, rhododendron, multiflora and beach rose, northern bayberry, and pussy willow. Rhode Island also has a fair number of pick-your-own farms. The most recent forest inventory for the state of Rhode Island, completed in 1985, showed that the state is about 60 percent forested, with slightly more than 400,000 acres of forest land.

Hundreds of varieties of wildflower bloom across the state, beginning most vibrantly in June and remaining vital well into early fall.

INVERTEBRATES

Mammals, fish, and birds may get most of the attention when it comes to wildlife sighting, but the vast majority of critters crawling, flying, and swimming around Rhode Island are—as is true the world over—invertebrates, some of which are quite interesting to observe or, in the case of some mollusks and crustaceans, eat.

Coastal Rhode Island has long had a reputation for its abundance of shellfish, but during much of the 20th century pollution and overfishing combined to deplete or spoil the region as a source of seafood. Thankfully, immensely ambitious efforts to clean up the waters off Rhode Island, along with careful harvesting regulations, have restored the region's proliferation of these tasty creatures. Nevertheless, before collecting shellfish along the state shoreline, check first with the local town hall—in nearly all cases a license of some sort is required, and it's always a smart idea to ask about what's safe for consumption and what isn't.

A great range of marine invertebrates are found off Rhode Island's shoreline, including a number of jellyfish and sea anemone, most of which are harmless but for the large and extremely dangerous lion's mane jellyfish, which fortunately is more common in northern waters. Scour the beaches and rocks during low tide and you'll find marine mollusks of every ilk, from Atlantic dogwinkles and edible common periwinkles to large (up to a half-foot long) knobbed whelks that live in those pretty yellow-gray shells that kids are prone to hold to their ears in hopes of hearing the seashore. You'll also see tons of lively hermit crabs sidling about the beach line—living safely inside the mobile homes they've fashioned out of gastropod shells.

Tasty blue mussels cling to rocks and pilings. Bay scallops, Eastern oysters, razor clams, hard-shell Northern quahogs (which include the prized cherrystones and littlenecks, the latter often found minced in clam chowder and atop pizzas), Atlantic surf clams, softshelled "steamer" clams, sea urchins (dangerous if stepped on), common green crabs, rock crabs, sand fiddlers, and the famously delicious blue crabs are found mostly in shallow, sometimes brackish, waters usually burrowed in or scampering about sandy bottoms, rocks, and mudflats. Farther out, beginning in about 10 feet of water, sea scallops and lobsters make their homes, coming closest to the shore in summer.

Less engaging to most people are the many land invertebrates that slither and crawl about the state, and indeed some of these—ticks, mosquitoes, horse- and deerflies, carpenter ants, yellow jackets, cockroaches, Japanese beetles—are a genuine nuisance. But on summer nights it's a comfort for most of us to fall asleep to the distinct chatter, trill, and staccato of the zillions of katydids and tree crickets. Spiders munch on most pests and rarely bother humans, as is true of the many beautiful dragonflies and ladybugs that swarm

> *A great range of marine invertebrates are found off Rhode Island's shoreline—tasty blue mussels, bay scallops, Eastern oysters, hard-shell Northern quahogs (including cherrystones and the littlenecks often found in clam chowder and atop pizzas), Atlantic surf clams, and softshelled "steamer" clams . . .*

about our flower beds. And we can thank honey bees for one of the state's tastiest commodities.

Rhode Island swarms with butterflies, most species from about May through September or October, lying dormant in winter. An exception are the glorious monarch butterflies that show up in the state in the spring and lay their eggs, which develop first into yellow, black, and white–banded caterpillars before slowly metamorphisizing into brilliant orange-and-black butterflies. Two or three generations pass until colder weather inspires the monarchs to begin their migration south, where they'll winter in Mexico before returning again the following spring.

BIRDS AND FISH

Given the Ocean State's coastal location, many islands, and extensive shoreline, Rhode Island is rich with sea creatures and birdlife. Fishing and bird-watching are among Rhode Islanders' favorite pastimes, and a more detailed description of the state's most common species and the places where you'll most likely find them appears in the On the Road chapter. But the marine life most commonly associated with Rhode Island includes lobsters, oysters, mussels, and the state's famous (among seafood lovers) quahog clams, all of which live close to the state's shoreline. Still fairly close to shore—seasonally—are bluefish, striped bass, and cod. Many other varieties of fish are found in the deeper and farther reaches of the Atlantic. People sometimes overlook the fact that Rhode Island also has dozens of freshwater ponds, lakes, and rivers. Inland species common to the state include trout (many ponds are stocked with them), bluegills, bass, and perch.

Rhode Island lies smack in the middle of a common migratory route for many species of North American birdlife. The state's coastal areas and many wildlife preserves contain a veritable who's who from the bird world, especially in spring, as birds fly from warmer climes up toward Canada, and in fall, when they reverse this route. Large, dramatic species such as peregrine falcons and blue heron can be spotted throughout the year, while smaller species—such as warblers, sparrows, and thrushes—congregate at beaches and other low-lying areas during the summer and fall.

REPTILES AND AMPHIBIANS

There are 13 species of snake in Rhode Island, none of them poisonous. Rattlesnakes and copperheads, which are common to other parts of New England, are considered all but extinct in Rhode Island, although there may be some slithering around the western and northwestern hills. Note that many nonvenomous snakes resemble their venomous cousins; Eastern hognose snakes look like copperheads, for instance.

Turtles are the other class of commonly found Rhode Island reptiles, especially painted turtles, which are known to sunbathe in groups around rivers and swamps. Respect the space of the snapping turtle, whose sturdy jaws can leave you with a nasty bite. You won't see these very often, but they do love to swim and cavort about muddy-bottomed rivers and other bodies of water.

Among amphibians, newts and salamanders aren't easy to see, as they often blend in well with their surroundings, but the yellow-spotted and red varieties do stand out a bit. They tend toward creeks and living under rocks and logs, and are most visible from March through October during the day. Frogs we all know from the oft-loud choruses of ribbeting and peeping we hear on spring and summer nights, when these loquacious animals seek out mates. Spring peepers, bullfrogs, and Woodhouse toads frequent ponds and swamps, while common American toads and wood frogs prefer yards, fields, and wooded areas. Unfortunately, in spring, thousands of frogs and toads are hit by automobiles in areas where large numbers of them are headed toward popular breeding grounds.

MAMMALS

The mammals you're mostly likely to see around Rhode Island are white-tailed deer, raccoons, opossum, Eastern chipmunks, Eastern grey squirrels, and striped skunks. All of these species are common to both secluded woodlands and developed suburbs and even some urban areas, and most of them are not easily startled by the presence of human beings.

Skunks, opossum, and raccoons are primarily nocturnal, and if you see one during the day you should keep a good distance, as, especially if it's behaving erratically or aggressively, there's a fair chance it's carrying rabies. This is a disease that can make an otherwise harmless animal bite at will, and should you ever come into any physical contact with such a creature, you should immediately contact an emergency physician.

Happily, the state's mammal population poses few serious threats otherwise. White-tailed deer may forage through gardens, and raccoons through trash cans, but such is the price one pays for living in countrified suburbs.

Less commonly sighted Connecticut animals, which you have the best chances of seeing in state parks and preserves, include black bears (only rarely and in northwestern Rhode Island), Eastern cottontail rabbits, woodchucks, beavers,

meadow voles, coyotes (again, mostly in the northern part of the state, but they are becoming increasingly common in this state where they were once virtually extinct), gray and red foxes, fishers, mink, and river otters.

Whale-watching cruises operate off Rhode Island's coast—these dramatic sea mammals that were once hunted to near-extinction often inhabit the state's waters. Finback, humpback, and minke whales are most often sighted, as is the occasional school of bottle-nosed dolphins. Whales are most common spring through fall, with small numbers of them summering off the coast and the majority of them passing through in April and May on their way north and back down again in October, November, and December during their migration to warmer waters.

Both harbor and gray seals, which have always been fairly common from Maine to Cape Cod, have made a recent comeback along Rhode Island's shoreline, primarily in Narragansett Bay.

History

Rhode Island being a small area, the history of the state as a whole is tied very closely to the individual histories of its major communities, including Providence, Newport, Warwick, and Pawtucket.You'll find more in-depth information on state history in the subsequent chapters on each region.

BEFORE 1636

The land that is now Rhode Island was occupied by a handful of Algonquin indigenous tribes throughout much of the early part of the last millennium—Narragansetts, Niantics, Nipmucks, Pequots, and Wampanoags all lived here, and not always at peace with one another. The tribes shared a common genealogical heritage and similar languages and other cultural traits, but they also observed their own distinct rituals, laws, and other practices. Even today, many Rhode Island place names have Native American roots: Conanicut Island, for example (where Jamestown is now located), is named for the 17th-century

leader of the Narragansetts, Canonicus; Pawtucket translates as "place with the waterfall"; and Sakonnet means "land of the wild goose."

By the early 1600s, when European settlers began exploring Rhode Island waters and islands, the various Native American tribes had a viable system of currency exchange in place (utilizing sea shells and beads). They manufactured their own farming and hunting implements, traded regularly among themselves and with the few Dutch traders who passed through, and lived as subsistence farmers and hunters. Contrary to what some history books might have school kids believe, the colonists from England who arrived in the New World in the 1620s did not find an impenetrable wilderness but rather a network of Indian villages, staked-out fishing areas, and cleared and tilled fields.

Among the Rhode Island tribes, women took on many of the most labor-intensive tasks, from cultivating and harvesting the fields to tanning hides to maintaining order in rudimentary homes. In warmer months the tribes

WHAT'S IN A NAME?

Of all the 50 states, Rhode Island might have the loosest relationship to its actual name. After all, the state is neither an island nor has any strong ties to the name "Rhode." Most historians trace the naming of the state to one of the region's earliest explorers, Florentine navigator Giovanni da Verrazano. In 1524, on sailing around Block Island, off the coast, he noted that this small parcel reminded him somewhat of the Greek Island of Rhodes.

In a strange twist, later explorers, armed with Verrazano's description, sailed along the coast and mistook Aquidneck Island (now home to the towns of Newport, Middletown, and Portsmouth) as Verrazano's Rhodes-like island. Thenceforth, Aquidneck Island came to be known as Rhode Island, and the intended Rhode Island became known for the Dutch explorer Adriaen Block, who sailed around *it* in 1614 after exploring the Connecticut River. Eventually, as Providence and Newport developed

into political hubs and competing colonies, and then joined together to form one political entity, the entire colony came to be known officially as "Rhode Island and Providence Plantations." Over time, people started dropping the "and Providence Plantations" part of the name, so now everybody knows the glorious subject of this book as simply "Rhode Island." Still, however, the technical name for the state remains "Rhode Island and Providence Plantations"—and this is the longest official state name in the union.

How strange that the smallest state in the union would have the longest official name, and that the name by which it is generally known—Rhode Island—refers in fact to a relatively small island in Narragansett Bay (which, oddly enough, is now known exclusively by its Native American name, Aquidneck). And to think that Rhode Island truly refers to the even tinier Block Island. What a strange little mess Verrazano made.

settled in open fields, and with the coming of cold weather they moved to wooded valleys and other sheltered areas.

When Roger Williams and his followers settled in Rhode Island, the area was home to perhaps 20,000 indigenous peoples. And although Williams himself worked peacefully with the tribes he encountered near Providence, the effects of settlement by Europeans almost wiped out this population within half a century. The settlers spread smallpox and other diseases to which they were immune but the Native Americans were not; they systematically removed tribes from the best and eventually even the least desirable lands; they introduced alcohol to them, murdered many who fought to keep their lands, and sold a good many more into slavery. The definitive blow to New England's Native American population—King Philip's War—occurred mostly in Rhode Island and just over the border in the Massachusetts colony in 1675–76.

Before the first Europeans established a permanent settlement in Rhode Island, quite a few explorers passed near the shore or spent time on land here. Some of these men left accounts of

their time here. A few early state histories asserted that the Vikings were Rhode Island's first European inhabitants, but it's now believed that those settlements were made many miles north of present-day New England in the Canadian province of Newfoundland. One quite early explorer to survey the coast appears to have been Portuguese navigator Miguel Cortereal, who sailed through in 1511.

The most celebrated explorer, however, is no doubt Giovanni da Verrazano, a Florentine sailing in the New World under the French flag; in 1524 he explored the waters around New York City (the Verrazano Narrows Bridge, which connects Brooklyn to Staten Island, is named for him) and up to Rhode Island. Dutch traders later explored the coast, among them Adriaen Block, for whom Block Island is now named.

COLONIAL SETTLEMENT

The founder of modern Rhode Island's first permanent European settlement is Roger Williams, who arrived in what is now Providence in 1636. This happened a year after a by-all-accounts odd and reclusive Anglican clergyman named William Blackstone (for whom the river and valley are named) established a camp in what is now Cumberland, but Blackstone lived alone, largely as a hermit, and no true community emerged in his wake.

Roger Williams arrived with the intention of establishing a settlement, and he did so quickly. More remarkably, he arrived after having been banished from the Massachusetts Bay Colony, where his beliefs in a separation of Church and State and that the Puritans should completely break their ties with the mother country's Anglican Church greatly angered that colony's rigid and virtually autocratic powers. Faced with an arrest warrant and the threat of deportation, Williams gathered up a handful of sympathizers and traveled to the confluence of the Woonasquatucket and Moshassuck Rivers, which today form the center of downtown Providence.

Williams had come to the New World in 1630 because he could not reconcile his comparatively progressive religious views with those of the Anglican Church of England—and he had little patience for a colony whose leaders continued to hold communion with the Anglicans. Williams had briefly come to know the leaders of the two primary Native American tribes in Rhode Island—Massasoit of the Wampanoags and Canonicus of the Narragansetts—when both men traveled to the Plymouth Colony in 1631, where Williams was then living.

During his time in Massachusetts, he took virtually every opportunity to affront the authority of the Plymouth and Massachusetts Bay authorities. He refused to take oath as a citizen of the colony and rejected the right of the King of England to hand out parcels of lands that belonged to the Native Americans. He repeatedly rejected the notion that civil magistrates of the colony could make rulings and mete out punishments related to religious infractions. In 1635, he was banished once and for all from the colony, and in January 1636 he fled to Rhode Island, where he hoped to found a community that would function, theoretically, just like the great plantations of England.

He secured a tract of land through negotiations with his Narragansett friend Canonicus,

and within two years had convinced a group of about a dozen other settlers to encamp at this new plantation he called Providence (in recognition of "God's providence" to Williams during his time of distress). Providence grew quickly and adopted a civil democratic form of government, which tolerated all religious beliefs right off. In 1639 he and a fellow resident of Providence baptized each other and then 10 others in founding what has become America's modern-day Baptist Church. (Both the American Baptist Church and the Southern Baptist Church, as well as a number of smaller, regional Baptist bodies trace their origins to this congregation in Rhode Island). Williams himself actually left that church soon after, and ultimately came to be known as a Seeker—one who rejected the need for a single organized religion and rather drew from what he believed were the noble elements of several. By 1640, Providence functioned as its own independent political entity, with a board of governors who conducted local business according to the popular sovereignty of the entire community.

Providence came to be the most influential of four independent communities that would eventually unify as the Rhode Island colony. Like Providence, the three others—Portsmouth, Newport, and Warwick—were also formed by political dissidents from Massachusetts. John Clarke and William Coddington were banished from the Massachusetts Bay colony in 1638 for publicly asserting their differences with Puritan government and religious authority. They came to Providence, consulted with Williams, and decided to settle in the northernmost section of Aquidneck Island. Their friend and political inspiration in Massachusetts, Anne Hutchinson, joined them at this new settlement, originally dubbed Pocasset, later that year.

But Hutchinson and the pair of Clarke and Coddington could not resolve their respective power ambitions, and so the latter two ultimately left with a small group of allies to form their own settlement, Newport, at the southern tip of the island in 1639. Pocasset came to be called Portsmouth. While Hutchinson and the Clarke/Coddington groups maintained some autonomy, they also recognized their strength in numbers, and in 1640 agreed that their two communities would submit to joint rule, with Coddington as governor of this new "colony." A few years later the island then known as Aquidneck adopted the name accidentally assigned to it many years earlier, Rhodes—and in 1644 it officially took the name Rhode Island.

Warwick was settled in 1638 by yet another of the dissidents who originally came to Portsmouth, Samuel Gorton. An idealist and ideologue who made trouble everywhere he trod, Gorton was banished first from Plymouth and then ultimately from Portsmouth, where he drew ire from Hutchinson and her followers. He took up residence in Providence for a time, and then in 1645 moved with a small group to Pawtuxet, the original village of Warwick. He arranged a deal from the Narragansetts to transfer that land to the English Crown, and a year later sailed to England where he enlisted the aid of an old friend, the Earl of Warwick, to secure a royal guarantee of title from British parliament. In honor of the Earl of Warwick's assistance on Gorton's behalf, he named the settlement Warwick in 1648.

As the four individual settlements grew, Roger Williams began to recognize their respective and collective vulnerability, especially given the proximity of the two colonies in Massachusetts that so despised them all, and the growing colony to the west, Connecticut. In 1643 Williams sailed to England to secure a parliamentary grant that would guarantee all four communities the legal basis for existence—it was this grant, which he secured from the Earl of Warwick in 1644, that first named the new colony as "The Incorporation of Providence Plantations in the Narragansett Bay in New England." Originally, the grant referred only to Providence, Portsmouth, and Newport; Warwick was admitted to this new union during the colony's first legislative session in 1647. That first session met in Portsmouth, and subsequent ones met in different cities for a time, with Newporters typically serving as President of each session. At that time, Newport had the largest population (about 300), well more than Providence's 200 residents.

New towns were added to the Rhode Island colony throughout the rest of the 17th century,

including Westerly in 1661, Block Island in 1664 (incorporated as the town of New Shoreham), Kings Towne in 1674 (in 1723, it split into North Kingstown and South Kingstown), East Greenwich in 1677, and Jamestown (the town name for the island of Conanicut) in 1678. In Massachusetts during the years, the towns of Barrington, Little Compton, and Bristol were all formed; following the resolution of a boundary dispute these three communities would become part of Rhode Island.

COLONIAL RHODE ISLAND THROUGH THE AMERICAN REVOLUTION

Much of the next century in Rhode Island, and even a good many years beyond, centered on an amazing number and variety of border disputes, both internally and with neighboring colonies. Rufus Choate, a 19th-century Massachusetts political pundit, was described in the *WPA Guide* to Rhode Island as declaring that "the boundaries of Rhode Island might as well have been marked on the north by bramble bush, on the south by a blue jay, on the west by a hive of bees in swarming time, and on the east by 500 foxes with firebrands tied to their tails." A legacy of conflicting land deeds and purchases from area Native Americans created much of the trouble, but frequent claims on chunks of what is now Rhode Island from Massachusetts and Connecticut caused many problems, too.

Within the first two decades of Rhode Island's formation, religious dissidents from around the world began to learn of the tolerant reputation of the small colony. Quakers arrived in the New World in 1657 with the hopes of spreading the word through the colonies. Their efforts to spread the word in Massachusetts were met with fiery resistance, to the point that one proselyte, Mary Dyer, was hanged in Boston in 1660 for attempting to make converts out of Puritans. But they were welcomed in Newport, many of whose residents actually joined the Society of Friends during the city's first several decades. Providence and Roger Williams were less enthusiastic about the Quakers, but as was consistent with their beliefs, they made no efforts to curtail this freedom of religion (Williams even engaged in a three-day debate with a Quaker spokesperson in 1671).

Jewish settlers from Holland came to New-port in 1658 and swiftly established Jeshuat Israel congregation there. The community thrived for more than a century, until Britain occupied New-port during the American Revolution. The set-tlement's Touro Synagogue, still in use, is the oldest such place of worship in the United States.

A major shift in political power in England, the restoration of King Charles II in 1660, made the leaders of the young Rhode Island colony a bit nervous, so a group sailed to the Mother Country in 1663 and success-fully secured a royal charter to supersede the parliamentary grant issued by the Earl of War-wick in 1644. Interestingly, this charter—which fully asserted the religious tolerance of the state—remained in effect well after the United States secured her inde-pendence from England, until 1843 to be exact.

Rhode Island developed a rep-utation as a rather ruthless little shipping powerhouse during the latter half of the 17th century. Newport and other communities outfitted a number of privateer-ing ships, mostly during the myr-iad colonial wars of that time—the Anglo-Dutch trade wars of the 1650s, '60s, and '70s, and the French and Indian Wars of the following century. Privateering, where private ships armed with sea-men were enlisted to attack and capture enemy ships, was not even formally outlawed by the Rhode Island Assembly until the very end of the 17th century. And even then, illegal privateering, which is really just a nice word for pirating, took place regularly at the hands of Rhode Island crews.

From the late 1600s onward, Rhode Island de-veloped into one of the world's busiest trading hubs, establishing commercial ties with virtually every other colony and many countries, including England, the islands colonized by Portugal, west-ern Africa, and the West Indies. Most colonists

Rufus Choate declared "the boundaries of Rhode Island might as well have been marked on the north by bramble bush, on the south by a blue jay, on the west by a hive of bees, and on the east by 500 foxes with firebrands tied to their tails."

still made their living as farmers until well into the 18th century, but increasingly and especially in port communities such as Providence, Newport, Bristol, Westerly, Wickford, and Pawtuxet, many residents made their living in merchant trade or re-lated professions such as shipbuilding.

Slave-trading was easily the most lucrative form of commercial enterprise during this pe-riod, and Rhode Island raked in more money through this abhorrent practice than just about any other state. (Despite the colony's infamy as a slave-trading hub, Rhode Island in 1774 be-came the first state to ban slave trade; in 1784, the state outlawed owning slaves entirely.) A huge percentage of the New World's slave ships during the late 17th through late 18th cen-turies were registered to Rhode Island. Generally these ships sailed to Africa with rum and other goods in exchange for slaves, who were mostly brought to the West Indies or to South Carolina, where they were sold and distributed across the South. Many slaves were brought directly to Rhode Is-land and forced into domestic or agricultural service there. From the West Indies, the ships brought molasses to Rhode Is-land, where it was distilled into the rum that ships carried to West Africa to obtain more slaves. The process came to be known as the Triangle Trade.

With its prominent shipping interests, Rhode Island was one of the first New World colonies to object strenuously to the many trade regulations and taxations imposed by Great Britain through-out the mid-18th century. Some laws put limits on the manufacturing of goods in Rhode Island, forcing colonists to engage in expensive trade for such items, while other edicts placed onerous duties on molasses and other imported wares. Another practice that enraged the colonists was that of British ships whose "press gangs" ran-domly kidnapped Americans and forced them to enlist in the English navy.

THE DORR REBELLION

Rhode Island governed according to its colonial charter, granted in 1663, for longer than any other northern state. By the 1840s, the governing principles laid out in this document had become a poor fit for the state, especially given Rhode Island's rapid industrialization and growing immigration. What rankled many citizens was the antiquated criteria for voting rights—only men owning land worth $134 (a goodly amount in 1663 — and in 1840) were permitted to participate in the electoral process.

The unjust effect of these rules seemed particularly appalling given Rhode Island's track record on freedom of religion—and its vehement protests against taxation without representation during the American Revolution. Here, more than 60 years after the United States secured her independence, Rhode Island was letting a comparatively wealthy minority set policies and laws for the general population. Of course, the state legislature was made up chiefly of well-to-do landowners who knew that any concessions toward universal men's suffrage would severely diminish their power and influence. They fought tooth and nail to keep this enormous chunk of the population disenfranchised.

A resident of the still-rural village of Chepachet, in western Rhode Island, Thomas Dorr decided it was time for Rhode Island's lawmakers to recognize the changing times and extend full voting rights to all male state residents, as neighboring states had done. (Of course, women would not be empowered to vote in Rhode Island or in any U.S. state until well into the 20th century, so even were Dorr's best intentions carried out, half the adult population would continue to be excluded from the political process.)

Interestingly, Dorr was from neither an immigrant nor an industrial background. Born in 1805 to a wealthy Rhode Island family, he became a successful lawyer and around 1840 began rallying for popular legal reforms that would greatly liberalize the state's voting laws. Dorr's People's Party, frustrated with the lack of headway they were able to make against the state's incumbent conservative legislators, called its own constitutional convention in October 1841 in an effort to amend the antiquated state constitution. During this convention, his party ratified what would be called the People's Constitution. Of course, this entire process went technically outside the laws of Rhode Island, and not a word of the new constitution was recognized by the sitting legislature, which voted down the Dorrites' referendum's overwhelmingly.

In effect, Rhode Island suddenly found itself with competing legislatures each acting in total defiance of the other. The federal government decided not to intervene and rather en-

By 1765, the resentment had turned to outright hostility, and on one particular night in June, a posse of nearly 500 Newport men and boys cut loose a boat attached to a British ship that had been used for impressing colonists, dragged it to shore, and set it afire. A few years later another band of Newporters destroyed a British revenue ship, the *Liberty*, and in 1772 perhaps the most notorious of these acts of insurrection further intensified anger between the British and the Rhode Island colonists. On a warm June evening, a group from Providence snuck out to the British revenue ship the *Gaspee* and set it on fire. This event galvanized support in Rhode Island for a full-scale war against the mother country—the *Gaspee* incident has been described by some as the colony's ownBattle of Lexington. Rhode Island's governor of the time, Newport's Joseph Wanton, walked a tightrope following the *Gaspee* incident, issuing a warrant for the arrest of the men who burned the ship but making little effort to capture them.

But the actual Battle of Lexington in April 1775 stirred Rhode Island into a formal—and fervent—state of war. Within 24 hours of news concerning the Lexington and Concord battles reaching Rhode Island, the tiny colony put together a force of some 1,500 militia. Governor Wanton, sympathetic to the colonial cause but skeptical that war would bring about positive change, declined to officially sanction military action. The assembly convened in October

couraged the dual governments to work things out on their own. Matters only worsened, however, when on April 18, 1842, Dorr's party elected him the new governor of Rhode Island, while the opposing state government re-elected incumbent Samuel H. King. By May, Thomas Dorr had rallied a team of supporters to stage a coup on the Providence Armory, in hopes of turning the military on his side and ultimately taking over the State House and other official state offices.

In fact, relatively few Dorrites partook of the mission on the armory, and Thomas Dorr and his followers were handily turned back. Several weeks later, Dorr decided to call his new government to assembly at Sprague's Tavern in Chepachet (which still operates as a restaurant today, the Stagecoach Tavern). Governor King sent the Rhode Island militia to silence this rebellion. Dorr's own small militia waited at Acote's Hill, about a quarter-mile south of where present-day U.S. 44 crosses through Chepachet, but on realizing that King's troops were far greater in number and in firepower, Dorr and his group retreated to the tavern.

King and his men marched to Sprague's Tavern, where they ordered the Dorrites out at gunpoint. There was a standoff of sorts, during which more words were exchanged than firepower, although one of King's men did manage to fire a

shot through the keyhole of the locked tavern, striking a Dorrite on the thigh.

In despair, Thomas Dorr fled the state. Many of his followers were arrested. The rival government had been completely shut down. The appropriately named governor King took a rather autocratic approach to restoring order: He declared martial law and had Dorr arrested and charged with high treason.

Although disgraced by the state's official government, Thomas Dorr was hailed a hero by many, and the goals of the so-called Dorr Rebellion were largely accomplished. Fearing a backlash and continued civic unrest, the conservative state legislature caved in and amended the constitution, dramatically liberalizing the requirements for voting rights. In 1843 Rhode Islanders took to the polls and approved the new Rhode Island constitution.

The rest of Dorr's life was quite sad, however. He was found guilty of the treason charges against him in 1844 and sentenced with an amazingly harsh punishment: hard labor for the rest of his life. Again, many Rhode Islanders and even some dignitaries rallied for his pardon, which was granted after just one year of time served. Still, Dorr was demoralized and physically weakened by this ordeal. He died just a few years after taking his famous stand on behalf of voting rights.

1775, voted to depose Wanton, and immediately replaced him with Providence assemblyman Nicholas Cooke, who authorized Rhode Island's participation in the military campaign against Britain.

On May 4, 1776, the Rhode Island Assembly become the first colony in the New World to formally declare its independence from England—some eight weeks before the Continental Congress in Philadelphia issued the unified Declaration of Independence. Rhode Island, therefore, can and does claim to be the oldest independent state in the United States. On July 18, 1776, the General Assembly convened and officially named their former colony the State of Rhode Island and Providence Plantations.

Rhode Island's shipping prowess became yet again evident during the American Revolution; Esek Hopkins, the brother of noted statesman and 1750s governor Stephen Hopkins, was the first commander-in-chief of the Continental Navy, and many in the colony served at sea during the campaign. Warwick son General Nathanael Greene successfully turned around the colonists' failing efforts in the South when he led his troops to victory over the British in March 1781 at Guilford Courthouse, northwest of Greensboro, North Carolina.

Meanwhile, Newport—which was occupied by British troops from December 1776 through October 1779, when the whole lot of them abandoned the city to provide reinforcements in New

York City—played an important role toward the end of the war. It's here that General Rochambeau and his French troops encamped in March 1781, and where he conferred with General George Washington to plan out the sneaky and successful assault on Yorktown. A detachment of the Rhode Island regiment, led by Captain Stephen Olney, also partook of the Yorktown battle.

The British occupation of Newport, however, proved devastating to that city, which prior to the Revolution had been well on its way to becoming one of the nation's most dynamic and important ports. The population of the city declined by nearly 50 percent following the war, in part because many Tory sympathizers had lived there during the British occupation—as the war drew to a close, they fled permanently to Canada, mostly Nova Scotia. In general, Rhode Island's economic prospects were gloomy for the first couple of decades following the war, and shipping trade was reduced to a trickle.

STATEHOOD AND THE INDUSTRIAL REVOLUTION

Although Rhode Island made the earliest declaration of independence of any colony, it also took the longest to agree to join the union. From 1776 through 1787, it existed essentially as an independent state. Almost wholly dependent on trade, its residents resented having to conform to trade restrictions and controls set by the entire union. The notion of joining with the other colonies struck at least some Rhode Islanders as no better than having to submit to British rule. The idea of having to funnel a portion of state shipping revenues, in the form of taxation, to the federal government was totally unacceptable.

At the Constitutional Convention in Philadelphia in 1787, it was decided that Rhode Island would be made to join the Union—the colony itself sent no delegates to the convention, in something of an act of protest. It was not until May 29, 1790—after much internal debate and external pressure from the newly formed U.S. Congress—that the state assembly convened in Newport and ratified the Federal Constitution by an extremely close vote of 34 in favor, 32 against.

At this time, the new state of Rhode Island comprised 30 towns and had a population of nearly 70,000 (nearly 10 times greater than the population of the previous century).

Rhode Islanders remained divided on a number of issues facing the state and the young nation for the decades following the war. Lines split over whether to support Alexander Hamilton's Federalist agenda or Thomas Jefferson's Republican—and pro-French—stance. Sympathies were split, too, during the War of 1812, which, because of its stifling effect on maritime trade, hurt Rhode Island financially more than it did almost any other state. But one Rhode Island military star did make a name for himself during this war: South Kingstown's Oliver Hazard Perry, who commanded the victorious U.S. fleet during the Battle of Lake Erie in 1813. Having secured America's control of Lake Erie, Perry paved the way for General William Henry Harrison's shortlived invasion of Canada. Perry's younger brother, Matthew, earned fame by negotiating America's first commercial trade agreement with Japan in 1854. Bristol native General James De Wolfe also contributed admirably against the British during the war.

While the state's shipping economy declined following the revolution and its agricultural prowess had been dropping over the past century, Rhode Island was about to to become a different kind of economic superpower. In early 1790s Pawtucket, Moses Brown—one of the Providence Brown brothers, after whom the university is named—financed a young textile worker from England who had secretly traveled to America in hopes of profiting from his extensive knowledge of Britain's advanced mill technology (at this time it was illegal for British citizens to share their knowledge of English technology with other nations).

Samuel Slater almost single-handedly oversaw the formation of America's textile industry, and in so doing played as important a role as anybody in sparking America's Industrial Revolution. Within a few years, several powerful and highly mechanized mills had sprung up in Pawtucket and neighboring towns of the Blackstone River Valley, a superb source of water power.

Textile mills opened in Warwick, Coventry, and other cities within a few years. A quarter century after Slater designed the first water-powered textile mill in Pawtucket, Rhode Island employed some 25,000 workers in textile production, and was spinning some 30,000 bales of cotton annually into nearly 30 million yards of cloth. The boom continued right through the 19th century, with Rhode Island's capital expenditure in cotton textile production rising from about $7 million in 1850 to more than $30 million in 1880.

Following on the heels of Rhode Island's cotton-textile milling success, the state developed into a leader of woolen and worsted material production, too. By 1850 extensive worsted woolen mills ran in Cranston, North Kingstown, Hopkinton, Peace Dale, North Providence, Pawtucket, Woonsocket, and Providence. Innovations such as the carding machine, developed in Peace Dale by Rowland Hazard, and steam power, used in Providence at the Providence Woolen Manufacturing Company, further established the state's industrial preeminence. By 1890, Providence was second only to Philadelphia in woolen manufacturing.

MODERNIZATION AND INDUSTRY

Inventor George H. Corliss developed a proper steam engine for the Providence Dyeing, Bleaching, and Calendering Company in 1848, and soon the Corliss Steam Engine was famous all over the world for its time- and labor-saving devices. Eventually, Corliss would become the largest steam engine producer in the country. Numerous related industries, especially machine-tool making, sprang up during the textile boom.

Another industry that excelled during the 19th century, especially in Providence, was the manufacture of jewelry, especially the costume variety. Seril and Nehemiah Dodge, brothers from Providence, had developed a cheap and fairly easy way of electro-gilding metal, thus enabling them to produce popular jewelry at extremely low prices. Nehemiah later expanded his business greatly, employing journeyman gold- and silversmiths and apprentices, to become the nation's first mass producer of discount jewelry.

One of the Dodge apprentices, Jabez Gorham, went from making silver spoons and selling them door-to-door to founding the now-famous Gorham Manufacturing Company in Providence. The early 19th century saw a rapid increase in jewelry production, with dozens of shops making that and silverware by 1810. By 1880, Rhode Island led all U.S. states in the percentage of residents employed in jewelry manufacture.

Rhode Island didn't revise its constitution, which had been in place since the Royal Charter of 1663, until 1842, by which time a growing number of residents had begun to recognize the unfairness of a governing document that allowed only owners of more than $134 worth of land to vote. Slavery had been banned 60 years earlier and sentiments in favor of egalitarianism had been intensifying. The new constitution was therefore revised, after the constitutional crisis known as the Dorr War, to grant universal suffrage to all men in Rhode Island. Women remained without a voice, as they did throughout the United States, until 1920.

At the onset of the Civil War, Rhode Islanders actively supported the Union efforts, furnishing thousands of troops early on, the first regiment under the noted Colonel Ambrose E. Burnside (who later moved permanently to Rhode Island). The state governor of that time, William Sprague, served in the Battle of Bull Run. And all told, 14 Rhode Island regiments went to battle during the Civil War, including the one consisting entirely of black men that was immortalized in the 1989 film *Glory*. Rhode Islanders participated in nearly every major battle. The Civil War legacy is an interesting one in a state that profited from slavery for so many years.

Throughout the 19th century, as the state's industrial prowess grew, economic and technological advances followed. Gas lighting was introduced to the streets of Newport and Providence in the early 1900s, several state banks were chartered, steamboats connected Providence to Newport and then to many other locations, the Blackstone Canal was dug between Providence and Worcester, and railroad tracks linking Providence and

Boston, southeastern Connecticut, and Worcester were laid between 1835 and 1847. In 1880 the state received telephone service, and around the end of the 19th century, Providence houses were illuminated with electricity. Also around this time, the present State House in Providence was constructed, with the first General Assembly convening there on New Year's Day in 1901. Since that day, Providence has been the sole capital of Rhode Island—before then, Newport and Providence alternated.

Rhode Island's economy, and its intake of immigrant workers, grew precipitously following the Civil War. In addition to producing large quantities of textiles and jewelry, Rhode Island factories by the turn of the 20th century specialized in various types of metal manufacture (wire, hardware, stoves, fire extinguishers), rubber goods and footwear, paints, yacht and ship equipment, sewing machines, chemical and drug products, and baking powder. By the turn of the 20th century, the Providence-based manufacturer Brown and Sharp (it moved to North Kingstown in the 1960s) was the nation's largest producer of machine tools. There were some 150 machine shops in Rhode Island by 1900, and 250 costume-jewelry manufacturers.

Conditions in factories were miserable, in some cases brutally inhuman, throughout the 19th century. In the early 19th century, men earned about $5 per week in mill jobs, women less than half that, and children a little over $1. A work week consisted of six 12- to 14-hour days. Workers lived in tightly supervised mill villages—employers supplied the houses, schools, hospitals, churches, and shops; they effectively controlled every aspect of their employees' lives. And at least early on, these villages were bleak and depressing.

A few mill owners, notably the Hazards of Peace Dale, made an effort to promote culture and education within their communities, but this was the exception rather than the rule. As early as 1836, the Children's Friends Society of Rhode Island was formed to rally on behalf of child workers' rights, and in 1840 a state law was passed requiring that children under 12 attend at least 12 months of schooling prior to beginning their "careers" in the mills.

Other unions formed gradually during the 19th century, as an increasing number of local workers began to rebel against the horrid conditions. But mills simply imported foreign workers, who were less organized and able to unionize and more willing to accept harsh conditions. Immigration drew heavily from French-speaking Canada, Ireland, Britain, Italy, Poland, and Portugal. It was not until 1909 that the state actually formed a board to oversee and regulate labor conditions in Rhode Island factories, but even this organization had little success in improving working conditions until 1923, when the state Bureau of Labor was established. Strikes occurred regularly throughout the early 20th century, and some of these were intensely bitter and violent.

World War I, to which Rhode Island sent some 29,000 troops (of which 600 perished), interrupted Rhode Island's steadily growing industrial power for a time. Following World War I, as companies grew frightened of the increasingly strong labor unions throughout New England, Rhode Island began losing textile factories to the cheap labor of the South. But by the 1930s, even with the Depression in full force and an increasing number of companies leaving the Northeast, Rhode Island had become the most highly industrialized state in the Union—more than half of the working population of 300,000 in 1930 was employed in manufacturing.

By 1940, the population of Rhode Island had grown to nearly 700,000. World War II interrupted everyday life here as it did all over the world. About 92,000 Rhode Islanders served in the war, and 2,157 were killed. The Ocean State, with its many factories, contributed tremendously to the war effort with the production of boots, knives, parachutes, munitions, and other supplies.

WORLD WAR II TO THE PRESENT: DECLINE FOLLOWED BY REGENERATION

Following the war, the advent of cheap suburban housing, a fast-growing and convenient interstate highway system, and a steady decline in urban industry inspired a rapid out-migration from Providence and other cities into neighboring towns. Even where jobs remained in the cities, at least for a while, workers no longer had to live near their places of employment. The 1950s marked the beginning of nearly four decades of wretched economic decline, high crime, and deterioration in Rhode Island's urban areas. Providence's 1950 population of about 250,000 dropped by 75,000 over the next 20 years. Economically, the state stagnated badly from the 1950s through the 1970s, and by the 1980s it had one of the least favorable climates for doing business in the country.

Suburbs like Warwick, Cranston, Johnston, and North Kingstown blossomed over this period, and today as you drive through these communities you'll see thousands of suburban homes built between World War II and the 1970s, not to mention scads of shopping centers and a handful of large indoor shopping malls that also date from this period. In cities, urban renewal efforts led to the clearance of many so-called slums, some of them with wonderful Victorian housing. But Providence, and Rhode Island in general, did a better job preserving its most important historic homes and neighborhoods than many other parts of New England. The Point District in Newport and College Hill in Providence, both of which fell into disrepair

for a time, now rank among the most beautiful historic districts in the nation.

One industry that thrived in Rhode Island following World War II was the military—the U.S. Navy was the state's largest civilian employer during the 1950s and 1960s. The naval shipyard just outside Newport was responsible for building America's cruiser-destroyer fleet. But this industry crashed in 1974 when the Navy moved these operations to the South. Yet again, the relatively high operating costs and wages in New England sent a company packing. Newport was left reeling, but the city rebounded by turning itself into a full-scale, year-round tourist destination. That industry remains the most important one in Newport today.

The tourism rebound of Newport and the general renaissance in Providence have been important factors in Rhode Island improving its image greatly over the past two decades. There have been failings, too, such as a slew of extremely embarrassing political scandals (almost all to do with bribery, extortion, misuse of funds, and other unethical misdeeds) that shattered the public's faith in state and local government during the 1980s. But the reforms that grew out of these incidents ultimately helped to clean up government, at least to a degree.

Government

Rhode Islanders have long marched to their own drummer when it comes to politics. The colony was founded by Massachusetts Bay Colony dissidents who believed strongly in religious freedom and the separation of Church and State. From the very beginning of the colony's settlement, there was tension between the southerners on Aquidneck Island and the northern residents of Providence.

The state operated under a Royal Charter issued in 1663 until well into the 19th century. Though this document proved antiquated and awkward by that time, it was only replaced, in 1842, after a near–civil war, the Dorr Rebellion.

Early on, Rhode Island was represented by a General Assembly comprising six men from

each of the original towns. As new towns incorporated, the Assembly grew. Sessions were held at private homes until the first colony house was constructed in Newport in 1690, but for some time after that the assembly often met in homes in other parts of the state. Even the revised state constitution of 1842, which finally granted suffrage to all male adult Rhode Islanders, authorized that General Assembly meetings could convene in Newport, Providence, South Kingstown, Bristol, or East Greenwich. In 1854, the Assembly pared this list of towns down to two, and from then until 1900 the legislature met alternately in Newport and Providence. It wasn't until 1900, at which time Providence had grown to become the state's hub of economics, education, and population, that it became the definitive state capital.

ORGANIZATION

As was true in a number of states well into the early 20th century, Rhode Island's method of filling the General Assembly, which consists of an upper house of senators and a lower house of representatives, greatly protected the power of individual towns against the power of the citizens in general. There are many reasons that Providence and other Rhode Island cities with dense populations suffered during the middle of the 20th century, most of them having to do with national economic trends, the development of affordable suburban housing, factories moving south and west in search of cheaper labor, and so on. But one likely and often overlooked factor was that state governments operated primarily according to the agendas of towns with relatively low populations, which meant that legislation often favored big business and low taxes among the wealthier residents over workers' rights, better urban housing laws, and other services that would benefit city residents.

Until the 20th century, the General Assembly was made up of equal numbers of representatives from every town in the state, meaning that the few people living in a rural and comparatively wealthy town like Little Compton or Charlestown had as much clout in the legislature as the many tens of thousands of working-class residents of Providence and the significant numbers of blue-collar workers in Pawtucket, Woonsocket, and East Providence. By the early 20th century, a city like Providence had nearly 40 percent of the state population but the same one vote in the state senate as a town with fewer than 500 residents.

In 1928, an article was finally passed that stipulated that the Senate would balance its representation. After that, the Senate consisted of one member from every town or city with a population of 25,000 or less. Towns with greater than this population were allowed to have one additional senator per 12,500 residents above that number, with no town allowed more than

Rhode Island State House

six senatorial representatives. Eventually the law was changed so that the Senate's representation came to be based purely on population distribution, although districts are drawn in such a way that no one senator is the lone representative for more than two towns (and coverage is only this thin in very sparsely populated sections of the state) out of 50 seats.

In the lower house, it was voted in 1909 that the state congress should contain a maximum of 100 representatives. The breakdown has since then been determined by entirely by population, greatly increasing the power of the state's urban areas.

In 1994, in an effort to streamline government and speed up debate, the House and Senate passed a bill to reduce the number of state representatives from 100 to 75, and the number of state senators from 50 to 38. These changes take effect in 2003. Opponents of downsizing cite several potential problems, including a higher concentration of power into fewer hands and a greater influence of special interests, but it appears these changes will take effect as planned.

Prior to 1992, the governor of Rhode Island held office for a term of just two years, but this was extended to four at that time; the governor may serve a total of two full terms.

Rhode Island has two U.S. Congresspersons, in addition to its two U.S. Senators.

POLITICAL PARTIES

Generally speaking, Rhode Island is politically more like a lot of Northeastern cities than it is like a state, in the sense that popularly elected officials tend to be socially rather progressive—fiscally they're more varied but still pretty liberal. Like its neighbor Massachusetts, Rhode Island tends to vote overwhelmingly Democratic: the most recent General Assembly consisted of 85 Dems and 15 GOPers in the House of Representatives, and 44 Dems and 6 GOPers in the Senate. The Governor as of this writing, Lincoln Almond, is a Republican. The most recent U.S. Senators were Lincoln Chafee (a Republican) and Jack Reed (a Democrat), and the most recent U.S. Congressmen were Democrats James R. Langevin and Patrick Kennedy (son of Sen. Ted Kennedy). The vast majority of the state's elected Republicans have been considered quite moderate in relation to the national party as a whole.

Of course, many people think of the long-time mayor of Providence, Buddy Cianci, when they discuss Rhode Island politics. For a brief look at Cianci's colorful career, see the Providence chapter.

The Economy

Rhode Island, with its history of wealthy shipping magnates and ostentatious summer cottages, coupled with its legacy of industry and manufacturing, is a state with quite a few extremely rich citizens and a huge core of working-class wage earners. The median household income of $36,699 is about the national average, and indeed the state's positive and negative economic attributes tend to balance each other out.

MANUFACTURING

The state's industrial clout continues to decline even today, but a rapid increase in the number of retail and service-oriented jobs has contributed to an overall economic boom not seen in Rhode Island for many decades. Benefiting especially has been Providence, which has become a poster child for the urban renaissance that has swept across many American cities over the past 15 years or so.

Manufacturing jobs in Rhode Island still continue to drop—from the 1990 to the 2000 censuses, the number of state residents employed in manufacturing dropped from 110,000 to 82,000 (a drop of more than 25 percent), although this area remains the state's second most important economic sector. Other major areas include wholesale and retail trade (77,000 employees); education, health, and social services grew (the leader at 115,000); arts, entertainment, recreation, accommodations, and food services (43,000); professional, scientific, management, administrative, and waste management services (41,000); finance, insurance, and real estate (35,000), and construction (27,000). Rhode Island also continues to have a prolific commercial fishing industry.

In the manufacturing sector, the main business endeavors are primary metals, fabricated metals, machinery, and electrical equipment. Jewelry and silverware production remains a manufacturing force (and still more so than in any other U.S. state), and Rhode Island still employs many people in textile production, even if the numbers are but a whisper of those a century ago.

TOURISM, EDUCATION, AND HEALTH CARE

As noted above, nearly 50,000 Rhode Islanders work in the arts, entertainment, recreation, accommodations, and food services industry, collectively known as tourism. After the Navy moved

RHODE ISLAND ON THE BIG—AND SMALL—SCREEN

Rhode Island has lobbied as hard as almost any state in New England to attract filmmakers to the state, and the results have been impressive. Many notable movies have been set in the Ocean State in recent years, and the television show *Providence* has also done a great deal to promote the capital city. The hit show, which debuted in 1999 and stars Melina Kanakaredes, Mike Farrell, and Paula Cale, is filmed largely in Los Angeles, but the show shoots a number of scenes each year on location in Providence and towns nearby—about twice each year the cast and crew travel to Rhode Island to shoot on-site footage. Even Vincent "Buddy" Cianci made a cameo on the show. (The animated Fox TV show *Family Guy* was also set in Rhode Island and even featured a fictitious Buddy Cianci High School.)

Rhode Island's history as a filmmaking fave is rather recent, although a handful of classics were shot here. Newport, for instance, was the film locale for the 1956 Grace Kelly, Bing Crosby, and Frank Sinatra movie *High Society*. Newport, in fact, has been a famous location for a number of pictures, perhaps most notably the 1974 adaptation of F. Scott Fitzgerald's *The Great Gatsby*, starring Robert Redford, Mia Farrow, and Sam Waterston. The mansion scenes were shot at Rosecliff Mansion. Other Newport-filmed movies include *The Betsy* (1978, starring Laurence Olivier, Robert Duvall, and Katharine Ross), *True Lies* (1994, starring Arnold Schwarzenegger and Jamie Lee Curtis), *Thirteen Days* (2000, starring Kevin Costner), *Mr. North* (1988, starring Anthony Edwards, Robert Mitchum, and Lauren Bacall), *Heaven's Gate* (1980, starring Kris Kristofferson, Christopher Walken, and John Hurt), and *Amistad* (1997, starring Morgan Freeman, Nigel Hawthorne, and Anthony Hopkins). *Amistad* also had scenes shot in Pawtucket and in Providence, including one at the Rhode Island State House.

One last Newport-filmed movie was *Me, Myself & Irene* (2000, starring Jim Carrey and Renee Zellweger), which was directed and written by perhaps Rhode Island's most famous movie-making

out of Newport in the 1970s, that city especially turned to tourism as its leading industry. Block Island also relies chiefly on tourism, although plenty of Block Islanders still make a living the same way that they have for generations: fishing. To a lesser extent, parts of South County—specifically the beach communities—are heavily dependent on tourism.

In recent years, with its vastly improved reputation, even Providence has come to depend heavily on tourism, a notion almost unthinkable during the city's worst years in the 1970s and 1960s. Still, Providence has a ways to go in building its tourism infrastructure to accommodate large numbers of visitors, and outside of the Northeast, many people remain unaware that the city has much to offer. Changes are under way—several hotels are planned, which will alleviate the crunch on in-city accommodations (it's a seller's market, with Providence claiming one of the highest hotel occupancy rates in the nation).

Rhode Island's other big service sectors are health and education. The former is especially significant in Providence and its suburbs, where there are many hospitals and health providers. Education, on the other hand, is a big contributor to the economy in both Providence and several other parts of the state. The University of Rhode Island, in Kingston, has the highest student enrollment in the state, while in Providence there's Brown University, Johnson & Wales, the Rhode Island School of Design, and Providence College. Other notable schools in Rhode Island include Bryant College in Smithfield, Salve Regina University in Newport, and Roger Williams University in Bristol.

team, brothers Bobby and Peter Farrelly. The Farrellys have became rather notorious for reinventing the "gross-out" genre with such ribald films as *There's Something About Mary* (1998, starring Ben Stiller, Matt Dillon, and Cameron Diaz), which was shot in part in Providence, and *Dumb & Dumber* (1994, starring Jim Carrey, Jeff Daniels, and Lauren Holly). And although they didn't direct it, the Farrelly brothers wrote and produced the Alec Baldwin and Shawn Hatosy movie *Outside Providence* (1999), which was indeed shot outside Providence, specifically in Woonsocket. *Me, Myself, & Irene,* by the way, also had filming locations in Jamestown, Galilee, and Narragansett.

Outside Providence was directed by another Rhode Island son, Pawtucket's Michael Corrente, who also directed *Federal Hill* (1995, starring Corrente himself), which traced the lives of five young men living in Providence's famed Little Italy, Federal Hill, and the screen adaptation of David Mamet's *American Buffalo* (1996, starring Dustin Hoffman and Dennis Franz), which was filmed

in Pawtucket. Corrente's movies offer an especially gritty and realistic look of urban Rhode Island.

Keep your eyes open while watching a few other Rhode Island–filmed movies, including *Mystic Pizza* (1988, starring Julia Roberts, Lili Taylor, and Annabeth Gish), which was shot mostly over the border in southeastern Connecticut but also had scenes in Watch Hill and Westerly; *Meet Joe Black* (1998, starring Brad Pitt and Anthony Hopkins), which was filmed in part at Warwick's Aldrich Mansion; *Reversal of Fortune* (1990, starring Jeremy Irons, Glenn Close, and Ron Silver), based on the true-crime book by lawyer Alan Dershowitz about the attempted-murder trial of Claus von Bulow—much of it was filmed in Newport; and *Wind* (1992, starring Matthew Modine, Jennifer Grey, and Cliff Robertson), which was shot in Jamestown.

Incidentally, the film adaptation of John Updike's *The Witches of Eastwick*— a book said to have been based on Wickford, Rhode Island— was actually filmed chiefly in Massachusetts.

The People

Although it's the smallest state in the Union, Rhode Island has more people living within its borders than Montana, Delaware, either of the Dakotas, Alaska, Vermont, or Wyoming. Roger Williams and the other early settlers in the area hailed from England, and from the 1630s through the 1850s, the population was largely white, of British descent, and Protestant. Within 50 years of Europeans settling in Rhode Island, the Native American population almost disappeared. The colony did possess at least a slightly more diverse population even in the 1600s than others in New England. The founding doctrine protecting the worship of all religions contributed to an early influx of Quakers (most of these practitioners came from England) and Jews (mostly from Spain and Portugal). Catholics, mostly from France, began settling in Rhode Island in small numbers after the American Revolution, during which locals became

quite appreciative and fond of the French troops stationed in Newport under Rochambeau.

During the past 150 years, the industrialization of Rhode Island has led to another dramatic change in demographics.

DEMOGRAPHY

The mills and factories throughout Rhode Island, which would later employ immigrants from several nations, began by hiring from the ranks of local farmers and small-time tradesmen in search of steadier employment and income. But over time, native Rhode Islanders grew unhappy and restless with the horrible working conditions of early factories in the state—they expected more, both better treatment and income. The factory owners thought of their workforce as just another factory part, and when this element stopped performing

THE FIVE INDIGENOUS TRIBES OF RHODE ISLAND

When Europeans first began to explore what is now Rhode Island in the 1500s, there were five indigenous tribes living on this land: the Pequots, the Nipmucks, the Niantics, the Narragansetts, and the Wampanoags.

Among the five, the Pequots—who lived mostly in what is now southeastern Connecticut but also in southwestern Rhode Island—exercised the greatest degree of autonomy and defiance against the settlers. This warlike mentality quickly led to their near-extinction, as colonists endeavored to silence them and even turn friendlier tribes, such as the Narragansetts and Connecticut Mohegans, against them.

The Pequots left their first calling card in the 1630s when they killed a pair of British merchants whom they encountered sailing up the Connecticut River on a trading mission. They further raised the ire of the settlers when they murdered the respected explorer John Oldham off the coast of Block Island in 1636, an act that led almost immediately to reprisals by way of burnings and raids by British troops. The Pequots continued to strike out, attacking and murdering several Wethersfield families during the winter of 1636–37, and unsuccessfully attempting to establish a warring pact with their neighbors, the formidable Narragansett Indians of nearby Rhode (Aquidneck) Island.

These tensions escalated the following spring into the great Pequot War of 1637, during which about 130 European settlers from the Connecticut River towns, along with 70 allied Mohegans, developed a plan to destroy their enemy. Believing it wise to approach from the least likely side, the group attacked from the east, sailing to Rhode Island's Narragansett Bay and marching west, with a force of about 400 Narragansetts looking on.

The Pequots were concentrated into a pair of encampments near what is now Norwich, Connecticut, each of these comprising a several-acre enclosure of a few dozen wigwams. The settlers, led by John Mason, struck the largest Pequot community at dawn and virtually obliterated its in-habitants, burning the wigwams and shooting any who attempted to flee. The second Pequot encampment attempted to thwart the invasion but was easily driven to retreat. Over the next two months, the remaining members of the severely crippled Pequot league edged their way west toward New York but were met in a massive swamp in what would become Fairfield by Mason and his battalion. Again a great slaughter was carried out, with the remaining 180 Pequots being taken hostage and brought to Hartford.

The Pequots could not have been subdued without the assistance of the Mohegans and the Narragansetts, with whom the English signed a treaty of friendship in 1637. But peace between the Native Americans and the English would last for only a few decades, until King Philip's War.

The Nipmuck Indians lived principally in central Massachusetts but also occupied some land in Northern Rhode Island. Their fate following King Philip's War, in which they participated against the colonists, is little documented, but it's believed that most survivors fled west into Canada, and those who remained joined with the few Indian tribes that remained friendly to the colonists.

Rhode Island's Niantics, which were different from but related to the Niantics of southeastern Connecticut, lived in the southern part of mainland Rhode Island, where the coast runs now through Westerly and Charlestown. Their ruler, Ninigret, managed to prolong the tribe's viability by keeping a distance from those Native Americans who rebelled against the colonists. Ninigret met on several occasions with colonists, and he even refrained from participating in King Philip's War. This tribe of Narragansetts (as colonists increasingly came to call all Rhode Island Indians)continued to live on their land through the late 1800s. By that time, their numbers had dwindled and their final bits of land were taken from them.

Rhode Island's modern-day Narragansetts are mostly of Niantic descent, but they're joined by some who descend from the actual Narragansett nation, which was perhaps the most pronounced and prolific tribe in Rhode Island during the 17th century. By the time of King Philip's War, there were some 5,000 Narragansetts living throughout Rhode Island—their significant numbers are explained in part by their not succumbing to the diseases that brought down the more powerful Wampanoags, who lived mostly in southeastern Massachusetts but also in part of eastern Rhode Island. As the Wampanoags declined, the Narragansetts actually took over the islands of what is now Narragansett Bay—land that the former had previously occupied.

It was with Narragansett and Wampanoag leaders that Roger Williams first socialized and negotiated a land treaty on his arrival in the 1630s. Canonicus was the sachem, or ruler, of the Narragansetts and would become a close friend of Williams until his death in 1647; Massasoit headed the Wampanoags, and Williams assisted in bringing about some degree of peace between these two nations—and he also made peace between the Native Americans of Rhode Island and the colonists of Massachusetts, the very ones who had arrested and banished Williams in the first place.

By the 1670s, the Narragansetts were led by a descendant of Canonicus, Canonchet. At this time, the leader of the Wampanoag tribe, Philip (the son of Massasoit), sought to unify New England's many Indian tribes in an ambitious and perhaps desperate conspiracy to overthrow the Puritan lock on the region. A Christian Indian loyal to the settlers betrayed King Philip's intentions and was quickly rubbed out by Philip's men in a move that could have easily been played out in a Mario Puzo novel. As with the Pequot situation in 1637, the settlers upped the ante by capturing and executing the murderers of the Christian informant, and so began King Philip's War, an infamous campaign that would ultimately seal the fate of Native Americans in the northeastern United States.

The war took place principally near the Rhode Island and Massachusetts border, where Philip's tribe occupied a fort at Mount Hope, which is today part of the Rhode Island community of Bristol. After several residents of the town of Swansea were murdered by the tribe, thousands of colonial troops descended upon Mount Hope. At the same time, the Native Americans managed to completely destroy about a dozen colonial settlements and significant damage another 40—all told roughly half the English villages in New England during the 1670s were damaged. More than 800 colonists and some 3,000 were killed.(To put this in proper perspective, it's worth noting that the Indians lost about 15 percent of their total population, while the colonists lost perhaps 1.5 percent.)

In the end, although a great many colonists were killed in the debacle, the raid was successful for the settlers, and all of the region's Indian tribes were ultimately contained. At the onset of the war, Canonchet and his Narragansetts adopted a neutral stance, but they could stand by no longer after the colonists went after the Wampanoags at Mount Hope. By this time, it had become apparent to even the Narragansetts that the settlers had every intention of completely destroying their way of life. The English struck first against the Narragansetts, fearing that they would join with the Wampanoags anyway. In fact, it was Canonchet who led several of the violent raids against the colonists (destroying many houses in Providence and Warwick) while King Philip spent time in northern New England attempting to unify other tribes to form a greater resistance. Canonchet was captured and executed near Stonington, Connecticut, in 1676. Soon after, King Philip was captured and killed near Mount Hope. The last remaining Narragansett royal, Quaiapen—a sister of Niantic leader Ninigret—died shortly thereafter in a battle at Warwick. By summer 1676, the Narragansetts had been virtually broken and the Wampanoags decimated (Philip's surviving family members were sold into slavery). The end of King Philip's War signified the end of Native American Rhode Island as it had existed prior to European settlement.

effectively, the owners simply looked to import new workers.

Immigrants of the Industrial Age

By the mid-19th century, Ireland was a nation whose residents faced famine, poverty, and blight—they moved to the young United States in search of better opportunities, and they, along with a number of Scottish and English immigrants, became the earliest foreigners to work Rhode Island's factories.

As of around 1850, Rhode Island's population included quite a few foreign-born citizens; about 97 percent of these hailed from Ireland, Scotland, Wales, and England. Assimilation into general society was fairly rapid, and in the general sense, Rhode Island still was culturally an Anglo state. Most of the communities that took in the early Irish and English immigrants were textile hubs, such as Pawtucket and Central Falls.

The next big wave of immigrants, from Québec, first arrived during the Civil War, in part because many Rhode Island residents left to fight. From this point through the end of the 19th century, many thousands of French-Canadians moved to work in mills in northern Rhode Island, the vast majority of them settling in Woonsocket. As of the 1930s, the height of the state's industrialization, about 20 percent of all foreign-born residents were French-Canadian. In the eyes of their employers, they were model workers—willing to work for low wages, eager to please, and suspicious of labor unions or any organizations that required that they assimilate into a larger group. The French-Canadians of Woonsocket and a few other nearby towns would remain a tight-knit and prolific force for many years, and even today, you'll find a strong and vibrant French-Canadian community in Woonsocket. As the mills have largely died away, however, many younger people from this area are moving elsewhere for better opportunities.

Perhaps the most pronounced immigrant group to settle in Rhode Island are the Italians, and Italian culture continues to this day to be highly important to the social fabric of the state. The biggest wave of Italian immigrants followed just as the French-Canadian migration slowed, from about

LIBERIANS IN RHODE ISLAND

One of the more recent immigrant groups of people to make their presence known in the state has been Liberians, an ironic turn of events given that Liberia was established by freed slaves who had returned to Africa following emancipation—and that Providence prospered hugely during colonial times through slave trade. Modern-day Liberia has been ravaged economically and politically by a devastating civil war throughout the 1990s. In 1991 the U.S. State Department drafted a law that granted provisional immigration status to Liberian refugees, and since that time more than 4,000 of the roughly 10,000 persons to receive this status have chosen to settle in Rhode Island.

1900 through 1915, but they arrived in smaller numbers for many years after—the majority from Sicily, Naples, and other southern Italian regions. Many Italians settled in mill communities, and many others in Providence where they took a variety of jobs, from shopkeeping to unskilled labor. But unlike some other immigrant groups, Italians—while still living in tight and insular groups—also assimilated actively into the general community. It wasn't long at all before a number of Italian immigrants and those born to them rose to important positions of influence, both professionally and politically.

Today, Rhode Island's most pronounced Italian-American communities are in Providence, especially the Federal Hill area, which has a Little Italy–style restaurant and shopping scene that's on par with any in the Northeast. There are other Italian enclaves in other parts of Providence, such as the North Side and Silver Lake, some of them dating back to the early 1900s, as also large contingents in East Providence, Barrington, Bristol, and Westerly.

Other immigrant groups that have contributed largely to Rhode Island's eclectic population of today include Poles, who arrived in the greatest numbers between 1895 and 1905 and settled heavily in Central Falls, Providence, Pawtucket, Cranston, Johnston, Warren, and Woonsocket; and Portuguese, especially those from the Azores, Madeiras, and Cape Verde island groups, who were recruited by the state's whaling industry in the 1850s and '60s. As the whaling industry died out, many of the Portuguese settled in fishing communities, while others worked as farmers and both skilled and unskilled laborers. Little Compton, East Providence, Pawtucket, Providence, Newport, and Tiverton all had high numbers of Portuguese immigrants at one time, and you'll still find excellent Portuguese restaurants and bakeries all over the state, especially in and around Providence. In smaller but still significant numbers, Swedes, Germans, Armenians, Greeks, Lithuanians, Finns, and Syrians settled in the Ocean State during the early 20th century.

As the United States began severely to limit immigration during the middle of the 20th century, the flow of Europeans to Rhode Island trickled to nearly a halt. A lack of manufacturing jobs, as mills and factories moved elsewhere, also diminished these numbers. In the second half of the century, a great number of Latin Americans, especially Puerto Ricans, as well as African-Americans and some Asians have moved to Rhode Island, the majority of them settling in Providence and to a lesser extent East Providence, Pawtucket, and Woonsocket. There has also been a gradual resurgence of Portuguese immigrants.

Providence's international population is reflected by its tremendously rich variety of ethnic cuisines—there are very good restaurants in the city specializing in everything from Polish to Sicilian to West African to Portuguese to Indian food. Many shops and galleries also specialize in crafts, artwork, clothing, and other goods from different parts of the world.

Recent Demographic and Population Trends

Outside of the big cities, Rhode Island is a state of predominantly Caucasians, chiefly of English, Irish, and Italian ancestry. Today, about 85 percent of all Rhode Islanders identify themselves as being white; another 5 percent identify as African-American, and 2 percent are Asian.

About 9 percent of Rhode Islanders are of Hispanic or Latino origin.

As of the 2000 census, the state population stood at 1,048,319. The state population has doubled since 1900, but increased only slightly since 1970, when it stood at 950,000. As is true all over the Northeast, cities in Rhode Island have mostly lost population over the past half century, while suburban areas have seen tremendous growth. Providence, for instance, had a population of nearly 250,000 around the time of World War II—that number dropped to just 160,000 in a matter of 25 years. In 1900 Providence was the 12th-largest city in the nation; today it ranks 121st. Between 1990 and 2000, however, Providence saw a nice bounce back up to 173,000. The 8 percent growth is greater than any major city in New England except Stamford, Connecticut, which grew 8.4 percent.

Towns just outside Providence have grown rapidly since the migration from the cities to the suburbs that began after World War II. Since that time, the population has nearly quadrupled in Warwick, doubled in Cranston, tripled in Barrington and Johnston, and increased more than six-fold in North Kingstown.

Rhode Island was one of the few states in the country to lose population during the 1980s, so the recent, significant growth is a welcome indicator that Rhode Island's economic future looks promising. It appears the state economy has bounced back a good bit too, since the recession of the early 1990s, and has for now at least weathered the more recent economic woes. Of course, this is the second most densely populated state in the Union, with just over 1,000 people per square mile (only New Jersey's is higher, and not by much). Of Rhode Island's 39 towns, 18 of them have population densities greater than 1,000 per square mile. So this will probably never be a state that growths at an enormous rate—there simply isn't room to put a lot of new people.

On the other hand, if you're looking for a sparsely settled part of the state, fear not. Block Island, West Greenwich, and Foster all have fewer than 100 persons per square mile. (although Block

Island bursts in the summer with part-time visitors) Little Compton, Exeter, Glocester, Hopkinton, Richmond, and Scituate have plenty of breathing room, too.

RELIGION

Still true to the principles of its founder Roger Williams, Rhode Island continues to embrace religious diversity. Interestingly, the most well-represented religion in the state, Catholicism, is the one that was actually tolerated the least for the longest time. But the huge influx of Irish, Italian, and French-Canadian immigrants between the 1850s and the 1930s, and the fact that Catholics often produced larger families than non-Catholics, has contributed to Rhode Island's—and northern New England's—overwhelmingly Catholic character.

Rhode Island was never a Puritan colony, as Massachusetts was. Where this fact is most apparent is in the village centers of most Rhode Island towns, which are not—as they tend to be in neighboring Connecticut and Massachusetts—anchored by a Congregational church and cemetery. Early Rhode Island towns observed a strong division between Church and State, and so churches also rarely served as meetinghouses for political gatherings. The few towns where this is not the case are in the East Bay and Sakonnet sections of the state, which were originally established as parts of Massachusetts. Little Compton's village center has the look and feel of a traditional New England town that could just as easily be in Vermont or Cape Cod.

Nevertheless, you'll find large numbers of Protestants all over Rhode Island, the majority of them belonging to the Congregational Church (which is true throughout much of New England). Various other Protestant sects and other Christian groups have congregations scattered throughout the state.

Ironically, although Rhode Island is home to the oldest synagogue in the United States, the Ocean State has a relatively small Jewish population. Things might have been different had Newport not been occupied by the British during the American Revolution, as this event forced the majority of the city's thriving and growing Jewish population to flee to other areas. Most Jews were loyal to the colonial cause, in part because many of them were engaged in merchant interests that stood to gain through independence from the Mother Country. Any remaining Jews in Newport who were loyal to the Crown no doubt left following the Revolution along with the most of the city's Tories.

For many years following the American Revolution, Newport's synagogue was hardly used. Over time, the congregation has built back up its numbers, but Jews are still a minority in Newport. Providence and other towns in the state do have Jewish congregations, and Providence—because of its strong ethnic diversity—also has mosques and other places of worship that serve the many non-Christians living in and around the city.

In keeping with Rhode Island's rather socially left-of-center reputation, even though religion plays a vital role in the lives of many or even most residents, the state does not have a markedly conservative religious tone. Fundamentalist or conservative Christians and others appear to be in the minority in this state that routinely favors political candidates who tend to vote progressively on such controversial issues as abortion, school prayer, gay rights, and school vouchers.

On the Road

MUSEUMS AND ATTRACTIONS

Rhode Island has 15 to 20 must-see indoor attractions, ranging from art museums to historic homes—the sorts of places that qualify as destinations unto themselves. Many visitors will build their vacations around one or two of these major sites, especially if a special exhibit is on, or a festival is scheduled. These attractions—The Breakers in Newport, the John Brown House and the Rhode Island School of Design Art Gallery in Providence, the Rhode Island Historical Society Museum of Work and Culture in Woonsocket, the Gilbert Stuart Museum in Saunderstown, to name but a handful—are typically open year-round and often charge a relatively substantial admission ($5 to $10 per person or more), not because they are operated by greedy trustees but more because these kinds of attractions tend to have high operating costs.

At the opposite end of the spectrum are dozens of smaller and often underrated attractions, including local historical societies and

house-museums and museums that focus on fairly specific topics, such as the Whitehall Museum in Middletown (where noted philosopher George Berkeley lived briefly in the 18th century) or the Pettaquamscutt Historical Society in West Kingston. Many of these lower-profile places rank among the most fascinating in Rhode Island, as their existence tends to rely more on the devotion and enthusiasm of their staff than on commercial potential. You're also more likely to receive personal attention at smaller attractions, and less likely to have your enthusiasm dampened by overcrowding, long lines, or a sense that you need to rush around and see every last exhibit to feel that you've gotten your money's worth.

In addition to the headliners and the sleepers, there are dozens

seagull on pier in Wickford

of attractions that fall somewhere between these extremes, and whose hours, admission, and visitor appeal vary greatly depending on any number of factors, from location to subject matter.

Hours and Admission

Hours at many smaller attractions can be very complicated and can change frequently throughout the year. For this reason, the *Moon Handbooks Rhode Island* lists an attraction's hours only when they're fairly straightforward and reliable; in all other cases the hours are listed as either "limited" or "seasonal," which means that you should phone ahead to ensure that the place will be open on the day that interests you.

As a general rule, the very smallest house-museums and historic attractions are open only on weekends (usually afternoons) from about Memorial Day to Columbus Day—especially likely in the colder and more rural inland communities and on Block Island, where the low off-season visitation and high cost of heating the buildings makes regular hours impractical. Except for Block Island, in towns along the coast—where there are more visitors and warmer temperatures—many smaller museums stay open April through November or Christmas, and may open from two to five days a week, late morning to late afternoon.

Don't be put off by limited hours either—in most cases, if you phone a week or two ahead and ask to see one of these smaller attractions by appointment, you'll be encouraged to set up a private visit. Most of these smaller establishments are operated by volunteers and curated through bequests and gifts; they typically charge a nominal entrance fee or perhaps request a donation.

Those attractions with a fairly steady flow of visitors offer the same hours you might expect of most local businesses and shops: 9 A.M. to 5 P.M., from five to seven days a week (Mondays or Tuesdays are the most common days when attractions are closed). In many cases, hours are reduced on Sundays. In summer some of these attractions stay open as late as 6 or 7 P.M., and in winter some of them close at 4 P.M. or don't open until 10 or 11 A.M.

The admission fee given for each attraction in this book is for adults. At the vast majority of the attractions in the state, very young children are admitted free; grade-school kids, college students, and senior citizens very often receive discounts of 25 to 50 percent. Some places also give discounts to holders of AAA cards or military IDs—it's always a good idea to ask about discounts before paying.

Whatever these general rules of thumb, and whatever hours and admission are listed in this book, remember that hours (and other policies) may change with no notice. It's highly advisable that you phone ahead before visiting any attraction in Rhode Island.

For additional information on attractions across the state, get a free copy of the *Rhode Island Travel Guide* from the state tourist board, 401/222-2601 or 800/556-2484. You can find Web links to many museums and attractions at the state Internet address, www.visitrhodeisland.com.

THEATER, DANCE, AND MUSIC

Rhode Island has a surprisingly limited range of performing arts venues, especially given the generally artsy buzz of Providence, which does at least have quite a few clubs and bars presenting live music. That city is the high point in the state when it comes to theater, live music (both popular and classical), and dance, but there are esteemed performance spaces in other communities.

There are excellent theaters in Matunuck, Providence, and Westerly; and acclaimed music festivals or performance halls in Kingston, Newport, and Providence. Providence has easily the greatest reputation for theater of any Rhode Island city; the Providence Performing Arts Center is one of the Northeast's premier performance facilities.

Several universities in the state present a varied and impressive array of musical and dramatic productions to which the public is welcome, including Brown and Providence College, in Providence, University of Rhode Island, in Kingston, and Roger Williams University, in Bristol.

For general information, listings, and calendars pertaining to the arts, contact the **Rhode Island State Council of the Arts,** 83 Park St., 6th floor,

Providence, 02903, 401/222-3880, website: www.risca.state.ri.us.

ARTS AND CRAFTS

While there are no particular artistic or crafts forms specific to just Rhode Island, the state has a long and prolific history of nautical and maritime art, from oil paintings and watercolors of ships and sea scenes to different kinds of sculpture, woodworking, and metalworking relevant to the ocean and seafarers. You'll especially find these kinds of works in Newport, which has many galleries, and the towns of the East Bay and South County. Several towns in Rhode Island have artists' co-ops, including very good ones in Kingston, Little Compton, Westerly, Wakefield, Wickford, and Newport, and on Block Island.

The state's other arts and crafts gallery hub is Providence, which has several of them, in part owing to an arts district established by the city government that supports artists through tax breaks. Providence throws a once-monthly art-gallery hop, during which a free trolley shuttles passengers among the dozen or more arts spaces downtown and on College Hill. Brown University and, of course, the Rhode Island School of Design have a great many artists among their student bodies, and you'll find several galleries near campus. Other downtowns with strong concentrations of arts and crafts galleries include Watch Hill and Bristol.

FESTIVALS

Rhode Island's most enduring festivals seem to involve one or more of the following three things: music, seafood, and the fine arts. As you might expect of a state whose tourism booms in summer and slacks off during the colder months, the most popular festivals occur from late spring through early fall. Some of the state's most famous events and festivals are mentioned below, but you'll find a wealth of additional listings, along with phone numbers and sometimes websites, listed in the Festivals and Events sections of this book's individual chapters.

Winter

Providence is one of a number of U.S. cities that ushers in the New Year with a rollicking **First Night** celebration, which occurs at several locations around the city and includes music, food, and other activities. Providence's Rhode Island Convention Center hosts several big events throughout the winter, including the celebrated **Providence Boat Show** in mid-January and the **Southeastern New England Home Show** in February.

Throughout December, Pawtucket's Slater Park presents a **Winter Wonderland** that includes a miniature winter village. The village of Wickford puts on a colorful **Festival of Lights** throughout December, and Block Island puts on a fun Christmas Stroll and also has one of the most celebrated St. Patrick's Day observations in Rhode Island. Newport has made a valiant effort to keep the city exciting during the colder months by throwing the **12 Weeks of Winter,** which includes a different theme each week from January through the end of March—these include Black Heritage Week, Cultural Arts Week, and a Winter Festival.

Spring

One of the top Little Italy neighborhoods of the Northeast, Providence's Federal Hill has a huge (and delectable) **Feast of St. Joseph** each May along bustling Atwells Avenue; food vendors, games, and music are among the diversions. That same month, Woonsocket kicks off the warming weather with the **Annual Riverfest and Friends of the Blackstone Canoe/Kayak Race**—the 4.2-mile course runs from downtown Woonsocket to Mannville. Later in the month, many locals attend the **Jubilee Franco-American Weekend,** which recognizes that city's proud French-Canadian heritage. Westerly recognizes a different heritage popular in Ocean State with the **Rhode Island Scottish Highland Festival,** while fans of sailing crowd into Newport for the **Bank of Newport Memorial Day Regatta.**

Summer

As the warmest days of the year heat up in Rhode Island, the festival season really starts to boom.

ON THE ROAD

Foodies let their mouths water a bit at the **Best of Rhode Island Party** at Providence's Rhode Island Convention Center; here some 80 recipients of *Rhode Island Monthly* magazine's "best of" food awards serve tasty samples of their goodies. Look to the skies over South County in late July, when the **South County Hot Air Balloon Festival** invites some 20 hot-air balloons to give rides and present demonstrations. August is the time for the **Charlestown Seafood Festival,** a must-do for quahog lovers. Later that month, South County's **Wickford Arts Festival** has been presenting the juried works of leading artists since the 1960s, while the **Block Island Arts Festival** is similarly appreciated out at sea. Ninigret Park in Charlestown puts on the phenomenally popular **Rhythm Roots** festival each August—it's a renowned showcase for blues, zydeco, Cajun, bluegrass, and other boot-stomping tunes.

Newport is party central for acclaimed summer events, including the **Great Chowder Cook-off,** when local kitchens compete for chowder bragging rights; the **Newport Music Festival,** which runs for two weeks with chamber music and other classical performances at Bellevue Avenue mansions; the **Newport Folk Festival,** which has been booking top folk music acts for years, including Bob Dylan and Shawn Colvin; and the **JVC Jazz Festival,** an equally prestigious celebration of music that has drawn the likes of Tony Bennett and New Orleans' Preservation Hall Jazz Band in recent years. If you're feeling patriotic, consider that no town in the United States has a longer-running **Fourth of July celebration** than Bristol—this is a huge event, with some spectators camping along Main Street as early as 4 A.M. to get a good seat.

Fall

Festival-wise, activities don't much slack off until mid-October. September is a hugely popular time to visit Providence, Pawtucket, and other Rhode Island towns to celebrate **Convergence,** a three-week arts and entertainment festival of increasingly huge proportions. This dynamic gathering shows the artwork and performance pieces of photographers, painters, musicians, dancers, filmmakers, and other artists from all over the

world. Events are at different venues throughout the state. At the end of the month, members from about 30 of Providence's ethnic communities gather on the State House lawn for the **Annual Rhode Island Heritage Festival.**

The **North Smithfield Harvest Festival** in Slatersville includes food, live music, hayrides, crafts demonstrations, and llama petting and feeding. Westerly hosts one of Rhode Island's best-attended **Columbus Day** parades, while Block Island throws a convivial **Harvest Festival and Antique Car Parade** in mid-October. Labor Day weekend is Newport's high-season swan song, during which you can watch the **Classic Yacht Regatta and Parade Day,** which features some 100 vintage sailing vessels taking to Narragansett Bay. One last **Harvest Festival** of note is that held in Bristol at Coggeshall Farm Museum.

NIGHTLIFE

When Rhode Islanders get serious about partying, they often head for Boston and sometimes even New York City, but Providence has an exceptionally trendy and hip club scene, from pulsing warehouse discos to big-name live-music clubs. Newport also has its share of hangouts, as does South County, the East Bay, and—in summer—Block Island, although the latter is pretty low-keyed as nightlife goes.

For the latest scoop on live music at local clubs and discos, check out the *Providence Phoenix,* which is free and has a helpful website: www.providencephoenix.com. This paper also lists the state's best dance clubs, from tribal to swing, and also notes poetry readings, open-mic sessions, and every other conceivable sort of nightlife option. After Boston, Providence is New England's top city for gay and lesbian nightlife, with nearly a dozen such clubs.

There's far more to do at night in towns along the coast and along Narragansett Bay than in the western and northwestern interior, or down on Sakonnet Peninsula. In places like Chepachet and Little Compton, the dance scene might consist of jitterbugging to old Glenn Miller records in your bed-and-breakfast's parlor, and the singles scene might center around the local luncheonette or, if you're lucky enough to be near one, coffeehouse. Many coffeehouses, especially in Providence, stage readings, open-mic sessions, and the like.

As a general rule, club cover charges of $2 to as much as $10 are assessed at some of the most popular dance and live-music clubs in Providence and Newport—this is especially the case on weekends, and at places frequented by college students. You're less likely to be charged admission at suburban bars, and also less likely to be charged at clubs without dancing or live music.

The Great Outdoors

For such a small and densely settled state, Rhode Island possesses an exceptionally well-developed variety of outdoor diversions. Among the miles of rivers and streams and countless lakes and ponds, you'll discover numerous boat launches and more than a dozen state parks and forests, not to mention municipal parks and privately administered nonprofit nature preserves and sanctuaries. Hiking and bird-watching are encouraged at most of these facilities, and many of them also welcome mountain-biking, cross-country skiing, boating, fishing, and camping.

While Rhode Island is densely populated and urbanized, residents work hard to preserve the state's rural integrity. One organization behind these efforts is the **Farm and Forest Coalition of** **Northern Rhode Island,** website: www.windsorbrookfarm.com/ffc, which works to educate the public about the virtues of preserving Rhode Island's agrarian ways. One way to learn more about this organization and appreciate the state's natural resources is to drop by the coalition-organized **Foster Farmers Market,** which runs from late June through September at the intersection of U.S. 6 and Route 94.

GENERAL RESOURCES

There are several excellent resources for learning more about the state's wealth of outdoor diversions. A good way to begin is by contacting the **Rhode Island Department of Environmental**

ON THE ROAD

© ANDREW COLLINS

Management (DEM), 401/222-6800. You can write or phone to request brochures on the state parks and on any of the aforementioned activities, or visit its useful website, www.state.ri.us/dem. The DEM also has an ice-safely 24-hour hotline with information on when it's safe to walk or skate on frozen water within the state-park system; 401/222-2632

For the lowdown on each of the state's 21 parks and beaches (including bike paths), contact the **State of Rhode Island Division of Parks and Recreation,** Snake Den State Park, 2321 Hartford Ave., Johnston, 02919, 401/222-2632, website: www.riparks.com. The division's website has a helpful interactive map locating state parks—click on the park in question, and you'll learn its acreage, history, facilities, parking and usage fees, hours, and distinctive features. In 1998 Rhode Island did away with admission fees for all parks; however, the state beaches still assess parking fees, and all parks collect a variety of fees for renting picnic and camping facilities and recreational equipment (boat rentals, playing fields, etc.).

As for beach parking fees, these are collected only from May 1 through September 30; nonresidents pay $12 per car on weekdays and $14 on weekends (those over age 65 pay $6 weekdays and $7 on weekends). Nonesidents' season-parking passes, which allow entry to all state beaches, cost $60 ($30 for senior citizens). Residents pay half for all of the aforementioned parking fees and passes. Rhode Island's state parks and beaches are usually open from dawn to sunset, year-round.

A wonderful way to learn about Rhode Island's outdoors and become involved with keeping them clean and desirable is to join the Rhode Island chapter of the **Nature Conservancy,** 159 Waterman St., Providence, 02906, 401/331-7110, website: www.tnc.org/states/rhodeisland. This highly respected and influential organization was founded in 1951, and the Rhode Island chapter has been instrumental in preserving some 15 of the state's most precious natural settings. You're welcome to visit any of the preserves from an hour before dawn to an hour after sunset, provided that you stay on marked trails, refrain from using bikes or vehicles (and from camping), and observe the conservancy's common-sense regulations concerning litter, bird-nesting sites, and so on.

Conservancy properties are all around the state, but the most noted include several parcels on Block Island, where the organization has worked closely with the Block Island Conservancy, the Block Island Land Trust, and town and state officials to secure roughly one-quarter of the 6,400-acre island, including some 25 miles of magnificent hiking trails. The island's Clay Head Preserve is renowned for its bird-watching, as is Rodman Hollow, a classic example of a maritime shrubland ecosystem. Other favorites include Quicksand Pond and Goosewing Beach Preserve in the Sakonnet town of Little Compton, where once-near-extinct piping plovers now breed; Exeter's densely forested Sodom Trail Preserve, a fall-foliage watcher's delight; and the Headwaters of the Wood River in West Greenwich, where hard-to-find species like the wood turtle and golden heather thrive.

AGRICULTURAL TOURISM

The state that once fostered a largely agrarian economy has relatively little private farmland today—there are about 600 farms statewide (working some 20,000 acres of farmland), and this number will most likely decrease over time as farming profits dwindle and real-estate developers buy up these desirable tracts of mostly cleared land. The farms that remain in business do so largely through the hard work and dedication of a small number of proud owners, some of whom are 10th- or 12th-generation descendants of settlers who long ago tilled the land. Many have increased revenues and the public's interest in their survival by welcoming visitors to partake of many activities.

You might pick your own produce or buy milk and homemade ice cream, cut your own Christmas tree or pick up a quart of fresh maple syrup. Pick-your-own farms make for an especially fun outing, whether alone or with a group. From early spring through late fall, you'll find fresh fruits and vegetables for your kitchen table.

RHODE ISLAND BIKE TRAILS

There are four designated bike trails in Rhode Island: the East Bay Bike Path, which runs 14.5 miles from Providence to Bristol; the Blackstone River Bikeway, which runs 17.1 miles from the Massachusetts border in Woonsocket to Lincoln (it will eventually run clear to Providence and connect with the East Bay Path); the Washington Secondary Bike Path, which runs 13 miles from southwest Providence to West Warwick (and will eventually run a total of 25 miles); and the South County Bike Path, which runs four miles from West Kingston to Peace Dale but will eventually extend a full eight miles to Narragansett. The state has become very proactive in its support of bicyclists, and in addition to the bike trails, many major streets have also been given designated bike lanes. Some of these streets are part of shared-use bike trails.

The **Rhode Island Department of Transportation,** 2 Capitol Hill, Providence, 02903, 401/222-2481, website: www.dot.state.ri.us/webtran/bikeri.html, has a wealth of information on bicycling in Rhode Island. The DOT's website has links to several pdf maps and other pages that show the state's bike trails, give advice and information on cycling in the state, and link to other useful sites. The DOT also has detailed construction updates regarding the extension of bike paths and the construction of bike lanes on more streets.

Certain produce, such as apples, potatoes, honey, carrots, cabbage, and other hearty edibles, are also available, to a limited extent, during the off-season. Regional specialties include apples, fresh and dried herbs, peaches, pears, pumpkins, raspberries, squash, blueberries, strawberries, rhubarb, sweet corn, and tomatoes. For a list of farms (listed by type—apples, berries, roadside stands, Christmas trees, etc., with contact information, addresses, and hours/months), call the **Rhode Island Department of Environmental Management—Division of Agriculture,** 401/222-6800, or download the list from the Web at www.state.ri.us/dem/topics/agricult.htm.

Another way to support local farming while also obtaining wonderful produce, fish and game, jams and jellies, cheeses and yogurts, flowers and shrubs, syrups and honeys, and other specialty-foods is to visit any of the dozen farmers markets held year-round across the state, usually once a week. This activity has grown enormously in popularity in recent years. For information, contact the Division of Agriculture, above, or visit the website, www.state.ri.us/dem/programs/bna-tres/agricult/markets.htm.

The division's website also has pages on the following Rhode Island agricultural topics: honey and maple-syrup producers, Christmas tree farms, roadside stands, certified nurseries, turkey farms, and many others.

BIKING

Most of Rhode Island is excellent biking terrain, generally flat and extremely scenic. The only real drawback is the relatively high amount of auto traffic, even in the state's most scenic areas, and the many narrow and winding roads. Rhode Island drivers also tend to speed around quite a bit, as is the case throughout southern New England.

The **Rhode Island Public Transit Authority,** Bike Coordinator, 401/222-4203, ext. 4042, website: www.ripta.com, produces a free booklet on bicycling titled *A Guide to Cycling in the Ocean State*. Additionally, the RIPTA buses that traverse the state are equipped with bike racks; the rack on the front of each bus holds up to two bicycles. There is no fee, beyond the standard bus fare, for using this service. You can download the guide from the DOT website (above) as a pdf file, or email or call for a print copy.

Another useful resource is *Short Bike Rides in Rhode Island,* published by Globe Pequot Press, 888/249-7586.

BIRD-WATCHING

From yuppies to senior citizens, families to singles, every kind of Rhode Islander seems to be taking up bird-watching these days, especially those folks who live around the coastal regions. The popularity makes a lot of sense, for as hobbies go, this is one of the least expensive and most educational. Best of all, birds are abundant in the state year-round, though of course the individual species you're likely to see depends on the season.

More than 400 species of birds live throughout Rhode Island. Much of the best birding is along the coast, where you'll see myriad waterfowl year-round and magnificent blue heron from October through April. Peregrine falcons and hawks regularly fly about marshes and estuaries, and in August and September you'll see warblers and thrushes. A huge population of sparrows descends on the coastal points during the fall. Owls are not easy to find, but they do live around the state.

For further information on specific species that live in Rhode Island, visit the website www.nenature.com/birds.htm, which has detailed information on and photos of hundreds of birds common to Rhode Island and the rest of the Northeast.

The Rhode Island chapter of the **Audubon Society,** 12 Sanderson Rd., Smithfield, 401/949-5454, website: www.asri.org, is also a useful resource. The society's website has helpful links for birders, and with the Rhode Island Ornithological Club, the society produces a bimonthly publication called *Field Notes of Rhode Island Birds* ($10 per year). At the society's headquarters in Smithfield, the **Hathaway Library** houses a vast collection of books, publications, videos, and software related to birding in general and in Rhode Island. You can also pick up books, tapes, and other birding materials at the two Audubon Society gift shops in the state, one at the headquarters and the other at the Audubon Environmental Education Center, 1401 Hope St., Bristol, 401/245-7500.

The society owns or oversees some 9,000 acres of preserves throughout Rhode Island, several of them open to the public and excellent for bird-watching. **Kimball Wildlife Sanctuary,** off U.S. 1 adjacent to Burlingame State Park, Charlestown, is a 29-acre property with a 1.5-mile hiking trail through fields and forests. Another birding Valhalla is the **Emilie Ruecker Wildlife Refuge,** Seapowet Ave., Tiverton, just off Route 77, overlooking the Sakonnet River. The salt marshes here are a favorite spot for ob-serving migrating birds during the fall and spring; there are blinds set up for watching and photographing the wildlife.

Another excellent spot is the **Crandall Swamp Preserve,** Boy Scout Dr., off U.S. 3, Westerly, a 150-acre site administered by the Nature Conservancy. It's the northernmost section of the 2,200-acre Crandall Swamp wetlands, parts of which were one of Westerly's famous granite quarries for many years. These days a network of trails cuts through the preserve, which is bisected by the Pawcatuck River (there's a canoe launch). Commonly sighted birds include turkey vultures and osprey. Another Nature Conservancy preserve that's ideal for bird-watching is the **Headwaters of the Queen's River,** Henry Bowman Rd., reached via New London Turnpike and Rte. 102, a remote woodland that connects Fisherville Brook Refuge (owned by the Rhode Island Audubon Society) to the state-administered Big River Management Area. Walking along trails here you're apt to see many kinds of forest interior birds, including hawks. Contact the Rhode Island chapter of the **Nature Conservancy,** 159 Waterman St., Providence, 401/331-7110, website: http://nature.org/wherewework/northamerica/states/rhodeisland, for directions to and descriptions of these and seven other pristine preserves around Rhode Island.

On Block Island, the Nature Conservancy works in partnership with several local organizations to preserve a huge portion of the island from ever being developed—these preserves are among the state's most exceptional venues for bird-watching.

CAMPING

There are two basic forms of camping in Rhode Island, the more primitive tent-and-backpack activity that's offered at both commercial grounds as well as at the state-operated Fisherman's Memorial State Park Campground and George Washington Management Area and Ninigret Conservation Area, and the somewhat cushier RV camping that's offered mostly at commercial sites but also at the state parks. There's also tent camping at three municipal facilities: **Fort**

RHODE ISLAND CAMPGROUNDS

Burlingame State Park, follow signs from Burlingame Picnic Area exit from U.S. 1, Charlestown, 401/322-7337 (campground information) or 401/322-8910 (park information).

Charlestown Breachway, follow signs from Charleston Breachway exit from U.S. 1, Charlestown, 401/364-7000.

Fisherman's Memorial State Park Campground, 1011 Point Judith Rd. (Rte. 108), Narragansett, 401/789-8374.

Fort Getty Recreation Area, Fort Getty Rd., Jamestown, 401/423-7211.

George Washington Management Area, 2185 Putnam Pike (U.S. 44), West Gloucester, 401/568-2248 or 401/568-2013.

Melville Ponds Campground, 181 Bradford Ave., Portsmouth, 401/849-8212.

Middletown Campground, 474 Sachuest Rd., Middletown, 401/846-6273.

Ninigret Conservation Area, E. Beach Rd., Charlestown 401/322-0450.

Getty Recreation Area, Melville Ponds Campground, and **Middletown Campground.**

The charge for camping sites at most state parks is $8 per night for residents, $12 for nonresidents; it's $14 per night for residents, $20 for nonresidents at Fishermen's Memorial. There are additional fees for sites with water, electrical, and sewer hookups, and for use of septic dump stations. Some parks have camping cabins available, too. For details on which state parks have camping and accept reservations, contact the **Rhode Island Department of Environmental Management,** Attn: Parks and Recreation, 2321 Hartford Ave., Johnston, 02919, 401/222-2632, www.riparks.com.

There are private commercial campgrounds throughout the state, most of them in the rural western and northwestern section of the state. You can obtain a directory that lists a dozen of these facilities by contacting the **Ocean State Campground Owners Association, Inc.,** c/o Oak Embers Campground, 219 Escoheag Hill Rd., West Greenwich, 02817, 401/397-4042, www.ricampgrounds.com.

FISHING AND HUNTING

Among the state's many great fishing holes and swift rivers, the Wood, Pawcatuck, Moosup, and Falls Rivers are among the best sources of trout-fishing. There are also a number of stocked ponds throughout the state designated only for kids under 15. Stocked trout ponds are closed for fishing from March 1 through the second Saturday in April, which marks the beginning of trout-fishing season. For a complete list of trout-stocked ponds and rivers in Rhode Island, and for other details about fishing in the Ocean State, contact the **Division of Fish & Wildlife,** 4808 Tower Hill Rd., Wakefield, 401/789-3094, website: www.state.ri.us/dem/programs/bnatres/fishwild/index.htm. The website also has links to all state fishing and hunting regulations, lists legal minimum sizes and possession rules, provides information on obtaining licenses, lists all of the state's fresh- and saltwater boat launches (and regulations concerning these launches), and provides tidal charts, lengths of fishing seasons, and scads of additional information.

Other common freshwater catches (some tasty and some usually thrown back) include banded sunfish, black crappie, bluegills, smallmouth and largemouth bass, and yellow perch. Largemouth bass and certain varieties of trout may be found also in brackish waters, and some species of anadromous fish (those that spawn in fresh water but live most of their lives in salt water) can be found here, notably shad and herring, which were recently reintroduced to the Blackstone River, where they thrived before mills and dams rendered these waters inhospitable in the mid-19th century.

Along Rhode Island's shoreline, bluefish, sturgeon, striped bass, and cod are popular game fish, as are a variety of shellfish, including mussels, oysters, lobsters, crabs, and Rhode Island's most famous saltwater treasure, the quahog clam, which are found up and down the Eastern Seaboard but are especially prevalent in the Ocean State. The quahog (pronounced "co-hog" in these parts but "kwah-hog" in some other places), also known as a steamer, is a hard-shelled, vaguely round clam that can be found in many sizes; the little ones are typically called cherrystones, the midsize variety are littlenecks, and the largest ones are called—and used to make—chowders (they're also used in clam cakes, fritters, and other delicacies). For a chance to fish for these and New England's many deep-sea species—such as haddock, black sea bass, bonito, mackerel, bluefin tuna, and swordfish—consider booking a trip on any of the state's many private fishing charter boats.

Recreational saltwater fishing does not require a license except for shellfishing ($200 for the season or $11 for 14 days), and then only for nonresidents—just be sure to observe all rules on minimum size limits. Recreational lobstering is permitted only for Rhode Island residents (and then only after buying $40 a license). Freshwater (and anadromous) fishing, if you're age 15 or older, requires a seasonal license, which costs $9.50 for residents ($31 out-of-state). Or, for just $16, out-of-state visitors can buy a three-day fishing license. These may be obtained at town halls and a number of bait-and-tackle shops. Fishing licenses expire on the last day of February each year, regardless of when purchased. If you're fishing for trout, salmon, or charr—or fishing in a catch-and-release or fly-fishing only area, you must purchase a trout conservation stamp along with your license; the cost is $5.50.

GOLFING

Rhode Island's number and variety of courses—from winding, relatively flat, and rather tight links to lush, narrow, and hilly woodland layouts—has increased rapidly over the years, especially in South County, which has become Rhode Island's golfing capital.

If you live or play regularly in Rhode Island, it makes sense to join the **Rhode Island Golf Association,** 1 Button Hole Dr., Suite 2, Providence, 401/272-1350, website: www.rigalinks.org. The association's website lists some 40 member clubs, upcoming local tournaments, and many additional resources.

For visitors just wanting to learn a bit about the ins and outs of the state's roughly 25 public or semi-private courses, **Rhode Island's Online Golf Source,** website: www.rigolf.com, is an outstanding resource containing detailed information on course and driving-range fees, hours, statistics, difficulty, terrain, and layout—there's even a link to miniature golf courses.

HIKING

Rhode Island has hundreds of miles of trails for hiking and biking, and you don't have to travel to the most remote reaches to find the most rugged and pristine scenery. Wonderful parks and trails are within a 10-minute drive of every city and town in Rhode Island.

Probably the greatest hiking asset in Rhode Island is the magnificent **North-South Trail,** which twists and turns for some 72 miles through eight rural towns in the western third of the state, beginning at the Massachusetts border and terminating down by the ocean in Charlestown. The website, http://outdoors.html planet.com/nst/nst_map00.htm, has a very nice detailed map of the trail as it runs through the state. You can also contact the Warwick Land Trust, 401/781-8117, for maps and information on events along the trail.

Other popular venues for hiking include Block Island, which has more than 25 miles of walking and hiking trails across the island; you can contact the Nature Conservancy office on Block Island, 401/466-2129, to order a trail guide (the cost is $9.99, plus shipping).

TAKING TO THE WATER

Rhode Island loves boating, so much that the purchase of boats (along with any equipment bought the same day) is tax-free. There are aquatic outfitters and tour providers throughout the state, with the most popular river sports (such as canoeing and kayaking) along the Wood River, the Seekonk River, sections of Narragansett Bay, and many of the salt ponds in South County. For information on boating safety and regulations throughout Rhode Island, visit the website www.boatsafe.com/Rhode_Island.

Contact the **Rhode Island Party and Charter Boat Association,** Box 3198, Narragansett, 02882, 401/737-5812, website: www.rifishing.com/charter.htm, for a full list of private fishing, sightseeing, and sailing charter boats throughout the state. Another good website, both for fishing and boating, is **Ocean State Angler,** www.oceanstateangler.com, which lists marinas, charters, bait-and-tackle shops, marine retail and rental operations, and countless additional resources for enjoying your time on Rhode Island's waters.

Many of the state's lakes and ponds allow boating, and there are marinas and launches strung along the shore, from Westerly to Little Compton. For a complete list of public boat launches, contact the **Rhode Island Depart-** ment of **Environmental Management (DEM),** 401/222-6800, or visit the following website, www.state.ri.us/dem/programs/bnatres/fish-wild/boatlnch.htm. For tidal charts, licensing information, and tips and information on Rhode Island boating safety, call the DEM or visit www.state.ri.us/dem/topics/boating.htm.

Kayaking is a major pastime in Rhode Island, with its hundreds of miles of shoreline, much of it along relatively calm bays, inlets, and rivers. There are kayak rentals in several places around the state, including **Ocean State Scuba,** 79 N. Main Rd., Jamestown, 401/423-1662, website: www.scuyak.com; **Narrow River Kayak,** 95 Middlebridge Rd., Narragansett, 401/789-0334; and **URE Outfitters,** 1009 Main St., Hope Valley, 401/539-4050. The **Kayak Centre,** with three South County locations—Brown and Phillips Streets, Wickford, 401/295-4400; 562 Charlestown Beach Rd., Charlestown, 401/364-8000; 93 Watch Hill Rd., Watch Hill, 401/348-2800—also 888/SEA-KAYAK, website: www.kayakcentre.com, rents (and sells) kayaks and also offers tours, lessons, and advice.

Accommodations

Most of Rhode Island has a healthy variety of lodging options, although some regions tend more toward smaller inns and bed-and-breakfasts, and others serve up chain motels and hotels. As you might expect, the most densely populated areas—along the interstates, in cities, and near industrial and corporate campuses—favor the larger properties. Only in the nontouristy western and northern interior will you find a dearth of accommodations, but hotel-rich greater Providence, Newport, and South County are close enough to virtually every point in Rhode Island to be excellent bases for any tour of the state.

Many of the smaller inns and B&Bs in Rhode Island close either seasonally or at will, according to the needs or the whims of their owners. It's always a good idea to book your accommodations as far ahead as possible, and it's imperative that you do so when planning a stay at an inn or B&B.

PRICE CATEGORIES

Accommodations in this book are grouped according to the following price categories: Under $50, $50–100, $100–150, $150–250, and over $250. These ranges are based on the cost of an establishment's standard double-occupancy room, during high season. Expect to pay the higher rate during holidays or a few popular weekends (i.e., weekends in October during peak foliage), for suites or rooms that sleep more than two, and for rooms with amenities such as fireplaces, hot tubs, and decks. Expect to pay less (often as much as 50 percent less) off-season (e.g., winter along the shore), during the week at leisure-oriented country inns and B&Bs, on weekends for urban hotels and motels, and for rooms with fewer amenities (shared baths, twin beds, brick-wall views, no TVs, etc.).

ON THE ROAD

© ANDREW COLLINS

Shelter Harbor Inn

WHAT IT WILL COST

Accommodation rates are based on supply and demand, and they are usually not set in stone. The price ranges in this book reflect the highest standard double-occupancy rates, during the most expensive times, so don't be put off if you see a hotel listed in the $150–250 range when you're seeking something under $100 nightly. There are hotels in Rhode Island whose rates in-season hover around $200 nightly but drop to as low as $70 during slow times—it's always a good idea to phone ahead or visit a property's website and ask about special packages and seasonal, weekday, or weekend discounts. You are more likely to see dramatic rate swings at upscale properties than you will at low-end or moderate ones.

No matter what it says in a property's brochure, remember that nothing at your hotel—breakfast, a pool, an exercise room, turn-down service, local phone calls—is truly free. These extras may be included in the rate, but this means that rates at properties with oodles of perks, amenities, and facilities are going to be higher than rates at properties without them. These extras are all well and good provided that you're really going to take advantage of them, but think seriously about book-ing a room at a country inn that's renowned for its lavish full breakfasts or an upscale hotel whose business and conference facilities are extensive. Do you eat breakfast? Are you in town on business?

At properties that rely principally on leisure travelers, rates are nearly always seasonal and always lower on weekdays than on weekends. This category includes bed-and-breakfasts, country inns, and a small number of larger hotels and motels in the more tourism-dependent sections of the state, such as Newport and South County. In much of the state, rates tend to be highest from late spring (anywhere from Easter to Memorial Day) until late October (following the peak foliage periods). The rest of the year you can sometimes find price breaks of anywhere from 30 to 50 percent, although the most popular establishments (particularly around Providence) often stay busy year-round and so don't necessarily reduce their rates much. Also, some hotels keep their rates up until January, as tourism (at least on weekends) can remain fairly strong through the Christmas holidays.

In the most desirable regions during peak season it's next to impossible to get a weekend room at the last minute—book as early as possible (at least two weeks ahead) and expect to find two- to three-night minimums in shore locations in summer. Typically, once you make a reservation, whether through a reservations service or directly through an inn, you'll be required to leave as much as a 50 percent deposit, the refund of which is contingent upon the property being able to rebook your room—at the least you'll be assessed a significant "processing" fee. Note the rules of deposit and payment carefully (not all accept credit cards, either) when placing your reservation (especially when doing so through orbitz.com, expedia.com, or other Web booking sites), and don't expect anybody to bend on these policies once you've booked your room. Remember, the laws of accommodations depend entirely upon supply and demand.

At properties that rely principally on business travelers, rates are the least affected by the season and the most influenced by the day of the week: On weekdays, when corporate travelers descend on the place, rates are at their highest, but on weekends they drop anywhere from 30 to 70 percent. This rule holds most true in Greater Providence, but with relatively few accommodations in downtown Providence and a strong mix of leisure and business travelers there, rates often don't vary much no matter what day of the week.

CHOOSING AN ACCOMMODATION

As the old real estate cliché goes, location is everything—even if you're just staying the night. Once you've established what you're willing to spend and what level of accommodation will suit you, think about where you plan to spend most of your visit. Are you looking to hide away with your mate in a romantic suite, rarely emerging until check-out? Or will you be spending as little time as possible in your room or even in the town where you're staying? Does a view matter? Being with walking distance of shops and restaurants?

One major caveat before relying heavily on state- or regionally produced travel planners and brochures: The organizations that produce these publications are funded by a hotel tax that is added onto your room rate. As long as a lodging pays this tax, it is entitled to be included in any literature published by the state and local tourist boards. This means that these brochures and publications cannot refuse a listing to even the seediest, dreariest, and most horrible establishment.

What does this mean in practice? Having anonymously inspected a great number of the properties listed in Rhode Island travel planners, I can say that 10 to 20 percent of them are highly suspect, and several of them make the hotel in *The Shining* look like a Ritz-Carlton. You would think that some sort of ratings system would be in place to keep properties that are truly unsanitary, substandard, or unsafe from being recommended unconditionally by organizations aiming to promote tourism, but such are the mysterious ways of governmental bureaucracies.

This is not to suggest that establishments omitted from this book are substandard—there are simply too many hotels to review in this guide, and thus what you'll find is a representation of the most appealing properties in the state, in every price category. In areas with an unusually high number of similar chain motels, I've selected those representing the greatest value, which is figured roughly by considering the rates, the location, the facilities, and the level of cleanliness and staff professionalism I encountered. A change in management can raise or lower the quality of a property almost overnight, but it's safe to say that at press time I'd have recommended every single property in this book to my mother (and that's saying a lot).

B&Bs and Country Inns

To get a real feel for the area you're visiting, consider choosing a B&B or country inn over the typical cookie-cutter chain property. It's sometimes believed that chains offer better rates, more consistent standards, better amenities for business travelers, and greater anonymity, but this is far from always—or even often—the case. Some smaller B&Bs, especially those that offer shared baths, have among the least-expensive rooms in Rhode Island (if fewer than three rooms, they're exempt from the state's 6 percent hotel tax), and most of them have higher-quality furnishings and amenities than similarly priced chains.

Furthermore, staying at a small historic property need not involve socializing with either your hosts or fellow guests, or placing phone calls and sending faxes from a common area. An increasing number of higher-end inns (this is less true of B&Bs) have recognized the needs of business travelers and begun installing in-room direct-dial phones, data ports, cable TVs, VCRs, and even high-speed Internet access. If privacy is important to you, ask if any of the rooms have separate outdoor entrances. You might be surprised how many places do, often in carriage houses or outbuildings set away from the main house.

All of this is not to suggest that warm and welcoming B&Bs and country inns are not plentiful—the kinds of places where guests compare notes on their finest antiquing conquests before a roaring evening fire, or conspire together to attack the area's most challenging hiking trails over a four-course full breakfast. The most successful innkeepers have learned to leave alone the independent travelers but gently direct the ones seeking local advice and connections, like hard-to-score dinner reservations and directions to secret fishing holes that you'll never find in brochures or even in this book. If it's your wish, a B&B can offer both camaraderie and a personal concierge—and these perks come with no extra charges.

In the broadest sense, B&Bs are smaller than country inns. At B&Bs there tend to be fewer than 10 rooms (sometimes only one or two), the owners often live on the premises, breakfasts tend to be intimate and social, common areas small and homey, and facilities and amenities minimal (rarely are there phones or TVs in guest rooms, or is there a restaurant or exercise room). At inns you may find anywhere from several to 100 rooms, a full staff of employees (the owners often live off-property), breakfasts served in dining rooms and often at your own private table, spacious and more formal common areas, and an array of facilities and amenities.

More often than not, breakfast at a country inn is Continental and breakfast at a B&B is full (with a hot entrée and often three or four courses). It's less of a rule, but country inns typically charge more than B&Bs and, although they're often less personable and quirky, they maintain a

higher standard of luxury and offer a greater degree of privacy. These are general differences, and in many cases the lines between country inns and B&Bs blur considerably. Regardless of these distinctions, inns and B&Bs share many traits: usually they are historic or designed in a historic style, rooms typically vary in layout and are decorated individually in period style, and settings are often rural or scenic.

The smallest variety of B&B is generally not covered individually in this book, because these places are very often operated discreetly or part-time (many are not licensed nor seek the publicity of guidebook coverage) and are best booked by contacting a B&B reservations service. The smallest B&Bs are closer to one- or two-room private homestays, where you may find yourself interacting closely with your hosts. It's important that you explain your privacy preferences when speaking with reservations services. These booking services cover a variety of properties, and some even represent larger hotels.

Hotels and Motels

The majority of the state's hotels and motels are perfectly nice, and a few are downright homey and charming. However, most of the unacceptable accommodations in Rhode Island are lower-end chain motels, many of them located off interstate or busy roads. There are exceptions, of course, as there are some truly awful B&Bs out there and some surprisingly unkempt and poorly run moderate to upscale hotels. You can increase your odds of picking a good property by keeping a few things in mind:

Look for *recent* stickers in lobby windows that indicate the hotel has been approved by AAA or the Mobil guides and really check credentials of motels on busy roads within earshot of a major highway (they're not only apt to be noisy, but they're more likely to be rendezvous points for any number of illicit activities). Motels that rent rooms by the hour are usually not very savory.

At any property with which you're unfamiliar, ask to see the room before you check in, and if the front desk refuses or even hesitates, you can safely assume they're harboring secrets that shall be revealed to you only after you have left a credit card imprint (like the postage stamp–size guest towels are frayed and threadbare, and the air-conditioner is broken). If you see plants or personal effects on the sills of guest room windows, or rusty cars in the parking lot, you have no doubt stumbled upon a residential hotel with facilities that are probably not up to the expectations of most travelers (this may sound like a joke, but a few of these places are listed in the brochures produced by tourist boards).

A few chains are consistently reputable or have especially good products in Rhode Island, including most of the high-end ones. Of economical and moderately priced chains, best bets include Comfort Inn, Courtyard by Marriott, Four Points, Hampton Inn, Holiday Inn Express, Motel 6 (the best bare-bones chain in the state), and Quality Inn. Independently operated budget motels are inherently no better or worse than chain properties—don't rule them out just because you've never heard of them. But do check them out carefully ahead of time.

Food

Like so much of America, Rhode Island's culinary scene has been blessed with an unparalleled wave of inventiveness and sophistication over the past decade or so. Eating out, in diners and pizza parlors or in upscale bistros and trattorias, yields pleasurable results across the state, with the greatest concentration of high-caliber eateries found in Providence and Newport. South County, Warwick, Cranston, and the East Bay are also rife with memorable dining options.

The variety and high standards that characterize the state's dining scene can be traced to several factors. First, the aforementioned regions of Rhode Island have large contingents of upper middle class and even wealthy residents with the discretionary income to dine out regularly. It also helps that Rhode Island lies between two of the nation's hot spots for fine dining, Boston and New York City. Rhode Island feels the influences of both of these world-class cooking capitals, yet it's refreshingly out of the hustle and bustle of either place.

Newport is the swankest of Rhode Island cities when it comes to dining, with a number of

FOODS OF THE OCEAN STATE

Rhode Island may be tiny, but the state has a big appetite, and it claims more regional culinary specialties than many states vastly larger. Most people know about quahogs, the local clam that's featured in just about everything but ice cream—from pies and fritters to chowders and stews; you can also try stuffies, which are stuffed quahogs.

Jonnycakes or johnnycakes—debates about the correct spelling date almost as far back as the delicacies themselves—have a loyal following among fans of hearty breakfast fare. The cornmeal cakes are cooked on a griddle and carry considerably more character and flavor than their wheat-based cousins, pancakes. The stone-ground cornmeal imparts a faintly earthy, sweet flavor. Jonnycakes are typically served silver-dollar size, but some cooks prefer to make larger cakes. There are adherents of thick and eggy cakes, which have plenty of heft, while others favor thin crepe-style jonnycakes. They're generally served with maple syrup, but some people prefer them with honey, powdered sugar, fresh fruit, or virtually any other topping you might also enjoy on traditional pancakes.

Coffee cabinets, Awful-Awfuls, coffee milks, or frappes—whatever you call these milk drinks flavored with coffee syrup and sometimes ice cream, they're a local favorite at ice-cream stands and short-order restaurants dating back to the 1920s. The local ice cream shop–cum–luncheonette chain, Newport Creamery, makes very good ones, but just about every mom-and-pop dairy store in the state makes them, usually with Autocrat brand coffee syrup. The simple version is just the consistency of chocolate milk, but with the addition of ice cream, these elixirs become rich and creamy milkshakes. In 1993, the state legislature voted to declare the coffee milk Rhode Island's official state drink.

If you're seeking a lighter and more refreshing alternative to a coffee cabinet, consider another of the state's most popular drinks, a Del's Frozen Lemonade. Supposedly, this favorite summertime thirst quencher was developed in Naples, Italy, in the mid-19th century, but it was a Rhode Islander named Angelo Delucia (hence the name Del's) who developed the local product. He opened his first lemonade stand in Cranston in the late 1940s, and now there are nearly three dozen franchises around the state.

Sometimes it's hard to tell from the name that a certain dish is unique to Rhode Island. Take New York System Wieners, for example, which are sold all around the state but especially in urban areas like Providence, Pawtucket, and

high-end, acclaimed restaurants—it's easy to spend $20 or more per entrée even at seemingly ordinary restaurants. Because Block Island is almost exclusively seasonal, it too tends to be pricey, even for basic seafood, burgers, and pub fare. On the plus side, Block Island and Newport have both changed for the better in terms of dining lately, with a mix of new restaurants and older ones receiving ambitious menu makeovers.

Providence is unquestionably Rhode Island's dining capital, and really the second-best restaurant city in New England, after Boston. Prices have risen steadily here, but you can still eat very well here without spending oodles of cash. Elsewhere in the state, beyond the immediate Providence suburbs, the East Bay, and parts of South County, dining options are limited but prices are also fairly low.

And what if you've got kids in tow, or you've been out hiking or beachcombing all day and are neither dressed for nor especially inclined toward dinner at a big-name restaurant? First, remember that all but a handful of even the best restaurants in the state welcome casual attire, put up with if not wholly accept children, and eschew fanfare and formality. Next, consider the plethora of outstanding cheap and casual eateries set around the state.

Rhode Island is where America's love affair with diners first developed more than a century ago, and the state still has a bevy of them, some open 24 hours. The largest ones—with the streaks of neon tubing and the shimmering stainless-steel facades—are sometimes Greek-owned and so feature a few Hellenic specialties plus just about every variety of sandwich, breaded fish, omelet,

Woonsocket. These are named New York Wieners in reference to that Queens bastion of hot dog making, Coney Island. Luncheonettes and cafés in Rhode Island dress their hot dogs with something called hamburg sauce (a seasoned blend of finely ground hamburger meat), along with onions, celery salt, chili sauce, and mustard (for the full effect, order your wiener "all the way"). The dogs aren't large and are first steamed and then stuffed inside fluffy little whitebread buns that have also been lightly steamed.

Rhode Island–style clam chowder (or chowdah, with the local accent) differs from New England chowder (which has heavy or light cream) and Manhattan clam chowder (which has a tomato-based broth). Here the chowder has a clear broth and either no cream or just a touch of it. Clam juice is the main component of the broth, but some places use other kinds of fish or even chicken stocks. Some Rhode Island chowder recipes do call for milk or cream, and at some restaurants, your clear chowder will come with a small side of warm milk, which you're free to mix in for thickness (although purists never do). You can also expect to find chopped potatoes, diced celery, onions, and some of the other seasonings you'd find in a typical New England chowder.

To make stuffies, you take big and juicy quahog clams and stuff these shells with a mix of ground, baked, or steamed clams, along with sautéed onions, hamburger rolls or other day-old bread, bell peppers, garlic, cayenne pepper or Tabasco sauce, parsley, saffron, and other spices. Once the quahogs are stuffed, they're baked for 10 or 15 minutes. It's a rather rich dish.

Clam cakes (or clam fritters) are not too unlike their counterpart, crab cakes, but more with the look and consistency of Southern hushpuppies—they consist of chopped clams rolled into small "cakes" with a batter of beaten eggs, milk, flour (the best are made with stone-ground cornmeal, the way jonnycakes are), baking powder, and salt and pepper; these are then deep-fried to a golden brown.

The traditional shore dinner is less a Rhode Island–specific thing than it is a regional New England favorite. These filling smorgasbords consist of clam chowder, steamers (littleneck clams, which are quite a bit smaller than quahogs), clam cakes (a twist that's unique to the state), chorizo or other baked and smoked sausages, corn on the cob, lobster, watermelon, and Indian pudding (an acquired taste, this steamed pudding consists of cornmeal and molasses).

and blue plate special (e.g., liver and onions, chicken parmigiana, pork chops with apple sauce) known to humanity, plus the requisite Greek salads, side plates piled high with french fries or hash browns, "dieter's delights" consisting of cottage cheese and canned peaches or pears, and glimmering, shimmering glass bowls of Jell-O in both expected and disturbing day-glo colors.

Rhode Island is not unlike other parts of New England when it comes to inexpensive local staples: the Americanized order-by-number Chinese restaurant, the sports bar or English-style pub with TGIF-style munchies and bar snacks, the family-run red-sauce Italian restaurant with predictable but ultimately satisfying pasta and veal dishes, and the venerable Colonial tavern complete with creaky wide-plank floors, dark-wood tables and bentwood chairs, Revolutionary War

kitsch, and a long list of Old Yankee favorites: pot roast, broiled haddock, clam chowder, filet mignon, and peach cobbler à la mode. These sorts of mid-priced independent restaurants are widespread if not necessarily of a higher quality than the better chain eateries lining the state's busiest roads.

Seafood is an obvious regional strength. There are dozens of fish eateries along the coast, many with "in the rough" seating either on or near the water, and a surprising plethora of fine seafood restaurants inland. Rhode Island has a number of specialties, including the state's delicious quahog clams, which star in Rhode Island–style (clear broth) clam chowder, stuffies (stuffed quahogs), clam cakes, and clam fritters.

The state of ethnic cooking in Rhode Island varies regionally. For the most part, restaurants offering Asian cuisine are quite good if a

THE BIRTH OF THE DINER

The simple, humble diner—often with a few counter seats and vinyl or wooden booths and the dimensions of a small railroad car—is a source of great adulation in many parts of the country, perhaps nowhere more so than in Rhode Island. A museum on diners will even be installed the new Heritage Harbor Museum complex in Providence in 2004.

The ancestor to today's modern, and often garish, diners was a simple wagon that a young entrepreneur named Walter Scott used to push along Westminster Street in downtown Providence in 1872. He sold nickel sandwiches and a few other basic foods to an all-night trade of mostly shipping and factory workers. The cart appeared each evening at sunset and was removed by the time the sun rose the following morning. Though they served food only during the night, people started calling them lunch wagons, because sandwiches and other light, lunch-like fare was typically served.

About 10 years later, just up the Blackstone River in the similarly industrial city of Worcester, Massachusetts, a man named Sam Jones improved upon Scott's mobile culinary triumph by developing a true eat-in diner, in which patrons could actually grab a stool at the counter and seek shelter from the elements along with good coffee and camaraderie. This concept flourished and spread like wildfire, so that soon there were hundreds of lunch wagons in just about every city in the Northeast.

The concept changed dramatically one last time—still in the early 1900s—as a way of circumventing laws that had been passed making it illegal for lunch wagons to remain on many city streets during daylight hours. This prompted some smart owners to start renting a bit of land and plopping their portable wagons down there, where in effect they became restaurants.

Many of these early diners were set inside old horse-drawn trolleys and streetcars that had been put to pasture with the advent of electric power. Over time, factories began to produce these small, usually rectangular diners. Many came to be called railroad diners not because they were actually fashioned out of discarded railway cars but because they were built to dimensions that would make it possible for factories to ship them on flat railroad cars.

With the age of Art Deco, diners increasing-

bit tepid when it comes to seasoning, but in Providence you'll find several Indian, Thai, Japanese, and Chinese restaurants that could hold their own anywhere on the Eastern Seaboard. For a while, you couldn't get Yankees to sample exotic or spicy food unless you toned down the more biting ingredients and cooked food as quickly and efficiently as possible—this sensibility encouraged chefs to pan-fry and deep-fry many dishes that would never have been drowned in hot oil if prepared in their native lands. But Providence is a youthful city with adventuresome diners, and authentic ethnic restaurants have done well here and have gradually started opening in the nearby suburbs, like Cranston and Warwick. For a major dining hub, Newport still lags well behind Providence when it comes to ethnic dining, but a handful of good options have opened since the late 1990s.

Many contemporary menus offer dishes with a Latin American or Mexican bent, but it's difficult to find authentic regional Mexican or Southwestern fare in Rhode Island.

In the end, while many of the ethnic eateries in the state fall short in terms of authenticity and subtlety of seasoning, they nevertheless offer food that is reasonably tasty and ingredients that are fairly fresh. If you can forget that the food you're eating at the vast majority of the state's "cantinas" is supposed to be Mexican, you may actually enjoy your meal—if this kind of food is no better than your average all-American cheeseburger or fried chicken, it's really no worse either.

Restaurant Prices

Following the phone number of most restaurants included in this book, the average range of the cost of dinner entrées has been provided

ly came to be spruced up with elements of that period, from stainless-steel facades and interiors to bits of neon to even more elaborate finials and ornaments. During America's diner heyday, these studies in Formica and vinyl truly excelled. They also changed in many cases to provide food into the late morning and even lunch hours. In fact, the idea that 24-hour diners opened as a way to feed late-night workers and eaters is not quite right; in fact, 24-hour diners opened as a way to accommodate daytime workers and eaters.

A number of factors helped to end the proliferation of diners by the 1960s, among them the advent of fast-food restaurants and the high commercial rents of downtown business districts. Still, many old-style diners have survived, including a number of great ones in Rhode Island—from the Modern Diner in Pawtucket to Providence's own Haven Bros. Diner, one of the few that still sits on wheels and is wheeled onto Kennedy Plaza only from the hours of 5 P.M. to 3 A.M.

Efforts to preserve diners have intensified. Another of Providence's most famous greasy spoons, the Silver Top Diner, nearly fell to the wrecking ball when developers sought its valuable land adjacent to I-95, almost behind Providence Place Mall. Restorers purchased the diner and had it moved to Pawtucket, where, as of this writing, plans are under way to reopen it.

Many of the newer knockoffs of old-style diners seem a bit disingenuous; others have been embraced because their owners have taken this time-honored concept and developed into an often fun or original idea. The Down City Diner, on Weybosset Street in Providence, is just such a place—this hip spot with a swank lounge serves updated contemporary American fare but still at fairly reasonable prices.

And then there are the hybrids. The Commons Restaurant in Little Compton sits by the town green of a charming colonial village and has been a favorite place to gather and eat since it opened in 1966. It looks like a storefront café from the outside, but once inside you'll fine a small counter, burgundy-color booths, linoleum floors, and—best of all—real homestyle diner cooking, from local favorites like jonnycakes and stuffies to famed diner standbys such as meat loaf and liverwurst sandwiches.

in parentheses (ie.g., $5–15). This is a general range that does not take into account the occasional high-priced special or unusual dish on a menu. For coffeehouses, gourmet markets, and some of the fast-food eateries in the book, no range has been given. And for restaurants where dinner is not served, the price range of lunch entrées has been given.

Shopping

In some parts of Rhode Island, shopping is nearly as serious a pastime as surfing is in Hawaii or skiing in Vermont. The state is home to many outstanding art galleries (especially in Providence and Newport). You'll find some quite daring contemporary galleries across the state; galleries near the water tend to emphasize traditional maritime art and landscapes. You'll also find a decent number of antiques stores. And all other forms of shopping proliferate around the state, with the exception of especially cutting-edge and out-there clothiers—New York and, to a lesser degree, Boston still maintain a stronghold where European boutiques and runway wear are concerned.

MAJOR SHOPPING REGIONS

There are several shopping malls in Rhode Island, but only a few of them are large and exciting enough to truly inspire excitement among tourists—the rest, while containing the usual chain shops, are no different than you'll find elsewhere in the nation. The four with the greatest cachet are the glitzy Providence Place, Lincoln

Mall (a few miles northwest of Providence), Warwick Mall, and Rhode Island Mall (which is also in Warwick). Warwick is Rhode Island's center of chain shopping, with not only the two malls listed above but also dozens of large shopping centers and outdoor strip malls. If it's chain shopping that interests you, head here.

As far as urban shopping is concerned, Providence has an engaging retail streetscape, most of it set around downtown, but also on the East Side (along Wickenden, Main, and Thayer Streets). This is a great city for books (both new and antiquarian), records, and cheap funky clothing—owing largely to the significant student population.

Newport is less urban in feel but is clearly a major retail hub with a nice variety of shops, from antiques stores to upscale clothiers to crafts galleries. Other downtowns with especially engaging and walkable streets for browsing and window-shopping include Block Island's Old Harbor, Bristol, Chepachet, North Scituate, Wakefield, Warren, Watch Hill, Westerly, and Wickford.

ANTIQUES
Organizations and Publications
Whether you're a novice or an expert, your antiquing success will be enhanced greatly if you consult a few publications before setting out. The country's leading resource is *Antiques and the Arts Weekly,* The Bee Publishing Co., P.O. Box

5503, Newtown, CT 06470, 203/426-3141, a mammoth 200-page feast of detailed auctions (with photos), museum and gallery exhibits, book reviews, antiques show calendars, shopping tips, and engaging features. Subscriptions are $65 annually. The paper has a fine website, www.antiquesandthearts.com, whose most helpful and unusual resource is an exhaustive list of antiquarian books and their authors.

Although based in Massachusetts, the monthly *New England Antiques Journal,* P.O. Box 120, Ware, MA 01082, 800/432-3505, website: www.antiquesjournal.com, has some coverage on Rhode Island (subscriptions are $17.95 annually). On the Internet, **New England Antiquing,** www.antiquing.com, has links to shows and events, dealers, towns that are good for antiquing, and other useful stuff.

A Regional Overview
You'll find a smattering of antiques shops in nearly every community, but a few regions stand out in particular. The East Bay, especially in the town of Warren (the state's antiquing capital), is a hot spot. You'll find some very fine, high-end antiques shops in Newport (especially around the intersection of Franklin and Spring Streets) and Providence. And a few quirky villages in the western and southern reaches of Rhode Island—Chepachet, North Scituate, Westerly—have a very nice selection of antiques shops.

Getting There and Getting Around

Rhode Island is tiny, crossed by a major interstate and railway tracks, served by New England's third-largest airport and within a two-hour drive of three other major ones, and easily reached from every major city in the Northeast. Few other states in America are more easily accessed, from corner to corner, than Rhode Island.

For general information on commuting, getting to and from Rhode Island, and getting around the state, contact the **Rhode Island Department of Transportation,** 2 Capitol Hill, Providence, 02903, 401/222-2481. Its website, www.dot.state.ri.us, offers extensive information

on numerous publications, traveler resources and road conditions, licenses and permits, upcoming roadwork and projects, legal notices, and construction bid notices. The site also discusses the current plans to relocate I-195 in Providence, so that it will cross at a point farther south than it does presently, thus improving the appearance and user-friendliness of the India Point and Wickenden Street areas.

An excellent resource for online transportation information in the state is www.apta.com/sites/transus/ri.htm, which has links to countless sites.

DRIVING DISTANCES FROM PROVIDENCE

Albany, New York	185 miles		Philadelphia, Pennsylvania	274 miles
Anchorage, Alaska	4,614 miles		Portland, Maine	162 miles
Atlanta, Georgia	1,050 miles		Providence, Utah	2,388 miles
Burlington, Vermont	267 miles		Toronto, Ontario	565 miles
Boston, Massachusetts	50 miles		Washington, D.C.	407 miles
Chicago, Illinois	971 miles		Westerly, Rhode Island	44 miles
Cleveland, Ohio	640 miles		Worcester, Massachusetts	39 miles
Concord, New Hampshire	119 miles			
Fort Providence, Northwest Territories, Canada	3,364 miles			
Hartford, Connecticut	73 miles			
Hyannis, Massachusetts	75 miles			
Mexico City, Mexico	2,873 miles			
Miami, Florida	1,471 miles			
Montréal, Québec	361 miles			
Nashville, Tennessee	1,071 miles			
New Haven, Connecticut	102 miles			
Newport, Rhode Island	34 miles			
New Providence, Iowa	1,300 miles			
New York, New York	180 miles			

Interestingly, few state capitals are closer together than Providence and Hartford, but they are not directly connected by an interstate highway. You either have to drive down I-95 to the coast and then continue east to Route 9 in Connecticut, or take any number of surface-road combinations.

Five cities that share Providence's approximate latitude: Salt Lake City, Utah; Beijing, China; Baku, Azerbaijan; Ankara, Turkey; Madrid, Spain.

Three cities that share Rhode Island's approximate longitude: Québec City, Québec; Santo Domingo, Dominican Republican; and Cuzco, Peru.

DRIVING
Road Names and Labels
Rhode Islanders invariably refer to all numbered roads, whether interstate or local, as "routes." It would be typical, for instance, for a local describing the best way from Providence to Narragansett to suggest taking "Route 95 South to Route 4 South to Route 1 South." Look on a map and you'll find that you actually need to take I-95 South to State Route 4 South to U.S. Highway 1 South. Because you the reader may or may not be from around the Northeast, this book follows what should be the clearest format in referring to numbered roads. All interstate highways are indicated with an "I" before the number (e.g., I-95, I-295), all U.S. highways are referred to with a "U.S." before the number (e.g., U.S. 1, U.S. 44), and all other numbered state and local roads are referred to with "Rte." before the number (e.g., Rte. 1A, Rte. 138).

Scenic Versus Dreary Drives
Little Rhode Island has a good many scenic drives. Alas, there are also plenty of major routes that make for lousy sightseeing and suffer from heavy congestion.

Of interstate highways, I-95 is a convenient if rather dull road that runs from the southwestern corner of the state in a northeasterly direction through Providence before exiting into Massachusetts. A bypass highway, I-295, cuts around the west side of Providence, from Warwick up nearly to Woonsocket and then east to Attleboro, Massachusetts. I-195 cuts east from Providence through the northern tip of the East Bay and into Massachusetts. These roads will get you where you need to go but are, especially around Providence, prone to the usual rush-hour traffic jams.

Route 146 is a convenient limited-access highway running northwest from Providence, and U.S. 6 is similarly fast heading west from Providence, but both of these become regular four-lane roads once they're out of the metro vicinity. But U.S. 6 and parallel U.S. 44 are generally fast roads with little commercial development that pass through the pretty wooded countryside of western Rhode Island; they're a smart way to get to Connecticut, even with the occasional traffic light. U.S. 1, the main shore road in South County, runs from Westerly east to Narragansett and then north to intersect with Route 4 in North Kingstown—the latter then leads back up to I-95. This route is generally fast, with some limited-access stretches. U.S. 1 north of North Kingstown is a slow, heavily developed road through Warwick, Cranston, Providence, and Pawtucket—it should only be used for local traffic, not as a way to get quickly from point to point.

Of other highways (U.S. and state routes), top picks for scenery include Route 102 (from North Smithfield south to North Kingstown), Route 138 (from the Connecticut border at Exeter east to Newport and then northeast up through Tiverton), Routes 77 and 81 (up and down the Sakonnet Peninsula), Route 122 (from Pawtucket through the Blackstone River Valley to Woonsocket), Route 94 (from Chepachet south through Foster), Route 14 (from Providence west over Scituate Reservoir through Kent to the Connecticut border), and Route 1A, which hugs the coast intermittently through South County, both along the ocean and then up beside Narragansett Bay.

Speed Limits

Speed limits along I-95 and I-295 are most 65 mph but drop to 55 mph in congested areas and even lower in a few spots. Other limited-access highways tend to range from 45 to 55 mph, depending on congestion. As in most states, however, officers typically don't pull over offenders who keep with 5 or 8 mph of the posted limit. Popular wisdom suggests that the police most heavily target drivers who fail to slow down when passing from the 65 mph zones into slower ones. Also heavily patrolled are U.S. 6 and U.S. 44, in the western sections of the state, where the speed limits are usually as high as 50 mph, but many drivers go a lot faster.

MASS TRANSIT

Because Rhode Island is small, and a significant chunk of the state is urban, mass transit is quite useful and efficient here, at least in terms of buses and to a limited extent ferryboats. There are no subways, commuter trains, or light-rail services based in Rhode Island, although Amtrak makes stops in a few towns and the Massachusetts Bay Transit Authority (MBTA) provides commuter rail service connecting Providence with Boston's South Station.

It's quite possible and economically feasible to visit some parts of the state without using a car. If, for example, you're going to Block Island, Providence, Newport, parts of South County, and parts of the East Bay, you could get into town from Boston or New York City by a combination of bus, train, and (for Block Island) ferry, and then use a bus or cabs to get around locally—in some of these towns you can cover quite a bit of ground on foot. To make the most of western or northwestern Rhode Island, or the more remote coastal areas (Sakonnet, Jamestown, upper Aquidneck Island), you really need a car—it's also most practical to use one in Providence's suburbs, from Pawtucket to Woonsocket down to Warwick, although buses do serve all of these towns and are fine in a pinch.

For optimum convenience and freedom to explore, a car is your best bet for covering the state as a whole. Even Providence has a fair amount of street parking and plenty of garages. In summer, Newport is almost congested enough that a car defeats its purpose, but if you're planning to explore the outlying areas and your hotel or inn provides off-street parking, it's a good idea to bring one. Block Island, especially in summer, is best visited without a car. It's a small island with good public transportation, and it's excellent for biking; almost all hotels are within walking distance of Old Harbor or New Harbor, where you'll find most of the island's shops and restaurants. If you're staying for a while, your accommodations offer off-street parking, or it's off-season, a car can make sense and give you a little more flexibility, but it's really not a necessity at any time of year. And everybody living on Block Island will be quite pleased if you arrive without bringing a car over and adding to the already heinous traffic.

Amtrak

Amtrak, 800/872-7245, website: www.amtrak.com, runs trains through the state daily. This is a fairly hassle-free way to get to the state from Boston, New York City, Philadelphia, and other major metro regions. There is one basic Amtrak route in Rhode Island, and it passes through en route between Washington, D.C., and Boston, with stops at Providence, Kingston, and Westerly. From Boston, it's just about 40 minutes to Providence, another 10 minutes to Kingston, and another 20 minutes to Westerly. Many of the Amtrak runs are Acela express trains that stop at Providence but not Kingston or Westerly. Coming from the south, train times to Providence are as follows (the shorter times are for high-speed trains): about 6 to 7 hours from Washington, D.C.; about 4.5 to 5 hours from Philadelphia; about 3 to 3.5 hours from New York City; and about 1.5 to 2 hours from New Haven.

Massachusetts Bay Transit Authority

The **Massachusetts Bay Transit Authority,** 617/222-5000 or, for route and schedule information, 617/222-3200, website: www.mbta.com, the nation's fourth-largest public transportation system, offers weekday commuter rail service between Boston's South Station and downtown Providence, with many stops in southeastern Massachusetts along the way. Trains depart Providence on weekdays about a dozen times daily, from 5:30 A.M. through about 9:30 P.M.; the ride takes about an hour and 10 minutes, and the fare is $5.75 one-way. On weekends, there is no service from Providence; however, the train does run about 7 A.M. until 10 P.M. from South Attleboro, Massachusetts, which is right at the Rhode Island border, just a 10-minute drive or cab ride from downtown Providence. South Attleboro Station is at Newport Ave. (Rte. 1A) and Colvin Street, just off Exit 2 of I-95. It's also possible to take buses from either South Attleboro

or, just a stop closer to Boston, Attleboro Station, to downtown Providence.

Extensions to the MBTA commuter rail service are in the works. One proposal would extend the Boston-Providence line all the way to T. F. Green Airport in Warwick. Another would extend the present Boston-to-Stoughton, Massachusetts, line to Fall River, which would put you a short drive from Bristol and Newport.

Interstate Bus Providers

If it's been a while since you traveled by bus, be prepared for a surprise: onboard movies and other improvements can make the ride quite comfortable (and far less expensive than Amtrak). **Bonanza Bus Lines,** 401/751-8800, website: www.bonanzabus.com, runs from Rhode Island to a number of New England cities. Examples include a run from Newport to New York City, with one stop in Narragansett, which runs Friday through Monday only, twice per day, and takes about four hours. The fare is $35 one-way, $53 round-trip. Service from Boston to T. F. Green Airport with a stop in Providence runs several times daily, takes about 90 minutes each way, and costs $9.25 one-way from Boston to Providence and $19 from Boston to T. F. Green.

Other routes include a daily New York–Providence–Cape Cod run, a daily Providence–Springfield–Pittsfield–Albany run, a daily Providence–Foxboro–Logan Airport run, regular service from T. F. Green Airport to cities all over New England, a daily Providence–Hartford–Waterbury–Danbury–New York City run, and a daily Boston–Fall River–Newport run.

Bonanza bus terminals in Rhode Island are in Newport at 23 America's Cup Ave., and in Providence at both 1 Bonanza Way (which is in the northern end of town, off Exit 25 from I-95) and downtown at 129 Washington St.; the stop served in Providence depends on the route, so check ahead.

Another option, if you're coming from New York City to Block Island, Newport, or Westerly, is taking the shuttle service offered by **Adventure East,** 401/847-8715 or 718/601-4707, website: www.adventureeast.com. Going this way can be a little confusing, because the shuttle determines which ferry terminal it will drive to based on the number of passengers, the time, and where everybody is headed. Most of the time, this is a shuttle between Manhattan and Newport, with a stop at Point Judith ferry terminal (and also, on request, at Westerly Airport, which has flights to Block Island). However, if there are no passengers for Newport, the shuttle will often take passengers to the Montauk ferry or the New London ferry instead, as these terminals are much closer to New York City. Whatever the details, the regular round-trip fare is $95, or $55 one-way (the price is the same regardless of which ferry terminal is used, or whether you're going to Newport or Westerly Airport). Adventure East often runs specials at significantly reduced rates.

You can pick the shuttle up from either Manhattan's Upper East or Upper West sides. Weekdays, there are two departures (early morning and late morning); Saturday departures happen early mornings; Sundays there are limited runs (call for availability). Returning from Rhode Island, there are mid-morning and mid-afternoon departures on weekdays, morning departures on Saturdays, and early evening departures on Sundays. Runs can be added or canceled on demand, so it's best to reserve well ahead.

Intercity Bus Providers

Rhode Island is small enough that much of the entire state is served by Providence's city bus system, operated by the **Rhode Island Public Transit Authority (RIPTA),** 401/781-9400, website: www.ripta.com. Most buses originate in Providence, but others start and end in other parts of the state. To give an idea, you can use RIPTA buses to get from Newport to Providence or the University of Rhode Island in Kingston; from Bristol to Providence; from Providence to Burrilville; or from Coventry to Providence. The base fare is $1.25 per ride; charges increase as you travel through different zones. RIPTA's website is very useful in terms of plotting your exact trip.

One other potentially useful resource is the **Greater Attleboro Taunton Rapid Transit Authority (GATRA),** 508/222-6106, website: www.gatra.org. On weekdays and Saturdays, Bus 19 runs from the commuter rail stations in Attleboro and South Attleboro to Emerald Square Mall, near which you can switch to RIPTA Bus 77 into Rhode Island (from which other RIPTA connections are possible). Also on weekdays and Saturdays, Bus 12 runs from Taunton, Massachusetts, into the RIPTA bus terminal in downtown Providence.

Airports

Rhode Island is served by **T. F. Green Airport,** 2000 Post Rd., Warwick, 401/737-8222, website: www.pvd-ri.com, which is eight miles south of downtown Providence off I-95, exit 13—it's rapidly become a significant alternative to Boston's Logan Airport, having completed an ambitious expansion and renovation in recent years. This is a pleasant, easy-to-use facility that readers of *Condé Nast Traveler* magazine voted the third-best airport in the United States and ninth-best in the world. It's served by 10 airlines (including Air Canada/airOntario, American Airlines/American Eagle, Cape Air, Continental Airlines/Continental Express, Delta Airlines/Delta Express/Delta Connection/Business Express, Northwest Airlines, Southwest Airlines, United Airlines, USAir/USAir Express) with flights to numerous U.S. cities, plus the Caribbean and Canada. About 180 nonstop flights fly in and out of Green Airport.

Green's expansion has resulted in lots of extra parking spaces; rates at the on-site garage range from $19 per day self-park to $27 per day valet; just south of the airport, the long-term parking lot costs $13 per day and $56 per week. For official airport parking, call 401/737-1220. There are also a number of commercial lots near the airport, several of which provide free shuttle service to and from the airport.

Transportation to and from the Airports

Rhode Island Public Transit Authority (RIPTA), 401/781-9400 or 800/244-0444, website: www.ripta.com, provides frequent daily service (Bus 12) from T. F. Green to downtown Providence; the ride takes 30 minutes and costs $1.25 one-way. **Airport Taxi and Limousine**

Service, 401/737-2868 or 888/737-7006, website: www.airporttaxiri.com, serves Warwick and neighboring communities and also provides regularly scheduled shuttle service from the airport to downtown Providence hotels, colleges, the convention center, and the train and bus stations. The cost is $9 per person to Providence for the shuttle; the cost of taxis varies according to the destination. **Cozy Cab,** 401/846-1500 or 800/846-1502, provides service from the airport to Newport; the cost is $20 per person.

Transportation from T. F. Green to South County, Newport, and some of the farther-reaching sections of Rhode Island is covered in detail in individual chapters of the book.

Prestige Limousine, 2329 Post Rd., Warwick, 800/736-8382, website: www.prestige-limo.com, offers all manner of ground transportation from T. F. Green Airport, from chauffeured limos to shuttle vans.

Car Rental Agencies

Major car rental agencies at T. F. Green Airport include **Alamo,** 401/738-1475 or 800/327-9633; **Avis,** 401/736-7500 or 800/331-1212; **Budget,** 401/739-8986 or 800/527-0700; **Dollar,** 401/739-8450 or 800/800-4000; **Enterprise,** 401/732-4000 or 800/325-8007; **Hertz,** 401/738-3550 or 800/654-3131; **National,** 401/732-0907 or 800/227-7368; **Payless,** 401/736-8503 or 800/729-5377; and **Thrifty,** 401/739-8660 or 800/367-2277.

Information and Services

HEALTH AND SAFETY

Crime

As with any part of the country that is densely populated, concerns about crime and traffic are germane to planning a trip to Rhode Island.

Without generalizing, Rhode Islanders have a reputation for being fairly aggressive on the roads and in a hurry to get from place to place—if you're driving in parts of the state that are unfamiliar to you, and slowing down to read street numbers or admire the scenery, you will no doubt incur the wrath of the drivers behind you. It is a very good idea to pull off the road from time to time to allow others to pass you, whether you feel their rush is justified or not. There are few roads with passing lanes in this state of hilly and winding terrain, and you stand to gain nothing by inciting road rage in either yourself or other drivers. Whenever possible, back down and let the speed demons around you get by.

Crime is not a major problem in Rhode Island, although random acts of both serious violent crime and petty theft are about as common in the state's urban areas as they are in New York City or Boston. In other words, most crime occurs in the rougher parts of town, well away from tourist attractions and the heart of downtown. It's

a good idea when walking in Providence, Pawtucket, Woonsocket, and to a lesser degree in the suburbs around them, to keep your eyes forward and carry yourself discreetly, without shows of jewelry or cash. The crime rate has dropped sharply in every major city in the state, just as it has elsewhere in the Northeast, and virtually no community in Rhode Island is so dicey that you shouldn't feel safe driving around and walking major thoroughfares.

If you have a cell phone, bring it along in the car with you, as it's always a comfort to know you can phone for help should you end up lost or with a disabled vehicle. In an emergency, you can reach the appropriate dispatcher by dialing 911. There are hospitals in every city and quite a few smaller regional hospitals in some of the more remote parts of the state.

Hospitals and Health Care

Because of Rhode Island's high population density, you're never terribly far from a hospital when you're in the Ocean State. Some major hospitals and their phone numbers include: **Kent Hospital,** 455 Toll Gate Rd., Warwick, 401/737-7000, website: www.kentri.org; **Memorial Hospital of Rhode Island,** 111 Brewster St., Pawtucket, 401/729-2000, website: www.mhri.org; **Mirium**

Hospital, 164 Summit Ave., Providence, 401/793-2500, website: www.lifespan.org/partners/tmh; **Newport Hospital,** 11 Friendship St., Newport, 401/846-6400, website: www.lifespan.org/partners/nh; **Rhode Island Hospital,** 593 Eddy St., Providence, 401/444-4000, website: www.lifespan.org/partners/rih; **Roger Williams Medical Center,** 825 Chalkstone Ave., Providence, 401/456-2000, website: www.rwmc.com; **Our Lady of Fatima Hospital and St. Joseph Hospital for Specialty Care,** 200 High Service Ave., North Providence, for Out Lady of Fatima, Peace St., Providence, for St. Joseph, 401/456-3000, website: www.saintjosephri.com; **South County Hospital,** 100 Kenyon Ave., Wakefield, 401/782-8000, website: www.schospital.com; and **Westerly Hospital,** Wells St., Westerly, 401/596-6000, website: www.westerlyhospital.com.

Pharmacies

You'll find pharmacies, many of them open to 9 or 10 P.M., throughout Rhode Island, the only exceptions being the more remote towns in the western and northwestern part of the state, and in Sakonnet. The leading chain in Rhode Island is CVS, website: www.cvs.com. Pharmacies open 24 hours include **Cranston CVS,** 681 Reservoir Ave., Cranston, 401/946-3960; **East Providence CVS,** 640 Warren Ave., East Providence, 401/438-2256; **North Providence CVS,** 1919 Mineral Spring Ave., North Providence, 401/353-0580; **Johnston CVS,** 1400 Hartford Ave., Johnston, 401/861-0312; **Woonsocket CVS,** 1450 Park Ave., Woonsocket, 401/762-3174; **Coventry CVS,** 733 Tiogue Ave., Coventry, 401/821-2068; **Wakefield CVS,** 684 Kingstown Rd., Wakefield, 401/783-9396; and **Westerly CVB,** 150 Granite Ave., Westerly, 401/348-6088.

Travel Insurance

Purchasing travel insurance makes sense if you've invested a great deal in a trip with prepaid accommodations, airfare, and other services, especially if you have any reason to be concerned about your ability to make the trip (if you have medical concerns, however, check the fine print regarding pre-existing conditions). It's a good idea to purchase insurance from a major provider,

such as **Access America,** 800/346-9265, website: www.etravelprotection.com, or **Travel Guard International,** 800/826-1300, website: www.travelguard.com. Typically these policies can cover unexpected occurrences such as trip cancellations, interruptions, and delays, as well as medical expenses incurred during your travels.

Water Safety

As the Ocean State is obviously a likely spot for activities on the water, it's a good idea to supervise children and exercise caution when boating, swimming, even fishing. Common sense applies here—use life vests and/or other flotation devices, avoid swimming in areas that don't have lifeguards (which is the case at many of the state's smaller beaches), and observe local regulations concerning boating, sailing, and fishing.

Motion sickness can be a serious, and sometimes unexpected, problem for passengers of boats. If you're at all concerned about this, or you've had bouts with seasickness in the past, consider taking Dramamine, Bonine, or another over-the-counter drug before setting sail; you may even want to consult with a physician before your trip, especially if you're interested in the Transderm Scop patch, which slowly releases medication into your system to prevent seasickness but is not without potential side effects. In general, try to avoid sailing on an empty stomach or too little sleep, keep your eyes on the horizon and avoid reading or focusing intently on anything that's small or moving with the rock of the boat, stick as close as possible to the center of a ship, and consider staying above deck (if weather permits), as breathing fresh air often helps.

Wildlife Encounters

Rhode Island, because it has relatively few truly wild areas, presents relatively few chances to encounter dangerous or menacing animals. Rabies is a relatively rare but persistent problem, occurring most often in skunks, opossums, raccoons, and other mostly nocturnal animals. If you see one of these animals during the day you should keep a good distance as, especially if it's behaving erratically or aggressively, there's a fair chance it's carrying rabies. This disease can make an oth-

LYME DISEASE

It's been well-documented that southeastern New England has one of the highest per-square-mile deer populations of any humanly settled area in the country, and it is the close proximity of deer with human beings that contributes ultimately to a painfully debilitating disease named for the small Connecticut town, just 25 miles west of the Rhode Island border, in which it was first diagnosed: Lyme disease. It was around 1975 that Yale-New Haven Hospital's Section of Rheumatology first diagnosed this strange bacterial disease that was causing severe arthritic pain in people of all ages.

Evidence finally linked the victims to bites from infinitesimal deer ticks carrying spiral-shaped bacterium called spirochete—while identified in New England, it's speculated that Lyme disease was actually carried to the United States from Europe sometime during the early part of this century. Symptoms, unfortunately, vary considerably from victim to victim, and one common problem is delayed diagnosis—the longer you go without treating this problem, the more likely the severity of its effects.

In most cases, a victim of Lyme disease will exhibit a red ring-shaped rash around the bite from the deer tick, somewhat resembling a little bull's-eye and appearing from a week to many weeks after the incident. Flu-like symptoms often follow—fever, achy joints, swelling. If left untreated for more than a couple months, chronic arthritis may set in. Lyme disease may also attack the nervous system, causing a loss or reduction of motor skills, severe headaches, paralysis of some facial muscles, and general fatigue—and in somewhat rare cases, patients have also developed heart problems. This is in no way a disease to be taken lightly.

Unfortunately, testing for Lyme disease is a sketchy business at best, as no definitive method has yet been developed. Doctors typically rely on a series of blood tests and more often than that rely simply on observation of symptoms. Research is under way to come up with new and more reliable tests, but in the meantime you should consult with your health care provider the very second you develop any of the symptoms outlined above—especially if you've been spending time in areas where ticks, and deer, are commonplace: wooded terrain, meadows, and coastal scrub.

When spending time in areas where tick infestation is a problem, wear a long-sleeved shirt or jacket and long pants, tuck your pant legs into your boots and/or socks, apply tick and insect repellant generously, and check yourself carefully for signs of ticks or bites. It's a good idea to don light-colored clothing, as you'll have an easier time sighting ticks, which are dark. Remember that the more commonly found wood ticks do not carry the disease, and that deer ticks are extremely small—about the size of a pinhead.

Should you be found to carry the disease, you'll most likely be treated with a fairly standard round of antibiotics, such as doxycycline and amoxicillin. And if you're diagnosed early enough, these treatments will, in most cases, do the job. Research over the past few years has also led to some vaccines, both for human beings and for animals such as dogs and horses. These vaccines vary in their availability and their suitability for different types of patients, and it's best to speak with your doctor if you're curious about whether you'd make a good candidate. In any case, the vaccines are purely preventative and will not help you once you're infected with the disease.

erwise harmless animal bite at will, and should you ever come into any physical contact with such a creature, you should immediately contact an emergency physician.

Rhode Island has no poisonous snakes (although it's theoretically possible to encounter a rattlesnake or copperhead, these species are considered all but extinct in the state). The state is rarely visited by bears or other potentially dangerous mammals such as coyotes and moose. Insects can be a problem in summer, but fortunately the state is without the nasty black flies that so commonly ruin the days of late spring in colder northern New England climes. Do watch out for ticks, however, and also be alert to the recent spread of West Nile virus throughout the United

States, carried by mosquitoes. If you feel at all feverish or sick after having been nibbled on by mosquitoes, and this condition persists, it's a good idea to consult with a physician.

SPECIAL INTERESTS

Gay and Lesbian Travelers

Serving all of New England but with some specific coverage of Rhode Island is Boston-based *In Newsweekly,* 617/426-8246, website: www.innewsweekly.com. This publication is free and distributed at most of the state's several gay bars, and at some bookstores and restaurants.

Close to such gay-popular vacation spots as Provincetown (MA), Fire Island (NY), Ogunquit (ME), and Northampton (MA), and several major cities with visible and vibrant gay neighborhoods, Rhode Island is a relatively progressive and accepting state when it comes to gay issues. Discrimination on the basis of sexual orientation is illegal (as it is on the basis of race, religion, gender, and age), and the vast majority of the restaurants, hotels, inns, and businesses in the state are quite accustomed to and comfortable with the presence of same-sex couples.

In the Providence chapter you'll find listings of bars and clubs with a specifically and predominantly gay following—on the whole, this city has a dynamic and pronounced gay scene, and Rhode Island School of Design (RISD), Brown, and Johnson and Wales all have active gay student groups. Other than this, there's one gay bar in Smithfield (the Loft) and another in Woonsocket (Kings and Queens). Newport presently is without a gay bar but has had one off and on over the years and is a very gay-friendly city; a few of its inns have an especially gay following. For information on Rhode Island's annual Pride festival, which is in mid-June by the State House in Providence, visit website: www.prideri.com.

Senior Citizens

Rhode Island is less famous as a destination among senior travelers than Cape Cod or certain parts of coastal Maine that draw many visitors in their senior years, but it's definitely a place where travelers over 50 or even 65 years old will

not feel at all out of place, excepting perhaps a few student-infested neighborhoods of Providence, where being over 30 can draw stares. Rhode Island is a family-friendly state, and as multigenerational travel has become increasingly popular—grandparents traveling with grandkids, or several generations of families vacationing together—the Ocean State's most family-oriented areas, such as South County and greater Newport, have become popular for these kinds of travelers.

Depending on the attraction or hotel, you may qualify for certain age-related discounts—the thresholds can range from 50 to 65. It can also help if you're a member of the **American Association of Retired Persons (AARP),** 800/424-3410, website: www.aarp.org. For a nominal annual membership fee, you'll receive all sorts of travel discounts as well as a newsletter that often touches on travel issues. **Elderhostel,** 877/426-8056, website: www.elderhostel.org, organizes a wide variety of educationally oriented tours and vacations geared toward 55-and-over individuals or couples of whom one member is that age.

Students

Providence is one of the most student-friendly big cities in the country, whether you're studying there or visiting. Especially along Thayer and Wickenden Streets in Providence, you'll find cafés, shops, and other businesses catering toward and sometimes run by area students. You'll also find all kinds of resources and like-minded and -aged company at the libraries and student unions of Brown, Rhode Island School of Design, the University of Rhode Island (in Kingston), and other schools across the state.

STA Travel Providence, 220 Thayer St., Providence, 401/331-5810, website: www.counciltravel.com, caters to student travelers and is a great resource when you're looking for deals. Oddly, there are no youth hostels in Rhode Island; however, **Hostelling International— American Youth Hostels,** 202/783-6161, website: www.hiayh.org, is a useful general resource for learning about hostels elsewhere in the United States.

Many Rhode Island museums and attractions offer student discounts; always bring your university or school I.D. card with you and ask even if such reduced prices or admissions aren't posted.

Travelers with Children

Rhode Island is an excellent, if not quite stellar, state for families and travelers with children. The only real drawback is that the most visited destination in the state, Newport, is more geared toward adults than children. This is not to say that kids won't enjoy touring some of the city's mansions, or that you won't find family-friendly hotels, cottage rentals, and restaurants. But do keep in mind that many Newport inns and higher-end hotels tend to frown on children as guests, as do some of the rowdier or more sophisticated restaurants and bars.

Providence and the metro region has some terrific attractions that may be of more interest to kids than lavish Newport mansions, such as the Museum of Work and Culture in Woonsocket, Slater Historic Site in Pawtucket, and—of course—the Rhode Island Children's Museum right in downtown Providence.

The hands-down capital of family travel in Rhode Island, however, is South County. From Watch Hill to Misqaumicut to Narragansett, you'll find great beaches, mini-golf and amusement parks, events tailored toward kids, and family-friendly accommodations (such as mid-priced motels and hotels with efficiency and other kitchen units, and also a vast selection of cottage rentals). Block Island is a little more sedate and less commercially kid-oriented, but it, too, has both hotels and cottage rentals that are perfect for families.

Many chain hotels and other accommodations throughout Rhode Island allow kids to stay in their parents' rooms free or at a discount, and many restaurants in the state have kids' menus. The local chain, Newport Creamery, is great fun for kids because of its huge ice cream and dessert selection, and you'll also find a number of clam shacks and ice-cream stands, especially in the state's coastal regions. Fear not if you're headed to a seafood house with finicky kids who aren't wild about fish or clams—it's the very rare restaurant that doesn't offer a few chicken, burger, or grilled cheese options. Many museums and other attractions offer greatly reduced admission.

Travelers with Disabilities

Rhode Island is on par with other Northeastern states as far as the degree to which establishments conform to the guidelines set by the Americans with Disabilities Act (ADA). With new hotels, larger and recently built restaurants, and most major attractions, you can expect to find wheelchair-accessible restrooms, entrance ramps, and other necessary specifications. But Rhode Island has many hole-in-the-wall cafés, historic house-museums with narrow staircases or uneven thresholds, tiny B&Bs, and other buildings that are not easily accessible to persons using wheelchairs. If you're traveling with a guide animal, always call ahead and even consider getting written or faxed permission to bring one with you to a particular hotel or restaurant.

A useful resource is the **Society for the Advancement of Travel for the Handicapped,** 212/447-7284, website: www.sath.org.

MONEY
Banks, ATMs, and Credit Cards

Banks are plentiful throughout Rhode Island although fewer and farther between in rural areas, including Sakonnet and the western and northwestern parts of the state. There, finding a bank that's open can require looking around a bit. Most banks are open weekdays from 9 A.M. until anywhere between 3 and 5 P.M., and on Saturdays 9 A.M. until noon.

ATMs are abundant in Rhode Island; most of those found at banks are open 24 hours and accept a wide range of bank cards (typically Cirrus and/or Plus) and credit cards. You'll also find ATMs in airports and at many bus and train stations, in many convenience stores and gas stations (especially larger ones that keep late hours), hotel lobbies, and increasingly in some bars and taverns. ATMs typically charge a fee ranging from about $1 to $2, the exception being those using bank cards issued by the bank whose ATM you're using. While crime is not a huge problem in Rhode Island, you should exercise discretion—especially if you're alone—when using ATMs late at night, especially in Providence and other urban areas. Walk away and choose a different machine if you see anybody suspicious lurking nearby or loitering inside the vestibule in which the machine is located, and never leave your car unlocked and running while you step out to use the machine.

Credit cards, and, increasingly, bank cards are acceptable forms of payment at virtually all gas stations and hotels, many inns and B&Bs (but definitely not some of the very small ones, which will take traveler's checks and sometimes personal checks), most restaurants (the exceptions tend to be inexpensive places, small cafés, diners, and the like), and most shops (again, the exception tends to be small, independent stores).

Currency

Rhode Island receives very few international visitors directly from their countries of origin—at T. F. Green Airport, flights are handled only from Canada and a few Caribbean nations. Therefore, currency exchange booths and services are limited in the state. It's best to make these changes in whatever city you fly into from your country of origin. Rhode Island is far enough south of Canada that Canadian currency is not generally accepted in the state.

Currency exchange rates may change during the lifetime of this book, but here are a few very approximate samples from some major English-speaking nations: 1 British pound equals about US$1.50, $1 Canadian equals about US65 cents; $1 Australian equals about US55 cents; $1 New Zealand equals about US45 cents; and 1 Euro equals about US$1.

Costs

Compared with other parts of the United States, no part of Rhode Island could be called inexpensive. Newport, especially during the summer high season, has some of the highest hotel rates in the country, with rooms at top properties easily exceeding $300 nightly. However, if you search a bit or consider some of the chain properties out in neighboring Middletown, you can find rooms as low as $70 per night on summer weekends. Top restaurants are pricey in Newport, but you can also find a number of both independent and chain eateries with rates similar to those found just about anywhere in the Northeast (which, in general, is perhaps 10 percent to 20 percent more costly than the average region in the United States). In the off-season, hotel rates in Newport drop a great deal, and the city can be a relatively affordable place to visit. Block Island has comparably priced accommodations and, relatively speaking, the most costly restaurants (and groceries) in Rhode Island. This is true for two reasons: the economy is seasonal, so businesses have to earn what they can during the summer high season; and every morsel of food, equipment, and material has to be ferried onto Block Island from the mainland, thereby increasing wholesale costs, which are passed on to retail customers.

Providence can be quite costly owing to the relatively few hotel rooms and the city's increasing popularity, especially when area universities are in session. Room rates are still typically 25 to 40 percent less than for comparable accommodations in Newport or Boston, but this varies greatly according to when there are events in town. It's fairly easy to eat well in Providence without spending a bundle; in that sense, the city is actually quite a bit less costly than Boston or New York.

Cost-wise, towns elsewhere in Rhode Island are priced similarly to the rest of southern New England, with low-end chains charging as little as (but rarely less than) $50 or $60 nightly, and better-class properties charging as much as $200 per night.

Shopping in Rhode Island is not markedly pricier or cheaper than in other parts of New England, although you'll find some very upscale boutiques and galleries both in Newport and Block Island. Gas stations in Rhode Island charge about the same as neighboring states, and often a bit less than in Connecticut.

Sales Tax

The Rhode Island state sales tax is 7 percent.

Tipping

Tipping practices are fairly constant and widely observed in the tipping-oriented United States, but in larger cities and especially in the more urbanized Northeast, people customarily tip slightly higher than the national average, especially at restaurants and hotels. This means that you might want to edge toward the higher end of the usual 15 to 20 percent range that Americans use to tip waiters at restaurants, obviously factoring in the level of service you receive. You might round up your change or leave as much as $1 when ordering a drink at a bar or a cup of espresso at a coffeehouse (some coffeehouses and cafés have "tip jars" on their counters and appreciate, but don't necessarily expect, you to drop a little change in); if you're ordering multiple drinks, tip more along the lines of 15 percent of the total bill. At nightclubs, the theater, or other places with this service, tip the coat-check staff $1 per coat or bag.

Tip taxi drivers 15 to 20 percent, as well as hairstylists. At hotels, tip your parking valet $1 or $2 each time they retrieve your car; tip bellhops 50 cents to $1 per bag, and leave $1 or $2 for hotel housecleaning staff in your room each day. If the concierge performs any special tasks for you, tip $5 to $10. Room-service gratuities are typically built into the total bill, so leaving an additional tip should only be done at your discretion; tip the local pizza or other food delivery person who brings dinner to your hotel room $2 or $3 depending on the total bill. At small inns and B&Bs, it's customary to leave somewhat more than this for cleaning and other staff, especially in seasonal places like Newport and Block Island, where the workers rely on tips to survive their summers. You may find an envelope left in your room especially for the purpose of tipping the staff. There seems to be no consensus about what to leave at small properties like this, but aim for a minimum of $2 or $3 per day, and anywhere from $5 to $10 per day if you received a great deal of personal service and attention (such as help with sightseeing and restaurant reservations) or you stayed in an especially big and luxurious suite that required a great deal of cleaning. At small B&Bs that are cleaned and serviced by the owners themselves, it is not necessary or even appropriate to leave a tip.

If you use the services of an individual tour guide, consider tipping 10 to 15 percent of the total cost. The practice varies greatly on package tours, but drivers and guides generally expect to receive anywhere from $3 to $10 per person per day, unless gratuities have already been included in the total price of the tour.

COMMUNICATIONS AND MEDIA

Phones and Area Codes

For the time being, Rhode Island has just one area code, 401, although there's talk of introducing a second code. When dialing within the state, it's unnecessary to use the area code. Outside of your local calling region, you need to first dial 1 and the area code. For directory assistance, dial 1, the area code, and 555-1212—the charge for directory assistance calls is typically 50 to 75 cents.

Note when reading about establishments in this book, where there is one, the local telephone number always precedes any possible toll-free number. Toll-free numbers may have area codes of 800, 866, 877, or 888.

Pay phones generally charge 50 cents for local calls, and they also add a 25-cent surcharge for calls placed collect or using a calling card. Most hotels charge anywhere from a 50-cent to $1.50 surcharge for local calls, toll-free calls, or just about any other kind of call placed from their phones; long-distance rates can be outrageous at many hotels, and it's generally a good idea—if you don't already have a cell phone with an economical calling plan—to use your own calling card or buy a prepaid one. The latter are available at many convenience stores and gas stations, and at a wide range of prices. If you're a member of Costco, Sam's Club, or another wholesale discount store, consider buying one of the prepaid Sprint, MCI, or AT&T phone cards sold at these stores—often you can find cards that end up costing just 2 or 3 cents per minute.

Cellular Phones

Cell phones are part of life in the United States, and few frequent travelers go anywhere without one. If you're a subscriber on one of the nation's major networks, such as Sprint PCS, Verizon, or AT&T, you'll find full coverage throughout most of Rhode Island, with only a handful of rural areas (Sakonnet, western and northwestern Rhode Island) being exceptions. Even in rural areas, you should have no trouble receiving the more expensive "roaming" service.

It's legal to jabber away on your cell phone while driving, but it's not a good idea, especially if you're unfamiliar with where you're going and driving on local surface roads. When possible, try to pull off to the side of the road; if traveling on a multilane highway, try to stay in the right and center lane and drive defensively if you must talk on your cell phone. And even if you're not speaking on your phone, be alert to drivers around you who are. Some states and cities in the United States have banned cell phone use while driving, and the trend seems to be in this direction. You can, legally, circumvent this trend by purchasing a hands-free attachment.

You can avoid the ire of those around you by either turning off your phone or setting its volume to "off" or "vibrate" when in restaurants, hotel lobbies, shops, and other confined spaces; do not talk on your cell phone in libraries or fancy restaurants, and avoid doing so when you're in shops or even fast-food or casual venues. If you must do so, try to keep the call short and speak quietly.

Internet Services and Computers

There are an increasing number of places throughout the United States, especially in fairly urbanized states like Rhode Island, where you can check the Internet—even some airport pay phones are now providing this service. The best and most convenient place to check email and surf the Web is the public library; there's one in virtually every Rhode Island town, although only those in larger communities tend to have public computers. Libraries at Rhode Island's several universities and colleges are also open to the public, but their policies vary regarding computer use; some only allow computer access to students, faculty, and staff. Libraries generally allow you to use their computers for short periods, ranging from 15 minutes to an hour.

A handful of cafés around the state have pay Internet stations, as does **Kinko's**, which has branches in Warwick (1020 Bald Hill Rd., 401/826-0808), Middletown (7 E. Main Rd., 401/848-0580), downtown Providence (160 Westminster St., 401/331-8200), and Providence's East Side (236 Meeting St., 401/273-2830); all are open 24 hours. Kinko's is an excellent traveler's business and work resource, as it's also a place to make copies, buy some office supplies, use Federal Express and other shipping services, and rent time on computers (whether to surf the Internet, print-out copies, scan photos, etc.).

If you're traveling with your laptop computer and looking to go online from your hotel, keep a few things in mind. First, check with your Internet service provider (ISP) about how to access them from outside your local area; if it's a local provider, you'll most likely have to call long-distance. Some ISPs issue toll-free numbers or have local access numbers in other regions. Major U.S. Internet service providers (such as Earthlink and America Online) have several local access numbers in Rhode Island; if you subscribe to one of these providers, you'll probably be able to access them making a local call in Providence/Pawtucket, Newport/Middletown, North Kingstown, South Kingstown, Warren, Westerly, and Woonsocket, but there are some exceptions.

These days it's easy to plug your laptop computer into the phone jack at virtually any motel or hotel, whether they have phones with dedicated data ports or not. It's a good idea to bring your own phone cord and cord coupler, which enables you to extend an existing hotel-room phone cord on the chance that it's very short or inconveniently located. Additionally, some of the major mid- and upscale hotel chains now offer high-speed Internet service—for a daily noon-to-noon fee (often $8 to $10), you'll enjoy unlimited high-speed access. this service generally works on any recent-model laptop with a USB or Ethernet port (cables are typically provided in the hotel rooms).

If logging on using your laptop is important to you, ask about phone policies before booking a room at a B&B or small inn. It's usually not an issue if you have a phone in your room, but in smaller places, more than one guest room may be sharing a line, which means that you won't be able to log on for long periods without inconveniencing fellow guests. Some inns have only a common phone, and innkeepers are often very accommodating of guests who wish to log onto the Internet using their laptops if it's just a brief call, but if you're planning to be online a great deal, it's best to avoid staying at properties that don't offer in-room phones.

Media

Rhode Island has about 20 newspapers, five TV stations, and nearly 40 radio stations. A few local magazines and periodicals cover individual regions within the state, some of them distributed free at tourism offices and in hotels.

Rhode Island Monthly, 401/277-8200, website: www.rimonthly.com, has good dining, arts, and events coverage. The *Providence Journal,* 401/277-7300, website: www.projo.com, has an outstanding and highly informative website with information on local dining, arts, music, travel, kids-oriented activities, and so on. An excellent resource for metro Providence arts, dining, shopping, clubbing, and similar such diversions is the decidedly left-of-center *Providence Phoenix* alternative newsweekly, 401/273-6397, website: www.thephoenix.com.

PRACTICALITIES

Business Hours

Most city and suburban restaurants serve lunch from 11 A.M. or noon until 2 or 3 P.M. and dinner from 5 or 6 P.M. until 10 P.M. In some of the more rural parts of the state, especially the western and northwestern sections, expect lunch to end by 2 P.M. and dinner by 9 P.M. The post office is usually open 8 A.M.–5 P.M. on weekdays and also on Saturday mornings.

There's no rule on typical shop hours, except that they seem to be getting gradually longer over time, to the point that major chain shops and stores in big shopping malls often stay open from 9 or 10 A.M. until 9 or 10 P.M., typically with shorter hours on Sundays. Local, independently operated boutiques and shops often don't open till late morning (especially in resort areas), and they often close by 5 or 6 P.M.; these same shops may not open at all on Sundays or even on Mondays or Tuesdays. In some densely populated areas you'll be able to find 24-hour full-service grocery stores, and 24-hour gas stations

and convenience stores are found in several parts of the state, especially near exits of major interstate highways. Because shop hours vary so greatly, it's especially important to phone ahead if you're concerned about any one particular business being open when you arrive.

Electricity

The standard in Rhode Island and the rest of the United States and Canada is AC, 110 volts/60 cycles. Plugs have two flat, parallel prongs.

Time Zone

Rhode Island falls entirely within the Eastern Standard Time (EST) zone. Chicago is an hour behind, Los Angeles three hours behind. The Canadian Maritimes are an hour ahead; London, England, is five hours ahead; and Israel is seven hours ahead.

Remember that hours behind and ahead are affected by the fact that Rhode Island, like most but not all American states and Canadian provinces, observes Eastern Daylight Time (EDT): on the last Sunday in October, clocks are set back one hour through the first Sunday in April, when they are set forward ahead an hour.

When to Go

Keeping in mind special events and festivals, which may influence when you plan your visit, Rhode Island is increasingly a year-round destination. If you're planning to take advantage of the Ocean State's vast access to the water, whether it be in the form of boating or beachcombing, you may want to focus your visit around the warmest months, generally from mid-May through mid-October, but especially from mid-June through Labor Day. Keep in mind, however, that in ocean resort areas like Newport, Block Island, and South County, you'll be competing with throngs of other sea-lovers for space and parking at the beach, a table at restaurants, and hotel rooms. In recent years, Newport and parts of South County have made an effort to attract off-season visitors. Museums have begun keeping longer winter hours, and many hotels and other organizations offer special rates and deals in the off-season. This can be a pleasant time to tour coastal Rhode Island, as the crowds are at a minimum, and the restaurants and bars can be quite cozy and inviting during the colder months. Block Island has few hotel options and even fewer dining options in winter, but it's nonetheless stunning.

Elsewhere in the state—even in the East Bay towns, which are on the water but have a greater variety of indoor diversions—Rhode Island is very much a year-round destination. Because the colleges in Providence infuse downtown and College Hill with an abundance of energy when schools are in session, some visitors actually prefer fall, spring, and even winter in the state capital, which can seem a bit empty in summer when there aren't as many students. Providence, like other New England cities, can also be uncomfortably hot in July and August. Winters are not brutal compared with northern New England, but the state does get socked with the occasional snow or ice storm, and the wind and frigidity can be uncomfortable from December through March.

For many, the most bewitching and scenic seasons in Rhode Island are spring, when the entire state is abloom with greenery and flowers, and fall, when the foliage turns.

What to Pack

Packing for a trip to Rhode Island is not unlike planning for a trip to any city or town with a four-season climate and an oceanfront setting. This is a small, somewhat industrialized state without a great many opportunities for true wilderness hiking and camping, so unless you're planning a very specific adventure of this kind, it's not necessary to think much in terms of advanced camping gear. Also, virtually nowhere in the state are you very far from almost any kind of household, clothing, food, or travel supply—distances in Rhode Island between gas stations, grocery stores, and department stores are very short.

Winters are not as brutally cold here as they are in northern New England, but it can snow as early as November and as late as April or rarely even in early May, so especially when visiting during the spring or fall, prepare for a wide range of weather. You could need shorts and short-sleeved shirts in October or April, and you might want to bundle up at these times, too.

If you're headed toward the shore, as so many vacationers in Rhode Island are, bring your sandals, swimwear, and a windbreaker (even in summer, as it can be very cool if you're out on the water sailing). Also, while it's easy to find sunscreen, film, and other conveniences at shops all throughout the shore towns, it's more economical to bring these supplies yourself.

TOURIST INFORMATION

The state of Rhode Island is broken down into six distinct tourism regions: Blackstone River Valley (which includes northwestern/western Rhode Island), Block Island, East Bay, Providence (which includes Warwick and the suburbs), Newport (which includes Sakonnet Peninsula), and South County. Each has its own tourism office, brochures, and staff. It's wise to work directly with these offices when planning a trip to a specific area within the state. In many cases, the towns that make up a particular section of this book fall into more than one tourism region, meaning you may want to call two or three local offices to best plan out your itinerary and cull advice on upcoming events, attractions, and such.

The statewide information bureau is the **Rhode Island Office of Tourism,** 1 W. Exchange St., Providence, 02903, 401/222-2601 or 800/556-2484, website: www.visitrhodeisland.com, which can send you a free Rhode Island travel planner.

There are also a number of visitor centers located throughout the state, some of which are unstaffed and others that are open only Memorial Day through Columbus Day. These all contain an array of brochures and range from quite helpful to not very—they're nice in a pinch or for basic questions, but you're always better off phoning ahead and obtaining local brochures and advice from the extremely useful regional boards.

Providence

The story of Providence's renaissance over the past two decades has been well documented in the media and by local boosters, but many people still have little sense of this hilly city of 175,000—the second-largest metropolis in New England. Travelers tend to focus on Rhode Island's coastal half, it being, after all, the Ocean State. But Providence has grown into a distinctive and dynamic destination of its own. It's the state's culinary as well as visual-and-performing arts hub. And Providence possesses a larger and better-preserved district of colonial architecture than any other city in the United States. For many travelers, it's reason enough to spend time in Rhode Island, and as a destination the city's rise in popularity has really only just begun.

Beginning in the early 1980s, Providence invested many millions of dollars to reinvent its downtown, recover and landscape the long-ago-buried river system, and turn itself into a first-rate city. Plenty of U.S. cities have attempted the same sort of comeback in recent years. Few have done a better job of it than Providence, especially in terms of what the city now offers visitors. Indeed, the clichéd Cinderella stories about the city speak more about its quality today as a place to visit than as a place to live. The population has declined steadily over the past few decades, with no immediate end in sight, and Providence still has plenty of rough neighborhoods, cracks in its public-school system, and image problems concerning its notoriously

Providence skyline

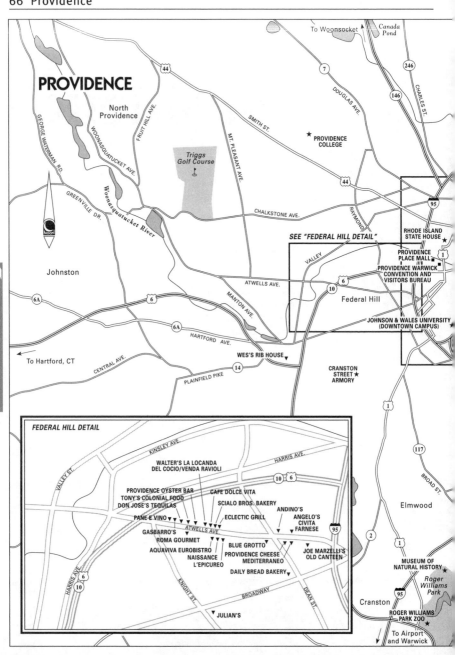

PROVIDENCE

PROVIDENCE

North Providence

Triggs Golf Course

★ PROVIDENCE COLLEGE

Johnston

To Hartford, CT

WES'S RIB HOUSE

SEE "FEDERAL HILL DETAIL"

RHODE ISLAND STATE HOUSE ★

PROVIDENCE PLACE MALL
PROVIDENCE WARWICK CONVENTION AND VISITORS BUREAU

Federal Hill

JOHNSON & WALES UNIVERSITY (DOWNTOWN CAMPUS)

CRANSTON STREET ★ ARMORY

Elmwood

MUSEUM OF NATURAL HISTORY

Roger Williams Park

Cranston

ROGER WILLIAMS PARK ZOO ★

To Airport and Warwick

FEDERAL HILL DETAIL

KINSLEY AVE.

HARRIS AVE.

VALLEY ST.

WALTER'S LA LOCANDA
DEL COCIO/VENDA RAVIOLI

CAFE DOLCE VITA

PROVIDENCE OYSTER BAR
TONY'S COLONIAL FOOD
DON JOSE'S TEQUILAS

SCIALO BROS. BAKERY

ANDINO'S

ANGELO'S CIVITA FARNESE

PANE E VINO

ECLECTIC GRILL

ATWELLS AVE.

GASBARRO'S
ROMA GOURMET

AQUAVIVA EUROBISTRO
NAISSANCE
L'EPICUREO

BLUE GROTTO
PROVIDENCE CHEESE
MEDITERRANEO

JOE MARZELLI'S OLD CANTEEN

DAILY BREAD BAKERY

HARRIS AVE.

KNIGHT ST.

BROADWAY

DEAN ST.

JULIAN'S

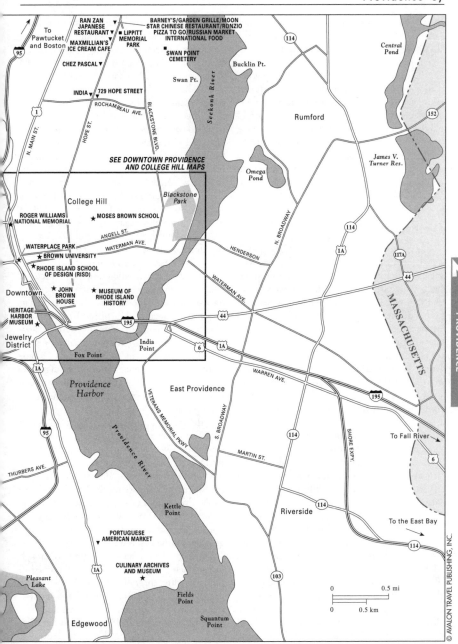

To Pawtucket and Boston

RAN ZAN JAPANESE RESTAURANT ▼
MAXMILLIAN'S ICE CREAM CAFE ■
LIPPITT MEMORIAL PARK

BARNEY'S/GARDEN GRILLE/MOON STAR CHINESE RESTAURANT/RONZIO PIZZA TO GO/RUSSIAN MARKET INTERNATIONAL FOOD

SWAN POINT CEMETERY

CHEZ PASCAL ▼

INDIA ▼ 729 HOPE STREET

ROCHAMBEAU AVE.

HOPE ST.

N. MAIN ST.

BLACKSTONE BLVD.

Swan Pt.

Seekonk River

Bucklin Pt.

Central Pond

Rumford

James V. Turner Res.

Omega Pond

SEE DOWNTOWN PROVIDENCE AND COLLEGE HILL MAPS

College Hill

Blackstone Park

★ ROGER WILLIAMS NATIONAL MEMORIAL
★ MOSES BROWN SCHOOL

ANGELL ST.

WATERPLACE PARK

WATERMAN AVE.

★ BROWN UNIVERSITY

★ RHODE ISLAND SCHOOL OF DESIGN (RISD)

Downtown

★ JOHN BROWN HOUSE

★ MUSEUM OF RHODE ISLAND HISTORY

HERITAGE HARBOR MUSEUM ★

Jewelry District

Fox Point

India Point

HENDERSON

N. BROADWAY

WATERMAN AVE.

44

195

6

1A

1A

114

114

117A

44

MASSACHUSETTS

Providence Harbor

East Providence

WARREN AVE.

195

To Fall River

VETERANS MEMORIAL PKWY.

S. BROADWAY

SHORE EXPY.

114

6

Providence River

MARTIN ST.

95

THURBERS AVE.

Kettle Point

Riverside

114

To the East Bay

PORTUGUESE AMERICAN MARKET ▼

114

Pleasant Lake

1A

CULINARY ARCHIVES AND MUSEUM ★

Fields Point

103

0   0.5 mi

Edgewood

Squantum Point

0   0.5 km

PROVIDENCE

© AVALON TRAVEL PUBLISHING, INC.

shady—at least historically—city government. Granted, the same is true of many urban locales that have undergone a major revitalization in recent years.

What Providence has done successfully is encourage the development of a fabulous arts district through far-sweeping tax incentives for artists and galleries, help develop a phenomenal restaurant scene by assisting in the financing of such ventures, dismantle a dreary downtown rail system, uncover and restore two rivers long ago forgotten, and put forth plans to open an ambitious museum and cultural complex called Heritage Harbor.

ORIENTATION

While it's the Ocean State's largest city, Providence lies a good 25 miles north of where Narragansett Bay opens to the Atlantic. Still, water has a major effect on the city's appearance, especially in recent years. Much of the water that rushes down through the river valleys of central Massachusetts into Narragansett Bay does so by way of Providence.

The eastern boundary of the city is formed largely by the broad Seekonk River, which separates Providence from East Providence, and then feeds into Providence Harbor. The main feeder waterway for the Seekonk is the mighty Blackstone River, which for two centuries has powered factories and mills through the valley that bears its name (all the way north to Worcester). Two smaller rivers run through downtown Providence: the Woonasquatucket (meaning "where the tide ends") River, which meanders about 20 miles down from the west-northwest town of North Smithfield, and the Moshassuck (meaning "moose hunt") River, which comes down from the Lincoln Woods area in the northwest. The confluence of these two waterways, at approximately Thomas and Canal Streets, begins the Providence River, which continues south paralleling Water and Dyer Streets before emptying into Providence Harbor, which is really the head of Narragansett Bay, just west of where the Seekonk comes in.

In the 19th century, in an attempt to discourage epidemics and health crises and to maximize downtown's limited acreage, city planners decided to cover up significant spans of the Woonasquatucket, Moshassuck, and Providence rivers. The three rivers were capped with massive concrete covers, and for more than a century they were forgotten and neglected as they trickled beneath downtown. Fortunately, in the mid-1980s, plans were introduced to reverse the procedure by uncovering the Providence River and slightly rerouting the Moshassuck and Woonasquatucket Rivers. Today, pedestrian promenades run alongside the revitalized rivers where they pass through downtown. The four-acre WaterPlace Park is a lovely promenade spanned by graceful bridges and lined with benches and paths. Work continues along the southern reach of the Providence River, where the Heritage Harbor complex will eventually house numerous museums. Eventually, the ugly span of I-195 that crosses the river up close to downtown will be rerouted to south of the massive Hurricane Barrier at the mouth of the river, thereby uniting the city's Jewelry District and harborfront with the rest of downtown. But even today you can sail or motor a boat from Providence through Narragansett Bay out to the ocean, and ferry service connects Providence with Newport, Point Judith (in South County), and Block Island.

Although it's a large river, the Seekonk affects the overall look and feel of Providence less than the smaller Woonasquatucket and Moshassuck rivers, as it's visible from only a few parts of the city (and not at all from downtown). It's also dominated by industry on the East Providence banks. Still, you can catch a nice glimpse of the Seekonk both from Swan Point Cemetery and Blackstone Park, two picturesque patches of greenery on the East Side.

Providence is said to rise on seven hills, though one of them, Weybosset Hill, was flattened in the early 18th century for its valuable clay (used to make bricks). The others, which still stand—some more prominently than others, are College Hill, Constitution Hill, Tockwotten Hill, Smith Hill (on which the State House is perched), Federal Hill, and Christian Hill.

For all practical purposes, the Providence River, and then north of it the Moshassuck River, separates the city into the East and West Sides. As soon as you cross the rivers, College Hill rises sharply to form almost a palisade on the East Side, with Brown University and the Rhode Island School of Design anchoring its slopes, along with homes, school buildings, and churches from the colonial through Victorian eras. From the crest of College Hill east to the Seekonk River you'll find some of the city's most desirable, newer neighborhoods, laid out mostly in the 19th and early 20th centuries. This rule holds true north to the Pawtucket border. The south boundary of the East Side is Fox Point, a thriving Portuguese community that's also home to many students and academics from nearby Brown and RISD; its southern tip, India Point, is where Seekonk River flows into Providence Harbor.

In general the East Side feels less like a big city and more like its own kingdom of trendiness, history, and academia. It's rife with restaurants, shopping, great strolling, and a handful of museums, and any leisure visitor to Providence should expect to spend more than half of his or her time over here.

You could throw a rock from the eastern edge of downtown (aka Downcity) over the Providence River to the foot of College Hill, but this relatively flat network of curving streets and both new and vintage office towers feels worlds apart from the East Side both in appearance and pace. In many regards, it's a classic business district of a typical U.S. city—the sidewalks roll up at night and on weekends in some sections, but up closer to Providence Place Mall and the State Capitol Grounds, and also to the southwest near Johnson & Wales University and the nightclub-strewn Jewelry District, you'll usually find the sidewalks teeming with pedestrians night and day.

Downtown contains the bulk of the city's hotels, a considerable number of shops and restaurants, some performing arts spaces, but rather little in the way of formal attractions. Still, it's within walking distance of College Hill and most of the city's walkable neighborhoods, and it's an excellent base, particularly because most of the hotels are close to the WaterPlace Park and Providence Place Mall.

The Jewelry District has been one of the most changed Providence neighborhoods of the past two or three decades. Mostly a patch of warehouses and industrial concerns from the mid-19th through the mid-20th centuries, it's where the city's reputation as the jewelry-manufacturing capital of the nation was built. Some of these buildings still house jewel-making concerns, but many others now house dance clubs, restaurants, and a handful of retail concerns. And the old electricity plant at Point and Eddy Streets is currently being transformed into the Heritage Harbor development.

Right now the neighborhood is cut off from downtown by I-195 to the north, a branch of I-95 that shoots off into East Providence and continues all the way through Massachusetts South Shore nearly to Cape Cod. When the I-195 is shifted in the next few years, the personality of the neighborhood should change dramatically. You'll be able to walk easily between here and the rest of downtown, and gentrification will no doubt accelerate, where already it's been increasing steadily in this district over the past several years.

I-95 snakes north-south through Providence and effectively separates downtown from the many mostly working-class residential neighborhoods that form the city's West Side. The most interesting of these areas, in terms of there being a lot to see and do, are the "Little Italy" enclave of Federal Hill, which is immediately west of downtown across the interstate, and Roger Williams Park and Zoo, which lies about four miles southwest of downtown and is best visited either by car or public transportation. However you get to the park, do make the effort to go—it's a marvelous little slice of the country in an otherwise densely settled and urban environment.

THE PEOPLE

Providence, from its early days as a refuge from the oppressive religious and political doctrines of the Massachusetts Bay Colony, has always heartily embraced persons from all backgrounds and all walks of life. The blue-blooded exclusivity or wary stand-offishness that people often think they'll find in New England has never been present here. At the forefront of America's industrial revolution, Providence welcomed workers from Canada, Ireland, Italy, Portugal, and many other countries well before this was the trend elsewhere. True, these groups didn't always get along with one another, and the state's voting laws misrepresented the state's urban dwellers and therefore the majority of foreign-born residents until well into the 20th century. Nevertheless, you can't deny the city's long tradition of cultural plurality.

Providence is an international hub of education, the state's political center, and a sprawling enclave of tight-knit, working-class ethnic factions, and these three factors endow the city's population with a worldly sensibility. The presence downtown of major colleges and universities—Brown University, Rhode Island School of Design (RISD), Providence College, Johnson & Wales—accounts for the many offbeat and inexpensive shops and eateries, hip nightclubs, and stylish-looking twentysomethings slinking about. Politicians, lawyers, bankers, and downtown office workers imbue Providence with a slightly more grown-up, upscale appeal that manifests itself in high-end restaurants and the relatively high rates at the city's handful of mostly upscale hotels. Finally, the pockets of Hispanic, African, Asian, and Central, Eastern, and Southern European immigrants keep Providence culturally and socially varied and without airs.

Densely populated, free-spirited, and progressively tolerant Providence is one of the more politically liberal cities in the United States, and its most famous institution, Brown University, is one of the more politically liberal schools in the world. Many people think of Boston as left-of-center, which it is by many measures, but Providence cultivates a significantly more bohemian arts, music, and political scene. It's less buttoned-down than its neighbor 50 miles to the north, and the high percentage of creative types (RISD is an arts school, and Johnson & Wales is famous for its culinary programs) infuses the city with an edgy, countercultural demeanor that you'd expect more of New York City or San Francisco than you might of a New England state capital.

THE PROVIDENCE BANNER TRAIL

In 1996 the city christened the Providence Banner Trail, a walkable system of cultural, historic, and architectural sites throughout downtown, the State House grounds, and the East Side—virtually every site along the trail is within a mile or so of downtown. This is an easy way to get a quick feel for the city's layout and history—the Providence Convention and Visitors Bureau and many hotels and attractions distribute free Banner Trail maps, and the trail commences and ends at WaterPlace Park. Leaving from the Westin Hotel (which is also the headquarters of the CVB), you can tour the Banner Trail by trolley on Wednesday through Saturday, June through October. Trail brochures are available at sites along the way, from the Providence CVB information kiosk at the Westin Hotel, or by calling the CVB at 401/274-1636 or 800/233-1636.

This is especially true in the more visitor-oriented parts of town, most of which lie close to the campuses of the aforementioned colleges. Providence has well established gay, feminist, and ethnic communities, each with their own favored hangouts, and yet as New England cities go, the crowds you'll encounter at clubs, restaurants, and simply strolling the sidewalks represent a highly varied range of backgrounds, styles, ages, and looks. It's not a very ghettoized city, and so people from all different walks of life seem to find each other.

Whatever a citizen's politics, just about everybody in Providence has a serious opinion on the city's mayor and unabashed cheerleader, Vincent "Buddy" Cianci, who's been caught up in all kinds of controversies during his tenure, which began in the late 1970s. This is the guy *Boston Magazine* described as a "born politician who could schmooze Satan." But Cianci began with a determined vision to make Providence a destination, and while his megalomaniacal style rubs many people the wrong way, he seems to have a remarkable knack for getting things done. Cianci deserves a great deal of credit for much of downtown dramatic renewal.

PLANNING YOUR VISIT

If you're visiting Rhode Island for the first time, or you're seeking a seaside vacation, you should probably think of Providence more as a day trip or at the most a weekend getaway than as the primary focus of your trip. For such a dynamic city, at least until Heritage Harbor opens, Providence has relatively few formal attractions and no major-league sports teams—you could see the best of the city's museums in one well-

planned day. But if you're a shopper, a foodie, an aficionado of historic preservation, a theatergoer, a gallery hopper, or live-music fan, you'll easily find plenty here to keep you busy for several days.

For anybody who lives in or spends a fair amount of time in the surrounding region, whether it be the towns along the shore, Cape Cod, Boston, or even New York City, Providence makes for an enchanting and easily accessible diversion. It may be smaller and lower-profile than several other major destinations on the Eastern Seaboard, but in terms of big-city sophistication and culture, Providence ranks with the best of them.

History

The history of Providence closely links that of the state of Rhode Island, so for a further discussion of the issues that precipitated the city's settlement and the lives of the Native Americans who occupied the land originally, refer to the book's introductory chapter.

EARLY SETTLEMENT

You don't hear the phrase so much these days, although a bed-and-breakfast downtown uses it as its name, but the greeting "What cheer, netop?" is supposedly what helped convince religious and political dissident Roger Williams to drop anchor—figuratively and literally—at the confluence of the Woonasquatucket and Moshassuck Rivers. That year was 1636, and this point we now know as Providence.

"Netop" can be translated loosely to mean "friend." An amiable Native American cast out the greeting to a no-doubt dejected but determined Williams, who was paddling down the Seekonk River in search of a place to build a new settlement. After spending five years as an assistant minister first in Salem, then in Plymouth, and then back in Salem, Williams had alienated himself from the Puritans on two major grounds. First, he condemned the Puritans' unwillingness to split completely from the Anglican Church

of England, a bold step the founders of the Massachusetts Bay and Plymouth Colonies could not bring themselves to take. And second, he believed that the colonies' governing bodies had no business whatsoever monitoring and controlling the religious beliefs and practices of its citizens. Essentially, Williams was one of the world's earliest proponents of the separation of Church and State, and a further practitioner of unconditional religious tolerance.

His insistence on articulating these then radical and seditious views eventually forced the hand of the Massachusetts Bay Colony powers, who convicted him for his contrary and dangerous beliefs in 1636 and put forth plans to deport the minister back to England. In February 1636, with arrest imminent, Williams and his wife, Mary, fled the colony, first spending time with the allied Wampanoag Native Americans who lived in the region of what is now Massachusetts, between the Plymouth and Providence regions.

After making a brief stab at forming a settlement in East Providence, Williams sailed down the Seekonk River, where he received the encouraging greeting from a Narragansett Indian, or so this tale goes. He continued south and then west around India Point and turned north around Fox Point up the Great Salt (now Providence) River. Here Williams and five compatriots encountered a gurgling fresh spring, and thenceforth sprung the rather rapid rise of Providence, Rhode Island.

The land comprising most of present-day Rhode Island was the domain of the Narragansett Indians for the centuries preceding Europe's swift and unflinching consumption of the continent. Williams encountered an amiable and wholly encouraging people. From the tribal chiefs, Canonicus and Miantonomi, Williams immediately secured verbally the rights to settle the lands surrounding the two rivers, and acquired a written deed in 1638. To the east of this point at the head of Narragansett Bay rises today's College Hill, and to the west lies downtown.

Roger Williams then penned the following edict, "Having of a sense of God's merciful providence unto me called this place Providence, I desired it might be for a shelter for persons distressed for conscience." The city founders set about establishing property lots, which they offered new settlers pending their approval by the community's members.

Streets were laid out across Providence, many—Hope, Benevolent, Peace, Friendship, Faith, Benefit—with names that reflect the progressive principles on which Williams established the city. Within the first three decades, about 50 families had settled in Providence, each with a rudimentary home and ample pastureland. The inhabitants chose mostly agrarian pursuits, along with a limited degree of fishing and fur trading. There was a gristmill, operated by one of the six founders, John Smith (the others, in addition to Roger Williams, were William Harris, Francis Wickes, Joshua Verein, and Thomas Angell), located at roughly what is now North Main and Mill Streets. Other early community concerns included a tavern, jail, cattle pound, and tannery, and a bridge spanned the Moshassuck River as early as 1663, approximately at the point of today's Smith Street Bridge.

By the end of the 1670s, Providence had some 1,000 residents. Roger Williams maintained close and respectful ties for the rest of his life with the Narragansetts. In fact, on his deathbed, chief Canonicus asked to be buried in cloth given him by Williams, and that his old friend attend the funeral. Williams decried attempts by settlers at christianizing the indigenous persons, and at various times acted as an intermediary between the very Puritans who had pushed him out of Massachusetts and both the Narragansetts and the Wampanoags.

In general, however, the English throughout the New World set about systematically diminishing the land holdings of Native Americans, and by the time of Williams' death in 1683 there was little good faith left between the two sides. In 1675, the leader of the Wampanoags, King Philip, began what some say was a last-ditch drive to unify all of the region's Indian tribes in defiance of encroaching settlement and control by the colonists. King Philip's War drew quite a few residents of the city into the fray, which was centered nearby in Swansea, on the border of the Rhode Island and Massachusetts colonies. During the conflict, the once-friendly Wampanoags descended on Providence and burned about a third of the 70-some houses.

Providence really came into its own shortly after this troubled period, when in 1680 resident Pardon Tillinghast built a wharf—and so the city's destiny as a commercial center was sealed. New England's famed Triangle Trade, in which rum and slaves and molasses were traded among Africa, the West Indies, and the colonies, played a vital role in the city's growth—ironic, given that the city was founded on principles of tolerance and human rights. Indeed, the city's most famous sons—the Brown brothers, John, Joseph, Nicholas, and Moses—secured their fortunes largely through slave trade.

In the most general sense, the whole of Providence prospered intensely from the late 17th through late 18th centuries. Immense homes grew up along the East Side, filled with lavish art and furnishings. The Brown brothers endowed schools and religious institutions, William Goddard began the *Providence Gazette and Country Journal* in 1762, and arts-minded individuals established a short-lived theater shortly after. In 1770, Rhode Island College (which we now know as Brown University) moved from its original home in the East Bay community of Warren to Providence, where it grew rapidly in prestige.

COLONIAL PERIOD

The residents of Providence, so heavily dependent on trade, took a particularly keen interest in the financial demands leveled by the English crown on Rhode Island. In 1772, John Brown and a group of citizens plotted the burning of the British tax ship the *Gaspee,* which had become snagged at low tide in Narragansett Bay. Providence held its own tea party, after Boston's—on March 2, 1775, a heap of tea was burned before a large gathering of citizens in Market Square as a protest of Britain's unreasonable taxation policies. And on May 4, 1776, the legislature passed the Rhode Island Independence Act, signing the bill in the Old State House.

Despite these events, no battles of the American Revolution occurred in Providence, although the city contributed significant numbers of men—as well as ships, supplies, and money—to the war effort. University Hall at Brown College quartered French troops under Count de Rochambeau prior to and following his march to take over Yorktown.

During the American Revolution, the city became a significant dry-goods supplier of the Continental Army, and following the war, trade here expanded greatly throughout the world. Ships embarked on lengthy and often risky journeys to the Mediterranean, through the Middle East, and to China and the Far East. The War of 1812 embargo effectively shut down the city's port for several years. Exacerbating things was a massive hurricane (called the Great Gale, as this occurred long before such storms were given cute little names) in 1815, which ripped much of the city to tatters and destroyed dozens of tall ships.

INDUSTRIAL REVOLUTION TO WORLD WAR II

By 1820, Providence's population stood at about 12,000, having doubled since the Revolution—it was the seventh largest city in the young republic. Even with the troubles of storms and embargoes, it remained a commercial powerhouse, in part because of the early industrial successes in textile mills in Pawtucket, just north of

the city, which began in the 1790s and developed rapidly. This movement toward industrialization would transform Providence, the farming village and later shipping center, into a bustling factory and mill town by the time of the Civil War (to which, once again, Providence contributed numerous troops).

One rather unusual industry that developed shortly after the American Revolution, jewelry manufacturing, remains a staple of the city's economy to this day. Brothers Nehemiah and Seril Dodge developed a way to plate metal with gold, and thus a fairly cheap and quick way to mass-produce costume jewelry. Over the next three decades about a dozen jewelry factories opened in Providence, and by the Civil War the city's nearly 100 such manufactories employed more workers than any other industry in Rhode Island. All kinds of costume jewelry and related products were and are still produced here—about 20,000 people earn their living today working in the jewelry business, and another 25,000 in support industries.

In addition to jewelry and textiles, banks, insurers, and transportation concerns developed to support factory growthThe city opened its doors increasingly to immigrants, mostly of Italian, Portuguese, French-Canadian, and Swedish descent. Close-knit ethnic enclaves grew up throughout the city, and in particular the Italians and Portuguese continue to this day to identify closely with certain sections of town. By the mid-1930s about 20 percent of the city's residents were of Italian descent, and so developed the city's lively and engaging Federal Hill community, still one of the most vibrant Little Italys in the United States.

A CITY REINVENTED

Providence endured a steady economic decline beginning with the Depression and lasting through World War II and well into the 1970s. Factories shut down, many workers lost jobs and those who didn't moved out to the suburbs, and entire neighborhoods fell into severe states of decay. The city had nowhere to go but up by the time a plucky and ambitious new mayor named

BUDDY CIANCI AND THE PROVIDENCE RENAISSANCE

In the minds of many observers and political pundits, the Providence of today is almost a singular realized vision of longtime mayor Vincent "Buddy" Cianci. There's no question that a good bit of the credit for the city's so-called renaissance, as Cianci himself often referred to it, goes to this Huey Long–like mayor who was convicted in summer 2002 of, according to the *Providence Journal*, one "racketeering conspiracy charge accusing him of masterminding a criminal scheme that took bribes for favors, including tax breaks, jobs, and sweetheart deals on city-owned land." It was the culmination of an investigation of city officials that the FBI called Operation Plunder Dome. Given this conviction, Cianci decided in June 2002 not to run for another term.

The colorful, controversial, stocky politico has had his hand—or his strong arm, some might say—in Providence politics since his dark-horse election to the mayor's office in 1974 (he won by fewer than 1,000 votes, becoming the first Republican to make it to the Providence mayor's office since the 1930s). Given Providence's relative prominence vis-à-vis the rest of the state, and that the Rhode Island State House is just a matter of blocks from Providence City Hall, it's easy to understand why Cianci has obtained power and attention that seems more fitting of a state governor than a city leader. That being said, it's worth noting that Rhode Islanders soundly rejected his bid for governor in 1980.

What Cianci largely spearheaded, at a time when Providence and virtually every other Northeastern city with working-class roots was down in the dumps, was an effort to recover downtown from the throes of urban blight and turn the city into a bona fide tourist and business destination. He believed, when a lot of people thought this idea was crazy, that Providence could compete with Boston and even New York for tourism dollars and for corporations—and on some level he's succeeded.

Many things have helped Providence to recover, and Cianci is only responsible for some of these. But you really can't help but admire the ge-

nius of certain moves, like offering low-interest city financing to restaurateurs in order to lure them into the city and out of the wealthier suburbs. In America's age of eating out, this trend has helped bring droves of suburbanites and visitors into the city, helping to infuse new blood into once-dowdy areas, and to support a slew of related businesses, from hotels to art galleries to nightclubs. He also drove the efforts that led to the formation of an Arts District, in which self-employed artists are exempt from paying local income taxes. Cianci has supported the construction of new parks and a massive new shopping mall and a similarly ambitious convention center, the renovation and landscaping of the Woonasquatucket and Moshassuck (which had actually been paved over for many decades), and the preservation of several faltering historic neighborhoods.

With the crude enthusiasm and gusto of a used-car salesman, and with plenty of bravado, determination, and innovation, he's largely accomplished his aims. But there is a troubling side to this charmingly raffish character.

Cianci was not only convicted of racketeering in 2002 and sentenced to a prison term of five years and four months, he has watched as one political crony after another has gone down on city corruption and bribery charges under his watch. City politicians have been nailed for all sorts of grievous acts, some of them reflecting an almost shocking degree of chutzpah. It sometimes appears as though the FBI simply has to stand there shining a flashlight down City Hall's darker corridors and boom, they've caught another politico embezzling, bribing, or extorting. Heads of the Board of Tax Assessment Review were busted on extortion, State Supreme Court justice Joseph Bevilacqua had to resign after getting caught trysting with his secretary at a motel allegedly owned by the mob, his successor was charged with writing off luxury personal items, ex-governor Ed DiPrete went to jail for racketeering and other corrupt acts, and many others have been indicted and forced to resign. Cianci may not be linked directly to any of these other crimes, but he is connected to a number of fallen politicians, and as the saying goes—at least in the eyes of many observers—"where there's smoke, there's fire."

Most infamously, in 1984, Buddy himself was convicted of wrongdoing. This was no mere "gentlemen's" crime of dodgy taxes or making sweetheart deals—the guy was nabbed for (and pleaded no contest to) kidnapping and then beating up his then-estranged and now-ex-wife's boyfriend with a fire log and burning him with a lighted cigarette. The loveable emperor of Rogue's Island, as the Ocean State is sometimes mockingly called, clearly revealed an unpleasant side of himself.

He spent the term of his suspended sentence, five years, as a radio talk-show host, and drew fantastically high ratings. The ratings continued when, in 1991, Buddy ran again for mayor and won, this time capturing an astounding 97 percent of the vote—this for a convicted criminal, and for a Republican in a mostly Democratic and mostly liberal state (although on most social issues, Cianci has a thoroughly progressive record). Keep in mind that Cianci has not only endured a conviction, he also weathered a different storm in 1977, when a woman accused him of raping her at gunpoint while both were students at Wisconsin's Marquette University in the mid-1960s. The woman faded away after Cianci paid her $3,000, maintaining his innocence the entire time, and charges were never filed.

But Providence, not only in spite of its and Buddy's political antics but some say because of them, has risen from ashes and reinvented its image. It's got a hit TV series named after it, and local filmmakers like the Farrelly brothers (*There's Something About Mary, Outside Providence*) and Michael Corrente (*Federal Hill, American Buffalo*) are turning it and the rest of the state into a favorite Hollywood shoot locale by emphasizing rather than hiding the city's and the region's quirky personality and peculiar politics. In fact, it's remarkable how similar Providence's theatrical rise has been to another working-class East Coast port city that has also experienced a rejuvenation in recent years, Baltimore. That city also has a notoriously bizarre political history, an up-and-coming waterfront, two noted filmmakers—John Waters and Barry Levinson—and its own TV show, *Homicide*.

Critics will point out that, as is also the case in Baltimore, Cleveland, and other comeback kids of the urban landscape, the great turnaround in Providence has largely helped visiting suburbanites and other tourists more than it's helped actual residents. This is true and not true. Providence's population increased more between 1990 and 2000 than that of any major city in New England except Stamford, Connecticut (which beat it by only a fraction of a percent), so maybe it's enough that Cianci presided over the city as it grew.

But the city still has a lower per-capita income than any other Rhode Island city does, and poverty remains a major problem. Providence is a fairly large city, and yet visitors only deal with the gussied-up parts—College Hill, the nightclub district, the area near the mall and state house. There are several Providence neighborhoods that visitors rarely set foot in, and in which welfare recipients are as common as not. Providence has sky-high property taxes and an ailing, though some say gradually improving, school system. It would be a gross oversimplification to say that Buddy Cianci and his devotees have merely put a fresh coat of paint on a junker and called it new—Providence is improved in countless ways. But the city still has a long way to go before it's the sort of thriving metropolis where workaday folks make a comfortable living and send their kids to decent public schools.

Following his conviction for racketeering, Buddy Cianci was sentenced to five years in prison. He resigned as the Mayor of Providence a few days later. City voters elected Democrat David Cicilline to become the city's new mayor (in the process, Providence became the largest city in the United States with an openly gay mayor). In December 2002, Cianci began serving his sentence at Elkton Federal Correctional Institution in Ohio.

Vincent "Buddy" A. Cianci, Jr. took office in the late 1970s. Cianci envisioned and subsequently spurred a renaissance that many old-school East Coast cities have only recently begun to emulate (and few so successfully). Not everybody agrees that Cianci deserves as much credit for the city's happy reversal of fortune as he claims, but it's hard to argue that the mayor galvanized greater and broader support for downtown civic projects than anybody might have dreamed before he took office.

The plans for bringing back Providence centered around the city's rich maritime history. It was theorized then—and very evident today—that the cornerstone of any urban comeback should always be the waterfront. In the case of Providence, reclaiming the city's waterways meant a great deal more than simply sprucing up the banks of a river—here planners had to come up with a way to fully uncover two rivers that had been paved over a century ago, and to reconstruct the rivers' original courses. Providence long claimed to possess the world's widest bridge—really a lid built to cover both the Moshassuck and Woonasquatucket Rivers, whose confluence lay in the center of downtown. The "bridge" was dismantled, and landscaped pedestrian ways created alongside the riverbanks. Attractive Venetian-inspired foot- and auto bridges were constructed over the rivers, too, linking downtown with the East Side and the area just south of the State House grounds. The Rhode Island Convention Center opened in 1993, drawing in a healthy number of conventions and business groups, and Providence Place Mall followed in 1999. With additional museums and recreational developments under way, and the highest hotel-occupancy rate of any city in the nation, the future of Providence couldn't look better.

Downtown Providence Sights

THE STATE HOUSE AND THE RIVERWALK

A good place to begin a walk around the city is to begin at the grounds of Providence's white-marble-domed **State House,** bounded by Francis, Gaspee, and Smith Streets, 401/222-2357. High above the new Riverwalk and WaterPlace Park, the State House strikes a dramatic pose over downtown. Built over a few years in the late 1890s by the then-ubiquitous firm of McKim, Mead, and White, the leviathan work in white Georgia marble dominates grassy and hilly grounds of several acres. The enormous dome ranks among the largest freestanding domes in the world—it is otherwise without excessive decorative work, its key traits being simplicity and enormity. Open weekdays 8:30 A.M.–4:30 P.M., with guided tours at 10 and 11 A.M.

WaterPlace Park

The part of downtown that extends south from the State House for the next few blocks defines the vision city planners and politicos have for Providence. Walk down Francis Street and on your right you'll pass along the imposing facade of Providence Place Mall, which faces out over the 4-acre WaterPlace Park and Riverwalk. The mall and the park are the anchors of the city's much-touted renaissance, and indeed a stroll alongside the Moshassuck and Woonasquatucket Rivers allows you to grasp both Providence's colonial past and its postmodern present—at one end you can admire the 18th- and 19th-century buildings that fringe Main Street just east of the Providence River; at the other end, the mammoth mall rises high over the waterway.

The part of WaterPlace Park just down the hill from the State House and east of the mall occupies what was once a large tidal basin, about where the Woonasquatucket joined the Moshassuck. During the second half of the 19th century a landscaped cove was installed by the Providence and Worcester Railroad, and for decades a wide expanse of rail tracks effectively cut downtown off from the State House and the neighborhoods around it. The cove and surrounding park was filled in 1892 and then laid over with more rail lines and yards. You'd never believe the area's industrial past today: A newly created pond now lies approximately where the northern end of the basin once did, and various entertainment, mostly rock and pop music, is presented at an adjacent outdoor amphitheater (alternative rock radio station WBRU hosts concerts all summer long).

Today, WaterPlace Park celebrates the city's two rivers (which form one, the Providence River). These waterways weren't always appreciated, and even today, despite major efforts to clean them, they suffer from moderate pollution that results from decades of allowing industrial discharge to enter the rivers. Metals and hazardous wastes have settled on the river bottoms. In the mid-19th century, at the height of the Industrial Revolution but before Providence had developed a sewer system and a sewage treatment plant, both the Moshassuck and Woonasquatucket Rivers flowed a thick and murky brown comprising human and factory waste, decomposing animals, and garbage. It's hardly surprising that cholera epidemics were widespread during these years, nor is it any mystery why city planners rerouted and then decked over the rivers for many decades.

One of the more unusual ways to take in the revitalized riverfront is by gondola. Contact **LaGondola, Inc.,** WaterPlace Park, next to Citizens Plaza, 401/421-8877, www.gondolari.com, for a ride aboard one of its Venetian-style gondolas. There are two gondolas to choose from— the *Cynthia Julia* dates to 1996 and is believed to be the first true Venetian-style gondola, with a 19th-century design and hand-sculpted ornamentation, built outside Venice itself. The second gondola, *Cynthia Jacob,* was built a year later in Venice and shipped here. It's worth walking over even if just to catch a glimpse of the 250 feet of solid brass trim running the length of these 36-foot-long works of art—each with a capacity of some 2,000 pounds. On the chance you're fantasizing about becoming a gondolier yourself, start getting your upper body into shape now— it's just you and a 16-foot oar to move the gondola up and down the city's rivers.

The gondola ride runs the length of the landscaped waterwalk (roughly a 45-minute tour). You supply the beverage (alcoholic or not) and a date (actually up to six persons, which is nice if you can't decide on one), and the gondolier will serenade you with schmaltzy but endearing love songs. It's a very good idea to make reservations, especially on weekend evenings (the fare is about $65 for the first two persons and $15 thereafter for each passenger in your group). It's still possible to ride without reserving ahead—just show up at the landing by Citizens Plaza, and if the gondola is available you're free to book a 15- to 20-minute excursion (the price for this shorter trip is $30 for up to three persons and $10 per person thereafter). It's customary to tip your gondolier 15 to 20 percent.

On about 20 evenings (generally Saturdays) from March through November, **Waterfire Providence,** 401/272-3111, website: www.waterfire.org, dazzles spectators who come to marvel at the more than 100 bonfires set in cauldrons on pylons along the rivers. The fires, which burn from sunset to midnight, seem actually to dance above the water's surface, the flames choreographed by artist and creator Barnaby Evans to the sounds of classical and evocative world-beat music. The aroma of burning cedar, oak, and pine lends a distinct ambience to this ritual. Written descriptions fail this highly unusual multimedia presentation—try to check this one out in person.

To the immediate west of Providence Place Mall and the State House neighborhood, across I-95 (which has one exit that feeds almost directly into the mall parking garages), you can see vestiges of the industry and commerce that once characterized much of downtown. The most prominent structure west of the interstate is the **Foundry,** Promenade and Holden Streets, a sprawling redbrick complex with ranks and ranks of windows and one massive hemispherical window that earned the building its nickname, the "Big Bubble." The structure has been retrofitted in recent years to include offices on its upper floors, most notably the Rhode Island Department of Environmental Management. The basement of the building has housed nightclubs over the years, including the Living Room Club (now on Rathbone Street); it's currently the home of Charlie Hall's Stage, a small theater.

To Woonsocket 146
To Pawtucket
and Boston

7
95
OLNEY ST.
Moshassuck River
ORMS ST.
44
BARNES ST.
JEWETT ST.
SMITH ST.
BOWEN ST.
RHODE ISLAND
STATE HOUSE
★
ROGER WILLIAMS
NATIONAL MEMORIAL
★
★CATHEDRAL OF
SAINT JOHN
PROSPECT
TERRACE ★
MEETING ST.
FOUNDRY ★
PROMENADE ST.
PROVIDENCE
PLACE MALL ■
OLD STATE HOUSE ★
SHAKESPEARE'S
HEAD ★
BROWN UNIVERSITY ■
BOOKSTORE
College
Hill
Woonasquatucket
OLD ARSENAL ★
ANGELL ST.
River
LAGONDOLA, INC. ★
WATERPLACE ★
PARK
FIRST BAPTIST CHURCH
IN AMERICA ★
★ RISD ART MUSEUM
RHODE ISLAND SCHOOL
★ ★ OF DESIGN (RISD)
WATERMAN ST.
BROWN
UNIVERSITY
6 10
EXCHANGE TER.
FLEET
★ SKATING
CENTER
OLD
MARKET
HOUSE ★
LIST ART CENTER
PROVIDENCE ATHENEUM
★ JOSEPH BROWN HOUSE
GEORGE ST.
★ STEPHEN HOPKINS HOUSE
THAYER ST.
95
Kennedy
Plaza
PROVIDENCE WARWICK
CONVENTION AND ★
VISITORS BUREAU
PROVIDENCE ■
CIVIC CENTER
SABIN ST.
WASHINGTON ST.
EDDY ST.
THE ARCADE ★
PROVIDENCE COUNTY
■ COURTHOUSE
★ JACKSON-GARDNER PARK
THOMAS POYNTON
★ IVES HOUSE
POWER ST.
ATWELLS AVE.
To
Federal
Hill
BROADWAY
Downtown
6
DORRANCE ST.
BAER'S RIVER
WORKSHOP
S. MAIN ST.
★ JOHN BROWN HOUSE
S. WATER ST.
BENEFIT ST.
44
PROVIDENCE
PUBLIC LIBRARY
GRACE CHURCH ★
WEYBOSSET ST.
PROVIDENCE
★ PERFORMING
ARTS CENTER
ARNOLD ST.
195
FOUNTAIN ST.
EMPIRE ST.
GREEN ST.
WESTMINSTER ST.
BENEFICENT
CONGREGATIONAL
CHURCH
★ ★
JOHNSON & WALES UNIVERSITY
(DOWNTOWN CAMPUS)
DEAN ST.
WESTMINSTER ST.
PINE ST.
HERITAGE
HARBOR
MUSEUM ★
1A
EDDY ST.
S. MAIN ST.
Providence River
BROAD ST.
BASSETT ST.
ELM ST.
CHESTNUT ST.
RICHMOND ST.
Jewelry
District
POINT ST.
S. WATER ST.
Fox
Point
1
CAHIR ST.
HURRICANE
BARRIER

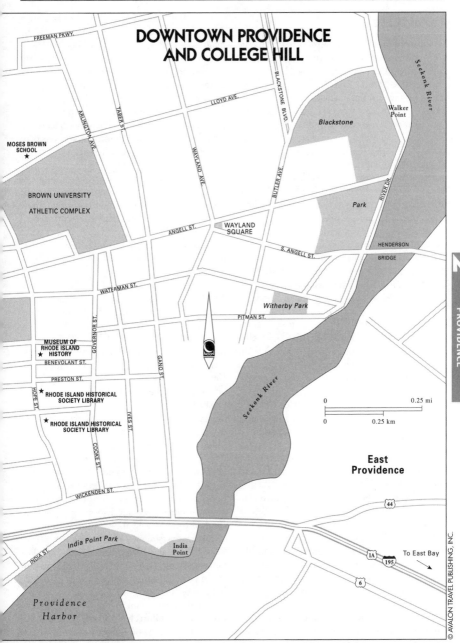

DOWNTOWN PROVIDENCE AND COLLEGE HILL

FREEMAN PKWY.

LLOYD AVE.

BLACKSTONE BLVD.

Seekonk River

Walker Point

Blackstone

ARLINGTON AVE.

TABER ST.

WAYLAND AVE.

BUTLER AVE.

MOSES BROWN SCHOOL
★

BROWN UNIVERSITY

ATHLETIC COMPLEX

Park

RIVER DR.

ANGELL ST.

WAYLAND SQUARE

S. ANGELL ST.

HENDERSON

BRIDGE

WATERMAN ST.

Witherby Park

PITMAN ST.

GOVERNOR ST.

GANO ST.

MUSEUM OF RHODE ISLAND HISTORY
★

BENEVOLANT ST.

PRESTON ST.

HOPE ST.

IVES ST.

★ RHODE ISLAND HISTORICAL SOCIETY LIBRARY

★ RHODE ISLAND HISTORICAL SOCIETY LIBRARY

Seekonk River

COOKE ST.

0   0.25 mi

0   0.25 km

East Providence

WICKENDEN ST.

44

INDIA ST.

India Point Park

India Point

1A 195

To East Bay

6

Providence Harbor

N

PROVIDENCE

© AVALON TRAVEL PUBLISHING, INC.

DOWNCITY

The part of Providence that most resembles the downtown of any Northeastern city lies just south of the WaterPlace Park area, bounded by the Providence River, on the west by I-95, and on the south (at least until it's relocated) by I-195. The northern and eastern fringes of the neighborhood have met with the wave of the city's gentrification, especially the commercial area that borders WaterPlace Park. Here just in the last decade have opened the Providence Convention Center, the adjacent Westin Providence hotel, and across the street the Courtyard by Marriott hotel. Next to that, the former train station and nearby buildings now contain restaurants and offices.

Kennedy Plaza

To the immediate south, across from Exchange Place, a grassy park extends across Kennedy Plaza, which is home to the city's bus terminal (the hub through which virtually every bus in Rhode Island seems to pass) and faces **Providence City Hall.** Here, too, is the **Fleet Skating Center,** which contains a rink and offers ice and roller skate rentals. Currently receiving a facelift, Kennedy Plaza is slowly being transformed into downtown's social anchor, although beyond the skating center there's not a huge amount to see or do here. On the southwest corner of Kennedy Plaza, at Dorrance and Washington Streets, note the grand Providence Biltmore Hotel, which was constructed in 1922. A plaque on the facade shows the high-water mark reached during the devastating Hurricane of 1938, which ravaged all of southern New England.

Even with all the improvements made downtown, the city—like other so-called comeback cities such as Cleveland and Baltimore—has had difficulty finding ways to convince residents to move downtown. Many neighborhoods on the periphery, especially on the East Side, have vibrant residential communities, but downtown itself, despite attempts to develop housing here, struggles in this regard. Most people point to Downcity, the nickname for the city's downtown commercial core, as the most likely candidate for developing a mixed commercial-residential core.

Extending south from Kennedy Plaza are a network of mostly one-way urban streets, the main east-west ones being Washington, Westminster, Weybosset, and Pine; and the main north-south ones being Dorrance, Eddy, Mathewson, and Empire. There are few attractions on or near these streets, just banks, office buildings, and mostly workaday retail concerns and undistinguished eateries and bars that cater to the neighborhood's 9-to-5 workers and the mix of students and regular joes who spend time here. Visitors should see in this neighborhood during the day, not so much because it's unsafe at night but more because there's little to see or do at that time. The neighborhood's main draw is its wealth of fine 19th- and early-20th-century commercial architecture (though quite a bit of it, especially on the floors above street level, has been for years vacant).

The Arcade

The lower portion of downtown is slowly becoming more lively—and it feeds into the burgeoning Jewelry District, which lies immediately south on the other side of I-95. As you walk over this way, consider strolling by way of Weybosset Street. If you walk down Dorrance from Kennedy Plaza and make a left on Weybosset, you'll soon come to perhaps the most distinguished architectural gem in downtown Providence, The Arcade, 65 Weybosset St., 401/598-1199, which dates to 1828 and is the oldest indoor shopping center in the nation. This magnificent example of Greek Revival architecture, designed by James C. Bucklin and Russell Warren, is made of granite and rests under a dramatic glass skylighted roof, its two entrances fronted by a dozen 13-ton Ionic columns. Inside there's also a great food court with Italian, Greek, vegetarian, and other foods.

Walk back along Weybosset Street past Dorrance and continue west (really southwest) in the opposite direction. Although the East Side holds most of the city's historic places of worship, downtown is home of the **Beneficent Congregational Church,** 300 Weybosset St., 401/331-9844, an 1809 structure that is the oldest building in this neighborhood. The parish formed in 1743 after about half the membership of the present-day First Congregational Church split off on its own and began worship in a new and fairly modest building that would become the heart of downtown. The current church is notable for its massive gilded dome, which was added on in 1836. Only a bit newer but quite famous because of its design by famous church architect Richard Upjohn, **Grace Church,** Mathewson and Westminster Streets, 401/331-3225, may remind you of some of his other structures, such as Trinity Church in New York City and the chapel at Bowdoin College— Upjohn also designed the outlandish and flamboyant Connecticut State Capitol in Hartford. This Gothic Victorian of somber brownstone is presided over by an octagonal spire, and its chimes resound throughout downtown.

Downcity, while it still hasn't realized its full potential (nor the expectations of boosters and politicians who would like to see it become a true mixed-use residential-commercial neighborhood), does contain a smattering of hip shops and some eateries, plus the **Providence Public Library,** 225 Washington St., 401/455-8000 or 401/455-8090, which has an art gallery with rotating exhibits and is part of the city's popular Artrolley Gallery Night.

Johnson & Wales University

Just around the corner from the Providence Public Library, you'll also find the always-daring **AS220** artspace, plus the downtown campus of **Johnson & Wales University,** Weybosset and Empire Sts., www.jwu.edu. Begun by Gertrude Johnson and Mary Wales as a business-education school in Providence in 1914, Johnson & Wales has become a world leader in its technology, hospitality, and culinary arts programs throughout the country; there are additional campuses in Miami; Charleston, South Carolina; Denver; Norfolk, Virginia; and Goteborg, Sweden. Television chef Emeril Lagasse, who grew up just over the border in Fall River, is among the most famous alums.

You need to call for an appointment, but if you're something of a foodie don't miss the **Culinary Archives and Museum,** 315 Harborside

Blvd., 401/598-2805, website: www.culinary.org, which is located at Johnson & Wales Harborside campus. Hours are based on the academic calendar, but generally you can schedule one of the excellent hour-long guided tours for Tuesday through Saturday 10 A.M.–4 P.M. Admission is $5. This, the world's largest such archive, contains every imaginable bit of food minutiae, including an exhaustive and fascinating cookbook collection, including titles dating back to the 1500s. Another strength is the collection of more than 4,000 menus. Exhibits trace different types of food and how, when, and where they became popular over time, as well as shedding light on the evolution of kitchen gadgetry and equipment, as well as how restaurants have changed over the years. All told the archives contain more than a half-million items. Note that the archives are well south of the downtown campus, a short drive away, on the Providence/Cranston border.

JEWELRY DISTRICT

Fairly quiet during the day, except for the handful of factories that still operate here, the Jewelry District comes alive at night as a dynamic district of nightclubs and a handful of eateries. The neighborhood is cut off from the rest of downtown by I-195, which forms its northern boundary; it's marked by I-95 to the west, Point Street on the south, and the riverfront to the east. At the moment, unless you're a big club craver, this neighborhood may not hold a huge amount of interest, but come back in two or three years and you'll see the whole district transformed.

Heritage Harbor

What's sure to put the neighborhood on the map is the new multi-museum plex at Heritage Harbor, which is slated for completion by roughly 2005 and will eventually contain some 15 museums. There have been some delays in construction and funding, so the exact opening date of this facility remains a bit uncertain. The project will eventually contain some 14 museums. The complex is being developed inside a neoclassical turn-of-the-20th-century power plant on the Providence River (at Eddy and Point

© ANDREW COLLINS

looking across Providence River toward the future Heritage Harbor Museum

Streets), which was donated to the city by the Narragansett Electric Company—there are also a few attached outbuildings. The structure is within walking distance of downtown and the East Side (opposite the river, reached easily via a short bridge) After I-195 is relocated to the south, access will be even greater.

Heritage Harbor Museum, website: www.heritageharbor.org, will comprise several distinctive museums, a facility for booking boat excursions, and theater and performing-arts venues. This ambitious and ingenious reuse of a dramatic light-filled space with vaulted ceilings, skylights, and high arched windows will include Corliss Hall, a state-of-the-art visitors center with ticketing and reservations booths for area events, attractions, and accommodations. A permanent exhibit, "La Survivance," will tell the turbulent and moving story of the thousands of mill workers who came to Rhode Island (and other New England states) throughout the 19th century from rural life in Québec to seek a better life. (For more on this, be sure to see the Museum of Work and Culture in Woonsocket, one of the best interpreters of industrial history in the nation.) Engaging and interactive mixed-media dioramas and displays will bring to life the state's founding, and the life and travails of Roger Williams. There will also be a Diner Museum, honoring Rhode Island's much-adored invention. Heritage Harbor planners are working with ethnic groups from throughout Providence as well as with representatives from the Smithsonian to create this state-of-the-art facility.

For the foreseeable future, Heritage Harbor has one attraction that's open, the **Rhode Island Children's Museum,** 100 South St., 401/273-5437, website: www.childrenmuseum.org, which moved several years ago down from Pawtucket. This engaging hands-on facility offers a range of cool exhibits, including a children's garden that takes visitors through a touch-friendly tour of trees, shrubs, and plants native to Rhode Island; a funhouse of mirrors with a walk-through kaleidoscope; a miniature animal hospital sponsored by the Providence Animal Rescue League; and an infant-oriented area called Littlewoods in which participants can scamper through simulated caves and climb trees. One of the more innovative exhibits takes visitors through a manhole beneath the city streets, where kids can ride on an actual steamroller and learn up-close how streets are made. One area that may sound more daunting than fun is Teeth!, but this is actually one of the museum's most popular draws: here you explore the teeth of humans and several types of wild animals and kids get to brush an enormous larger-than-life mouth. Open Tues.–Sun. 9:30 A.M.–5 P.M.; $5 for adults and children.

FEDERAL HILL

Go ahead, make those jokes about crime bosses and imagine characters from *The Sopranos* or a Mario Puzo novel sauntering along Atwells Avenue, the main drag of Providence's own Little Italy, **Federal Hill.** Just keep your jokes quiet, and don't spend a lot of time staring at guys who fit the image of a modern-day mob boss. Maybe there's a mafia presence here these days, maybe there isn't—unquestionably there have been mob-related busts here in the past.

What you will find along Atwells Avenue, and also surrounding the charming neighborhood hub **Depasquale Square,** are terrific restaurants and food shops that seem right out of a Roman streetscape. Local filmmaker Michael Corrente has brought considerable fame to the neighborhood by shooting the movie *Federal Hill* here. (Corrente also shot *Outside Providence* and the cinematic adaptation of the David Mamet play *American Buffalo* in and around the city.)

The neighborhood begins just west of where Atwells Avenue crosses I-95, and you'll know you've found it the second you pass under the lighted **Federal Hill Arch,** from which an Italian pine cone hangs as a gesture of welcome. For about 15 blocks you'll find shops and eateries proffering various delectables, not to mention dry-goods stores and a surprising number of tattoo parlors. This is one stroll on which you probably won't burn any calories.

College Hill and the Riverfront Sights

The city's East Side is marked by the Moshassuck River north of about Thomas Street and then the Providence River, below that. Rising precipitously to the east just past the river is College Hill, the home of both Brown University and the Rhode Island School of Design.

Providence Preservation Society Heritage Tours, 21 Meeting St., 401/831-8586, website: www.ppsri.org, offers both guided and self-guided walking tours of the neighborhood. Certain times during the year the general public gets a glimpse inside some of these exceptional examples of colonial through Victorian homes, and sometimes the elaborate gardens that surround them. In mid-June, you can attend the **Festival of Historic Houses,** 401/831-7440, a two-day event of house and garden tours along Benefit Street. Then in December, come for the **Holiday Festival of Historic Homes,** 401/831-8587, a Benefit Street ramble that includes carolers and street performers in period garb, and tours of several of the neighborhood's most prominent homes.

ALONG THE RIVERFRONT

You can get a real sense of modern Providence's humble origins by visiting the site of the original natural springs at which Roger Williams established a settlement, now the **Roger Williams National Memorial,** 282 N. Main St., 401/521-7266, website: www.nps.gov/rowi. This is a small 4.5-acre plot (open daily dawn–dusk) and visitor center (open daily 9 A.M.–4:30 P.M.) with free admission; it's very accessible from downtown hotels and lies just a few blocks east of the State House via Smith Street—it's also right at the lower slope of College Hill. And it's a fine place for a brief stroll or lunchtime picnic. In the visitor center a small but well-executed exhibit details the travails of Roger Williams, and the manner in which his novel ideas influenced America's present-day policies and beliefs.

Outside the visitor center in the park, the **Bernon Grove** of trees and plantings commemorates the life of Gabriel Bernon, a French Huguenot who fled persecution in Europe in

PROVIDENCE

the 17th century for Providence, where he helped found the Cathedral of St. John (just across the street from the park). Marking what is believed to be the exact spot where the natural springs once flowed, the **Hahn Memorial** is a well-shaped sculpture named for the first Jewish citizen of Providence to hold elected office. (The colony had been a welcome refuge to many 17th-century Jews forced from Spain and Portugal—the General Assembly of Rhode Island dissented, as usual, from their neighboring colonies by declaring that the refugees "may expect as good protection here as any stranger residing among us.")

Just across from the Roger Williams National Memorial stands an elegant example of Georgian ecclesiastical architecture, the Episcopal **Cathedral of St. John,** 271 N. Main St., 410/331-4662, which also contains a number of Gothic elements, from tall lancet windows to a Gothic belfry. John Holden Greene designed the church in 1810, but the congregation dates to much earlier, when Huguenot Gabriel Bernon fled Europe in the early 18th century and established King's Chapel here with Nathaniel Brown. The adjoining cemetery contains graves of many of the city's early luminaries.

Persons unfortunate enough to be found guilty of serious crimes in colonial Rhode Island were for many decades pilloried nearby, at the southwest corner of North Main and Haymarket Streets. The pillory stood until 1837, long after this form of punishment had been done away with. The home of Roger Williams stood behind what is now 235 North Main Street, nearly overlooking the spring at which the state's founder decided to establish the city of Providence in 1636. As you might guess, the site of the city's first mill was at the corner of North Main and Mill Streets—here John Smith operated the facility in 1646.

The Providence Preservation Society is headquartered at the distinctive wooden three-story building known quizzically as **Shakespeare's Head,** 21 Meeting St., 401/831-7440. The 1772 house has enjoyed a colorful history, having served originally as the print shop for the city's first newspaper, the *Providence Gazette and Country Journal,* and then as the city's post office.

Postmaster John Carter, who had been appointed by U.S. Postmaster-General Benjamin Franklin, not only oversaw mailing here, he sold books and writing materials. A sign depicting the head of William Shakespeare hung outside the front door to advertise the house shop. The Preservation Society tends to a delightful restored colonial herb and flower garden behind the house (it's open to the public).

First Baptist Church in America

It may lack the height of the downtown skyscrapers, but the First Baptist Church in America, 75 N. Main St., 401/454-3418, nevertheless affects a more dramatic influence on the city's skyline than any other building. Roger Williams established this parish in 1638, making it the nation's first such congregation. Interestingly, within just a few years, Williams parted ways with the Baptist Church, unable to reconcile his membership of any "earthly church" with his own devout beliefs in the New Testament. In 1700, member Pardon Tillinghast (who built the city's first wharf) constructed a meeting house for the congregation—at his own expense— along North Main Street. This structure was succeeded by a larger church in 1726, and in 1775 by the present Baptist church whose triple-tiered spire rises to 185 feet. It continues to draw attention, in part because of its exquisite design, but also owing to its regal landscaping and prime location atop a bluff on North Main Street. The most architecturally inspired of the famous Brown brothers, Joseph, designed the building. A glimpse inside reveals the remarkable craftsmanship of the times, the five-bay vaulted ceiling rising majestically above rows of wooden pews. The building is barely altered since it was constructed, and it's one of relatively few major structure (especially among those down by the riverfront) that withstood any major damage during the Great Gale of 1815. This is one building that was built, emphatically, to last.

Pause to wonder exactly how the builders were able to hoist the church bell, which was cast in London and weighs two and a half tons, to the belfry. Other notable elements include a massive crystal chandelier built in Ireland and brought over in 1792 and an elaborate organ that was installed in 1834. The congregation has been highly influential throughout the country and the world, and it also helped to start up some 12 additional Baptist churches throughout greater Providence during the 19th and early 20th centuries. In 1806, the Women of First Baptist Church founded the Female Mite Society, which became the state's first missionary organization.

The **Providence Art Club,** 11 Thomas St., 401/331-1114, occupies a pair of late-18th-century houses right around the corner. Here you can visit the free galleries, which present rotating exhibitions of club members' works—this is a popular stop on the monthly Providence Gallery Night. Seril Dodge designed these stately brick houses; in the main structure, Seril and his brother Nehemiah developed a technique for silver- and gold-plating that marked the beginning of the city's costume-jewelry industry. The Art Club formed nearly a century later, in 1880. Open weekdays 10 A.M.–4 P.M., Sat. noon–3 P.M., and Sun. 3–5 P.M.

Thomas Street ranks among the city's most charming, offering historic residential architecture on a steep grade. A couple doors over from the Providence Art Club, the half-timbered **Fleur-de-Lys Building,** 7 Thomas St., was the home of prominent Rhode Island painter Sidney R. Burleigh until his death in 1929. Edmund R. Willson created the medieval-inspired structure, which has housed artists' studios since Burleigh's passing. At No. 9 Thomas St., the **Deacon Edward Taylor House** dates to 1790 and was the residence of the deacon of the First Congregational Church for many years. The building is regarded for its steep-pitched roof.

If you wonder why a road called Canal Street runs up alongside what is actually the Moshassuck River, beginning in 1828 the Blackstone Canal was built to connect Providence with Worcester, and it paralleled the Moshassuck through downtown Providence. The canal was a financial burden that encountered frequent structural problems, as were most canals in the northeast. Once railroads came along, the canal lost favor, and it closed for good in 1843.

Just down the hill from Brown University, directly on the Providence River, you'll find the beautifully preserved 1773 **Old Market House,** in Market Square, built as the city's agora, where farmers from outlying areas met to sell their goods in town. French soldiers were quartered in the building during the American Revolution. The building was designed by Joseph Brown and Stephen Hopkins.

An odd sight along North Main Street, right at Waterman, is the opening of a large road tunnel. This tunnel runs under College Hill and opens again onto Thayer Street, and your only chance of passing through is to take a bus across the East Side. In 1914 the tunnel was dug by the East Side Electric Car company to compete with the counterweighted grip buses that ran up and down steep and slippery College Hill. Rollerbladers and skateboarders, at least a few courageous ones, sometimes sneak through the structure, but such activity is highly illegal. The North Main Street entrance to the tunnel marks the very spot where Roger Williams traditionally gathered townspeople for meetings and discussions on local government.

College Street marks the transition from North to South Main Street. South Main contains a curious mix of historic residences, funky and increasingly swanky restaurants and a few shops, vintage redbrick commercial structures, and new offices. Structures worth noting as you stroll along include the **Joseph Brown House,** 50 S. Main St., the 1774 home of one of the four famous Brown siblings. Joseph took well to architecture and designed this staunch city home of red brick with a widow's walk on the roof—he also designed the First Baptist Church and the Old Market House. At No. 86, note the **Old Stone Bank,** former home of the **Providence Institution for Savings,** which was the city's first savings bank and one of America's oldest. The imposing gilt-domed neoclassical building dates to 1898. No. 112 is the private **Cooke House,** named for resident (and grandson of Governor Nicholas Cooke) Benoni Cooke. The Federal mansion dates to the 1820s and is considered one of John Holden Greene's finest residential architectural accomplishments. Brown

University bought both the Old Stone Bank and the Cooke House in 1995 with the intention of moving the Haffenreffer Museum of Anthropology—currently in Bristol—to Providence. Brown later decided the Old Stone Bank lacked sufficient space for the museum, and now uses it for special functions. Current plans are for Brown to build a brand-new structure on campus to house the Haffenreffer.

Jackson-Gardner Park

Around the Westminster and Pine blocks of South Main Street, you can take a break or even have a little picnic along the river at Jackson-Gardner Park, a small landscaped patch of land shaded by tall oak trees and with benches, as well as the inspiring 75-foot-tall World War I monument. The park is named for F. Ellis Jackson, who in 1933 built the **Providence County Courthouse** across the way at 30 South Main, and Henry B. Gardner, a naval officer of note in World War II. The courthouse replaced the original Superior Courthouse and before that the Providence Towne House, which served the function from the 1720s through 1860. The formidable eight-story neoclassical structure, built of red brick and limestone, covers a full city block. Its main ground-level entrance on is Main, with a rear entrance up on Benefit Street level with the building's fifth floor—it's on quite a steep hill. A four-stage squared tower crowned by a cupola stands sentry over the vast structure, notable for its stepped, flanking gabled wings. Few buildings on the East Side command more respect, both architecturally and practically speaking, than the courthouse.

As civic centers go, the South Main Street neighborhood is unusually charming and historic, with relatively few modern structures—although the massive glass tower at Providence Washington Plaza (it's the home of Hemenway's seafood restaurant) fails to respect the scale and aesthetic of this otherwise walkable and enjoyable street.

BENEFIT STREET

The city's "Mile of History," Benefit Street runs parallel to North and South Main Streets, just a

© PROVIDENCE WARWICK CONVENTION & VISITORS BUREAU

famous Benefit Street

block east but in most places many feet higher in elevation. As the previous tour along Main runs north to south, this next excursion runs the opposite direction. From lower South Main Street, cut east up one of the cross streets, preferably James or Transit Street.

During Providence's heyday as a colonial shipping center, and then throughout the 19th century's industrial periods, wealthy city residents built their homes along or just off Benefit Street, which remained fashionable well into the early 20th century. Following World War II, however, and coinciding with the so-called white flight to the suburbs that affected most large U.S. cities, the neighborhood rapidly lost its prominence. Many of the old homes along Benefit were boarded up, and others were subdivided into boarding houses and cheap apartments. During the 1960s and 1970s, few visitors set foot in these parts.

It was during the city's renaissance, which began in earnest in the late 1970s, that the Providence Preservation Society set forth to restore

Benefit Street, house by house. Walking through the neighborhood today, it's hard to believe that it was ever blighted—all told you'll find about 200 18th- and 19th-century buildings along Benefit Street, which is strung with vintage gas lamps and lined by brick sidewalks.

One of the first prominent structures you'll come to as you walk north from Transit or James Streets is the immense **Nightingale-Brown House,** 357 Benefit St., 401/272-0357. Colonel Joseph Nightingale built the prodigious, square, hip-roofed house in 1792. Brown University founder Nicholas Brown bought the house in 1814. Here his son John Carter Brown amassed an unrivaled collection of artifacts and documents tracing the New World's early history. (This collection is now contained within the walls of the library at Brown University that bears his name.) The house remained in the Brown family into the 1980s, and now, appropriately enough, contains the John Nicholas Brown Center for the Study of American Civilization, named for John Carter Brown's son. Open Fri. 1–4 P.M.

John Brown House

Arguably the most imposing of the neighborhood's many impressive homes is just up the block along Power Street, the Rhode Island Historical Society's John Brown House, 52 Power St., 401/331-8575, website: www.rihs.org. The sixth U.S. president, John Quincy Adams, described this as "the most magnificent and elegant private mansion I have seen on this continent." This grand home, exquisitely restored and furnished top to bottom, still looks swanky today—few American house-museums from this period rival it. Inside you'll find a first-rate assemblage of colonial furnishings and decorative arts. John Brown, a fabulously successful merchant and one of the masterminds of the *Gaspee* incident, began construction on the three-story Georgian mansion in 1786, on a bluff along Benefit Street, facing downtown and the riverfront.

Drawing the greatest interest on this redbrick mansion with white wood trim and stone lintels is the ornate balustraded parapet over the cornice. Members of the Brown family occupied the house until 1901, adding a Victorian-style ser-

vants' wing in the mid-19th century. For many decades during the building's first century, a party at the Brown House was a must-attend occasion among society types and academics—in fact, Brown University's commencement dinners were held here for some time. In 1941 the house was bequeathed to the Rhode Island Historical Society, which set about reproducing the interior's original colors and French wallpapering. Furnishings include many created by local artisans William Clagget (a clockmaker) and Goddard–Townsend (a Newport firm that specialized in high-quality colonial wood furnishings). The art collection is well regarded, too. Former mayor Buddy Cianci once lived in the estate's former carriage house, adjacent to the property. Open Tues.–Sat. 10 A.M.–5 P.M., Sun. noon–4 P.M. (limited hours Jan.–Feb.); admission $7.

Up the street, note the private **Thomas Poynton Ives House,** 66 Power St., one of the city's most important and impressive colonial mansions. The Georgian colonial home dates to 1811 and is notable for its finely crafted rail running along the roofline and semicircular portico, which was added in the 1880s. Another nearby private house of considerable note, the **Edward Carrington House,** 66 Williams St., reveals the shift around the early 1810s from Georgian colonial to Federal (or Adam) architecture. Built in 1811, the three-story brick mansion (the final story was added shortly after the home's original construction) with heavy stone corner quoins and lovely elliptical fanlights above the front door, stayed in the Carrington family well into the 20th century.

Known as a governor and then U.S. Senator of Rhode Island, before that as a prominent Civil War general, Ambrose Burnside may be known best for lending a variation on his name to what we commonly call facial hair extending from just in front of the ears down the side of the face. Yes, it's after Burnside (who wore a prominent pair of them) that the term "sideburns" derives. The Rhode Island native lived for many years at the now private 1850s redbrick Victorian at 314 Benefit Street, between Power and Charlesfield Streets, a dramatic edifice with wrought-iron work around it.

GENERAL AMBROSE BURNSIDE

Although a native of Indiana, Civil War general Ambrose Everett Burnside (1824–1881) is most closely associated with the Ocean State. Burnside worked as a tailor's apprentice as a young man before gaining admittance to West Point Academy, from which he graduated in 1847. He then spent several years in the army, including tours of duty fighting the Apaches in the New Mexico territory, but eventually resigned from the military and settled in Rhode Island to become a gun manufacturer.

Burnside had developed a breech-loading carbine gun, which he had patented and hoped to produce in Providence. Unfortunately, he was unable to secure a contract to provide these guns to the U.S. Army, and he ended up assigning his patent to creditors to cover some of his debts. During these years in Providence, he became involved with the Rhode Island state militia, and this affiliation would lead him into the Civil War.

History has taken a rather unfavorable view of Burnside's role during the Civil War—he enjoyed few successes as a commander. Things began auspiciously enough, as Burnside arrived in Washington, D.C., with his Rhode Island troops very early in the war, and quickly developed a friendship with President Abraham Lincoln. Early success came as he led his troops during the First Bull Run attack and organized successful military endeavors along the North Carolina coast, at Roanoke Island and New Bern. He was a two-star general at this point and was even offered the command of the Union Army, which he refused, citing his own relative lack of military experience at this level.

Eventually, Burnside became the reluctant commander of the Army of the Potomac and, in fact, only accepted the post because he felt obligated to obey his commanders and please President Lincoln. In this capacity he led the advance on Fred-

ericksburg, but Confederate General Robert E. Lee took advantage of myriad delays and handily fended off the Union approach. Profoundly disappointed, Burnside offered to retire, seeming almost vindicated by his failure, since he had, after all, claimed all along that he was not fit to serve in this capacity. His superiors refused his resignation.

Success continued to elude General Burnside, and for a time he was, at his request, reassigned to lead the Department of Ohio, where he went after Confederate raiders and other troublemakers. He soon found himself in good standing again, following a successful maneuver at Knoxville, and this time he commanded troops under General Grant in Virginia, with only limited success. He endured a rather monumental failure during the march on Petersburg.

Following these debacles, Burnside finally earned his leave from the military and formally resigned on April 15, 1865. A congressional investigation following the war cleared Burnside of much blame concerning the ill-fated Petersburg incident, but his military reputation remained tarnished. Nevertheless, back in Rhode Island, he found almost instant political and business success. He was elected governor three times (1866, '67, and '68), and he served as president of several manufacturing corporations. In 1874 he was elected to the U.S. Senate, where he served until his death in 1881. He is buried in Providence's Swan Point Cemetery.

Burnside's most lasting legacy, however, has nothing to do with his contributions to politics, the military, invention, or manufacturing. Rather, most people speak of him today, often unknowingly, in reference to a hairstyle of sorts. Burnside grew his whiskers thickly down along the sides of his face, a look that we now call "sideburns."

Undoubtedly the most kindly and generous-sounding street intersection you'll ever come upon, the corner of Benefit and Benevolent streets is the site of John Holden Greene's **First Unitarian Church,** 401/421-7970, a work that many consider even finer than his arguably more famous Cathedral of St. John. It's the third church building on this site to serve the congregation

that dates to 1723; this structure with its tall steeple and magnificent Classical Revival detailing is known best for containing within its belfry the largest bell ever cast by Paul Revere's foundry.

A particularly fine example of a mid-18th-century colonial home, the **Stephen Hopkins House,** Benefit and Hopkins Streets, 401/751-1758 or 401/884-8337, has been around the block a couple times. In 1804 it was moved from its earlier perch down the hill at Hopkins and South Main Streets, and it was pushed farther up Hopkins in 1928 to accommodate construction of the Providence County Courthouse. Here the noted colonial governor Stephen Hopkins resided during his 10 terms at the helm of Rhode Island; other posts during his distinguished political life included being a member of the Colonial Congress (he signed the Declaration of Independence), serving as Chief Justice of the Supreme Court, and being the first chancellor of Brown University. Exhibits and artifacts in the house document the life and times of this eminent statesman, as well as the lives of some of his guests (including George Washington). On warm days be sure to stroll out back through the museum's exquisite parterre garden. Open Apr.–mid-Dec., Wed. and Sat. 1–4 P.M.

Providence Atheneum

Among the oldest libraries in North America, the **Providence Atheneum** 251 Benefit St., 401/421-6970, dates to 1753 and contains such rare and fascinating works as the seven volumes of the original double elephant folio edition of John J. Audubon's *Birds of America.* Another specialty of the Atheneum's holdings is its Roycroft collection consisting of about 300 items produced between 1895 and 1915 by the distinguished Roycrofters press, famous for its Arts and Crafts prints and illustrations. Rare works by Robert Burns, a Napoleon-commissioned early-19th-century study of Egypt titled *Description de l'Egypte,* and several books from 14th-century Europe are additional highlights of the Rare Books Collection.

The Atheneum was established in 1831; a few years later Providence Library Company (established in 1753) combined with it, and the two collections were moved to the second floor of the Arcade on Weybosset Street; in 1838 the Atheneum moved to this majestic Greek Revival structure, which was designed by Russell Warren and the Arcade's architect, James C. Bucklin. In the late 1840s Edgar Allen Poe and Sarah Whitman spent many an hour discussing literature and admiring one another's works in the Atheneum's corridors.

In addition to priceless original literary volumes and a comprehensive modern collection that can be viewed by any visitor (and taken out on loan by members), the Atheneum houses several rare artworks, including *The Hours,* a famous painting by Newport-born miniature painter Edward G. Malbone. There are also about 50 books here that date from the original 1753 library collection—the first library building burned in 1758 and all of the 350 books inside lost—but for about 70 that happened to be out on loan at the time. Lectures, concerts, and other events are held regularly at the Atheneum. Membership (which confers borrowing privileges and allows regular visitation) is open to anybody (resident or not) for $85 per year for individuals and $150 for households. Strengths within the collection of some 150,000 works include biography, travel, poetry, mystery, current fiction, and history. Open Mon.–Thurs. 10 A.M.–8 P.M. and Fri.–Sat. 10 A.M.–5 P.M. (closed Sat. mid-June–early Sept.).

Rhode Island School of Design (RISD)

The campus of the prestigious **Rhode Island School of Design** occupies much of the blocks along Benefit Street from College to Waterman Streets (there are buildings down the hill along Main Street and up a block on Prospect, too). Indirectly, RISD owes its very existence to the success of Samuel Slater, who more than any other person is responsible for the development of the Blackstone River valley into North America's premier center of textile manufacture. The school opened with a very practical vocational aim: to verse students in the ways of textile arts and design, and also in related fields notable in Providence, such as jewelry design and manufacture, and machine works and design. Over the years, the school has gained considerable prestige not only for its applied design courses but for training some of the nation's leaders in fine and graphic arts, interior design, costume-making, and the like. An artsy buzz permeates the campus and nearby streets, and no doubt has helped to influence the similarly alternative tone of its neighbor Brown, which is quite possibly the most countercultural of the Ivy League universities.

PROVIDENCE

RISD was founded in 1877 and occupied a single building downtown on Westminster Street before moving to new digs in 1895 on the block bound by Waterman, Benefit, College, and Main Streets—directly down the slope of College Hill from Brown University. The two campuses, at least in the eyes of most visitors, seem to blend almost imperceptibly—indeed, they both share stellar reputations. F. Ellis Jackson and his crew, the same group responsible for the nearby Providence County Courthouse, designed one of the school's best-known structures in 1937, the sprawling Helen Adelia Rowe Metcalf Building. It's fairly easy to see similarities of style and design in both RISD's campus and the courthouse.

Keep an eye out for signs marking RISD's Office of Admissions, which occupy a brilliant Italianate edifice called the **Woods-Gerry Mansion,** 62 Prospect St., 401/454-6140. The building contains galleries with rotating art exhibits, and in back you can walk through a small sculpture garden. Open Mon.–Sat. 10 A.M.–4 P.M., Sun. 2–5 P.M.

Be sure to stop by the **RISD Art Museum,** 224 Benefit St., 401/454-6500, website: www.risd.edu/museum.cfm. As it's an educational facility, the museum here offers a true survey of works from around the world, and spanning many centuries. There's no particular concentration here, but several works by Monet grace the French Impressionist area, and there's also an excellent collection of mostly 18th- and 19th-century American furniture and decorative arts contained in the adjoining Pendleton House—these rooms are themed to reflect the wares of different periods and styles, such as "Rhode Island and the China Trade," Two Generations of Providence Cabinetmakers," "Dining in Federal America," and so on. Contemporary collections take up several galleries, and there's also a small center for the study of photography. Other areas include galleries covering Greek and Roman, Medieval, Renaissance, Asian, Egyptian, and Buddha art (including the Heian Buddha, which is the largest wooden sculpture in the United States), plus Asian textiles and Japanese prints. Rotating exhibitions vary considerably but have included in

recent years "Contemporary Jewelry" and "Fashion, Art, and the Tirocchi Dressmakers' Shop, 1915–1947." Guided tours (free with the $6 admission) are given most weekends at 2 P.M. Open Tues.–Sun. 10 A.M.–5 P.M.

A distinct departure from the many fine residences along Benefit, the formidable concrete **Old Arsenal,** 176 Benefit St., was designed by the same architect as downtown's Arcade and the nearby Providence Atheneum, James Bucklin, in 1840. Behind the imposing Gothic Revival facade of white stucco with a giant green batten door that looks like something out of *Jack and the Beanstalk,* it housed troops during both the Dorr Rebellion and then later the Civil War.

Until the construction of the present-day State House near Providence Place Mall, Rhode Island's General Assembly met at the **Old State House,** 150 Benefit St., 401/277-2678, the surprisingly humble-looking brick-and-sandstone structure constructed in 1762—its wooden predecessor burned in 1758. Dignitaries of the nation's early years, including the first three U.S. presidents, paid visits here. And on May 4, 1776, the young assembly passed what is considered the first Declaration of Independence in the United States, the Rhode Island Independence Act. For two months, little Rhode Island functioned as its own free republic, until on July 4 representatives of all 13 colonies signed the Declaration of Independence in Philadelphia. Open weekdays 8:30 A.M.–4:30 P.M.

A short distance up Benefit at No. 109 stands a lavish private home known as the **Sullivan Dorr House,** one of the city's most admired early-19th-century structures. The three-story mansion, built largely with fortunes accrued through overseas trade by the home's namesake, contains a magnificent Palladian window—the design is loosely modeled on that of the British villa owned by the poet Alexander Pope. It was Sullivan Dorr's son Thomas whose noble aim of universal suffrage inspired the infamous uprising in 1842 now known as the Dorr Rebellion.

Note the private home at 88 Benefit Street. Here in this 1790 colonial lived the object of Edgar Allen Poe's affection, a young widow named Sarah Helen Whitman, to whom the poet dedicated the famous works "To Helen" and "Annabel Lee." Poe had corresponded with Whitman—herself a poet—for a few years and finally met her when he came to lecture at the Franklin Lyceum. The two became immediately and seriously smitten with one another, but Whitman objected to Poe's habitual carousing and boozing—ultimately, she broke off their engagement to be married and left him because of his inability to distance himself from the bottle. Shortly thereafter, the penniless and drunken Poe was found dead in Baltimore.

Retrace your steps back down Benefit Street a few blocks, and then turn left onto Angell Street and climb to Congdon Street (another left) to reach perhaps the most romantic outdoors space in the city, lofty **Prospect Terrace,** Congdon and Bowen Streets, a grassy rectangle with a wrought-iron fence that's perched high up above downtown and the State Capitol grounds. It's also the burial site of Roger Williams, whose image is carved in granite above his grave. Surrounding the park are more of the neighborhood's comely houses, and it's a relatively short walk east and then south to Brown's commercial strip along Thayer Street (meaning you could walk off your dinner and woo your sweetheart with a few blocks' stroll to the park).

Brown University

BROWN UNIVERSITY

Few educational institutions can claim a greater degree of recognition, both nationally and internationally, than Brown University, whose stately—if somber—campus dominates the upper slope of the East Side's College Hill.

The seventh college founded in what became the United States, Brown was begun in 1764 in the East Bay community of Warren, with the name Rhode Island College, under the guidance of Reverend James Manning. It was established by prominent Rhode Island Baptists, and its first commencement—in fall of 1769—saw the graduation of just seven students. Despite its Baptist leanings, an early edict related to the school's operations was that "into this Liberal and Catholic Institution shall never be admitted any Religious Tests but on the Contrary all the Members Hereof shall forever enjoy full free Absolute and uninterrupted Liberty of Conscience." No educational institution of that day so strongly encouraged religious freedom and liberty, but this doctrine seemed only natural given the circumstances under which both the city of Providence and the state of Rhode Island were founded 130 years earlier.

In 1770, a permanent location for the college was established on the east side of Providence on eight acres of what is now College Hill. University Hall was constructed, and Rhode Island College grew rapidly in prestige despite shutting its doors during the chaos of the American Revolution, from 1776 to 1782 (during which Rochambeau's French troops, and at other times Patriot rebels, used the building as a barracks). During this interruption, the library collection was stowed safely away in nearby Wrentham, Massachusetts. In 1790 the college presented the nation's first president, George Washington, with an honorary degree. It wasn't until 1804 that Brown University assumed its present name, in

WHO WAS JOSHUA CARBERRY?

Brown University has matriculated a great many prominent students, from famous writers and performers to illustrious business leaders and politicians. But perhaps the most distinguished alumnus and former professor you'll hear mentioned at Brown is one Josiah S. Carberry. A vast trove of records exist dating back to the late 1920s, noting that Carberry, a professor of psychoceramics(the study of cracked pots) has given important lectures, published valuable scholarly essays, and altogether changed the course of Brown's academic history.

He has been listed in the cast of university plays, served as the subject of more than a few newspapers articles (including one by the *New York Times* that described him as "The World's Greatest Traveler" in 1974), and even been awarded the Ig Noble Prize (a playful take on the Nobel Prize) for, according to an article by a Brown University archivist, being a "bold explorer and eclectic seeker of knowledge, for his pioneering work in the field of psychoceramics.

Perhaps the most amazing thing about Josiah "Joshua" Carberry is that no such person actually exists. Indeed, it appears that Carberry was dreamed up as a hoax, some say by an actual professor at Brown, John Spaeth. Carberry's history is traced back to a notice on a bulletin board in 1929 that read: "On Thursday evening at 8:15 in Sayles Hall J. S. Carberry will give a lecture on Archaic Greek Architectural Revetments in Connection with Ionian Philology."

This minor event gradually snowballed to the point that Carberry became larger than life. He was cited as having a wife, a daughter, and a clumsy research assistant. In 1955, an unnamed person sent a donation of about $100 to Brown with the instructions that it be used to form the Josiah S. Carberry Fund. A stipulation is that every Friday the 13th, change be collected in brown jugs to bolster the fund. So the next time you hear somebody cite the considerable credentials of Joshua Carberry, think fondly of his legend—and consider how soon it is until the next Friday the 13th, your next opportunity to contribute to the Carberry fund.

appreciation of the enormous $5,000 gift that merchant magnate Nicholas Brown bestowed upon the facility.

Brown presently enjoys a reputation for being a jet-set, flashy school of hipsters and poseurs. Not everybody appreciated the article in the February 1998 issue of *Vanity Fair* that painted the student body in a particularly glib Euro-trashy light, but plenty of students bathed in the attention, deserved or not. The media hype aside, if you look around campus and the adjoining neighborhoods, dining at local restaurants and browsing at area shops, you may be surprised just how much students in these parts look, dress, and behave like those of other large urban universities. Designer duds and flashy sports cars have their place at Brown, but no more so than at other high-profile schools throughout the country.

Brown fosters a deeply liberal and somewhat countercultural collective philosophy, one that's evidenced by an enormously successful and popular lesbian and gay student union. It's a place where avant-garde arts and studies of on-the-edge literary and social theories thrive. The school first admitted African-American and Asian students in the 1870s, and the Women's College in Brown University opened in 1894 (and was later renamed Pembroke College). The student body presently identifies itself as approximately 75 percent Caucasian, 15 percent Asian-American, 6 percent African-American, and 6 percent Hispanic American. In 2000, Brown named Ruth Simmons the new school president; she is the first African-American to assume the helm of an Ivy League school.

Campus Buildings

On Brown's central hub, the **Main Green,** you can still admire the elegant Georgian architecture of **University Hall.** But the university's picturesque hilltop campus incorporates nearly every popular civic architectural style of the past two centuries. Colonial and then Greek Revival architecture (note James C. Bucklin's 1835 Manning Hall and also the 1840 Rhode Island Hall) dominates the style of those buildings created up until about the late 1880s, when the aesthetic was shifted to accommodate the Victorian movement. Imposing Romanesque buildings such as **Sayles Hall** and **Wilson Hall** also front Main Green, as does the John D. Rockefeller–endowed **Faunce House,** which the firm of McKim, Mead, and White executed in 1904.

A new spate of building during the 1960s produced the colonial-style **Wriston Quadrangle,** and more modern structures like the **Rockefeller Library** and **List Art Building** went up. Philip Johnson designed the latter structure in 1971; in it you'll find the **David Winton Bell Gallery,** List Art Center, 64 College St., 401/863-2932, website: www.brown.edu, which is open every afternoon, showing both contemporary and historic exhibitions. While it's not especially attractive, the 14-story **Sciences Library,** because it's perched on College Hill well above downtown, has the tallest reach in Providence.

Other buildings worth noting (and in some cases visiting) include the **John Hay Library,** Prospect and College Streets, 401/863-2146, which dates to 1910 and serves as the repository for Brown University's rare collections. These include a substantial trove of manuscripts attributed to Abraham Lincoln, more than 400,000 pieces of sheet music, the correspondence of early horror writer H. P. Lovecraft, many items from the life of Napoleon, an impressive collection of rare miniature soldiers, some 50,000 postage stamps, Elizabeth Barrett Browning's tea set, and many more unusual collectibles and artifacts. The four-story, marble, Georgian Revival structure is named for the Secretary of State under presidents McKinley and Theodore Roosevelt, who graduated from Brown. Free; open weekdays 9 A.M.–5 P.M.

History buffs should visit the neoclassical 1904 **John Carter Brown Library,** George and Brown Streets, 401/863-2725, whose collection of artifacts and documents pertaining to the history of the New World from the days of Columbus until the American Revolution is among the world's most important. Brown (who began the collection himself) was the son of Nicholas Brown and the grandson of colonial postmaster and printer John Carter. Free; open weekdays 8:30 A.M.–5 P.M., Sat. 9 A.M.–noon.

Just about every visitor to Brown notices the imposing and elaborate **Van Wickle Gates,** which were constructed in 1901 and stand guard over the university's Front Campus. In case you're wondering, the gates are always closed, except on two days—on Convocation Day in the fall, the gates are opened inward toward the Main Green to welcome incoming freshmen. And on Commencement Day in the spring, the gates are faced outward as a "see ya" gesture to graduating seniors.

Brown's commercial college strip centers on **Thayer Street,** from about Bowen south to Waterman Street. Even in summer when relatively few students are on campus, Thayer remains lively, cerebral, and youthful—there are coffeehouses, sandwiches shops, ethnic restaurants, bookstores, a few school buildings, and a decidedly counter-cultural buzz that befits the entertainment district nearest Brown—plenty of students from nearby RISD also hang out in these parts.

FOX POINT AND INDIA POINT PARK

You'll find another corridor of artsy, student-frequented shops and eateries along **Wickenden Street,** which runs east-west across Fox Point (at the southern end of College Hill), which fronts Providence Harbor. India Point, at the southeastern tip of this neighborhood, has for many years been the center of the city's Portuguese community and because of its fine restaurants and shops draws folks from all over. The crowd along Wickenden is less exclusively identified with Brown: here you'll find just as many RISD students, as well as other teens and twenty- and thirty-somethings from throughout the city.

Eighteen-acre **India Point Park,** accessible either from Exit 3 off I-195 or by heading south on Gano or South Main Streets from Wickenden Street, provides the city's only frontage on Narragansett Bay, right at the bay's head, where it meets with the Seekonk and Providence Rivers. The point owes its name to its maritime heritage—in the 18th century merchant ships debarked from here en route to China, India, and other faraway lands. During much of the 20th century, industry dominated the waterfront, but

H. P. LOVECRAFT

Like the more celebrated and earlier Gothic horror writer Edgar Allan Poe, who also lived in Providence for a time, the writer H. P. Lovecraft died in relatively obscurity and on the brink of poverty. The Providence native's own life is, in many ways, as strange and as tragic as those of the many bizarre characters he invented in his works.

Born in 1890 in Providence, Howard Phillips Lovecraft lived in a large Victorian home at 454 Angell St. His father died several years after his birth, after suffering a nervous breakdown and countless subsequent mental attacks. The precocious Lovecraft was raised largely by an overbearing mother and two aunts, along with his grandfather, a noted Providence businessman (his mother also died under extreme emotional duress, when Lovecraft was 29). He took to poetry and writing at an early age, but he also endured an isolated and awkward childhood, one largely lacking in close friendships.

As an adolescent and throughout his 20s, Lovecraft produced countless amateur fictions, poems, and other writings, most of them sharing a penchant for the macabre, the tragically ironic, and the otherworldly. In today's literary vernacular, he'd have been described as a science-fiction writer, and indeed, in the years since his early death, Lovecraft's works have inspired countless practitioners of this genre. His studies of astronomy and the scientific world—he actually produced several journals and publications on science himself—also influenced his unusual art forms. For a time, he wrote columns on astronomy for the *Pawtuxet Valley Gleaner* and later for *The Providence Journal.*

Lovecraft endured several early failures, including an inability to gain admission to Brown University, the fall of his family from financial success to rather poor circumstances, and various personal difficulties that culminated in a nervous breakdown and thoughts of suicide—all this before his 20th birthday. But gradually, during his 20s, Lovecraft's odd writings, especially his verse, began to gain a small following. He was invited to join the United Amateur Press Association (UAPA) in 1914, and later served as the organization's president. Lovecraft made a number of literary liaisons as an active member of UAPA, and during this period he wrote a handful of notable works, including *The Tomb* and *Dagon*. He also corresponded heavily with a number of like-thinking writers of the day, and wrote many essays.

Lovecraft finally began to earn some professional notice after moving from Providence to Brooklyn, New York, where he began writing stories for a pulp fiction magazine *Weird Tales*. He married Sonia Greene while living in Brooklyn, but this marriage didn't last long. In 1926 Lovecraft moved back to Providence, taking up residence near Brown University at 10 Barnes St. Here he wrote some of his best-known works, including *At the Mountains of Madness* and *The Shadow out of Time*.

In 1932 Lovecraft moved to behind Brown's John Hay Library, but his professional writing career had by now peaked, and he supported himself largely through ghost-writing. In 1936 he took ill with intestinal cancer, a disease that would kill him in March 1937. He is buried at Swan Point Cemetery.

Lovecraft enjoyed relatively little acclaim during his lifetime, but having encouraged the careers of many young writers, and also having corresponded so enthusiastically with a great many men of letters, the reclusive and sad author's career enjoyed a renewal of interest well after his death. Eventually his stories were published posthumously in several volumes, among them *The Outsider and Others* and *Haunter of the Dark and Other Tales.* "The Case of Charles Dexter Ward," "The Shunned House," and "The Haunter of the Dark" are each set in Providence.

in 1974 the city cleared out the by-then shuttered industrial buildings and opened India Point as a park. Today it's where you'll find the Brown University Boathouse, from which crew members row in season. It's the northern terminus of the East Bay Bike Path, and the park has a small network of paved trails similarly suitable for biking or strolling, plus meadows ideal for tossing a ball or Frisbee about. Families appreciate the playground, and it's also a good spot for fishing.

At the west end of the neighborhood, South Water Street runs south along the east bank of the Providence River. There's a small park at the end and parking along the street, and from here you look out south down the river and see the hulking gates of the city's Hurricane Barrier, which was built from 1961 to 1966. On the opposite side of the Providence River, via Globe Street, which is off Allens Avenue, you can get a closer look at this roughly 700-foot-long structure whose massive doors are kept open except when the city is threatened by major storms (which to date has only been on a handful of occasions). Devastating hurricanes in 1954 and 1938, to name a few, have brought the city to its knees, and in 1815 the Great Gale pushed a huge flood surge up through Narragansett Bay, leveling Providence and destroying hundreds of buildings, plus ships, wharves, and bridges. Keep your eyes open when strolling around downtown for plaques on many buildings that record the high-water marks of the larger storms that have struck Providence over the past two centuries.

NORTH AND EAST OF COLLEGE HILL

The lower and later upper slopes of College Hill developed during the 17th and 18th centuries, during which time the land east of the hill's summit extending to the Seekonk River consisted mostly of undeveloped woodland and later farm fields. This all began to change as Providence grew larger and more prominent following the American Revolution, and during the 19th century many fine homes went up along the East Side's primary north-south avenue, Hope Street. Residential development of the streets intersecting Hope continued, and in the 1890s broad Blackstone Boulevard was built roughly parallel to Hope to the east. Even during the city's toughest economic times during the middle part of this century, the streets on or near Blackstone Boulevard have been the wealthiest and most prestigious—it remains a favorite area to gawk at grand mansions and beautifully landscaped yards.

The area east and north of College Hill covers a substantial distance and while safe and pleasant is more difficult to cover on foot than College Hill itself, Wickenden Street, and downtown. You might consider driving or taking a bus to Blackstone Boulevard or Blackstone Park and walking, or consider riding a bike through this area—it's one of the few neighborhoods within Providence city limits that's highly conducive to cycling.

Beginning at the intersection with Wickenden Street and heading north, Hope Street contains several cool shops and eateries, plus some fine old homes—this section of the street was developed earlier than the northern reaches. A few blocks north of Wickenden you'll come to the **Rhode Island Historical Society Library,** 121 Hope St., 401/331-8575, website: www.rihs.org, worth a stop if you have even a casual interest in genealogy or early state history. Documents—including all manner of birth, death, and marriage records pertaining to Rhode Island—date back to the days of Roger Williams. You'll also find prints, paintings, photos, and other historical items. The society sponsors 90-minute city walking tours from July through mid-October, with the focus on history, the waterfront, architecture, art, and such. Open Wed.–Sat. 10 A.M.–5 P.M. (and Tues. noon–8 P.M. in summer).

In the same neighborhood, history buffs should visit the **Museum of Rhode Island History,** 110 Benevolent St., 401/331-8575, in the 1822 Federal-style Aldrich mansion. Exhibits here, in four galleries, rotate regularly but typically touch on regional architecture and decorative arts. The early-20th-century U.S. Senator from Rhode Island who once lived here, Nelson Aldrich, established the nation's Federal Reserve system. His daughter, Abby, married John D. Rockefeller, Jr. Open Tues.–Fri. 8:30 A.M.–5:30 P.M.

Up Hope Street a few more blocks, note the

decadent **Governor Henry Lippitt House Museum,** 199 Hope St., 401/453-0688. A sterling example of a high-style Italianate Victorian mansion from the 1860s, the building reveals the fine craftsmanship of the day with ornately carved Renaissance Revival woodworking, meticulous stencil work, and myriad faux finishes. Even if you've but a faint interest in interior design and restoration, the Lippitt Museum is a must-see. Many of the furnishings in the house belonged to Lippitt family members, and the museum throws events, teas, and dinners periodically that offer an intimate glimpse of life in this house during the Victorian era. Open Tues.–Fri. 10 A.M.–4 P.M. (shorter hours in summer).

Another block north, at Lloyd Avenue, you'll pass by the prestigious **Moses Brown School,** 250 Lloyd Ave., 401/831-7350, a Quaker prep school notable for its tree-shaded lawns and fine old buildings. The school has been in existence since 1784, having opened in the only state in the young United States that tolerated Quakers. Begun down near the coast in Portsmouth as the New England Yearly Meeting Boarding School, it faltered soon after opening, closing its doors for some 31 years. The school's founder, Moses Brown, continued to champion the institution and finally, following the War of 1812, he donated 43 acres of his Prospect Hill farm on College Hill to develop a new site: in 1819, it finally reopened, and in 1904, the school assumed its present name in honor of the man who helped found it. Interestingly, while many private schools admitted only boys until rather recently, Moses Brown stopped admitting them in 1926 (breaking with the school's coeducational policy, which had dated to its origins). At that time, coeducation fell out of popular favor throughout the United States. In 1976, the policy was repealed and coed admissions continue today. The curriculum here is broken down into three schools, the Lower serving nursery through fifth grade, the Middle School welcoming sixth through eight graders, and the Upper School teaching 9th through 12th graders. Visitors can wander the pretty campus of Moses Brown School, visiting the **Krause Gallery,** Jenks Center, Friends Hall, which shows the works of noted local and national sculptors, painters,

and photographers. Open weekdays 8 A.M.–4 P.M., Sun. 1–4P.M.; closed Saturdays.

Return back down Hope a block and make a left onto Angell Street; head east a few blocks (you'll pass the enormous Brown University Athletic Complex on your left). You'll soon come to a short little strip of shops and a handful of cheap eateries, including the engaging Providence Bookstore, which has a lively café and is a great place for a break or a shopping trip. This tiny commercial district, **Wayland Square,** serves the many residential blocks nearby, home largely of young professionals and students and faculty of Brown, RISD, and the city's other universities.

Blackstone Boulevard

Continue east down Angell Street and on your left, shortly after you cross Butler Avenue, you'll reach hilly 40-acre **Blackstone Park.** Here along River Drive you can walk alongside the Seekonk River, which narrows just south (where the Angell Street bridge crosses the river); across the water you'll be looking at the mostly industrial western shore of East Providence. Grassy, tree-shaded Blackstone Park is ideal for a stroll—it has a couple ponds and several walking paths, plus some nice spots for a picnic. There's ample parking along River Drive, up past the Narragansett Boathouse.

The mostly upper-middle-class residential neighborhood surrounding the park contains many fine stucco, wood-frame, and redbrick homes from the early part of this century, all with neat gardens and perfectly manicured lawns. Just south of the park, down East River Street, you'll come to an old industrial complex (at the end of Waterman Street) that's been converted to offices.

From the northern end of Blackstone Park, cut west on Irving Avenue, and you'll come to the southern end of **Blackstone Boulevard,** a broad tree-lined avenue with a wide grassy median that's usually abuzz with joggers, walkers, bladers, and cyclists. Along Blackstone, and also on side streets such as Freeman Parkway and Laurel Avenue, you'll pass the city's most impressive mansions.

A little more than a mile north on Blackstone you'll come to the entrance (on the right) of the gracious 210-acre **Swan Point Cemetery,** which was laid out in 1875. This is one of America's foremost garden cemeteries, and visitors are encouraged to bicycle (slowly), walk, or drive the grounds, which are laced with beautiful gardens—out of respect you're asked to wear proper attire, jogging is permitted only 7:30–9 A.M.; of course, you're to steer clear of graveside services. This is a serene and tranquil place, a real unsung gem that deserves a visit. Some of the paved lanes through the cemetery lead down alongside the Seekonk River, and you'll see some highly elaborate monuments and headstones. In addition to having miles of paved lanes with flower beds and trees of every variety, this is an interesting spot for bird-watching—more than 150 species of birds have been observed here, with spring migration the most popular, and enjoyable, time to visit. Warblers, vireos, and thrushes are common, while you might see a screech owl or great horned owl if you're lucky. Among the famous Rhode Is-

landers buried here are horror writer H. P. Lovecraft and Civil War general Ambrose Burnside

Back on Blackstone, continue north a short ways, noting **Lippitt Memorial Park,** a pretty little slice of greenery with a grand old central fountain and ample seating. The jogging path up the median of Blackstone Boulevard terminates at where Hope Street becomes East Avenue, almost suspiciously across the street from Maxmillian's Ice Cream Cafe. At this point you're a short walk from Providence's northeastern border with Pawtucket—this is a part of Providence many visitors never see, and yet it's extremely charming and diverse. Yuppies, families, gays and lesbians, and students and academics have settled here, taking advantage of the low-keyed and quiet pace yet proximity to bustling downtown. With I-95 just up the road, it's also an appealing neighborhood among commuters to as far away as Boston.

Sights Elsewhere in Providence

Much of the rest of Providence—the neighborhoods south, west, and northwest of downtown—is dominated by lower-income residential neighborhoods and industry, which is not to say many of these areas aren't interesting from an architectural perspective. But you'll find few attractions elsewhere in Providence, and little beyond mundane eateries and shops.

One particularly fascinating site just southwest of downtown is the **Cranston Street Armory,** 125 Dexter St., a massive yellow-brick and granite 1907 building that housed the Rhode Island National Guard for many years but now is threatened with being torn down. The long, dramatic structure with crenellated six-story towers at either end was built by William R. Walker and Son for a princely sum of $650,000—it's more than 150,000 square feet, and prior to the opening of downtown's convention center it was the frequent site of major events. Architecturally, while there's nothing subtle or quaint about it, the building can be appreciated for its ornate copper trim and extensive corbeling. This centerpiece of the gradually gentrifying West Broadway neighborhood is on the National Trust for Historic Preservation's

list of most endangered structures. Much talk has centered around turning the building into a state-of-the-art performing arts center; it provided the soundstage for the film *Outside Providence,* directed by Michael Corrente. This neighborhood has enormous potential, with many striking—but often dilapidated—Victorian homes, from Second Empire to Greek Revival especially.

In the northern part of the city you'll find the campus of **Providence College,** Eaton Street and River Avenue, 401/865-1000, website: www.providence.edu, which was begun in 1917 by the Right Reverend Matthew Harkins, the city bishop credited with helping restore harmony during a time when differing ethnic groups often clashed politically and ideologically. About 3,800 undergraduate students (some 85 percent of them Catholic) attend Providence College, which is anchored by the elaborate 1919 Harkins Hall, the school's main administrative building. About 50 Dominican Friars reside on campus, most of them in the St. Thomas Aquinas Priory. It's relatively new, as are most of the buildings on campus, which while pleasant offers little of the architectural splendor of Brown and RISD. To reach campus, follow Smith Street (US 44) west from the State House grounds for several blocks, turning right onto River Avenue. A block north, you'll reach the main entrance on the right.

ROGER WILLIAMS PARK

You'll want either to drive or take the bus the roughly four miles south of downtown to reach the city's largest and most treasured urban oasis, 430-acre Roger Williams Park, Elmwood Avenue., 401/785-3510, the home, too, of **Roger Williams Park Zoo,** 1000 Elmwood Ave., 401/785-3510, www.rwpzoo.org, admission $7. Visitors can bike, blade, or walk along nearly 10 miles of paved road (note that these roads are open to auto traffic, but only at low speeds, and there's usually ample room for all persons and vehicles to maneuver). Unpaved trails also meander into the verdant greenery, around the 10 lakes (many where you can rent small boats). The great-great-granddaughter of Roger Williams, Betsey Williams donated the land for this park in the 1870s, and it retains its splendid Victorian layout created by designer Horace W. S. Cleveland in 1878. The look and ambience borrows heavily from the most famous of 19th-century park designers, Frederick Law Olmsted.

Roger Williams Park looks terrific these days, as it's recently completed an ambitious 15-year, $20 million, acre-by-acre renovation that earned it a National Preservation Honor award in 2000 from the National Trust for Historic Preservation. The park had become decrepit and unsafe, damaged by vandals and diminished by severe budget cuts—it's hard even to comprehend the improvements today. The park and all of its buildings are protected on the National Register of Historic Places.

One of the most architecturally significant structures in the park, the **Casino** dates to 1896. This imposing redbrick colonial revival building has impressive views from its veranda over the restored music bandstand and Roosevelt Lake. With a ballroom crowned by 20-foot ceilings and ornate plaster friezes and trim, the building is a fine example of the park's success in restoration and a favorite place for weddings and parties. Surrounding the casino and extending throughout several parts of the park are lovely rose and flower gardens, as well as a Japanese Garden. The **Charles H. Smith Greenhouses,** which date to 1937, house cactus, rain forest, and herb gardens.

You can catch live music events at the **Benedict Temple to Music,** an amphitheater. Kids enjoy the reproduction vintage carousel at **Carousel Village,** which also has a miniature golf course, bumper boats, and other rides and amusements. You can also visit the **Betsey Williams Cottage,** a small history museum that preserves the legacy of the city's first family. Open mid-Apr.–mid-June and mid-Sept.–Oct., Sun. 1–4 P.M. The park grounds are open daily 9 A.M.–9 P.M. The greenhouses and Carousel Village are open daily 11 A.M.–5 P.M.

Museum of Natural History

The park is also home to the Museum of Natural History, 401/785-9457, website: www.osfn.org/museum, which contains a planetarium and more than 250,000 objects and artifacts collected over the past two centuries—at any given time, a mere 2 percent of the museum's holdings are actually on display. These include preserved mollusk shells, birds, mammals, rocks, minerals, and—a particular strength—fossils from the region's Coal Age. The museum displays cultural artifacts, mostly from North America, including baskets, textiles, tools, and carvings. Rotating exhibits come on line every few months. This grandiose but intriguing chateau-esque building dates to 1895 and was built by the firm of Martin and Hall. This, the state's only museum of natural history, holds an impressive collection, but the overall feel and appearance of the place seems to be of another era—it's not the most dynamic museum in the city. Considerably more titillating is the attached Cormack Planetarium, where a dazzling computerized star projector offers a memorable lesson in astronomy; these 35-minute shows are presented weekends at 1:30 and 3 P.M. Museum admission $2 ($3 for museum and planetarium); open daily 10 A.M.–5 P.M.

Roger Williams Park Zoo

The Roger Williams Park Zoo, 1000 Elmwood Ave., 401/785-3510, website: www.rwpzoo.org, has more than 900 animals and is open year-round—it's the third-oldest zoo in the nation, and *Travel & Leisure* magazine has ranked it among the nation's ten best. Indeed, this is a fantastic facility, and one that's surprisingly underrated in the northeast. There are seven main habitat here; the first one you'll come to after passing through the ticket gates is the Plains of Africa, where elephants, masai giraffes (a baby boy came into the world, and the zoo, in August 2000), zebra, cheetahs, ostriches, and bongo antelopes prance about a large area meant to resemble something you might experience on a safari. From here it's a short walk to the African Pavilion, which has smaller and more varied animals from the dwarf mongoose to emperor scorpions. Continuing on you'll soon come to Australasia, the home of kangaroos, wallabies, and many more Down Under species. Across the way you'll get a somewhat more localized lesson at the North America habitat, where polar bears (whom you view almost face-to-face through protective glass), bison, and wolves roam about, and there's also a large sea lion and penguin pool.

In Madagascar, one of the world's most beautiful islands but one whose rain forest is seriously endangered, you'll see many species of lemur, plus the radiated tortoise. One of the favorite exhibits is the Marco Polo Trail, an interactive walk through habitats of Asian animals (such as moon bear, snow leopards, and camels) and botany. The final habitat, Tropical America, takes you inside and across a swaying rope bridge through a re-created rain forest of playful monkeys, alligators, bats, two-toed sloths, milksnakes, and silver-beaked tanagers. Smaller but still very popular exhibits include the African Fishing Village, a farmyard petting zoo, the Natural Wetlands Trail, and the educational zoo laboratory.

Conservation efforts are a major mission of this zoo, which has earned considerable kudos as a participant in the global Species Survival Plan. In this capacity, the zoo works to help save species from extinction through breeding programs and attempts to reintroduce animals into the wild. One success has been helping with the comeback of the American red wolf. Admission $7; open mid-May–mid-Oct., 9 A.M.–5 P.M.; mid-Oct.–mid-May, 9 A.M.–4 P.M.

Shopping

For several reasons, Providence offers an uncharacteristically good selection of unusual shops, as well as the chains you'd find anywhere. First, a nice thing about the city's Gaps and Victoria's Secrets: the vast majority of them are contained within one of the better-designed and better-located urban shopping malls you'll ever find, Providence Place. This mammoth structure anchors downtown and overlooks the brilliantly landscaped riverfront—it's close to several hotels and within walking distance of the universities. And there are several good restaurants on the ground floor, plus a top-level food court that's better than most, as well as a movie theater and IMAX. If malls are often guilty of sucking the life out of cities and forcing people out to bland suburban retail compounds that could be anywhere, Providence Place at least draws people to the heart of downtown.

Beyond the mall, Providence has a number of funky and hip design shops, galleries, art-supply stores, indie book and record shops, vintage clothiers, and home-furnishings and gift boutiques. These are geared as much toward nonlocals as they are the city's artists, students, academics, and hipsters. Providence lures creative types, and these very people often end up opening offbeat and innovative businesses. And while this isn't necessarily an ideal city for bargain hunters, commercial rents are much, much lower than in Boston or New York City, Block Island or the Cape. You'll often find decent deals on antiques and art, and at any of the student-oriented spots you'll have no trouble homing in on discount threads, used books and CDs, and low-priced bric-a-brac.

PROVIDENCE PLACE MALL

Opened in 1999, **Providence Place Mall,** 1 Providence Pl., 401/270-1000, website: www.providenceplace.com, is an immense four-

GALLERY-HOPPING IN PROVIDENCE

Providence has an impressive fine-arts scene, with galleries set throughout downtown and College Hill. Among the better-known downtown venues is one at the historic Arcade at 65 Weybosset St.: **CenterCity Contemporary Arts,** 401/521-2990, www.home.ici.net/~iridi/ccaart.html, which focuses primarily on the works of Rhode Island artists. Also check out **Tilden Thurber Co.,** 292 Westminster St., 401/272-3200, www.stanleyweiss.com, known throughout the Northeast for its phenomenal selection of museum-quality antiques and silver jewelry and accessories; as well as the **Bush Gallery,** 212 Weybosset St., 401/578-7304, and the **Tse Tse Gallery,** 101 Orange St., 401/453-3337. One of the most innovative and popular spaces in the city is **AS220,** which is also a very nice restaurant and a place to listen to readings and live music. The **Rhode Island Foundation Gallery,** 1 Union Station, off Exchange Terrace, 401/274-4564, www.rifoundation.org, which is a former cafeteria in the old Union Station, shows rotating art exhibits. The Rhode Island Foundation is a center for philanthropy that acts as a liaison between donors and grantees both in the public and private sector, in education, health care, and the arts. Works shown in the gallery focus heavily on local artists in all media.

On the East Side, three galleries are clustered around the Fox Point neighborhood. These include **Peaceable Kingdom,** 116 Ives St., 401/351-3472, where you'll find carved masks and figurines, lavish textiles, and paintings from around the world; **Peck Gallery,** 424 Wickenden St., 401/751-0017; and **Helianthus,** 398 Wickenden St., 401/421-4390. Further west on Wickenden you'll find **JR's Fine Art,** 218 Wickenden St., 401/331-4380, which represents a number of reputable painters and potters; and **Picture This,** 158 Wick-

---

story atrium mall with a 16-screen Hoyt's Cinema multiplex and an IMAX theater, and a fairly standard upscale mix of apparel, home-furnishing, and other chain shops. The top-floor 700-seat food court is unusually good, with Ben & Jerry's, Johnny Rockets, Subway, Japanese/sushi that's excellent by mall standards, Italian, and Chinese eateries. The ground level is lined with sit-down restaurants that are mostly upscale looking if not genuinely expensive; most of them are jam-packed weekend evenings. The mall has been successful in drawing visitors from the –burbs, but some question how much it's gotten folks to see more of the city—you can exit from I-95 directly into the mall parking garages, barely touching city surface streets. On the other hand, the mall is within walking distance of the riverfront, state house, convention center, and even College Hill—especially on warm days, plenty of shoppers wander out and explore the city. Major shops include Filene's, Lord & Taylor, and Nordstrom; you'll also find chain shops like Abercrombie & Fitch, Restoration Hardware, Bed, Bath, & Beyond, Brooks Brothers, J. Crew, Lindt Chocolate, Yankee Candle, Borders Books, Music & Cafe, and all the myriad siblings in the ubiquitous Gap family—about 150 stores total.

THE EAST SIDE

There are several commercial strips on the East Side, beginning at the base of College Hill along North and South Main Streets., and also on the Brown University retail corridor along Thayer Street. Wickenden Street, at the southern tip of the East Side, also makes for great window-shopping, and you'll find a small but lively district around Wayland Square, just east of Brown University and Hope Street.

At the base of College Hill, **Comina,** 245 S. Main St., 401/273-4522, is a delightful home-furnishings shop with emphasis on country British and French furnishings. It has a branch in Connecticut, too. Farther down the block you'll find very fine antiques and decorative arts at **Camden Passage,** 359 S. Main St., 401/453-0770. Don't be alarmed by the excessively friendly staff of the fine men's clothier **Briggs Providence,** 200 S. Main St., 401/453-0025, whose owner is a throwback to the shopkeepers of yore—he'll practically come out and invite you in off the

enden St., 401/273-7263, www.picturethisgalleries.com, a respected frame and print shop; and down by India Point **Bert Gallery,** 540 S. Water St., 401/751-2628, whose paintings are mostly by notable 19th- and early-20th-century Rhode Island artists (it's an excellent place to get a lesson in local art history). Finally, there are two spots near RISD and Brown: the **David Charles Gallery,** 263 S. Main St., 401/421-6764, which has fine maritime art, beautiful framed photos of the Providence skyline, and numerous depictions of noted New England landmarks; and the historic **Providence Art Club,** 11 Thomas St., 401/331-1114. This is America's second-oldest art club—it occupies the 1790 Obadiah Brown House, where members still carry out the tradition of munching on jonnycakes in the vintage dining rooms.

The third Thursday of every month, the city sponsors a free **Gallery Night ArtTrolley,** 401/751-2628, www.providenceri.com/gallerynight. From 5 to 9 in the evening, you can ride one of three trolleys (departing from Citizen's Bank, 1 Citizens Plaza) on a historic loop through downtown and the East Side, stopping at some 20 art galleries and museums—on hand to mingle with visitors at most of these events are local artists and gallery owners. Each of the three trolleys plies a different route (one through the East Side, one through the West Side, and one making the entire loop); on board, volunteer guides from the Providence Preservation Society offer commentary on the sights and neighborhoods along the way. Sakonnet Vineyards donates free wine (and other refreshments are also provided), and there's live music at some venues. Keep in mind that Rhode Island has exempted sales tax on all galleries located within Providence's downtown arts district—you'll find some very good art buys in these parts.

street if you browse his window displays for a few moments. This upscale shop has been a favorite for business and sports suits since the 1940s.

With art students strolling around every corner, it's no surprise that Providence has some excellent sources for supplies, including most prominently the **RISD Store,** 30 N. Main St., 401/454-6465, which also has one of the best selections of art books and periodicals in the city. It's fitting that Providence would have several exceptional jewelry stores—among the best-known is **Martina & Company,** 120 N. Main St., 401/351-0968, a contemporary gallery that occupies a dramatic space. A more daring possibility along trendy North Main is **Miko Exoticwear,** 653 N. Main St., 800/421-6646, website: www.mikoexoticwear.com, which has a strong student following for its club gear and racy lingerie, plus oils, lotions, and the like.

Wickenden has a number of antiques stores, including **Providence Antique Center,** 442 Wickenden St., 401/274-5820; **Antiques & Artifacts,** 436 Wickenden St., 401/421-8334; and the whimsically named **This and That Shoppe,** 234 Wickenden St., 401/861-1394, a multi-dealer establishment with about 50 sellers. Most of the businesses along this funky stretch (including the scads of eateries) are set in wood-frame and brick Victorians and a few Colonials. Just off Wickenden, **Rustigian Rugs,** 1 Governor St., 401/751-5100, has an astounding selection of fine rugs, mostly from Far and Middle Eastern locales. Where there are college students, you can always find used CDs—among the several such shops in town, **Round Again Records,** 278 Wickenden St., 401/351-6292, ranks among the best.

In trendy Wayland Square, **Providence Bookstore and Cafe,** 500 Angell St., 401/521-5536, is an atmospheric East Side shop with a cool little restaurant attached—it's open till 1 A.M. most nights (till 2 A.M. Sat.). Also check out **Books on the Square,** 471 Angell St., 401/331-9097, which has a broad section of fiction and nonfiction, particularly strong on feminist, gay/lesbian, political, and children's books. You can sit in a comfy armchair and flip through books before buying them. **Claytime,** 13 S. Angell St., 401/421-5456, is a cute paint-your-own-pottery place with an enormous selection of bowls, mugs, frames, and decorative pieces. The decidedly upscale **Opulent Owl,** 195 Wayland Ave., 401/521-6698, specializes in crafts, tableware, jewelry, stationery, and

PROVIDENCE

other fine knick-knacks. Christmas collectibles are a big part of the business, but you'll also find dinnerware, crystal, table lamps and clocks, frames, and just about every other sort of gift imaginable.

You'll find a great selection of titles at the **College Hill Bookstore,** 252 Thayer St., 401/751-6404, which sits along the busy college strip just a couple doors down from the larger but more impersonal **Brown University Bookstore,** 244 Thayer St., 401/863-3168, which also sells college sweatshirts and other logo'ed items. GenYers and club kids stock up on edgy gear at **Trend Clothing,** 224 Thayer St., 401/273-7999, while **Apropos,** 269 Thayer St., 401/621-7745, carries stylish women's attire. Designer labels at designer prices are the hallmark of the exclusive women's clothier **Simone,** 245 Meeting St., 401/273-9500. Since you're in the jewelry capital of the nation, you might want to poke your head inside **Details,** 277 Thayer St., 401/751-1870, a top purveyor of both high-end and less pricey costume pieces of all kinds and styles. A funky local favorite, **Oop!,** 297 Thayer St., and in Providence Place Mall, 401/281-4147, website: www.oopstuff.com, offers a cool range of home furnishings (including a distinctive line of rustic furniture fashioned out of sticks), gifts, objets d'art, toys, crafts, and jewelry, much of it made locally. The reputation is for fun, fairly inexpensive items, but Oop! sells some pricier antiques, and the management has a keen marketing sense, presenting all kinds of special theme events, from free face painting days to birthday parties celebrating the natal days of stars from Judy Garland to Mick Jagger. One of the best independent record stores in town, **In Your Ear,** 286 Thayer St., 401/861-1515, also sells tickets to many of the live-music venues around town. To get a full sense of Thayer Street's myriad offerings, contact or browse the website of the **Thayer Street Business Association,** 401/273-5422, website: www.thayeronline.com. There are about 22 eateries along here, and numerous boutiques, inexpensive and funky clothiers, and a great movie theater.

Up Hope Street where it meets with Blackstone Boulevard, **Herbalicious,** 1080 Hope St., 401/421-7770, is an all-natural store of foods, vitamins, herbs, soaps, essential oils, and homeo-pathic remedies. Also check out **Green River Silver Co.,** 735 Hope St., 401/621-9092, which custom-makes fine sterling-silver jewelry. **Studio Hop,** 810 Hope St., 401/621-2262, carries a wide and unusual range of gifts from all over the world, including Asian and Mediterranean skin and beauty products, candles, framed photos and artwork, carved wooden bowls and utensils, and other hand-crafted items.

DOWNTOWN

Apart from Providence Place Mall, downtown's most engaging retail spots are scattered about, in many cases down quiet little streets where you might not expect to find something. If shopping is a sport to you, it's worth covering downtown block by block to discover its gems.

Few shopping venues in the United States possess the charm and history of **The Arcade,** 65 Weybosset St., 401/598-1199, which dates to 1828 and contains cafés and eateries, plus local shops, from a toy store to a palm-reading salon to art galleries, a florist, and photography shop. Also check out **Copacetic,** in the Arcade, 401/273-0470, where you'll find a colorful array of clever, if at times surreal, jewelry, clocks, candlesticks, and other cool hand-crafted accoutrements. RISD students and other arts-and-crafts aficionados frequent the **Art Supply Warehouse,** 14 Imperial Pl., 401/331-4530, set in an imposing old knife factory (that's also the site of CAV restaurant) on a quiet side street in the Jewelry District.

Since 1910, **Axelrod,** 251 Weybosset St., 401/421-4833, has been crafting fine musical instruments. **Cellar Stories Bookstore,** 111 Mathewson St., 401/521-2665, website: www.cellarstories.com, is the largest used and antiquarian bookstore in the state, specializing not only in hard-to-find and out-of-print books but also magazines and periodicals. Much smaller but with a fine selection of rare, vintage titles, **Tyson's Old & Rare Books,** 334 Westminster Ave., 401/421-3939, also specializes in historic maps and prints. High-end menswear is found at **Philip Wolfe Fine Men's Apparel,** 84 Dorrance St., 401/331-6532, which has an on-premises tailor.

Sports and Recreation

By virtue of its being such a hilly city, merely maneuvering around Providence on foot qualifies as a recreational pursuit. Beyond that, within the city limits you'll find a smattering of venues for sports and enjoying the outdoors, but with so many large parks and recreation areas within a 15-mile radius of Providence, many residents get their exercise elsewhere. In addition to the activities described below, also keep in mind the city's many exceptional parks. These include Roger Williams Park, India Point Park, and Blackstone Park.

BICYCLING, JOGGING, AND BLADING

There aren't any great spots for mountain-biking within Providence city limits (although you'll find several good spots nearby), but the city does have some neat routes for conventional biking. Just keep in mind that this is a busy city, in many places with narrow streets and high auto-traffic volume—and particularly on the East Side, you'll have some very steep hills to contend with.

Joggers and bladers face some of the same issues but can enjoy one span that bikers will find less useful. Beginning either by the Capitol grounds or at nearby Providence Place Mall, you can enjoy a marvelous stroll along the restored riverfront, a two-mile loop if you take it all the way down to Bridge Street.

Within Providence, few roads seem better suited to cyclists, joggers, and bladers than wide, tree-lined Blackstone Boulevard, which runs about 1.5 miles from Hope Street south down to Blackstone Park, past handsome old homes and the entrance to Swan Point Cemetery. You can make a nice triangular loop out of this area, using Blackstone Boulevard as the hypotenuse, Hope Street as the longer leg (it meets with Blackstone up near the Pawtucket border), and any of the many cross streets down closer to Brown University as the shorter leg.

From Providence you can access the 14.5-mile **East Bay Bike Path,** a flat, 10-foot-wide,

and wonderfully scenic asphalt trail that hugs many portions of eastern Narragansett Bay, from India Point Park clear to Bristol. The path also welcomes joggers, strollers, bladers, and just about anybody with a yen for scenic rambles. The path, which follows an old rail bed, encounters a tremendously varied landscape, from undeveloped waterfront to the lively commercial districts of Warren and Bristol to Haines and Colt State Parks, in East Providence and Bristol—both parks have picnic areas, and at several points on or just off the path, you'll encounter places to stock up on snacks, deli sandwiches, and drinks. The path begins at India Point Park.

You can rent bikes on College Hill (fairly close both to Blackstone Boulevard and India Point Park) at **Esta's,** 257 Thayer St., 401/831—2651. Another excellent source of equipment and bikes is **Providence Bicycle,** 725 Branch Ave., 401/331-6610, which is in northern Providence but worth the trip if you're a devotee of cycling. Rates run from about $15 per half-day to $20 for a full day.

BOATING, CANOEING, AND KAYAKING

Although not the boating hub that is Newport, the East Bay, or South County, Providence does contain some access points that lead right into Narragansett Bay. A prime resource is **Baer's River Workshop,** 222. S. Water St., 401/453-1633, from whom you can rent kayaks and canoes (May–October), take classes or personalized instruction, and ask for ideas about where to paddle. The shop organizes some sea-kayaking and other boating trips along the Seekonk River, on the Woonasquatucket River right through the heart of downtown, and off India Point. You can take sailing classes (geared to all levels of ability and experience) at the **Community Boating Center,** 25 India Point Park, 401/454-7245.

GOLF

Donald Ross, known for designing municipal courses in cities throughout New England, laid out **Triggs Golf Course,** 1533 Chalkstone Ave., 401/521-8460, in the 1930s. It's a relatively affordable, reasonably well-maintained course with cart and club rentals.

ICE-SKATING

A favorite spot in the winter months (October–March) is the **Fleet Skating Center,** Kennedy Plaza, Dorrance and Washington Streets, 401/331-5544, website: www.fleetskating.com, which has public skating daily 10 A.M.–10 P.M. weekdays, 11 A.M.–10 P.M. on weekends. This outdoor rink twice the size of the famous one in Rockefeller Center anchors downtown Providence, right by the bus station and close to the Riverwalk—it's good fun as much for taking to the ice as it is for watching skaters on a brisk day. Late spring through early fall, the focus here shifts to roller-skating. Year-round, lessons in both of these balancing arts are given; you can also rate equipment at the large pavilion

and admission booth at the end of the rink, which also contains lockers, a pro shop, a snack bar, and some private party rooms that revelers sometimes rent for birthdays and special events.

SPECTATOR SPORTS

Providence has but one pro sports team, the **Providence Bruins,** 401/273-5000, website: www.provbruins.com, an American Hockey League farm club that's a feeder for the NHL's Boston Bruins. The season runs from October through early April, and tickets cost $10–20. Games are held at the Providence Civic Center, 1 LaSalle Sq., 401/331-6700 (for ticket office).

With all the schools in Providence, you'd think there would be more opportunities to catch live college sporting events, but few of these institutions have notable athletic programs. A major exception to this rule is **Providence College,** whose Friars basketball team, 401/331-0700, frequently ranks near the top of the Big East Basketball Conference. Games are held at the Providence Civic Center. The college's hockey team, 401/865-2168, is also quite accomplished and plays at Schneider Arena, Admiral and Huxley Streets.

Accommodations

When it comes to hotels, Providence is seller's market. There simply aren't many properties given the city's size and rapidly growing popularity—Providence has among the highest occupancy rates in the nation. What hotels you'll find here are uniformly excellent, many of them opened within the past decade and most within walking distance of great shopping, dining, and culture. You'll also find several historic inns, from high-end luxury spots to a few that serve travelers with a somewhat limited budget. However, for truly affordable accommodations, you'll have to venture outside of town, to nearby Warwick or Pawtucket, or even as far as Woonsocket, Bristol, or across the border to Seekonk or Fall River.

It's fairly easy to get in and out of Providence, so do consider choosing a hotel in the outlying region—after all, Rhode Island is a tiny

state, so even communities in the Blackstone River Valley or the East Bay are relatively convenient to exploring the capital. Staying in one of these nearby areas might save you $50 to $100 per night for a room that's comparable to what you'll find in Providence proper, depending on the time of year. Providence is a commercial, educational, and political hub—it hosts a fair share of conventions and can be especially busy during weekends throughout the school year and weekdays any time. Generally, the farther ahead you book a room in this city, the better you'll do rate-wise.

DOWNTOWN

$100–150

The relatively new **Courtyard by Marriott,** 32 Exchange Terrace, 401/272-1191 or 888/887-

7955, website: www.courtyard.com, closely resembles the historic tan-brick structures on Exchange Street beside it—aesthetically, it's a marvelous property, and it couldn't be more conveniently located either. Predictably, the hotel has been phenomenally popular since it opened, with relatively reasonable rates for downtown but high as the Courtyard brand goes. The 216 rooms are large and airy, and many have unobstructed views of the State House, Providence Place Mall, and WaterPlace Park. All have high-speed Internet access, two-line phones, and large work desks. Common amenities include a business center/library, indoor pool with hot tub, fitness center, and a small café. It can get a little harried in the small lobby, but that's a minor quibble. It's an excellent property all around. A towering brown-clapboard tenement house in a funky, gradually gentrifying neighborhood just west of the State House and Providence Place Mall (via Smith Street over I-95), the **State House Inn,** 43 Jewett St., 401/351-6111, website: www.providence-inn.com, offers sunny rooms done with Shaker and colonial furnishings, country-style quilted bedspreads, and in some cases four-poster beds, fireplaces, and original hardwood floors. The hosts are friendly and easy-going, and all rooms have cable TV and phones. While Jewett Street is on the up, this part of town lacks the charm of the East Side. Full breakfast is included.

By no means unpleasant, the 274-room **Providence Holiday Inn,** Atwells Avenue and Broadway, 401/831-3900 or 800/HOLIDAY, is nevertheless one of the city's less inspired efforts, with a drab modern facade and a convenient but loud and rather unattractive location at a busy intersection west of the convention center, just off I-95. You can walk to downtown attractions and Johnson & Wales. The management has pumped a bit of money into sprucing up the lobby and guest rooms, but service isn't always on the ball and little about the place stands out (although many rooms have plum skyline views). There's a full fitness center, indoor pool, and whirlpool tub. Rates are lowest on weekends, and at busy times they creep up as high as about $200 for the largest units.

$150–250

The **Providence Marriott,** 1 Orms St., 401/272-2400 or 800/937-7768, has a superbly trained and extremely warm staff, plush rooms with desks and armchairs with ottomans, upscale bath amenities, a very nice health club and indoor/outdoor pool, and a good restaurant (along with an outdoor pool deck and grill that's open in summer). There's free parking, too. It's a terrific property in every regard but for the fact that it's slightly north of downtown attractions and restaurants—a 10-minute walk, which is only unpleasant if it's cold or wet outside. This 351-room hotel does, however, lie just a short walk north of the State House, and it's right off I-95. The **Providence Biltmore,** Dorrance and Washington Streets, 401/421-0700 or 800/294-7709, website: www.providencebiltmore.com, dates to 1922 and is unquestionably the city's grande dame. Each of the 289 rooms is quite cushy, and 181 of them are suites with sitting areas. There's a full health club, a car-rental agency next door, and a very good restaurant (Davio's, 401/274-4810, which serves upscale Italian fare), but it's the sense of history and the perfect location that draw most guests back again and again. The hotel is worth visiting just to admire the elaborate lobby with its soaring three-tiered atrium, vaulted gilt ceiling, and gurgling fountains. At one time rooms here had become somewhat less fabulous than the public areas, but an impressive and expensive rejuvenation in the late 1990s changed all that—accommodations are warm and atmospheric, with elegant bathroom fixtures, fine linens, and other cushy amenities. The location couldn't be more central, either. Many of the top rooms, especially at busy times, run well over $200 nightly.

One of the most distinctive and admired new constructions in downtown Providence in the 1990s was the 364-room **Westin Providence,** 1 W. Exchange St., 401/598-8000 or 888/625-5144, website: www.westinprovidence.com, a dramatic neoclassical skyscraper with peaked gables and a redbrick facade. Interior elements carry out the elegant theme, from the massive glass-dome rotunda to public areas of marble, polished dark woods, and recessed

PROVIDENCE

To Woonsocket

To Pawtucket
and Boston

146

7

95

PROVIDENCE
MARRIOTT

ORMS ST.

Moshassuck River

OLNEY ST.

TORTILLA
FLATS

HOPE ST.

44

JEWETT ST.

STATE HOUSE INN

CAPITOL HILL

STATE ST.

SMITH ST.

1

BARNES ST.

WHAT CHEER!
BED & BREAKFAST

HOLDER ST.

PARK ST.

FRANCIS ST.

BENNETT ST.

PROSPECT ST.

BOWEN ST.

PROMENADE ST.

1

OLD COURT B & B

SPIKE'S
JUNKYARD
DOGS

CAFE ANDREA'S

MEETING
STREET CAFE

MEETING ST.

KEBOB-
N-CURRY

CHEESECAKE
FACTORY

NAPA VALLEY
GRILLE

Woonasquatucket

River

FRANCIS ST.

XO

BELLA
VISTA

CAPITAL GRILLE

OLIVES

NUOVO

MILL'S
TAVERN

N. MAIN ST.

CAFE PARAGON GRILL/
VIVA BAR & EATERY

GEOFF'S

SURA

ANGELL ST.

College
Hill

LA CREPERIE

THAYER ST.

WATERMAN ST.

BROWN
UNIVERSITY

6   10

FIRE + ICE

JOE'S AMERICAN BAR

RAPHAEL BISTRO AND BAR

COURTYARD BY MARRIOTT

AGORA

WESTIN
PROVIDENCE

RI-RA

EXCHANGE TER.

HAVEN BROS. DINER

UNION STREET
ALE HOUSE

Kennedy
Plaza

GEORGE ST.

PARKSIDE
ROTISSERIE
AND BAR

HEMENWAY'S SEAFOOD
GRILL & OYSTER BAR

95

ATWELLS AVE.

To
Federal
Hill

BROADWAY

PROVIDENCE
HOLIDAY INN

SABIN ST.

1

1

MURPHY'S
DELICATESSEN

TRINITY
BREWHOUSE

WASHINGTON ST.

EDDY ST.

DORRANCE ST.

PROVIDENCE
BILTMORE

POT
AU FEU

TEN PRIME STEAK
AND SUSHI

RED FEZ

Downtown

DOWN CITY
DINER

CABLE CAR CINEMA

POWER ST.

S. WATER ST.

S. MAIN ST.

BENEFIT ST.

6

PAKARANG

44

ARNOLD ST.

FOUNTAIN ST.

EMPIRE ST.

GREEN ST.

1

COOKIE PLACE CAFE

AS220
CAFE

EMPIRE
PROVIDENCE

WESTMINSTER ST.

BOSPHORUS
KEBAB

WYBOSSET ST.

INDIA

INTERMEZZO

195

BRICKWAY

TASTE OF
INDIA

THE COFFEE
EXCHANGE

O-CHA

DEAN ST.

WESTMINSTER ST.

BROAD ST.

CAHIR ST.

1

PINE ST.

BASSETT ST.

RESTAURANT PROV.

CAV

ELM ST.

Jewelry
District

RICHMOND ST.

CHESTNUT ST.

POINT ST.

EDDY ST.

1A

GRAPPA

Providence River

AL FORNO

S. WATER ST.

S. MAIN ST.

Fox
Point

HURRICANE
BARRIER

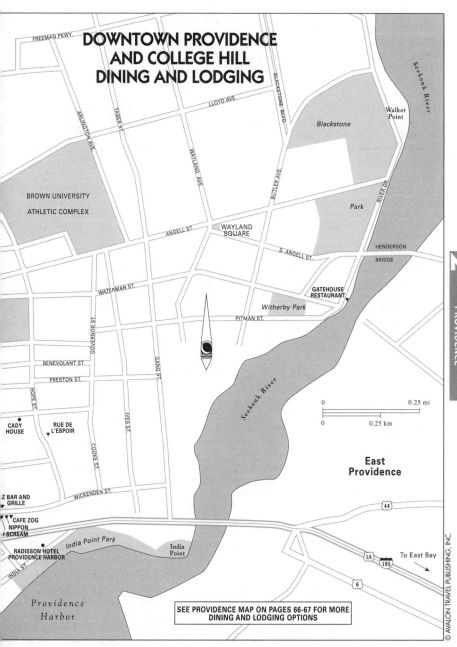

DOWNTOWN PROVIDENCE
AND COLLEGE HILL
DINING AND LODGING

FREEMAN PKWY.

LLOYD AVE.

ARLINGTON AVE.

TABER ST.

WAYLAND AVE.

BLACKSTONE BLVD.

Seekonk River

Walker
Point

Blackstone

BROWN UNIVERSITY
ATHLETIC COMPLEX

Park

BUTLER AVE.

RIVER DR.

ANGELL ST.

WAYLAND
SQUARE

S. ANGELL ST.

HENDERSON
BRIDGE

WATERMAN ST.

GATEHOUSE
RESTAURANT

Witherby Park

PITMAN ST.

GOVERNOR ST.

GANO ST.

BENEVOLANT ST.

PRESTON ST.

Seekonk River

HOPE ST.

IVES ST.

CADY
HOUSE

RUE DE
L'ESPOIR

0   0.25 mi

0   0.25 km

COOKE ST.

East
Providence

Z BAR AND
GRILLE

WICKENDEN ST.

CAFE ZOG
NIPPON
I SCREAM

44

India Point Park

India
Point

RADISSON HOTEL
PROVIDENCE HARBOR

1A

195

To East Bay

INDIA ST.

6

Providence
Harbor

SEE PROVIDENCE MAP ON PAGES 66-67 FOR MORE
DINING AND LODGING OPTIONS

PROVIDENCE

© AVALON TRAVEL PUBLISHING, INC.

lighting. Guest rooms mix reproduction French and British antiques with rich fabrics and wallpapers, and the oversized bathrooms boast plush fixtures and fancy soaps and shampoos. Units in a level of rooms called Westin's Guest Office contain business-oriented perks like ergonomically designed seating and desks, in-room fax/printer/copiers, and two-line speakerphones (all rooms have two phones). The rooftop health club, under a cavernous glass dome, ranks among the top such facilities at any hotel in New England. In addition to the simple and airy Cafe for lunch and breakfast, the Westin claims one of the city's top eateries, Agora. There are also three lounges, including a favorite date spot, the dark and inviting Library Bar & Lounge (with an extensive selection of cognacs, wines, and aperitifs), as well as the more casual International Yacht & Athletic Club—despite the cheesy name, this is a festive sports bar with a great casual-munchies menu. Another plus is the central location, with enclosed elevated walkways that connect the hotel both to the Providence Convention Center and Providence Place Mall. The Westin may lack the tradition of the nearby Biltmore, but in every other regard it's comparable or better.

Named for the famous greeting a Narragansett Indian allegedly uttered to Roger Williams upon his first trip to this land, **What Cheer! Bed & Breakfast** 73 Holden St., 401/351-6111, website: www.providence-suites.com, is run by the same folks who operate State House Inn, and it lies just around the corner with the same proximity to the State House and Providence Place Mall. This graceful, meticulously restored red Victorian house with green and tan trim overlooks the historic redbrick Foundry industrial complex and has somewhat more romantic and frilly guest and public rooms than its sister—all have phones and cable TV, tiled private baths (most with whirlpool tubs), four-poster beds, air-conditioning, and private sitting rooms (all with pull-out sleepers and work tables). A nice touch are the many rooms with vintage photos of the city. Full breakfast is included. Most rooms are under $180 nightly.

COLLEGE HILL AND THE WATERFRONT

$50–100

A very informal, almost secretive inn with no sign, extremely laid-back hosts, and rates beginning around $80, the **Cady House,** 127 Power St., 401/273-5398, website: www.cadyhouse.com, has an outstanding location by Brown and the great shopping and dining of Thayer and Wickenden Streets and Wayland Square. This large Classical Revival home with considerable character dates to 1839. The rooms all have private bath, TV, and phone. Folk art—a specialty of collectors and owners Bill and Anna Colaiace—and Victorian antiques and Oriental rugs fill the rooms, and there's a lovely garden on the grounds. A pair of friendly dogs greet guests. In warm weather you can read or relax on the garden patio, surrounded by well-tended flower beds and plantings, as well as mature trees—with grounds so lush you'd hardly know you were in a city. Just down the street is the famed John Brown House and the "mile of history" along Benefit Street. Continental breakfast is included.

$100–150

Radisson Hotel Providence Harbor, 200 India St., 401/272-5577 or 800/333-3333, with 140 rooms and an enviable location overlooking Providence Harbor, is a very good mid-priced chain property that enjoys equal popularity among leisure and business travelers. Its location wedged between I-195 and an exit ramp may sound off-putting, but you can't beat the convenience to India Point Park, the hip restaurants on Wickenden Street and down by Fox Point, and the campuses of Brown and RISD. Rooms themselves are fairly traditional and cookie-cutter, but they are clean and bright, half have water views, and for an extra $10–20 you can get one with a Jacuzzi. There's an exercise room with whirlpool, an outdoor pool whose terrace has water views, and a functional restaurant. The **Old Court B&B,** 143 Benefit St., 401/751-2002, website: www.oldcourt.com, has about the most wonderful setting in Providence, in the heart of the historic Benefit Street neighborhood. Built as a rectory in 1863, it's right beside the old Rhode Island courthouse and nearly across from the original state house. Rooms contain truly museum-quality antiques, collectibles, and chandeliers mostly from the Victorian era and early 20th centuries, and are themed after specific styles or mood-setting furnishings: one room has Chippendale pieces, another Eastlake Victorian antiques. The Stove Room is anchored by, as you might guess, an antique stove—it's original to the rectory. The rooms are refreshingly free of clutter or cloying tchotchkes, allowing the inn to strike a pleasing balance between a traditional B&B and a small luxury hotel. This is one of the priciest B&Bs in inland Rhode Island, but considering the lavish furnishings, delightfully scenic and convenient location, and modern amenities (phones, TVs, and private bath in every room), the Old Court represents a very smart value.

Food

You're wise to be suspicious of any city these days that promotes itself as some sort of dining mecca—*every* U.S. city's restaurant scene has improved by leaps and bounds since the 1980s. We've all witnessed the nation's big culinary revolution, and most of us know it takes more than a few trendy-looking eateries fusing various Asian and Mediterranean cuisines to make for a stellar dining experience. So why does Providence truly deserve to be called one of the nation's finest small restaurant cities?

Well, in the first place, Providence had great restaurants well before Alice Waters and Wolfgang Puck began revolutionizing the way chefs approached cooking. The city has long harbored many ethnic groups with rich culinary traditions, from Italians to Portuguese to Latin Americans to Asians. Providence's own Little Italy, on Federal Hill, ranks among the best in the world (well, outside Big Italy). It's less blue-blooded than many New England destinations, and so folks here seem less married to old regional standbys like broiled haddock and Yankee pot roast. Indian and Thai restaurants flourished here long before they became commonplace; same with sushi. Providence is on the water, just inland from the ocean—fishing is in its blood. Seafood plays a vital role in local cuisine. And as an international port, Providence has always had access to exotic ingredients.

The city's arty element and many students have created a desire, if not a need, for cheap and innovative foods—and don't forget, quite a few of those students (and professors) are affiliated with the fabulous culinary arts program of Johnson & Wales University, home to the world's largest culinary archive. Providence diners are open to trying new things, to dining in style without spending a huge amount of money, and to lingering over a hot bowl of soup or steamed chai while browsing a fashion magazine or discussing literary theory with fellow culture vultures. Café society is alive and well here. Dining out is about more than mere sustenance—it's about seeing and being seen, talking and observing, laughing and listening to music.

Finally, the city government knows that Providence restaurants bring legions of hungry foodies into town, and it's passed some unusual legislation to promote noshing. It presently provides financing to new restaurants, which as a result seem to open almost constantly throughout the city.

As the trends of contemporary American cooking have evolved in recent years, from the garlic-mashed-potato and sun-dried-tomato phases of years gone by to today's obsession with everything from kumquats to pomegranates to ostrich meat to caramelized everything, Providence chefs have moved with the trends. The already exceptional seafood, Italian, Asian, and regional New England menus have expanded, intermarried, and updated. But on the road to culinary innovation, Providence has remained happily true to its roots. Ask most residents whether they'd rather have a plate of scallion pancakes with kiwi salsa and nori-wrapped sea urchin, or a stack of good old-fashioned jonnycakes with a side of clam chowder, and they'll usually opt for the latter. The trends come and go, but Providence's tradition of culinary excellence spans the ages.

DOWNTOWN
Upscale

A warm and romantic eatery down a quiet alley downtown, **Pot au Feu,** 44 Custom House St., 401/273-8953 ($16–21 in the Bistro, $22–32 in Salon—three-course prix fixe also offered), is the city's seminal French restaurant. It opened in the early 1970s and has grown more popular seemingly each year. Depending on your mood, or your budget, opt either for the classic bistro fare of the cozy basement space, where a classic bouillabaisse and a signature dessert of crème brûlée vie for your attention (this is the better place to dine with a group of friends), or for the suave upstairs Salon, which fosters the rarified ambience you might seek if celebrating a more formal or special occasion. Here try roast duckling (the accompanying sauce changes frequently but may be anything from apricot to orange), foie gras, and similarly rich French standbys. The restaurant holds one-day cooking seminars that deal with both food preparation and wine selection—certainly the caliber of cuisine here speaks well for the staff's teaching abilities.

A favorite for its storybook location overlooking the swans and gondolas gliding along the river, as well as a backdrop of downtown office towers and the stately Biltmore Hotel, **Bella Vista,** 1 American Express Way, 401/272-1040 ($16–30), makes especially good sense in warm weather, when you can grab one of the outdoor seats. Any time of year this cavernous bilevel space is ideal for first-rate contemporary Italian fare such as snail salad chopped with celery and onions and tossed with a light and simple blend of extra virgin olive oil, lemon juice, and herbs, followed by fettuccine tossed with veal, prosciutto, sage, and minced vegetables with a marsala wine sauce and parmesan cheese. A lengthy list of grills, seafood specialties, and pastas are offered—and while the view may be this restaurant's claim to fame, the food lives up to the setting. Although it's a chain, the upscale **Capital**

Grille, 1 Cookson Pl., 401/521-5600 ($17–31), feels distinctly local, a favorite haunt of politicos from the nearby State House, plus business execs from surrounding office buildings. Steaks (the dry-aged Porterhouse steak keeps carnivores coming back again and again) are the main draw, plus broiled fresh lobster and obscenely large sides of baked potato, creamed spinach, asparagus with Hollandaise, and so on. The dark, clubby interior has an almost oppressively masculine feel, but that's part of the Capital Grille's gimmick. The entrance lies steps from Riverwalk and a very short distance from Providence Place Mall.

If you can pardon the mall location, the Providence branch of the upscale **Napa Valley Grille,** Providence Place, North Tower Entrance, 401/270-6272 ($17–30), works well as both an elegant setting for a special occasion and as simply a natty spot for a tasty sampling of creative California-style cooking. Murals of the California wine country, wine-glass chandeliers, and subdued amber lighting convey the theme, and the restaurant's wine list offers a nice balance of regional California wines. As for the menu, consider the likes of crab-crusted Maine cod with zucchini noodles, Yukon gold potatoes, and orange-ginger sauce; and maple-walnut chicken breast with crème fraîche mashed potatoes, broccoli rabe, and a natural reduction. **Empire Providence,** 123 Empire St., 401/621-7911 ($15–27), presents a broad and varied range of contemporary American and Italian dishes. From the pasta side of the menu, sample pappardelle with boneless pork rib ragu and parmigiano; larger entrées include roasted chicken breast wrapped in smokehouse bacon with braised endive and herbed potatoes, and griddled Delmonico steak with onion crema, crispy potato torta, and roasted peppers. Cheese fondue for two, with garlic rostini, is an excellent starter. This is one kitchen staff that knows what it's doing, and it has risen above most competitors in a city where it's not easy to make waves—of course, it doesn't hurt that husband-and-wife team and owners Eric Mosier and Loren Falsone are alums of the kitchen at Al Forno. In their first year (1999), *Food and Wine* named the two among the nation's 10 best new chefs.

Agora, 1 W. Exchange St., 401/598-8011 ($18–28), at the Westin Providence, is run by Frank McClelland, famous for L'Espalier in Boston. Seafood is a top pick at this eatery that by leaps and bounds transcends conventional hotel dining. The menu changes fairly often but has included a starter of wood-grilled lobster with apple and pumpkin salsa and a pomegranate glaze, as well as similarly far-out but well-executed entrées like seared coriander-rubbed yellowfin tuna with annato rice, tempura beans, and a chanterelle reduction, and grilled beef tenderloin with a port-basil reduction and chevre-scallion mashed potatoes. Great food aside, pluses include a spacious and uncluttered dining room of fine china, crystal, and silver, and almost overly solicitous service by a relatively attitude-free staff. There's live piano weekend evenings, and free valet parking. Another of Providence's favorite power-lunching venues, **Nuovo,** 1 Citizens Plaza, 401/421-2525 ($16–28), presents an appropriately dazzling (and long) menu of rich and elaborate contemporary American dishes, such as caramelized sea scallops, lobster ravioli, and a show-stopping Dover sole prepared tableside. The wine list reads like a who's who of top vintages. The restaurant occupies the ground floor of a fancy office tower at the confluence of the Moshassuck and Woonasquatucket Rivers—some seats are right on the river terrace. **Ten Prime Steak and Sushi,** 55 Pine St., 401/453—2333 ($18–$32), has been a white-hot culinary star since it opened in 2001, serving up tasty portions of Asian-inspired steaks and seafoods. Sushi is artful and delicious here, but not every item has an Asian spin—a formidable veal chop, for instance, is served with Portobello mushrooms and shaved parmesan. As interesting as the food is, Ten Prime has been most successful because of its lavish decor, fancy (and huge) martinis, extensive sake list, and sexy attitude. Drawbacks are the occasionally haughty, or in some cases just flaky, service and certain dishes which sound interesting but are executed unevenly. Note that it has the same owners as XO, which also walks a tightrope between snazzy and silly.

Creative but Casual

The quirky hangout **CAV,** 14 Imperial Pl., 401/751-9164 ($13–20), occupies a characterful old knife manufactory in the Jewelry District and offers coffee, antiques, and victuals—the first letters of these three words spell the restaurant's name. So you can drop in to sip espresso and nosh on fresh baked goods, or hunker down for a substantial meal. And all the while, check out the considerable selection of vintage furnishings and goods. The menu tends toward fresh pastas (you can mix-and-match them with several sauces), but a number of innovatively prepared fish and meat grills, salads, and desserts show up, too. CAV has folk and jazz music many weekend evenings, too. This is a popular spot—book ahead when possible. Another inviting hangout in the same neighborhood is the **Restaurant Prov,** 99 Chestnut St., 401/621-8888 ($15–22), formerly known as the Atomic Grill, which books live bands, too. Here you might try kicky Asian-fusion concoctions like seared sesame-crusted tuan over lobster noodle salad and wontons with mango dressing and rooster sauce. You're apt to see culinary students from nearby Johnson & Wales congregating at the art deco **Down City Diner,** 151 Weybosset St., 401/331-9217, ($12–23), a stylish take on a traditional greasy spoon. The little cocktail bar has an artsy following, and is a favorite spot for a drink before continuing out to one of the neighborhood's several gay and mainstream bars; it's also a hot spot for brunch on Saturday and Sunday. Tasty dinner offerings include lobster-and-leek chowder with scallion-and-parsley crisps; roasted French rack of pork with apricot-guava glaze and mashed sweet and Idaho potatoes; and forest mushroom and port wine ravioletti with artichoke hearts, goat cheese, and arugula salad. Great desserts, too.

A quirky popular bistro serving mod-Californian cuisine, **Julian's,** 318 Broadway, 401/861-1770 ($11–18), offers uncomplicated, soul-warming fare that might include roast duck with a honey-walnut risotto cake; or pappardelle pasta with veal, peas, and parmigiano-reggiano cheese. The dining rooms are filled with unusual objets d'art and decorations. Breakfast is served all day—and the eggs Hussard (poached eggs with hollandaise sauce, tomatoes, and Italian toast with home fries) is irresistible. At lunch, check out the long list of specialty sandwiches. BYOB. Reasonably priced **Intermezzo on Weybosset,** 220 Weybosset St., 401/331-5100 ($10–18), spans the Mediterranean and Southeast Asia to bring patrons a creative array of grills, salads, and most notably desserts, which are a specialty here—in particular the rich, decadent kind: try a roasted-hazelnut fudge tart with a shortbread crust, or the signature New York–style cheesecake with fresh berry compote. You're as welcome to drop by for a full meal or for coffee and a light bite as for a full meal; the restaurant adjoins the Providence Performing Arts Center and counts quite a few pre- and post-show-goers among its devotees. Yuppies and see-and-be-seen types appreciate the cool colors and postindustrial lighting fixtures of chic **Raphael Bistro and Bar,** 1 Union Station, 401/421-4646 ($11–29), a loud and convivial spot near Providence Place Mall and the riverfront. The kitchen puts a worldly spin on Italian fare with such tasty antipasti as cornmeal-fried calamari over fresh watercress with cherry-pepper aioli, and main dishes like grilled eggplant ravioli primavera with grilled field greens, vegetables, pan-roasted black truffle oil and sun-dried-tomato tapenade; and a rich grilled beef tenderloin with sautéed spinach, balsamic demi glace, and crisp fried sweet onions. A newcomer to downtown, the laid-back **Red Fez,** 49 Peck St., 401/272-1212 ($6–14), is a dark and intimate space that offers excellent light fare, including hefty and creative sandwiches, in the bar, and more substantial dinners in a separate downstairs space, where you might sample orange-chipotle-marinated pork tenderloin with seared kale and chipotle mashed sweet potatoes; or balsamic-glazed grilled salmon topped with tomato-caper relish, served with grilled, stuffed tomatoes and orzo-pesto salad.

Pizzas, Pastas, and Pub Grub

The loud, high-ceilinged **Cheesecake Factory,** 94 Providence Pl., 401/270-4010 ($8–23), suffers a bit from crowds upon crowds (and that means obnoxiously long lines, especially on weekends), but the staff here takes it all in stride and remains consistently personable. If this seems like a lot of fuss for a national chain restaurant on the ground floor of a shopping mall, well, it is. Still, the many-paged menu suggests an amazing variety of foods, offering more appetizers than most restaurants do total items, plus pizzas, burgers, stir-fries, tacos, chicken and biscuits, pastas, seafood, steaks, and massive salads and sandwiches. Of course, plenty of people come simply for the cheesecake, which is available in about 35 varieties, from Dutch apple-caramel to lemon mousse. Another of the popular chain eateries at Providence Place Mall, Boston-based **Joe's American Bar,** 148 Providence Pl., 401/270-4737 ($10–20), has a strong following for dependable—if rather predictable—comfort cooking favored by "regular Joes" (and Janes): meat loaf (in this case flame-grilled with mashed potatoes and sautéed spinach), milkshakes, barbecued baby back ribs, and Cobb salads.

Vintage signs and memorabilia lend a festive air to **Ri-Ra,** 50 Exchange Terr., 401/272-1953 ($9–15), a dapper Irish eatery along Exchange Terrace. Try traditional standbys prepared with considerable flair, such as corned beef and cabbage, salmon boxty (char-broiled salmon with diced tomato, scallion, and cream cheese in a potato pancake with an Irish parsley sauce), and beef-and-Guinness pie—you'll find a smattering of vegetarian options as well. An oft-requested finale is Kelly's Cake, a dark-chocolate confection layered with Bailey's-chocolate mousse and coated with a milk-chocolate glaze. As you might guess, Ri-Ra is a hit with the after-work happy hour set. An atmospheric subterranean haunt along Exchange Street, the **Union Street Ale House,** 36 Exchange Terrace, 401/274-BREW ($10–17), serves a fairly typical but reliable mix of pizzas, dinner salads, ale-battered fish-and-chips, hickory-smoked ribs, and more unusual foods like baked crabmeat-stuffed tilapia over saffron rice with fresh corn, asparagus, and red pepper ragout. Another favorite among fans of this genre, the **Trinity Brewhouse,** 186 Fountain St., 401/453-BEER ($5–15), brews six beers and serves an impressive range of snack foods and light entrées, including pulled-pork barbecue sandwiches and shepherd's pie. You'll find great burgers, too, and also some veggie options like falafel and grilled Portobello sandwiches.

Ethnic Fare

Many of the city's Asian eateries lie across the river on the East Side, but **India,** 123 Dorrance St., 401/278-2000; also on the East Side at 758 Hope St., 401/421-2600 (and in the East Bay town of Warren, at 520 Main St.), brings excellent Indian fare to downtown. In addition to the standbys, India offers some unusual options like mussels steamed in garlic, lemon juice, and chat masala (tomato, cream, cardamom, fenugreek, and fresh cilantro); chicken in sweet-and-sour mango sauce; fiery green-pea and chickpea pulao (with jalapeños, onions, cilantro, and mustard seed). One of the best eateries of this genre in New England—partly it's the food, and partly it's the imaginative and bold decor, with bright paintings, hanging Oriental rugs, and elegant light fixtures. Look to **Bosphorus Kebab,** 286 Westminster St., 401/454-3500 ($3–7), for affordable and tasty Middle Eastern and Mediterranean victuals, from pizzas to salads to fresh-made soups.

Under the category of "Eat-ertainment," **Fire + Ice,** 48 Providence Pl., 401/270-4040 ($15.95 fixed price all-you-can-eat, less for brunch and lunch), looks like a Pee-wee's Playhouse homage gone horribly awry, with dangling multicolored chandeliers and brilliantly hued furnishings of all shapes and sizes. There's no set menu; what you do here is walk over to the various veggie, meat, and seafood stations, fill your bowl with whatever interests you (could be swordfish, pork, scallops, shallots, portobello mushrooms, black olives, leeks, jalapeños, you name it), and then continue on to a sauce station where again you get to pick (will it be Jamaican jerk, rosemary, roasted corn-and-tomato, Thai-basil cream, or one of the dozen others?). You move on to a large grill, where you get to watch a chef cook up your chosen ingredients. It's noisy and usually packed, but if the gimmick works for you, try it—there's no arguing that it's a great value for big eaters (return trips for extra helpings are free).

Quick Bites

Haven Bros. Diner, Kennedy Plaza, 401/861-7777 ($2–5), open 5 P.M.–3 A.M., is another of the favorite late-night greasy spoons in town, famous for its hearty breakfast food. This loveably gruff hangout is actually a diner on wheels, which the owners park outside City Hall into the wee hours.

On the second level of the acclaimed and provocative AS220 arts space, **AS220 Cafe,** 115 Empire St., 401/831-9190 ($3–8), serves healthful sandwiches, smoothies, salads, and creative entrées, and it's open till 1 A.M. most nights. **Cookie Place Cafe,** 158 Washington St., 401/351-8789 ($2–5), serves a nice variety of sandwiches (the Cajun seafood salad and bacon cheeseburger are popular options), but it's best known for its addictive chocolate-chip cookies, plus other baked goodies like Heath bar toffee crunch brownies and cinnamon rolls. And if chocolate isn't your thing, the lemon-butterscotch cookies are delicious. Cookie Place, Inc. is a not-for-profit organization that aims to provide supportive employment opportunities for persons with psychiatric illnesses; it's closed weekends. Since 1929, downtown office workers have relied on **Murphy's Delicatessen,** 55 Union St., 401/621-8467 ($3–6), for filling sandwiches. Favorites include the lobster salad roll; the artery-clogging corned beef, pastrami, salami, and Swiss; and Murphy's Reuben (with Irish corned beef). Several burgers are offered, too, as well as some veggie options.

FEDERAL HILL

In addition to the several very good Italian restaurants and food shops detailed in the "Eating Your Way Through Providence's Little Italy" callout, Federal Hill has a number of additional great restaurants serving several types of food.

Creative but Casual

Departures from traditional Italian fare are becoming increasingly commonplace on the Hill: take **AquaViva EuroBistro,** 286 Atwells Ave., 401/273-8664 ($5–14), whose cloyingly catchy name can be forgiven thanks to an absolutely stellar menu of more than 60 tapas. Since open-

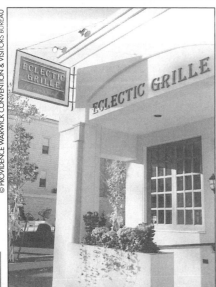

© PROVIDENCE/WARWICK CONVENTION & VISITORS BUREAU

Eclectic Grille on Federal Hill

ing in 1999, fans of the small-plate genre have flocked here with near religious fervor for onion-anchovy-olive tarts; sautéed chicken breast served cold with asparagus, onions, olives, and slices of orange; skillet-sauteed zarzuelas (paella-like rice casseroles with myriad ingredients); and roast pork loin with stewed apples and Calvados. While the theme is Spanish, the tapas here span the European continent, as does an extensive list of wines and imported beers. This loud and festive eatery with an airy postmodern feel is an especially good option when dining out with a group of friends—plate-sharing is almost de rigueur here. Look to **Eclectic Grill,** 245 Atwells Ave., 401/831-8010 ($15–20) for a change of pace, as the cuisine here varies considerably what you'll find at most of the neighborhood's eateries. There are Italian influences to be sure (this is evidenced partly by the huge portions), but mostly the menu offers sophisticated, artfully seasoned Continental cuisine, such as grilled pork wrapped in bacon with a brandy-cream sauce. The wine bar here is one of the best in the neighborhood. A rather new (fall 2000) non-Italian contender on the Hill, **Naissance,** 242 Atwells Ave., 401/272-

9610 ($8–15)—like AquaViva—gears its menu toward plate-sharing and at very reasonable prices. A group of a few friends, or even just two of you out on a date, can nosh away on cheese and antipasto platters, any of several artfully presented fondues (the Asian warm plum–ginger version with tempura veggies and mini spring rolls is especially tempting), salads of goat cheese and baby greens, and plates of grilled eggplant stuffed with ricotta. There's a lounge with occasional live entertainment in the back of this softly lighted spot with sponge-painted blue and gold walls. Shellfish devotees should also consider **Providence Oyster Bar,** 283 Atwells Ave., 401/272-8866 ($12–21), which offers a great deal more than its name suggests—although the half-dozen varieties of oyster on the half shell are always fresh. The rest of the menu offers a fairly typical array of seafoods, from baked Chilean sea bass with a light citrus butter to platters of fried clams and scallops. There's an excellent oyster stew, too, which alone qualifies as a pretty substantial meal. The menu may suggest a bare-bones spot with butcher's paper on the tables, but in fact this chatter-filled eatery is warmly lighted with dark-wood trim and a handsome long bar.

Ethnic Fare

Federal Hill also has an excellent Mexican restaurant, **Don Jose's Tequilas,** 351 Atwells Ave., 401/454-8951 ($8–13), with a mix of Americanized and authentic regional dishes. The little dining room is modest but cheerfully decorated, with small tables and black bentwood chairs; extremely friendly and helpful waiters and waitresses deliver service with a smile, along with platters of chiles rellenos stuffed with mashed potatoes and jack cheese, chicken quesadillas, swordfish burritos, and chips with a smoky chipotle salsa.

COLLEGE HILL AND THE WATERFRONT

Upscale

Al Forno, 577 S. Main St., 410/273-9760 ($16–28), occupies a squat warehouse near Fox Point with two-story-tall dining room windows that offer views across the Providence River, at the ominous power plant across the river, and at the Hurricane Barrier. This restaurant put the neighborhood on the culinary map in 1980, and its reputation has further raised the city's reputation as a dining destination—Al Forno's list of awards is almost unbelievable when you consider that it's not in one of the nation's larger cities. Among the high praise, the *International Herald Tribune* named it the world's best restaurant for casual dining. So what's all the fuss? Chef-owners (and married couple) Johanne Killeen and George Germon have made a study of Northern Italian cuisine, which they prepare using—whenever appropriate—wood-burning ovens or open-flame grilling. Classic dishes include the clam roast with fiery hot sausage, tomato, endive, and mashed potatoes; and angel-hair noodles in fennel broth with roasted ocean catfish and peppery aioli. Pumpkin-cappuccino soup is one of the more innovative starters. As you might guess, reservations are not easy to score here—book well ahead if you can. **Gatehouse Restaurant,** 4 Richmond Sq., 401/521-9229 ($18–26), serves up live jazz on Fridays and Saturdays. In addition to more substantial fare, the restaurant has a less pricey pub menu. A lengthy list of creative martinis keeps trendsters happy. A big plus here is the location in a lovely old building on the Seekonk River. The art-filled dining room has floor-to-ceiling windows overlooking the water, so whether you come day or evening it's exceedingly romantic—weekend brunch is another great time to eat here. The menu emphasizes lavishly prepared, traditional Continental recipes with innovative twists, such as braised veal osso bucco with garlic-mushroom demi-glaze and cereliac mashed potatoes; and slow-roasted boneless duck with a Grand Marnier glaze and espresso sauce, praline–sweet potato hash, and sautéed and roasted vegetables.

Hemenway's Seafood Grill & Oyster Bar, 1 Providence Washington Plaza, S. Main St., 401/351-8570 ($15–23), is the place to go for fresh seafood. There's little pretentious or contrived about the food here—just fresh and simply prepared fish like shrimp scampi over linguine, fried shrimp dinners, broiled Florida grouper, baked scrod with seafood crumbs, just about every kind of fish imaginable. It's in an immense office building, but the nicest tables overlook the river. The oyster bar draws fans of the bivalve from all over the Northeast—14 varieties are served here.

Creative but Casual

Probably the most upscale and popular of the restaurants along Thayer (and it's still relatively affordable), **Cafe Paragon Grill,** 234 Thayer St., 401/331-6200 ($7–14), occupies an airy street-corner space with funky hanging lamps and tall French door–style windows overlooking the varied pedestrian traffic. There's lots of sidewalk seating in warm weather. The menu emphasizes pastas, pizzas, sandwiches, and fairly simple grills—good bets include the pie topped with basil, pear tomatoes, mozzarella, and parmesan; the six-cheese ravioli; and the swordfish sandwich with a lemon-oregano sauce. **Parkside Rotisserie and Bar,** 76 S. Main St., 401/331-0003 ($10–20), is a terrific little neighborhood restaurant, just across from Jackson-Gardner Park and drawing a more adult and less sceney crowd than many of the restaurants this close to Brown and RISD. The staff is accommodating and fun, too. Inside this warmly lighted, narrow and long dining room, tables are set with crisp white napery and fringed by small wooden chairs or plush banquettes. The food is creative without going overboard, with an emphasis on pastas and rotisserie chicken, as well as some excellent seafood grills. There's a nice selection of wines and beers, too. A trendy, riverfront space just off funky Wickenden Street, **Grappa,** 525 S. Water St., 401/454-1611 ($10–$20), presents an eclectic menu that includes grilled pizzas, clam chowder, creative salads, and vaguely Continental—but contemporary—grills like salmon with dill aioli and jasmine rice. The ambience is casual but inviting, but the view of the river, especially during the warmer months when windows are open, is the key drawing card.

Guppies and students love to crowd the trendy bar at **Rue de L'Espoir,** 99 Hope St., 401/751-8890 ($13–22), almost as much as they delight in supping here on sublime New American,

EATING YOUR WAY THROUGH PROVIDENCE'S LITTLE ITALY

On Federal Hill, Providence has one of the most prominent Little Italy neighborhoods in the country, and if you're a aficionado of great food from this culinarily blessed nation, you could easily spend a week or so sampling the specialties of every delightful grocery, trattoria, pizza place, and food shop in the district. Here's a roundup of some of the best Italian eateries along Federal Hill's main drag, Atwells Avenue.

If it's a special occasion, you might consider planning for a long, leisurely dinner at **L'Epicureo,** 238 Atwells Ave., 401/454-8430 ($16—25), which may be the most sophisticated Federal Hill eatery of the bunch. What began years ago as one of the neighborhood's top butcher markets (in the 1940s) has evolved slowly but surely into a dark and romantic setting for special occasions and very special food. This is refined Italian cooking with light and simple sauces (or none at all), from black-peppercorn-crusted beef tenderloin with feathery sweet-potato gnocchi to wood-grilled portobello mushrooms over braised spinach with grilled shrimp. Subtle seasonings and deft hands in the kitchen ensure consistently superb meals enhanced by L'Epicureo's warm and accommodating wait staff. Another upscale favorite is the **Blue Grotto,** 210 Atwells Ave., 401/272-9030 ($15–25), a dignified restaurant whose polite, tux-clad waiters glide about the somewhat formal dining room serving plates of gnocchi with a light basil-tomato sauce and fresh mozzarella, and lobster meat and littleneck clams in a spicy marinara over risotto. Federal Hill isn't all about tradition, other than the seemingly annual rite of some glittery new restaurant opening amid the old standbys. In 2002 it was **Pane e Vino,** 365 Atwells Ave., 401/223-2230 ($14–$24). Upscale in feel more than in price, this Italian restaurant took the place of an ancient hardware store, perhaps not to everybody's pleasure (Federal Hill doesn't exactly need more dining options). However, nobody seems to be arguing about the high caliber of cooking, from a starter of littleneck clams with a garlic-tomato broth and cannellini beans, to a main course of gnocchi with a rich port-wine wild boar sauce. Desserts here are excellent, and the wine list includes more than two-dozen varieties by the glass.

Tavern-like **Mediterraneo,** 134 Atwells Ave., 401/331-7760 ($14–22), is a loud and fun place with a youngish crowd. Tall French windows overlook the street—making it a prime spot to watch the world go by (everybody gravitates toward the sidewalk seating in summer). From all the hype around town, you'd think this place crawls with A-list celebs every night of the week; more likely you'll simply find a lot of well-dressed patrons hoping to spy somebody even more fabulous than themselves. Don't think the glitzy ambience is merely a cover for so-so food: this kitchen knows

Italian, and French fare—dishes like homemade ravioli filled with spinach, mushrooms, smoked gouda, and ricotta. For its delicious food and warm and romantic dining room, the restaurant nevertheless maintains a friendly, low-attitude ambience. And as it's slightly off the beaten tourist path, it has cultivated a strong following among locals since it opened back in 1976. It's just a great all-around neighborhood eatery, and a smart spot for brunch, too. A snug and super-trendy café with exposed brick, tall gilt-frame mirrors, and walls that have been graffitied by patrons, **XO,** 125 N. Main St., 401/273-9090 ($12–29), tends toward the outlandish, although it employs a waitstaff that can be snippy. The food combinations and preparations here can be overwrought—even silly—and not always executed successfully, but more often than not you'll come away from here having enjoyed a memorable and tasty meal. Before you try any food, check out the sprightly and spunky drink list—the prickly pear margarita is a nice way to start things off. At XO it's recommended that you order dessert first (hazelnut-spiked French toast brulée with raspberries and Chartreuse berry sorbet is a popular option). Few patrons appear keen on this strategy and instead opt for the more expected (though unusual) starters like the roasted

what it's doing, presenting superb regional Italian fare like a double-cut pork chop stuffed with spinach, prosciutto, and fresh mozzarella; and both straightforward and complicated pasta dishes like fusilli with a pink vodka sauce of plum tomatoes, onions, pancetta, and heavy cream. Late at night, the place switches gears and becomes a Euro-trendy (or -trashy, according to some) dance club with a sneering, velvet-rope door policy. On reputation alone, **Angelo's Civita Farnese,** 141 Atwells Ave., 401/621-8171 ($4–9), could survive on any street in Providence, but here on Federal Hill it's a star among the cheaper eateries—expect heaping portions of traditional red-sauce fare in this boisterous place with communal seating. There's not much in the way of ambience, but it's fun—and Buddy Cianci loves it. Try **Andino's,** 171 Atwells Ave., 401/421-3715 ($10–20), for signature dishes like chicken Andino (boneless chicken baked with artichoke hearts, sliced pepperoni, and sweet peppers with a white wine sauce; linguine with whole clams; and veal Zingarella (veal medallions sautéed with marinara sauce, roasted red peppers, sliced onions, and white mushrooms). A practitioner of authentic Etruscan-style cooking, all of it done in terracotta bakeware, is **Walter's La Locanda del Coccio,** 265 Atwells Ave., 401/273-2652 ($18–23), which faces vibrant Despasquale Square. Favorites here include soft polenta with stewed sausages, and roasted filet of beef with a sauce of gorgonzola, rosemary, and raisins.

Joe Marzelli's Old Canteen, 120 Atwells Ave., 401/751-5544 ($9–13), is an elegant white mansion (made only slightly less elegant by its pulsing pink neon sign), a dependable middle-of-the-road option with reasonably priced fare. A memorable spot for desserts, especially on a warm summer evening, is **Cafe Dolce Vita,** 59 Depasquale Square, 401/331-8240, a coffeehouse, pastry shop, and gelateria whose outdoor tables are shaded with umbrellas. You can buy fantastic handmade ravioli in some 75 varieties at **Venda Ravioli,** 265 Atwells Ave., 401/421-9105, one of the most inspired delis in any Italian neighborhood in the country; here you'll find fresh sausages, sauces, oils, vinegars, cheeses, and so on. A century-old wine and liquor shop, **Gasbarro's,** 361 Atwells Ave., 401/421-4170, sells some wonderful Italian imports, including about 150 varieties of chianti, and almost as many of grappa. **Tony's Colonial Food,** 311 Atwells Ave., 401/621-8675, is a tempting *salumeria* with just about every kind of gourmet grocery imaginable. **Roma Gourmet,** 310 Atwells Ave., 401/331-8620, across from Tony's, has imported cheese, olives, sauces, and pastas, as well as hot dishes ready for take-out. Cheese lovers should be sure to stop by **Providence Cheese,** 178 Atwells Ave., 401/421-5653. Family-owned since 1916, **Scialo Bros. Bakery,** 257 Atwells Ave., 401/421-0986, fires up its brick ovens daily to produce delicious Italian bread, biscotti, cakes, and pastries.

pulled-duck tamale with cumin-scented masa, ancho-pepper mole, and goat cheese in banana leaf; or the pizza topped with mushrooms, thyme, and faux-boursin cheese. A typically dazzling entrée of whole-friend yellow-tail flounder, stir-fried coconut-basmati rice, and soy sake dipping sauce appeared on a recent menu, but the kitchen is always toying around with new ideas. Though it's less pretentious than XO, **Z Bar and Grille,** 244 Wickenden St., 401/831-1566 ($11–19), nevertheless strikes a sophisticated pose on the otherwise shabby-chic Wickenden Street restaurant row. Here you'll typically find a well-put-together crowd hobnobbing behind the long

polished-wood bar, or dining at tables in the loud but comfy dining room with exposed brick and air ducts—when the weather cooperates, you can escape the din on the lovely brick courtyard in back. Sup on creative pizzas, large salads, appetizers like mushroom ravioli with shiitake mushroom–tasso cream, and entrées with a contemporary bent, such as filet mignon with garlic mashed potatoes and asparagus; and chicken, broccoli rabe, tomatoes, garlic, cannellini beans, and capers tossed over angel-hair pasta. Creative "Zangwiches" (groan) include oven-roasted turkey, cranberry sauce, and seasonal stuffing served on lavash.

PROVIDENCE

Steaks, Seafood, Pizzas, and Pub Grub

Olives, 108 N. Main St., 401/751-1200 ($10–18), caters to a fashionable crowd of pre-nightclub crawlers, post-work revelers, and variations thereof. The loud and lively tavern-like eatery with high pressed-tin ceilings and French doors opening onto North Main Street serves an eclectic menu of better-than-average comfort foods, including pasta pomodoro, sesame-or-ange salmon, filet mignon, and gourmet burgers. Also catering to a sceney (some say Euro-trashy) set, **Viva Bar and Eatery,** 234 Thayer St., 401/272-7600 ($6–13), is a sophisticated lounge space with parquet floors and a large semicircular bar. People come here to drink and look bored as much as to nibble on fairly standard bar victuals like honey Dijon chicken, burgers, and lobster ravioli. If you don't look the part at this Brown University near-campus commissary, you may feel a bit out of place.

Ethnic Fare

Another of the many eateries along South Main Street, **Pakarang,** 303 S. Main St., 401/453-3660 ($7–14), is a reliable option for Thai; it's a lively, cleverly decorated spot with mounted fish "swimming" against a brick sea. House specialties include Choo Choo curry with snow peas, pineapple, peppers, zucchini, summer squash, and tomato; and sliced sautéed salmon with ginger, asparagus, onion, carrot, black mushroom, red pepper, and scallion. **O-cha,** 221 Wickenden St., 401/421-4699 ($5–16), is a cute little Asian eatery on the ground floor of a handsome old Wickenden Victorian—it's tiny but cozy with an almost familial-seeming staff that aims to please, and there's some outdoor seating on the side deck. The menu mixes Thai recipes (spicy duck topped with Thai herbs in wine sauce, beef with coconut curry, pad-Thai) with traditional Japanese sushi. On the college strip, **Kebob-n-Curry,** 261 Thayer St., 401/273-8844 ($7–14), presents an ambitious menu of Indian specialties, from the usual tikka masalas and vindaloos to less predictable creations like lamb chops marinated in mint and white wine, and chunks of cod baked with cumin. **Taste of India,** 230

Wickenden St., 401/421-4355 ($9–15), is one of the very best bets in town for fine Indian cooking. Soft pink walls brighten an otherwise plain dining room, but you choose this restaurant for its exceptionally well seasoned and fresh food. The menu runs a fairly traditional course, with the usual tandooris, meat with spiced spinach, nan and kulcha Indian breads, pakora deep-fried vegetables, and the like.

A departure from the slick contemporary interior of so many Japanese restaurants, **Nippon,** 231 Wickenden St., 401/331-6861 ($9–15), almost feels a bit cluttered (in a good way), set inside a grand old rambling wood-frame house with creaky wide-plank floors. Sushi rolls include dragon maki with eel, cucumber, rice, and avocado; and a crispy kirin maki that's lightly fried and filled with tuna, salmon, and white fish. Entrée favorites include barbecued beef rolled with scallions, tuna teriyaki, and several tasty udon and soba noodle dishes. Up near the Pawtucket border at the north end of Blackstone Boulevard, **Ran Zan Japanese Restaurant,** 1084 Hope St., 401/276-7574 ($7–16), is a hole-in-the-wall with a young and accommodating staff and a low-keyed ambience that replicates the experience of eating over at a friend's house (assuming you have a friend who cooks very good Japanese food and prepares fresh sushi). Pork katsu, shrimp yakisoba, and various sushi combos are offered at quite reasonable prices. **Sura,** 182 Angell St., 401/277-9088 ($10–17), is a cozy Korean and Japanese restaurant just off Thayer's commercial strip—you won't find especially noteworthy decor but the service is very friendly and the sushi (many, many varieties—from fluke maki to a plum paste roll to sea scallop sushi) prices are easy on the wallet. Sura also serves a number of Japanese and Korean specialties, including broiled freshwater eel on a bed of rice; Korean sweet-potato noodles stir-fried with beef and fresh vegetables; and spicy stir-fried octopus. There's a second branch in Johnston, at 300 Waterman Road.

Cafe Andrea's, 268 Thayer St., 401/331-7879 ($3–7), is a cheap and inexpensive meze (appetizer) bar with decent if rather ordinary Middle Eastern food—there's lots of outdoor seating. It's been around since the 1960s. **Tortilla Flats,** 355

Hope St., 401/751-6777 ($7–12), serves pretty tasty Mexican food, including a house specialty called the cactus flower, a tortilla basket stuffed with lettuce, tomato, cheese, guacamole, and olives, topped with grilled steak or chicken breast. It's no better or more authentic than most Mexican restaurants in Providence, but it has a pleasant ambience and serves consistently fresh food.

Quick Bites

Geoff's, Thayer and Angell Streets, 401/751-9214; 163 Benefit St., 401/751-2248 ($4–6), your source for hefty sandwiches along Thayer, suffers from indifferent service and a dull little dining room. But you eat here for the amazing sandwiches: try the Chicken George, with chicken salad, bacon, melted Swiss, hot spinach, tomato, onion, and Russian dressing; or the Mike Schwartz, with tuna, hot pastrami, Muenster cheese, Russian dressing, lettuce, and tomato. More prosaic varieties are offered, too, but it's the massive and elaborate creations that have earned Geoff's its sterling reputation. **La Creperie,** 82 Fones Alley, 401/751-5536 ($3–5), is a tiny spot down an alley off Thayer, but this homey little place serves very good sweet and savory crepes, and it stays open late (one wonders how, as so few people walk by it). Fresh fruit smoothies are another house specialty. Of all the quasi-fast-food eateries along Thayer, **Spike's Junkyard Dogs,** 273 Thayer St., 401/454-1459 ($2–6), most deserves the chance to harden your arteries—the dogs here are exquisite, especially the chili-and-cheddar dog. Subs, too. Just off Thayer, the **Meeting Street Cafe,** 220 Meeting St., 401/273-1066 ($3–7), serves immensely satisfying scones, pastries, pies, cookies, and light breakfast and lunch fare.

A hit with students from nearby RISD and Brown, **Cable Car Cinema,** 204 S. Main St., 401/272-3970 ($3–6), is known as much for its cheap and cheerful dining as for its art-film theater. White-tuna and other sandwiches, homemade soups, bagels and spreads, fresh-baked cookies, coffees, and all sorts of sweets are served in this quaint café with the black-and-white-striped awning. Sun-filled **Brickway,** 234 Wickenden St., 401/751-2477 ($4–7), which has an

inviting little brick terrace, is a casual spot with outstanding breakfasts and lunches in heart of Wickenden's dining area. About 10 kinds of pancakes and French toast are offered (from chocolate-chip to Caribbean—with pineapple, banana, and kiwi), plus great omelets and other egg dishes. Lunch options include curried chicken and pasta salad, veggie- and hamburgers, and hot and cold sandwiches.

Get fresh cheesecake and coconut–almond bar ice cream at **I Scream,** 227 Wickenden St., 401/621-7974, the annoyingly named but very good parlor on Wickenden Street. Up at the northern end of Blackstone Boulevard and lovely Lippitt Memorial Park, **Maxmillian's Ice Cream Cafe,** 1074 Hope St., 401/273-7230 ($3–6), is a good spot for snacking. This dark and cozy little parlor has frozen treats of many, many flavors, plus wraps, BLTs, soups, and other savories.

Java Joints

The Coffee Exchange, 207 Wickenden St., 401/273-1198 (under $4), occupies an attractive Second Empire Victorian house on Wickenden filled with bric-a-brac, coffee-related goods, and such. There's also an attractive patio. The coffeehouse donates a portion of its take to needy workers, many of them children, who struggle to make a scant living employed on coffee farms in poor countries. **Cafe Zog,** 239 Wickenden St., 401/421-2213 ($3–6), serves healthful salads, prepared foods, and chai teas to patrons tucked in around closely spaced tables, watching the world stroll by on Wickenden. Zog offers what might be one of the best bargains in the city: $3.95 gets you an omelet with your choice of numerous fillings and a bagel (a nice bagel, not some stale plain old thing) with cream cheese or butter. How they make money on this is anybody's guess.

Gourmet Goods and Picnic Supplies

Indigent college students have for years been throwing what little money they have after the delectable baked goods at **729 Hope Street,** 729 Hope St., 401/273-7290, a bakery-cum-gourmet food shop almost across the street from the similarly enticing Trent Bistro. White-chocolate Cage Cake is the house specialty. Coffees

© ANDREW COLLINS

PROVIDENCE

The Silver Top Diner, originally located in an industrial neighborhood in Providence, has since been moved to Pawtucket.

and sandwiches are available also. At nearby Wayland Square, consider the freshly made goodies at **Daily Bread Bakery,** 188 Broadway, 401/331-4200, a good place to pick up a picnic lunch for a sojourn in Blackstone Park. Also near the park, the **Pastry Gourmet,** 149 Elmgrove Ave., 401/273-1700, serves some of the tastiest sandwiches, bagels, and—as the name suggests—desserts you'll find in the city. In Fox Point, fans of Portuguese cooking shouldn't miss either the **Fox Point Bakery,** 208 Taunton Ave., 401/434-3450 (famous for their Portuguese sweet bread), or the **Friends Market,** 126 Brook St., 401/861-0345, which carries imported delicacies from the mother country.

ELSEWHERE

Technically in Pawtucket but literally a few steps from the Providence border, there's a prosaic shopping center that has several delicious options for cheap eats. The top picks are **Barney's,** 727 East Ave., Pawtucket, 401/727-1010 (under $4), a

cheerful and upbeat deli with outstanding bagels. Next door is an attractive little veggie eatery called **Garden Grille,** 727 East Ave., Pawtucket, 401/726-2826 ($3–8), with a full juice bar, healthful goat cheese and arugula salads, fresh sandwiches, and all manner of great food. Others in this shopping center include **Moon Star Chinese Restaurant,** 727 East Ave., 401/728-0710 ($5–11), and **Ronzio Pizza to Go,** 727 East Ave., 401/722-5330 ($6–11), which are both rather ordinary, but fine in a pinch. Sandwiched between them, however, is **Russian Market International Food,** 727 East Ave., 401/723-9870)—the mother lode for authentic Russian caviar, cheese, breads, chocolates, jams and jellies, and baked goods; there's also a deli with luncheon meats from Brooklyn. This is something of an unofficial community center for the local Russian population—rarely will you hear folks speaking anything but Russian.

Well west of downtown in the Olneyville neighborhood, **Wes's Rib House,** 38 Dike St., 401/421-9090 ($6–16), is a down-home Missouri-style barbecue spot that's worth the trip.

Savor the Show Me platter (comes with your choice of four meats, plus cole slaw, barbecue beans, and cornbread), or try the individual ribs, chicken, beef, and other plates. Well south of downtown, the **Portuguese American Market,** 896 Allens Ave., 401/941-4480), is the place to stock up on fava beans, linguica, salt cod, and fresh-baked sweetbreads.

Entertainment

ARTS AND CULTURE

Providence enjoys a highly developed and richly endowed performing arts scene, with a slew of theaters that range from big-time showcases of pre-Broadway shows and national touring acts to inexpensive, avant-garde local workshops that will challenge your sensibilities. It's a good destination for people who like to push the envelope and take chances—here there's no shortage of educated and progressive, even a bit jaded, audiences. And so not an evening passes in Providence when you won't have the opportunity to watch some out-there abstract dance piece, or catch an obscure foreign film at one of the art cinemas or a courageous new dramatic work by the next wunderkind in the city's theater scene.

Theater

The **Providence Performing Arts Center,** 220 Weybosset St., 401/421-2787 or 800/445-8587, website: www.ppacri.org, ranks among New England's top venues for concerts, children's theater, and Broadway-style musical comedies—plus ballet, opera, and classical music. Throughout the year top recording stars (and a smattering of comedians) ranging from Ray Charles to George Carlin to the swoon-inducing Englebert Humperdinck perform here. In recent years Broadway and national-touring musicals have included *The Scarlet Pimpernel, Godspell,* and *Annie,* while *Cinderella* and *Sesame Street Live* have graced the children's stage.

One of the city's most innovative venues for all kinds of arts, from visual to performing, **AS220,** 115 Empire St., 401/831-9327, website: www.as220.org, has cultivated a following for undiscovered, experimental works. It occupies a large space with about 25 artists-in-residence, and it's the home of various local theater groups.

The upstairs space houses art galleries and also the **AS220 Cafe.** Dance classes, poetry readings, live music of just about every variety, open-mic nights, and film screenings keep all different types coming and going. The **Sandra Feinstein-Gamm Theatre,** 31 Elbow St., 401/831-2919, website: www.sfgt.org, presents four plays a year, including works by up-and-coming playwrights as well as established icons like Tom Stoppard and Anton Chekhov. The Tony Award–winning **Trinity Repertory Company,** 201 Washington St., 401/351-4242, website: www.trinityrep.com, presents seven classic and contemporary plays annually with a season running from September to June. Additionally, there's an annual production of **A Christmas Carol,** which runs during the holidays.

Music and Dance

The **Rhode Island Philharmonic,** 222 Richmond St., 401/831-3123, website: www.ri.philharmonic.org, has been a cultural mainstay in Providence since 1945, pulling in notable guest conductors from time to time, plus pop artists like Debbie Reynolds and Marvin Hamlisch. The Philharmonic presents a classical series, three fully staged operas, a pop series, and several family-oriented pieces.

Film

Try to catch a movie at the **Avon Theater,** 260 Thayer St., 401/421-3315, which shows both popular and art movies (and serves Häagen Dazs), with midnight screenings some nights. Another art house is the **Cable Car Cinema,** 204 S. Main St., 401/272-3970. At Providence Place Mall you'll find a 16-screen **Hoyts Cinema,** plus the **Feinstein IMAX Theatre,** 401/453-4629, website: www.imax.com/providence, which shows these larger-than-life features on a six-story screen with a mind-blowing (perhaps ear-splitting) 12,000-watt surround-sound system.

NIGHTLIFE

Students, students, students . . . need anybody say more? They're everywhere you look, and they've created a vibrant market for pulsing nightclubs, swanky lounges, and singles joints. Providence has the usual dive bars, with regular joes quaffing Bud tall boys and smoking Marlboro Lights, shooting pool and sucking down buffalo wings, watching **Monday Night Football.**

But for a relatively small city, it also has a surprising number of high-profile, sophisticated, and in some cases snobby boîtes where the city's fabled collegiate Euro-rubbish hold court and cast snide glances around the room. Actual velvet ropes are the exception rather than the rule, but a number of bars in this town set up invisible velvet ropes—if you don't fit the look or the style, you may feel rather left out.

Downcity and in the adjoining Jewelry District you'll encounter the lion's share of the city's nightspots, from big and brawny dance clubs that simmer with the libidos of drunken college kids and revelers from the suburbs to cool live-music clubs drawing the latest and strangest alternative rock and jazz acts. Providence also has a highly pronounced gay scene, with several extremely popular clubs that pull in patrons from all of southern New England as well as the many lesbian and gay students in town.

Dining and Drinking

Many of the restaurants reviewed under Food also have a strong following as nightspots; these include the **AS220, Atomic Grill, Bella Vista, CAV, Down City Diner, Gatehouse** (which has live jazz on weekends), **Hemenway's, Intermezzo, Joe's American Bar and Grill, Naissance, Olives, Parkside Rotisserie and Bar, Raphael Bar and Bistro, Ri-Ra, Rue de L'Espoir, Trinity Brewhouse, Union Street Ale House, Viva Bar and Eatery, XO,** and **Z Bar and Grille.** Serving creative and superb contemporary American fare in a riotously loud but inviting dining room, **Mill's Tavern,** 101

N. Main St., 401/272-3331 ($18–$29), opened in 2002 to tremendous acclaim. Dishes like crisp-grilled salmon with French lentils and sweet-and-savory tomato-citrus jam have helped this stately spot on increasingly trendy North Main Street develop into one of the city's top venues for celebrating a special occasion. An unassuming gem on the north side of Hope Street, overlooking Lippitt Memorial Park, **Chez Pascal,** 960 Hope St., 401/421-4422 ($16–$25), prepares stellar authentic French bistro fare: coquille St. Jacques, confit of duck with garlic potatoes, hangar steak with a shallot demi-glace, escargot in puff pastry with Roquefort, and baked goat cheese over baby spinach and sliced apples. There's nothing avant-garde about either the ingredients or the preparation, and that's why loyalists love the place. Romantics appreciate the cute, dimly lighted dining room and unrushed pace.

Hangouts

For pre- or post-dinner drinks with a special someone, consider the Westin Providence's plush **Library Bar & Lounge,** 1 W. Exchange St., 401/598-8000. Even if you disdain hotel bars, you might give this upscale, inviting bar a chance—it's close to everything downtown, and the menu of fine wines and drinks is impressive. Keep in mind that it's also a favorite of cigar smokers. The same hotel is also home to **IYAC,** short for "International Yacht and Athletic Club." Here there's live music and often dancing Thursday through Saturday, but the clientele is mostly guests of the Westin and other nearby hotels. **Charlie Hall's Stage,** 235 Promenade St., 401/621-4141, occupies a large space inside the historic Foundry Building just west of Providence Place Mall. The complex consists of three areas, one a show lounge decked with caricatures of Rhode Island celebs, and shows range from magic to comedy dinner theater to live jazz. There's also a Sunday night cabaret series.

Blake's Tavern, 122 Washington St., 401/274-1230, draws the after-work set for cocktails and tasty bar fare—wings, nachos, and the like. Students from area colleges cruise each other up and down at **Oliver's,** 83 Benevolent St., 401/272-

8795, which is within spitting distance of Brown's and RISD's campuses. **Liquid Lounge,** 165 Angell St., 401/454-3434, is a sexy pick-up spot off Thayer with a mostly Brown crowd—arty, countercultural types favor this one. A young and casual crowd roots for New England teams and tosses back beer after beer at the aptly named **Keg Room,** 101 Richmond St., 401/274-1070, a cavernous sports bar and pool hall with large-screen TV monitors. Among the several Irish pubs in the city, **Muldowney's,** 103 Empire St., 401/831-6202, scores significant crowds owing to its proximity to AS220.

Suave and romantic L'Elizabeth, 285 S. Main St., 401/621-9113, is a sit-down bar pouring international coffees, single malts, cognacs, and similar after-dinner treats in a lavish drawing room of armchairs and sofas; soft jazz is piped in, and a handful of desserts are offered (including a delicious white-chocolate cheesecake). Expect to find the city's artier, bookish types lazing around the bohemian basement lounge at the **Providence Bookstore Cafe,** 500 Angell St., 401/521-5536, a seductive underworld of students and intellectuals with goatees and wire-rim glasses. There's live jazz on Saturday nights; other times come and enjoy the well-edited wine list, or even make it a meal (some great desserts are also offered).

At Providence Place Mall, you'll find a 40,000-square-foot branch of the national shrine to grown-ups who refuse to grow up. **Dave & Buster's,** 401/270-4555, pulses with the sounds of high-tech video games and similar-such amusements; there's a huge bar, and the crowd here likes to party and party late. At **Snookers,** 145 Clifford St., 401/351-7665, shoot pool to your heart's content—this sprawling place has many tables, and there's live music here on weekends in the adjoining **Green Room.** The **Living Room,** 23 Rathbone St., 401/521-5200, is another popular warehouse dance club.

Live Music and Clubbing

The city's main venue for major touring music acts is the **Providence Civic Center,** 1 LaSalle Square, 401/331-6700, at Broadway and Atwells, in the western end of downtown. Down toward Fox Point, **Fish Co.,** 515 S. Water St., 401/841-

5510, pulls in a mix of local and nationally known alternative and rock music acts, playing mostly to a collegiate crowd. It's also a big draw for happy hour earlier in the evening.

The obnoxiously named **Jerky's,** 73 Richmond St., 401/621-2244, is another standby on this strip of clubs, slightly mellower than most of the establishments nearby—it's basically a lounge, and it can be a meat market on weekends. Below, you'll find the considerably louder Goth club **Hell,** 401/351-1977, where the pierced, black-mascara set convenes for sneering and hanging around. The sceney Federal Hill restaurant **Mediterreaneo,** 134 Atwells Ave., 401/331-7760, also has a dressy and rather exclusive nightclub where you'll hear mostly a Latin beat—that is, if you're able to get in. It's a very cliquey place.

Downtown, **Lupo's Heartbreak Hotel,** 239 Westminster St., 401/272-LUPO, is one of the top music venues in the city, booking rock, folk, country, and blues.

Suburbanites and college students from schools throughout Rhode Island make the drive into the city to cut loose at **The Complex,** 180 Pine St., 401/751-4263, a massive maze of dance clubs and crowded bars. Check the local papers to see which (mostly local) bands are booked at the **Green Room,** 145 Clifford St., 401/351-7665, a reliable Jewelry District option no matter your age or style; there's decent bar food here, too.

Few venues draw a more impressive range of alternative and rock acts in Providence than **The Call,** 15 Elbow St., 401/421-7170. Also consider the neighboring **Century Lounge,** 150 Chestnut St., 401/751-2255, a cozier basement boîte with sofas and loungy seating, dim retro lighting, and down-home (often blues) music. The restaurant **Leon's,** 164 Broadway, 401/273-1055, has a big following for its jazz Wednesdays—it's close to downtown on an unassuming street corner on the West Side.

Gay Bars and Clubs

Deville's, 150 Point St., 401/751-7166, is a terrific women's club that moved into an attractive new space late in 2002; it has a large dance floor, lots of nooks for sitting and talking, and a friendly staff. In a historic industrial neighborhood south of downtown, **Gerardo's,** 1 Franklin Sq., 401/274-5560, is one of the longest-running hot spots in New England, with a totally eclectic and very lively crowd—from students to yuppies to regular janes and joes. There's a large dance floor, but almost everybody, at least in warm weather, congregates out on the side patio.

A handsome bilevel space close to the bevy of straight and wild discos on Richmond Street, **Mirabar,** 35 Richmond St., 401/331-6761, is the definitive men's stand-and-model bar with a small dance floor and a cozier cocktail bar with a pool table upstairs. It tends to draw a fairly young and professional crowd. The city's largest and most happening gay dance club, **Pulse,** 86 Crary St., 401/272-2133, brings in some of the Northeast's top DJs and tends to draw quite a few groovy straights, too. It's 18-and-over some nights. The sound system is impressive. It's tricky to find-in an industrial area just south of downtown. **Yukon Trading Co.,** 124 Snow St., 401/274-6620, on a desolate side street on the edge of downtown, is an appropriately shady location for a hard-core cruisy disco and hangout popular with leather men and other butch types.

Festivals and Events

SUMMER

In mid-June, come to Roger Williams Park for an earful of music at **Hear in Rhode Island Festival,** 401/949-0757, which features four stages of musicians from across the state playing simultaneously—there's also arts, crafts, food, and family-oriented activities. One of Providence's most pronounced ethnic groups throws an **Annual Cape Verdean Independence Day Celebration,** India Point Park, 401/222-4133, which gives attendees a chance to sample authentic Cape Verde foods, observe arts and crafts exhibits, and listen to music and storytelling. In early August foodies descend upon the **Best of Rhode Island Party,** Rhode Island Convention Center, 401/781-1611, during which more than 80 winners of *Rhode Island Monthly* magazine's "best of" food awards dole out portions of the kibbles that made them so popular. Begun in 1997, the **Rhode Island International Film Festival,** various locations in Providence, 401/861-4445, website: www.film-festival.org, has grown into a highly prestigious event.

FALL

Now a statewide festival, Providence-based **Convergence,** India Point and WaterPlace Parks, 401/621-1992, runs for three weeks in mid-September at locales throughout Rhode Island. This is a dynamic convergence of performing and visual artists, many with an innovative and provocative bent, from all over the world—events include film screenings, interactive media, contemporary music and dance performances, and art installations. As you walk around the city you'll also discover some 40 sculptures, as well as encountering street performers and muralists. This is a tremendously festive and engaging event.

Also in the middle of September, about 30 of the city's ethnic communities gather for the **Annual Rhode Island Heritage Festival,** State House lawn, 401/222-2678, to share traditional song and dance, arts and crafts demonstrations, and foods. In early November, bring out your inner decorator at the **Annual Fine Furnishings-Providence,** Rhode Island Convention Center, 401/846-1115, which focuses mostly on the handcrafted furnishings and decorative arts of New England artisans. You'll find a nice range of both traditional and contemporary wares, in all price ranges. In mid-November, the Leukemia Society of America hosts the **Ocean State Marathon,** 401/943-8888, a rigorous 26.2-mile run that starts in Warwick and ends in Providence.

WINTER AND SPRING

Like many U.S. cities do, Providence ushers in the new year with **First Night,** various sites downtown, 401/521-1166, with family-oriented theater, music, art, and dance performances. Yachting and sailing enthusiasts gear up for the coming season in mid-January at the **Providence Boat Show,** Rhode Island Convention Center, 401/458-6000, where dealers show off the latest sail and power boats and equipment. A week later at the same venue, you can hunt for cars at the **Northeast International Auto Show,** 401/458-6000. In mid-February, the convention center hosts the **Rhode Island Spring Flower & Garden Show,** 401/458-6000. Later in the month it's the site first of the **RV & Camping Show,** 401/458-6000; a week later the **Southeastern**

New England Home Show, 401/458-6000; and in early March the **Rhode Island Pet Show & TICA (The International Cat Association) Cat Show,** 401/458-6000. One of the most popular events at the convention center is the **Business Expo,** 401/521-5000, which comes in early April and hosts some 400 exhibitors and 80 professional development workshops.

Nobody with an interest in great food should miss the city's **Feast of Saint Joseph,** along Atwells Avenue on Providence's mostly Italian Federal Hill. It's held in May and features food vendors, games, music, and plenty of laughter and loudness.

Information and Services

VISITOR INFORMATION

Pamphlets, brochures, and tourism information are available from the **Providence Warwick Convention and Visitors Bureau,** 1 W. Exchange St., Providence, 02903, 401/274-1636 or 800/233-1636; website: www.providencecvb.com. You can also stop by the **Providence Visitors Center,** at WaterPlace Park, 401/751-1177, another vast repository of brochures and information.

GETTING AROUND

For information on getting to Providence (and Greater Providence) by train, plane, bus, or car, see the On the Road chapter. Within Providence, as congested New England cities go, it's not a terribly difficult place to get around by car, although if the weather's decent you should definitely consider striking out on foot. The city also has an extensive network of bus and trolley routes.

Buses

Bus travel is inexpensive and relatively convenient throughout the state via **RIPTA (Rhode Island Transportation Authority) buses,** 401/781-9400 or 800/244-0444, website: www.ripta.com. Kennedy Plaza, in the heart of downtown, is the clearinghouse for bus routes all over Rhode Island. Fares start at just $.50 for

any ride within a mile of downtown to as high as $1.25 for rides to other towns and cities in Rhode Island (Transfers are an additional $.25). Have some coins with you, as exact change is required. There are student discounts as well as monthly passes. Buses run generally from 6 A.M. till 7 P.M., and the Providence Visitors Center and the Convention and Visitors Bureau distribute free maps detailing popular routes. Useful as the bus system is, like most municipal transportation in most U.S. cities, it's used considerably more by locals and commuters than by tourists—this is partly due to the ease and relative affordability of renting cars, navigating the region's streets, and finding parking.

However, both locals and visitors have taken a shine to the city's newest form of local transit, the **LINK trolley,** which started running in the mid-1990s and is also operated by RIPTA. This pleasant and inexpensive way to get around comprises a pair of well-placed lines. The Green line runs from Fox Point up through College Hill past Thayer Street and then west across downtown and over to colorful Federal Hill. The Gold line runs from the State House south through downtown and the Jewelry District (with a stop at the Providence ferry landing), terminating in the Southside at Blackstone. The fare is $.50 for any ride on the system, and monthly and 10-ride discount passes are offered. LINK trollies make their appointed stops every 10 to 15 minutes and run much later than RIPTA buses: Weekdays 7 A.M.–10 P.M., Sat. 9 A.M.–11 P.M., and Sun. 11 A.M.–6:30 P.M.

Driving and Parking

Traffic inside Providence is tight at the obvious rush-hour times but no worse than in other major New England cities. One-way, narrow, and crooked streets proliferate and can be confusing and frustrating (charming as they are to walk). Cyclists are a common sight throughout the city, especially around the universities—be very alert to both bicycles and pedestrians. The pace of driving here is less chaotic than in Boston, but this is still a Type A kinda place: People drive fast and use their horns. Overall, though, if you're fairly used to driving and parking in urban environments, Providence is reasonably amenable. For information on renting a car, see the On the Road chapter.

Parking garages abound downtown but can be rather expensive. A smart strategy is to park at the 5,000-space, nine-level Providence Place Mall, which is within easy walking distance of most downtown attractions and is extremely economical, but only if you get your parking ticket validated at a shop in the mall. You don't have to buy anything pricey/tk to get the validation—any store or eatery there can stamp your ticket. On the southern side of downtown, around the Jewelry District and the new Harborside area, you can usually find metered street parking without much difficulty. And at night, when the clubs and restaurants are going strong, you'll find both street parking (limited and tough to score on Friday or Saturday nights) as well as open (but staffed) lots that charge $5 to $8 for the entire evening. On the East Side, parking is pretty easy to find around Brown and RISD, on or just off Wickenden and Thayer Streets, and in any of the neighborhoods on the East Side. You may have to circle the block a couple times, but you'll almost always find something unless there's a major event going on.

As for the safety of your auto, if you're concerned at all—or if big cities give you the willies—go with the downtown garage/staffed lot options.

If you're staying at a hotel downtown, leave your car there the whole time and walk—at the properties on the city's outskirts, you can still manage pretty well with taxis and even local buses if you don't feel like walking. If you decide to park on the street, follow the laws of common sense (empty expensive belongings from your car, or at the very least hide them or stow them in the trunk; park in a busy and well-lighted area, use The Club or another anti-theft device, read the parking signs posted on *both* ends of the block you've chosen). This is a relatively safe city, and you don't often hear of car theft or break-ins, but it certainly can and does happen. You'll save a lot of money opting for street parking over garage or supervised-lot parking, but you also open yourself up to the risks of theft.

Taxis

Cabs are not used commonly in Providence for basic errands and trips, but they are a great resource if you're trying to get to the airport, coming home late from a bar or restaurant, or needing to make it to an out-of-the-way part of town. The fare is $2 per mile (or $7 per every three miles). You don't hail cabs here on the street (although you may, occasionally, find them outside clubs late at night). Popular companies include **Checker Cab,** 401/944-2000; **Corporate Taxi,** 401/231-2228; **Rhode Island Taxi,** 401/272-1222; and **Yellow Cab,** 401/941-1122.

Ferry Service

The 49-passenger **Pawtucket-Providence Ferry,** 171 Main St., 800/619-BOAT, runs daily between the two cities. The ferry stops in Pawtucket at Town Landing (off Roosevelt Avenue Extension), and in Providence both at Point Street Landing (off Point Street by India Point) and Dyer Street Landing (corner of Dyer and Crawford Streets).

MEDIA

The city's (and the region's) daily is the *Providence Journal,* 401/277-7300, website: www.projo.com. The paper has an outstanding and highly informative website with information on local dining, arts, music, travel, kids-oriented activities, and so on. An excellent resource for metro Providence arts, dining, shopping, clubbing, and similar such diversions is the decidedly left-of-center *Providence Phoenix* alternative newsweekly, 401/273-6397, website: www.thephoenix.com.

TOURS

Providence River Boat Co., 140 Larch St., Providence, 401/274-8377 or 401/458-BOAT,

offers water-taxi service, sightseeing cruises, and charter tours of the Providence waterfront and out into Narragansett Bay. **Conway Tours/Gray Line Rhode Island,** 10 Nate Whipple Hwy., Cumberland, 401/658-3400 or 800/888-4661, website: www.conway-tours.com, runs all kinds of bus and boat tours of the region, from daily trips to Connecticut's Foxwoods Casino out of Providence and Newport to narrated trolley tours of Newport to cruises on Providence harbor.

Greater Providence

You could make the case that just about every town in Rhode Island, with the exception of Providence itself, qualifies as Greater Providence—in fact, parts of southwestern Massachusetts and even eastern Connecticut are essentially Providence suburbs. For the purposes of this book, the Greater Providence chapter takes in all those Rhode Island communities fringing Providence, as well as all the towns north, west, and southwest of the city clear out to the state border. It's not a knock to say that most of these areas draw relatively few of the state's tourists, although many charming and often uncrowded parks, museums, accommodations, and eateries await travelers who venture out to Rhode Island's off-the-beaten-path communities.

Many of the towns covered in this chapter are sparsely settled, with few businesses and attractions—this is especially true along Rhode Island's western border with Connecticut and its northern border with Massachusetts. The historic mill city of Woonsocket is the one exception, as it has several good restaurants and one of the state's best museums. Closer-in suburbs like Warwick, Cranston, and Johnston—while not exactly tourist meccas—do possess a bounty of good eateries and many chain hotels; these towns are a more affordable and less hectic alternative to staying right in Providence or down in the coastal resort areas of Newport and Narragansett, and yet they're convenient to just about any town in the state.

The one part of Greater Providence with a distinct cultural and historic identity is the Blackstone River Valley, which extends from Woonsocket south down through

Blackstone River

the towns that form the state's northeastern border with Massachusetts and on through the small but vibrant city of Pawtucket. It was in this valley that America's textile industry took flight around the turn of the 19th century. It may lack the pizzazz of Providence and coastal Rhode Island, but the Blackstone River Valley provides a fascinating glimpse into the nation's industrial history.

Because attractions in Greater Providence are few and rather far between, the coverage of this chapter differs a bit from that in the other regional chapters in the book. Towns are described, for the most part, as self-contained destinations rather than stops along a grand tour of the region—although suggestions about noteworthy drives are given where applicable, and towns are organized loosely in geographical order, moving roughly counterclockwise, beginning with Pawtucket.

The Blackstone River Valley

In the Blackstone River Valley you can get a sense of how this nation shifted from being an agrarian land of farmers, independent artisans, and skilled craftsmakers to a full-fledged industrial powerhouse. Shortly after America's successful battle for independence, the young nation's first factory opened on the banks of the Blackstone River in Pawtucket—a still-industrial community immediately northeast of Providence. Complete mill communities—with worker housing, community halls and churches, and massive mill buildings—sprung up all along the Blackstone and its tributaries, from Pawtucket north through Woonsocket and across the Massachusetts border clear to Worcester, nearly 50 miles away. First-rate museums in both Pawtucket and Woonsocket, set aptly inside old mills, provide a detailed and fascinating history of the region's industrial flourish.

In the course of its 46 miles the Blackstone plummets about 450 feet (a rate of 10 feet per mile, more than the Colorado River drops as it passes through the Grand Canyon). Were it not for this steep descent and powerful flow, it's hard to say whether or not the American Revolution would have germinated in northern Rhode Island. As early as 1665 settlers began damming sections of the river, harnessing its energy to run mills. By the late 19th century, the once crystal-clear Blackstone had become one of the hardest-working, most heavily dammed,

and most polluted rivers in North America. In 1986 Congress designated the river as the John H. Chafee Blackstone River Valley National Heritage Corridor, and since that time major efforts have been put forth to clean it up and preserve both its pristine and industrial elements.

Although Pawtucket and Woonsocket are bustling—if rather small—cities, and giant mill buildings and dams line the region's rivers, the Blackstone River Valley nevertheless contains a surprising number of areas with low population density and an almost rural character. There are quite a few places in this part of the state where it's almost impossible to imagine that a city as large as Providence lies just a few miles south (and, for that matter, cities as large as Worcester and Boston lie just 40 and 50 miles northwest and northeast, respectively).

If you live in or near Rhode Island or are spending more than a week visiting the area, try to take at least an overnight trip through this often-overlooked part of the state. Even if you're only in the area for a few days, it's quite easy to make an afternoon trip up to the exceptional museums that detail the region's history, one of them in Pawtucket and the other in Woonsocket. Anybody with a keen interest in history (especially our industrial heritage), immigration (especially of French-Canadians), and mill architecture should make a tour of this region a priority. But there's plenty to see and do even for a traveler with a casual interest in regional history.

PAWTUCKET

Pawtucket, population 75,000, is a classic river town, its eastern and western boundaries formed by the Ten Mile and Moshassuck Rivers. The river for which it's most famous, however, is the Blackstone, which cuts right through the center of the city and played a major role in making Pawtucket the cradle of the Industrial Revolution. As the Blackstone tumbles down over Pawtucket Falls, it becomes the Seekonk River, which in turn forms the northern point of the Narragansett Bay tidewater.

In colonial times, the Blackstone formed the east-west border between Rhode Island and Massachusetts. Early Pawtucket was part of North Providence, on the west side of the river, from 1765 onward. The east side of the river changed names several times—from Rehoboth to Seekonk to Pawtucket—but always was part of Massachusetts until 1862, when portions of land east of river were ceded to Rhode Island. In 1874 the communities on both sides of the Blackstone formed into one community, which incorporated in 1885 as the city of Pawtucket (at that time covering 10 square miles and with 18,500 inhabitants). The state border of today wasn't completely finalized until 1899.

Pawtucket has a densely packed little downtown of crooked and narrow side streets, most emanating from the main drags, Main and Broad Streets and East Avenue. Complicating the flow is I-95, which makes an S shape as it snakes northeasterly from Providence through Pawtucket and over the Massachusetts border into Attleboro.

To the south, Pawtucket forms almost a seamless border with Providence—you can't tell you've left one city for the other but for street signs noting the transition. Likewise, Providence nearly encircles the tiny city of Central Falls, and here again the neighborhoods on either side of the town lines are nearly indistinguishable.

Pawtucket has always had a hard-nosed, working-class personality, but at the same time it's without much urban blight and decay. Modest double-decker and triple-decker tenement

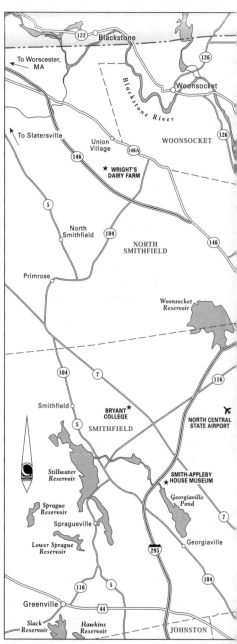

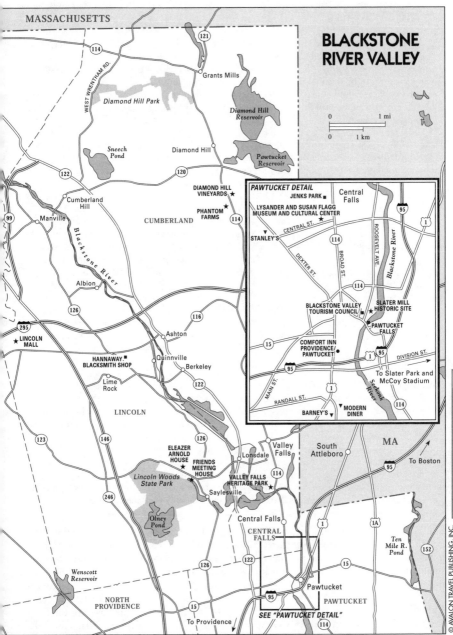

MASSACHUSETTS

BLACKSTONE RIVER VALLEY

114

121

Grants Mills

Diamond Hill Park

WEST WRENTHAM RD.

Diamond Hill Reservoir

0   1 mi
0   1 km

Sneech Pond

Diamond Hill

Pawtucket Reservoir

122

Cumberland Hill

120

DIAMOND HILL VINEYARDS ★

99
Manville

Blackstone River

CUMBERLAND

PHANTOM FARMS ★

114

PAWTUCKET DETAIL

JENKS PARK ■   Central Falls

LYSANDER AND SUSAN FLAGG MUSEUM AND CULTURAL CENTER

95   1

CENTRAL ST.

▼ STANLEY'S

114

DEXTER ST.

ROOSEVELT AVE.

Blackstone River

Albion

BROAD ST.

126

114

BLACKSTONE VALLEY TOURISM COUNCIL ★

SLATER MILL HISTORIC SITE ★

295
★ LINCOLN MALL

116

Ashton

15

★ PAWTUCKET FALLS

Quinnville   Berkeley

COMFORT INN PROVIDENCE/ PAWTUCKET ●

1   95

DIVISION ST.

HANNAWAY ■ BLACKSMITH SHOP

To Slater Park and McCoy Stadium

Lime Rock

122

MAIN ST.

95

1

Seekonk River

114

LINCOLN

123

146

ELEAZER ARNOLD HOUSE ★

126

FRIENDS MEETING HOUSE ★

RANDALL ST.

BARNEY'S ▼   ▼ MODERN DINER

Lonsdale

Valley Falls

South Attleboro

MA

To Boston

Lincoln Woods State Park

VALLEY FALLS HERITAGE PARK ★

114

95

246

Saylesville

Olney Pond

Central Falls

1   1A

CENTRAL FALLS

Ten Mile R. Pond

152

Wenscott Reservoir

126   122

15

NORTH PROVIDENCE

15

95

Pawtucket

PAWTUCKET

To Providence →   **SEE "PAWTUCKET DETAIL"**

114

N

GREATER PROVIDENCE

© AVALON TRAVEL PUBLISHING, INC.

SAMUEL SLATER AND THE INDUSTRIAL REVOLUTION

One early history of Rhode Island, written in the 1880s, commented that the "life of Samuel Slater is more worthy of honor than that of many a statesman or warrior whose renown is worldwide. His triumphs were peaceful, but they produced changes greater than the downfall or up-building of an empire."

This unqualified praise of the man whom many credit with almost single-handedly kicking off America's Industrial Revolution oversimplifies both the person and the events surrounding his life. Apprenticed at an English textile mill at the age of 14, Slater did apply his considerable knowledge of both the technical and business workings of British mills to the facilities that employed him in Rhode Island. And his helping to make a textile mill in Pawtucket in 1793 did ultimately push the United States toward industrialization. Slater, however, was just one of several factors that helped to make northern Rhode Island the birthplace of the nation's textile-milling industry.

Slater was born in 1768 to a successful farming family of considerable means in Derbyshire, England, the very place where a shrewd protoindustrialist named Richard Arkwright had perfected and patented a number of new machines that would revolutionize textile production in Britain. Slater's father became a close business associate of one of the area's mill owners, Jedediah Strutt, and this connection enabled him to secure an apprenticeship for his son, Samuel. For seven years working under Strutt, Slater learned not only the technical workings of an Arkwright mill, but also how such a facility was managed and how profits were most effectively increased. Slater completed his apprenticeship and obtained his indenture papers in 1783, and at this young age of 15 he already knew that his best

prospects in applying his training and mill knowledge lay overseas, in the New World.

At this period just following America's independence from England, the young United States found itself increasingly reliant on its former mother country for finished goods. The 13 colonies had developed a great tradition of trade, and of providing raw materials, during the past two centuries, but not of actually developing the means to manufacture products. England, on the other hand, had progressed dramatically in this regard through the late 18th century.

By the late 1780s, a number of American entrepreneurs began experimenting with ideas about mass manufacture. Areas with shipbuilding traditions, where one could already find plenty of workers skilled in forging and other kinds of machinery making, were likely places for these manufacturing ideas to take hold. Towns that also had excellent supplies of water and strong traditions of milling were similarly desirable. Pawtucket was a logical place for investors to start thinking about creating a textile factory—it had water power from the Blackstone River, and a number of workers versed in shipbuilding, tool-manufacture, and milling. Pawtucket was one of several New England cities that developed small and somewhat low-tech textile manufactories during the late 1780s.

Moses Brown, one of the highly successful Brown merchants of Providence, began a small textile mill in 1789 along with his son-in-law William Almy, who operated the business with Brown's nephew, Smith Brown. The Almy and Brown Company enjoyed limited early success, and Brown spent a great deal purchasing the latest machines and seeking out skilled employees who could not only work these machines but also im-

housing proliferates in many neighborhoods, and large numbers of Italians, Portuguese, Puerto Ricans, and African-Americans—along with smaller factions of myriad other ethnicities—make up the population.

Early History

Roger Williams first referred to Pawtucket, meaning "land by the falls," in a deed that iden-

tified the then heavily wooded and boulder-strewn landscape as the northern boundary of a purchase from the Narragansett Indians—a land purchase that ultimately became Providence.

Joseph Jencks, formerly of Lynn, Massachusetts, established a meager settlement here in 1671. Jenks realized the power of the Blackstone and used the dense woodland for fuel almost immediately on settling here. The town's

prove upon them. In particular, Almy and Brown hired a number of immigrant workers who had experience with more advanced mills elsewhere in the world. But none of them possessed the complete industrial knowledge—in both technology and management—that they were seeking. That is, until a young immigrant worker in New York City, Samuel Slater, contacted Moses Brown after hearing of his endeavors to develop a large-scale textile mill in Pawtucket.

Slater had left England with the intent of marketing his knowledge of Arkwright mills elsewhere. In Britain, people with such industrial knowledge were forbidden to even leave the country, much less bring with them plans, papers, or other documents that might compromise England's stronger hand in technology. Slater let virtually nobody back in England know his plans, and he boarded his boat to America dressed as a farm laborer.

With nothing committed to paper, Brown hired Slater based on what he said he knew about Arkwright mills. Slater shrewdly refused to divulge everything he knew of mill operations without first securing a long-term contract that would assure him a nice cut of any profits, and Brown—just as shrewdly—refused to commit to Slater until convinced that the young man truly possessed the means and ability to move the Almy and Brown mill into the industrial age. During this break-in period, Slater oversaw a team of mechanics already employed by the mill, and together they upgraded an existing spinning frame into a far more efficient Arkwright-style machine. After gaining full employment and a degree of partnership in operations, Slater went on to help develop other machine parts necessary to run the mill.

In his short history *Samuel Slater: Father of American Manufactures,* historian Paul E. Rivard argues that it was actually through "Slater's management work . . . rather than in his machine building, that he was to make his biggest contribution to the development of the textile industry." Slater argued that mills must produce to their fullest capacity, not according to demand for products. He argued against trying to produce a little of everything but rather for specializing in specific products. If the mill manufactured large quantities of a limited number of finished products efficiently and cheaply, the mill's owners could then find emerging markets for these finished materials. And right from the start he advocated hiring young children, some not even 10 years old.

In the end, it was these management philosophies, along with a number of others, that made the Almy and Brown factory profitable and inspired other entrepreneurs up and down the Blackstone River Valley, from Woonsocket to Pawtucket, to open similar operations. Slater had given birth not only to incredibly productive textile mills, but also to the horrid working conditions—especially those applied to children—that would eventually drive workers to unionize and then factories to seek cheaper labor elsewhere.

Slater was a brilliantly analytical and shrewd manager and businessman, and it might not be fair with today's hindsight to blame him for helping to develop a system that dehumanized and ultimately broke down its workers, but it's interesting to contrast the praise his accomplishments received in the 1880s versus the more complex characterization of his life and works reported in more recent years.

industrial beginnings started innocently enough: Jenks built a small iron forge just below Pawtucket Falls, on the west side of the river (about where Main Street crosses the river today). Jenks crafted fine tools, and soon a handful of fellow manufacturers opened in the vicinity. Only for a short time in the 1690s, during King Philip's War, did the industrial powers of the little settlement slow down—

most of the village buildings were destroyed during the uprising. But Jenks and the others returned just as soon as the war had ended.

Throughout most of the 1700s, Pawtucket served as a small but prolific community of metal forgers, which provided the larger city of Providence with metal farm tools, bells, ship parts, and various utensils. Later in the century, during the American Revolution, the same forges produced ammunition, muskets, and other war goods for the Continental Army.

The Industrial Revolution

Following the Revolutionary War, Great Britain sought to cut its losses by preventing the export of technology and industrial innovation to America. Passengers on U.S.-bound ships were forbidden from taking with them blueprints, books, and materials containing the information that had made England into an industrial superpower. Also prevented from leaving the country were workers with considerable experience in English factories.

Samuel Slater, a 21-year-old who had worked as a manager in England's technologically advanced Arkwright Mills, found a way around this policy. As the story goes, he snuck aboard a ship in attire and with baggage that gave no hint of his social and professional standing and sailed to the United States, arriving first in New York, where he found few worthy opportunities for employment. A newspaper employment ad placed by Moses Brown (of the famous Providence Brown family) caught Slater's attention, and off he traveled to Pawtucket. Brown had sought an individual with experience in textile manufacture. With Slater's knowledge and Moses Brown's capital, Pawtucket quickly became the site of the nation's first textile factory. The new enterprise prospered well beyond anybody's wildest expectations.

With the success of Slater's mills, investors quickly began pumping money into the region, building new cotton and wool mills, as well as factories for tool manufacture, textile production, and hat and shoe making. The tremendous competition spurred constant innovation and technological improvement, and in this hothouse of industry, America came of age as an industrial nation. Farmers with unsteady income subject to the whims of Mother Nature were lured to these fast-growing mill villages with the promise of constant, albeit difficult, work. On the flip side, mill owners ran their operations like fiefdoms, exploiting workers, hiring young children and women for some of the most difficult and dangerous jobs, establishing inhumane working conditions, and controlling just about every aspect of the mill workers' lives. Help were expected to attend church, to remain sober, and to buy all goods from a company store. Owners controlled the housing, the schools, the roads, the churches, and the shops. Whereas life on the farm was financially erratic, mill workers could count on steady wages and the basic shelter and food to ensure survival. But their lives were monotonous and brutal. This practice of employing and providing for entire families to work the mills came to be known as the Rhode Island System of Manufacturing.

The child-labor practices of the day seem almost unbelievable in the 21st century. Many of the mill workers were as young as 6 years old. In 1826, for instance, the superintendent of the Providence Thread Company was a 19-year-old young man; what's all the more remarkable is that he had about 11 years of experience in the factory by this time. Children generally worked 12 to 14 hours per day, suffered frequent injury and illness, and—being small and nimble—were often assigned those dangerous jobs that involved fast-moving machine parts. For this, they were compensated perhaps $1 per week.

Through the early 19th century, cotton mills and machine shops huffed and puffed along the banks of the river in tremendous numbers. In 1809 President Madison gave a great boost to the local textile industry when he wore a woolen suit manufactured in Pawtucket. In the diaries of Dr. Timothy Dwight (the early president of Yale College), which detailed his travels throughout young America, the author observed in 1810: "There is probably no spot in New England, of the same extent, in which the same quantity of variety [and] manufacturing business is carried on."

By 1815 there were 16 cotton mills in Rhode Island, Connecticut, and Massachusetts, with 119,310 spindles (there were said to be about 350,000 spindles in the nation as a whole at that time). The number of spindles in the nation grew to 1,500,000 by 1830, and 2,300,000 by 1840. By then, the leading cotton-manufacturing states were Massachusetts (278 mills, 666,000 spindles) and its much smaller neighbor, Rhode Island (209 mills, 519,000 spindles).

With the growth of factories all over northern Rhode Island and elsewhere in southern New England, means of transportation improved rapidly and radically. A canal was opened in 1828 alongside the Blackstone River, and the Providence & Worcester Railroad followed in 1847, spelling the end of the canal business. Road improvements continued all the while.

Since 1900

Because it attracted families from all over Europe and the New World, the Rhode Island System of Manufacturing encouraged a tremendous diversity of ethnicity and religion, a mix unheard-of in Puritan New England prior to the Industrial Revolution. Rhode Island had already been a haven of religious freedom and practice, having hosted New England's first significant communities of Quakers, Catholics, Baptists, and Jews. As mills ran out of local farmers to populate their mill villages, they began recruiting from afar. Over the decades, workers arrived from Ireland, Scotland, England, Germany, the Netherlands, Italy, Greece, Portugal, the Ukraine, Sweden, Armenia, Poland, Lithuania, Finland, and Syria. And perhaps most prominently in northern Rhode Island, huge numbers of job-hungry French-Canadians came down to work these enormous factories. During the middle half of the 20th century, Black Americans came to the region from the southern states, as well as Latin Americans and Asians.

By the 1940s, about 75 percent of Pawtucket's 75,000 residents were foreign-born. By then there were about 50 textile mills in Pawtucket, but these were outnumbered at this point by some 60 general factories producing everything from machine parts to metal goods and jewelry.

The mills raised the bar worldwide for industrial productivity by the late 19th century, as production soared to all-time highs. But by the early 20th century, cheaper labor, more land, and better water sources in the South began to set an industrial decline in motion in New England. Labor problems caused disruption and closures, and fed-up mill owners began investing their capital in more hospitable parts of the country. By the 1920s, the South accounted for half of America's industrial output. The downward spiral in the Northeast translated to less capital, outmoded factories and machines, increasingly disgruntled workers, and more mill closures. Only about 10 percent of the textile mills in operation at the tail of World War II remain open today. Many of the former mill villages of the Blackstone River valley appear downtrodden and dispirited today, and quite a few of the old mills have been abandoned or demolished. However, a new interest in vintage mill architecture has resulted in the restoration and retrofitting of at least some of the most important buildings in the valley.

Still today in Pawtucket a number of textile factories produce specialty products like lace and elastic-woven materials, but most of the industry here is dominated by makers of toys, jewelry, silverware, and metal goods.

Exploring Pawtucket

Downtown Pawtucket, while industrial and working-class, is clean and well kept, with an especially walking-friendly area around the preserved **Slater Mill Historic Site,** along the Blackstone River. Across from the mill, a contemporary, 10,000-square-foot visitors center contains an enormous amount of information that's useful for exploring not only Pawtucket but the entire Blackstone River Valley.

Inside the visitor center you purchase tickets for the 90-minute guided tour of the Slater Mill. Included with admission is an informative 18-minute video, shown in a small theater inside the visitors center. The movie, though narrated in a fairly rosy tone, does offer a stark view of mill life in Rhode Island, with especially good focus on the harsh child-labor practices and myriad labor struggles. In the visitor center you'll find an extensive gift shop of books and locally made crafts, music, and other local goods.

In total, the Slater Mill Historic Site encompasses 5.5 acres and offers a fascinating look into Pawtucket's role as the birthplace of America's industrial revolution. You'll hear how the young British immigrant Samuel Slater took a job in Ezekiel Carpenter's clothing shop, and by recalling the exact blueprints

© ANDREW COLLINS

GREATER PROVIDENCE

a church near Old Slater Mill

for water-powered textile machinery, developed the nation's first such textile factory.

The site comprises several buildings. The three-story **Wilkenson House,** which was built in 1810 on the site of an old metalworks, contains on its ground-level floor a full machine shop. Just outside the basement you can take a close-up look at the head race, into which water from the Blackstone is diverted. The raceway enters the ground level of the mill and powers a massive waterwheel that weighs 16,000 pounds dry and 20,000 when wet. A gate is raised to regulate the flow of the water, which determines the wheel's speed, and therefore its power. What you see in the basement today is an authentically rendered reproduction of the original wheel. After the water powers the wheel it empties through a tail race (more on that later). The power created by the wheel is generated through a series of gears that lead up to the building's upper two floors.

During the tour, you actually watch as the wheel turns and spreads the power through the building, the gears turning a series of pulleys, which in turn power individual tools and machines. You'll notice that the Wilkenson House is narrow, with high ceilings; tall windows line the

walls. This is typical of mill buildings of this period, as these structures were designed to maximize natural light, and also to distribute the power of the one main gear as efficiently as possible throughout the building.

About 20 men worked in the Wilkenson House's first-floor machine shop, from woodworkers to metalworkers. During the tour a guide demonstrates exactly how a drill is powered by the mill race. In this very shop owner, David Wilkenson—often called the father of America's tool industry—created a number of important tools that helped foster the success of Rhode Island's textile industry. All told, the mill operated with water power for about 30 years, when it was converted to steam power.

Perhaps the most striking of the site's structures, the **Old Slater Mill** is a sturdy 1793 wooden structure commissioned by William Almy, Obadiah Brown, and Samuel Slater, and built by local Pawtucket laborers. Sunlight rushes through the building's many soaring windows. Within just a few months of its construction, the factory had turned out the first cotton yarn produced in the New World. The building's graceful architecture established the standard style for similar mill construction throughout the Blackstone River Valley, as well as in eastern Connecticut and other parts of Massachusetts. Almy, Brown, and Slater ceased operations in 1829, but subsequent owners continued to operate a cotton factory here until 1905. Its appearance today resembles the mill roughly as it looked and functioned around the 1830s.

The 1793 invention in Georgia of the cotton gin, by Connecticut resident Eli Whitney, played a vital role in the region's manufacturing prowess. The gin separated the seeds from the cotton at a rate many, many times faster than could human hands. Cotton, shipped to Rhode Island from the South in 500-pound compressed bales, was loaded into a bale breaker on its arrival there. The bale breaker broke out debris and waste from the cotton mass, after which the material was put through a carding machine, which untangled it into coarse strands that were fed into the looms for further refining. A roving machine twisted the cotton onto bobbins, and a throstle spinning frame wove the material into fine thread.

In the Old Slater Mill, you'll find a few original machines from the period and many more authentic replicas that provide a clear sense of how these factories operated during the earliest days. Many of the machines were either designed or modified by Samuel Slater himself. You'll see several kinds of carding machines and example of most of the others mentioned above. As you see how each one works, you also get a clear sense of why so many workers contracted "white lung," an ultimately fatal disease caused from inhaling cotton dust and debris over many years. At one end of the building a small gift shop sells penny candy and small gifts.

The economic depression of 1829 that contributed to the dissolution of Almy, Brown, and Slater also closed down the machine and textile shops in this building, but new owners ran a cotton and woolen mill here for much of the 19th century. In later times tenants here included makers of coffin trim and jewelry tools, as well as an electrical generator.

Moved here in 1962, after having been spared destruction when I-95 was brought through Pawtucket, the 1758 **Sylvanus Brown** house, a nicely restored gambrel-roof colonial, is also part of the tour. Often demonstrations of flax-weaving are given inside—a garden of flax was installed behind the house in 2000. (The golden-colored debris left after flax has been combed through a large metal hackle is called tow, hence the term "tow-head" to describe a blond-haired boy or girl.) Millwright Sylvanus Brown ran the house as a carpenter's shop during the late 1700s. It has been fully restored to its original appearance.

The massive dam that runs across the Blackstone River from the Old Slater Mill dates to 1792. The construction of the dam caused a bit of controversy, as various property owners along the river claimed water rights at certain points. Miller John Bucklin and blacksmiths Stephen and Eleazer Jenks, who operated water-powered workshops downstream from the dam, destroyed parts of the original structure shortly after it was built, claiming—correctly—that the dam had diminished the water power through their section

of river. The dam was eventually rebuilt by original investors Oziel Wilkinson and the firm of Almy, Brown, and Slater.

Running from above the dam and under the Old Slater Mill and to the front of Wilkinson Mill, **Slater's Trench** (aka the Great Flume) siphoned water from the river to power the machinery of the two mills. The water then continued into Sargeant's Trench, which sent the water down below the falls and back into the Blackstone. Battles over fishing and water-power rights surrounded the trench and nearby river until in 1826 Judge Joseph Story assigned specific water rights to the different lots of land along the waterways.

Crashing down below the Main Street Bridge, Pawtucket Falls were a natural formation that were improved upon with man-made damming in 1718. These days the falls are faced in brick, and they continue to provide power to the Blackstone Valley Electric Company, which stands just downstream. The double-arch, cut-stone **Main Street Bridge,** from which you can get great views of the entire Slater Mill Historic Site, dates to 1858, but a bridge has crossed at this point since 1714. Ezekiel Carpenter's original clothing shop stood just on the southwest corner of the Main Street bridge and the river; it's where Samuel Slater first worked on his arrival to Pawtucket.

The Slater Mill Historic Site is at Main Street and Roosevelt Avenue, 401/725-8638, www.slatermill.org. Admission is $8. Guided tours are given June through November three times daily Monday through Saturday, and twice on Sundays. From December through May, tours are given daily on weekdays, three times on Saturdays, and twice on Sundays.

Another noteworthy site in Pawtucket is the **Arboretum at Riverside,** 724 Pleasant St., 401/724-8733, where you can explore 80 acres of beautifully landscaped pathways and gardens along the Seekonk River, into which the Blackstone flows below Pawtucket Falls. Among the varieties of tree you're apt to find while strolling through are black oak, eastern red cedar, ginko biloba, wild black cherry, big-tooth aspen, and white ash. Shrubs from as far away as Japan and central Asia thrive here, plus impressive stands of azalea and rhododendron. The management tends the arboretum organically, using only natural fertilizers and pesticides. In late May, come to attend Azalea Day, when these lovely shrubs bloom in a riot of colors. The Arboretum borders historic Riverside Cemetery, which was established in 1874 and laid out using the teachings and philosophies of landscape guru Frederick Law Olmsted. Open Tues.–Sun. 10 A.M.–2 P.M. Admission is $5.

In the northeastern section of town, near the Massachusetts border, lies Slater Park, which has entrances on both Newport Avenue (Rte. 1A) and Armistice Boulevard (Rte. 15). Here you'll find 18 picnic sites, plus tennis courts, ballfields, gardens, and—an obvious favorite with kids—pony rides. These are given in what had been an old zoo, which has now been transformed into a mini-farm area. Call Daggett Farm Riding Academy, 401/725-3686. Slater Park also contains the historic **Daggett House,** 401/722-2631, the oldest standing house in the city, furnished in the period style with fine antiques, vintage pewter, and Revolutionary War–era china. Some eight generations of Daggetts lived in this house over the years. Admission $2; open June–Sept. weekends 2–5 P.M.

Also at Slater Park there's a **Looff Carousel,** 401/728-0500, ext. 252, which dates to 1895. Charles I.D. Looff ranks among the earliest and most distinguished designers of carousels, and Slater Park's ride contains 50 whimsical characters. There's another Looff nearby in East Providence's Crescent Park. Hours vary greatly, but the carousel is generally in operation from June to early September.

East Providence

From downtown Pawtucket, drive south four miles along Route 114 and you'll find yourself in the center of this semi-industrial suburb that's just over the I-195 bridge across the Seekonk River from Providence. The town is often thought of as little more than an extension of Providence itself, a reputation it's held since nearly its very inception in 1862. A history from the late 19th century offered the following prediction "[East Providence] will, doubtless, in course of time become one of the wards of the city of Prov-

idence. Every day its relations with the principal capital of the State become more intimate. Its final annexation to its powerful neighbor is only a question of years." So far, East Providence remains wholly independent. But then the prognostication in question never specified exactly how many years this transformation would take.

Instead, East Providence became a small industrial city like its neighbor to the north, Pawtucket, in this case producing baking powder, refining petroleum, and engaging in other light industry.

There are a few notable sites in East Providence, especially toward the north part of town. From Route 114, bear left onto Route 114A and make a right turn onto Hunt Mills Road. Just a few yards from the Massachusetts border, the **East Providence Historical Society,** Hunt Mills Road, Rumford, 401/438-1750, makes its home in the Georgian-style John Hunt House in the historic Hunt Mills neighborhood of Rumford, a village within East Providence. The five-bay, center-chimney colonial was constructed in 1750, and then added to significantly in 1790. Inside, it is furnished as an upper-class country house of the day would have been; you'll find a varied collection of memorabilia, tools, documents, and photographs (most of them donated by residents over the years) that paint a picture of East Providence's history. Every couple of years changing exhibits are installed. Also note the Harold Flint library room, which contains a photo archive and genealogical records. Free; limited days and hours.

From downtown East Providence (or I-195, Exit 7), take Route 103 South along the waterfront through the Riverside section; bear right onto Bullocks Point Avenue and down along the narrow peninsula for which the road is named. At Crescent Park, kids and any adult with fond childhood memories of carousels will get a kick out of the **Charles I.D. Looff Carousel,** at the end of Bullocks Point Avenue, 401/435-7518 or 401/433-2828. This 1895 wooden structure has long been recognized as one of Charles Looff's most beautiful and ornate designs. On it there are 62 figures carved of wood and four chariots. Beveled mirrors, faceted glass, and twinkling lights add further sparkle to the clanging contraption that circles about to the sounds of Wurlitzer organ music. The hours vary greatly over the year but you can pretty much count on being able to ride on weekends from about Easter to Columbus Day, from noon to about 7 P.M.; but call if you're visiting on a weekday, as in summer it's sometimes open then, too. Rides are just $.75. There's a small food concession where you can snack on clam cakes, chowder, and other traditional short-order favorites.

Central Falls

Little Central Falls lies but a mile north of downtown Pawtucket along Route 114; it's just a mile square, making it the smallest community in the nation's smallest state. There are also few communities in the nation with a higher population density (it currently stands at nearly 14,000 residents per square mile). Although a village was established here in 1730, Central Falls didn't incorporate until 1895. The town began its foray into industrialization with the formation of a chocolate factory in 1790 (for many years this area was called simply Chocolate Mill). Central Falls played a prominent role in King Philip's War—a band of Indians ambushed Captain Michael Pierce and his company of colonists here, killing the majority of them, in 1676.

Such a small city formed because in 1871 the territory in these parts was split up so that Central Falls, which by then had become its own fire district, became a section within the much larger and more sparsely populated town of Lincoln. Residents of the rest of the town complained that this small pocket of industry and population bore an unusually hefty tax burden and petitioned the legislature to set Central Falls apart as its own city. This was granted in 1895.

Gold and silver electrolytic extraction was an industry for a time, as was textiles. A large branch of Corning Glass Works produced light bulbs here at a factory on Broad Street. By about 1940, nearly eight in ten residents were foreign-born, half of them French-Canadian, and many others English, Irish, and Scottish. The city continues to be a manufacturing center.

Right in the center of the village, a couple blocks north of Central Street, you'll come to four-acre **Jenks Park,** Broad Street (Route 114), 401/727-7480, home of the four-faced 1904 Cogswell Clock Tower. Park anywhere around here to explore the rest of this tiny town on foot. The tower stands atop Dexter's Ledge, which Indians used as a watchtower during King Philip's War. You can climb the tower and take in excellent views of the valley. Central Falls holds concerts here during the summer months on Sundays. You'll also find some walking trails ideal for a light stroll.

Walk south and turn right onto Central, where you'll find the **Lysander and Susan Flagg Museum and Cultural Center,** 205 Central St., 401/727-7409. This stately colonial revival home contains maps, newspapers, paintings, and photos relevant to the city's history, as well as a collection of locally produced textiles.

A couple blocks east, from High Street you can access the **Pierce Park and Riverwalk,** 401/727-7480. Open year-round, dawn–dusk.

Cumberland

At 28 square miles and with a population of 28,000, Cumberland offers a quieter and more rural vision of the Blackstone River Valley. The town was settled in 1747 when a Royal Decree transferred the land from Massachusetts to Rhode Island. Extensive mineral deposits (mostly iron and copper) provided early revenue for the town, but today Cumberland prospers with revenues from mostly light manufacturing and retail. It's also a popular suburb for workers in Pawtucket, Providence, and Woonsocket.

In Valley Falls, an old mill community in the southwest section of Cumberland, you can visit the **Valley Falls Heritage Park,** 45 Broad St., 401/728-2400. This free self-guided historic trail occupies the site of the former Valley Falls Company, which from the 1810s through the 1930s produced great numbers of textiles. During most of this period, there were stone and brick mill buildings on both sides of the Blackstone River, along with housing and numerous outbuildings—all of it made up Valley Falls Mills. The portion of the compound that sat on the east side of the river, in Cumberland, was demolished in 1934, shortly after the mill closed, so that its owners could avoid the hefty property taxes. The land sat vacant until 1991, when it was incorporated into part of the Blackstone River Valley National Corridor. Today, while there's no formal museum or guided tours, a network of paths, ramps, and bridges traverses the property, and interpretive signs tell you what you're looking at and how different parts of the mill functioned.

Over on the Central Falls side, the mill buildings were eventually converted to senior citizen housing, and portions of the stone buildings were covered in stucco. You can still get a sense from walking through this complex, however, of the original property and its use. The gatehouse through which water entered a trench from the river and powered the mills still stands.

From here, it's a five-mile drive north on Route 114 to reach family-owned **Diamond Hill Vineyards,** 3145 Diamond Hill Rd., Cumberland, 401/333-2751 or 800/752-1505. Since 1976, the winery has been producing acclaimed pinot noir, as well as traditional New England wines made with blueberries, peaches, and apples. You can tour the grounds and winery, which is anchored by an 18th-century farmhouse, Mon–Sat. noon–5 P.M.

Also nearby, just 3.5 miles farther north, is **Diamond Hill Park,** Route 114. You're just a couple miles from the Massachusetts border from this point, and also just four miles east of downtown Woonsocket via Route 114. Here you'll also find a mile-long face of veined quartz, which was deposited by mineral-laden hot water flowing along a fracture in the earth's crust. This is a great spot for a light hike, jogging, picnicking, or just taking in the scenery. At the summit of Diamond Hill you'll be rewarded with very nice views of the Rhode Island and southern Massachusetts countryside. This had been a ski slope some time ago, and the trails lead to the small peak.

More than most Rhode Island towns, Cumberland looks and feels like the hilly, hardwood-dominated terrain of points north and makes for lovely country driving, especially when fall foliage season kicks in. Just drive along the many back roads through town, especially Route 114 and the roads off of it.

Lincoln

Named for the 16th U.S. president in 1871, Lincoln was once the home of Narragansett Indians and later the settler William Blackstone, for which the river and its valley are named. The town encompasses seven villages, Albion, Fairlawn, Lime Rock, Lonsdale, Manville, Quinnville, and Saylesville. The manufacture of jewelry, silverware, and other traditional Rhode Island metal products continue to be a big source of revenue for this suburb of about 18,000.

In Lonsdale, a large industrial bakery once thrived, as well as textile concerns. The village is the seat of government for Lincoln township. There are a couple of noteworthy historic sites along Route 126 in this part of town. First you'll reach the **Friends Meeting House,** 374 Great Rd., 401/245-5860, parts of which date to 1703 (the main portion is from 1745). There's a small graveyard here with many very old headstones.

Nearby is the **Eleazer Arnold House,** 487 Great Rd., 617/227-3956. This tall, classic wood-frame house with a massive stone chimney and a steep wooden roof was once a tavern along the Great Stage-Coach Road. This house looks nothing like the later and more prevalent Georgian and Federal-style houses that most of us associate with colonial America; it has tiny unadorned windows, an austere batten door, and an absolutely massive fireplace and stone chimney. It was built in 1687. This lies along the town's Great Road Historic District, which runs about 4.5 miles along Route 123 and contains a number of fine buildings from the 17th to 19th centuries.

Three miles north via Route 126 in the center of Lincoln, you'll find the **Hannaway Blacksmith Shop,** 100 Old River Rd., 401/333-1100, ext. 289. This single-story barn dates to the 19th century and has been fully restored as a period blacksmith shop; demonstrations are given to the public one Sunday per month, April–Nov.

Along Old Louisquisset Pike (Route 246), the **North Gate Toll House,** 401/725-2847, served as a working tollhouse during the early 19th century and then as a wayside hotel. It now contains a local-history library and a small museum with period colonial furnishings. It's open by appointment.

While the big-name gaming in southern New England takes place just over the Rhode Island border in Connecticut, you can play the slots, bet on live greyhound racing, and grab a meal at the food court at **Lincoln Park,** 1600 Louisquisset Pike, 800/720-PARK, www.lincolnparkri.com.

From Lincoln, it's about six miles north to Woonsocket, via either Route 126 or Route 99.

WOONSOCKET

Barely a blip on the radar screen during Rhode Island's first 200 years, Woonsocket developed during the mid-19th century into one of the nation's great hubs of woolen manufacture. The industry thrived well into the 1940s before succumbing to increased costs and competition from cheaper labor in the South. Today this city of 45,000, which fits snugly into a nine-square-mile swath of hilly country on the Massachusetts border, celebrates its labor history and strong French-Canadian heritage with the Rhode Island Historical Society Museum of Work and Culture, one of the most fascinating and well-executed museums in the Northeast. Apart from this, and the city's abundance of nicely preserved mill buildings, there are relatively few formal attractions in this working-class city, but

THE FRENCH-CANADIANS OF WOONSOCKET

By the 1870s, the bustling mill town of Woonsocket had virtually no unemployment and an almost desperate need for new workers. And many factory owners had become disenchanted by, or at least nervous about, hiring more American workers, as this kind of employee was starting to speak up loudly and angrily about the mills' brutal working conditions.

Owners felt compelled to look elsewhere for new employees. Across the border from northern New England, rural Québec, Canada, was the perfect place to seek workers. Here was a land whose population depended largely on farming but had a short growing season. French Canadians were hard workers in search of better employment, and the long hours and poor living conditions of mill towns were accepted without much complaint. The intensely close-knit French Canadians mingled little with workers from other backgrounds, which weakened the solidarity among Woonsocket's factory employees. Many Irish, Scottish, and English immigrants came to work Woonsocket's mills, too, during these years, but now if they complained too much about jobs, their bosses could easily sack them and hire more French-Canadians.

Most French-Canadian workers in Woonsocket hailed from small Québec towns, but large numbers also moved down from Québec City and Trois Rivières. In Woonsocket thrived one of the largest French-Canadian populations in the United States. Local Yankees, and many other immigrants, continued to disparage the French-Canadians for accepting work for the lowest wages, thus filling most of the jobs.

This insularity continued to keep the community tight for many generations. The social hub of close-knit French-Canadian Woonsocket was the appropriately named neighborhood of Social.

If you'd walked through town during the early 1900s, you'd have seen as many French and Canadian flags hanging from the front stoops of houses and business as you would have U.S. ones. By 1940 the overall population of Woonsocket was three-fourths of French-Canadian descent, and the majority of residents spoke with one another in French. Until 1942 the city produced *La Tribune,* a French-language newspaper. And radio WOON (then WWON) broadcast in French into the mid-1960s. Still today, on some local radio stations, you can hear programs spoken in the local Québecois-French dialect.

The city celebrates its heritage in other ways—there are a handful of restaurants serving authentic French Canadian fare such as poutine—French fries with hot chicken gravy and cheese—and ragout de pattes—fresh pork hocks browned with flour and served with vegetables. In August, Woonsocket celebrates the region's French and French-Canadian heritage with Jubilee Franco-American Weekend, a festival of storytelling, living-history exhibits, food, boat tours, and music.

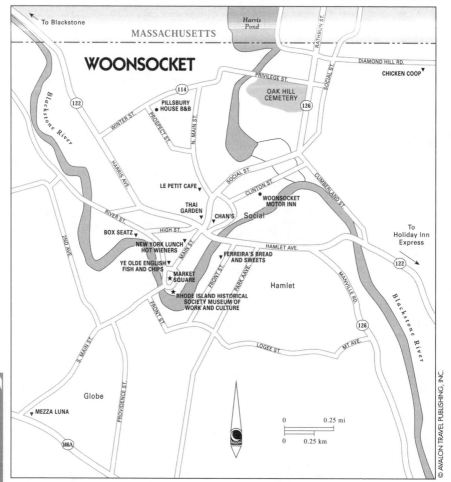

Woonsocket does offer visitors a glimpse of an industrial community relatively little changed in the past century.

Woonsocket lies just over the Massachusetts border, about two-thirds of the way downriver from Worcester to Providence, bordered in Rhode Island by the towns of Cumberland on the east and southeast, and North Smithfield on the west and southwest. The city incorporated in 1888 and comprises six distinct villages: Globe, Bernon, Social, Hamlet, Jenckesville, and Woonsocket, most of them set along the Blackstone River, near the dramatic Woonsocket Falls.

Walk around downtown and the residential neighborhoods surrounding it and you'll see blacks, Asians, Portuguese, Latin Americans, French-Canadians, and all manner of ethnicities. This is not a major tourist destination, but the city abounds with grand, often formidable, stone-and-redbrick industrial architecture, the framework of a once vibrant factory town. You can still hear a distinct French-Canadian accent in these parts, although distinctive intonations and words fade a little with each generation. Along many streets you'll pass by imposing stick, Queen Anne, and gingerbread Victorian houses, most of them subdivided, as well as hundreds of southern New England's trademark triple-decker houses.

Early History

The history of Woonsocket bears a resemblance to that of many other New England mill towns. The name probably meant little or nothing to anybody outside the immediate region prior to the Industrial Revolution, although—like the towns of eastern Rhode Island—it figured centrally in years of vitriolic border disputes with Massachusetts. From the late 17th century well into the first two decades of the 18th, the land that today comprises Woonsocket evidently meant a great deal to the governing bodies of both colonies. The town, however, had little going for it.

Woonsocket may take its name from the Indian word "nisowosaket," which translates roughly as "thunder mist," but there's some debate as to the legitimacy of this derivation. Mills have played a role in Woonsocket's fortunes since 1666, when Richard Arnold (the son of one of Roger Williams's exiled colleagues) built a sawmill along the Blackstone River about where the Woonsocket Falls roar today. Grist and fulling mills, and then an iron forge, soon followed. But agriculture dominated the landscape until well into the 19th century, when the boom in textile production kicked off in earnest, peaking in the 1840s.

The Industrial Revolution

As trade among southern New England's major metro areas began to flourish in the early 1800s, Woonsocket's star began to rise, first as a major stopover on the stage road from Hartford to Boston. In 1829, the short-lived Worcester-Providence Blackstone Canal opened, bringing further fame and fortune to the hilly river town. The canal closed 20 years later, as the Providence & Worcester Railroad, built in 1846, quickly rendered canal transport obsolete.

The fast-flowing Blackstone and its numerous tributaries provided power for dozens of Woonsocket mills during the city's peak years of production, as it did in Pawtucket and the towns in between the two cities. Sluiceways branched out from the rivers and ran alongside streets and rail tracks, over viaducts, and into the basements of factory buildings. Following an especially acute industrial boom after the Civil War, Woonsocket found itself with more factories than it could fill with workers. It welcomed workers from Québec and then from many other countries.

Exploring Woonsocket

You can get a real sense of the city's industrial heritage around **Market Square,** which overlooks Woonsocket Falls and lies within steps of numerous old factory buildings. Because of horrendous floods over the years, mechanical flood barriers were installed in 1955 by the Army Corps of Engineers—these now diminish the original view of these 30-foot falls, at least as they appeared before man first began to harness their powers. But as they rush below the Main Street Bridge, they still make quite a racket and produce a cool mist. Across the bridge, you'll see the building containing turbines, where the Blackstone Electric Company's Thunder Mist Plant produces hydroelectric power. The falls produce more than seven million kilowatt/hours of electricity per year. You can also see one of the old yarn mills, just off Market Square. In many places around here, the names of shops and on the sides of buildings bear out the city's French-Canadian ties.

The **Rhode Island Historical Society Museum of Work and Culture,** 42 S. Main St., 401/769-WORK or 401/331-8575, www.rihs.org/visitone.htm, anchors Market Square and provides a wonderfully vivid glimpse into the industrial history both of Woonsocket and southern New England. The curators have designed imaginative, interactive exhibits that capture the spirit and reveal the hardships of the city's history—the museum is beautifully designed.

Specifically, the museum traces the history of Woonsocket's French-Canadian immigration movement. You can get a very good sense of this insular community—its proud labor history, and its ardent preservation of customs and languages.

Exhibits re-create, among other things, a 1920s textile mill shop, a farmhouse in rural Québec, and a circa-1900s Catholic church.

One of the better exhibits takes you into a triple-decker—these three-story tenements were built mostly from the 1890s to about 1930 and are notable for their three-story, stacked exterior porches; they're a common sight throughout urban Rhode Island, as well as in many other parts of New England. Here you can ring the three different doorbells of the three tenants who lived in this building—Harry Lariviere, Anita L'Etoile, and Laura Martineau—and listen to engaging and colorful descriptions of working-class life in Woonsocket during the early 1900s. Living in triple-deckers was an often fleeting existence. Families moved dozens of times over the years from tenement to tenement, as jobs ended or rents were raised. Tenants had few rights and no written leases or guarantees. About 90 percent of the original occupants of Woonsocket's triple-deckers were French-Canadians.

You can sit inside the re-created classroom of a late 1920s parochial school and listen to a tape of a priest answering common questions children might have asked at these times. Many of the political and social complexities of the day are hashed out during this informative exchange—especially provocative is a retelling of the Sentinelle Affair, which tore Woonsocket in two. This was a classic debate between French-Canadian assimilationists and nationalists (or Sentinellists), and the argument remains surprisingly germane today as these same factions debate whether provincial Québec should secede from or remain a part of Canada.

The museum tour ends with a presentation inside a re-created 1930s Independent Textile Union Hall. The ITU was founded in Woonsocket in 1931 by Joseph Schmetz, a Belgian worker and socialist; it preceded the now ubiquitous AFL-CIO and had a membership as high as 18,000—representing every craft and every industry—at its peak. In the union hall you hear the typical plight workers faced during these years. Challenges ranged simply from low pay and long hours to female employees being forced to performed sexual favors in exchange for continued employment.

Local textile mills were dangerous places of work, all of them with treacherous belt-driven machinery, and most of them employing risky and exploitive labor practices that seem almost unbelievably cruel today. Some mills, like French Worsted, were seasonal, which meant that workers were only assured of employment for a short period, and were never guaranteed rehire from year to year. Cotton mills were the major force here until about 1900, when their output was surpassed by factories producing woolen yarns.

All told, the museum contains eight real-life interactive exhibits, 200 period photographs, and many additional hands-on displays. Many of the tapes and interactive exhibits are narrated by older town residents who lived through the city's labor strife of the early 20th century. You're able to read some of the touching letters immigrants here sent back to their families still living in rural Québec. Other exhibits discuss some of the popular forms of recreation, such as baseball, which occupied the relatively little free time of workers in the Blackstone Valley. Major League Hall of Fame baseball legends Nap Lajoie and Gabby Hartnett hail from these parts; Lajoie was born in Woonsocket. In one important respect, the Museum of Work and Culture succeeds where many of the famous mansions and historical societies elsewhere in the state fail: it actually talks with its visitors, rather than merely showing them static displays or reeling off unrelated facts. Open weekdays 9:30 A.M.–4 P.M., Sat. 10 A.M.–5 P.M., Sun. 1–5 P.M. Admission $5.

Running east from Market Square, Bernon Street brings you alongside **River Island Park,** where a walking path traces one of the old trenches that carried water from the falls to factories decades ago. This is the heart of **Old Woonsocket Falls Village;** downriver a bit, a left from Bernon onto Front Street leads to **Old Bernon Village,** which contains several fine old cotton mills. Over the Court Street Bridge, you can take in a very nice view of the old Bernon Mills. Note the path of Allen Street, which runs alongside the west side of the river—it retraces the path of the old Blackstone Canal. The area may seem fairly quiet and pedestrian these days, a far cry from the bustle of commerce and manufacturing that shook this area for decades prior to World War II, when the city's blue-collar industries began their steepest decline.

The Providence & Worcester rail bridge, supported by the original 1847 stone pillars, crosses the Woonsocket River down a ways from the Court Street Bridge. At Depot Square you'll see the 1882 **Worcester Railroad Depot,** which replaced the wooden original, lost to a fire. Trains no longer stop here (although two freight trains pass by nightly), but the impressive station still functions, now as the headquarters of the Blackstone River Valley National Heritage Corridor Commission. Inside you'll find exhibits and documents about the Blackstone River Valley; park rangers can answer questions about the area's history. At its prime, about 25 Providence & Worcester trains chugged by each day. Near the station stands the 1855 **Harris Warehouse,** a curving stone building inside which the old train tracks ran, so that wool could be loaded and unloaded even in the rain.

Many of industrial Rhode Island's most notable commercial buildings line Woonsocket's Main Street, including the imposing **City Hall,** at No. 169, where Abraham Lincoln once spoke.

It was begun in 1856 and added onto in 1891. Several vintage early-20th-century three- and four-story buildings line the street nearby. Some of these buildings have been restored, others have not. But the potential for a full restoration is great. Many of the city's mills now house light industry and service-oriented companies.

North Smithfield

Just west of Woonsocket and a rural community during its earliest years, North Smithfield incorporated in 1871, but by then it was an industrial stronghold, just like the rest of the region. Within the present town limits you'll find several villages, notably **Slatersville,** its seat of government, and Forestdale, Branch Village, Union Village, and Primrose. This last is a little bump of a hamlet that still has a remarkably rural character—at the intersection of Grange Road and Rocky Hill you'll come to the seemingly abandoned Primrose Grange, along with a handful of pretty and in some cases historic homes.

North Smithfield is most notable, however, for its historic mill towns, such as **Union Village,** which is just southwest of the Woonsocket border off Route 146A (just 1.5 miles north of

© ANDREW COLLINS

countryside near Smithfield

the intersection of Rtes. 146A and 104). This was the first part of North Smithfield to be settled, and it contains a number of fine old homes and makes for a pretty drive—most of the oldest buildings date to the 1790s and early 1800s.

From Union Village, continue northwest along Route 146A about two miles, making a left turn onto Green Street to reach historic Slatersville, the first planned industrial community in America. It and nearby Forestdale—a once mostly Polish and Portuguese factory hub that produced everything from scythes to flannel blankets— were among the most prolific mill villages of their day. Slatersville was a continuation of the region's "great experiment" in mill industrialization.

Whereas the Slater mill complex in Pawtucket required no construction of housing and village buildings, because it sat in the middle of an already established urban enclave, Slatersville was created in a then-rural area west of Woonsocket. John Slater, the younger brother of Samuel, had come to America in 1803; Samuel hired him to scout out a site along a strong source of water power that would be suitable for the creation of a full-fledged mill village. He chose to build around a small existing settlement, then known as Buffum's Mills, which comprised a sawmill, grist mill, and blacksmith shop—it sat along the Branch River, a tributary of the Blackstone. The firm of Almy, Brown, and Slater started buying up the land and water rights, and in 1807 they opened a mill. They also constructed a village of worker housing. Today this charming little mill village remains remarkably intact, offering a glimpse of the blueprint for so many villages set all around New England.

Generations of Slaters continued to own and run Slatersville until 1900, when James R. Hooper bought the compound and ran the by-now-languishing community as an operation for bleaching and dyeing cloth. Henry Kendall took over in 1915 and set about renovating many of the mill buildings and residences, as well as adding the attractive landscaping that still distinguishes Slatersville. Kendall also gave many of the buildings and houses in town white clapboard siding to give the village more of a traditional New England sensibility.

Slatersville is set around a traditional New England common, which is almost unheard-of in Rhode Island outside of the towns in the southeastern part of the state that were once part of Massachusetts. The Slater family laid out the Green in 1838, the same year they constructed the Greek Revival **Congregational Church,** which remains one of the most elegant in the state. An octagonal three-tier belfry rises high over the main structure; it replaces an even larger spire that toppled in 1938 during the great hurricane that devastated southern New England. You can relax for a bit on one of the several benches that surround the Slatersville common.

The village stands just northeast of Slatersville Reservoir, which the Branch River empties into after passing over two small man-made waterfalls. The dams provided the powerful rush of water that fed through a sluice gate and into a trench— or raceway—that powered the Slatersville Mill.

Just above the river, along Main Street, you'll see several fine examples of workers' housing. Some of the original mill buildings stood just across the street from the housing. One of these 1820s structures has housed the **North Smithfield Public Library** since 1966; this building gives a good sense of what the other mill structures along here looked like. The main **Slatersville Mill** still stands at the corner of Main and North Main Streets; this massive 1826 building with a five-story tower replaced the original 1807 structure, which burned. As of 2003 the mill is vacant, but the owners are seeking a tenant and planning to restore the building. Sitting quite close to the workers' housing, the **Slatersville Commercial Block** dates to 1850 (with the second half of this four-story gambrel-roofed block of brick storefronts dating to 1870).

In Harrisville, you'll drive by the old Stillwater Worsted Mills, today surrounded by chain-link fence crowned with barbed wire. Weeds grow over the fences like wisteria on an arbor. It's quiet and desolate, yet eerily enchanting.

GREATER PROVIDENCE

They have housed all kinds of village businesses over the years.

One of the more dramatic buildings in the village, the Greek Revival **Dr. Elisha Bartlett House** stands at 2 Green St. Bartlett was born here in 1804, graduated from Brown University with a medical degree in 1826, and was the mayor of Slatersville in the 1830s. Nearby, at 16 School St,, you'll see the 1810 residence of town founder John Slater.

From Slatersville, take Main Street west to Route 102, which leads southwest into Burrillville.

Burrillville

Established in 1730 and incorporated as a town in 1806, Burrillville today is one of the largest towns, geographically, in the state, occupying some 55 square miles and taking in several old mill communities. It had been a part of Providence until 1731, and then a section of Glocester until its own incorporation. The town is named for James Burrill, Jr., who served as state attorney general from 1797 to 1814 and then as a U.S. Senator for a term after that. Burrillville is the state's north-westernmost town, the only one to border both Connecticut and Massachusetts. Rivers including the Pascoag (pronounced pass-coh), Nipmuck, Branch, and Clear have long powered mills and factories in several little industrial burgs throughout this otherwise sparsely populated and hilly woodland community, which is also notable for having several fine stone quarries.

By the 1850s, Burrillville was the state's most prolific producer of wool goods. Production peaked around the turn of the 20th century and then declined steadily over the next few decades. Most of the mills had packed up and moved south by the 1960s, and today these little vestiges of industrial life look rather dated and even deserted, although commuters from as far as Providence and Worcester still occupy much of the local housing. The town is also a center of recreational activity, thanks to its several lakes and nature preserves. As in Woonsocket and North Smithfield, Burrillville is home to many French-Canadians.

These humble, working-class communities have relatively few offerings of interest to trav-elers—just a smattering of local bars and simple eateries, and no hotels or inns. The locals are generally friendly but perhaps slightly surprised when strangers penetrate their midst. Oakland, Harrisville, Pascoug, Mapleville, and Bridgeton are the main industrial centers.

Some of the abandoned mills are interesting just to look at. In **Harrisville,** for instance, you'll drive by the old Stillwater Worsted Mills, today surrounded by chain-link fence crowned with barbed wire. Weeds grow over the fences like wisteria on an arbor. It's quiet and desolate, yet eerily enchanting. And you can stand there imagining the bustle of this village when hundreds of workers toiled and moved about. Harrisville is one of the more attractive villages in Burrillville, the home of the town library, main post office, courthouse, and such.

Every little village has its own distinct story and ambience. **Bridgeton** was home to the White Mill Park, begun in 1834 as a worsted wool mill. **Oakland,** too, was a center of worsted wool manufacturing, as was its insular neighbor **Mapleville**—you can still see much of the old mill housing in these villages. Pascoug, a center of Irish immigration during its mill heyday, is another little hard-luck town with shops like Moonshine Liquors, Fishin' Stuff Live Bait & Tackle, and Palmisciano's TV. Neon beer signs fill the windows of several taverns.

Burrillville's mills are famous for having clothed a huge chunk of the Union Army during the Civil War and dressing U.S. soldiers during World War I and II. Quite a few Providence buildings were made with granite quarried from Burrillville. It's one of the better towns in Rhode Island for leaf-peeping in the fall.

Smithfield

Not to be confused with North Smithfield, Smithfield—which was settled as a Quaker enclave—lies just to the south and is its own incorporated entity. It, too, contains a few small mill villages but it's more of a middle-class bedroom community (pop. 20,000) for Providence commuters, as well as being the home of **Bryant College,** 1150 Douglas Pike, 401/232-6000 or 800/622-7001, www.bryant.edu, known to football fans as the summer training camp for the New England Patriots. Although the town developed heavily during the Industrial Revolution as a textiles center, it's always had strong agrarian roots and a reputation for apple farming. There are still quite a few apple orchards in town today. More recently, big-name corporate concerns have built modern offices in Smithfield, the largest being Fidelity Investments.

The government seat of Smithfield is **Georgiaville,** just northeast of where U.S. 44 intersects with I-295. Smithfield was incorporated as a town in 1731, at that time taking in what are now parts of North Smithfield, Lincoln, and Woonsocket. It was mostly a farming village in these early days, until the Industrial Revolution, at which time French-Canadians, Irish, Italian, and Portuguese laborers moved here in significant numbers. The village takes its name from the Georgia Cotton Manufacturing Company, which formed here on the Woonasquatucket River in 1813.

Smithfield's historical society is based at the **Smith-Appleby House Museum,** 220 Stillwater Rd., 401/231-7363, www.smithfield-history.org, a 12-room farmhouse, portions of which date to 1696. At that time the rambling structure was much simpler, just one room with a loft upstairs. Elisha Smith, the grandson of one of the six men who joined Roger Williams in his initial settlement of Providence, built the house. Today it contains fine 18th- and even 17th-century furnishings, although the original family pieces were auctioned off when the last family member, Myra Appleby, passed away in 1959. The house is open by appointment and on Saturdays May–Sept., noon–4 P.M. Admission is $2. Fundraising socials are held every month from May through December, usually themed after a meal or snack (e.g., admission to the Apple Social includes a homemade apple dessert and beverage).

In the southwest end of town, little Greenville is a pretty, largely undeveloped village that's home to **Powder Mill Ledges Wildlife Refuge,** 12 Sanderson Rd., Smithfield, 401/949-5454, www.asri.org.

SHOPPING

Pick-Your-Own Farms and Other Edibles

A longtime favorite in Cumberland, **Phantom Farms,** 2920 Diamond Hill Rd., 401/333-2240, has a greenhouse gift shop and offers pick-your own veggies, pumpkins, apples, and other fruits seasonally, along with fresh-baked pies, apple crisp, candied apples, and other gourmet goodies. During the holidays, it's also a great source of Christmas trees, wreaths, and other decorations, and there are Easter eggs hunts and other family-oriented events in the spring.

In North Smithfield, **Wright's Dairy Farm,** 200 Woonsocket Hill Rd., 401/767-3014 or 800/222-9734, is a working farm where you can view cow milking daily 3–6 P.M., and buy fresh milk, whipped cream, cream-filled pastries, and baked goods from the on-site shop. In the early 1970s this farm started a bakery, which has supplemented the farm's income.

In North Smithfield, **Pearl's Candy and Nuts,** 4 Eddie Dowling Hwy., Park Square, 401/769-1166, is known for miles around as the source for fun retro candies, from Squirrel Nuts to Necco Wafers, plus fresh-roasted nuts and fancy boxed chocolates. You can also satisfy your sweet tooth at **School House Candy,** 280 Rand St., Central Falls, 401/726-4500, an outlet shop set inside a vintage brick factory building and proffering all kinds of tasty sweets.

One of the more unusual ways to enjoy a bit of Rhode Island when you're miles away is to contact **Clambakes to Travel,** 800/722-CLAM, www.clambakeco.com, a Pawtucket-based company that will ship up to eight authentic clambake meals to anywhere in the continental United States. Each meal includes a 1 1/4 pound lobster, steamed clams, mussels, chourico sausage, corn on the cob, red bliss potatoes, and onions packed with rockweed inside a reusable pot. It's $99 for one meal but just $289 for six meals, which is a pretty reasonable price divvied up among a large group.

Outlets and Antiques

It's only appropriate that Pawtucket would have

one of the better fabric shops in the state. **Lorraine Mills Fabrics,** 593 Mineral Springs Ave., 401/722-9500, offers thousands of bolts of fabric and is set inside a historic brick mill building. Knitters and darners will also want to check out the **Yarn Outlet,** 280 Rand St., Bldg. 4, Central Falls, 401/722-5600, which has needles, books, and yarns and fabrics.

In Cumberland, **Planet Garden,** 30 Martin St., 401/334-4443, is a factory outlet for birdbaths, benches, and both indoor and outdoor statuary for gardens, greenhouses, patios, and terraces. In Smithfield, the **Lenox-Gorham Factory Outlet,** 270 Jenckes Hill Rd. (Rte. 123), 401/334-1943, is a great source for bargains in crystal stemware, china, and the like.

In the Greenville section of Smithfield, the Greenville Antique Center, 711 Putnam Pike (U.S. 44), 401/949-4999, displays the wares of some 140 dealers, offering everything from furniture, toys, china, and glassware to vintage prints and paintings.

SPORTS AND RECREATION

A favorite spot in the area for strolling, jogging, swimming, and having fun is **Lincoln Woods State Park** (also known as Lincoln Woods Reservation), 2 Manchester Print Works Lane, off Route 123, 401/723-7892. Established in 1909 on Abraham Lincoln's birthday, the heavily wooded, gently rolling 627-acre park surrounds Olney Pond, which is popular for swimming, trout-fishing, and—when weather permits—ice-skating. Other features include playing fields, a snack bar, picnic tables and shelters, fireplaces, a bathhouse with changing rooms and showers, and a boat ramp.

Baseball

All New Englanders root for, often futilely, the Boston Red Sox, but Rhode Islanders get behind their scrappy **Pawtucket PawSox,** McCoy Stadium, 1 Ben Mondor Way, Pawtucket, 401/724-7300, www.pawsox.com, with particular fervor. For a fraction of what they're charging up in Beantown, you can score great seats for a game of this Triple-A farm team that has witnessed the rising stars of Mo Vaughn, Roger Clemens, Wade Boggs, Nomar Garciaparra, and countless others. The regular season runs from April through early September. You can also hear the games on the radio, at 790 AM The Score, which airs from Providence.

Bicycling

Opened in 1998, the **Blackstone Bike Trail** follows parts of the Blackstone River and the old Blackstone Canal—it currently runs from Pawtucket 17 miles north to Woonsocket but will someday connect clear to Worcester. You can access it in several places, and park your car at lots in Lincoln (at both ends of Front Street, along the river), and at Blackstone State Park at the end of Lower River Road. It's a hit not only among bikers, but also in-line skaters, joggers, and strollers. You'll pass by some of the great old mills of the region, as well as vast meadows and some fairly mundane suburban stretches.

Boating

In an effort to familiarize the public with the Blackstone River, the staffs of the National Heritage Corridor, Paddle Providence, and the Rhode Island Canoe and Kayak Association have created the **Blackstone Valley Paddle Club,** 401/762-0250. You can get further information through **Paddle Providence,** 401/453-1633, www.paddleprovidence.org; and the **Rhode Island Canoe and Kayak Association,** www.ricka.org. The club offers kayak and canoe lessons and organized excursions led by park rangers, and also advice and information on taking to the river in these parts. You can also participate in water-quality monitoring projects, river and canal cleanups, and other activities that promote the health of this valuable resource. Guided paddles are typically given through the summer on Tuesday evenings at 6:30 P.M. Putting-in points along the river change each week, so call ahead for details. On Saturdays, you can come by for lessons or to improve your kayaking and canoeing skills.

The Blackstone is a complex waterway for paddlers; you'll encounter dams, which require portaging, as well as unmarked spillways that can greatly alter the river's water level. The ranger staff offers a great deal of information on how to make the most of canoeing and kayaking along here, as well as how to do so safely. You can also learn a great deal about the river's history, and the flora and fauna encountered along it. Before boating on the river, log onto the website of the United States Geological Survey monitoring station (http://waterdata.usgs.gov), which is in Northbridge, Mass. From here you can get a good indication of whether the flow is safe.

Golfing
In the Nasonville section of Burrillville, golfers can test their skills at the **Country View Golf Club,** 49 Club La., off Colwell Road, 401/568-7157.

Hiking
On Earth Day each year, in mid-June, Blackstone River State Park hosts "Spruce Up," a volunteer clean-up of the historic Blackstone Canal and its adjoining tow path. Call 401/724-2200 for details.

ACCOMMODATIONS
There aren't a whole lot of places to stay in the Blackstone River Valley, and even fewer in the smaller towns west of Woonsocket. It's very easy to use Providence or Warwick as a base for exploring this part of the state, and you can see much of this area on one- or two-day excursions. On the other hand, the few hotels and inns in these parts generally charge rates far lower than in points farther south—you can save a good bit of money booking a room in Woonsocket or Smithfield and using these towns as your base for exploring Providence, Warwick, and even South County. Such are the benefits of visiting the nation's smallest state: you can stay at one end of the state and easily daytrip to the other.

Hotels and Motels
$50–100: Woonsocket got a nice little hotel boost in 2000 when the **Holiday Inn Express,** 194 Fortin Dr., 401/769-5000 or 800/465-4329, www.hiexpress.com, opened in a convenient, downtown location. This clean and efficiently run 88-room property has an indoor pool, Jacuzzi,

and health club—there are also 16 suites. The no-frills **Woonsocket Motor Inn,** 333 Clinton St., Woonsocket, 401/762-1224, is a basic if dated motel in the center of town; its rooms are unmemorable but have large TVs and clean bathrooms. It's decent, considering the price (you can sometimes get rooms for under $50, but rack rates are $55 and up). In Smithfield, the **Fairfield Inn,** Route 116, Smithfield, 401/232-2400 or 800/228-2800, is another inexpensive, low-frills property. It has 117 rooms and an outdoor heated pool; rates include Continental breakfast.

$100–150: Just off I-95, the **Comfort Inn Providence/Pawtucket,** 2 George St., Pawtucket, 401/723-6700 or 800/228-5150, www.choicehotels.com, has standard rooms in a typical midrise building; amenities include an outdoor pool, guest laundry, Nintendo, and Continental breakfast. Attached is the Ground Round Restaurant. One of the better chain properties in the region, the 84-unit **Comfort Suites,** 1010 Douglas Pike (Rte. 7), Smithfield, 401/231-6300 or 800/228-5150, www.choicehotels.com, has business services, a gym, and rooms with microwaves, refrigerators, coffeemakers.

Country Inns and B&Bs
$50–100: A gorgeous Second Empire Victorian with a green mansard roof, the **Pillsbury House B&B,** 341 Prospect St., Woonsocket, 401/766-7983 or 800/205-4112, www.pillsburyhouse.com, is one of the most appealing inns in northern Rhode Island and one of the better values in the state. The 1870s house with a big leafy yard sits along one of Woonsocket's most prestigious streets, lined with large homes that were once the domain of mill owners. It's an easy walk from downtown. Rooms are spacious and bright with mostly Victorian antiques that include ornate chandeliers, plush beds made up with either country quilts or fine white linens, and myriad antiques—most of the rooms have soaring 10-foot ceilings and period wallpapers. Certainly one of the most distinctive accommodations in New England, the English-made **Samuel Slater Canal Boat B&B,** Central Falls, 401/724-2200, www.tourblackstone.com, was brought to Central

Falls in winter 2000; the 40-foot boat offers a look back into the era when canals drove the economy in this region, from about 1828 to 1848. The boat can be chartered by up to 12 passengers for tours along the river, or up to four can use the boat as an overnight B&B.

A gracious colonial homestead in a historic section of Lincoln, the **Whipple-Cullen Farmstead B&B,** 99 Old River Rd., 401/333-1899, dates back nearly 300 years, having been built by the grandson (Job Whipple) of one of the state's founding fathers, Thomas Angell. A stay here offers a glimpse back to the colony's earliest days—the house has eight fireplaces, three beehive ovens, and its original crown molding and mantels and wide-plank pine floors. There are four guest rooms decorated with early colonial pieces. The present owners can trace their lineage in the house back five generations. While the house is just a short drive off I-295 (by the Lincoln Mall), it's also within walking distance of the Blackstone River and Canal. **Willingham Manor,** 570 Central St., 401/568-2468, an 1840s Victorian on 2.5 acres in Pascoag, is really the only lodging option in northwest Rhode Island. The house is furnished with period antiques and retains its original hardwood floors. Plenty of families choose this option—guests have use of their own dining room, kitchen, and living room, plus a phone and TV/VCR. The two bedrooms share a bath, but one has twin beds and the other a queen-size bed.

Camping

Camping options in Burrillville include **Echo Lake Campground,** 180 Moroney Road, Pascoag, 401/568-7109 or 401/568-5000; and **Buck Hill Family Campground,** 464 Wakefield Rd., Pascoag, 401/568-0456.

FOOD

The region is dominated by fairly simple and affordable restaurants that emphasize steak, pastas, and the region's famous "family chicken dinners," which you can read more about below. With such a strong ethnic presence in the region, you'll also find several fine purveyors of authentic Portuguese, Italian, and

French-Canadian food. Gourmet dining workshops are held at **Aaron Smith Farm,** 264 Victory Hwy., Mapleville, 401/568-6702. Part of the fun of taking cooking classes here is having the opportunity to learn, and then dine, in a restored 1730s colonial home with Greek Revival details. The emphasis here is on historic Early American recipes.

Upscale

It's one of the few restaurants in northern Rhode Island that could be called dressy, but even at **Bella,** 1992 Victory Square, Burrillville, 401/568-6996 ($9–24), you can get by with casual attire. The spacious dining room of this Italian restaurant looks and feels like a banquet hall; the ambience is not especially distinctive, but it's pleasant nonetheless. The menu reveals a tremendous variety—specialties include grilled New York sirloin brushed with rosemary-infused oil and grilled marinated chicken over tossed field greens with balsamic vinegar. Pastas are, of course, a great option here: homemade lasagna and gnocchi are favorites, and you can mix-and-match several types of pasta with about 15 kinds of sauce (red or white clam, vodka, primavera, and so on).

Pizzas and Pub Grub

Justly famous for introducing northern Rhode Islanders to the communal concept of "family chicken dinners," **Wright's Farm Restaurant,** 84 Inman Rd., Nasonville, 401/769-2856 ($8–13), presents family-style meals—the heaping platters of chicken, green salad, fries, rolls, and pasta sides can feed armies. The concept is so simple, so all-American—all-you-can-possibly-stuff-down-your-throat dinners that bring legions of family members and friends together in a homey ambience. It's a huge place, with banquet seating for some 1,600 patrons, plus a gift and toy shop that sells house-made specialties like Italian dressing, barbecue sauce, fudge, and pasta sauce. It's become increasingly famous every year since it opened in 1972. It's a pretty amazing operation—75 ovens work away in the kitchen. Another of the excellent chicken-dinner purveyors in northern Rhode Island, **Village Haven,** 90 School St., Forestdale, 401/762-4242

GREATER PROVIDENCE

($8–14), scores high marks for its down-home American cooking, such as prime beef and baked stuffed jumbo shrimp. The cinnamon buns are the stuff of legend. It's a very lively spot, with a friendly staff and dependable food. A popular option for pastas and more substantial Italian fare is Smithfield's **Bella Luna,** 566 Putnam Pike, 401/949-0182 ($9–17), which has an attractive, intimate dining room that's a refreshing change from institutional-looking red-sauce Italian joints around the region.

Packed on weekends and with baseball and other sports memorabilia lining the walls, **Box Seatz,** 360 River St., Woonsocket, 401/762-0900 ($5–14), is a jumping sports bar and tavern with a remarkably long menu of quite well-prepared pub food: burgers, barbecued ribs, Philly cheese steaks, veal parmesan, calamari rolls, and blackened chicken fettuccine Alfredo with mushrooms. Karaoke on Thursday nights pulls in a big crowd of yuksters.

At **Ye Olde English Fish and Chips,** Market Square, Woonsocket, 401/762-3637 ($2–7), you can grab your food and eat it on a bench overlooking the Blackstone River and falls, or eat in the casual sit-down dining room. This place has been serving up fresh seafood since 1922, and its proximity to the Rhode Island Museum of Work and Culture makes it a hit with visitors. Of course, fish-and-chips are the menu favorite, but you might also try a fish burger, stuffed quahogs, baked scallops, baked stuffed shrimp, or Manhattan-style clam chowder. The **Chicken Coop,** 828 Diamond Hill Rd., Woonsocket, 401/769-2667 ($7.95 dinner buffet), is a favorite for rotisserie chicken, mashed and oven-roasted potatoes, chicken wings, chicken stir-fry, and so on. This is a nice choice if you've got a large group of kids with you.

Set in a grove of towering pine trees in North Smithfield, the aptly named **Pines Restaurant,** 1204 Pound Hill Rd., 401/766-2122 ($7–16), is another favorite for chicken family-style, as well as traditional American standbys like lobster, prime rib, baked haddock, king crab legs, and chops. It's family run and tends to draw a local crowd. Slatersville's best dining option is

Pinelli's Cucina, 900 Victory Hwy., 401/767-2444 ($10–16), where you might sample both classic and contemporary Italian fare, such as shrimp scampi over cappellini, veal topped with prosciutto and mozzarella with a mushroom-marsala sauce, and grilled Italian pork chops with sautéed vinegar peppers and Tuscan potato wedges.

A humble pizza place serving prodigious portions of hearty Italian chow, **Mezza Luna,** Route 146A, at the intersection of South Main Street and Great and Smithfield Roads, Woonsocket, 401/769-7654 ($4–11), charms patrons with its super-friendly staff and gooey pies piled high with addictive ingredients like spinach, hamburger, and lobster. Meatball grinders, pasta shells, and salads round out the menu. Families pack the place on weekends. The **Mad Dog Saloon,** 98 Main St., Pascoag, 401/568-9448 (under $8), is a real no-nonsense tavern with sports on TV, cold beer, and greasy pub fare. But the crowd is friendly and good-natured. A festive little deck out back overlooks the Pascoug River and is strung with twinkling lights. It's a real bikers' hangout on weekends.

On the Woonsocket/Cumberland border, **Moon's Restaurant,** 4077 Mendon Rd. (at Rtes. 122 and 99), 401/658-0449 ($6–14), has been serving tasty New England seafood since the late 1970s; the fried clam platters and half-pound scrod dinners are among the favorites from the seven-page menu. In Cumberland, **Tuck's,** 2352 Mendon Rd., 401/658-0450 ($5–10), is a reliable option for burgers, salads, chicken wraps, homemade soups, and other tavern fare; it's open to 1 A.M. most nights. The bar also serves 12 kinds of beers on tap, making it a favorite watering hole for locals.

Ethnic Fare

It may not be as trendy-looking as many Thai eateries in Providence and Boston, but the diminutive **Thai Garden,** 280 Main St., 401/765-7010 ($6–14), a simple dining room in downtown Woonsocket, serves excellent Thai food. The fact that many patrons are Thai themselves attests to the kitchen's dedication to authenticity. Dig into spicy vegetable tempura and hot-and-sour chicken soup. Other specialties include sea bass deep-fried and topped with a sauce of hot chilies, onions, red peppers, and scallions; tofu pad thai; and beef with fresh mushrooms and asparagus in oyster sauce. Everything can be spiced authentically if you specify. More Americanized but plenty of fun is **Chan's,** 267 Main St., Woonsocket, 401/765-1900 or 401/762-1364 ($5–12), an elaborate, almost campy Chinese restaurant that since 1905 has been noted perhaps more for its live entertainment than anything else. It's well-regarded enough that people will drive 30 minutes or more to check out the scene here, sample the tasty Szechuan fare, and listen to the line-up of hip jazz greats and other musicians. The menu is encyclopedic with nods to just about every Chinese culinary tradition you can think of. Specialties include roast pork egg foo yong, beef sautéed with pickled ginger, egg drop soup, lobster with fried rice, and the inevitable Tahitian Delight (fresh sea scallops and tender chicken stir-fried in a light sauce with straw mushrooms, broccoli, carrot slices, and water chestnuts on a bed of pan-fried noodles).

At the Lincoln Mall, **Asia,** off Route 146 and I-295, 401/334-3200 ($5–10), serves a well-prepared if fairly standard range of Chinese specialties, such as hot-and-sour soup, shrimp with almonds, and General Tso's chicken. It's an attractive spot with hanging Chinese prints, tapestries, and regional artwork.

East Providence has one of the state's several outstanding Portuguese restaurants, **Madeira,** 288 Warren Ave., 401/431-1322 ($10–21), a classy spot with a super-solicitous staff. Here you can try flame-grilled Portuguese sausage; kale, chorizo, and potato soup; filet of scrod topped with the restaurant's secret Madeira sauce; paella Valencia; and boiled dried codfish served with boiled potatoes, chickpeas, and hard-boiled egg. Everything is cooked to order, which means you'll often have to wait 30 to 40 minutes for your dinner, but it's worth the wait for such authentic fare. Vegetarian entrées are available on request.

Quick Bites

Grab lunch in Smithfield at **J's Delicatessen,** 285 George Washington Hwy., 401/231-0823 ($3–8), where favorite sandwiches include the Portfolio (hot pastrami, melted cheddar, and tangy buffalo sauce). Right on Main Street in Woonsocket, **New York Lunch Hot Wieners,** 114 Main St., 401/769-2799 (under $4) has eight little diner stools and serves juicy hot wieners (with a small drink) for just $1.65. The best way to eat them is smothered in hamburg sauce (a seasoned blend of finely ground hamburger meat), onions, and mustard. You can get basic diner fare here, too. East Providence isn't known for food, but you will find similarly esteemed wieners at **Sparky's Coney Island System,** 122 Taunton Ave., 401/434-9826 (under $4).

Modern Diner, 364 East Ave., Pawtucket, 401/726-8390 (under $7), a crimson-and-cream Sterling Streamliner steel railroad-car diner attached to a Victorian house, serves excellent home-style food. It's a short drive from Slater Mill, and breakfast is served all day. Plenty of the state's diner aficionados rank this place among the best around. Cranberry-almond pancakes are a highlight, but you'll find a full slate of typical diner favorites. No dinner; cash only. For several decades, devotees of burgers and fries have been cramming into **Stanley's,** 535 Dexter Ave., Central Falls, 401/726-9689 ($3–7); the patties here are fresh-made and wonderful, grilled with several toppings (cheddar, mushrooms, onions); the French fries are prepared with just the right crispness.

Bagel devotees swear by the holy holey discs at **Barney's,** 727 East Ave., Pawtucket, 401/727-1010 ($2–7), a fine kosher deli that shares the same shopping center as a few other excellent and affordable purveyors of good food on the Providence/Pawtucket border. **Horton's Seafood,** 809 Broadway, East Providence, 401/434-3116 ($4–11), serves up tasty lobster rolls that can be admired for both their heft and lack of filler. In summer you can dine on the screened-in porch.

Get ice cream kicks at **Sunshine Creamery,**

© ANDREW COLLINS

Modern Diner in Pawtucket

305 N. Broadway, East Providence, 401/431-2828, which dishes out nearly 40 flavors of the sweet, frozen treat. **Ice Cream Machine,** 4288 Diamond Hill Rd., Cumberland, 401/333-5053, is one of the top homemade ice cream shops in the state, also known for its ice-cream pies. It's closed November through March. At **Phantom Farms,** 2920 Diamond Hill Rd., 401/333-2240, great desserts are served.

Java Joints
Le Petit Cafe, 38 Blackstone St., Woonsocket, 401/765-7466, is a sunny café on the ground floor of an elaborate Queen Anne Building downtown—stop in for espresso, teas, bagels, and light sandwiches. It's a nice little break near center of town.

Gourmet Goods and Picnic Supplies
You'll find excellent house-made pastas and Italian groceries at **PastaWorks,** 2 Whipple Ave., Smithfield, 401/232-9136, where you can buy both fresh and frozen varieties. The lobster ravioli is some of the best around, but any of this stuff when prepared at home will have you looking like a gourmet chef. Drop by **Ferreira's Bread and Sweets,** 107 Front St., Woonsocket, 401/762-5295, for linguica-and-spinach pies, Portuguese bread, coconut custard pastries, flan, bismarks, éclairs, and orange sponge cake. It's a treat for the senses just to stand in this little storefront bakery and smell the treats in the oven. Or check out the delicious goodies and sweets at **Pastry Gourmet,** 570 Putnam Pike, Smithfield, 401/949-1441; there's also a branch in Cumberland, 2001 Mendon Rd., 401/333-5535. It's fun just to stroll in and admire the wedding cakes. **Creative Pies and Cakes Bakery & Coffee Shop,** 459 Chapel St., Harrisville, 401/568-7117, anchors downtown Burrillville. In this sun-filled dining room of mismatched tables and chairs, expect good hearty breakfasts and, of course, fresh muffins, sweets, and cookies. It's also the place to hear local scuttlebutt—it's not cute or created, but a genuine slice of a small blue-collar town.

ENTERTAINMENT AND NIGHTLIFE
For nightlife, it's hard to find a more unusual and entertaining venue than **Chan's,** 267 Main St., Woonsocket, 401/765-1900, www.chans

eggrollsandjazz.com, which brings in a great variety of jazz bands and musicians, usually on Wednesday, Friday, and Saturday nights—call ahead or check the website for details. **Gator's Sports Pub,** 1402 Victory Hwy., North Smithfield, 401/769-2220, also hosts live music regularly and can be a fun hangout for drinks or to play volleyball. It's a bit of a singles scene. The kitchen serves chicken fajitas, nachos, pastas, and such. Otherwise, there's not a tremendous amount in the way of nighttime activities in these parts, as most folks just head down to Providence.

Currently under restoration in Woonsocket is the 1926 **Stadium Theatre Performing Arts Centre,** Monument Square, Main Street, 401/762-4545, www.stadiumtheatre.com, which seats 1,100. The **Blackstone River Theatre,** 549 Broad St., Cumberland, 401/725-9272, www.riverfolk.org, is a nonprofit cultural center that presents music, dance, and folk arts, usually in the traditions of the many different ethnic groups that have settled in the Blackstone River Valley. Many presentations are geared toward children. The theater occupies a vintage former Masonic Lodge, which had been slated for demolition until the theater company took over the space in 1996.

FESTIVALS AND EVENTS

One of the main events in the region is **Convergence Pawtucket,** 401/724-2200, which runs through two weekends in mid-September at various locales throughout Pawtucket. The first weekend's festivities are mostly around Slater Mill, and the second weekend by Slater Park. Eat a French-Canadian meat pie as you browse everything from wood-carving to photography exhibitions. In early September, the region's largest **Arts and Crafts Show** is held at Burrillville, 401/568-4300, on the Assembly Grounds on Route 107. Local-history walks through the Harrisville section are offered during the festival.

Around the first weekend of October, the **North Smithfield Harvest Festival,** Homestead Gardens, 200 Industrial Dr., Slatersville,

401/765-4847 or 401/766-5909, kicks off with food, live music, hayrides, crafts demonstrations, llama petting and feeding for kids, and other family fun. In Woonsocket, **Autumnfest** takes hold in early October at World War II Memorial Park, Social Street, Woonsocket, 401/762-6400, with four days of live music and entertainment, amusement rides, fireworks, a Columbus Day parade, and foods of all kinds.

Through most of December, you can attend the **Winter Wonderland at Slater Park,** Armistice Blvd., Pawtucket, 401/728-0500, ext. 251; a miniature winter village is set up on the park grounds. This includes live entertainment, clowns, snacks, and hayrides at the Looff Carousel. In early May, a similar day of festivities kicks off the spring opening of the Looff Carousel. On Christmas Eve, Slatersville comes alive with holiday lights and luminarias for an evening stroll through this picturesque village.

In mid-May, head to Woonsocket's lively River Island Park, at Market Square, for the **Annual Riverfest and Friends of the Blackstone Canoe/Kayak Race,** 401/762-0440 or 401/766-6262. The 4.2-mile race runs from downtown Woonsocket to Mannville, and the park hosts food stalls, live music, and crafts. **Cumberlandfest,** Diamond Hill Park, Route 114, Cumberland, 401/728-2400, draws visitors for amusements, concerts, food, and games for four days in early August—it's always a big hit with kids. Later that month, Woonsocket celebrates the region's French and French-Canadian heritage with **Jubilee Franco-American Weekend,** various locations, 401/861-4445 or 401/847-7590, with storytelling, regional cuisines, riverboat tours, living-history exhibits, and live music. This is a terrific time to visit the city, and also to check out the fascinating Museum of Work and Culture. Few festivals of this kind in the United States offer such a detailed and colorful glimpse into French-Canadian culture. In early September Pawtucket is the site of the **Rhode Island Labor and Ethnic Heritage Festival,** Slater Mill Historic Site, Roosevelt Avenue,

401/725-8638. Local music, tours, even foods tell the story of the region's immigration, union-organizing, and industrial history over the past two centuries.

INFORMATION AND SERVICES
Visitor Information
Pamphlets, brochures, and tourism information are available from the **Blackstone Valley Tourism Council,** 171 Main St., Pawtucket, 401/724-2200 or 800/454-2882, www.tourblackstone.com.

Getting Around
This is definitely a part of the state that's easiest to get around by car, although you can take a bus to several areas, among them Pawtucket and Woonsocket. It's fairly easy to get to Slater Mill from Providence using public transportation—Bus 99 is your best bet; it runs regularly between Kennedy Plaza in Providence and downtown Pawtucket. Bus 54 runs from Kennedy Plaza through Lincoln (stopping at the Greyhound Park and Lincoln Mall), then continuing on to downtown Woonsocket. If you're driving, note that I-295 cuts across the southeastern half of the Blackstone River Valley as it loops from I-95 south of Providence back up to I-95 north of it in Attleboro, Massachusetts. From Providence, Route 146 is a quick limited-access highway northwest to Woonsocket.

The West

The largely rural and sparsely populated towns of western Rhode Island, like those just across the border in eastern Connecticut, have relatively few attractions and notable sights. You will find a handful of enchanting small villages, characterized mostly by rolling woodland, obsolete but often-handsome mills, and fast-growing tracts of suburban housing. There are very few accommodations in these parts and extremely limited public transportation. But it is an ideal region for relaxing country drives, bike rides, or moderately hilly strolls.

Glocester
One of the state's largest towns, Glocester takes in about 56 square miles, even more than its large neighbor to the north, Burrillville. It was once part of Providence, which occupied most of northern Rhode Island until the 1730s. Coal-mining, potash making, iron-forging, marble quarrying, felt-hat making, and cotton-seed-oil manufacture were among the eclectic industries this town supported, along with farming, which remains in force to a small extent today. There are just under 10,000 residents in town, making the population density among the lowest in the state.

From Providence, U.S. 44 cuts west up through Glocester and into its most notable village, Chep-achet, which lies at the crossing of Rtes. 100/102 and U.S. 44. This pretty village embodies the sleepy pace of northwestern Rhode Island while also defying the stereotype that there's little to see or do in these parts. Main Street abounds with antiques and other unusual shops, and you can also get a brief lesson in state history by visiting the bronze plaque marking the site of the 1842 Dorr Rebellion, an event that threw Rhode Island politics into a state of chaos.

Chepachet has always been a bit more refined than some of the industrial villages in this part of the state, it having been a summer colony in the 19th century popular with visitors far and near, as well as a dairy-farming hub.

In Chepachet you can visit the **Job Armstrong Store,** 1181 Main St. (U.S. 44), 401/568-4077, which had been the largest of 13 dry-goods stores in this village in the early 1800s. Today it has been converted to a living museum, where you can watch crafts, spinning, quilting, and rug-hooking demonstrations. It's also the headquarters of the Glocester Heritage Society and a visitor center with information on the area's few local attractions. Open noon–4 P.M., Saturdays only. You'll also find the oldest (though no longer in use) animal pound in the United States, on Chopmist Hill Road; this stone-walled enclosure that's 50 feet square contained stray cattle and other livestock and pets from 1749 on. Owners paid a small fee to retrieve their animals, or else the beasts were auctioned off.

Just south of Chepachet you'll find **Sprague Farm,** Pine Orchard Road, 401/588-9124, a 291-acre site administered by the Glocester Land Trust and containing mature evergreens, striped maples, and Atlantic white cedars. There are also flower gardens and shrubs, and several stone bridges of note.

Johnston

A fast-developing suburb just five miles west of Providence, Johnston had been a part of the larger city until incorporating in 1759, taking its name from Rhode Island attorney general Augustus Johnston. It's a lightly undulating town with several ponds and a mostly residential landscape—there are also quite a few restaurants along Route 6A near the Providence border. Light industry hummed here during the 19th century, but less so than in the Blackstone River Valley towns. The biggest factories manufactured worsted yarn. Those imposing granite columns at either end of the famous Arcade shopping center in downtown Providence were built with stone quarried at a vein in Johnston known as Bear Ledge.

Scituate

From Johnston, U.S. 6 continues west into Scituate and then on to the Connecticut border via Foster. It's a fairly nondescript drive through these parts but for a stop in the town's administrative center, North Scituate, an endearingly unfussy village of mostly white clapboard colonial houses. North Scituate is entirely ingenuous—unsullied by development and still totally free from banal attempts at gentrification. There's nothing cutesy here, just a few historic buildings that seem always in need of a fresh coat of paint.

Scituate, named for the town in Massachusetts from which its earliest settlers came in 1710, incorporated in 1739. Light industry dominated the town during the 18th century, from saw- and gristmills to small factories producing corset laces and cotton clothing. One of the town's best-

known features is six-mile-long Scituate Reservoir, a narrow waterway that terminates at the immense Scituate Dam, which is 3,200 feet long. The state created the reservoir in the 1920s by relocating some 1,600 residents of seven villages—Kent, South Scituate, Ashland, Richmond, Rockland, Saundersville, and Ponganset—and flooding the entire basin. It's now the state's largest body of freshwater, and the reservoir provides water for about two of every three Rhode Island households. You can drive around parts of the 60-mile shoreline, but recreational activity—including fishing, boating, and hiking—is strictly forbidden.

James Angell (born 1829) is among the town's most notable sons, having graduated from Brown University (where he later taught), edited the *Providence Journal,* and served as president of the University of Michigan and University of Vermont. He went on to become the U.S. Envoy to China, where he helped negotiate the treaty that opened up trade there with the United States. Rhode Island statesmen Stephen and Ezek Hopkins spent part of their childhood in Scituate as well.

Foster

Still farther west, Foster formed in 1781 from Scituate. Little Foster Center is the civic hub of this large but sparsely populated township. By Rhode Island standards it's quite hilly and rugged, its slopes feeding into the Moosup and Ponagansett Rivers. Anchoring this village is the **Foster Town House,** 180 Howard Hill Rd., 401/392-9200. This 1796 two-story building was built and used as a Baptist church until the 1840s.

Coventry

Extending from the busy suburbs of Cranston and West Warwick, you can follow Route 117 to reach the quiet township of Coventry, which at 62 square miles is the second largest town in the state. The village of Washington is its civic seat. The village itself went by the name of Coventry from the time of its incorporation in 1741 until it was renamed in 1809 for the local Washington Manufacturing Company. During the 19th century, Washington was the site of mills specializing in lace, cotton, and wool.

NATHANAEL GREENE

General George Washington might have been the most celebrated American military figure of the Colonial era, but plenty of scholars will argue that Rhode Island's own Major General Nathanael Greene was the leading strategist of that time. In rank during the American Revolution, Greene was second only to Washington, who made it clear that should anything happen to himself he would most want his young protégé to succeed him.

Born in 1742 in the Potowomut section of Warwick, Greene studied military science as a young man, much to the consternation of his pacifist Quaker friends. In 1775, as a member of the Rhode Island company militia, Greene was sent to join the Continental Army in Boston, and within a year his prowess as a leader earned him the rank of major general in charge of the Continental troops on Long Island. He was barely 24 years old.

He rose to quartermaster general at Valley Forge during the infamously harsh winter of 1778, helping keep in line troops on the verge of mutiny over the lack of provisions and warm clothing. He went on to lead his troops with distinction at Princeton, Brandywine, and Germantown.

In 1780, he became General of the Southern Army and so successfully managed his charge that the states of South Carolina and Georgia gave him land grants as an expression of gratitude. In towns such as Guilford Courthouse, Ninety-Six, and Eutaw, Greene triumphed over the British troops, and these efforts greatly helped to turn the course of the American Revolution in favor of the colonies.

Greene died in 1806 at the age of 44; he's buried at Johnson Square in Savannah, Georgia, where an obelisk commemorates his life and career.

In the Anthony section of town, just north of Washington, lived the famous colonial military statesman Nathanael Greene. Born to Quaker parents in 1752, the distinguished general lived in the **Nathanael Greene Homestead,** Greene Street off Laurel Avenue, 401/821-8630, website: http://members.aol.com/JonMaltbie/Homestead.html, from 1770 to 1776, after which it was owned by his brother, Jacob.

The two-and-a-half-story frame house has two chimneys and sits on a bluff by the south branch of the Pawtuxet River. Every room in the house contains a paneled fireplace and three double-hung windows; it's been a museum since it was restored in 1924. It now contains furnishings and artifacts from the Greene family. It's believed that the cannon in front of the house was made at the Greene family forge in Potowomut. Open April–Oct., Wed.–Sun., and by appointment.

West Greenwich

From Coventry, Route 117 leads west to Route 102; heading south will lead you into the village of West Greenwich, through which I-95 passes. West Greenwich was, right into the early 20th century, the least densely populated town in

Rhode Island, but I-95 transformed it into a bedroom community for Providence and environs.

Exeter

Route 102 continues beneath I-95 and then east into little Exeter, which is the administrative center of West Greenwich Township. It had been a part of North Kingstown until 1743, when it split off and incorporated. This hilly town dotted with small ponds is quite pretty but, like much of metro Providence, fairly quiet. A few small factories operated here over the years. The entire town is nearly 60 square miles but has a population of just around 6,000, making it one of western Rhode Island's typically rural and sparse communities.

Hopkinton

While Hopkinton and Richmond don't abound with formal attractions, they do possess some of the state's best hiking, canoeing, fishing, and camping areas, as well as several excellent golf courses.

The town of Hopkinton comprises some 16 villages, three of them—Hopkinton City, Wyoming, and Carolina—designated National Historic Districts. Stroll through any of these small communities, and you'll see numerous examples of colonial and Victorian architecture. Bisected by Route 138, Wyoming (civic seat of the township of Richmond) was once a stagecoach shop anchored by the Dawley Tavern. Here you'll find the Richmond Town Hall and a small village with a few noteworthy shops. Wyoming was settled in 1758 as the site of an iron works; woolen and carding mills later thrived here.

Head just west on Route 138 to enter Hope Valley, one of the more prominent little towns in western Rhode Island. In 1770 this village took hold when Hezekiah Carpenter built a dam here and used the power to build a sawmill, gristmill, fulling mill, and carding plant. For quite a while the town was known as Carpenter's Mills.

Among Richmond's many villages, Shannock, Kenyon, and Woodville are quaint old mill communities, still with their clapboard and redbrick buildings. Shannock Village, with its Shannock Mill Complex and Horseshoe Falls, is especially scenic—some of its buildings date back well into the 18th century. The **Richmond Historical Society,** 401/539-7676, bases its operations in the historic **Bell School House,** Rtes. 112 and 138, a one-room schoolhouse still with many of its early furnishings, plus documents and memorabilia pertaining to the region's history.

A short way southwest along Route 138 and you'll hit the actual village of Hopkinton, which had been part of Westerly until separating as its own town in 1757, named for then-governor Stephen Hopkins. It has been planned as a major town, as it sits along what had been the main turnpike from New London to Providence and Newport, but is largely an agrarian area. In the mid-19th century the main business here was a sleigh and carriage manufacturer

SHOPPING

You'll find none of the sprawling superstores and shopping centers common in Warwick and coastal South County in these parts—nor are there many commercial districts of any significance. However, there are several excellent pick-your-own farms, and a few villages, especially Chepachet and North Scituate, have become notable hubs for antiques shopping.

Richmond Antiques Center, 318 Kingstown Rd., Wyoming, 401/539-0350, is popular for its auctions—there are two floors of dealers. The **Hope Valley Antiques Center,** 1081 Main St., 401/539-0250, is a large, expansive showroom in a redbrick building. There are three floors of wares, and a penny

KENYON'S GRIST MILL

Rhode Islanders love their jonnycakes, and probably the most famous purveyor of the stone-ground cornmeal that's the main ingredient of jonnycake batter is the ancient Kenyon's Grist Mill, Old Usquepaug Rd., just off Rte. 138, five miles east of I-95 Exit 3, 401/783-4054 or 800-7-KENY-ON, www.kenyongristmill.com. Kenyon Corn Meal Company has been milling grist since the early 1700s, and the current operations are in a charmingly raffish clapboard building from 1886, with peeling red paint. It looks about as one imagined it must have more than a century ago, and the staff still grinds the meal the traditional way, using a massive granite millstone—it's great fun for visitors to watch the staff make the meal using a process that's remarkably similar to that which the indigenous tribes of New England used for centuries before Europeans arrived.

The mill employs ancient techniques but is often coming up with new meals and grains, which it grinds without any preservatives or additives. So whether you're an amateur baker or a real pro, or you just want to try making jonnycakes at home, this is the definitive source for meals and flours. Some favorite Kenyon's Grist Mill products, in addition to jonnycake meal, include buckwheat flour, scotch oat flour, buttermilk-honey pancake mix, quince jam, cinnamon apple jelly, whole quinoa, Rhode Island flint corn, Indian pudding, and local honey.

© ANDREW COLLINS

Hack and Livery General Store, Hope Valley

GREATER PROVIDENCE

candy section that keeps the younger customers happy. **Hack and Livery General Store,** 1006 Main St., 401/539-7033, is a typically locals-oriented business in little Hope Valley. Inside you can shop for penny candy, gifts, odds and ends, pottery, and all sorts of interesting collectibles and one-of-a-kind items. **URE Outfitters,** 1009 Main St., Hope Valley, 401/539-4050, in a brick warehouse, is an excellent source of outdoors gear and clothing and is close to several of western Rhode Island's recreation areas.

In a cavernous, vintage red barn in Glocester, **Cherry Valley Herb Farm,** 969 Snake Hill Rd., 401/568-8585, www.cherryvalleyherbfarm.com, sells a wide array of mostly country French collectibles, home furnishings, and garden accoutrements, plus gourmet jams and sauces and, as you would expect, a long list of herbs and spices. Another nearby spot with both a year-round Christmas Shop and also a wide array of toys, teddy bears, dolls, and gifts is **Johnson's Farm,** 33 Money Hill Rd., 401/568-1693. Inside the former post office of the village of Harmony (in

Glocester), the **Frogg's Nest,** 199 Putnam Pike (U.S. 44), 401/949-3791, houses several unusual shops that sell antiques and gifts.

Pick-Your-Own Farms

John and Cindy's Harvest Acres Farms, 425 Kingstown Rd., 401/789-8752, is an extensive farmstead with fresh honey, maple syrup, sweet corn, tomatoes, mums, milk, eggs, fresh fruit and jams, and pumpkins. Pick fresh fruit, fall pumpkins and Indian corn, and other seasonal goods at **The Junction,** 1194 Putnam Pike, Chepachet, 401/568-1825, www.the-junctiononline.com. Here you can also browse the extensive selection of garden statuary, candles, antique furnishings, and plants and flowers. Fresh strawberries, raspberries, sweet corn, pumpkins, and hay are the order of the day all summer long at **Salisbury Farm,** Route 14 at Plainfield Pike and Pippin Orchard Road, Johnston, 401/942-9741, which was founded in the 1800s and has been presided over by five generations of the Salisbury family. The farm also contains an intricate corn maze, the

ANTIQUES AND CRAFTS SHOPPING IN NORTH SCITUATE AND CHEPACHET

The towns in western Rhode Island tend to be fairly rural, with few formal attractions and shopping districts, but two charming exceptions have developed over the years, North Scituate and Chepachet. Both of these small, historic villages contain a number of well-preserved 18th- and 19th-century buildings, and both of them have become quite well-known for their first-rate antiques shopping.

In the center of North Scituate Village you'll find a nice range of antiques shops, including **Elsie's Antiques and Collectibles,** 180 Danielson Pike, 401/647-3371; and, in the same building, **J & M Hobbies,** 401/647-7778, a delightful nostalgic shop with vintage model railroad equipment, die-cast toy cars, crafts, puzzles, rockets, and other paraphernalia that may bring you back to your childhood. **Village Antiques,** 143 Danielson Pike (at Rte. 116), 401/647-7780, specializes in furnishings and decorative and fine arts from the mid-19th through mid-20th centuries, from Victorian to Arts and Crafts to Art Deco. Primitive artworks and collectibles are the focus of the **Colonial Homestead,** 174 Danielson Pike, 401/647-4883 or 401/934-3015, which occupies a tiny pale yellow clapboard building across from the post office.

In Chepachet, you can take classes at **Holidaze Stained Glass,** 6B Money Hill Rd., Chepachet,

401/568-5140, www.holidazestainedglass.com, a studio where art and gifts in stained glass are sold (and also custom-made). **Magnolias and Memories,** 171 Danielson Pike, Chepachet, 401/647-3335, occupies a fading Greek Revival house and is piled high with collectibles, crafts, and country gifts. Most everybody who visits Chepachet makes it a point to stop by the **Brown & Hopkins General Store,** 1179 Putnam Pike (U.S. 44), 401/568-4830, which opened in 1809 and is alleged to be the oldest continuously operating store in the nation. It's a good place to buy local foods and gourmet items, baskets and pottery, fine upholstered furniture and antiques, and Christmas decorations (displayed year-round).

You can browse for locally made candles of every kind and scent at the **Olde Newport Candle Co.,** Pinewood Park, U.S. 44, about 1 mile east of Chepachet village, 401/568-4209. **Rhode Island Custom Furniture Plus,** 844 Putnam Pike, Chepachet, 401/568-6384, makes wonderful handmade oak gliders and other classic furniture, plus picnic tables, swing sets, and outdoor pieces. Drop by the **Adirondack Trading Post,** Pinewood Park, U.S. 44, Chepachet, 401/568-4209, to examine the beautifully crafted fiberglass and wood-trim canoes and kayaks, outboard boats, and other great vessels for taking to Rhode Island's waters.

first of its kind in New England. About a mile of pathways cuts through four acres of corn rows—it's no easy feat finding your way out. In the fall, hayrides are given.

SPORTS AND RECREATION

What western Rhode Island lacks in formal attractions, it more than makes up for in opportunities for hiking, biking, fishing, and enjoying the outdoors. The Arcadia area is best known for its **Arcadia Management Area,** a 14,000-acre preserve that passes through Richmond, Hopkinton, and Exeter. There are two freshwater beaches along Beach Road (off Rte. 165) and also one at Browning Mill Pond (off Arcadia

Rd.). You can pursue everything from hunting and fishing to hiking, mountain-biking, and horseback-riding in this preserve.

Hope Valley's best kids' amusement is **Enchanted Forest,** Route 3, 401/539-7711, a family activity center with boat rides, a roller coaster, Ferris wheel, batting cage, miniature golf, and recreated scenes from nursery tales. You can pick fresh berries here, and also pat tame animals in the petting zoo.

Boating and Fishing

Anglers should check out the **Wood River,** the state's best trout-fishing stream—it meanders down through Exeter and Hope Valley, passing through the southwestern corner of the state before emptying into the Pawcatuck River in Westerly and flowing south to the ocean.

It's a great river for several reasons. There are both rapid and comparatively gentle stretches; at various points you'll pass through ponds and swamps and under dense canopies of woodland. You'll also encounter a few portages at dams, but these are generally short and easy. Access to the river is from several points. If you tackle the full navigable length of the river, it'll take a good seven hours by canoe or kayak (the river is nearly 14 miles long). One of the most popular put-ins is located off Route 165 in Exeter (follow it west from Route 3, just south of the I-95 overpass) toward Beach Pond State Park until you reach the bridge over the Wood River. This upper stretch is relatively brisk but without any rapids.

Another popular access point is Hope Valley Road Landing, just off Route 3 in the village of Hope Valley. From here it's a quite smooth run for about six miles down to Alton Dam. This lower stretch is especially picturesque, the riverbanks lined with dense maple and oak woodland and groves of laurel—bird- and other wildlife-watching are great pastimes from this point. The upper stretch, nearest the Route 165 bridge, is one of Rhode Island's top spots for trout-fishing, especially in the spring, when there's decent water flow.

Golfing

Western and southwestern Rhode Island, with its low population and hilly and scenic terrain, is the state's hub of golfing. One of the newest and most popular area courses is **Fenner Hill Golf Club,** 33 Wheeler Lane, Hope Valley, 401/539-8000, opened in 1999 and has quickly developed a following for its rolling layout and well-kept grounds. **Foxwoods Golf & Country Club at Boulder Hills,** 87 Kingstown Rd. (Rte. 138), Richmond, 401/539-4653, which is run by the Mashantucket Pequot Tribal Nation in nearby Ledyard, Connecticut, offers a challenging and picturesque layout. It can get very crowded on weekends, as this is one of the state's top golfing draws. Greens fees are also among the state's highest.

Richmond Country Club, 74 Sandy Point Rd., Richmond, 401/364-9200, opened in 1991 and sharpens golfers' skills with several difficult water hazards. Towering evergreens line the fairways, punishing errant drives. **Foster Country Club,** 67 Johnson Rd., Foster, 401/397-7750, offers an open layout with relatively few sand traps and hazards; it's less difficult than most of the others in the region. It's also less crowded than most, making it a nice alternative. The back 9 requires a little more finesse, as the fairways are narrower. Charming for its covered bridges and picturesque waterways, **Exeter Country Club,** 320 Ten Rod Rd., Exeter, 401/295-8212, runs long and can get fairly crowded. But it's a pretty day of golf, if you don't mind slow playing conditions on weekends.

Hiking

Some of the best area hikes are in Hope Valley around **Blue Pond, Long Pond,** and **Ell Pond.** Marked trails meander around these lakes and through groves of hemlock and clusters of rhododendrons. Long Pond makes for an especially nice hike—just follow Route 138 west from Hope Valley, turning left at Rockville village onto Canonchet Road. After about a mile you'll come to a parking area for the Narragansett Trail, which leads west along the south shore of Long Pond. From the same parking area, a different walk cuts south toward Asheville Pond. The terrain in these parts is somewhat challenging, sometimes passing over steep rock ledges and leading to relatively high bluffs.

In Ashaway, **Crandall's Field** makes for a nice stroll and has an enormous playground for kids. This informal town common is also the site of the Swamp Yankee Days Festival and occasional crafts shows. There's a pond here, and woods beyond it.

Another excellent spot for a ramble is Exeter's **Beach Pond,** which lies half in Rhode Island's Beach Pond State Forest and half in Voluntown, Connecticut's Pachaug State Forest (access is off Route 165, about six miles west of Route 3). From the parking area you'll head to marked trails of varying lengths that climb up through hemlock and birch forest, around the north shore of the pond, and through some quite steep valleys. An additional network of trails meanders south of the pond, nearly as far as Route 138. These blazed trails cross several scenic stream beds and wooded glens. The pond is also a popular spot for fishing and boating. This is one of several popular hiking areas off Route 165, which cuts through some of the state's prettiest and least populated terrain. Other hikes to consider are the Mt. Tom, Bald Hill, and Stepstone Falls trails.

ACCOMMODATIONS

While there are a few run-down motels in this part of the state (avoid any place that advertises waterbeds, weekly rates, or—as if you need the warning—hourly rates), you're more likely to find good places to stay in South County, which is easily accessible from Hope Valley, Richmond, and Wyoming; and Warwick and Cranston, which puts you close to the rest of the region. Otherwise, there are a few decent hotels in West Greenwich, and a few smaller inns scattered about the region.

Hotels and Motels

$50–100: Best Western West Greenwich Inn, 101 Nooseneck Hill Rd., West Greenwich, 401/397-5494 or 800/528-1234, www.best-western.com, is one of the best lodging options in these parts. The 56-room hotel tends to have rates comparable to the local, less desirable Super 8. It's on attractive, wooded grounds and has a restaurant on-site. The **Super 8,** 101 Nooseneck Hill Rd., West Greenwich, 401/397-3381 or 800/800-8000, www.super8.com, another discount option, is just next door.

Country Inns and B&Bs

$50–100: A simple, relatively modern home in a lovely pine-shaded setting in the sparsely populated Carolina section of Richmond, **Country Acres B&B,** 176 Townhouse Rd., Richmond, 401/364-1800, has two rooms, which share a bath. There's a large outdoor pool

in back, as well as a barbecue pit. Full breakfast is included. A delightful 1790s home, **Millstone Farm B&B,** 410 Plain Meeting House Rd., West Greenwich, 401/397-7737 or 401/397-6517, www.intap/net/~rbutler, offers perhaps the most distinctive and historic accommodations in the region. The center-chimney, Cape-style home has antiques-filled rooms. One grand feature is the greenhouse, in which there's an in-ground swimming pool. You can wander some 24 acres of wooded grounds with impressive landscaping—ideal for hiking and fishing in warmer months and cross-country skiing and ice-skating in winter.

Campgrounds

Greenwood Hill Family Campground, Newberry Lane, Hope Valley, 401/539-7154, occupies a pastoral, secluded setting surrounding a pond and field in quiet Hopeville. It has full RV hookups, a general store, and children's activities.

FOOD

There are a handful of inviting little restaurants in this region, plus a fairly typical array of family-friendly restaurants, neighborhood pizzerias, and the occasional fast-food restaurant (especially in Johnston along Route 6A and in Wyoming just off I-95 at Route 138).

Creative but Casual

At the **Purple Cat,** in Stafford Yard, Rtes. 100 and 102 and U.S. 44, Chepachet, 401/568-7161 ($7–18), tempting blackboard specials are presented daily. This classy and distinctive country restaurant has been open since the late 1920s. It has several cozy dining areas with beamed ceilings, wooden booths and tables, a fireplace, and Colonial-style furnishings. Expect a long menu with everything from simple pasta with homemade meatballs to fresh seafood like snow crab-and-lobster pie, plus steaks, broiled lamb chops, and stuffed clams. A relative newcomer in inviting Harmony, **Chester's,** 102 Putnam Pike (U.S. 44), 401/949-1846 ($7–13), doles out estimable portions of comfort foods, many of the dishes with nouvelle tendencies, including veal saltimbocca, chicken sautéed with sun-dried tomatoes, mushrooms, and pasta with a pink cream sauce, and scallops Nantucket baked with bacon and cheddar. Burgers are a big hit, as is the fried calamari. A fieldstone fireplace warms the dining room.

Pizzas, Pastas, and Pub Grub

Gentlemen Farmer Restaurant, 2405 Nooseneck Hill Rd., Coventry, 401/392-0130 ($3–11), is a delightful little stone-and-timber pizzeria and diner where all the locals hang out, and the waitresses call you "hon." There's a long and varied menu and portions are huge and well-priced, with about 20 kinds of grinder, a variety of pizzas, seafood platters, bacon burgers, hot dogs, Greek salads, and barbecued pork sandwiches. Most of this stuff will give your arteries a good hardening, but it's tasty cooking. Also locations at 50 Danielson Pike, Scituate, 401/647-7774 or 401/647-7775; and 617 Putnam Poke, Chepachet, 401/568-3335 or 401/568-3336. The **Stagecoach Tavern,** 1157 Main St., Chepachet, 401/568-2275 ($8–16), serves mostly traditional American dishes (steaks, honey-roasted chicken, fried seafood, pizzas) plus some kicky Cajun specialties like pan-blackened scallops. Plenty of customers come here for a taste of history too; during the Dorr Rebellion, shots were fired through the keyhole of this early 18th-century tavern, where Dorr and his men sought refuge from the state militia. Old pots and pans and paintings and portraits are hung throughout the low-ceilinged, cozy dining rooms with wide-board floors and vintage furnishings.

T's Pizzeria, 1417 Atwood Ave., Johnston, 401/464-9700 (large pies $8–14, entrées and sandwiches under $6) is a wonderful little find in a shopping center off otherwise dreary Route 5 in Johnston. The festive dining room painted in earthy tones recalls a little country cottage in Tuscany, and the service is super-friendly. A popular specialty pie is the Charles Street (with Italian sausage, eggplant, pepperoni, meatballs, and mozzarella); also note the spinach-cheese-steak wraps, the chicken parmesan grinders, the lasagna roll calzone, and the steak sandwiches.

Ethnic Fare

Behind a striking red facade with ornate wood carvings, **China Jade,** 1511 Atwood Ave., Johnston, 401/273-6220 ($6–13), has a somewhat less-inspired dining room and fairly standard but decently prepared Cantonese fare: diced chicken with peanuts, sweet-and-sour squid, pork with onions and scallions, bean curd with oyster sauce, and the inevitable orange beef.

Quick Bites

You can't miss **Cindy's Diner,** 46 Hartford Ave., North Scituate, 401/934-2449 (under $8) with its glittering pink, blue, and yellow neon sign. It's a big hit with the breakfast crowd. **Shady Acres Restaurant and Dairy Bar,** 164 Danielson Pike, 401/647-7019 (under $6), in Foster, is a typical roadside short-order eatery with a long menu of delicious home-baked pies and ice creams. Burgers and fried seafood are also offered. **Sal's Pizza and Grinders,** 410 Kingstown Rd., 401/782-8855 (under $5) serves Del's Frozen Lemonade and ranks among the better options for a snack along Route 138. A homey little bakery that's champion of the local pastry delicacy known as the Bismarck, **West's Bakery,** 995 Main St., 401/539-2451, lies right in the heart of Hope Valley and also serves tasty grinders and excellent ice cream (the peanut buttah! parfait makes a memorable treat). If you find yourself hungry out near Arcadia Management Area, there's always the **Middle of Nowhere Diner,** 222 Nooseneck Hill Rd. (U.S. 3), Exeter, 401/397-8855 (under $6), a simple clapboard eatery with tasty short-order cooking.

Java Joints

Contempo Coffees, 1428 Hartford Pike, 401/272-1960, is a cheerful sun-filled coffeehouse at the busy intersection of Route 6A and U.S. 5, in Johnston.

Gourmet Goods and Picnic Supplies

If you've got kids in tow, definitely check out **Lickety Splits,** 39 Kingstown Rd., Wyoming, 401/539-9047, a sweets shop and ice cream stand with extensive selection of goodies. It's on Route 138 just east of I-95, occupying a pair of gray clapboard cottages. Take a break from shopping at the **General Store and Cafe,** 13 Putnam Pike (U.S. 44), Harmony Village, 401/949-0985 ($3–8), which offers light homemade sandwiches, soups, coffees, ice cream, and other sweet little delectables like fudge, biscotti, and cocoa. There's seating on a large country porch, out in the exquisite gardens, and also inside by the hot stove or in the tearoom. And if you simply can't take your mind off browsing, the General Store also carries a huge array of gourmet goods, repro and authentic antiques, folk paintings and crafts, and fine bath goods and toiletries.

FESTIVALS AND EVENTS

Befitting a region rife with arts and crafts galleries, the **Scituate Art Festival,** 401/647-5487, attracts more than 100,000 enthusiasts every Columbus Day weekend—about 200 stalls set up along the Village Green and the several handsome streets that emanate from the main drag, Route 116. Also come to enjoy the live music and great food.

INFORMATION AND SERVICES

Visitor Information

For information on the towns of Glocester, North Scituate, and Foster, contact the **Blackstone Valley Tourism Council,** 171 Main St., Pawtucket, 401/724-2200 or 800/454-2882, www.tourblackstone.com. For information on Coventry, Richmond, and Hopkinton, contact the South County Tourism Council, 4808 Tower Hill Rd., Wakefield, 401/789-4422 or 800/548-4662, www.southcountyri.com.

Getting Around

Although you can reach this area by Amtrak, 800/USA-RAIL, www.amtrak.com, using the stops at Westerly or Kingston, you'll need a car to explore most of this region, part of which is bisected by I-95, and other sections by U.S. 6 and U.S. 44. You'll rarely encounter traffic jams in this part of the state, but you should prepare for the occasional unpaved (though maintained) road, especially in some of the sections popular for hiking and canoeing.

Cranston and Warwick

Rhode Island's most densely populated suburbs, Cranston and Warwick lie immediately south of Providence and contain high concentrations of shopping malls and stripmalls, chain restaurants and motels, and busy roads lined with traffic lights. Warwick is also home to T. F. Green Airport, New England's third-busiest airport. Although it's crowded and in many places prosaic, these middle- to upper-middle-class bedroom communities are not without their charms. Both towns lie along Narragansett Bay and have several interesting and historic residential neighborhoods near the water. And, especially in Warwick, you'll find several villages with their own personalities, histories, and walkable commercial districts. The towns also contain the nearest public beaches to Providence, and just south of Warwick, the all-American community of East Greenwich has a delightfully charming downtown with hip eateries and a smattering of cool boutiques.

Cranston

Cranston lies immediately southwest of and is easily reached from the capital via I-95 or Route 10. The area was settled in 1638 by associates of Roger Williams who included William Harris, Zachariah Rhodes, and William Arnold (the progenitor of the traitorous Revolutionary War general Benedict Arnold). Harris waged a battle with Roger Williams asserting that his township was not under the jurisdiction of Providence. The land was then known as Pawtuxet, and in 1754 this and the adjacent settlements joined to form the town of Cranston (named for the governor of Rhode Island from 1698 to 1727, Samuel Cranston). It was incorporated as a city in 1910, having thrived as a textile-manufacturing center during the 19th and early 20th centuries.

It's almost impossible to tell the eastern reaches of Cranston from Providence, as they're

To Nicole's Bistro and
Carmine's Sub Shop

MARCHETTI'S

WEST END
CAFE

To Haven
Hill Cafe

To Twin
Oaks

Cunliff
Lake

12

10

Cranston

PROVIDENCE

EDGEWOOD
MANOR

Knightsville

To Pippin Orchard
Nurseries and Farms

12

Wayland

2

RAINBOW
BAKERY

Auburn

5

EFENDI'S
MEDITERRANEAN
GRILL

Meshanticut

CULINARY
AFFAIR

295

Garden
City

95

Fenner
Pond

1

Pawtuxet River

Lakewood

PAPA RAZZI

CRANSTON

1A

117

Posneganset
Pond

Oaklawn

BARNEY'S

37

MOTEL 6
FAIRFIELD INN

Norwood

Sand
Pond

Spring
Green

2

0   0.5 mi
0   0.5 km

HARUKI

Pawtuxet River

Lincoln Park

SHERATON INN
PROVIDENCE AIRPORT

COMFORT INN

Hoxsie

Pontiac

295

5

PONTIAC
MILLS

RESIDENCE INN
BY MARRIOTT

RADISSON AIRPORT HOTEL
LEGAL SEA FOODS

AIRPORT
CONNECTOR

HOLIDAY INN
EXPRESS

HAMPTON INN
MASTER HOSTS INN

JEFFERSON BLVD.

THEODORE FRANCIS GREEN
STATE AIRPORT

Warwick
Pond

117A

WARWICK
MALL

RHODE
ISLAND
MALL

95

East
Natick

2

CROWNE
PLAZA

113

WARWICK

1

Greenwood

MICKEY STEVENS
SPORTS COMPLEX

SANDY LN.

115

Gorton
Pond

Little
Pond

Wildes
Corner

117

Apponaug

WARWICK MUSEUM

WARWICK CITY HALL

117

PETER'S CONEY
ISLAND SYSTEM

To East
Greenwich

117

REMINGTON
HOUSE INN

To Ward's
Publick House

Nausauket

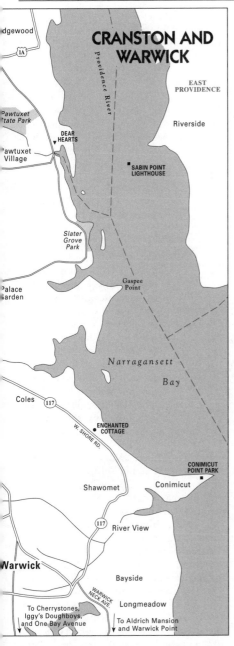

CRANSTON AND WARWICK

EAST PROVIDENCE

Riverside

DEAR HEARTS

SABIN POINT LIGHTHOUSE

Slater Grove Park

Gaspee Point

Palace Garden

Narragansett Bay

Coles 117

ENCHANTED COTTAGE

W. SHORE RD.

CONIMICUT POINT PARK

Shawomet   Conimicut

River View 117

Warwick

Bayside

WARWICK NECK AVE.

To Cherrystones, Iggy's Doughboys, and One Bay Avenue   Longmeadow

To Aldrich Mansion and Warwick Point

both densely settled with old homes and factories. Historically, major factories produced cotton, mill machinery, brass and copper tubing, and fire extinguishers. The city's earliest industrial enterprise of any significance was the Cranston Print Works, which went up in 1824 and printed finished textiles.

Warwick

It's almost incorrect to call Warwick a suburb—this full-fledged city is one of the state's most prominent communities, as it's home to Rhode Island's main airport and has a population of some 90,000 (second only to Providence). Like many of the state's communities, Warwick actually comprises several small village centers rather than one coherent core. It became a city in 1931. Borders of Warwick include West Warwick, Cranston, East Greenwich, and North Kingstown, along 39 miles of Narragansett Bay and its rivers and inlets. The eastern part of town fringes Narragansett Bay and has several fine beaches.

Through the early 20th century, mills—engaged in dyeing, bleaching, and finishing—employed many of Warwick's workers, but even back a century ago many residents commuted to Providence and other nearby towns, and it has remained a bedroom community ever since. From 1920 to 1930 Warwick boomed—it was the fastest-growing town in all of New England, growing from 13,000 to 23,000 residents.

Warwick was founded in 1641 by a determined political and religious dissident from Massachusetts named Samuel Gorton, who left a trail of insubordination wherever he ventured, from Boston to Plymouth to Pocasset (now Portsmouth), Rhode Island. By today's standards he comes off as a pretty rational guy—one move that earned him the wrath of authorities was his defense of a servant who had been censured for cracking a grin during a church service. The Puritans, of course, weren't much either for humor or humanity. Gorton made an effort to settle in Providence, the seeming haven of all renegades, but even there he could not conform to the relatively loose governing of Roger Williams.

Gorton was not without admirers, however; and on his departure from Providence he assembled a fairly loyal posse of like-minded rebels and, after participating in a riot in the fall of 1641, fled with his group to Pawtuxet (so named for the river that today divides Warwick from its northern neighbor, Cranston), which had but a handful of inhabitants.

As a means of evading the jurisdiction of the Massachusetts Bay and Providence Colonies, Gorton purchased land from the Shawomet and Miantonomi Indians, but he continued to incur the harassment of the Massachusetts Bay crowd, which challenged the legality of the purchase and ultimately arrested Gorton and brought him to Boston to be tried on a variety of trumped-up charges, all vaguely involving blasphemy. Gorton and his cohorts were found guilty and nearly condemned to death but instead served a fairly short time in prison; they were then expelled from the colony. Gorton and a colleague, Randall Holden, took up on Aquidneck Island for a time, before sailing to England in hopes of securing royal backing in their efforts to return to their Pawtuxet lands. It was abroad that Robert Rich, Earl of Warwick, chief member of the Parliamentary Committee of Foreign Plantations, warmed to the two iconoclastic colonists and interceded on their behalf. Gorton and Holden returned to their new Warwick Colony, whose existence had been guaranteed by the British crown.

The following year, 1647, the Rhode Island General Assembly convened in Portsmouth to organize a unified charter recognizing the settlements as Newport, Providence, and Portsmouth as forming one commonwealth. While they didn't name Warwick on the charter, they did agree that the new colony—with its British recognition—should have the same privileges as Providence.

A town meeting house wasn't erected in Warwick until the mid-1670s, the same decade that King Philip's War presented such grave danger that the residents fled for a time to Aquidneck Island. But by the end of the decade, mills had begun operating along the Pawtuxet River. Following U.S. independence, Warwick developed into a major center of textile production, particularly in the Anthony, Hope, Natick, Crompton, Phenix, and Arctic sections of the original town (parts of which are now West Warwick and Coventry).

The city's civic center is historic **Apponaug Village,** where you'll find the dramatic 1894 **Warwick City Hall,** 3275 Post Rd. (U.S. 1), 401/728-2000, which is crowned with an imposing six-story clock tower. Practically next door, the **Warwick Museum,** 3259 Post Rd. (U.S. 1), 401/737-0010, which was built in 1912 as the Kentish Artillery Armory, presents rotating art and some history exhibits throughout the year. There are more than 30 buildings of historic or architectural distinction in the village—you can learn more about them by obtaining the free "Walking Tour of Historic Apponaug Village" booklet distributed by the Warwick Convention and Visitors Bureau, which produces a similar booklet on Pawtuxet Village.

It is from Pawtuxet Village that a party of local patriots attacked the grounded British revenue schooner **Gaspee,** *one of several early acts of defiance against the Crown in New England that ultimately led to the American Revolution.*

Pawtuxet Village is Warwick's oldest village and contains a number of fine old colonial homes, most of them along Narragansett Avenue and the roads that intersect it. It is from Pawtuxet that a party of local patriots attacked the grounded British revenue schooner *Gaspee,* one of several early acts of defiance against the Crown in New England that ultimately led to the American Revolution. Since 1966 Pawtuxet has hosted the annual *Gaspee* Days celebration, held from May through June.

Warwick is perhaps best known as the home of **T. F. Green Airport..** The city's aviation history extends back many years. An airfield opened in 1928 and was dedicated the state airport just a few years later, at which time paved runways and a terminal were added. A new terminal went up in 1961, and an expansion in 1996 saw the creation of a second terminal.

Conimicut Village, an early fishing enclave that developed into a fashionable summer colony around the late 19th century, has gradually shifted into a laid-back, upper-middle-class suburb of attractive homes, many dating back to the early part of the 20th century. There's great strolling along the bay and by Conimicut Park and Lighthouse, which pokes out into the Narragansett Bay and overlooks Patience and Prudence Islands. Over Labor Day weekend, some 30,000 people attend the Conimicut Festival, a lively crafts and food festival. Sitting just offshore from the village, **Conimicut Lighthouse** sits along a rocky ledge by Conimicut Point Park. You can't visit this 1868 structure, but it cuts a dashing figure in the bay. In 1960 the lighthouse was changed from kerosene to electric power—it was the last lighthouse in the nation to convert to electricity.

Warwick has one other impressive lighthouse, at the tip of Warwick Neck. This 51-foot cast-iron tower was built in 1932, the last traditional lighthouse constructed in Rhode Island. It's now operated by the Coast Guard. Warwick Neck is one of the city's fanciest neighborhoods, the appropriate setting for one of the state's most imposing estates, even compared with those in Newport, the **Aldrich Mansion,** 836 Warwick Neck Ave., 401/739-6850, www.aldrichmansion.com. This 75-acre estate on Narragansett Bay was the home of one of Rhode Island's greatest political figures, Sen. Nelson W. Aldrich. On this estate, John D. Rockefeller Jr. married Aldrich's daughter, Abby, thus setting in motion one of the nation's more formidable political-industrial dynasties. The couple's son, Nelson Rockefeller, later served as Vice President of the United States. It took more than 200 craftsmen more than 15 years to build this lavish 70-room mansion, which was completed in 1912. Today the mansion is rented out for weddings, business meetings, and other functions—it con-

tains a fine collection of art, and all the original detailed woodworking has been carefully restored. The house starred alongside Brad Pitt in *Meet Joe Black* in 1997.

Potowomut

To reach one of the most interesting parts of Warwick, you have to get out of town. Potowomut occupies a peninsula south of Warwick proper, fringing the shoreline of East Greenwich. You reach it by driving south of U.S. 1 through downtown East Greenwich, and then make a left onto Forge Road, and another left onto Ives Road. Most of this land was used for raising cattle during colonial times, and Revolutionary War hero Nathanael Greene was born on the peninsula. At the tip of the peninsula is a small residential neighborhood with a mix of new and old homes, many of them overlooking the bay.

The big draw here is **Goddard Memorial State Park,** Ives Road, 401/884-2010, the site of an ambitious tree-growing project undertaken by the late-19th-century owner of this land, Henry Russell, and continued by the subsequent owner, Col. William Goddard. By 1920 the U.S. Forest Service declared it the most impressive example of private forestry in the nation. Goddard died in 1927 and left about 500 acres of this choice waterside forest to the state, and so the park was born. Today you can stroll or ride horseback through the park's many trails, admiring the fruits of Russell's and Goddard's labors. There's also a fine beach along Greenwich Bay, complete with changing facilities, as well as a nine-hole golf course. Concerts are given during the warmer months in the park's restored carousel pavilion, right by the beach. Admission is $3 per car in summer.

East Greenwich

Downtown East Greenwich is lined with pretty, mostly Victorian, buildings and has some good shopping and dining. There's not a whole lot to see and do here, but it's worth a detour just to stroll around.

SHOPPING

Warwick is a shopping hub for the state, although you won't necessarily find a huge number of independent stores. Still, if you're looking for the nearest outpost of your favorite chain, drive along Route 2, where—among more than 200 other shops—you'll find Filene's, Radio Shack, CompUSA, Home Depot, Sam's Club, Barnes & Noble, Pier 1 Imports, Pro Golf Discount, KMart, and a Christmas Tree Shop. Also along here are two large if fairly run-of-the-mill indoor shopping malls, **Warwick Mall,** 400 Bald Hill Rd., 401/739-6772, and **Rhode Island Mall,** Rtes. 2 and 113, 401/828-7651. More interesting, especially from an aesthetic perspective, is **Historic Pontiac Mills,** 334 Knight St., 401/737-2700. This former textile mill along the Pawtuxet River was the home of Fruit of the Loom underwear (the owners chose the name "Fruit of the Loom" as an easy-to-identify symbol that even illiterate consumers would remember). Today the several buildings contain a slew of intriguing, independent shops and galleries, most of them selling antiques and arts. Several of these offer fine metalworks, while others specialize in sculpture, cabinet-making and refinishing, interior design, pianos, photography, tapestries and wall hangings, caning, ceramics and pottery, guitars, watercolor, and custom framing. Of particular note is **Decorum,** Historic Pontiac Mills, 334 Knight St., Building 1, 401/732-8898, where you can browse through room after room of very cool reproduction antiques and unusual objets d'art, Oriental rugs, and housewares. Plans are under way to completely overhaul the Mills and add a hotel, a new restaurant, offices, and more space for shops.

Pick-Your-Own Farms

Pippin Orchard Nurseries and Farms, 1199 Pippin Orchard Rd., Cranston, 401/828-0358, offers some of the best blueberry picking around.

Miscellany

Another good shopping spot in Warwick is **Ferns and Flowers Tea House & Gardens,** 1094 Centreville Rd., 401/821-1447, www.ftd.com/fernsandflowers, where you can do more than browse for flowers, plants, and related gifts. In the sprawling clapboard Colonial house and its outbuildings you can also come for breakfast, lunch, and afternoon tea (reservations required). Special guest-chef breakfasts and luncheons are also given from time to time. Also stop by to check out the selection of handmade candies and rich cakes and sweets.

SPORTS AND RECREATION

Warwick has several beaches, including **Goddard Memorial State Park** and 126-acre **Warwick City Park,** which has a saltwater beach, changing facilities, bike paths, hiking, and ball fields. It's said, although not verified, that the very first clambake was held here in the late 1800s. Sheltered **Oakland Beach,** at the southern tip of Oakland Avenue, off Route 117, is a smaller swath of sand.

The **Mickey Stevens Sports Complex,** 975 Sandy Lane, 401/738-2000, ext. 6806 (ext. 6800 for events information), is Warwick's recreation facility, with a public ice-skating/rollerblading rink, a one-mile walking/jogging path, basketball courts, eight lighted tennis courts, and two volleyball courts, plus a public swimming pool.

Boating

Warwick is interior Rhode Island's boating capital, with more marinas, moorings, and slips than any other city in the state. Some of the larger marinas include **Apponaug Harbor Marina,** 17 Arnold's Neck Dr., 401/739-5005, 204 slips and 30 moorings; **Brewer Yacht Club,** 100 Folly Landing, 401/884-0544, 240 slips and 10 moorings; **C-Lark Marina,** 252 Second Point Rd., 401/739-3871, 350 slips; **Greenwich Bay Marina,** 1 Masthead Dr., 401/884-1810, 320 moorings; and **Norton's Shipyard,** foot of Division Street, 401/884-8828, 160 slips and 160 moorings.

Cycling

The **Cranston Bike Path** offers nearly five miles of pancake-flat terrain, extending along a former railway. Parking is on the Cranston/Warwick border just off Pontiac Avenue (below I-295).

Golf
Goddard Park Beach Golf Course, at Goddard State Park, Ives Road, 401/884-9834, is a nine-hole public course that's open mid-April through late November. A windswept, fairly level course that runs fairly long, **Cranston Country Club,** 69 Burlingame Rd., 401/826-1683, is known for its sizable greens that demand skillful putting.

ACCOMMODATIONS
Because it's just south of Providence and is the site of T. F. Green Airport, Warwick has a bounty of chain motels and hotels, most of them quite nice if somewhat nondescript. These places offer an affordable alternative to the few pricey properties in downtown Providence, but none of them occupy particular charming settings, nor can you walk to shops or restaurants from them. There are a few small inns as well, worth checking out if you're seeking a place with a little more personality.

Hotels and Motels
$50–100: Next to Hampton Inn at the airport, and with rates that average $50 less per night, the **Master Hosts Inn,** 2138 Post Rd., Warwick, 401/737-7400 or 800/251-1962, has 103 units, including a few suites with wet bars and refrigerators. The property's slogan, "luxury for less," is a bit optimistic, but the rooms are pleasantly decorated as far as economy chains go, and the staff is consistently helpful and friendly. Just three miles north of the airport, you'll find the region's two least expensive chain properties, the **Motel 6,** 20 Jefferson Blvd., Warwick, 401/467-9800 or 800/4-MOTEL-6, www.motel6.com, and the **Fairfield Inn,** 36 Jefferson Blvd., Warwick, 401/941-6600 or 800/228-2800. Both of these are perfectly fine if you just need a cheap clean bed for the night. The most impressive of the lower-priced properties in these parts, the **Holiday Inn Express,** 901 Jefferson Blvd., 401/736-5000 or 800/HOLIDAY, opened in

2001 just off the Post Road, west of the airport. There are 147 rooms, including 31 suites, plus full business services, an indoor pool, a small gym, and a hot tub.

$100–150: The only one of the upper-price chain properties that's not directly facing the airport, the upscale **Crowne Plaza,** 801 Greenwich Ave., Warwick, 401/732-6000 or 800/2-CROWNE, sits two miles southwest, near I-95's Exit 12, on an attractively landscaped 80-acre plot. Rates start below $150 but often climb into the low $200s (weekends are usually slightly less expensive), and business travelers make up the bulk of the clientele. They appreciate the many amenities, including free shuttle service to the airport, a popular wine bar with 24 vintages served by the glass, an indoor pool and fitness center, a full business center, and a sauna and whirlpool. The facilities are in tip-top shape, the rooms large and well-equipped, and the staff friendly if not necessarily more efficient than the employees at most of the less pricey chain properties by the airport. Weekend packages are sometimes offered, in which certain meals are included. And the restaurant presents a lavish Sunday brunch that's well-attended by both guests and nonguests. The Crowne Plaza's most obvious competitor, the 207-room **Sheraton Inn Providence Airport,** 1850 Post Rd., Warwick, 401/738-4000 or 800/325-3535, www.sheraton.com, occupies a rather dated-looking building within view of the airport and offers rates generally about 10 percent to 25 percent lower. Rest assured that once you're past the drab exterior you'll find a brightly furnished and well-managed contemporary property with about 200 nicely proportioned rooms, a restaurant, fitness center, and indoor pool.

Rates at the **Hampton Inn,** 2100 Post Road, Warwick, 401/739-8888 or 800/HAMPTON, www.hampton-inn.com, run about the same as the others along this stretch but sometimes creep a bit higher. Given this, and consider the beautifully kept guest rooms and public spaces, this is an excellent choice, whether you just need a night close to the airport or you're seeking out a good base for visiting the entire region. Rooms are homey, with high-quality furnishings, and a fireplace warms a lobby lounge that you'd feel comfortable reading or relaxing in (not the case of many hotel lobbies). Amenities include indoor pool, Continental breakfast, gym, whirlpool, business center, game room, two-line phones, and coffeemakers. Along the same stretch, the **Comfort Inn,** 1940 Post Rd., Warwick, 401/732-0470 or 800/228-5150, sits right next Bertucci's Pizza and Atwood Grill (casual American food) but has few other distinguishing features. Considering its rates are no lower, typically, than the Sheraton's or Hampton Inn's, it should be booked as a last choice. There's nothing especially wrong with it, but the decor, staff, and amenities are just so-so. Some rooms do have whirlpool baths, however. Nearly across the street from the airport entrance, the **Radisson Airport Hotel,** 2081 Post Rd., Warwick, 401/739-3000 or 800/333-3333, www.radisson.com, has rates that are comparable to or sometimes even better than its competitors. It nearly adjoins Legal Seafoods and also has its own decent restaurant, and about 40 suites have whirlpool baths and wet bars. There's also a business center. It's a fairly ordinary-looking building, but the big plus here is that the hotel is staffed by young and enthusiastic students from the Johnson & Wales hospitality program, which means you can usually count on highly responsive and cheerful service, as well as clean rooms.

There are a couple of properties in town better suited to longer-term guests (usually business travelers, but these can be good choices for families and leisure travelers, too). The **Residence Inn by Marriott,** 500 Kilvert St., Warwick, 401/737-7100 or 800/331-3131, www.marriott.com, lies a half-mile west of the airport, just off I-95. In West Warwick, **SpringHill Suites by Marriott,** 14 J.P. Murphy Hwy., 401/822-1244 or 888/287-9400, www.springhillsuites.com, also caters to long-term stays. Each unit has separate sleeping, eating, and working areas (as well as a sleeper sofa). Other amenities include in-room refrigerators, microwaves, coffeemakers, and wet bars; plus on-site exercise room and indoor pool.

Country Inns and B&Bs

$50–100: A great alternative to Warwick's many chain properties, the **Enchanted Cottage,** 16 Beach Ave., 401/732-0439, is a restored Cape Anne in charming Conimicut Village, overlooking Narragansett Bay. Choose from three rooms (which share a bath), each with fine British antiques, fine crystal and lace, handmade quilts and blankets, and well-chosen collectibles. The neighborhood features quiet, oak-shaded lanes and sidewalks—joggers and walkers are a common scene along these roads. It's just four miles east of the airport, and 10 miles south of downtown Providence, making it a good choice for experiencing the region.

$100–150: In Cranston, the 18-room **Edgewood Manor,** 232 Norwood Ave., 401/781-0099 or 800/882-3285, is a grand early 1900s Greek Revival mansion with five beautifully crafted fireplaces and ornate architectural detailing. Rooms and suites carry out the building's lavish theme, with plush linens, Oriental rugs, four-poster beds, neatly framed paintings and prints, paneled walls, and high-style Victorian antiques.

FOOD

Warwick has dozens of restaurants, many of them chains, and many of these along the busy retail strip of Route 2. Along here you'll find Pizzeria Uno, Red Lobster, Olive Garden, Lone Star Steakhouse, and Friday's, among many others. Warwick, Cranston, and East Greenwich are somewhat upscale suburbs, so quite a few notable chefs have opened restaurants in these parts in recent years, especially in East Greenwich's quaint downtown.

Upscale

One of the better known dining options in these parts, the **Post Office Cafe,** 11 Main St., East Greenwich, 401/885-4444 ($12–26), actually occupies the town's circa-1930 post office. It's a bright, high-ceilinged space with friendly, refined service. The same owners operate the Grille on Main, Pinelli's, and several other great Rhode Island restaurants. You might start with grilled rosemary shrimp with baby pear tomatoes and bocconcini, served with a champagne-garlic-butter sauce. The Post Office bouillabaisse has a loyal following, as does the slow-simmered porcini-mushroom risotto with truffle oil. The signature entrée is diver sea scallops saltimbocca, wrapped in prosciutto and served over parmesan whipped potatoes and sautéed spinach with crisp-fried sage and a fresh-garlic demi-glace. There's an impressive wine list, too. This place fills up fast on weekends—book well ahead. A dimly lit, snazzy space with an exhibition kitchen and a lively dining room with Oriental rugs, tile floors, and tables set with floral centerpieces, **Nicole's Bistro,** 555 Atwood Ave., Cranston, 401/944-2500; also 198 Putnam Pike (U.S. 44), Johnston, 401/231-2440 ($13–19), serves a fairly ambitious menu of Continental fare, including swordfish puttanesca, roasted cod over shiitake mushroom–scallion risotto in a roasted-tomato broth, lobster alfredo, braised lamb shank, and gourmet brick-oven pizzas. Excellent Mediterranean and Greek fare is served at **Efendi's Mediterranean Grill,** 1255 Reservoir Ave., Cranston, 401/943-8800 ($11–19), a laid-back restaurant with sophisticated cooking that rises above its casual environs. Specialties include rack of lamb confit with a fresh-herb red wine sauce; Turkish *izgara kofte* (ground beef with spices and vegetables served with tzatziki); and seafood kabobs. Pita sandwiches are offered at lunch, and the Sunday brunch draws a sizable crowd for a mix of traditional breakfast fare and more savory grills and egg creations.

Creative but Casual

The **Grille on Main,** 50 Main St., East Greenwich, 401/885-2200 ($8–14), is a swanky little eatery on this pretty village's dapper Main Street. Singles appreciate the long and comfy wooden bar, where you can also order from the menu. Tables in front look out through a bow-front window over the busy sidewalk outside. The urbane dining room, with lavender trim and tightly spaced wooden tables, is noisy and fun. The menu changes often, and highlights include foccacia stuffed with mozzarella,

vine-ripened tomatoes, fresh basil, and garlic; an excellent Buffalo chicken salad; and more substantial dishes like oven-baked haddock topped with Ritz cracker crumbs and a citrus vinaigrette, or chicken Vera Cruz with salsa, Monterey jack cheese, diced tomatoes, and jalapeños. It's a great value. Burgers and creative pizzas are also offered, plus lavish desserts. The famous Boston fish house **Legal Sea Foods,** 2099 Post Rd., Warwick, 401/SEA-FOOD ($11–23), has a popular branch across the street from T. F. Green Airport, and even with Rhode Island's many considerable seafood eateries, Legal draws plenty of kudos. Eat either on the casual deck from which you can watch planes taking off and landing, or in the clubby, masculine interior. Favorite starters include blackened sashimi tuna, bluefish pâté, marinated grilled calamari with white beans and grilled onions, and the restaurant's trademark clam chowder. Lobsters are the most popular entrée offering, but you'll find a large selection of grilled and fried fish platters.

Another excellent source of creative cooking in Cranston is **Haven Hill Cafe,** 20 Haven Ave., 401/942-1009 ($12–16), a modest-seeming spot with a BYOB policy and dazzling dishes like pork loin with spicy banana demi-glace, chipotle-smashed potatoes, and an orange-mango salsa. The chef loves mixing sweet and savory flavors, as further evidenced by the peach-ginger grilled chicken breast with a rice cake and snow peas. The cozy dining room of closely spaced tables with small bentwood chairs and terracotta walls can get noisy, but this is still a fine spot for a romantic tête-à-tête. The chef-owner has done stints at the noted Providence restaurants Cafe Nuovo and XO. A smart and contemporary space with light-wood furnishings, matte-green walls, and a couple of booths, **Culinary Affair,** 650 Oaklawn Ave., Cranston, 401/944-4555 ($8–14), serves both unusual and rather expected American and Italian dishes. Grilled squid over couscous with baby greens and an orange vinaigrette makes a tempting starter. Penne with grilled shrimp and plum tomatoes in a cracked pepper–Dijon sauce; or veal paillard grilled with broccoli rabe and carrot mashed potatoes are tasty entrées. A touch of Providence's trendy College Hill neighborhood seems to have been airlifted over to Cranston in the form of the **West End Cafe,** 39 Phenix Ave., 401/944-7770 ($15–22). Fine choices from the contemporary menu include sublime tuna spring rolls, and a pizza topped sliced black Angus beef. In a cozy lounge pretty types linger on plush couches over cocktails. You'll find superb, creative Italian fare at **Cafe Fresco,** 301 Main St., East Greenwich, 401/398-0027 ($12–18), a snazzy, high-ceilinged space with tall windows and banquette seating. A raw bar turns out oysters, littlenecks, and a house specialty called oyster Fresco, topped with raspberry vinaigrette, sour cream, and caviar. Bruschetta topped with shredded black Angus beef and a creamy shallot sauce; and seared-tuna sashimi over mixed baby greens are top-flight starters, while memorable main dishes include Portobello risotto; shrimp fra diavolo; and clams and sausage with tomatoes, onions, and garlic over mashed potatoes.

Pizzas, Pastas, and Pub Grub

People head to **Cherrystones,** 898 Oakland Beach Blvd., Warwick, 401/732-2532 ($8–18), as much for the remarkable views out over Narragansett Bay as for the superb seafood—including the usual Rhode Island delicacies: clam cakes, snail salad, clear-broth chowder, stuffies, baked stuffed lobsters—plus nonfishy fare like barbecued ribs and Cajun-spiced steak. There's live music many nights. Although it sits just off busy Huntington Expressway, **Twin Oaks,** 100 Sabra St., Cranston, 401/781-9693, ($9–19), overlooks Spectacle Lake and has a sedate, elegant dining room. Traditional American fare is served, including baby rack of lamb, black Angus steaks, sole Florentine, and lighter fare such as cheeseburgers and veal parmesan grinders. There's nothing trendy about this place, but it's a reliable option. In Cranston, head to **Papa Razzi,** Garden City Center, 1 Paparazzi Way, 401/942-2900 (pizzas $8–12, entrées $11–20), for pizzas and pastas. This is a classic trattoria with a couple of twists: on Monday nights they perform opera classics here, and on weekends there's a fantastic brunch. Stars from the kitchen include slow-roasted lemon-garlic chicken with wilted greens and roasted potatoes, a terrific rendition of spaghetti Bolognese (with pancetta, ground veal, mushrooms, and a light tomato-cream sauce), and the pizza topped with prosciutto, mozzarella, arugula, and balsamic tomatoes.

Marchetti's, 1463 Park Ave., Cranston, 401/943-7649 ($6–11), serves very good and large—almost preposterously so—portions of red-sauce Italian fare, the standard favorites, from pastas and grills to veal parmagiana and grilled calamari tossed with roasted red peppers, artichoke hearts, black olives, and a white-wine-and-butter sauce over pasta. Lively **Pinelli's,** 701 Quaker Lane, West Warwick, 401/821-8828 ($8–20), run by the same folks who own the Post Office Cafe and the Grille on Main in East Greenwich, plus other Pinelli's in North Smithfield and North Providence, ranks among the area's most reliable restaurants. Specialties are many but include shrimp fra diavolo, fettuccine in pink vodka sauce, grilled herb-encrusted Norwegian salmon served with parmesan mashed potatoes, grilled asparagus, and slow-roasted plum tomatoes, and the house signature dish: chicken alla Pinelli, served with white mushrooms, roasted red peppers, and artichoke hearts in sage, wine, and lemon butter, then finished with mozzarella. In historic Apponaug Village, the **Remington House Inn,** 3376 Post Rd., Apponaug Village, 401/736-8388, ($10–16), is a charming colonial inn marred only slightly by its very busy location. Inside you'll find an inviting spot with hanging brass pots, a dark timber ceiling, and a redbrick fireplace that glows all winter long. There aren't a lot of surprises on the American/Italian menu, but portions are large and the food well-prepared. You might sample chicken sautéed with roasted red peppers, garlic, onion, tomato, and fresh herbs, tossed with bowtie pasta in a mascarpone-cream sauce; or lamb tenderloin charbroiled and finished with a merlot sauce. Clams Remington is a worthy appetizer for the Ocean State—the tender bivalves come sautéed with Portuguese chourico sausage, fresh tomatoes, garlic, and onion. There are many draft beers offered, and there's an impressive wine list.

Ward's Publick House, 3854 Post Rd., Warwick, 401/884-7008 ($8–12), fits the bill if you're craving decent pub fare and a pint of imported draught beer (Harp, Guinness, Tetleys, Speckled Hen, and Murphy's are all on tap). For sustenance, try the stir-fried veggies, traditional Irish bangers and mash, shepherd's pie, or blackened salmon. There's traditional Irish music many evenings. Whether for a meal or drinks, this is a festive and atmospheric hangout with warm pub decor. **One Bay Avenue,** 1 Bay Ave., Warwick, 401/738-4777 ($8–16), a restaurant, raw bar, and fish market, sits on the bay a block north of Oakland Beach. It's a spacious place with high ceilings, tall windows, hanging plants, and a cavernous fireplace. On the surface, the menu looks pretty basic—mostly seafood classics, steaks, and chops. But the preparation and ingredients are consistently quite good and sometimes imaginative. Starters worth sampling include rock-crab cakes with white wine and a lemon-horseradish-cream sauce, and scallops rolled in bacon with a honey-Dijon glaze. Continue with blackened swordfish, shrimp casino, or Yankee pot roast slow-roasted with caramelized onion au jus. In East Greenwich, yuppies and yachting types flock to **Twenty Water Street,** 20 Water St., 401/885-3703 ($15–23 in main dining room; $9–15 in tavern and on deck), a festive waterside bar and eatery with a lovely deck overlooking the many sailboats and fishing trawlers on Narragansett Bay—it looks out over the water toward Goddard Park. The dining room, decked with hardwood floors, Windsor chairs, and dark-wood paneled walls, presents a somewhat upscale menu of seafood favorites, such as clams casino, seafood casserole with a sherry-wine lemon butter, and rack of lamb with garlic and rosemary. More casual fare is served on the deck and in the tavern, including grilled swordfish steak, lobster rolls, and Caesar salad. By most accounts, the tavern fare is both better tasting and a better value.

Ethnic Fare

Providence takes the prize in Rhode Island when it comes to fine Indian cuisine, but the 'burbs have caught up fast in recent years. Take the **Indian Club,** 455 S. Main St., East Greenwich, 401/884-7100 ($10–15), which serves commendable shahi baingan bartha (eggplant grilled over an open flame, mashed with spices, and sautéed with onions and green peas), lobster masala in a mild tomato-cream sauce, and spicy chicken vindaloo. Tomato-coconut soup makes a nice starter. Meals come to the table on authentic Indian serving dishes and copper pots, and calming Indian music hums in the background. You can get your sushi fix at **Haruki,** 1210 Oaklawn Ave., Cranston, 401/463-8338 ($9–17). You'll seldom dine alone at this phenomenally popular spot on busy Oaklawn Avenue. Dining is inside a bright, beautiful dining room with varnished wood trim and elegant Japanese murals. There's an extensive and reasonably priced sushi menu—unusual options include the yellowtail and scallion rolls, sea urchin, and spicy codfish roe. Specialties from the grill range from crispy fried catfish with wasabi and light pepper-onion sauce to scallops teriyaki and honey-barbecued pork ribs.

Quick Bites

The very same **Barney's,** 870 Oaklawn Ave., Cranston, 401/943-7050 ($2–7), that delights connoisseurs of bagels and kosher deli food in Pawtucket also gets the crowds going wild in Cranston. Barney's is named for Barney Kaplan, who came to the United States in 1905 from the Ukraine, hailing from a long line of bakers. His bagel-making ranks among the best you'll ever find, and his family continues to operate his restaurants. Several kinds of cream cheese are available, from cinnamon-raisin-walnut to chive- and lox-flavored. And the sandwich list includes kosher chopped liver, whitefish salad, corned beef, and many other deli favorites. **Iggy's Doughboys,** 889 Oakland Beach Ave., Warwick, 401/737-9459 ($3–9), might just serve the best clam cakes in the state—it's certainly fun to test them out against the many reputable competitors around Rhode Island. The original Iggy's opened in 1924 and has withstood hurricanes and recessions; the view, out toward Newport Bridge, Jamestown, and across to the East Bay, is outstanding—you'll actually feel as though you're down by the ocean. Standard fare includes chowder, stuffies, fried scallops, the famous Iggy Burger with sautéed peppers and onions, tuna grinders, meatball subs, and chicken wings. Iggy's also specializes in greasy little fried doughboys, which are dusted liberally with powdered sugar; an order of a half-dozen costs just $2.95. Click on the website for coupons discounting several items on the menu, http://iggysdoughboys.com.

You'll find a nice selection of tasty sub sandwiches at **Carmine's Sub Shop,** 310 Atwood Ave., Cranston, 401/942-9600 (under $5). Fillings include veal steak, meatballs, and a wide and tempting array of cold cuts. A stellar competitor is **Mario's Italian Deli,** 164 Gransett Ave., Cranston, 401/944-3130 (under $7), whose cold cuts and Italian meatball grinders are just plain delicious. Pick up a couple (or a few . . . or a plateful) of New York wieners at **Peter's Coney Island System,** 2298 West Shore Rd., Warwick, 401/732-6499 (under $4), one of the legions of exceptional purveyors of these addictive treats scattered about the state. A meager burger stand when Jigger Lindberg opened it in 1918, **Jigger's Diner,** 145 Main St., East Greenwich, 401/884-5388 ($5–11), serves some of Rhode Island's best diner fare, from the trademark gingerbread pancakes to more prosaic fare like eggs and bacon. This may not be fancy food, but it's definitely not your typical greasy-spoon cooking either—presentation verges on elaborate, with fresh and inventive ingredients, like the sandwich of fresh mozzarella, pesto, and vine-ripened tomatoes; or pan-roasted cod topped with salsa fresca (that's a dinner entrée, and this meal is served Fridays only, when the restaurant also allows patrons to bring their own wine or beer). The fries are hand-cut and homemade, as is the breakfast sausage. It's one of the oldest restaurants in town (although it was closed for a spell in the 1980s). The little railroad-car diner with a blue facade stands along the ranks of pretty shops in East Greenwich.

Head to **Sweet Temptations,** 450 Main St., East Greenwich, 401/884-2404, for fresh-made cakes and sweets, as well as deli sandwiches and light breakfast fare—always using this bakery's exceptional fresh breads. **Dear Hearts,** 2218 Broad St., Cranston, 401/941-5167, doles out about 50 varieties of delicious homemade ice cream.

Java Joints

Grab a light lunch, pastries and baked goods, or a cup of espresso at **SimonSays Cafe,** 96 Main St., 401/884-1965, a fun little coffeehouse in downtown East Greenwich.

Gourmet Goods and Picnic Supplies

Home of the intriguing and strangely satisfying stuffed pickle, **Pickles Gourmet Deli,** 135 Frenchtown Rd., East Greenwich, 401/884-1828 ($3–8), also serves up about 30 kinds of breakfast and lunch sandwiches, plus homemade quiche and stuffed eggplant tortes. Not long ago, *Rhode Island Monthly* magazine had a bunch of second-grade school kids in Barrington taste-test cookies from a few of the state's most reputable bakeries. **Rainbow Bakery,** 800 Reservoir Ave., Cranston, 401/944-8180, took the prize for the best chocolate-chip cookies. Hard to argue with such a reputable panel of experts.

ENTERTAINMENT AND NIGHTLIFE

With close proximity to Providence, which has scads of hip bars, performing-arts venues, and nightclubs, most folks in Warwick and Cranston head into the big city when they're seeking a night of revelry. Otherwise, they tend to have cocktails at some of the aforementioned restaurants with good bars—such as **20 Water Street, Remington House, Ward's Publick House,** and **Legal Sea Foods.** The local chain of bar-restaurants, **Chelo's Waterfront Bar and Grille,** 1 Masthead Dr., Warwick, 401/884-3000, overlooks the bay and serves casual seafood and American fare. Head to **Copperfield's,** 1551 Warwick Ave., Warwick, 401/738-7936, to shoot pool, watch a game on TV, belt out karaoke tunes, or listed to live bands—it's a large and popular hangout, sort of an adult's Chuck E. Cheese, with 10 pool tables and about a dozen large-screen TVs, plus dart boards. There's often live folk, R&B, and rock at the **Harp & Shamrock,** 557 Warwick Ave., 401/467-8998, a friendly, traditional Irish pub.

FESTIVALS AND EVENTS

Warwick's most celebrated event, *Gaspee* **Days,** 401/781-1772, takes place every May through June in Pawtuxet Village, in celebration of one of the American Revolution's earliest acts of defiance. Events include an arts and crafts fair, a gala ball in period colonial costume, a children's costume contest, a parade, and a mock battle reenactment. In September, **Apponaug Village Festival,** 401/737-9033, and **Conimicut Village Festival,** 401/738-3749, celebrate their respective communities with crafts, food, and celebration. The **Warwick Heritage Festival,** 401/738-3225, convenes in Warwick City Park in November.

Information and Services

VISITOR INFORMATION

Pamphlets, brochures, and tourism information are available from the **Providence Warwick Convention and Visitors Bureau,** 1 W. Exchange St., Providence, 02903, 401/274-1636 or 800/233-1636; www.providencecvb.com; and from the **Warwick Tourism Office,** Warwick City Hall, Warwick, 02886, 401/738-2000 or 401/738-6639, www.warwickri.com.

GETTING THERE

Warwick is the home of the state's main airport—specific transportation options to and from T. F. Green Airport are discussed in the On the Road chapter. In general, most of the hotels in the Warwick area have free shuttle service to and from the airport; you'll also find a full slate of rental-car agencies. Amtrak, 800/USA-RAIL, www.amtrak.com, stops in Westerly and Kingston, which makes it a convenient way to reach the southern half of the region. Greyhound, 800/229-9424, www.greyhound.com, makes regular stops at T. F. Green Airport.

GETTING AROUND

Cranston, Warwick, and East Greenwich are relatively compact and are traversed by some of Rhode Island's busiest roads, including U.S. 1 and I-95. It's very easy to get around the area by car, although traffic can be a nightmare on the key roads, especially at rush hour. Although this region is densely populated and fairly urban in character, it's still not nearly as conducive either to walking or using public transportation as is Providence. Nevertheless, you can easily park and explore East Greenwich's engaging downtown—there are metered spaces and several lots. Rhode Island Public Transit Authority runs several buses through the area, including Bus 31 from Providence with several stops in Cranston and Warwick (including Rhode Island and Warwick Malls); and Bus 12 from Providence to Apponaug Four Corners, T. F. Green Airport, and East Greenwich.

MEDIA

As these towns are fairly close to Providence, you can count on the *Providence Journal,* 401/277-7300, www.projo.com, as your best source of local information. The paper has an outstanding and highly informative website with information on local dining, arts, music, travel, kids-oriented activities, and so on. An excellent resource for metro Providence arts, dining, shopping, clubbing, and similar such diversions is the decidedly left-of-center *Providence Phoenix* alternative newsweekly, 401/273-6397, www.thephoenix.com. Other area papers include the twice-weekly *Warwick Beacon,* 401/732-3100, www.warwickonline.com; the *Kent County Daily Times,* 401/821-7400, www.ricentral.com; and the weekly *Cranston Herald,* 401/732-3100, www.cranstonherald.com. **Southern Rhode Island Newspapers,** 401/789-9744, www.ricentral.com, publishes several local weeklies including *The Chariho Times* (Wyoming), *The Coventry Courier, The East Greenwich Pendulum,* and *The Standard Times.*

TOURS

One interesting way to explore the region is on one of the cruises offered on the **Blackstone Valley Explorer,** 175 Main St., Pawtucket, 401/724-2200 or 800/454-BVTC, www.tourblackstone.com, a 49-passenger riverboat with a canopy roof that runs up and down the Blackstone River from April through October. Several different kinds of excursions are offered, leaving from Central Falls, Blackstone (Massachusetts), and Woonsocket. However, some of these are available only to groups and student tours, so it's best to call ahead for details. Rates are generally $5 per person. These tours give a particular strong sense of the mix of rural and wildlife-inhabited lands existing side-by-side with the great old mill villages of the past two centuries.

Another possibility is the **Blackstone River Valley Scenic Railway Tours,** Blackstone Valley Tourism Council, 401/724-2200, www.tourblackstone.com/tours.htm, which offers excursions from Cumberland, once in the spring and then again in the fall. The Spring Blossom Excursion departs in May and last six hours, working up through the valley to Worcester and then back down again through Connecticut to the town of Putnam, before returning to Cumberland. In mid-October, a Fall Foliage Tour lasts just four hours and runs to Worcester and back down to Cumberland. The cost is $32 per person for the fall excursion, and $35 for the spring one. Lunch is available, or you're welcome to bring your own picnic.

Conway Gray Line, 10 Nate Whipple Hwy., Cumberland, 401/658-3400 or 800/888-4661, www.conwaytours.com, offers narrated van tours of the valley that pass by the attractions both in Providence and by Slater Mill and the many industrial sites of the area. The cost is $49 for one passenger, $30 per person for two to three passengers, and $24 per person for four to six passengers. The same company also operates a 33-passenger vintage-style trolley that can be chartered for tours; call for schedule information.

Finally, the most intriguing option is a tour on the **Samuel Slater Canal Boat,** 401/724-2200, www.tourblackstone.com/canal.htm, a bright red-and-green vintage canal boat. The boat, which was built in Cambridgeshire, England, can be chartered for tours along the Blackstone and can also be booked as a bed-and-breakfast. There's seating for 12 and overnight accommodations for up to four guests. Charter rates are quite reasonable if you have a large group—it's $125 for the first 90 minutes and $50 each hour thereafter.

South County

Politically—even geographically—there is no South County. What Rhode Islanders refer to as such is really Washington County, which comprises 11 townships and even a bit of southern Kent County. This area makes up the lower third of western Rhode Island, but generally speaking, when people talk about South County, they really mean the shore towns, beginning with Westerly to the west, extending east to Narragansett, and extending north along Narragansett Bay to North Kingstown. And it is these townships that this chapter covers: Westerly, Charlestown, South Kingstown, Narragansett, and North Kingstown.

The inland communities of Washington County, such as Hopkinton, Hope Valley, and Exeter, are covered in the Greater Providence chapter, because the character, terrain, and histories of these towns are more like the others covered in that chapter than they are like the South County shore towns. At the risk of confusing anybody further, keep in mind that—just as it's the case all over Rhode Island—every

township is made up of a series of small villages. If you're looking for coverage of Watch Hill or Misquamicut, turn to the Westerly section, because those shoreline villages are part of that town. Wakefield, Peace Dale, Matunuck, Jerusalem, and Kingston are villages in South Kingstown; Saunderstown and Wickford are part of North Kingstown; and Point Judith and Galilee are part of Narragansett.

These towns that define lower South County also define the part of Rhode Island that appeals most to families and summertime shoregoers. Sure, Newport may be more famous, but it's also a largely adult city with an upscale reputation. Little Compton occupies a dazzling stretch of oceanfront but has relatively little public beach access and very few accommodations. South County is Rhode Island's kid-friendly, teen-popular beach retreat, with scads of low-key motels and inns, some of them owned by the same families for nearly a century. You'll find a few snazzy boutiques here and there, and the occasional luxurious B&B or swank bistro. But for the most part,

Watch Hill Point

this is the place to tuck into clam fritters at an in-the-rough seafood shanty, to Jet Ski or surf-cast into the sea or a salt pond.

South County has a youthful demeanor, which is not to say adults won't find plenty to keep them busy. It's just that minigolf courses and amusement parks are easy to find, and the style of accommodations lend themselves to families vacationing for several days—or even weeks. Especially in the oceanfront communities like Misquamicut and Narragansett, many visitors rent cottages during warmer months, and others stay at one of the many hotels that rent efficiency or cottage-style accommodations with kitchens and sitting areas. A whole different contingent of South County tourists include groups of twenty- and thirty-somethings from Providence and other inland areas who come down every weekend or for extended periods to rent these same places. Kingston's University of Rhode Island is a short drive from the beach, and you can count on seeing plenty of college kids lazing around on the area's magnificent beaches, which rank among the prettiest in the Northeast.

For all its youthful buzz, and with the exception of some moderate beachfront development in Misquamicut and Narragansett and to a lesser extent elsewhere, South County is strangely and happily old-fashioned and uncluttered by strip-mall excess. Nowhere do high-rise hotels and massive condo communities exist, and where high-density beach housing has been allowed, it's mostly tasteful and unflashy, in the traditional New England style of gray or white shingle houses, some of them on stilts to protect against tidal storm surges. Watch Hill, in Westerly, looks like the set of an old movie, its cute harbor and small shopping district without a single neon sign or modern chain shop. Punctuating the shoreline are vast tracts of protected wilderness preserves and sheltered saltwater ponds. Migrating birds love South County, and the people here love those birds—one senses that nobody in these parts is going to let anything happen that threatens the region's sweetly simple character or ecologically precious natural assets.

While beachfront fun is a major attraction of South County, the area is noted for several addi-

THE VILLAGES OF SOUTH COUNTY

As is the case throughout Rhode Island, each town in South County consists of several smaller villages, and in some cases, the village is better known than the town itself. South County's most notable villages are listed below, followed by the name of the town in which they are located.

Avondale, Westerly township
Cross Mills, Charlestown township
Galilee, Narragansett township
Jerusalem, South Kingstown township
Kenyon, South Kingstown township
Kingston, South Kingstown township
Matunuck, South Kingstown township
Misquamicut, Westerly township
Narragansett Pier, Narragansett township
Peace Dale, South Kingstown township
Point Judith, Narragansett township
Quonochontaug, Charlestown township
Quonset Point, North Kingstown township
Saunderstown, North Kingstown township
Wakefield, South Kingstown township
Watch Hill, Westerly township
Weekapaug, Westerly township
West Kingston, South Kingstown township
Wickford, North Kingstown township

tional attributes. The old ports of Galilee and, across the river, Jerusalem rank among the nation's leading fishing communities. These are charming but rough-and-tumble working ports that make for a fascinating visit, although there are no formal attractions in either place, just a few low-frills restaurants serving super-fresh seafood. Galilee is also the main port from which ferries run back and forth to Block Island. Up the coast on Narragansett Bay, in North Kingstown, the village of Wickford is one of the best-preserved colonial villages its size anywhere in America—you'll find scores of handsome 18th- and 19th-century homes here in this quaint hamlet that's also famous for shopping. Peace Dale, the site of America's first power loom, still contains a number of handsome granite and brick buildings from its heyday as a textile-mill town, and nearby Kingston is dominated by the many stately buildings of the University of Rhode Island. A final inland gem worth a look is Westerly, which is perched on the Connecticut border and has a lovely, walkable downtown replete with dignified civic buildings, a few inviting boutiques and antiques shops, and a leafy green park that's perfect for a stroll or picnic.

WESTERLY TO CHARLESTOWN

Westerly, so named for its position at the southwestern tip of the state, actually makes up about two-thirds of a community that straddles the Connecticut border. Just stroll across the Broad Street bridge a very short distance and, although the scenery or ambience doesn't change a whole lot, you'll find yourself in the village of Pawcatuck, Connecticut, part of the incorporated town of Stonington.

As with most Rhode Island municipalities, Westerly the town is a large area that takes in several small village, among them Westerly proper, Watch Hill, Misquamicut, Weekapaug, and Bradford. Hopkinton and Ashaway (see Greater Providence) lie just northeast. The parts of the area that most visitors spend their time in are Watch Hill, Misquamicut, and Weekapaug, three highly popular summer resort communities that fringe the Atlantic Ocean.

When indigenous peoples lived on these lands, the whole coastal area—on both the Rhode Island and the Connecticut sides—was called Misquamicut (which translates to "place for salmon-fishing"). Members of several different tribes called this area their home, and land disputes often arose among these Niantic, Pequot, and Narragansett Native Americans.

It's supposed that Adriaen Block got a good look at the coast while navigating Connecticut's and Rhode Island's early waters aboard the *Onrust* in 1614; he apparently called the Pawcatuck the East River. Early permanent settlers began arriving around 1650, in the form of a few homesteading Newporters. In 1660 this group of settlers formally purchased a deed to the Misquamicut Tract from a Pequot supposedly on the outs with his tribe, but disputes over the

rightful owners of the land continued almost unabated for many years. Massachusetts laid claim to it, as did the residents of Stonington, Connecticut, as did various Indian tribes. Eventually the Newport settlers successfully petitioned the Rhode Island Assembly to ratify their claim, and so Westerly became Rhode Island.

Well, sort of. Connecticut and Rhode Island continued to tussle over the exact state, and therefore town, boundary, until 1728—these skirmishes occasionally got ugly, with residents on either side destroying the others' property and sometimes pilfering possessions. At this time Westerly extended into present-day Hopkinton, which eventually broke off on its own, and also as far as Narragansett Bay, encompassing what we now know as Charlestown.

Westerly derived its income during these early years mostly from farming, and to a lesser extent from shipbuilding along the Pawcatuck, although this industry produced boats straight through the middle of the 19th century (the Pawcatuck was a deeper river back then than it is now). A few residents operated taverns on Queen Anne's Road, the old stage route that ran directly through town, connecting the ferry landing at Narragansett Bay (for Jamestown and Newport) with New London, Connecticut.

The town's vast granite resources were discovered in 1846; since that time a number of granite quarries have come and gone. The fine-grained stone quarried here has mostly been used for gravestones, but Westerly's handsome red granite has also been used in the construction of thousands of buildings throughout Southern New England and New York.

In addition to producing granite, Westerly made a name for itself during the 19th century as a producer of woolens, silk, and curtains; a handful of textile mills thrived along the Pawcatuck River, mostly north of downtown, as well as in Bradford. These sections of Westerly, on the northern side of town, still largely comprise modest communities of working-class housing. Descendants of the original Italian immigrants who came to work the mills still make up a good bit of the population.

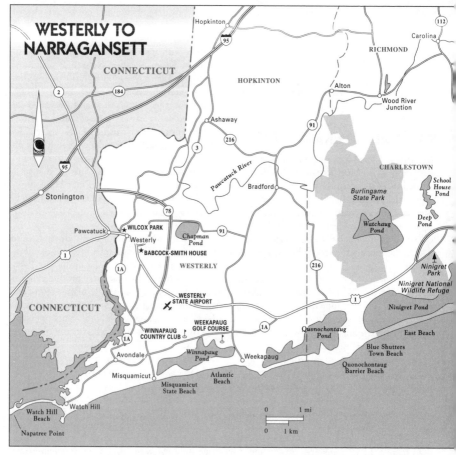

WESTERLY TO NARRAGANSETT

CONNECTICUT

Hopkinton

RICHMOND

Carolina

HOPKINTON

Alton

Wood River Junction

Ashaway

CHARLESTOWN

Pawcatuck River

Bradford

School House Pond

Burlingame State Park

Deep Pond

Watchaug Pond

Stonington

Pawcatuck

WILCOX PARK

Westerly

BABCOCK-SMITH HOUSE

Chapman Pond

WESTERLY

Ninigret Park

Ninigret National Wildlife Refuge

CONNECTICUT

WESTERLY STATE AIRPORT

Ninigret Pond

WEEKAPAUG GOLF COURSE

Quonochontaug Pond

East Beach

WINNAPAUG COUNTRY CLUB

Blue Shutters Town Beach

Avondale

Winnapaug Pond

Weekapaug

Quonochontaug Barrier Beach

Misquamicut

Atlantic Beach

Misquamicut State Beach

Watch Hill Beach

Watch Hill

Napatree Point

0   1 mi

0   1 km

Downtown Westerly is a pleasant town, marked by a number of distinguished buildings from the early 20th and late 19th centuries. Many of them are granite, and indeed Westerly's granite quarries have for more than 150 years been among the most prized in the United States. Most of the town's civic buildings, as well as several of its largest and grandest homes, are on or near gracious **Wilcox Park,** bounded by High, Broad, and Granite Streets and Grove Avenue, a broad and rolling 18-acre green with mature shade trees, a duck pond, and several distinctive sculptures and fountains—there are fewer more enchanting spots in Rhode Island for a picnic.

The park, named for early benefactors of the town, was laid out in 1898 by landscape designer Warren Manning.

Probably the most imposing building by the park is the **Westerly Public Library,** 44 Broad St., a lavish brick–and–red granite structure with a red-tile roof accented with terracotta trim. It was built in 1894 as a memorial to local Civil War veterans and originally included a bowling alley, gymnasium, art gallery, and community space for the Grand Army of the Republic. Also note the very handsome U.S. Post Office at the corner of Broad and High Streets; constructed in 1914, this dramatic space with a broad white marble fa-

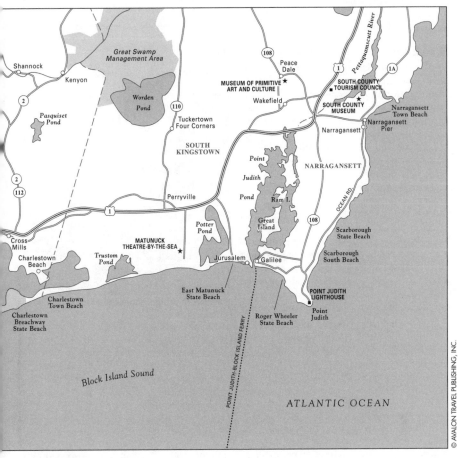

cade is decorated with fluted Doric columns. Inside, the lobby has a terrazzo marble floor and much bronze and cast-iron decorative work.

The **Babcock-Smith House,** 124 Granite St., 401/596-5704, website: www.babcocksmithhouse.com, is Westerly's de facto local history museum; the 1734 early Georgian–style house was built for physician Dr. Joshua Babcock, who made an even greater name for himself after being appointed the Chief Justice for Rhode Island. The building also housed the town's earliest post office, and in the 1840s it was the home of Orlando Smith, the man who first discovered and developed the town's rich

veins of granite. The massive central chimney rising over the gambrel roof accommodates the smoke from six fireplaces. Inside you'll find a superb collection of 18th-century furnishings, ranging from primitive pieces to an ornately wrought Federal sideboard and a towering highboy from Connecticut. Part of the home's collection of vintage textiles is also shown at certain times. Admission: $5. Open May–June and September, Sun. 2–5 P.M., and July–Aug., Wed.–Sun. 2–5 P.M.

Broad Street leads west over the **Pawcatuck Bridge** into Connecticut; this 115-foot-long bridge was built in 1932. There's a small grassy park on each side of the river, extending just south of the bridge.

Watch Hill

To the south of downtown Westerly, the town's personality changes entirely, as here along the water you'll find the aforementioned summer communities, which year-round draw a fair share of vacationers and second-home owners, plus some workers from other parts of Rhode Island; it's just a 45-minute commute to Providence, and even closer to the many businesses in Warwick, Cranston, and eastern Kent County.

From downtown Westerly, head south on Route 1A, following this as it winds along flat lands beside the gradually widening Pawcatuck River, until you reach the village of Watch Hill; it's about a six-mile drive and takes perhaps 15 minutes, depending on whether you stop along the way at one of the handful of shops between the two communities. About halfway along this journey you'll pass Riverbend Cemetery on your right; this tranquil spot along the river was dedicated in 1852 and contains many headstones of locally quarried granite.

In the tiny village of **Avondale,** which you'll pass through soon after, there are a few marinas and shipping concerns along the Pawcatuck River, just off Route 1A (via Avondale Road). This pleasant community retains a rural feel. As you turn off Route 1A and follow Watch Hill Road as it twists and turns down to the village, you'll pass a number of both grand and modest vacation homes, many of them perched on shady hillocks that afford stunning ocean views.

The commercial center of the village runs along Bay Street for just about 400 yards, and contains a mix of cafés and eateries, galleries and boutiques, and just a handful of accommodations. It's a tight-knit, familial little town with a friendly personality, and it's completely devoid of the modern development that characterizes South County's beach communities farther east. High above Bay Street, a parallel road called Bluff Avenue sits over the community and contains the grandest of Watch Hill's summer homes. In some ways, Watch Hill feels like

Pawcatuck Bridge, connecting Rhode Island to Connecticut

a little slice of Block Island clinging to the mainland—even though it's named for a geographically prominent point, it's a bit of a secret.

The very tip of Watch Hill, a long hook of sand, juts out into the water like a scythe and forms the boundary at which the very eastern end of Long Island Sound becomes the Atlantic. Although Rhode Island does not have a land boundary with New York, the two states do share a maritime boundary and are therefore neighbors (a nugget of trivia that may come in handy the next time somebody asks you to name every state that borders Rhode Island). From the tip of Watch Hill to what are technically New York State waters, it's just about a mile southwest; Fishers Island, New York, is but two miles from the tip of Watch Hill.

This watery location, which opens the town to constant ocean breezes, accounts for the fact that Watch Hill enjoys some of the coolest summer temperatures of any community in Rhode Island, and this in turn accounts for its popularity. It's just a 10- or 15-minute drive from here up Route 1A into Westerly's downtown, and yet the temperature on a summer day can be as much as 10 degrees cooler.

The beach at Watch Hill is quite well-known, at least among southern Rhode Islanders and others who live nearby—this long strand largely unblemished by development ranks among the prettiest beaches in southern New England. Jutting into Watch Hill's little harbor, which feeds into the mouth of the Pawcatuck, is the private **Watch Hill Yacht Club,** which sits along a wharf. The **Watch Hill Lighthouse,** 14 Lighthouse Rd., lies just south of the village center, down a sandy spit that extends off Bluff Avenue. Watch Hill has for nearly 200 years been known for its lighthouse, which was commissioned in 1806, thereby establishing the community as we now know it. In 1879 a life-saving station was commissioned following a disaster when two ships collided just offshore, claiming more than 70 lives. The lighthouse grounds are open 8 A.M.–8 P.M. and free; you can visit the small museum in the white-brick base of this granite tower on Tuesdays and Thursdays in July and August.

Misquamicut

You can return to Route 1A the way you came or jog along the waterfront, following Westerly and Niantic Avenues; after about three miles on Route 1A you'll find yourself in the Misqaumicut (pronounced "mih-*sqauw*-mih-cut), which has a gracious three-mile-long stretch of sand. Unlike Watch Hill, Misquamicut was not settled until the very end of the 1800s, and it really only began to flourish as a resort community around 1910 or so; originally it was named Pleasant View, but citizens changed it to Misquamicut in 1928 as a tribute to coastal Westerly's original inhabitants.

This community is a traditional shore strip of pastel-hued clapboard cottages, houses, and motels—the latter are fairly similar in amenities and styles, but they all vary a bit in decor. The larger places facing the beach offer clear ocean views and rooms just steps from the surf. Many have kitchenettes, and most have their own fairly predictable seafood/chops restaurants. There are no franchise restaurants or hotels in Misquamicut—instead, you'll mostly find proper-

ties that have been in the same family for generations, catering to successive generations of guests. Plenty of these hotel employees know their guests' names by heart, and vice versa. It's the sort of tight-knit community where kids grow up together as their families revisit summer after summer. There's an unpretentious air about Misquamicut, and a safe and familiar feel.

Behind, or north of the beach, extends the long salt pond, Winnapaug, which is popular for sailing, fishing, crabbing, and other activities because of its sheltered location. In the center of Misquamicut is the actual **Misquamicut State Beach,** 401/596-9097, with a large and attractive beach pavilion, a big playground, changing rooms, and other facilities. This is a beautiful and well-kept stretch of sand. The section of the community just east of the state beach is more honky-tonk and less pristine, but it is an excellent place to bring the kids, with go-kart tracks, minigolf courses, snack bars, and video arcades in abundance.

From here, follow the community's main drag, Atlantic Avenue, east to reach Dunn's Beach, a long swath of summer houses punctuated by just a few businesses.

Weekapaug

The Weekapaug area has older, grander, and more dramatically situated homes, most of them with shingle siding, multi-gabled roofs, and two or three chimneys. This is a wonderful section for a bike ride.

As you follow Atlantic Avenue along the beach it eventually crosses a small stream that feeds into Winnapaug Pond; bear right over the bridge and you'll enter the more upscale and secluded summer resort of Weekapaug. The shore along here is rocky and a bit more dramatic, and it's without the commercial development of Misquamicut, but for a couple of hotels. Weekapaug has its own large salt pond, called Quonochontaug; it and the **Quono-chontaug Barrier Beach** are enveloped by a vast nature preserve. At the beach, you'll find a boat launch on the salt pond and a very popular fishing area. It's also a great spot for a hike along the sand. Just keep in mind that parking is limited here.

Follow Noyes Neck Road north away from Weekapaug, and you'll soon reach Shore Road (Route 1A), onto which a right turn leads to U.S. 1 and the village of Haversham.

Charlestown

From Westerly, you'll enter Charlestown on U.S. 1 and soon pass alongside two large parks; first, on the north side of the road, signs point the way to Burlingame State Park. A bit farther along U.S. 1, on the south side of the road is a parcel divided into Ninigret National Wildlife Refuge and Ninigret Park—this land fringes another of South County's big saltwater ponds, Ninigret Pond.

Charlestown today is one of Rhode Island's great hubs of recreation—it has outstanding beaches as well as several extensive tracts of undeveloped and preserved land; if there's an outdoor activity that interests you, save perhaps mountain-climbing, there's a fairly good chance you'll find a venue for it here, along with like-interested new friends to pursue it with.

Shortly after passing by the parks, bear right from U.S. 1 onto Route 1A, toward Cross Mills and Matunuck Beach. You'll very soon come to the tiny village of Cross Mills, an utterly charming and sleepy community that's home to Fort Ninigret, for years thought to have been a Niantic fortification (today's historians believe that it was built by Dutch settlers). Cross Mills is the site of a pair of corn mills, the small Charlestown Town Hall, and the old Indian Burial Ground. Set inside a 19th-century one-room schoolhouse is the **Charlestown Historical Society,** on the grounds of the Cross Mills Library, 4417 Old Post Rd., 401/364-7507. The school operated until 1918 and was moved here in 1973. The building has been faithfully restored and decorated with 19th-century furnishings.

From the Old Post Road (Route 1A), a bit east of Cross Mills, turn right onto Matunuck School House Road, from which you can reach Charlestown Beach and, farther east, Grill Hill Beach—these areas are well-marked. Eventually Matunuck School House Road dead-ends with Matunuck Beach Road, onto which a right turn leads down to Matunuck Beach. This is a popular, long-time family resort area packed with fair-

ly modest cottages. You'll also find a few pubs and taverns at the beach, as well as the famous Matunuck Theatre-by-the-sea.

From here, return up Matunuck Beach Road to U.S. 1, turn right, and go a short way to Succotash Road. A right turn here will lead you down to the village of Jerusalem, which—with Galilee on the other side of the river into Point Judith salt pond, forms the western half of the massive fishing port of Galilee. There are a few places to buy fresh seafood here, and it's also just an interesting place to watch the boats chug in and out of the port.

NARRAGANSETT TO NORTH KINGSTOWN

From Jerusalem, retrace your steps back up Succotash Road to U.S. 1, cross up around Point Judith Pond, and you'll enter Narragansett. Narragansett was originally part of South Kingstown but spun off into its own town in 1901. The name of this small community preserves the legacy of the indigenous tribe that was driven away from here during King Philip's War. Narragansett is the easternmost of South County's coastal resorts—it runs along the very southeastern tip of the oceanfront and then up the western side of Narragansett Bay. As is true in the ocean towns, Narragansett also has several decent-size salt ponds that sit just inland—Point Judith Pond is the largest of these, and it separates the Point Judith section from the Galilee area.

The northern section of town along the bay is called Narragansett Pier, so named for the long pier that jutted out into Narragansett Bay before a Nor'easter tore it away. All along here there are sandy beaches and in many places large and stately summer homes, in others cottages and smaller residences. Other than the fishing and boating interests down at Galilee and Point Judith, Narragansett is almost entirely a tourist town, although plenty of folks also commute from here to Providence, which is just 30 miles north; Newport is a manageable commute, too.

From U.S. 1, make a right onto Point Judith Road (Route 108), and follow the road south. After nearly four miles you'll pass the turnoff

GILBERT STUART

You may not recognize his name, but you'd almost certainly recognize the most famous work of the famed Colonial portraitist Gilbert Stuart. For it's Stuart's stately painting of President George Washington that appears on the U.S. $1 bill, and has also appeared on several U.S. postage stamps. It is through Stuart's works that the world now imagines the expressive yet rather somber face of America's first commander-in-chief.

Gilbert Stuart was born December 3, 1755, in what is now the Saunderstown section of Narragansett. The house, which was also a working snuff mill, is now the Gilbert Stuart Museum. He lived here with his father until he was 7 years old, at which time the Stuarts moved to Newport (Stuart's Scottish father was married to Middletown's Elizabeth Anthony, whose family sold the property that Bishop George Berkeley moved to in the 1730s).

The young boy took an interest in art and painting at a very early age, and almost immediately his promise was recognized. In those early years he studied with Scottish portrait painter Cosmo Alexander, who was living in Rhode Island for a time. One of his very earliest works, a portrait of two dogs under a Goddard–Townsend table, still hangs in the Hunter House museum in Newport—the dogs belonged to the home's 18th-century owner, Dr. William Hunter.

In his early teens, Stuart was sent to London to train under esteemed artist Benjamin West and then with the master of British portraiture, Sir Joshua Reynolds. He later enrolled at the University of Glasgow, where he continued to study under Cosmo Alexander for a time.

He returned to the United States an established painter and lived in Philadelphia, New York, and Washington, D.C. He's most famous, of course, for the portrait of Washington, but Stuart also painted hundreds of prominent Colonials, among them Presidents Adams, Jefferson, Madison, and Monroe. Other noted subjects of Stuart's include Sir Joshua Reynolds and Kings George III and George IV. He lived the last part of his life in Boston, and died there in 1828.

---

for Galilee, a bustling port opposite Jerusalem. This whole area is more generally part of Point Judith, which is tiny as communities go; however, it ranks a formidable eighth in the nation among all fishing ports, producing annual fishing revenues of nearly $70 million. Approximately 250 boats call Point Judith home. You'll also find many of the area's summer homes, plus clam shacks, charter fishing operations, and some of the state's top beaches. From here you can book whale-watching tours and other excursion boats, and this is also where you catch the ferry to Block Island.

Back out on Route 108, the road leads a bit farther south, where a right turn onto Ocean Road leads to **Point Judith Lighthouse,** website: www.lighthouse.cc/pointjudith. Fans of lighthouses should explore the grounds of the 1857 lighthouse, the third incarnation to be built on this spot; the original Point Judith Lighthouse went up about a half-century earlier, and many a ship has been steered clear of the rocks and shoals off these shores. The lighthouse itself is not open to the public.

Ocean Road then becomes Route 108 and turns north following the shore. This five-mile road passes beautiful Scarborough State Beach and then through some very posh residential neighborhoods near the ocean before entering the village of Narragansett Pier, which came into its own as a Victorian resort, to which wealthy vacationers arrived in droves by steamship and train. The great site was, until it burned in a fire in 1900, the Narragansett Casino Resort, which was designed in 1884 by the esteemed architectural firm of McKim, Mead, and White. The casino's elegant towers still stand today. Numerous beach cottages and quite a few shops and eateries line the streets of Narragansett Pier.

Make a left turn onto Route 1A South (at this point called Narragansett Avenue), and follow it a short way until you reach Strathmore Street, and follow this to the **South County Museum,** Canonchet Farm, off Route 1A, 401/783-5400,

SOUTH COUNTY

website: www.southcountymuseum.org, whose myriad exhibits offer an engaging and useful overview of a gentleman's farm, carpenter's shop, blacksmith shop, general store, a one-room schoolhouse, and many other historic venues that you might find in colonial and then Victorian coastal Rhode Island—you'll find more than 20,000 period artifacts and implements spread among these exhibits. The museums organizes dozens of events, including apple-pie-eating contests, fall harvest fairs, Victorian teas, and quilt shows. Displays here are geared largely to kids and families and include an exhibit on the railroads of South County. Many rotating exhibits are also shown. The museum sits on 175-acre Canonchet Farm, which dates to the 18th century and was once the home of Rhode Island governor William Sprague. Admission is $4. Open June–Aug., Wed.–Sun. 11 A.M.–4 P.M.; April–May and Sept.–Oct., Fri.–Sun. 10 A.M.–4 P.M.

On Kingstown Road just past Strathmore Street, at Sprague Park, note the **Narragansett Indian Monument,** a 23-foot-tall wooden pole carved from a single Douglas fir; it's part of a series of such monuments throughout the country. Retrace your steps back to the beach via Route 1A and continue north.

From Narragansett Pier, keep follow Route 1A north along the shore toward the Route 138 Bridge to Jamestown. As you enter the village of Saunderstown, keep your eyes open as you pass **Historic South Ferry Road,** where you'll find the old South Ferry Church, the historic port and ferry landing, the World War I Fort Kearney, and a World War II POW camp. This is also home to the University of Rhode Island's Graduate School of Oceanography and the Coastal Institute Visitors Center, 401/874-1000.

A short way farther north you'll come to **Casey Farm,** 2325 Boston Neck Rd. (Rte. 1A), 401/295-1030, website: www.spnea.org /visit/homes/casey.htm, site of a Revolutionary War battle, beautiful ocean vistas, and lots of hands-on farming demonstrations. This circa-1750 farm, directly overlooking Narragansett Bay, was the site of several small battles during the American Revolution. Now this 300-acre working farm is a rare parcel that preserves the agrarian ways of colonial times in coastal New England—rare not only for Rhode Island but for the entire country. As a visitor you can tour what is run as a community-supported farm by the Society for the Preservation for New England Antiquities, and see how produce was grown organically in colonial times. Hiking trails lace the property. Special events throughout the summer and fall include hayrides, produce sales, and demonstrations. The SPNEA also runs nearby Watson Farm, 401/432-0005, website: www.spnea.org/visit/ homes/watson.htm, in Jamestown; the same admission fee applies there, and visitors can take self-guided tours. Admission is $4. Open July–mid-October, Sat. 11 A.M.–5 P.M.

From here, continue driving north until you see the left turn for Snuff Mill Road, which becomes Gilbert Stuart Road and is home to the **Gilbert Stuart Museum,** 815 Gilbert Stuart Rd., off U.S. 1, 401/294-3001, website: www.gilbertstuartmuseum.com. The house dates to 1751, and in it was born the famous American portraitist Gilbert Stuart. A gristmill was later operated in this building for about a century, and there's an original alewife fish ladder. In this large red gambrel-roofed colonial house, Gilbert Stuart was born in December 3, 1755. He only lived in the house until he was 7, at which time his family moved to Newport; soon after, people began to notice his prowess as a painter.

Stuart's father operated the first snuff mill in the United States on this site, and today the old snuff mill has been preserved and is one of several rooms you'll see while touring the house—here's where Stuart's father ground tobacco. The house has been preserved as it functioned—both as a home and a small colonial factory of sorts. Each room contains a corner fireplace, and many of the original details of woodworking and construction are still intact, from the wooden door latches to the hand-blown windowpanes. Reproductions of Stuart's works hang throughout the house. In the common room you'll see a display of colonial cooking utensils and tools. Costumed docents are often on hand to demonstrate colonial activities, like fulling wool and grinding meal.

The house occupies wonderfully scenic grounds near a pond and a stream; on the grounds is the restored gristmill in which two massive grinding stones made the cornmeal used in jonnycakes. There's an herb garden where plants commonly used during colonial times are raised, and a children's activity garden with educational and interactive outdoor exhibits. Also here, there's an authentic alewife fish ladder which a cornucopia of herring use each year to migrate to Pausacaco Pond. In April you can watch this fascinating phenomenon, when the museum and the Rhode Island Division of Fish and Wildlife sponsor "Fish on the Run." Admission is $3. Open April–Oct., Thurs.–Mon. 11 A.M.–4 P.M.

Wickford and North Kingstown

Retrace your steps back out to Route 1A, continue north under the Route 138 overpass (which leads over the bridge to Jamestown, and eventually to Newport), and continue a few miles into North Kingstown, in the direction of historic Wickford.

North Kingstown is what remains after South Kingstown split off in the 1720s and Exeter set off on its own in 1842. Wickford, one of New England's best-kept secrets, has scads of beautifully preserved colonial houses and lies just minutes east of busy U.S. 1, seemingly in its own little universe. Follow Main Street from the village's commercial district out to the town pier on Wickford Harbor, which opens out to Narrangansett Bay. Here you can walk alongside stacks of lobster traps, listen to the squawk of aggressive seagulls, breathe in the briny air, and look back over the dozens of masts in the harbor toward the colonial homes and businesses of town.

It's like a movie set for a film you'd imagine set many decades ago, and indeed, in 1987, the town served as the set for the movie adaptation of John Updike's novel, *The Witches of Eastwick.* Almost nothing about Wickford suggests the last half-century, except perhaps the occasional jet rushing overhead from nearby T. F. Green Airport. Main Street is dotted with 18th-century homes and a few churches, and it and the more commercial Brown Street are lined with park benches—the better shopping is along Brown.

Smith's Castle, 55 Richard Smith Dr., off U.S.

1, just north of Wickford, 401/294-3521, website: www.smithscastle.org, is North Kingstown's other big draw. You may think plantation homes only exist on the Great River Road in Louisiana or along the Ashley River in Charleston, but Wickford is actually home to America's oldest surviving plantation house. Guided tours are given of this neatly restored house, which came extremely close to demolition in the 1940s until local preservationists stepped in.

The history of the house mirrors the checkered history of Rhode Island; during the state's slave-trading heyday, the early 18th century, this manor was a slave-holding plantation. The end of slavery doomed it to some extent, and the onset of the Industrial Revolution led to a decline in agricultural production at this once 3,000-acre property. After lying nearly dormant during the 19th century, it did function again as a small dairy during the early part of the 20th century.

The lands on which the plantation were built were named Cocumscussoc by the Narragansett Indians who inhabited this area. According to some theories, Roger Williams came to this exact spot to trade with the local Indians; Queen Quiapen even lent him the island offshore, Queens Island, for him to keep his herd of goats. Williams operated a trading post on this land for a time, and in 1651 he sold the land and the operation to another trader named Roger Smith. Indians burned the trading post in the bitter aftermath of King Philip's War in 1676, but Smith's son Roger Jr. rebuilt an even more impressive home, which he operated as a plantation for many years. Eventually this passed on to the Updike family. Here the farm raised tobacco, grains, apples, vegetables, and the like—as well as all kinds of livestock, from sheep to cattle to pigs.

Admission is $5 to tour the house, free for the grounds. Open June–Aug., Thurs.–Mon. noon–4 P.M.; May and Sept., Fri.–Sun. noon–4 P.M., and other times by appointment. You can walk the grounds year-round, admiring the cove that looks across to Queens Island, and strolling through the lush gardens.

North Kingstown's **Quonset Naval Air Base,** Quonset Point, off U.S. 1, 401/294-9540, website: http://users.ids.net/~qam/qam, is home to the Quonset Air Museum, as well as the headquarters for the Rhode Island National Guard. Numcrous aircraft can be viewed at this facility, including Douglas Skyhawks, Hellcat fighter planes, and several helicopters. On open-cockpit days, the third Saturday of each month, you can climb inside many of the aircraft. The base hosts an air show each June, which features daredevil stunts by the Blue Angels. Admission is $3. Open Fri.–Sun. 10 A.M.–3 P.M.

SOUTH KINGSTOWN AND WAKEFIELD

From North Kingstown and Wickford, follow U.S. 1 south about six miles, turning right (opposite the Wooden Observation Tower) onto Route 138, which you can follow west into Kingston, which—confusingly—is part of the town of South Kingstown.

Before turning onto Route 138, you might also want to stop for a moment at the **Wooden Observation Tower.** This 100-foot-tall tower with an open-air observation deck sits on one of the county's higher points, MacSparran Hill, and affords stunning views of Narragansett Bay, Conanicut and Aquidneck Islands (and the bridges that connect them), and the South County shoreline.

Kingston was made the county seat in 1752 and was formerly known as Little Rest, some say because it was home during colonial times to several taverns providing room and board. It's one of the state's most famous towns today because it's home to the **University of Rhode Island (URI),** founded in 1892 as Rhode Island College of Agriculture and Mechanic Arts. URI has a student body of about 11,000 undergrads, plus 3,000 more graduate students. The campus is some 1,200 acres, and many of the ivy-covered granite buildings are quite notable. The most recent addition is the $54 million **Thomas M. Ryan Center,** a 200,000-square-foot athletic center and per-

Minutes off U.S. 1, Wickford is one of New England's best-kept secrets. At the town pier, walk alongside stacks of lobster traps, breathe in the briny air, and look back over the masts in the harbor toward the colonial homes and businesses of town.

formance space that opened in summer 2002. It seats 9,000. The former athletic center, the **Keaney Gymnasium,** was converted into the **New England Basketball Hall of Fame,** website: www.internationalsport.com/basketball, which opened in October, 2002.

This hall of fame is part of the larger **International Scholar-Athlete Hall of Fame,** Feinstein Bldg., 3045 Kingstown Rd. (Rte. 108), website: www.internationalsport.com, within walking distance just southeast of URI's campus. Exhibits focus on the black baseball leagues, posters of the Olympic games, historic baseball parks, and many other sports-related themes. The main exhibit hall contains memorabilia from past inductees, sports artwork from more than 125 countries, and a Rhode Island room that celebrates the achievements of noted scholar-athletes from the state. Admission: $2. Open weekdays 10 A.M.–5 P.M. and Saturdays 10 A.M.–3 P.M.

There aren't a lot of formal attractions related to URI, but the public is welcome to visit the **URI Fine Arts Center Galleries,** 105 Upper College Rd., 401/792-2775, website: www.uri.edu/artsci/art/gallery, which include the Main, Photography, and Corridor exhibit spaces. Admission is free, but the hours for each vary, so it's best to phone ahead or visit the website.

Apart from URI, Kingston is notable for its small but pretty village of Federal and colonial buildings. Across from campus stands the **Pettaquamscutt Historical Society,** 2636 Kingstown Rd. (Rte. 138), 401/783-1328, which can be visited by appointment. The dignified granite-block building dates to 1792, when it was built as the Washington County Jail; a cell-block was added in 1858. In 1960 the Rhode Island Assembly transferred ownership of the building to the historical society, and today it contains household goods and tools from the period, vintage toys and clothing, Native American arrowheads, and other implements; you can also tour the old cell block, which looks much as it did when in use. The society also houses a genealogical library, and the public is welcome to visit and conduct research here.

Just down the street, the Federal-style **Helme House,** 2587 Kingstown Rd., 401/783-2195, website: www.southcountyart.org, is headquarters to the South County Art Association. Art classes are given here, and there's a small gallery whose exhibits rotate frequently. Also headquartered here is the esteemed Potter's Cooperative Gallery, which includes a number of local photographers, sculptors, painters, and potters. The house, which dates to 1802, is one of the town's most stately Federal buildings.

Kingston has had a couple of impressive courthouses over the years, and both of them now function in different capacities. In the earlier of the two, an immense 1775 structure that also served on a rotating basis as the Rhode Island State House between 1776 and 1791, you'll now find the **Kingston Free Library,** 2605 Kingstown Rd., 401/783-8254. Take one good look at it and you may mistake this for a construction of the late 19th century—indeed, the mansard roof and central Gothic Revival tower were added on in the 1890s, as was much of the ornamentation. The building has a beautiful interior, having been top-to-bottom renovated in 1994.

Down the road a ways you'll find the second of the county's courthouses of note, now the **Courthouse Center for the Arts,** 3481 Kingstown Rd., 401/782-1018, a tall and imposing granite structure that was built in 1896. It houses art galleries and a shop selling locally produced arts and crafts, as well as classrooms for various visual and performing arts workshops. This is also the site of music concerts throughout the year.

Nearby is one of two Rhode Island train stations served by Amtrak, **Kingston Railroad Station,** 1 Railroad Ave., off Kingstown Road (Route 138). This handsome clapboard building, which is on the National Register of Historic Places, was built in 1875 in the Stick Victorian style, with the influences of a European chalet.

Back at the intersection of Route 138 and Route 108, follow Route 108 South into **Peace Dale,** a prosperous old factory town that is now

a bit quiet but has some impressive stone factory buildings. The mill buildings here once made up the Peace Dale Manufacturing Company, which began turning out fine woolens and shawls around 1800 and employed about 750 workers during the mill's heyday. Notable buildings around town include the **Peace Dale Public Library,** 1057 Kingstown Rd., 401/789-1555, a majestic Richardsonian Romanesque building designed in 1891 by Frank W. Angell; the stone building is notable for its huge chimneys, grand porte-cochere, and conical turret. Inside what was originally an auditorium you can see a detailed reproduction of *Cantoria,* a work by Italian Renaissance sculptor Lucca della Robbia, carved into a plaster frieze. On the grounds of the library is *The Weaver,* a bronze relief sculpture executed by Lincoln Memorial sculptor Daniel Chester French in 1920.

Nearly across the street you'll find the **Peace Dale Office Building/Museum of Primitive Art and Culture,** 1058 Kingstown Rd., 401/783-5711, which originally contained the mill's post office, company store, and housing for mill workers. Today it's South County's oldest museum, containing a collection of archaeological and ethnological materials culled from all over the world, including pottery, weapons, tools, and blankets. Donation of $1 requested. Open Tues.–Thurs. 11 A.M.–2 P.M. These are but a handful of the impressive structures set throughout this community.

Continue from Peace Dale down Route 108 into **Wakefield,** the administrative center of South Kingstown, home of the stately 1877 **South Kingstown Town Hall,** 180 High St., 401/789-9331. The township of Kingstown was established in 1674 and divided into two separate townships in 1723: South Kingstown and North Kingstown.

This is the main commercial center for South Kingstown and residents of Narragansett and Charlestown. Here you'll find the usual array of prosaic shopping centers and strip malls, but follow Main Street west away from U.S. 1 into downtown and you'll find a more attractive stretch of mostly late Victorian and early-20th-century shopfronts and buildings. One notable structure is the Campus Cinema at 297 Main St., which was built as an opera house in the 1890s. The Saugatucket River passes through the center of town, and it's around this area that a number of businesses have opened in recent years in an attempt to revitalize the downtown and make it more of a destination. The town is also working hard to develop a greenway along this historic, and once polluted and industrial, river.

Wakefield lies just northwest of Narragansett and north of Charlestown; a short drive east or south will return you to U.S. 1.

Shopping

Although South County is neither especially crowded nor famous for being a retail hub, each town in the county does contain a handful of notable shops, and a few areas—such as Watch Hill and Wickford—are quite respected for their boutiques and galleries. All of the county's better shopping areas are in good walking neighborhoods, making it easy to park your car and explore a few shops on foot.

Westerly and Watch Hill

The **Book & Tackle Shop,** Merchant's Square, 55 Beach St., Westerly, 401/596-1770; also in summer at 7 Bay St., Watch Hill, 401/596-0700, specializes in vintage books, including some quite rare finds. **Westerly Artists Coop Gallery,** 12 High St., Westerly, 401/596-2020, is another of South County's several cooperatives, with work by local artisans for sale. There are several good antiques shops in Westerly, among them **Riverside Antiques,** 8 Broad St., 401/596-0266, which occupies a nice space on the Pawcatuck River, and **Fine Consignment,** 43 High St., Westerly, 401/348-1818. At **Mary D's,** 3 Commerce St., 401/596-5653, you find stalls from several dealers selling an eclectic range of antiques. The **Black Duck Gallery,** 25 Broad St., Westerly, 401/348-6500, carries all manner of wood-carved birds, plus paintings and other fine art relating to animals of flight. **Paul's Music and More,** 5A Canal St., Westerly, 401/596-1185, specializes in impossible-to-find recordings of classical, jazz, and blues. You can listen before you buy. You'll also find posters, videos, children's music, and the usual pop and rock tunes.

At **Mo Books and Art,** 60 Bay St., Watch Hill, 401/348-0940, a curious little gallery-boutique, browse the out-of-print children's books, with an emphasis on art and local photography shot and framed by owner Mo. **Puffin's Too,** 64 Bay St., Watch Hill, 401/596-1140, open since the mid--80s, sells the jewelry, home furnishings, and works of about 150 American artists, many of them from Rhode Island and Connecticut. Items include paintings, pottery, chimes, and accessory furniture. **The Wise Owl Toys and Kites,** 56 Bay St., Watch Hill, 401/348-6663; also 50 High St., 401/348-9555, is a great spot for colorful games and toys, and there's no better kite-flying than in breezy Watch Hill. You can reward kids you've dragged into countless grown-up stores with a visit to the **Candy Box,** 14 Fort Rd., Watch Hill, 401/596-3325. **Comina,** 117 Bay St., Watch Hill,

Broad Street, Westerly

401/596-3218, which has several other locations in Connecticut and Rhode Island, carries imaginative home furnishings, collectibles, and gifts—including beautifully hand-crafted Mexican aluminum tableware. The **Country Store,** 19 Bay St., Watch Hill, 401/596-6540, carries garden accessories, dried floral arrangements, framed art, small painted furnishings, and other elegant wares.

Charlestown

The **Fantastic Umbrella Factory,** just off U.S. 1, 401/364-6616, is just down the Old Post Road from Ninigret Park and qualifies as a certifiable tourist attraction. At the whimsical complex you'll find shops, an art gallery, lavish gardens, a petting zoo, and a snack bar. Among the shops are Dave's Den, which sells incense, tapestries, oils, beaded curtains, Native American arts and crafts, and other odd goods. The main store carries a fairly bizarre assortment of collectibles culled from all different parts of the world—kites, jewelry, soaps, greeting cards, mugs, toys, wood carvings, and paintings are among the goodies here. At Small Axe Productions, craftsmen create hand-blown glassworks, stained glass, and stoneware pottery. You can also dine at the Spice of Life restaurant, which specializes in natural foods. The "factory" was founded in 1968, and it definitely still has a hippie sensibility.

At the **General Stanton Flea Market,** General Stanton Inn, 4115 Old Post Rd., off U.S. 1, browse for a wide variety of wares, collectibles, furnishings, and odds and ends; it's open May through October, weekends and holidays, and features more than 200 dealers. In Cross Mills two vintage Cape houses comprise **Simple Pleasures,** 4436 Old Post Rd., 401/364-6496, a great source of herbs, plants, gifts, antiques, and more. At **Charlestown Village,** U.S. 1 at Route 2, you'll find a smattering of eclectic shops selling everything from T-shirts to chocolates to nautical ephemera.

Narragansett

Narragansett Pier Marketplace, Ocean Road, is a small collection of tourist shops, including the Shell Boutique, which specializes in art and Native American gifts but also has an astounding selection of shells. There's a T-shirt shop in the market, a gift shop, and a wonderful ice-cream parlor called Nana's. Adjoining the market is the Coast Guard House restaurant. In Mariner Square, **Lion's Mane Antiques,** 140 Point Judith Rd., 401/789-7411, carries chests, mirrors, armoires, and other pieces chiefly from the Victorian era.

Wakefield, Peace Dale, and Kingston

Near URI, **Allison B. Goodsell Books,** 2538 Kingston Rd. (Route 138), Kingston, 401/792-8662, is a very fine source of rare and antiquarian books, with quite a few titles on Rhode Island history. The historic 1820s **Fayerweather House,** Rtes. 108 and 138, 401/789-9072, open from mid-May through mid-December, is the restored home of 19th-century blacksmith George Fayerweather. Today it contains a gift shop selling the wares of local artisans. It's open Tuesday, Thursday, and Saturday 10 A.M.–4 P.M. A few miles west of URI, off Route 138, **Peter Pots Pottery,** 494 Glen Rock Rd., 401/783-2350, has been an acclaimed shop and gallery since the 1940s; it's a source of beautiful yet functional stoneware, including coffee mugs, table accessories, wine decanters, lamps, and pitchers. The showroom is set inside a circa-1700 stone mill.

Thomas Ladd Pottery, 352 High St., Peace Dale, 401/782-0050, is a very nice little shop showing both contemporary and traditional styles in a quiet residential neighborhood.

Downtown Wakefield has a smattering of antiques shops and other independent stores and boutiques. The noted mail-order company **Kenyon Consumer Products,** 1425 Kingston Rd. (Rte. 108), Peace Dale, 401/792-8093, is a top seller of discounted outdoor gear, clothing, and sporting goods—you can also drop by its outlet store, near the Kenyon headquarters, in Peace Dale. The **Purple Cow,** 205 Main St., Wakefield, 401/789-2389, is an offbeat gallery with custom-made clothing, jewelry, greeting cards, and other gifts. At **Saywell's,** 326 Main St., Wakefield, 401/783-0630, you'll find a vast selection of antiques, books, handmade toys, decorative arts, home furnishings, and other such goods. Wakefield's **Hera Gallery,** 327 Main St., 401/789-1488, is a nonprofit artist's cooperative.

Wickford

Wickford has about 40 shops and boutiques, most of them independently owned. The vast majority of the shops are along West Main Street and Brown Street, the latter being Wickford's main drag.

Pet Peeves, 3 W. Main St., 401/295-5035 or 888/522-5035, is more than an animal-themed boutique. It has all kinds of delightful knick-knacks from pottery to toys to books. **Beauty and the Bath,** 11 W. Main St., 401/294-3576, sells upscale bath amenities, plush robes, soaps, gels, and shaving creams. At the **Grateful Heart,** 17 W. Main St., 401/294-3981, pick up New Age and other spiritual and holistic health–related books, incense, oils, crystals, music, and such. **Village Reflections,** 5 W. Main St., 401/295-7802, offers smart and stylish contemporary woman's clothes and beautiful jewelry. At the **Shaker Shop of Wickford,** 16 W. Main St., 401/294-7779, pick up reproduction Shaker furnishings and handcrafts. Foodies flock to **Wickford Gourmet Kitchen & Table,** 21 W. Main St., 401/295-9790 or 800/286-8190, for intriguing food items, cookware, and table settings.

The **Toy Cellar,** 7 W. Main St., 401/295-1772 or 800/815-1772, offers fanciful games and whimsies. **Studio Zwei,** 2 W. Main St., 401/295-5907 or 800/760-5907, has a remarkably extensive showing of local works, including Wickford sea- and landscapes. Owner Elsie Schaich Kilguss has taught and exhibited her works since 1980. Across the street is another excellent gallery and framer, **Five Main,** 5 W. Main St., 401/294-6280, a collective representing the photography and paintings of some 35 artists. **Nautical Impressions,** 16 W. Main St., 401/295-5303, sells appropriately sea-themed art and gifts.

Wickford Village Antiques and Collectibles, 93 Brown St., 401/294-1117, is a spacious shop with a "Chatchka" room filled with quirky knick-knacks; a garden courtyard shows lawn and outdoor pieces. There are quite a few nautical decorative arts, too. **Wilson's of Wickford,** 35 Brown St., 401/294-9514 or 800/371-9514, is a large department store selling casual yachtsmen's and beach bum wear, with a country-club casual aesthetic. **J. W. Graham,** 26 Brown St., 401/295-0757, has beautiful handcrafted glassware, lamps, home furnishings, and accessories with an emphasis on birds, fish, and the colors of the sea. The **Hour Glass,** 15 W. Main St., 401/295-8724 or 800/585-8724, has a fairly amazing selection of timepieces, including ship's clocks and hourglasses; you'll also find kaleidoscopes, thermometers, sundials, and barometers.

You can browse for art at the **Wickford Art Association Gallery,** 36 Beach St., Wickford, 401/294-6840, a nonprofit cooperative with some 300 members. For information on the many other shops and businesses in Wickford, check out the website of the **Wickford Village Association,** website: www.wickfordvillage.com.

Sports and Recreation

South County, both near the beach and inland a short ways, contains a vast cache of preserved, undeveloped lands, especially in the town of Charlestown. These dedicated green spaces are excellent for hiking, sailing, beachcombing, kayaking, and watching wildlife.

The largest of these parks are in Charlestown. Nearest the shore, there's the **Ninigret National Wildlife Reserve,** off U.S. 1, 401/364-9124, a broad rolling space that leads down to the shores of Ninigret Pond, one of the shore's several massive salt ponds. The preserve has almost no facilities but some excellent hiking trails, including a gentle 1.4-mile loop that ends at Grassy Point, where you can climb to an observation platform and gaze out over Ninigret Pond. The Foster Cove Nature Trail is a 1.1-mile loop that also leads to an elevated platform. There are great opportunities for wildlife viewing at this park, which is home to more than 250 species of birds throughout the year, and dogs are welcome if you keep them on a leash.

Adjacent to the Preserve and with an entrance off Route 1A (which is just off U.S. 1) a short

SOUTH COUNTY FAMILY AMUSEMENTS

As it's a tremendously popular family destination, South County has a wide assortment of amusement centers, minigolf courses, driving ranges, and other activity parks geared toward the zillions of kids who visit here, especially in summer (most of the places below are open spring through summer). Popular options include **Adventureland of Narragansett,** Point Judith Road, 401/789-0030, which has batting cages, bumper boats, a go-kart track, and one of the county's best minigolf courses; **Atlantic Beach Park,** Atlantic Avenue, Misquamicut, 401/322-9298, which includes a "kiddie" amusement park and a carousel; **Bay View Fun Park,** Atlantic Avenue, Misquamicut, 401/322-0180; and **Old Mountain Lanes,** 756 Kingstown Rd., Wakefield, 401/783-5511, which is open year-round and has bumper bowling, billiards, a game room, and two restaurants. There's a skating center at the **Narragansett Ocean Club,** 360 S. Pier Rd., 401/783-1711.

If you're visiting with kids, keep in mind that South County has a couple of YMCA summer camps run weekly sessions. In Charlestown, **Camp Watchung,** 401/596-2894, is open to boys and girls ages 4 to 14 and sits along 60 acres overlooking Watchung Pond; it offers a full slate of athletic and outdoors activities. A related half-day and full-day **Kiddie Kamp,** 401/596-2894, in Westerly is geared toward kids ages 3 through kindergarten.

ways to the east, **Ninigret Park,** 401/364-1222, is the more activity-oriented section of the Ninigret lands. One of the first things you'll notice upon driving into the park are the many acres of abandoned tarmac, now overgrown with grass in some places. From 1943 through 1973, this park was the home of the Charlestown Naval Auxiliary Landing Field—thousands of infantrymen trained for flight in several wars at this facility. It's the old runways that you'll see in some parts of the park. Some are now popular as jogging and bicycling tracks, although they lend a slightly eerie "ghost airport" effect to the park.

Near the park's entrance, a granite marker, the **Charlestown Naval Air Station Memorial,** notes some 60 men who trained here and perished in World War II, Korean, Vietnam, and other military conflicts.

Facilities at the park include athletic fields, public tennis courts, an impressive children's playground, a paved bike trail, hiking areas, fishing in Ninigret Pond and a small freshwater pond with a beach, and picnic groves. Another feature is the **Frosty Drew Nature Center,** 401/364-9508, website: www.frostydrew.org, which throughout the summer offers week-long nature programs for kids 6 to 10; it's open to the public July and August and contains exhibits on natural history. Nature Center staff regularly give walks, talks, and other programs. A final feature near the nature center is the **Frosty Drew Observatory,** 401/596-7688, a nonprofit center that hosts many programs open to the public, usually on Friday nights. A retractable roof allows the observatory's powerful telescope to peer up into the brilliant night sky. In summer the observatory is open according to when it gets dark, while during the fall you can typically visit at about 6:30 P.M.

Burlingame State Park, Sanctuary Road, follow signs north from U.S. 1, Charlestown, 401/322-8910, 401/322-7337 for campground, 401/364-8910 for picnic area, was established in 1927; it's an enormous reserve of some 2,100 acres. This is a top pick for camping, as you'll find some 750 primitive sites here; you can stay as long as two weeks, and there are washing facilities and toilets near the sites. You'll also find a general store and excellent swimming. Other park facilities include a boat launch, ample picnic facilities (both covered and out in the open), and fishing. Picnic sites cost $2 per day, and the group picnic shelters cost $35. Otherwise, as is the case at all Rhode Island state parks (excepting beaches), there's no day-use fee here.

Another excellent spot for outdoors enthusiasts, especially if you're into canoeing, kayaking, or fishing, is **Great Swamp,** a dense swath of South County that has many parts you can't get to at all except by boat. The main route begins at the launch off Route 138 in West Kingston, known as Taylor's Landing. From here you enter a very narrow stretch of the Chipuxet River and paddle south; after a while the trickle of water opens to a much wider and more stable stretch of river. After about three miles of fairly easy paddling you'll enter one of the larger freshwater bodies in the state, Worden's Pond. There are all sorts of opportunities for wildlife sightings along this trip. There's also a put-in/take-out area at the south end, off Worden's Pond Road.

Beaches

A tourist brochure on South County gloats, "Charlestown's secluded beaches offer everything you can desire . . . surfing, kayaking, basking, sailing, walking, shelling, bird-watching, and swimming, in either rough or protected waters." Well, frankly, this probably goes a little too far, but Charlestown does have some of New England's best beaches, and while locals know this, a good many outsiders do not. Of course, Charlestown contains only a fraction of South County's many fine beaches, which extend from Watch Hill, by the Connecticut and New York border, to the lower, western edge of Narragansett Bay. It may not seem like a huge area, but South County has about 100 miles of shoreline, most of it accessible to the public.

This is a remarkable part of New England for beachcombing, but keep in mind that this is also an incredibly fragile ecosystem. Most of South County's sands are on barrier beaches, which are separated from the mainland by long salt ponds and connected by narrow lanes or causeways. It's important to adhere to any fences or signs regarding beach access, and to stay off the dunes whenever possible. Winter storms are constantly eroding and reshaping the shoreline, and efforts are constantly under way to reinforce the dunes, which protect the beaches that many of us take for granted.

Of the roughly 20 public beaches in South County, five of them are state beaches. At these facilities, note the following parking policies: Residents pay $6 per car on weekdays and $7 on weekends and holidays; nonresidents pay $12 per car on weekdays and $14 on weekends. Residents can buy a season pass for $30, and non-

residents for $60. These fees are only assessed on weekends Memorial Day through late June, and daily late June through Labor Day. There's no fee if you arrive by bicycle, on foot, or using public transportation.

As you move west to east in the county from the Connecticut border, you'll first come to the beaches of Watch Hill, which include **Watch Hill Beach,** off Route 1A, 401/596-7761 or 800/SEA-7636, which has restrooms and a bath house and occupies one of the prettiest stretches of sand in the state; the half-mile of beach here leads farther out to isolated **Napatree Point,** 401/596-7761 or 800/SEA-7636, which juts out into Long Island Sound. Parking at Watch Hill (there's none specifically for Napatree) costs $10 per day, and spaces are quite limited—for this reason, you won't typically find swarms of people here. Napatree has a well-deserved reputation for bird-watching, as many migrating shore birds frequent these sands at various times during the year.

Farther east, **Misquamicut State Beach,** 257 Atlantic Ave., off Route 1A, 401/596-9097, offers a half-mile of very popular and heavily used beachfront—it's among the most developed of any beach in the state, which is a turnoff for some but a plus for social butterflies. Within walking distance are minigolf courses, batting cages, and other amusements. Misquamicut has one of the largest parking lots of any beach in the state; facilities are extensive and include picnic tables, changing rooms, a snack bar, and lifeguards. The undertow here is slight, and the comparatively mild surf ideal for swimming. In mellow Weekapaug, to the east, there's shore access at **Quonochontaug Conservation Area,** off West Beach Road, which has very limited facilities but is overseen by lifeguards. A lot of people choose to swim in the eponymous salt pond that fringes the beach; like Napatree, this is a fine place for bird-watching.

A secluded and modest barrier beach with ocean on one side and the west end of Ninigret Pond on the other, **Blue Shutters Town Beach,** off East Beach Road, which is off U.S. 1, 401/364-3878, has a few parking spaces, a snack bar, and changing facilities with showers. Remote **East Beach** is reached on foot by walking farther along the shore from here; this is an uncrowded and largely unsupervised area that's nice for swimming, at your own risk, of course. **Charlestown Town Beach** off U.S. 1, 401/364-3878, is a good bet for beating the crowds, although avid outdoorsy types love it for its big crashing waves (note the surfers) and wide beach (note the volleyball court). The beach has full changing facilities, restrooms, picnic areas, and lifeguards. Parking costs about the same as at the state beaches.

A rather narrow stretch of South Kingstown cuts down to the ocean between Charlestown and Narragansett; here you'll find a pair of excellent beaches. By far the most popular is **East Matunuck State Beach,** off 950 Succotash Rd., 401/789-8585, which has a 700-car parking lot, lifeguards, and full changing facilities. This half-mile beach is close to **South Kingstown Town Beach,** Matunuck Beach Road, 401/789-9301, which is just over 1,000 feet but has sports facilities, grills and a picnic grove, changing rooms with hot showers, a playground, and other good stuff.

To the east, Narragansett is Rhode Island's beach-bumming capital, its crown jewel being **Roger Wheeler State Beach,** Sand Hill Cove Road, off Route 108, 401/789-3563, a typically packed swatch of golden sand at Point Judith with among the best facilities in the county, including an excellent playground, picnic area, and bathhouse. Just west of Roger Wheeler, in Galilee, is **Salty Brine Beach,** 254 Great Rd., 401/789-8374, a short span that's popular with area teens and young people. On the Narragansett Bay side of town, **Scarborough State (North) Beach** and **Scarborough South Beach,** both off Ocean Avenue, 401/789-2324 or 401/782-1319, connect and provide a total of about 3,000 parking spaces and roughly a half-mile of sand. These are both hot spots for college students, and the crowds can get a bit rowdy from time to time. Farther up Ocean Avenue, at Narragansett Pier, is **Narragansett Town Beach,** a broad beach with shallow bathing and a full slate of facilities and plenty of parking (though less of the latter than at the state beaches).

Bicycling

South County is mostly flat, especially the coastal sections. However, venture more than a mile or two inland, and you'll find the more jagged woodlands up toward Kingston and northern Westerly, and leading into the northern reaches of Washington County. From Watch Hill to Narragansett and then north along the shore to Wickford, you could largely follow any portion of the driving tour outlined earlier in the chapter on bike; just be careful on busy U.S. 1, and on some of the narrow stretches of secondary roads. By far the safest and most practical road for bicycling is Route 1A, especially from Wickford south to Point Judith. You'll be rewarded with wonderful beach views all along this stretch.

A very recent development is the impressive **South County Bike Trail,** which has been completed from Kingston Amtrak station, just off Route 138, down to Peace Dale, but will eventually twist through the county for some 11 miles, terminating at the South County Museum near Narragansett Pier. Other sites along or just off this trail, which runs over an easement of the old Narragansett Pier Railroad (it shut down in the late –60s), include the Courthouse Center for the Arts, the URI campus, and Peace Dale's Museum of Primitive Art & Culture. When completed, the trail will run along the Saugatucket River Corridor, through downtown Wakefield, and along part of the Pettaquamscutt River. It's not known just yet when the final portion of the trail will be completed, but depending on funding, it could be by 2004. To keep up with the trail's status and learn more about sites along the way, visit the website: website: www.south-county.com/bikepath.

You can get a bike to South County from just about anywhere served by Amtrak or RIPTA. RIPTA buses all have bike racks, year-round. Amtrak runs the "Bikes-on-Board" program on all of its routes serving the Northeast Corridor. Travelers with bikes can store them on a specially equipped baggage train. Just ask about this program when booking a ticket on Amtrak.

Boating, Kayaking, and Sailing

You've come to the right part of the Ocean State if you're intent on actually venturing out onto

© ANDREW COLLINS

Watch Hill piers and harbor front

the open waters. South County has boat and sailing rentals and charters of just about every kind, as well as some excellent spots for kayak rental and instruction.

The **Kayak Centre,** with three South County locations—Brown and Phillips Streets, Wickford, 401/295-4400; 562 Charlestown Beach Rd., Charlestown, 401/364-8000; and 93 Watch Hill Rd., Watch Hill, 401/348-2800; also 888/SEA-KAYAK, website: www.kayakcentre.com—rents (and sells) kayaks and offers tours, lessons, and advice. It's an excellent resource. Other sources of kayak rentals and instruction include **Narrow River Kayak,** 95 Middlebridge Rd., Narragansett, 401/789-0334; and **Quaker Lane Bait and Tackle,** 4019 Quaker La., North Kingstown, 401/294-9642.

Public boat launches are found all through the county, on both fresh- and saltwater sources. These include the launch on the Pawcatuck River on Main Street in downtown Westerly, and at Lotteryville Marina in Avondale (off Route 1A).

Popular boat charters include **Night Heron Harbor & Nature Cruises,** 401/783-9977, which offers trips that explore the great salt ponds of South County, plus snorkel/dive tours and sunset cruises, and the ***White Rose,*** 401/789-0181, which offers custom sails throughout

Rhode Island waters. The **Southland Riverboat,** 401/783-2954, website: www.southlandcruises.com, offers tours on an authentic riverboat that departs from State Pier in Galilee. The 11-mile narrated tour chugs along the South County shoreline and lower Narragansett Bay, by lighthouses and through prized fishing waters, passing about a dozen small islands and beside countless coves and peninsulas. This flat-bottom riverboat, built in Mississippi, holds about 150 passengers and has a full bar and snack area. Both standard sightseeing cruises and evening sunset sails are offered, with prices ranging from about $10 to $15 for adults; children are roughly half price. In Wickford, the Dutch sailing yacht, the *Brandaris,* 7 Main St., 401/294-1481, helped evacuate troops from the shores of Dunkirk during World War II and is now available for sightseeing excursions. The 63-foot ship accommodates up to 30 guests.

Near the Cross Mills section of Charlestown, **Ocean House Marina,** 60 Town Dock Rd., off the Post Road (Route 1A), 401/364-6040 or 888/211-1609, website: www.oceanhousemarina.com, was built as the town meeting house, and then came to be run as a summer resort. Today it's a marina renting all types of boats, as well as being a bait-and-tackle shop. It sits right on Ninigret's salt pond, from which you can access Block Island Sound.

For information on the more than 50 party boats that sail from South County, contact the **Rhode Island Party & Charter Boat Association,** 401/737-5812, website: www.rifishing.com/charter.htm. There's a full list of boats and phone numbers on the website, plus links to websites for many individual boats.

Fishing

Home to the second-most-profitable fishing port in New England, Point Judith, South County is nirvana for fishing enthusiasts, and not just the saltwater variety. Several clear and fruitful rivers and a handful of freshwater ponds are popular, including Bradford Landing, which is along the Pawcatuck River off U.S. 1. For sport fishing, Westerly is better suited to noncommercial fishing enthusiasts, as it has several great spots for casting a line into the surf, including Watch Hill Point, Misquamicut State Beach, Weekapaug Breachway (which is administered by the state and has stairs laid out conveniently to the waterfront below), and Napatree Point. In this part of the state you can also charter a boat to fish for blues, bluefin tuna, sharks, swordfish, and many other varieties.

Several companies in South County offer fishing charters. **Frances Fleet,** 2 State St., 401/783-4988 or 800/66-CATCH, website: www.francesfleet.com, hosts a variety of trips, from cod-fishing excursions at sunrise to nighttime bluefish and striped bass runs to tuna trips far out at sea. Frances also offers Rhode Island's only whale-watching cruises, from July through Labor Day, Mon.–Sat. 1 P.M. Other fishing boats include **Old Salt Charters,** 401/783-4805; **C-Devil II Sportfishing,** 860/267-9912; **Seven B's,** 401/789-9250; and **White Ghost Charters,** 401/828-9465.

If you're simply interested in casting a line into the surf yourself, try **Charleston Breachway State Beach,** 401/364-7000, in Charlestown, which is sheltered and extremely popular for this activity. Also note some of the boating charters mentioned above in Boating, Kayaking, and Sailing—some of these are good sources for renting your own boat, with or without a crew, and in some cases these marinas sell bait and tackle.

Golf

South County is Rhode Island's golfing capital, and a handful of excellent courses have opened just over the last couple of decades. Greens fees at South County courses are among the most reasonable you'll find in southern New England. Most of these are in the northern part of the county, covered in the Greater Providence chapter. But in the lower South County towns, consider the following courses.

Winnapaug Country Club, Shore Road, Westerly, 401/596-9164, is an attractive 18-hole course with very nice views of Winnapaug Pond. The layout was designed by acclaimed architect Donald Ross. There's also a very nice little restaurant here, open for both lunch and dinner. **Weekapaug Golf Course,** 265 Shore Rd. (Rte. 1A), 401/322-0840, is nearby and has just nine holes.

Fairly close to URI campus, **Laurel Lane Golf Course,** 309 Laurel La., West Kingston, 401/783-3844, is a short but pleasant 18-hole course; it also has a lounge and snack bar. This is an exceptionally well-cared-for course, with beautiful greens and fairways. Another option is **North Kingstown Municipal Golf Course,** Quonset Access Road, North Kingstown, 401/294-4051, which also plays to 18 holes and sits out on Quonset Point. Area nine-hole courses include **Rolling Greens,** Ten Rod Road, North Kingstown, 401/294-9859, the par-27 **Rose Hill Golf Club,** 222 Rose Hill Rd., 401/788-1088, and **Woodland Greens Golf Clubs,** 655 Old Baptist Rd., North Kingstown, 401/294-2872.

Hiking and the Outdoors

The western and northern parts of South County are more remote and less crowded, ideal for horseback riding, camping, and hiking. The 72-mile **North-South Trail** runs from the northern boundary of the state all the way through South County before ending at the coast; the trail enters lower Washington County up around where Routes 138 and 112 intersect, in Wyoming and a little east of I-95

Exit 3, and terminates at Charlestown's Blue Shutters Town Beach. Highlights and good access points along the trail include Burlingame State Park, Indian Cedar Swamp, and the Carolina Management Area. The website, http://outdoors.htmlplanet.com/nst/nst_map00.htm, has a very nice detailed map of the trail as it runs through the state.

Scuba Diving

Twin Dolphins, Inc., 60 Sportsman Rd., Charlestown, 401/322-9171, offers scuba-diving charter trips to various wrecks off the Rhode Island shoreline.

Tennis

In Charlestown, **Ninigret Park** has public tennis courts; another option is **Fishermen's Memorial State Park,** Route 108, Point Judith, 401/789-8374, which is right by the beach. The town of South Kingstown has public courts at several of its town parks, including **Brousseau Park,** Succotash Road; **Old Mountain Field,** Kingstown Road; and **West Kingston Park,** Route 138. Call South Kingstown's recreation department for details at 401/789-9301.

Water Sports and Parasailing

Bar Fly Parasail, 401/487-4137, offers safe and exciting soaring from 500 to 1,000 feet over the coast.

If you're a fan of boogie-boarding, head to East Beach in Westerly. The salt ponds behind the barrier beaches along the South Coast shoreline are ideal for any activities that are best in calm water, such as Jet Skiing. An excellent spot is **Winnapaug Pond,** by Misquamicut State Beach; at **Misquamicut Beach Jet Ski Rentals,** 401/596-9518, you can find all the equipment and instruction you need.

Accommodations

In some respects, South County is a throwback to another era when it comes to its accommodations. Of the more than 100 options in South County, the vast majority of them are within a mile, or even quarter mile, of the ocean. Almost none of them are chain properties, and very few offer the sort of upscale accommodations you'd find in Newport or Block Island. South County is a value-oriented community, and a place where family-run, comparatively simple hotels, motor lodges, and motels dominate the landscape. It's quite easy to find accommodations with kitchen facilities, that sleep four to eight guests, and that have plenty of social- and activity-oriented amenities, from playgrounds and expansive pools to shuffleboard courts and boat launches. Especially in Misquamicut, you'll find several properties that sit directly on the beach.

A drawback of sorts is that it's rather difficult to find seaside properties that possess a great deal of character; the expectation is that visitors to South County aren't likely to spend a whole lot of time in their rooms. There are a couple of historic properties in Watch Hill, and you'll find a smat-tering of atmospheric inns strung throughout the county, both near the shore and inland. Also, while accommodations here aren't fancy or super-expensive, they're generally not bargain-basement cheap in summer, at least near the water. During July and August, it can be tough finding accommodations, at least on weekends, for less than $100 nightly. The most economical deals tend to be hotels that have efficiencies or cottages available on a weekly basis—these are especially useful and economical if you're booking a unit that sleeps a few people.

HOTELS AND MOTELS

Under $50

An inexpensive, simple option near historic Wickford and also a good base for exploring metro Providence and even Newport, the **Budget Inn,** 7825 Post Rd., North Kingstown, 401/294-4888, website: www.budget-inn.net, is a one-story brick motel with clean rooms with phones, cable TV, and in some cases microwaves and refrigerators.

$50–100

Along U.S. 1 near Westerly Airport, the family-run **Ambassador Motel**, 201 Post Rd., 401/322-7995, is a cheap and cheerful little property that feels like it's from another time. Friendly owners take good care of this place, and rates dip below $50 on weekdays and in the off-season and aren't much higher on summer weekends. There are nine rooms, all with cable TV, tiled bathrooms, phones, and air-conditioning. A bargain option in Charlestown, the **Sea View Motor Court**, 3865 Old Post Rd. (Rte. 1A), 401/364-6212, doesn't actually have a sea view, but hey, why split hairs? Beaches are an easy bike ride away, and the freshwater swimming and fishing of Ninigret and Burlingame parks is even closer. The motel has just six very simple units, but there are also 14 efficiency cabins that have their own porches, fully equipped kitchenettes, TVs, and modern bathrooms—they sleep from two to six people, depending on the size of the cabin. Unusual for a motel, the Sea View has a big screened-in gazebo with a fireplace and stereo, and there are also picnic tables and gas grills. Spruce trees tower over the grassy grounds. This is an excellent value.

Short of pitching a tent on the sand, you can't really sleep much closer to Scarborough State Beach than by renting a room at the **Anchor Motel**, 825 Ocean Rd., 401/792-8550, anchor825@aol.com, a 13-room motel with some of the best rates of any near-ocean property in South County. Rooms are basic but pleasant enough, especially if you're planning to spend most of your waking time out on the beach. One of the best economy motels in Rhode Island, the **Hamilton Village Inn**, 642 Boston Neck Rd., North Kingstown, 401/294-0700, is a dapper white structure that sits along the road between Wickford village and the bridge to Jamestown—it's close to Casey Farm and the Gilbert Stuart Museum, and not far from beaches either. Rooms are immaculate, and suites have fully equipped kitchens. This is a cut above some of the more dated motels in South County—rooms have brand-new carpets and light-wood furnishings, and the kitchens and baths are modern and attractive. The grounds consist of nicely cared-for gardens and towering trees, and the diner-style on-site restaurant, Sea View Station, serves three meals a day. A fairly basic accommodation right by the ferry terminal for Block Island, the **Lighthouse Inn of Galilee**, 307 Great Island Rd., 401/789-9341 or 800/336-6662, website: www.lighthouseinn-ri.com, is a motor lodge with prosaic but comfortable rooms, heated indoor pool, a hot tub, a gym, and a restaurant and bar. It's a good base for exploring the area, and the location if ideal if you'd like to hop over to Block Island for the day but don't want to sleep there.

$100–150

Andrea Hotel, 89 Atlantic Ave., Misquamicut, 401/348-8788, website: www.andreahotel.com, is a good option for families and adults—it's right along the beach and has a lifeguard watching over the 300 feet of beachfront all summer long. The amusement parks and video arcades of Misquamicut are within walking distance, but this is far enough west of all that to be relatively mellow for adults. This is one of the more popular hotels along the beach, having been owned for more than 50 years by the Colucci family. There's a large restaurant and bar, both looking out at the sea, and the recreational facilities are extensive. The 25 rooms are pleasant, and many of them have received top-to-bottom overhauls in recent years; they all have decks, some of them overlooking the water, and some have individual climate-control. Street-view rooms start well below $100 nightly, even in summer, while deluxe units facing the ocean can go for as much as $175. The restaurant serves sandwiches, burgers, seafood grills, and pub fare. At the comparatively quiet west end of Misquamicut Beach, still an easy walk or bike ride from the Boardwalk and with glorious views of the ocean and plenty of beachfront, the **Pleasant View Inn**, 65 Atlantic Ave., 401/348-8200 or 800/782-3224, website: www.pvinn.com, is this community's largest hotel, with 112 rooms, many of them overlooking the ocean. Room price depends on the view, size, and amenities, but all rooms have color cable TV and most have private balconies; suites have microwaves, refrigerators, and wet bars. There's nothing at all fancy about the cookie-cutter chain-hotel-style decor, but the

RENTING A COTTAGE

Many visitors to South County rent cottages, either for weeks or entire summers. This option can be a great money-saver even if you're only planning to visit for a week, and it's definitely an economical and convenient way to go if you're visiting for longer. Weekly rentals typically begin and end on Saturday afternoons, although certain owners require Friday-to-Friday or even Sunday-to-Sunday agreements. Most rentals in South County and other shore locations in Rhode Island are available from May through September, although there are some properties available during the off-season.

Amenities and costs vary greatly, with much dependent on proximity to the beach, but here's a sampling of what you might expect to pay for certain properties around the area. On the high end, a five-bedroom oceanfront house in Misquamicut (sleeping up to 17) rents for $4,500/week, and an upscale three-bedroom house on the ocean in

Charlestown rents for $3,200/week. In the mid-range, a Watch Hill two-bedroom ocean-view condo a block from the beach goes for $1,600/week. In the most affordable range, one four-bedroom house on a pond that's a mile or so from Misquamicut Beach rents for just $700/week (the catch is that it has only one bathroom), while a two-bedroom house just a short walk from Green Hill Beach near Charlestown rents for $820/week.

Most real estate agents accept reservations on properties up to a year in advance, and as you might guess, the very best rentals get booked up quickly, often by January or February preceding each summer. Nevertheless, don't despair if you find yourself interested in a vacation rental and it's already early August—with so many rentals on the market each summer, you'll generally find something in your price range and with the amenities and location you're seeking. Once you make a reservation, you'll be asked to make a deposit, often as much as 50 per-

---

functional furnishings are generally well maintained and definitely appropriate for families. Another plus for kids are the extensive facilities: a heated outdoor pool, sauna, and exercise room; you can also rent VCRs for your room, as well as movies from the hotel's video library. The Pleasant View has a pair of restaurants, one more casual and serving lighter snacks, but neither of them overly formal. The **Breezeway Resort,** 70 Winnapaug Rd., Misquamicut, 401/348-8953 or 800/462-8872, website: www.breezewayresort .com, is an attractive family-oriented property with four acres of nicely manicured grounds with lush green lawns and Japanese maple trees and 48 super-clean rooms. It's not on the beach, but it's a short walk up the road. The same family has owned the resort since the early 1970s. Amenities include in-room refrigerators, phones with data ports, and whirlpool tubs in some units; there are also bicycles for guest use, a large heated pool with a sprawling sun deck, a shuffleboard court, a small playground, and hammocks. The resort also runs Maria's restaurant, down near the beach. In addition to standard rooms, you can book a suite in the nearby annex; several of these units

have kitchens. Villas that sleep four and have kitchens are rented on a weekly basis. Complimentary Continental breakfast features bagels delivered from the famous A&M Bakery in New York City. The entire resort is an excellent value.

One of only a handful of chain properties in South County, the **Holiday Inn South County,** 3169 U.S. 1, at Route 138, 401/789-1051 or 877/805-9008, website: www.holiday-inn.com, sits high on a hill by the Wooden Observation Tower on U.S. 1. It's representative of the chain, with pleasant if unremarkably furnished rooms. The location is extremely convenient to URI, as well as to South County beaches and Newport. The 107 rooms are spread over four floors, and there's a full-service restaurant, a lounge, business services, a pool, a pair of volleyball courts, and a fitness center. The hotel books up completely for many weekends during the school year (parents' weekend, homecoming, etc.). **Charlestown Willows Resort,** U.S. 1, Charlestown, 401/364-7727 or 800/842-2181, website: www.willowsresort.com, is an attractive small mustard-hued motel complex that faces Nini-

cent down by mid-January or -February (if you book later, 50 percent is usually requested within a week or two of placing the reservation). Always read the fine print carefully, especially those clauses that apply to cancellations and transfers—prepare to lose the 50 percent deposit you've made if you change your plans after April 1 or so. You may have some or all of this amount returned to you if the agency is able to rent the property during the period you had booked it, but even this policy varies among different agencies.

Most rental agencies accept only cash, bank check, or money orders—no credit cards—and most expect full final payment on check-in. You may also be asked to make a security or damages deposit. Agencies can be very strict about prohibiting house parties and excessive guests (student groups, frat brothers, and the like are frowned upon if not outright forbidden by some agencies). Check around if you want to bring your pet, as a few properties permit this by arrangement (and often after requesting an additional security deposit). Many units are nonsmoking.

Renting a cottage differs considerably from booking a room at a hotel. Housekeeping is not included, and renters are expected to take good care of their homes and leave them as clean as they found them (or forfeit the deposit).

Numerous real estate agents in South County specialize in beach rentals, among them **Charlestown Beach Real Estate,** 401/364-6926 or 800/800-6926, www.riliving.com/02483; **Durkin Cottages Realty,** 401/789-6659, www.durkincottages.com; **JBL Realty,** 401/783-5183, www.jblrealty.com; **Lila Delman Real Estate,** 401/789-6666, www.liladelman.com; **Properties Unlimited,** 401/364-6700, www.propertiesunltd.com; **Stanton Realty,** 401/596-2885, www.stantonrealty.com; and **Wallander Realty, 401/364-3616 or 888/RI-OCEAN, www.wallanderrealty.com.**

gret Pond. Opened in the early 1930s, it's family run and has a simple good-natured feel; there's nothing fancy about it, but rooms are spotless. Efficiencies, rented by the week, have stoves, sinks, microwaves, and refrigerators; there's a large pool and a tennis court, game room, shuffleboard, volleyball, two practice golf holes, and boat rentals. It nearly adjoins the Ninigret Wildlife Preserve, whose entrance and parking lots are just a short distance farther on the right on Foster Cove. You can also dock your own boat right behind the motel. The adjoining Mariners Fare Restaurant serves fresh-caught seafood and occasionally presents traditional New England clambakes, prepared in a pit outside.

A large clapboard hotel right on the bay in the heart of Narragansett Pier, the **Village Inn,** 1 Beach St., 401/783-6767 or 800/THE-PIER, website: http://villageinnatthepier.com/, has 61 fairly large and contemporary rooms with typical chain-hotel-style furnishings. The big reason to stay here is location: it's adjacent to the Towers at Narragansett Pier, and within walking distance of the beach, many shops and restau-

rants, and the South County Museum. Pluses include whirlpool tubs in most rooms, and a large indoor pool with a Jacuzzi. There's also a lounge and sun deck, and two restaurants. A modern, immaculately kept low-rise hotel less than a mile north of Misquamicut's beaches and adjoining Weekapaug golf course, the family-run **Winnapaug Inn,** 169 Shore Rd., 401/348-8350 or 800/288-9906, website: www.winnapauginn.com, is a terrific option if you're seeking moderately priced rooms and a low-keyed setting that's both greener and less chaotic than the beach properties. Some upper-level rooms do have distant ocean views, and many more look out over the fairways of the golf course; most have balconies. Rooms are spacious but simply furnished and come in a variety of sizes, including some fully equipped townhouse units with kitchens. Some have whirlpool tubs, refrigerators, and wet bars. There's a large heated pool to one side, plus a shuffleboard court, and guests receive free passes to the beach and complimentary breakfast. The owners also operate the excellent Venice Restaurant next door.

SOUTH COUNTY

$150–250

Paddy's Restaurant and Hotel, 159 Atlantic Ave., 401/596-4350, website: www.paddys-restaurant.com, is a smaller property with beautifully maintained rooms that are a cut above most along Misquamicut. Rooms have hardwood floors, fresh flowers, attractive light-wood furnishings, and very new and clean fixtures and bathrooms. Lifeguards patrol the beach out back, and the Misquamicut Boardwalk is just steps away. Paddy's also has a large and popular restaurant. A Victorian-inspired inn that actually dates to 1939, the **Weekapaug Inn,** 25 Spray Rock Road, Weekapaug, 401/322-0301, website: www.weekapauginn.com, was built to replace the original 1890s structure that succumbed to the tremendous hurricane in 1938. This long building, with a roofline punctuated by more than a dozen gables, overlooks pristine Quonochontaug Pond and the ocean just beyond that. Its refreshingly uncomplicated rooms are tidy and attractive, well-tended by the fourth generation of Buffum family innkeepers to run the place since it opened. However, you won't find TVs or phones in these rooms—guests who favor the Weekapaug do so because they're seeking the peace and quiet of the sea. Entertainment tends to revolve around playing board games in the lobby, or taking in one of the many guest lectures or story-telling events set up frequently by the innkeepers. Outdoor amenities are many: shuffleboard, lawn bowling, croquet, bicycles, canoes, sailboats, and tennis courts. Children's activities—from arts and crafts to nature walks—are organized each day. This is an all-inclusive resort, so while rates begin at nearly $400 per double-occupancy room per night, they include three very good meals each day, plus all activities and facilities (children are charged about $125 each per night). Alcohol is not sold in the dining room, but set-ups are provided and guests are welcome to bring their own. Credit cards are not accepted, smoking is allowed only outside, and men are asked to wear jackets at dinner each night. If the rules and simple attitudes seem off-putting, this may not be the best option for you—but the Weekapaug has a devoted following, and many more first-timers come here unsure what to expect and leave completely sold on the inn's wholesome and uncomplicated take on vacationing.

INNS AND B&BS

$50–100

On Route 1A near Winnapaug Pond and just a short drive from the ocean, the turn-of-the-century **Grandview B&B,** 212 Beach Rd., Misquamicut, 401/596-6384 or 800/447-6384, website: www.grandviewbandb.com, occupies a handsome white clapboard and stone house. The sun-filled house is furnished in tasteful and elegant pastels, white or floral bedspreads, wicker armchairs and rockers, and other well-chosen and understated furnishings. Some of the 11 rooms have private baths (some of these with showers but not tubs), while a few of the least expensive accommodations share baths. But everything is kept immaculately here, and if you can stand to share a bath, these rooms are an excellent value. There's only one room that costs more than $150 per night, a family suite on the third floor, which has a king bed, two twins, and a large sitting area. Named for King Tom Ninigret, the last of the crowned kings of the Narragansett tribe, **King Tom Farm,** 4740 Old Post Rd., Charlestown, 401/364-9535, website: www.kingtomfarm.com, has been a gristmill and then a potato farm before becoming an inn. This 1880s farmhouse sits along eight acres of gardens, lawns, and light woodlawn—land that once belonged to King Tom. The four guest rooms are smartly and simply decorated, with a warm contemporary flair—you won't find tchotchke-filled nooks and frilly curtains in this refreshingly unfussy inn. One room has an understated floral motif, while another has a brass bed and vibrant red walls. The only drawback, at least for some people, is that each room shares a bath—but this fact also accounts for the extremely fair rates. Guest cottages on the property are ideal for longer stays. A full breakfast is included for guests of the inn itself. A grand 1830s mansion with 13 rooms of its own and another six in the cozy Holly House annex across the way, the **Larchwood Inn,** 521 Main St., Wakefield, 401/783-5454 or 800/275-5450, website: www.larchwoodinn.com, sits right on the edge of Wakefield, a short drive from URI and area beaches. Rooms have original and re-production Victorian and colonial pieces, in-cluding pencil-post and brass beds. Many rooms can be joined to create two-room suites suitable for families or friends traveling together. The inn's restaurant, the Buttery, serves traditional Continental and American fare, and there's also a festive bar called Tam O'Shanter. The inn is nicely maintained and reasonably priced, if not especially fancy or luxurious.

There's only one private home on Westerly's Wilcox Park these days, and fortunately for trav-elers, it's now the **Kismet on the Park B&B,** 71 High St., 401/596-3237, website: www.kismet-bandb.com, which is also steps from many inter-esting shops and eateries. The tall clapboard-and-shingle house offers several rooms in varying con-figurations, including a suite, and also an apart-ment that's available long-term. Some upper-level accommodations have very nice views over the duck pond and grassy meadows of Wilcox Park. This informal property where guests have a good bit of independence is an excellent choice if you're planning to spend a lot of time in Westerly, al-though it's a bit more of a drive from the area's beaches than accommodations in or near Watch Hill and Misquamicut. Set on a couple of acres crisscrossed by stone walls and dotted with flow-ering shrubs and leafy trees, **Sugarloaf Hill B&B,** 607 Main St., Wakefield, 401/789-8715, web-site: www.sugarloafhillbandb.com, contains two sunny guest rooms and a large suite with a skylight and its own private deck; one room has a fire-place. Two rooms have private baths, and another has a separate bathroom down the hall. The decor in the guest rooms and common spaces is eclectic and charming. Full breakfast is included. It's a short walk into downtown Wakefield. **Four Gables Bed and Breakfast,** 12 S. Pier Rd., Nar-ragansett Pier, 401/789-6948, website: www.vir-tualcities.com/ons/ri/n/rin5702.htm, is a lovely gambrel-roofed shingle-style cottage that's just steps from the beach in Narragansett Pier, in an at-tractive residential neighborhood. The interior

has stunning Arts and Crafts furnishings, as well as four fireplaces. From the dining room you can take in terrific views of Narragansett Bay. A pair of guest rooms share one-and-a-half baths; each room contains a tasteful mix of well-chosen antiques and collectibles. Gardens, a brick patio, and a ve-randa fringe this beautiful house. Full breakfast is included.

Just a mile and a half south of Wickford vil-lage, **Crosswinds Farm,** 800 Boston Neck Rd., North Kingstown, 401/294-6168 or 888/349-3105, website: www.crosswindsbnb.com, is a dapper 1850s farmhouse with a pair of homey guest rooms, each with private bath. The own-ers will rent a third room, which shares a bath with one of the other rooms, but only when the guests of both units are traveling together and request this arrangement. Slanting ceilings, country furnishings, and heavy quilts create a cozy and warm feel in each room, and com-mon areas contain a smattering of antiques—this is a low-keyed property that's ideal if you're seeking a peaceful and convenient location and are traveling on a moderate budget.

$100–150

The Haddie Pierce House, 146 Boston Neck Rd., 401/294-7674 or 866/4-HADDIE, web-site: www.haddiepierce.com, is a traditional early-20th-century four-square clapboard home with five warmly furnished guest rooms, each with private bath. Decor is heavy on frill, one room named for and accented with stuffed teddy bears, another for the vintage dolls contained therein. More masculine is the Nautical Room, with blue and white curtains and bedspreads and framed nautical prints on the walls. Some rooms have whirlpool baths. The large common rooms are decked with elegant Victorian furniture. The inn is just a short walk from downtown Wickford. An appealing B&B down the road from the URI campus, the Kings' Rose, 1747 Mooresfield Rd. (Rte. 138), Kingston, 401/783-5222 or 888/230-ROSE, email: kingsrose@earthlink.net, is a grand colonial revival inn that sits on a couple of acres of beautifully landscaped English-style gardens. There are seven guest rooms, five with private bath, and all with air-conditioning, TV, and phone. Although the house dates only to 1933, it's listed on the National Register of Historic Places, recognized for its fine craftsmanship and Williamsburg Georgian–inspired detailing. Sun-filled common rooms include the library, sunroom, and living room, as well as a spacious terrace. Full breakfast is included, and dinner can be arranged with 48 hours advance notice. And, unexpected for such a beautiful home, pets are welcome in many cases—check when booking. A short walk from the beautiful beaches of Matunuck, the **Admiral Dewey Inn**, 68 Matunuck Beach Rd., 401/783-2090, website: www.admiraldeweyinn.com, is a towering 1898 summer beach house whose upper floors afford exceptional views of the ocean and Block Island Sound. The inn opened as a boardinghouse back at the turn of the 20th century; these days you can expect somewhat fancier accommodations, but the 10 rooms are still happily uncluttered and informal, with hardwood floors, brass and carved-wood headboards and beds, and Victorian furnishings and wallpapers. Most rooms have private baths, and half of them offer ocean views. A buffet breakfast is set up in the dining room or, when weather permits, on the porch. Just across the street is Matunuck's Theatre-by-the-Sea.

The **Shelter Harbor Inn,** 10 Wagner Rd., off U.S. 1, Weekapaug, 401/322-8883, website: www.shelterharborinn.com, is a grand old white inn down a long circular drive off a commercial-free stretch of U.S. 1. Adirondack chairs dot the beautifully manicured grounds. Inside is a creaky-floored warren of comfortable guest rooms and common areas, including a sunny bar and dining room, with working fireplaces throughout. There are nine guest rooms, some of which have fireplaces and private decks; the barn has been renovated to house 10 rooms, and a separate carriage house has four more rooms, each with its own working fireplace. Lush terraced gardens surround the house, and public rooms include a library and sun porch. Amenities include paddle tennis and croquet courts, a hot tub on a third-floor sundeck, and a private beach (which is a short drive away and has restricted parking; however, the inn provides either shuttle-bus service or beach parking passes)—this beautiful swath of

sand extends for about two miles along the shores of Quonochontaug Pond and the ocean. You can borrow beach towels and pick up a box lunch to bring with you down to the beach or wherever your travels are taking you. There's a fine restaurant on premises that serves three meals a day (breakfast is complimentary for inn guests), plus an excellent Sunday brunch. The massive, rambling inn was built in the late 19th century and converted to an inn nearly a century ago; it's part of a 200-acre community that was originally a gathering place for musicians and came to be known as Musicolony. Streets are named for famous composers—Rossini, Verdi, Handel, Grieg, and so on.

In the same lovely neighborhood, **The Richards,** 144 Gibson Ave., Narragansett, 401/789-7746, website: www.virtualcities.com/ons/ri/n/rin5501.htm, is an imposing 8,500-square-foot stone mansion that was once the anchor of the 200-acre estate. No luxury or degree of craftsmanship was spared in constructing this stunning house, which even has a working elevator. There are four guest rooms, each with a working fireplace and a private bathroom; two suites have large sitting areas. The house is filled with museum-quality antiques and is situated on a lovely parcel with beautifully kept gardens—this is Narragansett's most photogenic inn. In each room you'll find a decanter of sherry awaiting you, and a full breakfast is served each morning.

$150–250

A stately, gambrel-roof house near both Misquamicut and Watch Hill, **The Villa,** 190 Shore Rd., Misquamicut, 401/596-1054 or 800/722-9240, website: www.thevillaatwesterly.com. The house sits down a short driveway, at the end of which you'll find a beautifully landscaped circular drive and the grand entryway to this handsome house. The grounds are abundant with flower gardens, and an in-ground pool sparkles out back. The Mediterranean-inspired house contains six guest suites, some with whirlpool tubs, fireplaces, and private terraces; all have refrigerators, coffeemakers, microwaves, TV/VCRs, and CD players. These are cushy, couples-oriented rooms that are perfect for special occasions; one has a skylight situated directly above its two-person Jacuzzi, while the master suite's double whirlpool faces the gas fireplace. Rooms all have big fluffy queen-size beds and lavish fabrics and bedding. In warm weather, breakfast is served on the lanai overlooking the pool and gardens. A popular spot facing Narragansett Bay, the **Ocean Rose Inn,** 113 Ocean Ave., Narragansett Pier, 401/783-4704, website: www.oceanroseinn.com, offers a mix of new and vintage Victorian accommodations. The main inn dates to 1901 and contains nine gorgeous Victorian-style rooms with polished hardwood floors, four-poster beds, and Oriental rugs; some have private decks and fireplaces, and all enjoy fabulous water views; there's also a long veranda with wicker chairs looking out over the water. A second, contemporary building contains 18 rooms, many of which also enjoy very nice water views—these accommodations have less character but are more practical for kids. All rooms in both buildings have private baths. The Turtle Soup restaurant, on the ground floor of the main inn, serves very good contemporary fare.

An enormous estate home that began as a modest farmhouse in the 1690s but has been expanded ever larger and more magnificently several times since, **Brookside Manor,** 380-B Post Rd., Wakefield, 401/788-3527, website: www.brooksidemanor.net, is today an upscale bed-and-breakfast with five distinctive rooms, each themed after a different region. In the beamed Cotswold Chamber, you'll find paneled walls, a low ceiling, a fireplace, and country-house furnishings, while the French Toile Salon is decked out in toile fabrics and wallpapers. Rooms look out over several acres of lush green gardens and lawns and brick terraces. Rates include a full breakfast and afternoon tea, although you're welcome to enjoy a

Continental breakfast in the privacy of your room. Rooms at the 1845 **Watch Hill Inn,** 38 Bay St., Watch Hill, 401/348-6300 or 800/356-9314, website: www.watchillinn.com, have a slightly dated feel but are brightened by the afternoon sun, which streams through the front windows and afford excellent bay views. This is a perfect location in the heart of Watch Hill, with a very nostalgic feel. Recent renovations have greatly spruced up the rooms, which have high-speed Internet, cable TV, and climate control. This is one of the few South County coastal inns open year-round. Continental breakfast and parking are included.

CAMPING

In addition to the public campground at **Burlingame State Park,** South County has a handful of private campgrounds. Just three miles from the ocean is **Timber Creek RV Resort,** 118 Dunns Corners Rd., Westerly, 401/322-1877, website: www.timbercreekrvresort.com, which has 150 RV sites and another 200 for tent camping. Facilities include a big swimming pool, a driving range, horseshoes, baseball and soccer fields, volleyball and basketball courts, tennis, and a lodge with a fireplace, large-screen TV, and library. You can fish in a catch-and-release freshwater pond, which also has a beach and canoe and paddleboat rentals, and kids can use a well-outfitted playground. Inland a few miles but along a glorious freshwater body, **Worden's Pond Family Campground,** 416A Worden's Pond Rd., Wakefield, 401/789-9113, is a 65-acre spread with about 200 campsites nestled in the woods. Amenities include showers, restrooms, fishing, swimming, and a playground.

Food

Upscale

Intimate **Basil's,** 22 Kingstown Rd., Narragansett Pier, 401/789-3743 ($17–26), is a tiny spot that's very romantic and a favorite for special occasions. Here you can sample excellent, straightforward French Continental cuisine and order from an extensive wine list. There aren't a lot of surprises on this menu, but traditionalists never seem to tire of the expertly prepared frogs' legs, duck á l'orange, steak au poivre, escargot, and crème brûlée. The **Shelter Harbor Inn,** 10 Wagner Rd., off U.S. 1, Weekapaug, 401/322-8883 ($14–23), a sun-filled, elegant dining room inside the historic inn of the same name, serves traditional American and Continental fare. Specialties include crab-and-salmon cakes, horseradish-crusted scrod, cedar plank–grilled salmon, sautéed calf's liver, and tournados of beef. The inn is also a popular spot for breakfast and lunch. **Spain of Narragansett,** 1144 Ocean Rd., Narragansett, 401/783-9770 ($11–21), while unfancy, is one of the more dramatic dining spaces in South County—it high-ceilinged dining room is anchored by a gurgling fountain. This isn't a tapas restaurant per se, but you will find a number of nicely prepared starters, from clams casino to garlic-smoked chorizo sausage. Sole lightly egg-battered and pan-sautéed in a lemon chablis sauce and chicken Andaluza (stuffed with pine nuts, diced smoked ham, spinach, and Manchego cheese, topped with fresh cilantro and tomatoes) are excellent entrées. Some dishes are available for two, such as paella Valenciana with shrimp, sea scallops, clams, mussels, chicken, and calamari with saffron rice and spices, and solomillo al Jefe, medallion of beef tenderloin served with artichoke hearts and mushrooms in a rioja wine, Dijon, and garlic sauce.

Up River Cafe, 37 Main St., Westerly, 401/348-9700 ($18–34), could get away with serving so-so food based simply on its memorable setting inside an old mill on piers over the Pawcatuck River. Fortunately, the kitchen delivers just as impressively as the interior designers have. The restaurant serves updated renditions of classic supper club fare—consider a starter of roasted beet salad with Taleggio cheese fondue, candied walnuts, and sherry vinaigrette. Excellent main dishes include a Parisian-inspired grilled hanger steak with baby greens and frites; seared Stonington sea scallops with lobster home fries, sautéed spinach, and saffron; and the Up River Cafe clam bake, comprising steamed littlenecks, a steamed lobster, gratin potatoes, and corn pudding. The bar serves swanky cocktails, from classic Manhattans to sophisticated Sazeracs. The restaurant at the **Watch Hill Inn,** 38 Bay St., Watch Hill, 401/348-6300 ($17–28), is noted for its wonderful bay views, especially at sunset. You can dine in the rather upscale Seaside Grille or on the sunny Veranda and Patio decks. The kitchen serves fairly traditional seafood and American favorites, from grilled swordfish in olive oil with lemon-dill-Hollandaise sauce to golden neck clams sautéed with white wine, garlic, virgin olive oil, shallots, and fresh herbs.

Creative but Casual

Opened as a quaint lunch spot and ice cream parlor in 1916, the **Olympia Tea Room,** 74 Bay St., Watch Hill, 401/348-8211 ($9–21), has evolved gradually over the years into one of Watch Hill's most dynamic and inventive restaurants. The handsome dining room with a black-and-white-checked floor, salmon-pink walls, and lazily whirring ceiling fans serves a wide range of regional American cuisines, from grilled Kansas City sirloin to littleneck clams with sausage simmered in marinara with linguine. Specials change often and have included Connecticut River shad roe panfried with butter and baked in cream, and a Watch Hill fried oyster po'boy with spicy red tartar sauce, vine-ripened tomatoes, and shaved red onion. One of the largest dining rooms on the beach, **Paddy's Restaurant,** 159 Atlantic Ave., Misquamicut, 401/596-4350 ($12–22), serves surprisingly good and often creative food, especially considering the crowds that pile in here many summer weekends. Favorites include penne in a pink vodka sauce with lightly fried calamari and parmesan cheese; the "bucket" of mussels with a sweet-and-spicy Thai butter sauce and grilled focaccia; oven-roasted Alaskan jerk salmon; and pan-seared tuna served rare over mashed potatoes with a miso vinaigrette. The kitchen does a nice job balancing hearty and uncomplicated favorites with some nicely inventive fare. The fine ocean views from the restaurant make this a romantic choice. An attractive, somewhat upscale spot that's just southeast of URI toward Peace Dale, **Quattro Italian Grille,** 2095 Kingstown Rd. (Rte. 108), South Kingstown, 401/789-5300 ($12–20), serves a nice mix of designer pizzas, creative salads, and rather rich grills and pastas. One pie topped with prosciutto, wild mushrooms, scallions, soy sauce, and mozzarella and romano shows the kitchen's offbeat use of both European and Asian ingredients. Sample the superb tiramisu for dessert.

84 High Street, 84 High St., Westerly, 401/596-7871 ($10–18), is a small and snazzy restaurant that shows the work of prominent local artists on its walls. It's steps from Wilcox Park, and right in the heart of Westerly's pretty downtown. The kitchen prepares relatively simple but contemporary regional American fare, from grilled lemon sole in a light cucumber sauce to grilled pork tenderloin finished with an applejack brandy cream sauce, plus several well-executed pastas. There's a large assortment of grilled pizzas, appetizers, and salads, which are also available at lunch, arguably the more popular meal here. At lunchtime you'll also find a very long list of creative sandwiches. Smart decor, fresh ingredients, and cheerful service make **Maria's,** 132 Atlantic Ave., Misquamicut, 401/596-6886 ($12–24), one of the most sophisticated options at Misquamicut, and it's just across the street from the beach. Excellent starters include jumbo shrimp sautéed with apricots and a Grand Marnier sauce, and arugula salad with

goat cheese crostini. Starters include a wide range of pastas, among them a very nice lobster fra diavalo, and grills like filet mignon Florentine and chicken balsamico. This is a more adult-oriented restaurant than most in Misquamicut, but there is a small children's menu. A decent spot for creative American food, **Turtle Soup,** 113 Ocean Rd., Narragansett, 401/792-8683 ($12–18) occupies a distinctive twin-gabled Victorian beach hotel, the Ocean Rose Inn, with nice views across the street of the water—it's an elegant space, but unfussy, as one would expect of a beachy restaurant. The menu offers a nice range of reasonably priced entrées, including shrimp with a sweet mango-rum glaze served with herbed couscous, and lobster ravioli in a Skyy vodka cream. Less expensive sandwiches (burgers, chicken clubs) are also available, and you can order from a nice selection of appetizers to form a good meal—pan-seared crab cakes with a smoked jalapeño remoulade are a fave. Service is low-keyed and friendly.

Serving subtly seasoned and wonderfully executed Northern Italian fare, perhaps the best in the county, **Trieste,** 944 Boston Neck Rd. (Rte. 1A), Narragansett, 401/783-9944 ($14–23), occupies a sleek, unfussy space a short drive north of Narragansett Pier and not far from the bridge to Jamestown (and yes, even Newporters make the drive here for such stellar cuisine). There's much to like about this chef-owned restaurant: that pastas are available in full and half orders, that the staff is well-informed and friendly, and that the menu changes often to take advantage of what's fresh each season. Recent entrées include asparagus-and-ricotta ravioli with sun-dried tomatoes, peas, artichoke hearts, and spinach in a gorgonzola cream; and oven-roasted Chilean sea bass with an herb-crumb topping, served in a lobster-tomato broth with spring vegetables, fennel, and baby gold potatoes. Grilled vegetables with a warm goat cheese cake make a tempting starter, and you should try to save room for the dessert of blueberry bread pudding with cinnamon-Frangelico crème anglaise. A small drawback for some is that the restaurant has no liquor license; however, you are encouraged to bring your own bottle ($3 corkage fee). Set inside a snazzy 1700s inn with solarium-style bar, wraparound flagstone porches, and several cozy dining rooms, **Mary's Restaurant,** U.S. 1 at Route 1A, Haversham Corners, Westerly, 401/322-0444 ($11–22), has been a tradition since it opened in 1946. Traditionalists will appreciate the setting and the menu, which offers plenty of Italian and American standbys—jumbo shrimp cocktail, herb-marinated chicken breast over Caesar salad, shrimp scampi with a lemon-wine-Pernod sauce. Organically grown herbs, high-quality ingredients, breads delivered daily from A&M Bakery in the Bronx, and some relatively creative preparations sets Mary's apart from the dozens of other Italian restaurants in South County. Consider whole New Zealand rack of lamb with herb-infused risotto, sautéed Stonington (Connecticut) calamari with fresh garlic, jalapeños, and a spicy red sauce, or farm-raised tilapia pan-seared with a lemon-caper-shallot reduction. The dessert list is similarly impressive, and many excellent wines are offered. **Ginger's Cafe,** 333 Main St., Wakefield, 401/789-0914 ($5–18), is a bakery and eatery. In addition to being a full-service restaurant serving eclectic American fare, the kitchen also serves about 15 delicious sandwiches on fresh-baked bread, among them goat cheese and roasted red peppers with pesto and jerk chicken with peach chutney. Entrées include baked cod stuffed with crab and roasted garlic butter, and pork Veronique with a red-grapes-and-cream demi-glaze. Several hearty pastas are offered, too.

Pizzas, Pub Grub, and Seafood

Few such lovely buildings were ever constructed for more mundane purposes than the **Pump House,** 1464 Kingstown Rd., Peace Dale, 401/789-4944 ($6–14), which dates to 1888 and originally served as the pumping station for the water system that served Peace Dale, Wakefield, and Narragansett. Today the elegant stone building with a towering chimney contains this rather simple restaurant that serves traditional American food, such as fish and chips, steaks, and chowders.

There's also an extensive salad bar. This is a popular option for families. Okay, so you might not think to eat dinner at a bowling alley; in fact, **Camden's,** 756 Kingstown Rd., Wakefield, 401/782-2328 ($8–15), adjoins Old Mountain Lanes and serves a full range of no-surprises American fare including prime rib, seafood chowders, fish and chips, surf-and-turf plates, and so on. There's also a coffee shop that serves three meals a day and opens at 5:30 A.M. An easy-going tavern serving a fairly typical compendium of steaks, chops, seafood, burgers, and bar munchies, **Charlie O's,** 2 Sand Hill Cove Rd., Narragansett, 401/782-2002 ($5–16), is a reliable option, especially late at night, as the kitchen stays open until around midnight and sometimes later. The place is big with collegiate types, in part for its pool tables and sports-bar theme, and also because it's a short drive from the beach.

Just once, experience the sheer vastness of **Nordic Lodge,** 178 E. Pasquiset Trail, Charlestown, 401/783-4515. It is famous for its dinner buffets, which cost a not-insignificant $49 per person but include unlimited access to heaping platters of more foods than you can imagine. Favorites include nicely proportioned steamed lobsters, prime rib, broiled scallops, Asian pork ribs, filet mignon, shrimp cocktail, and dozens of massive cakes, pies, and other desserts. People drive here from miles around to experience this embarrassment of culinary riches. The restaurant sits in a remote, wooded area overlooking a lovely pond. It's rather tricky to find this place that's a goodly drive north of Charlestown's beaches—it's a good idea to call ahead for directions. The quintessential house of good cheer, **Mews Tavern,** 456 Main St., Wakefield, 401/783-9370 ($5–14), serves outstanding burgers along with dozens of other hearty rib-sticking dishes: scallops carbonara, seafood pie pizzas (scallops, shrimp, crab, smoked salmon, and a blend of cheeses), stuffed portobellos, Cajun steaks, teriyaki chicken wings, and beef-and-bean burritos. Of course, plenty of people descend on this rambling wood-frame restaurant in the center of downtown Wakefield for the huge liquor list, including 70 microbrews on tap, more than 200 single-malt scotches, and three dozen tequilas.

A spacious, light-filled restaurant in a 1911 redbrick building at the center of downtown Westerly, **Pizza Place Pie & Suds,** 43 Broad St., 401/348-1803 (pies $8–13), despite its prosaic name, serves some rather inventive pizzas. The scallops-and-bacon pie with chopped garlic, parmesan cheese, and olive oil is a favorite, but don't overlook the perfectly simple and wonderful fresh-spinach-and-gorgonzola version. Red and white pizzas are available, and the list of toppings is long and impressive. You can also order from about six pastas and several tasty salads.

Dylan's Restaurant, 2 Canal St., Westerly, 401/596-4075 ($12–18), is an old-fashioned steak and seafood restaurant with a dark-wood interior, vintage photos, and friendly service. You might dine on shrimp Diane (sautéed jumbo shrimp with scallions, wild mushrooms, fresh basil, fish stock, a touch of cream, and fettuccine), veal marsala, or fried scallops. The food at **Wilcox Tavern,** Old Post Road at U.S. 1, Charlestown, 401/322-1829 ($11–18), tends toward the tried and true (standard renditions of veal, chops, chicken, seafood, etc.), but devotees appreciate the tavernesque feel of the dining rooms in this 1730 center-chimney house. In an enormous building next to the Winnapaug Inn, which is run by the same owners, **Venice Restaurant,** 165 Shore Rd., Misquamicut, 401/348-0055 ($10–21), ranks among South County's most popular Italian restaurants, both for dinner and for the lavish weekend brunch spreads. Veal is a house specialty, prepared several ways, but also consider the vegetarian portobello parmagiana, the grilled filet mignon with a burgundy-mushroom sauce, or the linguine with clam sauce. You won't find a lot of surprises on the menu, but nightly specials sometimes venture a little more off the beaten path. The huge, warmly furnished dining room can get a little noisy, but otherwise it's a very nice restaurant.

The **Coast Guard House,** 40 Ocean Rd., Narragansett, 401/789-0700, has spectacular views. This is a favorite spot for brunch, as it offers an immensely varied all-you-can-eat buffet with Belgian waffles, omelets, seafood Newburg, sausage, and so on. There's nothing especially gourmet about the food here, but it's an enjoyable spot for an outing. The restaurant occupies a former lifesaving station that adjoins the towers of the old Narragansett Casino. **Seaport Tavern Restaurant,** 16 W. Main St., Wickford, 401/294-5771, is a festive eatery in the heart of historic Wickford, with nice water views and a bar serving more than 100 kinds of beer and many wines by the bottle and glass. Clam cakes, broiled, grilled, and fried seafood, burgers, and a fair number of veggie items are offered. As ambience goes, **HooffinFeathers Carriage Inn,** 1065 Tower Hill Rd., North Kingstown, 401/294-2727 ($12–21), earns praise for its warmed-by-the-fire feel, inviting circa-1760 quarters, and casual—if predictable—pub fare, from pizzas and pasta to steaks and seafood. The menu is long, and the kitchen does turn out a smattering of more innovative dishes, such as grilled salmon with a light raspberry sauce. There's also an excellent shelled and sautéed lobster served in a rich sherry cream. Tuesday night brings out plenty of long-time fans for the $9.95 stuffed shrimp and prime rib dinners, and early-bird specials are offered daily.

On the road to Jerusalem, **Cap'n Jack's,** 706 Succotash Rd., Wakefield, 401/789-4556 ($7–14), has been serving up big portions of seafood and pasta since 1972—the cavernous restaurant is always packed, and nobody seems to mind the rather dull decor. What you come here for is lobster bisque with a hint of sherry, broiled scallops in a lemon-butter sauce, shrimp fra diavolo, baked scrod with mussels, and a few nonfishy items like gnocchi with meatballs and chicken teriyaki. The restaurant also makes its own pastries and desserts, which are just as hefty as the seafood platters. If you're renting a cottage or staying somewhere with a kitchen, keep in mind that Cap'n Jack's has a take-out counter. A longtime favorite for seafood, **George's of Galilee,** Port of Galilee, Narragansett, 401/783-2306 ($8–15), has been serving up outstanding fish and chips, clam cakes, chowders, and lobster since 1948. Fame has made this a tourist favorite, but it's still a high-quality restaurant, and the views both from the dining room and the outside deck are fabulous—the restaurant looks clear out toward the fishing harbor.

Ethnic Fare

Many locals swear by the spicy and subtly seasoned Szechwan and Mandarin cooking at
Ocean View Chinese Restaurant, Mariner
Square, 140 Point Judith Rd., 401/783-9070
($6–11). House favorites range from hot-and-
sour bean curd with brown rice to string beans
with pork. Alas, the place lacks a bit in service and
ambience, but in a region with few Asian restaurants, it's a reliable pick. A spicy twist on a traditional Irish pub, **Pancho O'Malley's,** Mariner
Square, 140 Point Judith Rd., Narragansett,
401/789-2299 ($6–13), serves a mix of Mexi-
can and Irish dishes, margaritas and Irish stouts.
As you might guess, it's as popular as a drinking
hole as it is for food, and the place especially
rocks late on weekends. Earlier in the evening, it's
a good choice for families. A great deli specializing in Middle Eastern and Lebanese food, **Pick
Pockets,** 230 Old Tower Hill Rd., Wakefield,
401/792-3360 ($4–7), stays open through the
dinner hour each evening. It's a good place to
pick up sandwich supplies and other goodies.

Quick Bites

A cozy hole-in-the-wall that serves up excellent
breakfast and lunch fare, **Dad's Place,** 142 Boon
St., Narragansett, 401/783-6420 (under $5),
serves heavenly chorizo omelets, fluffy pancakes,
and a wide range of sandwiches at lunchtime.
The **Station House,** Route 138, 401/783-0800
($2–6), lies just a couple miles west of the Uni-
versity of Rhode Island campus, making it a good
option for folks traveling in the western part of the
state, too. This cheerful eatery serves a nice range
of breakfast and lunch foods, including heavenly
cinnamon buns, fluffy omelets, prodigious burgers, and a very nice Reuben sandwich. The stain-
less steel **Wickford Diner,** 64 Brown St.,
Wickford, 401/294-9058 ($3–7), is a retro greasy
spoon with similarly delicious food. It generally
opens at 4:30 or 5 A.M., and closes at 2 P.M. Meatball grinders, burgers, steak and eggs, corned-
beef hash, fluffy banana pancakes, and fish and
chips are among the more popular offerings.

Spice of Life, Fantastic Umbrella Factory, just
off U.S. 1, 401/364-2030 ($5–14), has organic
soups and salads, some south of the border fare,

ice cream and frozen yogurt, and even an organic espresso bar. **Waterfront Grille,** 83 Brown
St., Wickford, 401/294-1150 ($4–8), is an ex-
cellent spot for breakfast, bagels, deli sandwiches, pastries, coffees, and early dinner (it's open
until 8 P.M.). This casual storefront eatery has
counter service and a simple but pleasant ambience—lots of hanging plants. The best feature
is the small outdoor dining area, overlooking the
many sailboats and yachts in Wickford's harbor.

Just beyond Cross Mills across from the fire-
house, stop in for a sundae at **Tropic Frost Ice
Cream,** 4187 Old Post Rd., Charlestown,
401/364-0869, where toppings range from but-
terscotch to cherry to wet walnut. Several picnic tables are set out back. A popular short-order
seafood place on the Post Road, in Charlestown,
the **Hitching Post,** 5402 Post Rd. (U.S. 1),
401/364-7495 ($4–11), is the sort of place where
you order at the window and take your food
back to devour in your car, as you watch others
do the same. The food here is simple and mouthwatering: burgers, clam rolls, Rhode Island clear-
broth clam chowder, Italian ices, and Good
Humor ice cream products. You'll find a small
outdoor dining area with picnic tables, too.

Fra's Italian Gourmet, Shore Road and Crandall Avenue, Misquamicut, 401/596-2888 ($4–8,
large pizzas $10–14), is an excellent source of
fresh-made sauces, pastas, and delicious prepared
and packaged goods. The families who rent cottages in this area swear by this place. Specialties
include the calabria grinder (stuffed with mor-
tadella, genoa, capicola, soppresata, provolone,
lettuce, tomatoes, balsamic-marinated onions,
and dressing), ricotta-stuffed shells, chicken-cut-
let focaccia sandwiches, and fresh tomato-and-
basil bruschetta. And if that's not enough, check
out the selection of gourmet pizzas. A good place
to grab a sandwich before strolling through
Wilcox Park or heading out to the beach, **Kelley's
Deli,** 14 High St., Westerly, 401/596-9896
(under $6), is a cheerful little luncheonette serv-
ing everything from traditional cold cuts to more
unusual fare like Cajun turkey salad and pastra-
mi Reubens. **Bay Street Deli,** 112 Bay Street,
Watch Hill, 401/596-6606 (under $6), serves
superb Rhode Island clam chowder, lobster rolls,

bagels, ice cream, muffins, pies and cakes, espressos, soups, and salads. You'll find a handful of sidewalk tables, but this is mostly a place to pick up take-out vittles.

By the Weekapaug fishing area and Dunn's Beach you can gorge on more short-order eats at **Seafood Haven Snack Bar,** 688 Atlantic Ave., at the Misquamicut/Weekapaug Breechway, 401/322-0330 ($4–18), a two-story white shanty with some indoor seating and several more outside tables. Clam cakes are the house specialty, a claim made by many fish restaurants in South County—but they really are delicious here. Also consider the twin lobsters served with drawn butter, rich home-style chili with melted cheese, three styles of clam chowder, chicken teriyaki, Stonington scallops, and mussels in marinara sauce. The owners also run a fish market next door, which is open daily 10 A.M.–6 P.M.—you can purchase complete clambakes from the market or order the similar Shore Dinner combo in the restaurant. **St. Clair Annex,** 141 Bay St., Watch Hill, 401/348-8407 ($3–11), is a favorite option for ice cream, fried seafood, grinders, and other casual fare. It's been open since the 1880s. **Dockside,** 19 Margin St., Westerly, 401/596-6370 (under $6), is a quirky little diner where you can get eggs, bacon, raisin toast, cheap sandwiches, and other greasy-spoon fare. It's just south of downtown Westerly, by a small marina on the Pawcatuck River.

More than a few Rhode Islanders believe that **Aunt Carrie's,** 1240 Ocean Rd., Narragansett, 401/783-7930 ($7–19), serves not only the best clam cakes and chowders in South County, but the best in the state—maybe even in southern New England. This handsome little eatery on the bay in Point Judith, an American flag hoisted high on a flagpole over the roof, looks directly over a tidal pond, often the turf of a few graceful swans. The casual eatery has ample outdoor and indoor seating, but its immense popularity re-

Bringing the kids to Sweenor's Chocolates is a South County shopping tradition. Family-owned for four generations, these shops sell 25 flavors of hard candy, an enormous variety of hand-dipped chocolates and confections, and cream and butter fudge of every permutation.

sults in lines most summer days—though a bring-your-own-booze policy makes the wait a little more pleasant for some patrons. After putting your name on the invariably long list for a table, you can wander around the attractive grounds or even hike down by the beach, which is very close by. The brightly painted dining room buzzes with chatter every night, as satisfied customers gorge on fried lobsters with drawn butter, whole-belly fried clams, and other fruits of the sea. **Iggy's Doughboys,** 1157 Point Judith Rd., Narragansett, 401/783-5608 ($3–9), might also serve the best clam cakes in the state— it's certainly fun to test them out against the many reputable competitors around Rhode Island. The original Iggy's in Warwick opened in 1924 and has withstood hurricanes and recessions. This small Point Judith branch opened more recently. Standard fare includes chowder, stuffies, fried scallops, the famous Iggy Burger with sautéed peppers and onions, tuna grinders, meatball subs, and chicken wings. Iggy's also specializes in greasy little fried doughboys, which are dusted liberally with powdered sugar; an order of a half-dozen costs just $2.95. Click on the website for coupons discounting several items on the menu, http://iggysdoughboys.com.

Java Joints

Pop into the **Bean Counter,** Riverside Building, 2 Broad St., Westerly, 401/596-9999, for snacks, desserts, cappuccinos and espressos; this is a comfy place with cushy seating, a short walk from Wilcox Park. It overlooks the Pawcatuck River toward Connecticut. Another enjoyable Westerly coffee hangout is **Perks and Quirks,** 48 High St., Westerly, 401/596-1260, a living room–style café with plush sofas and armchairs and a slightly bohemian buzz. You can also order bagels, fresh-baked breads, and yummy desserts. **Cafe Expresso II,** 98 Bay St., Watch Hill, 401/348-0103, serves tasty coffee drinks, plus mouthwatering Italian cakes and cookies. It's close to the beach, on the commercial strip in Watch Hill.

Gourmet Goods and Picnic Supplies

In the tiny Avondale section of Westerly, very convenient to Watch Hill and Misquamicut, the **Cooked Goose,** 92 Watch Hill Rd., 401/348-9888, is one of the best sources in the county for gourmet foods, both prepared and packaged. You can also pick up take-out sandwiches, breakfasts, and the like. Specialties include H&H Bagels delivered fresh from New York City, quiche (the selection changes daily), curried chicken salad, and such gourmet sandwiches as the Avondale (smoked turkey, havarti cheese, and cranberry mayo on pumpernickel). Fresh-baked pies, Louisiana bread pudding, and lemon squares are among the dozens of desserts available each day. A bit down Charlestown Beach Road toward Charlestown Beach you'll pass a large complex containing the **Corner Deli,** Charlestown Beach Rd., 401/364-3560, with a bakery, ice-cream parlor, deli, and pizza parlor. It's mostly take-out, but there's also a large patio. At the same intersection, **Breachway Seafood Market,** 14 Charlestown Beach Rd., 401/364-3352, sells both fresh unprepared fish and seafood dinners to go. It's hard to find fresher seafood than at **Champlin's Seafood,** 256 Great Island Rd.,

Galilee, 401/783-3152, which overlooks the fishing fleet and harbor at this famous port. You can dine here on the open-air deck, or buy fresh fish from the retail market and cook it back at your rental. There's also a branch in Wickford at 170 Main St., 401/295-4600.

Stop by the **Bagel Bakery,** 11 Main St., Wakefield, 401/782-2295 (under $6), for fresh-baked goods (including about 15 types of bagel accompanied by many kinds of cream-cheese spreads), plus deli and wrap sandwiches, breakfast fare, chais and lattes, and cookies.

Bringing the kids to **Sweenor's Chocolates,** 21 Charles St., Wakefield, 401/783-4433; U.S. 1 at Route 2, Charlestown Village, 401/364-3339; or Garden City Shopping Center, 140 Hillside Rd., Cranston, 401/942-2720, ranks among one of South County's great shopping traditions. Family-owned for four generations, these shops sell 25 flavors of hard candy, an enormous variety of hand-dipped chocolates and confections, and cream and butter fudge of every permutation. Quench your desire for sweets at the **Baker's Rack,** Hamilton Plaza, 683 Boston Neck Rd., North Kingstown, which specializes in such knockout desserts as chocolate bourbon pecan tart, caramel apple cheesecake, and pumpkin pie. There's also a wide variety of coffees.

Entertainment and Nightlife

South County has a lot going on in the way of both performing arts and nightclubbing, especially for an area that is in no way urban, but much of this activity doesn't really start up until late spring and dies just as quickly by October. The one area institution that keeps South County lively during the colder months, is URI, which presents musical and theatrical events throughout the school year, and whose students keep several bars hopping all year-round.

Bars and Clubs

There are dozens of mostly low-key taverns along the shore in South County, plus a few spots inland in Westerly and Wakefield popular

with students of nearby URI. Especially in summer the bars and taverns near the shore can get pretty wild, with a mix of summer-breaking college students, youngish tourists and vacationers, and gruff fishermen, depending on the venue. Singles on the make will find plenty of cruisy hangouts, although South County has no gay nightlife to speak of. In Misquamicut, where you'll find the greatest number of beach hotels and motels, much of the action takes places in bars located at the resorts themselves. You can hear live music at a number of places, and sports pubs are also relatively common.

A favorite locals hangout in Wakefield, **Casey's,** 191 Old Tower Hill Rd., 401/789-9714, is a spacious tavern that's a short drive from the beaches and serves a long menu of American, Mexican, and Italian fare. There's karaoke on Sundays and live music on Wednesdays and Saturdays. A hugely popular nightspot with college students and everybody else in South County with a yen for microbrews and imported liquors from all over the world, the **Mews Tavern,** 456 Main St., Wakefield, 401/783-9370, may just be the most crowded building in southern Rhode Island on weekends.

Ocean Mist Beach Bar, 895A Matunuck Beach Rd., Matunuck, 401/782-3740, has live music and draws a rowdy bunch of sunburned beachgoers on summer nights; it's within walking distance of East Matunuck State Beach. Other sources of live rock, reggae, and the like include **George's of Galilee,** Port of Galilee, Narragansett, 401/783-2306; the **End Zone,** 1230 Ocean Rd., Narragansett, 401/789-0696; the **Oak Hill Tavern,** 565 Tower Hill Rd., North Kingstown, 401/294-3282; **Brewmasters,** 733 Kingstown Rd., South Kingstown, 401/782-6700; and **Sandy's Lighthouse,** 148 Atlantic Ave., Misquamicut, 401/596-1496. A spot popular with the college set, both URI students and others that age from around the area, is **193 Degrees Coffee House,** 2nd floor of Memorial Union, University of Rhode Island, Route 138, 401/874-5060. This java joint hosts mostly student bands performing everything from blues to acoustic rock to funk.

The bar at Misquamicut's **Paddy's Restaurant,** 159 Atlantic Ave., 401/596-4350, is a popular spot all summer long, and here you can order all sorts of froufrou tropical drinks, from banana rum runners to some vaguely hallucinatory sounding concoctions, including one called fish on acid (a shooter containing Jaegermeister, coconut rum, and pineapple juice). Paddy's hosts live bands throughout the summer, and has fun theme nights, such as reggae Saturdays.

Black Point Bar and Grille, 15 Burnside Ave., Narragansett, 401/789-2037, draws big crowds from the beach for guzzling brewskis, shooting pool, and listening to live bands. Near the beach in Narragansett, **Charlie O's,** 2 Sand Hill Cove Rd., 401/782-2002, draws a convivial mix for shooting pool, watching sports on TV, and drinking.

Performing Arts

South County has a number of small theaters, which present a great variety of dramatic and musical works.

Matunuck Theatre-by-the-sea, 364 Cards Pond Rd., Matunuck, 401/782-3644 or 401/782-8587, website: www.theatrebythesea.com, which is on the National Register of Historic Places, presents light dinner theater and cabaret from May through September. There are four shows each summer, and the emphasis is squarely on popular musical comedy—the 2002 season saw *Smokey Joe's Cafe* and *Anything Goes.* The grounds are abloom with gardens all summer long.

In Westerly, the professional **Granite Theatre,** 1 Granite St., 401/596-2341, website: www.granitetheatre.com, stages about eight classic plays from April through September, and then again from Thanksgiving through Christmas. The theater occupies a former church—this Greek Revival structure was built in 1849, but lost its spire during the 1938 hurricane. The **Colonial Theatre,** Westerly, 401/596-7909, hosts free Shakespeare in the Park productions at Wilcox Park each July.

Many of the arts events in South County revolve around URI, including the **University of Rhode Island Theatre,** Fine Arts Building, Kingston, 401/874-5843, website: www.uri.edu/artsci/the, which presents four plays a year, from musicals to classic works. The **Music Department,** Fine Arts Building, 401/874-2431, website: www.uri.edu/artsci/mus, presents a wide range of works during the school year, from choral programs to classical concerts to live jazz. The **South County Chamber Singers,** 401/783-0943, website: www.sccsingers.org, perform at different venues around the area.

The **SC Players Children's Theatre,** 401/783-6110, website: www.southkingstown.com/scpct/home.html, performs year-round and hosts a Children's Theatre Camp during the summer, for ages 5 to 8, and then for ages 9 to 13.

Festivals and Events

Summer and fall are major event seasons in South County, especially for seafood and, specifically, quahogs, which are celebrated with great fervor. But spring has its share of engaging festivals, too. Westerly hosts the **Rhode Island Scottish Highland Festival,** 401/596-7791, website: www.riscot.org, each May, which consists of an amateur Scottish athletics competition, a Highland Dance festival, and live Scottish music, plus numerous kids' activities; as well as the **Virtu Art Festival,** 401/596-7761, a performing and visual arts festival at Wilcox Park, over Memorial Day weekend.

In late June, attend the **Quonset Air Show,** Quonset Air Museum, North Kingstown, 401/295-5566, which features high-flying displays of several exciting planes, from fighter jets to bombers. Many planes are also exhibited on the ground and can be toured up close. Boating enthusiasts gather to watch the **Annual Blessing of the Fleet,** Galilee, 401/783-7121, each July. In mid-July, South Kingstown's Lions Club hosts the **South County Seafood Festival,** 401/783-2801, a great opportunity to sample the fruits of local waters. Later in the month, the sky fills with color during the **South County Hot Air Balloon Festival,** 401/783-1770, website: www.wakefieldrotary.com, which draws more than 20 hot-air balloons offering both tethered and untethered rides over the area for three full days. There are also concerts, crafts, a classic car display, kids' amusements and games, a petting zoo, a Revolutionary War re-enactment, and lots more going on.

In early August, the **Charlestown Seafood Festival,** 401/364-4031, draws hundreds of chowder and quahog aficionados to Ninigret Park. Activities range from helicopter tours to live mamba music; just about every type of seafood popular in the Ocean State is available, including raw oysters and clams, steamed lobsters, clam cakes, fish and- chips, and fried whole-belly clams. Around the same time, celebrations in the next town revolve around the **Narragansett Heritage Days,** 401/783-7121. The following weekend, dozens of artists and collectors converge upon the annual **Wickford Art Festival,** 401/294-6840, which has been going strong since the early 1960s. Late August there's more seafood fun at the annual **International Quahog Festival,** 401/885-4118, website: www.quahog.com/festival.html. If there's a food that could possibly be concocted with clams, you'll find it here, from quahog chili to stuffies to cakes and chowders.

At the end of August, the **Rhythm Roots** festival, Ninigret Park, 888/855-6940, website: www.rhythmandroots.com, has quickly grown to become one of Rhode Island's top music festivals, an eclectic mix of Cajun and zydeco, bluegrass, folk, and rockabilly. It's a festive event, with excellent food stalls carrying items from all over the world, plus arts and crafts vendors. Late September is the time for the **South County Firefighters Memorial Millennium Parade and Fair,** 401/789-3071. In early October, head to the South County Museum in Narragansett for the annual **Octoberfest and Apple Pie Contest,** 401/783-5400. Westerly hosts a large and popular **Columbus Day Parade,** 401/596-7761, each October. And throughout December, retail hub Wickford hosts the **Festival of Lights,** when the town is aglow with holiday lights and alive with holiday shopping.

Information and Services

VISITOR INFORMATION

For information on the area, contact the **South County Tourism Council,** 4808 Tower Hill Rd. (U.S. 1), Wakefield, 401/789-4422 or 800/548-4662, website: www.southcountyri.com.

In addition to the regional office, several towns in the area have their own offices of tourism with visitor centers: **Charlestown Chamber of Commerce Tourist Information Center,** 4945 Old Post Rd., 401/364-3878; the **Narragansett Chamber of Commerce,** Ocean Rd., Narragansett Pier, 401/783-7121, website: www.narragansettri.com/chamber; the **North Kingstown Chamber of Commerce,** 8045 Post Rd., 401/295-5566; and the **South Kingstown Chamber of Commerce,** 328 Main St., 401/783-2801.

GETTING AROUND
Airports
Westerly Airport, U.S. 1 and Route 78, Exit 92 (in Connecticut) off I-95 from the south, Exit 1 (in Rhode Island) off I-95 from the north, is South County's regional air facility. It's primarily used by private planes and charters, and it's where you can catch flights via several airlines to Block Island. **New England Airlines,** 800/243-2460, website: http://users.ids.net/flybi/nea, the regular airline between Westerly and Block Island, can be booked for charters from Westerly to many other parts of the country. Of course, as is true for all of Rhode Island, Warwick's T. F. Green Airport is the main way to reach South County by air.

Buses
Rhode Island Public Transit Authority (RIPTA), 401/781-9400, website: www.ripta. com, runs several buses through the area, including Bus 14, which runs from Providence to Narragansett and on some routes Jamestown, with stops at Warwick, Apponaug Four Corners, Wickford, and several other places along the west side of Narragansett Bay. Bus 64 runs across South County, connecting with the route for Bus 14; it begins at Kingston Railroad Station, stops at URI, Wakefield Mall, along Route 1A in Narragansett, and eventually cuts over to Jamestown and Newport. There is no public bus service serving the western shore towns of South County, such as Charlestown and Westerly.

Though **Bonanza Bus Lines,** 401/751-8800, website: www.bonanzabus.com, has no direct service to South County, it is useful if you're coming from Boston or several other Northeast cities, as it will take you to Newport or Providence, where you can catch a RIPTA bus.

Driving and Parking
I-95 skirts the upper half of South County and is the best way to reach the area from Connecticut and points south, but the main road through lower South County is U.S. 1, which runs west to east near the shore to Narragansett and then north near the bay through North Kingstown; from it, Route 4 cuts northwest and joins with I-95 as the most direct route from South County to Providence and points north. U.S. 1 is a busy four-lane highway through most of South County and a fairly quick route except on summer weekends and at rush hour. Route 1A is the more scenic route, running mostly parallel to U.S. 1 as it jogs along the coast, offering access to beaches and many of the quaint shoreline communities. Route 138 runs west-to-east through the county's midsection and then continues on to Jamestown and Newport.

Parking is only a concern in South County when you're going to area beaches, and only during weekends from late May through late June, and daily from then through September. During these times, all of the town and state beaches charge a fee for parking, and nonlocals are charged the most for this privilege. You can generally find a spot at most beaches, but during peak weekends in summer, get there early. Some area hotels and inns

Kingston Train Station near the University of Rhode Island

provide their guests with parking passes for certain beaches.

Most major car-rental agencies have branches at Warwick's T. F. Green Airport, but additionally in South County, you can rent from **Enterprise,** 800/736-8222, website: www.enterprise.com, which has locations in Wakefield, North Kingstown, and Charlestown; **Rent-a-Wreck,** Narragansett, 401/782-6663, website: www.rentawreck.com; and **Thrifty,** Westerly, 401/596-3441, website: www.thrifty.com.

Ferry Service

Point Judith contains the ferry terminal for Block Island; see the Block Island chapter for details.

Taxis

Taxi companies serving South County include **Eagle Cab,** 800/339-2970; **Wakefield Cab,** 401/783-0007; and **Wright's Taxi,** 401/789-0400.

Trains

Amtrak, 800/USA-RAIL, website: www.amtrak.com, stops in Westerly and Kingston, which makes it a convenient way to reach South County.

MEDIA

There are three newspapers in South County. The **Westerly Sun,** 401/348-1000, website: www.thewesterlysun.com, comes out daily; the **Narragansett Times,** 401/789-9744, website: www.ricentral.com, comes out twice weekly; and the **North Kingstown Standard Times,** 401/789-9744, website: www.ricentral.com, which comes weekly.

Block Island

About 200 years passed before the European colonists on Block Island built a proper dock to accommodate mainland visitors. Perhaps they were staving off the inevitable. Just more than a century later, 15,000 visitors descend upon the pear-shaped 6.5-by-3.5-mile isle in high season. You can't help wondering if the spirits of those earliest settlers aren't smarting indignantly over having let the cat out of the bag—once you give mainlanders a peek at Block Island, they don't ever want to return home.

Thankfully, while Block Island may never return to its original state of pristine forested wilderness, its inhabitants have taken remarkable steps to balance its growth with staunch land conservation, and to develop tourism without sacrificing the island's character. Still, mainlanders have long penetrated the chalky bluffs and bayberry-swaddled shores of Block Island, many owning or renting homes here. If you haven't visited yet, you're missing out on a place whose easy accessibility belies its otherworldly beauty and shy, almost reclusive, personality. Block Island doesn't buzz with amusement parks, sightseeing and fishing charters, and other high-profile attrac-

tions—it's the antithesis of seaside honky-tonk, and yet it is neither staid nor snobby.

You'll find a smattering of galleries and boutiques, but the retail scene is also low-key. People walk and bicycle about, and you can easily manage without a car. Try renting a bicycle and taking to the island's gently undulating roads; from any point on the island you're within a leisurely hour's ride of any other.

The island offers a cool and breezy respite, with temperatures usually 10 degrees cooler in summer than on the mainland—and 10 degrees warmer in winter. Gently rolling and largely bare hills cradling innumerable ponds punctuate this wind-shorn place, abundant with fragrant beach rose, blackberry, honeysuckle, and dense underbrush. The geological result of debris left in the wake of the last glacial recession, the island is strewn rather artfully with boulders and outcroppings, mostly of granite; note the more than 2,000 miles of stone wall.

Narragansett Indians occupied the island they called Manisses (pronounced *Man*-iss-eez) for many centuries before Italian explorer Giovanni da Verrazano first called upon it, reporting its size and

view south from Cooneymus Road

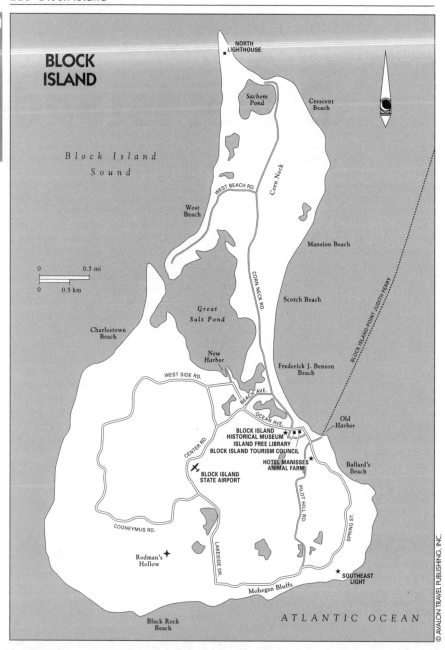

BLOCK ISLAND

BLOCK ISLAND

Block Island Sound

NORTH LIGHTHOUSE

Sachem Pond

Crescent Beach

Corn Neck

WEST BEACH RD.

West Beach

Mansion Beach

CORN NECK RD.

Scotch Beach

BLOCK ISLAND-POINT JUDITH FERRY

0   0.5 mi
0   0.5 km

Great Salt Pond

Charlestown Beach

New Harbor

Frederick J. Benson Beach

WEST SIDE RD.

BEACH AVE.

OCEAN AVE.

Old Harbor

BLOCK ISLAND HISTORICAL MUSEUM
ISLAND FREE LIBRARY
BLOCK ISLAND TOURISM COUNCIL

CENTER RD.

HOTEL MANISSES
ANIMAL FARM

Ballard's Beach

BLOCK ISLAND STATE AIRPORT

PILOT HILL RD.

SPRING ST.

COONEYMUS RD.

LAKESIDE DR.

Rodman's Hollow

SOUTHEAST LIGHT

Mohegan Bluffs

Black Rock Beach

ATLANTIC OCEAN

© AVALON TRAVEL PUBLISHING, INC.

character to be similar to that of the Greek isle of Rhodes, a comparison that eventually inspired the state's name, Rhode Island. The current and rather inelegant name, however, traces to Dutchman Adriaen Block, who visited in 1614, the same year he explored the Connecticut River Valley. About a half-century later, a group of 16 British colonial families purchased what was then a territory within Massachusetts, and from this group spring today's Block Islanders (although good luck finding a direct descendant amid all those who have settled in recent times—supposedly only two of the original surnames are found on the island today, Dodge and Rose).

Block Island's history is one of hardship and violence, a legacy that has contributed to a hardened insularity that to this day gives the place the personality of a faraway land, one that seems much farther away than the nine miles from the mainland that it is. During its first century of English settlement, pirates, privateers, and—horror of all horrors—Frenchmen invaded the island regularly, thieving and terrorizing islanders at will. With no suitable harbor and treacherous waters surrounding it, Block Island received few callers and maintained considerable autonomy well into the 19th century.

To this day, ships continue to have difficulties navigating the waters around Block Island. As recently as November 2000 a 78-foot fishing trawler out of Point Judith sunk off the southeast coast in heavy fog after crashing against rocks in shallow seas (the three-man crew and a dog named Shark Bait made it safely to shore in a life raft). It's estimated that about half of all the shipwrecks in New England have occurred off Block Island's waters—the total is put at roughly 500.

The island is vulnerable during wartime, while also maintained an odd sense of neutrality. During the American Revolution, General George Washington had all of the islanders' livestock shipped to the mainland, so any attacking British ships would be kept from snagging rations for their troops. During the War of 1812 it stood neutral, selling goods and produce at steep prices to enemy British, and it's persistently rumored that some islanders actually bartered with German submarine crews in World War II—it's quite

well-established that at the very least subs came within plain view of the island.

Tough years followed World War II, and Block Island's population plummeted, as did its popularity as a resort. It wasn't until the renewed popularity of New England's coastal islands and a nationwide embrace of historic preservation took hold, beginning during the 1970s, that Block Island began drawing major summer crowds again.

Temporary incursions were made from the sea into Great Salt Pond, a gaping body of water that bisects the island, several times during the colonial years in hopes of creating a permanent harbor, but the pond always found a way to seal itself. In the meantime, an anchorage called Old Harbor was created off the eastern coast in 1878, spurring a frenzied tourist boom, complete with the construction of leviathan wood-frame hotels with sweeping mansard roofs, towering turrets, and long wraparound porches. In 1900, New Harbor was finally established at nearby Great Salt Pond, when engineers dredged a permanent channel connecting it to the sea.

Today most ferries dock at Old Harbor, within a short walk of several fine beaches and the island's only significant concentration of hotels, restaurants, and businesses. New Harbor, a couple miles' walk away, welcomes just one ferry (from Montauk, Long Island—and it runs only in summer) but is also a large marina with slips for hundreds of yachts and sailboats, as well as a source of fishing charters and kayak and canoe rentals, and home to a couple of eateries.

Sunbathing and swimming are top activities on Block Island. Long and wide Crescent Beach, extending north from near Old Harbor, is a favorite. Canoeing or kayaking is another great way to experience the island. Great Salt Pond is safe even for beginners, while more seasoned boaters might explore the jagged coastal points. Hikers will find more than 30 miles of trails. The internationally respected Nature Conservancy, which in 1992 officially named Block Island one of the Western Hemisphere's "last great places," works in legion with the Block Island Land Trust to administer a network of preserves.

The island's dining scene resembles that of most other coastal New England towns, although because goods must be brought onto the island by air or boat, prices are slightly—but not unreasonably—higher than normal. And you'll find more than 50 hotels, inns, and B&Bs on the island, many of which book up fast on summer weekends.

Block Island's only sense of exclusivity is its proud preservation of nature and wildlife—this is an island that's absent of airs and also free from the crass commercialism that can so mar a small and highly desirable getaway. It's a credit to the generations who have cared for the island over the centuries that Block Island has managed overwhelming growth while still securing hundreds of acres of precious land, plus the legacy of countless endangered species. The ocean may keep on battering it and developers may eye it with avarice, but Block Island possesses an indefatigable resilience, and the promise of uncommon natural beauty for decades to come.

When to Go

There is no time not to visit Block Island, although zeroing in on the perfect season depends on several factors. The local tourist board goes out of its way to promote the island as a year-round destination, and this effort is more than just a marketing ploy. Granted, few hotels and even fewer restaurants remain open through the colder winter months, but the island possesses a brooding, rugged beauty at this time. Population and visitation decline precip-

itously—you'll almost never stand in lines or feel the uncomfortable crush of touristy mobs. In fact, winter visitors—especially those brave souls who venture to the island in January and February—are viewed as something of a curiosity, a pleasant one at that. There is much in this off-season to behold, views and scenery you might miss at other times.

Spring is a popular and breathtakingly scenic season on Block Island, with even more devotees than fall. In part this is because of Block Island's rolling terrain and relative absence of hardwood forest. There's less foliage drama on the island each fall than there is in the spring, when flower beds burst into form and beach shrubs and grasses turn an emerald shade of green. The greatest activity both in spring and fall is nature-watching, especially the opportunity to observe hundreds of species of birds passing north for the summer or south for the winter. The sheer numbers and variety of birds can be astounding.

Last, and obviously not least, there's summer—placed only at the end of this discussion to better publicize the off-season. For the vast majority of visitors to Block Island, this is the time to visit the island. Just about every business is open then, and certain activities, such as biking, sunning, and sailing, are ideal. Of course, in summer you'll pay dearly for accommodations (especially on weekends) and meals, and you may endure long lines at the ferry. But there's no denying the infectious joy of summering on Block Island.

Sights

What few formal sightseeing opportunities you'll find here evoke Block Island's topsy-turvy history of duplicitous privateers, rogue pirates, and brave seafarers (great ill-gotten treasures allegedly lie under the island's dunes and hills, perhaps even one buried by the infamous Captain Kidd). It doesn't take long to make a quick drive of the island, and even on a bike you can tour all of the major points of interest in one day.

OLD HARBOR

Most visitors begin their explorations of Block Island with a jaunt around Old Harbor—allowing minimal time for browsing shops, you can easily tour this charming waterfront commercial district in an hour or two. If you want to draw it out a bit, walk with an ice-cream cone in one hand. In Old Harbor, you'll find most of the island's commercial enterprises; it's also where most ferries dock from the mainland, and it's the site of the chamber of commerce visitor center. Businesses are concentrated mostly along Water Street, which sweeps alongside the harborfront; several lanes running perpendicular also contain a smattering of shops and eateries. The lovely old seaside inns that line the street and face out over the water make virtually every point in Old Harbor an ideal one for snapping a photo—the best views, though, tend to be from the deck of the ferry boats, a few hundred feet offshore.

For centuries, there was no harbor at all at Block Island, and landing a boat here on the mostly jagged beaches, booby-trapped by snags and rocks, proved exceptionally difficult and dangerous. The U.S. government finally installed two breakwaters here in the 1870s, and Old Harbor was developed with lightning speed. Today Old Harbor is a National Historic District, one of the best preserves of Victorian seaside architecture in the country. Outside of shopping, eating, and people-watching, there's little to see and do in Old Harbor—although keep the **Island Free Library,** 401/466-3233, in mind as a useful resource. In season most nights, the library presents an early-evening story hour geared toward children—a very nice event given that Block Island has no explicitly kid-oriented attractions.

Walk south (left as you leave the ferry parking lot) and you'll come to about the only major four-way intersection in Old Harbor, at Spring, Water, and High Streets. In the traffic island stands the **Statue of Rebecca,** a monumental fountain erected in 1896 by the Women's Christian Temperance Movement. Inspired by the biblical Rebekah-at-the-well, the statue was intended to encourage islanders to stay away from alcohol, this during a time when consumption on Block Island tended to exceed common standards, at least in many circles. While the island isn't as rowdy these days, you get the sense that few visitors or even locals heed Rebecca's message.

At the very southern tip of Old Harbor stood the island's most famous and immense Victorian hotel, the Ocean View, which burned accidentally in the 1960s. On its site now stands the **Ocean View Pavilion,** which looks out toward Crescent Beach and the ocean. It's a pretty spot for a stroll.

SAVING SOUTHEAST LIGHT

Formidable Southeast Light lies along the Mohegan bluffs, a constantly eroding fortification of sheer cliffs that forms Block Island's southern boundary with the sea. Wind and rain have chewed up huge chunks of the bluffs to the degree that in 1990 the Coast Guard predicted a grim, if ironic, fate for the lonely lighthouse: it would soon tumble from its imperious perch into the frothy waters below, pulverized by the same treacherous currents from which the light warned away ships for more than a century. After a determined fund-raising campaign, preservationists mustered up the cash to save the landmark, and in 1994 a crew of engineers painstakingly moved the massive structure, inch by inch, about 200 feet north from the perilous bluff's edge, thus preserving Southeast Light for generations to come (well, four or five generations anyway—the sea's steady onward march is, alas, inalterable).

EXPLORING SOUTH FROM OLD HARBOR

From Old Harbor, continue south along Spring Street. You'll quickly pass, on your right, distinctive Hotel Manisses, which is crowned by a squared-off central tower. It's worth poking your head inside to admire the interior common areas, and, particularly if you have kids along, be sure to make a visit to the hotel's **Animal Farm,** which is free and open to the public daily dawn to dusk. You can pet many of the llamas, sheep, donkeys, goats, and other farm animals here. The setting, a rolling meadow that slopes up toward several grand houses and hotels on High Street, pleases shutterbugs, too.

From here continue curving along the bluff that forms southeastern Block Island's natural boundary, and after about 1.5 miles you'll come upon the entrance, on your left, to **Southeast Light,** off Southeast Road/Mohegan Trail, 401/466-5009. The redbrick beacon, in the gingerbread Victorian style, was erected in 1873. At the time of its construction, with its power of 3,000,000 candles, this was the most powerful lighthouse on the New England coast. There's a small (free) museum documenting the lighthouse's history, and you can climb 50 feet or so up a narrow spiral staircase to stand inside the now-electric beacon lens. For a tour to the top, a donation of $5 per person is requested. Open Memorial Day–Labor Day, 10 A.M.–4 P.M.

Just beyond the lighthouse, you'll see a small parking lot that marks the entrance to the nearly 200-foot-high **Mohegan Bluffs,** the stretch of delicate outcropping that extends below nearby Southeast Light. The expanse of steep, crumbly cliffs derives its name from an infamous battle that took place centuries ago between the Mohegan and the Manisses Indians. You can hike down wooden stairs to the beach below—the journey is steep in places, so step purposefully. At the base you'll encounter far fewer crowds than at Block Island's more centrally located beaches—it's a contemplative, atmospheric spot to while away a sunny summer morning.

Do not walk along the edge of the cliffs themselves or anywhere off the marked trails—for two reasons: footsteps contribute to the ongoing erosion of these cliffs, and one false step on an unstable slab of earth and you could easily lose your footing and tumble onto the beach and rocks below. On sunny days the views from the cliffs are spectacular, taking in Southeast Light and, in the distance, the tip of Long Island's Montauk Point.

Continue west along Mohegan Trail, which hugs the island's southern shore, making a right onto Lakeside Drive, and then a left onto Cooneymus Road, and you'll soon come to unpaved Black Rock Road, which leads to the island's most famous nature preserve, **Rodman's Hollow.** All told it's about three miles to here from Southeast Light. This sunken glacial-outwash ravine has become an emblem of Block Island's crusade to preserve the island's natural spaces. In the early 1970s, the Block Island Conservancy purchased Rodman's Hollow, intercepting it before it could pass into the hands of residential developers. This inspired a major con-

servation movement that led to about a third of the island being permanently preserved. A network of trails traverses the hollow, and then leads down the cliffside to the sandy beach below. It's a popular spot for swimming, although the waters can be choppy and there's no lifeguard; exercise caution.

Near Rodman's Hollow, the **Smilin' Thru Greenway** is one of the more challenging hikes on the island, at least in terms of terrain. The trail is steep and rocky but offers back some great views of the ocean. Take the trail into the greenway from the intersection of Lakeside Drive and Cooneymus Road. You can connect from the greenway to Rodman's Hollow from a signed trail at the southern portion of the preserve.

Back on Cooneymus Road, by the entrance to Rodman's Hollow, continue west, and nearly a mile later make a right turn onto West Side Road. On your right you'll pass the ancient **Island Cemetery,** where headstones mark the passing of many of Block Island's earliest families. Names like Ball, Rose, Dodge, and Champlin appear on dozens of these markers, several of which date to the 1600s. It's a stunning location, with fine views north out over New Harbor and Great Salt Pond.

NEW HARBOR

From here it's an extremely pretty drive or bike ride north along West Side Road for about 2.5 miles to reach New Harbor, which is "new" only in the relative sense—it was developed in 1890s. Prior to this, Great Salt Pond had been a great freshwater pond, except when occasional storms breached the pond's land barrier and let in the ocean water. The breach was made permanent when a deep channel was dredged, and so opened the new harbor. Today, especially in summer, you'll see upwards of 1,500 boats tied up on 650-acre (about one square mile) Great Salt Pond, and you'll also see the ferry from Montauk, Long Island, sailing by daily. This sheltered setting is ideal for boaters and sailors who also take advantage of New Harbor's three fully equipped marinas, plus several inns and eateries. The entire Great Salt Pond was designated a Harbor of Refuge by the federal government in 1894.

© ANDREW COLLINS

marina at New Harbor

Just inland, at the corner of Old Town Road and Ocean Avenue, you can tour the **Block Island Historical Museum,** 401/466-2481, where exhibits—both permanent and temporary—illustrate the island's fanciful and fascinating history, with particular emphasis on the primary industries here, fishing and farming. This 1850s Second Empire building contains antiques donated by local families over the years. It's not a large museum, but it goes a long way to explain how Block Island developed into the community it is today. Admission is $2. Open 10 A.M.–5 P.M., daily late June–Aug.; weekends only late May–late June and September.

NORTHERN BLOCK ISLAND

You can easily cut back into Old Harbor along Ocean Avenue from New Harbor—the town districts are just under a mile apart. Or, where Ocean Avenue intersects with Beach Avenue, you can make a left, and then another left at the T-intersection with Corn Neck Road (which also leads directly into Old Harbor). At this spot you're poised to tour the narrow, northern tip of Block Island.

The reward for this 3- to 3.5-mile trip (depending on whether you start from the point described above or from Old Harbor) is a chance to visit the island's other great beacon, **North Lighthouse,** Sandy Point, north end of Corn Neck Road, 401/466-3220. At the northern tip of Corn Neck Road you'll reach a parking area, and from here it's an enchanting half-mile walk along the beach to the lighthouse. This granite beauty has stood guard here over a boulder-strewn beach since 1867, although other lighthouses had existed here before, each one destroyed by storms and erosion. North Lighthouse opened as a maritime museum in 1993 following many years of disuse and neglect. The exhibits inside detail the island's history of shipwrecks and dramatic rescues. The surrounding land falls within the Block Island National Wildlife Refuge and cannot be developed. It's an ideal habitat for some of the more unusual migratory birds that fly up and down the eastern seaboard each spring and fall; bird-watchers should be sure to bring along a field guide and a pair of binoculars. A favorite time to walk along the pebbly beach to the lighthouse is dusk, when the views of the sun setting over the horizon are magical. Admission is $2. Open 10 A.M.–4 P.M. on weekends in June and September, and daily July–Aug.

In the parking area for the lighthouse, note **Settler's Rock monument,** which marks the spot where the island's first English settlers came ashore in 1661.

Shopping

Though many businesses lie in either Old or New Harbor, there really aren't distinct shopping districts within Block Island—it's all one very colorful community.

GENERAL GOODS

Block Island Health and General Store, High Street, 401/466-5825, is something of a cross between a massive pantry and an offbeat variety store, stocking everything from snack foods and holistic vitamins to appliances and toiletries; the store also has a fax service. You can rent TVs, VCRs, and movies here too. Somewhat similar but with much more of an emphasis on gifts, beachwear, and touristy stuff, **Star Dept. Store,** Water Street, 401/466-5541, has a nice selection of men's and women's sportswear, T-shirts, sweats, and caps. Buy film and develop pictures at the **Photo Dog,** the National Hotel, Water Street, 401/466-5858, which also sells frames, postcards, artworks, T-shirts, and a smattering of gifts.

Old Harbor has a pair of small but very nice bookstores. Up a hill by the post office, **Island Bound,** off High Street, 401/466-8878, has a good children's section, stationery, some local history books, and a nice general selection of soft- and hardcover titles. This shop has the largest selection of books on the island. A bit smaller but with a great location across from the Old Harbor ferry and a thorough selection of books on and about Block Island, **Book Nook,** Water Street, 401/466-2993, stays open later in summer and sells newspapers and magazines, puzzles, painting kits, stationery, and arts and crafts, too. The **Salty Dog,** 226 Water St., 401/466-5254, sells a mix of beachy items: towels and flip-flops, saltwater taffy, coolers, T-shirts, boogie boards, and casual beachwear.

Pick up fashionable women's clothing and jewelry at the **Beach Plum,** next to Sharky's on Corn Neck Road, 401/466-8844. Look to **Pocketful of Posies,** Chapel Street, 401/466-5400, for gifts, fresh and dried flowers, gourmet foods, and wedding accessories (this island is a regular site of such occasions). And inside a charming little house on Dodge Street, **Scarlett Begonia,** 401/466-5024, is a terrific trove of crafts and fine arts, much of it locally produced. Pottery, painting, table linens, découpage lamps, and jewelry are among the distinctive wares. The clothier **Shoreline,** Ocean Ave., 401/466-5800, specializes in upscale clothing and accessories, especially Patagonia sportswear.

ART GALLERIES

There are a handful of art galleries on Block Island, a place where artists of all genres—many of them with international reputations—have been summering or living year-round for decades. **Greenaway Gallery,** Water Street at Fountain Square, 401/466-5331 or 800/840-5331, ranks among the most respected, it being the domain of contemporary photographer and island resident Malcolm Greenaway. There's a second branch of the gallery at **Block Island Glass,** Chapel Street, 401/466-2122, where the hand-blown works of islander Chris Baker-Salmon are shown.

Spring Street Gallery, Spring Street, 401/466-5374, is an artists' coop, with a wide range of media, from prints and photography to jewelry and textiles. Many of the island's most talented painters and sculptors show at the **Eisenhauer Gallery,** Water Street, Post Office Building, 401/466-2422. Andean sculptor Ccopacatty runs **Art Constructions, Studio, and Gallery,** 597 Corn Neck Rd., ground floor of the Beach House inn, 401/466-5562. On the lawn you'll see his compelling large-scale works executed in chrome and stainless-steel. Inside, his paintings and wall reliefs are displayed.

Sports and Recreation

BEACHES

Okay, maybe lying on the beach qualifies neither as a sport nor a form of recreation—there are still few activities more pleasurable on Block Island than finding a scenic stretch of golden sand and putting a blanket and cooler on it. Beaches abound here, as there are some 17 miles of them encircling the island. And beachcombers and solitude-seekers need not worry about excessive crowds, even in the height of summer—it's usually possible to find at least a small stretch of beach that's nearly or entirely deserted. Wherever you explore the shoreline, take great care not to trample Block Island's delicate dunes, which are constantly eroding.

Keep in mind that only Benson and Ballard beaches are staffed by lifeguards, and riptides are a serious problem in the waters surrounding Block Island. At any beach without lifeguards, you're swimming at your own risk; pay close attention to water and wind conditions before venturing into unfamiliar waters.

Perhaps the most famous but also most crowded swath of sand here is two-mile **Crescent Beach,** which begins just north of the Surf Hotel and consists of a few distinct sections. The main one, within an easy walk of both Old and New Harbors, is **Frederick J. Benson Beach**, off Corn Neck Road—here you'll find a large parking lot with bike racks, changing facilities and showers, chair and umbrella rentals, and a small snack bar. You can also rent boogie boards and ocean kayaks here. This town beach, formerly run by the state, tends to draw the bulk of day-trippers and tourists, especially on weekends.

If you continue up Corn Neck Road, or simply walk a quarter-mile farther north along the beach, you'll reach the somewhat more secluded **Scotch Beach** section, which tends to draw a lot of summer workers, local teens, avid volleyball players, and the like. It's less suitable for families than Benson. North of here, beautiful

Mansion Beach forms the northern end of this stretch. It lies beneath the remains of a mansion that burned in a fire long ago. There's not much parking here—many visitors arrive by bike. It's a very scenic and romantic spot, perfect for a picnic or some relative peace and quiet, and yet more accessible than some of the island's most tranquil beaches.

A lively—at night rowdy—spot at the southern tip of Old Harbor's commercial district, **Ballard's Beach** is right by Ballard's seafood restaurant, just beyond the harbor's southern breakwater. This attractive span is popular with younger singles and couples—waitstaff scurry about delivering beer and fruity drinks, revelers play volleyball, and rock bands entertain the masses on summer afternoons. Another reason this beach is better suited to adults than kids: the surf can be pretty intense at times, although it's perfectly safe for adults with swimming experience.

At the southern end of Crescent Beach, practically in Old Harbor, you'll find the shallow pools of **Kid Beach,** where families often bring children. It's a short walk from many hotels, and the tidal pools are fun for picking up fiddler and hermit crabs, collecting seashells, and swimming or wading. On just about any summer day, this beach is loaded with preteens.

A short drive or bike ride from Old Harbor, **West Beach,** West Beach Road, with parking just past the town transfer station, is a relatively peaceful beach that's ideal for a stroll, especially at sunset. From here you can hike up the entire western shore of the island, heading north to North Lighthouse. Part of this area is a bird sanctuary, and so dogs are not permitted and humans are asked to stay below the high tide line and avoid disturbing the dunes and wildlife.

There are several other smaller and more secluded beaches around the island, many of them known only among locals and accessible primarily on foot or by bike. Favorites among these include Black Rock and Vail beaches.

GREEN SPACES

To take a few steps on Block Island is to experience perhaps its most enduring pastime: hiking. This is by far the best way to appreciate the island's vast green spaces. Even simply walking along Block Island's roads is a relatively safe and quite scenic endeavor, particularly through the island's west side. There's really not a road on this island that doesn't offer wonderful views. More avid outdoorsy types will find trails that extend several miles, but the majority of the island's trails are easily navigated by persons of all ages and abilities.

This wind-shorn island is dominated by gently rolling and largely bare hills punctuated by numerous ponds—some say one for every day of the year. Because the island is the geological result of debris deposited during glacial recession at the close of the last Ice Age, it's also strewn with boulders and outcroppings, mostly of granite. As you hike across Block Island in summer you'll stroll beside fragrant bayberry, blackberry, honeysuckle, and dense underbrush. While you're welcome to pick blackberries, leave all other flora and fauna as you find it.

Interestingly, while Block Island claims quite a few endangered species, it is largely without mammalian wildlife, excepting deer and muskrats. Block Island has a significant deer population, and with it an abundance of deer ticks. Lyme disease is a relatively common occurrence, the risk of which can be greatly reduced if you follow some basic precautions. Poison ivy is another nuisance to look out for.

Bird-watching is a major activity along these trails. Ideal times for viewing are the spring and fall migrations, when you'll see hawks maneuvering across the moors and myriad wading birds along the shore. In September and October, the island teems with bird-watchers trying to get a look at the nearly 200 species that take advantage of Block Island's shoals, sheltered channels, beaches, sandbars, meadows, thickets of shrub, and light woodlands. Thermals rising from the oceanside cliffs on the south side of the island attract kestrels, peregrines, and merlins. In salt marshes, look for herons and egrets. Quite a few species nest here permanently in winter, too. In summer you'll see mainly shore birds.

Block Island has some 25 miles of nature trails; quite a few of them are linked through a comprehensive network called the **Greenway,** which can be accessed from 11 points. The Greenway runs through the southern half of the island, and highlights include Nathan Mott Park, the Enchanted Forest, the Turnip Farm, and Rodman's Hollow.

The **Elizabeth Dickens Trail,** which winds through open meadows and along high bluffs, is popular with bird-watchers. Its namesake taught natural history, conservation, and ornithology on the island, and was very involved in its preservation.

Another excellent walk for birders is **Clay Head Hill Trail.** You access Clay Head Hill Trail from the east side of Corn Neck Road, where you'll see signs pointing the way to the parking area and trailhead—you hit it shortly before Corn Neck Road ends at the parking area for North Lighthouse. About a third of a mile from the trailhead you'll come to a fork; make a right and you'll descend to a lovely beach; make a left and you'll rise to the bluffs and enter a famous section of the island known as the **Maze,** a vast and happily haphazard network of groomed walking paths—about 10 miles' worth—that run along and beside bluffs and hollows.

Of course, much of the best hiking on the island is along the windswept beaches—you can circumnavigate the entire island this way, excepting the channel at New Harbor and the commercial district of Old Harbor. Allow about eight hours to make this grand tour; you can begin such a walk from any beach.

Before setting out on any walk, you might want to stop by the **Nature Conservancy offices,** Ocean Avenue and Legion Way, New Harbor, 401/466-2554, where you'll find a detailed trail map and information on the wonderful nature walks the office sponsors throughout the summer.

The Block Island Sights section, above, describes some other ways to reach the beach.

BICYCLING

Few places in the Northeast are more ideally suited to bicycling than Block Island, where curving country lanes pass along rugged bluffs, past magnificent vistas, and alongside sweeping pastures and meadows. There are about 40 miles of road here, most with mild grades, as no point on the island rises to more than 250 feet; you will, however, find a handful of reasonably challenging hills and bluffs. There really aren't specific bike trails per se, as the entire island is appropriate.

Note: Do not ride on the hiking trails—the tires cause considerable damage to these fragile paths, and fast-moving bikes on narrow trails pose a danger, too.

BOATING AND SAILING

One of the yachting capitals of New England, Block Island has a couple of companies offering boat rentals. A popular and reliable company is **Sail Block Island,** Smuggler's Cove Marina, New Harbor, 401/466-7938, from which you can rent sailboats ranging in length from 15 to 30 feet. You can also hire captains to man boats on tours, and it's also possible to take sailing lessons here (either in groups or privately). Probably the most prolific source of boat rentals—of just about every kind—is **Champlin's Marina,** 401/466-5811, where you can take out pontoon boats, paddleboats, kayaks, bumper boats, and such.

CANOEING AND KAYAKING

Canoeing or kayaking is another great way to explore Block Island—take to Great Salt Pond, or venture out along the jagged coast. You can rent boats and pick up all kinds of great fishing and sporting equipment at **Ocean and Ponds,** the Orvis Store, Ocean Avenue, 401/466-5131. You can also rent kayaks at the concession at Fred Benson Town Beach, as well as from Oceans and Ponds and Champlin's Marina.

FISHING

There's more than saltwater fishing in these parts—many of the ponds on Block Island teem with perch, bass, and pickerel; you'll need a license from town hall, however, to fish these waters. In September, bonito swim up and feed off the shores of Block Island, delighting anglers who like a challenge. June is prime time for reeling in bluefish. Right in New Harbor Channel you can catch fluke, mackerel, and flounder. One of the best ways to fish out here is surf-casting from the beach, but there are also charters available for deep-sea fishing.

You can buy and rental tackle and fishing gear from **Oceans and Ponds,** 217 Ocean Ave., 401/466-5131, Block Island's local Orvis dealer. The store has information on local freshwater fishing and surf-casting, and also on boats that will take visitors out deep-sea fishing for striped bass, cod, marlin, and even tuna farther out. **G. Willie Makit Charters,** 401/466-5151, provides charters from Old Harbor on a 28-foot fishing boat. The specialty of G. Willie is bluefish during the day trips, and striped bass for night excursions. The *Kahuna,* 401/466-2184, provides sportfishing excursions for tuna, bluefish, marlin, shark, and other game fish popular in these parts.

HORSEBACK

Rustic Rides, West Side Road, 401/466-5060, provides many kinds of excursions on Block Island by horseback, from pony rides geared toward families with kids to guided trail rides through some of the island's most magnificent preserves and open spaces.

WATER SPORTS

Surfing is not uncommon on Block Island. It's also a popular place for scuba and snorkeling. You can rent boogie boards at several locations, including the kiosk at Fred Benson State Beach. The island's main diving company, **Island Outfitters,** Ocean Avenue, 401/466-5502, rents wetsuits, scuba gear, and snorkeling and spearfishing equipment.

Accommodations

Long three- and four-story hotels with sweeping verandas, grand staircases, and gambrel or mansard roofs with ornately trimmed gables, cupolas, and turrets were once ubiquitous up and down the Atlantic seaboard, from Bar Harbor, Maine, to Jekyll Island, Georgia. Here and there, they still stand, many of them renovated to their original glory. But the majority of these old hotels stand no longer.

The odds of one of these massive wooden structures—built well before there were comprehensive fire codes—surviving for more than 100 years without a major incendiary disaster were iffy to begin with. Indeed, arguably the most famous of Block Island's great hotels—the Ocean View—met exactly this fate in 1966. Hurricanes and eroded shoreline gobbled up plenty of others. But a more prevalent and certainly less dramatic grim reaper for the Victorian resort was simply economics—along the most desirable stretches of seashore, it became impractical for hotel owners to maintain these white elephants, especially in places where high-rise condos and hotels could generate better income with far fewer hassles. Bulldozers paved over hundreds of these structures, particularly during the 1950s through the 1970s, a period when America's sense of preservation fell largely by the wayside.

Block Island—in part because it catered to long-term guests during its Victorian and early-20th-century resort heyday—saw the construction of many of these lovely old hotels. Amazingly, about a half-dozen of these beauties still stand in or near Old Harbor; you won't find a greater concentration of better-preserved, operational, Victorian seaside hotels anywhere else on the East Coast. A sheltered and in many cases elevated location helped most of these properties weather the storms of the past century, and luck spared all but a few from conflagrations.

A dreary economy during the mid-20th-century and the high costs of bringing demolition crews in from the mainland are the major reasons you can still have a Victorian seaside vacation on Block Island. Nobody had the money to tear these beauties

down back when this was the trend elsewhere in the country, so these properties stood, boarded up and defunct. In more recent decades, as Block Island's popularity has skyrocketed and public opinion has begun to sway in favor of historic preservation, new owners have restored Block Island's remaining Victorian resorts to varying degrees.

Location, Location

While these famous old hotels—many of which grace postcards and coffee-table books on Block Island—receive the most attention, Block Island has seen an explosion of bed-and-breakfasts and smaller inns over the past 15 years or so. About 75 percent of these properties, which range from modest bungalows with three or four guest rooms to quite lavish mansions with 10 or more units, are within a 10-minute walk of Old Harbor—quite a few of them just up the hill from town, either on Spring or High Streets. The next greatest number is in or around New Harbor, which is just a 20- to 30-minute walk or easy bike ride from town. Perhaps a half-dozen additional properties dot the more remote parts of the island.

You don't need a car on Block Island no matter where you stay. It's a manageable walk from the ferry terminal to most inns and hotels, and a short cab ride otherwise. Similarly, the cab ride from the airport is short and simple. From all but a few hotels you'll be within walking distance of restaurants, shops, and beaches—and, of course, nowhere on Block Island are you especially far if you have a bike.

Amenities

Most of the larger hotels, about half of the inns, and a few of the B&Bs welcome families with kids; only about half the properties have televisions (and even fewer have in-room TVs), and most do not allow smoking, do not have air-conditioning (guests rarely find they need it, given the island's constantly cooling breezes), and do not comply with Americans with Disabilities Act guidelines. However, there are exceptions to all these rules.

BLOCK ISLAND'S HOTEL SEASONS

About a dozen of the nearly 60 or so accommodations on Block Island stay open year-round, but sometimes only on weekends in winter. The larger hotels in town are open mostly from early May through late October—some open or close a month earlier or later, and a couple stay open only from Memorial Day through Columbus Day weekends. They are staffed primarily by college-age students from abroad, often from Ireland, England, or occasionally Australia, although a fair number of U.S. teens also work the hotels of Block Island during their summer breaks.

In high season (July and August), virtually every accommodation has a two-night minimum on weekends, and many go as high as a four- or even seven-night minimum. These policies are based on supply and demand—on a slow week, or if there's iffy weather, you may get lucky and find a place willing to book you in for just a night. Accommodations generally let the Block Island Chamber of Commerce know when there are last-minute availabilities or cancellations. So don't give up hope, even on a busy weekend, of finding a room on short notice—just keep in mind that your options may be limited.

Compared with Newport, Nantucket, the Hamptons, or many other upscale seaside resorts in the northeast, Block Island does not have exorbitantly priced rooms. On a high-season weekend, you'll rarely see rooms with private bath letting for less than $100 nightly, but it's pretty easy to find them under $150. Only a few large suites at a few properties ever command more than $300 nightly, which while expensive is not at all out of line compared with many other desirable resort towns. On the other hand, budget travelers who don't mind a room with shared bath will find a substantial selection on Block Island—quite a few properties have at least some rooms with shared bath, and these can let for as little as $60 on high-season weekends.

Because so many of Block Island's visitors stay for four days or more during the high season, midweek rates generally don't fall by much, if at all. Expect a reduction of no more than 10 percent at most places. You should, however, have more luck booking a single-night stay or scoring a last-minute room during the week. During the spring and fall shoulder seasons, rates on weekends drop anywhere from 20 percent to 40 percent compared with summer; they can fall 30 percent to 50 percent at the few properties open in winter. Off-season weekdays usually see even more dramatic reductions in rates.

Reservation Services and House Rentals

An alternative to booking directly through a hotel, **Block Island Holidays,** 800/905-0590, website: www.blockislandholidays.com, arranges all-inclusive packages beginning around $120 per person that include accommodations, round-trip ferry, certain meals, and discount-shopping coupons. The hotels they work with are the Sheffield House, Dodge Cottage, the Gothic Inn, the 1661 Inn and Guest House, the National Hotel, the Harborside Inn, and the Hotel Manisses. There are also a handful of rental cottages and houses (from one to six bedrooms) available, with package rates starting at about $1,000/week in high season.

A similarly useful service is **Block Island Hotel Reservations,** 401/466-2605 or 800/825-6254,

website: www.blockislandhotel.com, through which you can book rooms at several hotels, inns, and private homes, or rent entire houses and cottages across the island. Rates vary greatly but can be quite reasonable, especially for rooms rented in private homes. The company has rooms all over the island, from the Water Street Inn and Water Street Suites (which are right by the ferry terminal) to the Highview Hotel (which overlooks New Harbor) to homes in some of the quieter and more out-of-the-way locations. Many of the rentals can accommodate two or three couples. And while it's a good idea to book ahead in high season, Block Island Hotel Reservations is another worthwhile option when you're trying to visit Block Island at the last minute.

Hundreds of Block Island property owners rent out their homes for part or all of the summer,

porch at the Surf Hotel, Old Harbor

either on a weekly or multi-weekly basis. In high season, expect to pay from about $600 for a small and basic cottage that sleeps two to nearly $5,000 per week for a mansion. Renting can be very economical, however, for groups of four or more—factor in money saved by preparing some of your meals at home and it can be a bargain. Real estate agents that specialize in rentals include **Ballard Hall Real Estate,** 401/466-8883, website: www.blockisland.com/ballard-hall; **Block Island Realty,** 401/466-5887, email: birealty@ids.net; **Sullivan Real Estate,** 401/466-5521, email: sullivan@riconnect.com; and **Phillips Real Estate,** 401/466-5521, email: phillips@riconnect.com.

HOTELS

$100–150

At one time, just about all of the old grandes dames on Block Island functioned in the way the **Surf Hotel,** Dodge and Water Streets, Old Harbor, 401/466-2241, does today. But most of the other hulking stalwarts around Old Harbor have been extensively remodeled in recent decades, the guest rooms enlarged and given private baths, TVs, and modern amenities. The Surf is very much the same family-friendly hotel it was when it opened more than a century ago. It was added onto a few times in the early years, but the most recognizable feature remains as it always was: a white-railed wraparound porch whose eastern sitting area overlooks Block Island Sound and Old Harbor. There are few more inviting spots on the entire island to while away an afternoon than on one of the wicker rockers on that porch. Behind the hotels, steps lead down to a small and scenic beach. The 47-room Surf stands at the corner of Dodge and Water Streets, a five-minute walk from several restaurants and shops as well as the ferry terminal. The rooms here, at least in the main building, are rather small, with functional furnishings, but many of them have tall windows and offer great water views; these rooms all share baths, which accounts for the very reasonable rates. An annex has newer and somewhat fancier rooms, including some with private baths. A light buffet breakfast is included. Run by the Cyr family since the late 1950s, the Surf draws a loyal repeat clientele. What it lacks in trendiness it makes up for in warmth and old-fashioned charm. Closed mid-October–late May.

Champlin's Marina, Hotel, and Resort, New Harbor, 401/466-7777 or 800/762-4541, website: www.champlinsresort.com, isn't one of the island's old beauties, but it is the ideal accommodation as far as plenty of sailors and boaters are concerned. Set along a beautiful stretch of Great Salt Pond, this full-service resort offers both pleasant—if fairly ordinary-looking—hotel accommodations and a formidable marina that can accommodate about 250 boats. The harbor depth is 30 feet, and yachts as long as 195 feet can dock here and pick up supplies, gas, marine equipment, and anything else a sailor could want. The hotel has 28 rooms, all with decks looking either onto the water or toward the island (which is by no means a bad view); many have convertible sofas and kitchenettes. On-site there's a casual restaurant and a rather campy lounge called the Tiki-Bar, where revelers sit around nursing their foofy cocktails, shooting pool, and ogling one another. Additional amenities include an in-ground pool, bike rentals, tennis courts, a children's playground, kayak rentals, a first-run movie theater, an ice-cream parlor, laundry facilities, a beach, and a bait-and-tackle shop. Closed Oct. 15–May 15. The **Samuel Peckham Inn,** 100 New Harbor, 401/466-2439, website: www.samuelpeckhaminn.com, is the only large hotel open year-round. It differs from the other large properties in several other ways, too: it's newer, with more modern furnishings and amenities, and it's a full-service resort with a large pool and Caribbean-inspired bar, tennis courts, an on-site bike- and car-rental service, and a conference center. It's less quaint and tranquil than the Old Harbor hotels, meaning that families with kids (especially teens) and even younger singles and couples tend to appreciate the Samuel Peckham. Many rooms can be joined to form two- or three-room suites, and all rooms have microwaves, cable TV, in-room phones (not a given on Block Island), and refrigerators (some have Jacuzzi tubs, too). Indeed, even many nonguests party in the hotel's lounge in season. Adjoining the property is a summer theater and a full-service marina. It's a bit of a walk into town from here, but a couple restaurants in New Harbor are close by, and the state beach is about a 10-minute walk.

$150–250

Considering its cheerful and friendly staff, breathtaking setting, and attractively furnished rooms, the **Atlantic Inn,** High Street, 401/466-5883 or 800/224-7422, website: www.atlanticinn.com, is arguably the cream of Block Island's hotel crop. This white, three-story hotel with a dark gray mansard roof and 21 guest rooms sits high on a hill a short walk from town—it's farther from the water than the other hotels in town, but because of its lofty elevation, ocean views are had from many rooms. Decor varies from room to room, but Victorian antiques abound. Lush flower gardens and well-manicured lawns surround the hotel. There are also two tennis courts and a croquet court. Closed Oct. 20–May 15. With its red mansard roof, striking cupola, and enviable setting on a bluff overlooking Old Harbor Point, few hotels on the entire eastern seaboard strike a more commanding and regal pose than the **Spring House Hotel,** Spring Street, 401/466-5844 or 800/234-0263, website: www.springhousehotel.com, which opened in 1852 to considerable excitement. This romantic hotel affords guests spectacular ocean views from many rooms (and the island views are nothing to sneeze at), and while it sits by itself on 15 green acres well away from town, you can walk to the ferry in about 15 minutes. The 39 rooms and suites in the main building are simply but attractively furnished with floral-print bedspreads, valances, and fabrics, pastel color schemes, and wicker dressers and nightstands; 10 similarly furnished additional rooms are next door in the Samuel Mott Building. If you're not staying or even dining here in the swank dining room, at least stop in to sip a cocktail and people-watch in the fabulously formal and rarefied Victoria's Parlor, the lavish lounge. Closed late Nov.–Mar.

Consisting of two inns and nearby smaller cottages, the **1661 Inn & Hotel Manisses,** 1 Spring St., 401/466-2421 or 800/626-4773, website: www.blockislandresorts.com, offers a distinctive and impressive range of historic accommodations, plus one of the island's finest restaurants. The pale gray Hotel Manisses, though smaller than the other classic hotels on the island, has plenty of admirers with its five-story central tower and admirable scale. Each of the 17 rooms is named for a famous Block Island shipwreck; generally, they are a bit darker and more elaborately decorated than rooms in some of the other large hotels. The presence of carpeting in many rooms and whirlpool tubs in several others, while adding a certain sumptuousness, may disappoint purists who prefer the austerity, hardwood floors, and pastel color schemes prevalent at other properties. There's no arguing that owners Joan and Justin Abrams have restored this hotel—along with the others they own—to absolute splendor. Behind the hotel, guests can wander through a lovely animal farm, where emus, pygmy goats, Sicilian donkeys, one very comely Brahman heifer, and several other engaging creatures roam about. Across the street, the imposing white 1661 Inn (seven guest rooms) and its adjoining contemporary guest house (nine rooms) offer a similarly plush experience, but with colonial instead of Victorian decor; four smaller units in the guest house share a bath and have considerably lower rates. Some rooms open onto a broad sundeck with stunning water views. If you're seeking more privacy and quiet, consider one of the three rooms in Nicholas Ball Cottage. This re-creation of the Gothic St. Anne's-by-the-sea Episcopal Church, which the great hurricane of 1938 razed completely, has wood-burning fireplaces in all units and lofts with spa tubs in two. On High Street, close to town, the turn-of-the-20th-century Dodge Cottage has nine rooms with Victorian furnishings, all of them comfortable but somewhat less distinct. And out on Ocean Avenue, a five-minute walk from Old Harbor (and a half-mile from the Hotel Manisses), the 1906 Dewey Cottage—though it's more contemporary in feel following a major 1994 renovation—has among the prettiest rooms of all six buildings. A lavish buffet breakfast, included in the rates (even for the cottages), is served daily in the 1661 Inn's breakfast room. Additional perks for all units include a guided island tour by van, a farm tour (given Saturdays only), late-afternoon wine and snacks, and a decanter of brandy in each room. When you factor in all the extras and the many types of accommodations, this well-operated resort can be considered a very good value. Open year-round.

With the same management, the **Harbor-side Inn,** Water Street, 401/466-2605 or 800/825-6254, website: www.blockislandhotels.com, and the **National Hotel,** Water Street, 401/466-2901 or 800/225-2449, website: www.blockislandhotels.com, are two of the most recognizable buildings in Old Harbor—the two wedding cake–like inns lie two doors apart, facing the ferry landing. The Harborside is the smaller and somewhat quieter of the two inns, but both have been completely renovated and modernized in recent years, with attractive and modern bathrooms and a mix of reproduction and a few authentic antiques. Rooms tend to be quite large, with high ceilings and large windows that let in plenty of light (especially the corner rooms, which tend to be the most sought-after)—and many of them have ocean views. The National Hotel, which was built in 1888 and has 45 rooms, has a more open feel, especially in its lobby and enormous veranda, than the 36-room Harborside—but the latter is a bit quieter. These are both good choices, however, if you want to be in the heart of the action. There are restaurants at both hotels and two bars as well as eight shops at the National. Closed late Oct.–early May.

INNS AND B&BS
$100–150

The quintessence of seaside simplicity, the **Sea Breeze Inn,** Spring Street, 401/466-2275 or 800/786-2276, website: www.blockisland.com/seabreeze, sits on a hillside overlooking marshes and swan ponds, and beyond that the ocean—this delightful little compound of weathered cottages sits low behind a row of hedges across from the Spring House Hotel. On thehe grounds you'll find aromatic and colorful perennial gardens and meadows carpeted with wildflowers. There are no TVs or in-room phones, not a single distraction—just the gentle crash of the surf behind these shingle buildings. The 10 rooms are airy, uncluttered, and tastefully furnished with well-chosen country antiques. You can borrow a kayak and paddle around the ponds behind the inn. Open year-round. On a hill a short walk up from Old Harbor, you'll be struck by **Sheffield House B&B,** High Street,

© ANDREW COLLINS

view from Gables Inn

401/466-2494 or 866/466-2494, website: www.blockisland.com/sheffieldhouse, an 1880s stick Victorian with pale blue clapboard siding and elaborate white trim. A crow's nest turret rises high over the gabled main roof. There are six generally cozy rooms, most with private baths and all with queen beds; furnishings are eclectic and well chosen, with a mix of antiques and newer pieces. In the downstairs living room, you'll find a common TV and phone and numerous games and books. Breakfast is served in the warmly lighted country kitchen, on the porch, or in the sunny garden in back. Open year-round.

It's hard to miss the distinctive **Gothic Inn,** Dodge Street, 401/466-2918 or 800/944-8991, website: www.blockisland.com/gothic, which is decked with frilly verge board, sharp pointed gables, and striking finials. The inn, set back from the road on a grassy lawn, backs up to Crescent Beach and is steps from Old Harbor restaurants and shops. Room decor is unfancy but pleasant, and from some windows you can enjoy views of the harbor. Also available are two-bedroom efficiency apartments, which are great for families and friends traveling together. Closed mid-Nov.–early Apr. Another reasonably priced option conveniently located on Dodge Street, the

Gables Inn and Gables II, 401/466-2213, is a compound of two attractive 1860s Victorian inns with many of their original details preserved, from pressed-tin ceilings to vintage floral wallpapers to Victorian rockers and wicker chairs. The Gables Inn's rooms are definitely the more romantic of the accommodations, as they contain most of the antiques—but the Gables II's more functionally furnished apartments and cottages are ideal for longer stays, families, or guests who appreciate dining or cooking in. Among the common amenities are barbecue grills and picnic tables, a laundry room, bike racks, and—never a given on Block Island—off-street parking. This is one of the relatively few properties on the island that not only allows children but actively welcomes them (cribs and strollers are available by advance request). Closed Dec.–mid-Apr.

$150–250

Victorian Inns by the Sea, 401/466-5891 or 800/992-7290, website: www.blockislandinns. com, consists of two main inns and a handful of smaller cottages, all of them quite upscale and with great locations. The late 1800s **Blue Dory,** Dodge Street, walks a nice balance between elegantly inviting and yet unstuffy and homey—from the back deck, a wooden doorway leads down the steps to the beach and crashing surf. You can relax or take afternoon tea in the small but attractive parlor munching on fresh-baked chocolate-chip cookies, and downstairs in an informal dining room a fairly perfunctory breakfast is served. The adjacent **Waverly Cottage** contains three large suites ideal for longer stays—each has either a wet bar or kitchen, a living area, and a Jacuzzi tub. As you might guess, the Waverly units are a favorite with honeymooners, but they also work well with two couples traveling together or families. A couple of blocks inland but on a hill looking out over Old Harbor, the **Adrianna Inn,** Old Town Road, has nine rooms and a lovely wraparound porch facing the rolling tree-shaded lawns. It's a bit more low-key and peaceful than the Blue Dory, and because it's not on the water the rates are lower. Additional properties include a three-bedroom oceanfront cottage and a restored four-bedroom farmhouse on the island's dramatic and rugged West Side. Typical in all the units are floral bedspreads and wallpapers, iron or brass beds (many of them four-posters), and period tables, chairs, and other pieces. If you have an aversion to Victorian frill, these inns may not be your cup of tea. Open year-round.

One of the quirkiest inns on Block Island, the early 1900s, pale rose **Beach House,** 597 Corn Neck Rd., 401/466-2924, stands about as close to long and sweeping Crescent Beach as you can get—it's a dream for beach lovers, as all of the guest rooms have dramatic water views. Rooms have an artsy feel. Art Constructions, Studio, and Gallery occupies the ground floor—many of the artworks can be viewed outside on the grounds. Down a quiet country lane off High Street (almost behind the Atlantic Inn), about a 10-minute walk from Old Harbor, the **Rose Farm Inn,** Roslyn Road, 401/466-2034, website: www.block-island.com/rosefarm, consists of two neighboring properties. The rambling 1890s Farm House contains 10 period-furnished guest rooms (eight with private bath and walk-in tile shower), a large southern-exposure sundeck, and a stone front porch. Across the lane, the gable-roofed Captain Rose House was built in 1993, and although some of the rooms here have double-whirlpool baths and a more modern feel, the decor, fabrics, and color schemes are authentically Victorian. Second-floor units in the Captain Rose House are perhaps the most romantic, as they have dormer windows and decks overlooking the 20 acres of pastoral grounds—a working farm until the 1960s, the property now acts as something of an unofficial wildlife preserve. Closed late Oct.–early May.

An inn since only 1999, the dramatic Second Empire **Hygeia House,** Beach Avenue, 401/466-9616, website: www.hygeiahouse.com, has been meticulously restored by the great-grandson (and

family) of the home's first owner, physician and hotelier Dr. John C. Champlin—the 1883 home has 10 guest rooms, most of them suites, and all with ocean views, fully updated bathrooms, and well-chosen Victorian antiques that impart a characterful yet uncluttered look. Guests can linger on a rocker on the porch or in one of the downstairs common areas; kayak rentals are available, and both New Harbor and Old Harbor are within a 10- to 15-minute walk. Open year-round. A huge American flag waves in the wind above the **Weather Bureau Inn,** Beach Avenue, 401/466-9977 or 800/633-8624, website: www.weatherbureauinn.com, not that this stunning Greek Revival building needs to call attention to itself. In fact, the tradition of waving a flag on the roof hints at the inn's original purpose—it was constructed in 1903 as a weather observatory, high on a hill visible from both Old and New Harbors. Here on Block Island, with treacherous seas in every direction, arriving ships needed all the help they could find. Depending on the weather forecast, different types of flags were hoisted above the flat roof, enclosed by a stately white wooden railing. These days, the Weather Bureau serves a new purpose—its four guest rooms resplendent with vintage wallpapers, upholstered chairs, and other dark-wood antiques, the building today is one of the island's most romantic inns. Views are impressive enough from the rooms, but head up to the third-floor roof deck and the panoramic vistas are simply breathtaking. Open year-round.

CAMPGROUNDS

Block Island has no campground and, in fact, camping is illegal throughout the island (but for a small tract of land owned by the Boy Scouts of America, on which only visiting scout troops may pitch tents).

Food

The island's dining scene resembles that of most other coastal New England resort towns, although because goods must be brought onto the island by air or boat, prices are slightly higher than on the mainland. There really aren't any specialties unique to Block Island, but seafood appears on virtually every menu and is consistently reliable.

Dress is casual everywhere, although at the handful of upscale hotel dining rooms you'll feel out of place if not dressed smartly (i.e., avoid print T-shirts, tattered jeans, and sneakers). Some places, especially the high-end spots, take reservations, but many others do not—on weekends, especially in season, it's worth phoning ahead either to book a table or ask about the wait. Off-season dining options are severely limited; from about mid-October to the end of December, and then from early April to Memorial Day, only a handful of places are open, and several of them only on weekends. From January through March, even fewer places remain open—on many weekdays your only option is the Beachhead.

Upscale

The lavish dining room at the **Spring House Hotel,** Spring Street, 401/466-5844 ($19–28), presents consistently fine contemporary Continental fare—past starters have included baby spinach and scallops wrapped in apple-smoked bacon with panfried goat cheese, as well as fresh buffalo mozzarella and beefsteak tomato salad. Main courses like crisp-seared half Long Island duck with a tangy blackberry-citrus sauce, and barbecued salmon with lobster mashed potatoes, have looked as good on the plate as they've tasted on the tongue. The dining room, with white napery and Windsor chairs, overlooks the ocean. Local opinions on the posh **Atlantic Inn,** High Street, 401/466-5883 ($42 prix fixe), run hot to cold, as some think the food stupendous while others claim the kitchen is resting on its laurels and the service doesn't always live up to expectations. There's no arguing that the food is creative—typical offerings from the four-course menu (dinners are prix-fixe only) include sautéed quail with an almond-couscous strudel and tahini sauce, and grilled striped bass with amaranth grain, a grapefruit-onion-beet salad, and watermelon broth. The malted crème brûlée makes for a memorable dessert.

Dinner at the **Hotel Manisses,** 1 Spring St., 401/466-2421 ($19–35) is another of the island's more lavish experiences. The creative regional American fare, such as baked Hudson Valley foie gras in puff pastry with caramelized onions, pancetta, and a raspberry-balsamic reduction, followed by grilled swordfish over a white-bean cake with a roasted-leek-and-tomato vinaigrette and sautéed escarole, may be the most daring—and richest—food you'll find on Block Island. Both á la carte and prix-fixe menus are offered. The flower-filled dining room of this stately old hotel makes a sublime setting for such a fine meal. For $250, you can also order one of the Hotel's special dinners for two to be prepared tableside and enjoyed (with fine linens and china) in your own room, on a deck, out on the beach, or virtually wherever you'd like it. The price includes a five-course meal, taxes, gratuity, transportation, and after-dinner drinks—it's hard to imagine a more romantic culinary interlude.

Creative but Casual

Consider yourself lucky if you're able to score a table at **Eli's,** 456 Chapel St., 401/466-5230 ($16–24), a hole-in-the-wall that locals speak of with solemn reverence. Expect enormous portions of such eclectic contemporary fare as peppercorn-pork tenderloin with spicy pineapple, orange, and apricot barbecue sauce; shallots and smoked gouda mashed potatoes; or crisp calamari with lemon-pepper breading served with a spicy cherry-pepper vinaigrette, cucumber coulis, and Cajun tartar sauce. Fortunately, everything on the menu may be ordered to go. The **Mohegan Cafe,** Water Street, 401/466-5911 ($12–20), which overlooks Old Harbor, is always a great bet for tasty lunch and dinner fare—it's also one of the island's best nightlife choices, with live music late many evenings. The food spans the

American culinary vernacular with some distinctive Asian and Southwestern influences. Good picks include the burgers, scallops with spinach tortellini, Buffalo-style chicken wings, and herb-roasted chicken with hoisin-rum barbecue sauce. The dining room is warmed by amber lighting and staffed by friendly, young folks. Some of the same lavish entrées served at the esteemed Hotel Manisses can also be ordered, in smaller portions, at the hotel's more casual **Gatsby Room,** 1 Spring St., 401/466-2421 ($9.50–17). Other possibilities include grilled barbecued shrimp over cheese grits; grilled flatbread pizza topped with figs, Stilton cheese, caramelized onions, and a roasted red pepper coulis; house-made rabbit and venison sausage with a spicy Dijon mustard; and selections from the raw bar. Or stop by for cocktails, aperitifs, or desserts.

Once just a burger joint better known for its drinks and homey nautical decor than for its culinary prowess, the **Beachead,** Corn Neck Road, 401/466-2249 ($5–18), revamped its kitchen a couple years ago and now serves very good seafood and American favorites. It's the only Block Island sit-down restaurant open daily year-round, making it a favorite of locals and visitors no matter the season. The food's hearty and tasty, including fantastic blue-cheese burgers and often inspired specials like shellfish bruschetta. Tasty crabcakes, outstanding chili, and spare ribs in hoisin sauce are quite good also. The staff is friendly, the service ranging from genial to a bit slow at times; and the decor of dark-wood tables, timber-beam ceilings, and TVs broadcasting Boston sporting events keep everyone in a happy mood. The restaurant is right by Crescent Beach and has water views from many tables.

Pizzas and Pub Grub

G. R. Sharky's, Corn Neck Road, 401/466-9900 ($13–27), is very good for steaks, seafood grills, hefty salads, chicken fajitas, fish and chips, and other casual dishes. The dining room is bright, attractive, and airy with high ceilings. There's a pleasant patio, too.

The National Hotel's **Tap & Grille,** Water Street, 401/466-2901 ($7–22), is justly renowned as one of the island's most memorable milieus—

seating is along the hotel's long and gracious covered veranda, which faces out onto Old Harbor and toward the daily parade of pedestrians strolling along Water Street. The food is pretty decent, too, with steaks, pastas, and seafood the specialties. Devotees swear by the Thai chicken salad, and the fish and chips also receives considerable praise. Just down the street, the restaurant at the National's sister hotel, the **Harborside Inn,** Water Street, 401/466-5504 ($8–21), serves an exceptional clam chowder, plus a fairly traditional roster of seafood, steak, poultry, and such. Outdoor seating is on a terrace on Water Street.

At the fancy **Spring House Hotel,** Spring Street, 401/466-5844 ($8–12), don't overlook the lighter menu available at lunch and dinner from the excellent, casual Verandah Cafe. Delicious gourmet pizzas are served, along with lobster rolls and sandwiches. Year-round, you can get tasty short-order fare from **Pizza Plus,** 401/466-9939, including calzones, subs, wings, salads, and sandwiches. This reputable parlor will deliver anywhere on the island. Seafood devotees linger blissfully around the raw bar at **Finn's,** by Old Harbor Ferry, 401/466-2473 ($10–22), which also serves hefty lobster dinners, rich chowders and stews, and heaping fried-clam platters. The bustling setting, by the ferry and overlooking the fishing boats sailing in and out of Old Harbor, is engaging—especially the seating on the patio, which fills up quickly on warm days.

Aldo's Italian Restaurant, Weldon's Way, 401/466-5871 ($6–22), attached to a wonderful little bakery and ice cream cafe, serves casual but reliable pastas, seafood grills, pizzas, and other Italian fare. Littleneck clams with drawn butter are an addictive specialty here, and pastas like penne á la vodka and seafood pesto (lobster, mussels, shrimp, scallops, and clams in a wine sauce over linguine) utilize fresh ingredients and old-world preparations. **Club Soda,** Connecticut Avenue, 401/466-5397 ($5–12), which stays open year-round and has been a bar since the 1940s, occupies the basement of the Victorian Highview Inn, and is best-known for serving delicious southern barbecue. Other pubby victuals include burgers, pizza, tangy Buffalo wings, and the like. There are open-mic nights, live entertainment, and always a sizable crowd on weekends. You can also shoot pool, watch football or baseball on a large-screen TV, or yuk it up with a mix of locals and tourists. By the bar you'll find a series of murals depicting local scenes painted by local artist George Wetherbee. A cheap and easygoing sister of the esteemed Hotel Manisses, **The Oar,** New Harbor, 401/466-8820 ($4–12), has a wonderful deck and dining room overlooking the sailboats and yachts on Great Salt Pond—a spectacular place for watching the sun set. Three meals are served here daily in season, and everything is available as take-out. Breakfast specialties include blueberry pancakes and egg sandwiches. A raw bar doles out smoked lemon-pepper mackerel, snow-crab claws, and similarly enticing fruits of the sea. Burgers, salads, sandwiches, fried chicken, and steaks are also served. The bar is renowned for its Block Island mudslides.

Quick Bites

Bethany Airport Diner, at the Block Island Airport, Center Road, 401/466-3100, is more than just a stopover for a light bite before or after a plane ride—plenty of locals swear by the hearty breakfast fare here, from flapjacks to breakfast burritos. Tasty burgers, sandwiches, and chowders are served at lunch (no dinner). Of course, reason enough to come here is the fun people-watching. From many seats you can see the planes landing and taking off, too. Another absolute favorite for breakfast is **Ernie's,** Water Street, 401/466-2473 ($3–8), which has occupied a ramshackle white building near the ferry terminal since the early 1960s.

For daytime sustenance, drop by **Aldo's Cafe,** Weldon's Way, 401/466-5871 ($6–22), for ice cream, muffins, Portuguese sweetbread, and designer coffees, and the all-you-can-eat country-style breakfast buffet weekend mornings. There's a row of outdoor tables and chairs in front, where on warm summer mornings locals nosh on eggs Benedict, French toast, and omelets (lots of fillings are available). Just watch yourself crossing Weldon Way with an ice cream cone in hand—this is a favorite street for riders to test rental mopeds from the nearby agencies. You can grab a light and refreshing meal at **Froozies,** back porch of National Hotel, Dodge Street, 401/466-2230 (under

$5), whose eponymous specialty is what most of us know as a smoothie—many flavors are available, and sandwiches and salads are also offered.

Java Joints

A snug coffeehouse around the corner from Water Street in Old Harbor, **Juice 'n Java,** Dodge Street, 401/466-5220, is one of the island's favorite social hubs, a place to meet up with old friends or make new ones, and to sample coffees, teas, and desserts from a vast list. More substantial fare—sandwiches, eggs, etc.—are also available. Shelves of board games and books keep snackers and sippers entertained, and there's live jazz some of the time.

Gourmet Goods and Picnic Supplies

Relatively close to Benson Beach and New Harbor, the **Old Post Office Bagel Shop,** Corn Neck Road and Ocean Avenue, 401/466-5959 ($2–7), is far more ambitious than its name suggests, presenting a wide selection of fresh-baked breads, along with the house-made bagels for which this sunny and cheerful café is named. Creative green and pasta salads, breakfast sandwiches, and healthful fruit cups complement the many types of bagels and spreads. An excellent source of gourmet foods and picnic supplies, **Daily Market,** Chapel Street, the Post Office Building, offers an ever-changing assortment of creative sandwiches and salads; healthful soft drinks, juices, chips, and snacks; fruit smoothies; hard-to-find cheeses and organic produce; soups made from scratch; bagels and pastries; and other breakfast dishes. There's a lot to munch on in this shop that you can't find in other shops on the island. Just down the hill by the ferry terminal, **Finn's Fish Market,** 401/466-2473, has the best selection of fresh creatures from the sea (in the tank, smoked, filleted, etc.), including fresh-prepared Rhode Island clam chowder to go. Get your food basics at **Seaside Market,** Water Street, 401/466-5876, and **Block Island Grocery,** Ocean Avenue, 401/466-2949. **Red Bird Package Store,** Dodge Street, 401/466-2441, has been the island's source of booze and beer since the end of Prohibition; it's open until 9 P.M. Mon.–Thurs., and to 10 P.M. Fri.–Sat.

Entertainment and Nightlife

This is not a major party island, even in high season, but you will find quite a few convivial hangouts, most of them frequented by young summer hotel employees and a fair share of islanders and tourists of all ages. Most of the bars are at or double as restaurants in town.

Captain Nick's Rock-N-Roll Bar, Ocean Avenue, 401/466-5670, brings in live music, throws a lively Disco Night on Mondays, and can drum up pretty substantial crowds on weekends. Adjacent is **Out Back Takeout,** Ocean Avenue, 401/466-5022, where pub food is served into the wee hours, and an outdoor bar serves fancy fruit drinks to a gabby crowd of tourists and locals. Another long-time favorite with the see-and-be-seen types is **McGovern's Yellow Kittens Tavern,** Corn Neck Road, 401/466-5855, which brings in hip live-music acts. The **Tap & Grille,** Water Street, 401/466-2901, at the stately National Hotel, is a great place to cocktails—the views out over the water are thoroughly enjoyable.

In **Victoria's Parlor,** Spring Street, 401/466-5844, the decadent sitting room and lounge at the Spring House Hotel, with Oriental rugs and Victorian settees and armchairs, you can order vintage port wines, specialty coffees, cognacs, and desserts. Similarly refined is the **Upstairs Parlor at the Hotel Manisses,** 1 Spring St., 401/466-2421, a dark and clubby room decked in Victoriana and wicker. Here you can sip fine drinks, play chess, and otherwise act like a fabled figure of coastal Rhode Island's gilded age.

The island also has a pair of movie theaters showing first-run films, the most interesting being the **Empire Theatre and Cafe,** Water Street, 401/466-2555, a lavishly restored venue that in addition to movies offers live music many evenings. Beer and wine are served before most performances. The other option is **Oceanwest Theatre,** Champlin's Resort, 401/466-2971.

Festivals and Events

Block Island has a broad range of events and gatherings through most of the year, with several good ones in the off-season, such as the fall Harvest Festival, Christmas Shopping Stroll, and Groundhog Day Census.

Another thing to keep your eyes and ears open for are the lectures and classical music concerts given throughout the high season by visiting performers, authors, and other notables. You can usually get the latest on upcoming events in the pages of the *Block Island Times* or by checking with the chamber of commerce.

The Fourth of July is a hugely popular time on Block Island—celebrations include a banjo concert and fireworks over Fred Benson Town Beach. An **Arts and Crafts Guild Fair** takes place at Esta's Park each year in early July. Later in the month, folks pile into St. Andrew's Parish for the **Annual Barbershop Quartet Concert,** which has been going strong since the early 1960s.

There are a number of races and athletic events on Block Island throughout the year, including early August's intensely challenging **Triathlon.** The Block Island Historical Society sponsors a well-attended and quite fascinating **House and Garden Tour** each August, while in the middle of the month the **Block Island Arts Festival,** spanning two days, has become one of the island's most crowded and lively weekends.

Birders and naturalists flock to Block Island the first weekend in October for **Audubon Weekend,** 401/949-5454. In the middle of the month, you can get in the spirit for the coming fall by attending the **Harvest Festival and Antique Car Parade.** And just when you think the island has all but shut down for the year, the weekend following Thanksgiving kicks off the **Annual Christmas Shopping Stroll,** during which several boutiques and shops display seasonal wares and gifts. That same weekend, there's a well-attended **Block Island Arts & Crafts Fair** held at Harbor Baptist Church.

The **Groundhog Day Census** is a fun way for islanders to gauge just how many residents are actually present on the island during about the bleakest point of winter, early February. So on the Saturday nearest Groundhog Day, everybody on Block Island registers with "census takers," at least some of whom are positioned at one of the few pubs on the island. Residents also enter a pool to guess what the official tally will be—the person who guesses closest takes home the prize. In 2002, the Groundhog Day Census recorded the highest tally in the island's history, 935. By the time the **St. Patrick's Day Celebration** comes and goes with some fanfare and a big party at McGovern's Yellow Kittens, Block Island's die-hards have generally sickened of the gray winter and seem eager for the spring thaw—even eager to welcome a new batch of tourists.

Information and Services

VISITOR INFORMATION

For tourism information, contact the **Block Island Tourism Council,** Box 356, Block Island, 02807, 401/466-5200 or 800 383-BIRI, website: www.blockisland.com. The council's offices double as the **Block Island Chamber of Commerce,** whose information center faces the Old Harbor ferry terminal. It's definitely worth popping in when you arrive on the island—brochures abound, and there's also an ATM, a fax/copier, and lockers for rent (ideal if you're day-tripping). You can also find out from the staff which hotels and inns on the island have vacancies. Next door to the chamber you'll find public restrooms (additionally, there are facilities at the fire/police station, the Island Free Library, and North Light).

A few practicalities to keep in mind: Block Island has a water shortage—the situation has been grave at times, and visitors are asked to make every possible effort to conserve water. Also do your best not to overuse electricity—the local utility company powers the island with diesel generators, and Block Island's electric rates are said to be higher than any other town's in the United States.

GETTING THERE

One way or another, you're going to have to get on a boat or a plane to make the final leg of your journey to Block Island.

By Plane

Flying to Block Island may not be as expensive as you think, and the time it saves (to say nothing of avoiding potential hassles) can make this option quite useful. The only regularly scheduled service is offered by **New England Airlines,** 800/243-2460, website: http://users.ids.net/flybi/nea, which offers frequent service out of **Westerly Airport,** U.S. 1 and Route 78, at Exit 92 (in Connecticut) off I-95 from the south, Exit 1 (in Rhode Island) off I-95 from the north. Hourly 12-minute flights are offered daily 7:30 A.M.–7:30 P.M. to Block Island, and 8 A.M.–8 P.M. back to Westerly. In summer, additional flights to Block Island are scheduled until 8:30 P.M. on Thursday, and until 10:30 P.M. on Fridays; additionally in summer, extra flights are offered back to Westerly on Mondays at 7 A.M. and Fridays at 10 P.M. The fare is $39 one-way, $69 round-trip, and children's and senior discounts are available. New England Airlines also offers charter service to Block Island from virtually any airport in the Continental United States.

You can reach Westerly Airport by **Amtrak,** 800/USA-RAIL, website: www.amtrak.com. Amtrak trains stop in the town of Westerly, from which you'll need to take a cab to the airport. Call **Eagle Cab,** 800/339-2970; the fare is about $15. Keep in mind, should you miss the last ferry (or should high winds or poor weather force ferry cancellation), that it's about a 20- to 25-minute drive from the ferry terminal in Galilee to the

BLOCK ISLAND BY FERRY

Getting to Block Island, especially in summer, takes a bit of preparation, plenty of flexibility, and a little luck. But making this trip is also, as the old cliché goes, part of the fun. Here's a roundup of how best to visit the island by ferry—there are many options, depending on where you're coming from. Keep in mind that reservations for passengers, motorcycles, and bicycles are not needed for any of the ferry services to Block Island.

Car Ferries: Cars can be brought over only on the ferries from New London and Point Judith. This can be a very tricky business, especially on weekends or virtually any day during summer. Unless you're hoping to obtain passage standby, make a reservation (book at least four to five months ahead of time for summer or holiday weekends). On the day of passage, be at the ferry dock and check in at the ferry window within one hour of ferry departure; if you're late, you risk losing your reservation to those waiting on standby.

If you're traveling off-season or you're flexible with time, consider going standby. In high season, standby is highly unreliable. Arrive at the terminal at least an hour before departure (a few hours ahead if you're trying to cross at a busy time). Once at the departure lot, check in with the attendant; he'll give you a ticket that establishes your place in the queue, and then you must remain with your vehicle if and until you're permitted to board (when it's not especially crowded, attendants sometimes let drivers leave their cars unattended for a bit). If in doubt about whether standby makes sense, phone the ferry company ahead of time and ask if they have an idea how crowded the ferry is expected to be on the date that interests you—nobody will make you any promises, but they will let you know if your chances are terrible. If you travel standby, you're not guaranteed return passage from Block Island—which means you may have to return at a different time (or on a different day) than you originally hoped.

From Point Judith: Most ferry travelers leave from Point Judith, the Narragansett fishing village just 10 miles or so from the northern tip of Block Island. This is the only point from which ferries sail during the off-season, from early September through early June, and it offers by far the greatest number of crossings. You also have a choice between conventional and high-speed ferry service from Point Judith.

Conventional service is provided by **Interstate Navigation,** 401/783-4613, www.blockislandferry.com. Service is offered year-round and changes from season to season, but there's always at least one (and usually two or three) sailings each day, even in winter (except for Christmas day, when there is no service at all). In fall and spring, service increases to four times most days and six times on weekends; and in summer there are eight or nine sailings per day. The times vary greatly, so call ahead or check the website for details. Keep in mind that even in high season, return ferries from Block Island never leave later than about 7 P.M. weeknights, and 9 P.M. Saturday and Sunday nights. In high season, the last ferry from Point Judith is usually 7 P.M., and 8 P.M. Friday through Sunday evenings.

The fare is $8.40 per passenger one-way ($13.50 round-trip, same-day), $26.30 for cars one-way, and $2.30 for bicycles. Round-trip tickets good for returning on a different day are available but they're usually no cheaper than buying two one-way tickets; and discounts apply for kids and seniors.

Summer 2001 saw the debut of **Island Hi-Speed Ferry,** 877/733-9425, www.islandhighspeedferry.com, a fleet of high-tech, passenger-only catamarans that reach speeds of up to 33 knots—the trip from Point Judith to Block Island takes but 30 minutes. These are sleek boats with climate control and airline-style seating. In summer, the ferry runs six times daily; in fall and spring service is cut to five times daily. You'll pay a little more for these boats, $14.50 each way for adults ($26.50 round-trip), but plenty of visitors feel the quick and comfy ride is worth the extra fee. Children's discounts also apply. Reservations are strongly recommended for these ships; currently you must make these over the phone, but the company plans to offer online booking.

Ferries depart Point Judith from Galilee State Pier, at the southern tip of the town of Narragansett. From points north, take I-95 to Route 4, following this south to U.S. 1, and then exiting in Narragansett at Route 108. If coming from points south, follow I-95 to Exit 92 in Connecticut, follow Route 2, turn right onto Route 78, and then follow U.S. 1 north to Route 108. From here, signs mark the way. There are numerous commercial parking lots within walking distance of the ferry, generally priced according to how close by they are. Driving times to Point Judith average an hour from New London, 50 minutes from Providence, and a little over 90 minutes from Boston.

There are several ways to reach the ferry terminal without driving there yourself. You can take **Amtrak,** 800/USA-RAIL, www.amtrak.com, to Kingston station, a 12-mile (20-minute) ride by taxi from the terminal. Kingston station is about three hours by train from Manhattan and an hour from Boston. Cab companies serving the area include **Best Taxi,** 401/781-0706 or 800/310-1127; **Eagle Cab,** 800/339-2970; and **Wakefield Cab,** 401/783-0007; the fare is about $25 from the station to Point Judith.

You can also get to Point Judith using **Rhode Island Public Transit Authority (RIPTA) buses** 800/244-0444, www.ripta.com. Buses run to the ferry terminal from Narrangansett, to which you can transfer to buses bound for T. F. Green Airport in Warwick, downtown Providence, and other parts of the state. This option requires a bit of planning and generally isn't worth the bother unless you're familiar with Rhode Island and used to regional bus systems.

Finally, if you're flying into T. F. Green Airport (which is served by most major U.S. airlines), you can always catch a cab to the ferry terminal (much, much easier than trying to take a RIPTA bus, but also much more expensive). Contact **Best Taxi,** 401/781-0706 or 800/310-1127; the fare is about $50.

Another option, if you're coming from New York City, is to take the shuttle offered by **Adventure East,** 401/847-8715 or 718/601-4707, www.adventureeast.com. Going this way can be a little confusing, because the shuttle determines which ferry terminal it will drive to based on the number of passengers, the time, and where everybody is headed. Most of the time, this is a shuttle between Manhattan and Newport, with a stop at Point Judith ferry terminal (and also, on request, at Westerly Airport, which has flights to Block Is-

land). However, if there are no passengers for Newport, the shuttle will often take passengers to the Montauk or the New London ferry instead of to Point Judith, as these two terminals are much closer to New York City). Whatever the details, the regular round-trip fare is $95, or $55 one-way (the price is the same regardless of which ferry terminal is used, or whether you're going to Newport or Westerly Airport). However, Adventure East often runs specials at significantly reduced rates.

You can pick the shuttle up from either Manhattan's Upper East or Upper West Sides. Weekdays, there are two departures (early morning and late morning); Saturdays, there are departures only early mornings; Sundays there are limited runs (call for availability). Returning from Rhode Island, there are mid-morning and mid-afternoon departures on weekdays, morning departures on Saturdays, and early evening departures on Sundays. Runs can be added or canceled on demand, so it's best to reserve well ahead.

From Newport, Rhode Island: Using this service, which is offered only late June–early September, to reach Block Island makes the most sense if you're driving from Cape Cod or somewhere east of Newport. It's also popular as a day trip with people vacationing in Newport. In all other cases, including from Boston, the Point Judith ferries make more sense (although the Newport ferry is a pretty boat ride through lower Narragansett Bay). Also, while Greyhound serves Newport, there's no service from Boston or Providence that arrives in Newport early enough to catch the ferry to Block Island.

As in Point Judith, service is provided by **Interstate Navigation,** 401/783-4613, www.blockislandferry.com. Ferries leave from Newport daily at 10:15 A.M. and return daily from Block Island at 4:45 P.M.—the sail time is about two hours. The fare is $8.25 for adults one-way ($11.85 round-trip, but only for same-day passage), and $2.30 one-way for bicycles. Children's and seniors discounts are available.

The terminal is at Fort Adams State Park, on Harrison Avenue; inexpensive water taxis run passengers back and forth between Fort Adams and

(continued on next page)

BLOCK ISLAND BY FERRY (cont'd)

downtown Newport (where there are plenty of lots and garages with long-term parking). Driving time to Newport is about 90 minutes from the Cape Cod canal crossing, and a little under two hours from Boston.

From New London, Connecticut: This is a popular summer-only option for the many Block Island visitors who hail from Connecticut and the Mid-Atlantic region, although it's not necessarily much faster in total trip time than driving to Point Judith and taking the ferry from there. Either way, it takes about two hours (from New London, depending on traffic, it's an hour's drive to Point Judith, and another hour or so by ferry to Block Island), unless you use the high-speed ferry, which is considerably quicker (but does not allow automobiles).

Ferry service, with **NELSECO Navigation Company,** 203/442-9553, www.blockislandferry.com, runs from early June through early September; departures from New London are daily at 9 A.M. (with one additional sailing each Friday at 7:15 P.M.); return passage from Block Island is daily at 4:30 P.M. The fare is $15 per passenger one-way ($19 round-trip, but only for same-day passage), $28 for cars one-way, and $3.50 for bicycles. Senior and children's discounts are offered, too.

The New London ferry terminal is right off I-95 (Exit 84S from the south, Exit 83 from the north)—just follow signs from the exit; it's right off Governor Winthrop Boulevard. You can park long- or short-term at the municipal **Water Street Parking Garage,** Atlantic Street, just off Eugene O'Neill Drive. Depending on traffic, you can expect the following drive times to New London: from Manhattan, 2.5 to 3 hours; from Hartford, about an hour.

The terminal is also just steps from New London's train station, which is served by **Amtrak,** 800/USA-RAIL, www.amtrak.com, with service from many major cities, including Manhattan (about 2.5 hours), Hartford (about 3.5 hours, with a change in New Haven), and Washington, D.C. (about 6 to 7 hours). **Greyhound,** 800/231-2222, www.greyhound.com, has service to New London from many major cities including Manhattan (3 to 4 hours), Hartford (2.5 to 3 hours), and Washington, D.C. (8 to 10 hours). The bus station is adjacent to the ferry terminal.

From Long Island, New York: Viking Landing ferries, 631/668-5700, www.pagelinx.com/bi-ferry, from Montauk, New York (at the eastern tip of Long Island's south fork) to Block Island runs late April to mid-October. Boats leave once a day from Montauk, at 9 A.M., and arrive in Block Island at 10:45 A.M. Return passage back to Montauk is at 4:30 P.M., arriving at 6:15 P.M. This is the only ferry to Block Island that arrives at New Harbor, rather than at the Old Harbor terminal. The fare round-trip is $40 adults, $20 children, and $10 per bicycle or surfboard—automobiles are not permitted. This service runs daily June–late September, and Fri.–Sun. (and sometimes Monday) April, May, and October.

If you're driving to Montauk (2.5 to 4 hours from Manhattan, depending on traffic), you can park at Viking Landing's lot for $5 per day. It's an arduous endeavor, but you could actually make it from New York City to Block Island using **Long Island Railroad,** 718/217-LIRR or 631/231-LIRR, www.mta.nyc.ny.us/lirr. Trains run between Penn Station in Manhattan and Montauk five times daily on weekends and 12 times on weekdays; the trip is three hours, and the fare ranges from about $10 one-way off-peak to $15 peak. The Montauk station is at Edgemere Street and Firestone Lane; it's a 2-mile taxi ride (call for a cab in Montauk at 631/668-6600) to the ferry terminal (at the end of Route 49). The catch is that ferries depart from Montauk for Block Island at 9 A.M., so you'll probably have to spend the night in Montauk—or if you're truly adventuresome, you could take the last train out of Manhattan (about half past midnight), arrive at Montauk at 4 A.M., and chill out for five hours.

If you'd prefer to take a car to Block Island from Long Island, keep in mind that you can take one of the frequent year-round car ferries from Orient Point (on the north fork of the eastern tip of Long Island) to New London (an 80-minute ride), and then take the car ferry from there to Block Island. For details about Orient Point to New London service, contact **Cross Sound Ferry Services,** 860/443-5281 or 631/323-2525, www.longislandferry.com. Cars cost $36 each way (including driver); it's another $10 per passenger.

airport in Westerly; from New London it's about a 35- to 40-minute drive.

A few other charter airlines fly frequently in and out of Block Island, often to regional Northeastern airports. These include a reputable Block Island–based option, **Resort Air,** 401/466-2000 or 800/683-9330, website: www.ultranet.com/block-island/resortair. Also, in summer, **Action Airlines,** 800/243-8623, flies out of Groton, Connecticut—minutes from New London's ferry terminal (which makes this a handy option if you miss your boat).

Block Island Airport sits atop a hill in the center of the southern half of the island. The 2,500-foot runway is lighted; and taxis usually greet regularly scheduled flights and can easily be phoned to meet charters. There's a funky little restaurant here, **Bethany Airport Diner,** that's quite fun, and both car and bike rentals are available in-season. You hardly even need that—it's a pretty, 20-minute walk into town from the airport (just turn right out of the entrance and walk down Center Road).

GETTING AROUND

You'll hear plenty of grumbling among islanders about the blight of mopeds—they are the frequent cause of accidents, often very bad ones. And as a means of transportation, they leave something to be desired. There aren't too many parts of the island that can't be managed on a bicycle, and if you are staying for more than a few days or traveling with a large group, you're better off bringing a car over anyway. Of course, islanders don't like visitors bringing their cars in high season either, but politically correct or not, there's no question that a car is convenient. If you're coming for fewer than four days, however, and staying anywhere within a 10-minute walk of Old or New Harbor (and about 90 percent of the island's accommodations are), you really need nothing more than a good pair of walking shoes to enjoy a vacation on Block Island. You can count on the island's fleet of taxis to move you about for longer trips, when you have luggage or shopping bags, or when several of you need to get somewhere.

If you do rent a moped, keep on the side of

the road, always rent a helmet, and do not travel on the island's dirt roads, where scars from wipe-outs are a constant reminder of the dangers. Keep in mind, too, that you may not take mopeds out after dusk. There are about 170 mopeds for rent on the island, but you may encounter a few stares or glares from islanders who count themselves among the "no-peds" contingent.

There are no street numbers in Block Island. The little signs mounted to the fronts of most houses and buildings are "fire numbers," used by the police and fire departments to locate buildings quickly in the event of an emergency. They mean nothing otherwise—their sequence has nothing to do with location.

Bike, Moped, and Car Rentals

Bike rentals are offered at several shops, with rates running $10–15 daily. Mopeds cost $30–60 daily. Many of these same agencies rent cars. Weekly rates are usually offered in all of these cases. All of these agencies take MasterCard and Visa, and some of them take American Express and Discover, too.

As you get off the ferry in Old Harbor, you'll find two rental agencies within steps of the terminal. **Island Bike & Moped,** Chapel Street, behind the Harborside Inn, 401/466-2700, rents six-speed beach cruiser bikes, 21-speed mountain bikes, tandems and tag-alongs, mopeds, and all the standard safety equipment. Offering a similarly extensive selection of bikes and mopeds, **Old Harbor Bike Shop,** 50 yards to the left of the ferry terminal as you disembark, 401/466-2029, website: www.oldharborbikeshop.com, also rents open-top Jeeps, vans, and other autos. With locations in New Harbor and at Block Island Airport, **Block Island Bike and Car Rental,** Ocean Avenue, 401/466-2297, has bikes, cars, and vans for rent. Also in New Harbor, **Boat Basin Car and Bike Rental** is right next to the Oar Restaurant; cars, vans, mountain bikes, six-speed beach cruiser bikes, baby seats, and similar equipment are available for rent.

Taxis

You'll see taxis lined up in Old Harbor and New Harbor, and also at the airport, waiting for passengers on scheduled ferry and plane crossings. You can also hail cabs on the street. Just hold out your right hand and wave as one passes, even if it looks full or doesn't appear to be slowing down much. If the driver can take you, the cab will pull over. If not, he'll often hold up his CB and wave it to you, indicating that he's calling for another cab to come get you.

Island cab drivers can be a font of information, and most of them offer hour-long tours of the island, usually for about $30 or $40, depending on how many of you come along for the ride. For simple rides, cabs charge a flat fee and do not use meters. Within the main taxi zone, which forms a triangle among Old Harbor, New Harbor, and the airport, the charge is $5 for the first two passengers and $1 more for each additional passenger. All but a handful of the island's businesses fall within this zone, so you'll rarely find taking a cab more complicated than this. Should you be venturing far, the fee will be a bit more, but it's always quite reasonable and fare rates are always displayed clearly in the cab. It's a simple policy, and these fares are firm; it's illegal to negotiate either higher or lower fares. Cabs can be fined for taking too many passengers, or for accepting passengers carrying open containers of booze.

If you need to phone a cab, try any of the following four companies: **Kirb's Cab,** 401/466-2928, run by local resident Avery Kirby, who has a loyal patronage of repeat customers; **Ladybird Taxi,** 401/466-3133, who drives a cool old Country Squire station wagon with wood paneling; **MinuteMan Taxi,** 401/466-3131; and **O. J. Taxi,** 401/741-0500, whose driver specializes in island history and photography tours. Others include **Bumble Bee Taxi,** 401/466-2807; **Rose Taxi,** 401/466-9967; and **Wolfie's Taxi,** 401/466-5550.

MEDIA

The weekly *Block Island Times,* 401/466-2222, website: www.blockislandguide.com, is an indispensable resource for anybody planning a visit of even a few days. Both the print paper and the online edition contain updated ferry information, news about upcoming events, and frequent features on local history.

TOURS

Other than taking a taxi tour of the island, boating excursions are a great way to get a different perspective on Block Island's enchanting scenery. A favorite tour boat is the *Ruling Passion,* 401/466-5131 or 800/ORVIS-01, a 45-foot trimaran that sails out of the Boat Basin thrice daily at 11 A.M., 2 P.M., and 6:30 P.M. On the last cruise, wine and cheese is served during sunset. The boat can take up to 29 passengers. Get tickets, information, and reservations at Oceans and Ponds, 217 Ocean Ave. *White Rose Custom Sail Charters,* 401/789-0181, gives full- and half-day sails on a 42-foot custom sloop. You can swim, sail, or sunbathe from or on deck. Overnight charters are also available.

Newport

But for historical happenstance, Newport might easily have become the largest city in New England—it's hard to imagine this elegant, almost quaint peninsula of colonial homes and lavish mansions instead studded with glass-and-steel skyscrapers, but Newport was headed in this direction until the Revolutionary War, and even for a time afterwards.

Newport began as one of early Rhode Island's typically tolerant colonies, as a haven for those disenchanted with the religious and political conformity, and ultimately oppression, so common in the Massachusetts colonies. With a strategic, sheltered harbor, however, it wasn't at all long before enterprising locals turned the young city into one of the New World's foremost ports. Particularly between 1720 and the American Revolution, countless shipping concerns flourished in Newport, which became a

corner of the infamous Triangle Trade with the West Indies and Africa. Much of Newport's early trading was slave-oriented—in fact, Newport surpassed even more Charleston during the early years. Rhode Island did, however, become the first colony to make slave-trading illegal, in 1774, thus ending that horrific practice—though the state did not actually ban the ownership of slaves until 1784, after several states already had.

The end of the slave trade did not greatly affect Newport's mercantile success; it continued to thrive in the trade of rum, molasses, indigo, and other wares. The blow to the city's economic clout, and also its colonist pride, came at the beginning of the American Revolution, when British forces decided to occupy Newport. Throughout much of the war, from 1776 through 1779, the city remained firmly under English control. Most of the population, which

boating in Narragansett Bay

© BILLY BLACK

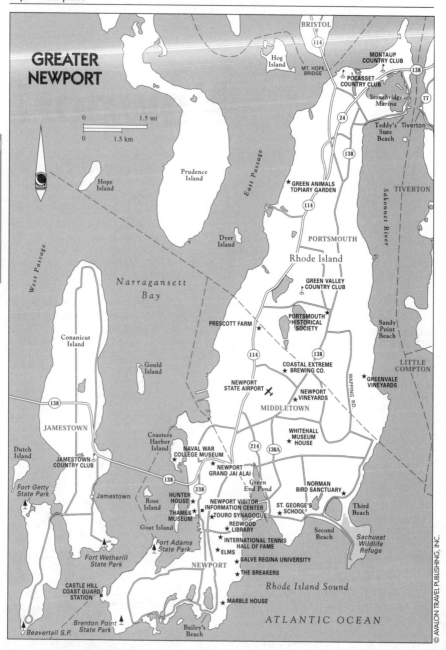

GREATER
NEWPORT

0   1.5 mi
0   1.5 km

BRISTOL
114

MONTAUP
COUNTRY CLUB
138

Hog
Island

MT. HOPE
BRIDGE

POCASSET
COUNTRY CLUB

Stonebridge
Marina

77

24

138

Teddy's
State
Beach

Tiverton

NEWPORT

Prudence
Island

East Passage

GREEN ANIMALS
TOPIARY GARDEN

114

Hope
Island

TIVERTON

Sakonnet River

PORTSMOUTH

Dyer
Island

Rhode Island

GREEN VALLEY
COUNTRY CLUB

Sandy
Point
Beach

West Passage

Narragansett
Bay

PRESCOTT FARM

PORTSMOUTH
HISTORICAL
SOCIETY

LITTLE
COMPTON

Conanicut
Island

Gould
Island

114

138

COASTAL EXTREME
BREWING CO.

Wapping Rd.

GREENVALE
VINEYARDS

NEWPORT
STATE AIRPORT

NEWPORT
VINEYARDS

138

JAMESTOWN

MIDDLETOWN

Dutch
Island

Coasters
Harbor
Island

NAVAL WAR
COLLEGE MUSEUM

214

138A

WHITEHALL
MUSEUM
HOUSE

JAMESTOWN
COUNTRY CLUB

138

NEWPORT
GRAND JAI ALAI

Green
End Pond

NORMAN
BIRD SANCTUARY

Fort Getty
State Park

Jamestown

Rose
Island

238

HUNTER
HOUSE

NEWPORT VISITOR
INFORMATION CENTER

THAMES
MUSEUM

TOURO SYNAGOGUE

ST. GEORGE'S
SCHOOL

Third
Beach

Goat Island

REDWOOD
LIBRARY

Fort Adams
State Park

INTERNATIONAL TENNIS
HALL OF FAME

Second
Beach

Sachuest
Wildlife
Refuge

Fort Wetherill
State Park

ELMS

SALVE REGINA UNIVERSITY

NEWPORT

THE BREAKERS

CASTLE HILL
COAST GUARD
STATION

Rhode Island Sound

MARBLE HOUSE

Brenton Point
State Park

Bailey's
Beach

ATLANTIC OCEAN

Beavertail S.P.

© AVALON TRAVEL PUBLISHING, INC.

was sympathetic to the war for independence, fled Newport. Tories from other parts of the colonies in turn moved here. Commerce as we know it ended, which was also true in New York City, Boston, and other East Coast ports. But because so little of the original population remained at the close of the Revolutionary War, Newport took longer to recover.

The city enjoyed a moderately successful final decade of the 18th century and some good years following that, but the shipping embargo imposed upon New England during the War of 1812 effectively sealed Newport's fate as nothing more than a small-time port city. For much of the 19th century, shipbuilding, naval exploits, and trade continued to play some role in Newport's fortunes, but the Industrial Revolution almost completely bypassed the city, while factories sprang up in and around Providence and in Rhode Island's northern areas, where rivers provided power to operate mills.

Newport's greatest commodity continued to be its marvelous location at the tip of Aquidneck Island, with its fine harbor and attractive, hilly layout that afforded excellent water views from many vantage points. Only now, Newport's location served not so much to attract merchants as to draw one of the earliest crops of America's vacationing leisure class. Wealthy factory owners, rail and shipping tycoons, and other solons of industry began summering in this town that rarely became as hot in the summer as other parts of the Northeast.

The area east and south of downtown, along Bellevue Avenue, became a summer destination for the rich and connected, as did parts of the jagged point that stuck out to the southwest and into the ocean. From about the Civil War up until about the Depression, the city enjoyed its renaissance as a pleasure village. As many fortunes fell during the 1930s and a spirit of fiscal conservatism continued to prevail during the Second World War, Newport's mansions fell empty. Many were sold and subdivided into apartments, while others were shuttered, the heirs of their original owners unable or unwilling to pay for their upkeep.

The rest of Newport continued to chug along as a fairly typical and undistinguished port city, but tourism was vital here throughout even the lowest points of the 20th century. As weeklong summer vacations became increasingly popular with middle-class families following World War II, an increasing number of visitors began spending summers in Newport and even more so in the several motels just over the border in Middletown.

Newport enjoyed a slow but steady resurgence from this point forward. Locals began to look around more and notice the city's incredible bounty of notable architecture, first by working toward the preservation of the city's grand "summer cottages." In 1967, tobacco heiress Doris Duke largely formed the Newport Restoration Foundation, which helped to preserve hundreds of important colonial houses. By the 1980s, one of Newport's oldest intact neighborhoods, the Point District, had become quite fashionable, its many 18th-century homes repainted and restored.

For at least the past 20 years, Newport has enjoyed a reputation as a yachting hub, an increasingly upscale vacation destination, and a favorite place for touring magnificent homes from just about every period of pre–World War II northeastern American architecture. Grand, rather formal inns and restaurants proliferated for many years—only recently have the decor and the menus at these places become noticeably trendy. The city is not growing, however; in fact, the population dropped more than 6 percent between 1990 and 2000.

Newport today remains fairly preppy, conservative in demeanor and style, although less so politically. This is a tolerant, socially progressive city, but without the youthful edge of Providence. College students from a number of Northeastern schools have made it a tradition for many years to summer here, as have many Irish and British young people, renting up downtown boarding houses and cheap apartments; working the restaurants, shops, and bars; and playing around during the time off, whether in sailboats, on beaches, or in taverns and clubs.

Newport is ideally suited to adult vacationers of almost any age, and although downtown hotels and inns will set you back a fair amount during

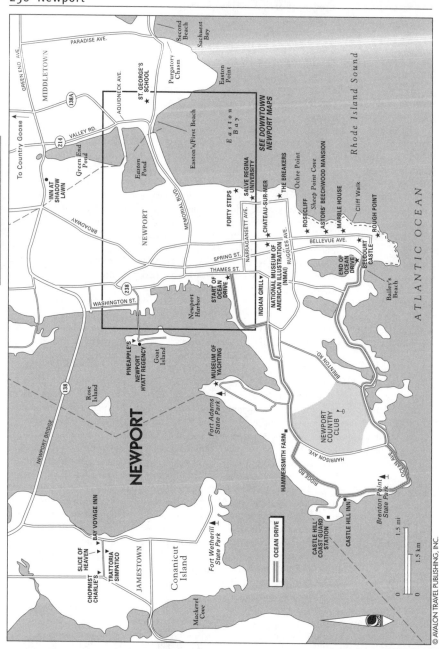

NEWPORT

© AVALON TRAVEL PUBLISHING, INC.

the high season, the region as a whole is not out of reach economically for most budgets. There are moderately priced motels and hotels in nearby Middletown, and it's not hard to find reasonably priced eateries. Still, to really see and experience the best of Newport, it helps to have plenty of discretionary income. This is the most expensive destination in the state, except perhaps Block Island during the peak of summer, and the admission costs to area house-museums add up quickly.

The kinds of diversions here—sailing charters, romantic inns and restaurants, posh boutiques, historic homes—lend themselves more to adults than to families, who may find a more child-friendly climate across Narragansett Bay in South County. However, Newport does have several family-friendly motels and hotels, as well as properties with kitchens and sitting rooms. And kids will enjoy some of the more colorful mansion tours, especially the Astors' Beechwood, as well as the beaches, the Newport-area branch of the New England Aquarium, and some other attractions.

Looking around this busy but small-scale city today, with its stunning parks and green spaces, its fine homes of all styles, and its low-key and friendly demeanor, it's easy to guess that most of the

city's residents and visitors are happy that fate chose not to turn Newport into another Boston or even Providence. There are big cities all up and down the Eastern Seaboard, but there are few places with the combined charms of Newport. These days the most apt comparison is with, oddly enough, Charleston, South Carolina—the two capitals of the 18th-century Triangle Trade share not only a common history but also the sophisticated appeal of small, historic, maritime cities.

Newport is really two cities in one—there's the tightly laid-out downtown with its narrow one-way streets and rows of colonial through Victorian buildings, and then there's the sweeping, wealthy peninsula that juts south and east of all this, where expensive homes on large plots of land dominate the landscape. Its dual nature extends to the change of seasons: in summer, the city's usual population of 26,000 climbs to well over 80,000, to the point that many Newport devotees won't even set foot here, preferring to visit during the mellow shoulder seasons. Summer is a favorite time to visit but an awful time for parking, getting a table quickly at restaurants, and enjoying the city's many house-museums and attractions without enduring long lines.

History

Newport occupies the southern tip, shaped like a jagged heel, of Aquidneck Island. It's a small city, with only about one-seventh the population of Providence. And yet, right up until the American Revolution, it appeared that Newport would grow to become one of the—if not *the* foremost metropolis and seaport on the Eastern Seaboard. Fate had different plans for the city, and its path since the 1780s has been less predictable—but at least interesting.

As with Providence, Warwick, Bristol, and just about every other early Rhode Island municipality, Newport was founded by iconoclasts who took issue with the tight governing grip of the Massachusetts Bay Colony. It takes its name, as far as anybody can tell, from the seat of government on the Isle of Wight, to which Aquidneck Island has been compared in size and physical character.

The first Europeans to establish a settlement here were John Clarke and William Coddington, a couple of Bostonians whose independent approaches to religion brought upon them the contempt of the Massachusetts Bay Colony's powers. They, with a cohort of about 15, called on Roger Williams and his dissident Providence clan in 1638; they enlisted Williams' aid in negotiating the purchase of Rhode Island proper. It's a little confusing, now that this name applies to the entire state, but the actual island that bore this name, now commonly referred to by its Native American moniker, Aquidneck, is wholly separate from the rest of the modern state of Rhode Island.

The northeastern end of Aquidneck had been settled by a differing group of Massachusetts exiles, led by Anne Hutchinson—this community would come to be known as Portsmouth.

EARLY NEWPORT'S QUAKER AND JEWISH SECTS

The fact of Newport's enviable strategic position and its—like the rest of Rhode Island's—complete religious and political tolerance was not lost on persecuted persons elsewhere in the New World and in Europe. Quakers were among the earliest and most prolific settlers; a ship of them arrived in 1657, and in a short time many of Newport's most prominent citizens joined the Friends movement, among them William Coddington and Governor William Brenton (for whom Brenton Point, at the southwest tip of the city, is named). While Rhode Island was founded by Baptists, the state's first two centuries saw the election of more Quakers than members of any other religious group.

Quakers were feared and despised elsewhere in New England. In fact, Mary Dyer, the wife of the secretary of Rhode Island, was hanged in Boston in 1660 during a visit, after having been warned to not to proselytize there in the name of Quakerism.

America's second-oldest Jewish congregation was established in Newport (the first was formed four years earlier in New York City). A ship containing 15 Sephardic Jewish families arrived from Barbados (having come originally from Spain and Portugal) and immediately formed a small congregation that would be formally named Jeshuat Israel a little over a century later. They worshiped in private homes for many years, until they built the Touro Synagogue in 1763, the oldest such place of worship in the United States. Newport's Jews also established what many people believe is the first Freemasons lodge in the New World. Jews also emigrated to Rhode Island during the colonial era from Curaçao and later from Portugal. New England's whaling industry was begun by Jacob Rodrigues Rivera, who fled Spain during the Inquisition in the 1740s.

Early Jews were among the earliest and most successful pioneers of Newport industry, and had the British not occupied the city during the American Revolution, they might very well have helped steer the city to unrivaled economic growth. Instead, industry died with British occupation, and most of the city's Jews fled to colonies loyal to the American Revolution.

So in 1639 Coddington and the others set out to occupy the southern end of the island. They first considered the present-day Newport Beach but then moved down the hill and west to the island's ideally sheltered harbor—its only drawback being that it was ringed by swampland. At about where West Broadway and Marlborough now intersect (very near city hall), Newport as we know it was born.

They declared that the land extending five miles north from the ocean, covering every point east to west, would constitute this new community. Housing lots were drawn, and the settlement's first thoroughfare, Thames Street, was laid out for one mile, running roughly parallel to the harbor. Later that same year, the founders of Newport met with those of Portsmouth and decided to create a joint government, composed of members from both towns, to rule the island. William Coddington was elected this new colony's first governor.

In 1644 the general colony of Rhode Island secured an English charter, thus uniting the entire colony—including Newport, Portsmouth, Warwick, and Providence—under one bureaucratic umbrella. John Coggeshall of Newport was appointed the first president, with his assistants being Coddington, John Sanford of Portsmouth, Roger Williams of Providence, and Randall Holden of Warwick. Confusion arose when in 1651 it became apparent that Coddington had, on his own, secured a separate English patent assuring him the governorship of Aquidneck—a fact that once again divided the young colony in two. Ironically, the two towns on Rhode Island were no longer political constituents of the Rhode Island colony.

The people of Newport and Portsmouth unhappily submitted to Coddington's authority, but they also immediately dispatched a team headed by John Clarke and Roger Williams to England to have Coddington's patent nullified. They succeeded, and in 1653 the two towns rejoined the greater Rhode Island colony. Clarke later helped to secure the King Charles Charter of 1663, which further validated the authority of Rhode Island, giving it the same weight as other nearby colonies like Connecticut and Massachusetts.

During these early years, Newport's principal trade—other than subsistence farming—was ship-building. As early as 1646 the colony was pro-ducing 100-ton ships for other New England communities. By the 1650s William Codding-ton had made commercial ties with islands in the West Indies, trading horses by ship with Barbados for sugar, molasses, indigo, and a variety of other sundries. These ties would ultimately seal Rhode Is-land's fate as the Northeast's most prominent hub of the slave trade, with Newport its capital. Other commerce involved the shipping of various goods to England, France, and other European nations.

One of the town's most prominent early citi-zens was Benedict Arnold, who became the first Rhode Island governor to serve after the restora-tion in 1660 of Charles II to the British throne. Benedict's great-grandson and namesake is better known today, as the most notorious traitor of the American Revolution. The earlier Arnold was one of many Newporters who served as gov-ernor during the colony's first 100 years.

Ben Franklin's brother James, as versed as his sibling in printing and newspaper publishing, left Boston for Newport in 1726, where he hoped to take advantage of the city's fervent support of freedom of the press. He had practically been run out of Massachusetts for printing the highly provocative *New England Courant*. In Newport, he started the *Rhode Island Gazette* in 1732; his son followed with the *Newport Mercury* in 1758, which—but for an extended shut-down during the American Revolution—has been published continuously to this day.

The Gilded Age Through the American Revolution

Newport prospered during the 18th century, grow-ing from a sleepy town whose economy was tied largely to shipbuilding, fishing, and farming into a bastion of merchant shipping. With the advent of Triangle Trade, successful sea captains began raking in fortunes in the commerce of molasses, rum, and African slaves. Sugar refining, brewing and distilling, and using sperm whale oil to make

candles grew as related industries. From about 1730 through the Revolutionary War, Newport hit its financial stride. By the 1760s, Newport had nearly 1,000 homes and some 500 warehouses and commercial businesses, making it one of the New World's most prominent colonies.

Newport's legacy as the slave-trading hub of the New World's most prolific slave-trading colony is a troubling one in hindsight—some 60 New-port-registered ships engaged in this activity dur-ing its peak. The importation of slaves reaped huge financial benefits, a fact not lost on the British Crown, which aggressively sanctioned this practice and, in 1708, instituted a tax of 3 pounds per incoming slave. Some of the spoils from this tax were used to pave Newport's streets and for other public works, but Great Britain also prospered significantly.

Privateering—basically, wartime piracy—sup-plemented or even became the primary income for many local sea captains. Two mid-18th-century military engagements, King George's War and the French and Indian War, proved especially prof-itable for Newport's fleet of some 50 privateers. En-gaged in this risky activity, ships sailed from Newport and challenged enemy sloops out at sea, securing them and returning to Newport with their cargoes. More than 100 merchant sailors were captured by enemy ships during these years, but Newport still prospered far more than it lost.

Newport's wealth made it a hotbed of high society, helping to fund the formation of the elaborate Redwood Library in 1730, and making the city fashionable with Southern aristocratic families looking for cooler climes during the summer months. These visitors were the precur-sors to the Morgans and Vanderbilts who would follow more than a century later; they tended to rent comparatively modest homes in the center of Newport, however, and did not construct the monuments to conspicuous consumption that the Gilded Age tourists would. Nevertheless, lav-ish parties and balls were held in Newport during these years, and a theater group performed Shake-speare. These years, however, would not last.

The earliest storm clouds appeared on the horizon toward the end of the 1760s, as the mother country England began enforcing tighter and more aggressive tax schemes and law enforcement on Aquidneck Island, which had become a jewel for Great Britain. Newport was eyed with avarice by European society types, who generally thought more of the sophisticated and highfalutin' city than they did Puritanical Boston or politically fervent Philadelphia.

Many Newport residents were at least moderately conflicted as talk of revolution began to sweep through the colonies. On the one hand, a war, and independence from the Crown, would severely disrupt commerce; on the other hand, England's taxes and harassment of merchants were disrupting commerce already. In Newport one might argue that the attitudes toward war were informed less by romantic issues of liberty and civil rights and more by what made sense economically (of course, this was the case all throughout the New World—though history books tend to focus on this motivation a bit less).

Ultimately, the financial controls enacted by England proved to be too much. In 1764, officers on a British ship in the Sakonnet River impounded a cargo of sugar from a merchant ship; locals on the shore gathered on the banks and hurled stones at the ship, and others actually took to arms. As subsequent incidents like this began to occur, increasing numbers of locals reacted hostilely. One particularly upsetting habit of the British was randomly impressing seamen from merchant ships—the English officers would stop the merchant ship for inspection and then take some of the crew and force them into British naval service. The British schooner the *Maidstone* sat in Newport Harbor for some months in 1765 impressing colonial crews from incoming merchant ships. Eventually a group of irate and rowdy locals secured one of the *Maidstone*'s dinghies and carried it to the town common, where they set it on fire. Nerves were frayed, and tension mounted through the close of that decade.

Things really began to get thorny in 1769, when the British *Liberty* brought a Connecticut merchant ship to Newport, where it impounded its cargo and crew. In the still of night, locals and cut the ropes tying the *Liberty* to shore—it drifted gradually toward Long Wharf, where the mob burned it. The British were not amused.

An English naval commander arrived in Newport soon after with a large fleet of ships to enforce order and punish the locals.

Tensions escalated for several years thereafter. In spring 1776, with talk of revolution rife throughout the 13 colonies, another gang of locals decided to mount an insurgence of sorts—a successful one, temporarily. They gathered at the harbor and opened fire on the British ships, driving the entire fleet out to sea for a time.

Just before Christmas of that same year, the British decided to put an end to the Newport nuisance once and for all. Commander Peter Parker sailed a force of some 9,000 English militia and Hessian mercenaries into the Newport harbor, by way of the Sakonnet River. This hostile maneuver stunned the city. Loyalists, of which there were a fair number, were thrilled; those sympathetic to the revolutionary efforts fled to other parts of Rhode Island and New England. Newport would never again look or feel quite the same. In a matter of months, the permanent population declined from about 9,200 to about 5,000.

Newport became a base of operations for the British army during the first half of the war. Troops resided in tent camps during the warmer months and were quartered in local homes as the weather turned harsh. Churches and civic buildings were turned into barracks and stables, every tree in sight was cut up for fuel, the wharves and harborfront were made a shambles, and hundreds of buildings were destroyed (especially homes and businesses of colonists who had fled). Such harsh treatment is typical of any military occupation, but clearly the British also sought to punish this community that had been such a thorn in their side.

Some of the British troops left for the even larger occupation of New York City in spring 1777. For most of the occupation, the British in Newport were led by a stuffed-shirt British commander, General Richard Prescott, who was generally despised by even his own troops. His leadership undoubtedly inspired further resentment among locals.

A glimmer of hope appeared in the form of French commander Count D'Estaing and a small but potent fleet of ships. D'Estaing sailed his group into Newport Harbor in summer 1778 and handily roughed around the British. It appeared that Newport would be rescued. A number of British ships were sunk or run aground, even burned. But England's Lord Howe and an even larger posse of British ships rushed to Newport to fend off the barrage. D'Estaing sailed out to cut off Howe's attack, but ultimately Mother Nature intervened to the benefit of the Brits. A huge storm fell upon Newport's waters, and both the French and British fleets were forced to disband and run for shelter. D'Estaing made one more stab at Newport, and anxious Continental militia soon grouped at the hills in northern Aquidneck Island, awaiting the opportunity to storm Newport and join the French in a full-scale attack.

This opportunity never came. D'Estaing, perhaps sensing the long odds of a successful engagement, retreated out to sea and then all the way back to Boston. The Portsmouth rebels were left at the altar; disheartened, they retreated farther inland, only to encounter an even larger group of British troops along the way. A skirmish ensued, during which the Americans did enjoy at least a small victory, killing quite a few of the British before making it to safety.

A retaking of Newport by American forces finally did happen, although in an almost anticlimactic way. In October 1779, the British decided they needed to bolster their defenses in New York and abandon Newport. All of the remaining English ships and troops on Aquidneck Island were ordered to leave. Like robbers leaving the scene of a hold-up, the departing Brits ordered the residents of Newport to remain indoors during their retreat. Of course, the minute the last of the British ships left the harbor—having pilfered numerous furnishings, church bells, all of the city's records, and countless volumes from the Redwood Library—the remaining Newporters ran to the shore and bid the Brits an appropriate good-bye, what we might today describe as a Bronx cheer.

Of course, quite a few Newport residents remained loyal to the British during the occupation; these residents either left with the Brits or fled to other parts of the New World, many to Nova Scotia and other Canadian towns. The day following the British evacuation, American troops returned to reoccupy what was left of Newport. Those homes and estates in the best condition, of course, had been owned by Tory sympathizers, and the Rhode Island authority spent a good bit of the winter of 1779–80 confiscating these properties and transferring them to American owners.

By summer of 1780, after enduring a harsh winter, Newport's residents prepared for a new occupation, and this time it was one they could embrace, at least relatively. On July 12, 1780, French General Rochambeau arrived in the city with more than 5,000 troops and a massive bounty of provisions. While this development was met favorably by most people, some residents had not yet forgotten or forgiven the abandonment of Newport by Count D'Estaing, and it took a little time for the French to earn the trust and appreciation of locals. General Rochambeau has long been viewed as one of the great statesmen of the late 18th century, and indeed he did nothing but contribute to this favorable reputation by conducting himself with grace and tact in Newport.

In some ways he had an even more difficult time earning the trust of colonists in other states, such as Connecticut, where strident religious intolerance made it tough for the mostly Catholic Frenchmen. Rhode Island was at least accustomed to exhibiting tolerance toward those of virtually any religious persuasion. The French, in turn, took quickly to Newport life—they appreciated the city's sophisticated ways and elegant homes.

Perhaps the most glorious day in Newport's still-young history occurred on March 6, 1781, when the commander-in-chief of the Continental Army, General George Washington, arrived by ship in Newport Harbor, debarking at Long Wharf clad—as a show of solidarity—in full French uniform. A huge crowd of locals greeted the commander, and an exhilarating military parade was held on what is now Washington Square. The following evening Rochambeau, Washington, and the many other dignitaries celebrated their cooperative war effort with a lavish ball held in the still-standing Colony House on the square.

Of course, Washington's visit was about much more than pomp and circumstance, or even diplomatic schmoozing. It was here that he and Rochambeau met more seriously at the latter's Newport quarters, Vernon House, to discuss military strategy. Washington left Newport having conferred with Rochambeau on a plan that would lead to one of the Revolutionary War's most important American victories, the Battle of Yorktown. A couple of months later, on June 9, Rochambeau and his troops marched forever from Newport.

1780–1850

After having endured some five years of upheaval, the bruised and battered port town was ready to return to normalcy. In 1784 Newport incorporated as a city. For the next decade or so, the financially depressed community, whose population had now fallen to 4,000, struggled to find its footing. The old lavish social customs of Newport had completely ceased, and city leaders instead enacted a policy of fiscal restraint. Gatherings, teas, and other parties were still held, but with much less fanfare than before the Revolution. The port of New York City had assumed prominence as America's new shipping center, and at least some Newport seamen moved there.

Comparatively limited efforts to reestablish the city's shipping interests met again with uncooperative historical circumstances. Tensions concerning trade and shipping were growing again between the young American nation and the British—these skirmishes ultimately led to a new military engagement, the War of 1812. The English formed their legendary blockade of southern New England, actually well west of Newport's waters, in 1812—but the blockade eventually spread east to include virtually the entire New England coast, and all merchant commerce in Newport effectively ended but for privateering. This latter industry did at least enjoy some success during the War of 1812, as local merchant ships set about intercepting and capturing any English vessels they could. Peace in 1815 came too late to help Newport return to its feet.

During the Industrial Revolution, which kicked into high gear in Rhode Island during the early 19th century, state commerce shifted from relying on trade and agriculture to manufacturing quickly and surely. The textile factories developed north

of Providence drew large numbers of immigrants to interior Rhode Island. But between 1812 and the 1830s, Newport's growth and fortunes stagnated almost entirely. You'll see almost no late Federal or classical revival structures in Newport today for the simple reason that so little was built during this era. Newport took a stab at joining in the good fortunes of cities like Providence, Pawtucket, and Woonsocket—a handful of textile works were opened here between 1830 and 1850, and one by one they failed. After about three decades of trying to convert to an industrial economy, Newport gave up—it had none of the advantages of most inland locations, such as swift-flowing rivers and convenient transportation; after all, it was on an island cut off from the rest of the state.

The idea of "vacationing" is a relatively new concept to America—it came about chiefly during the early 20th century, with the emergence of a middle-income working class and increased workers' rights that resulted from unions and collective bargaining, and with better forms of transportation and new highways. Before this time, only the extremely wealthy could afford to enjoy any kind of vacation, and because travel took such effort and such a long time, these trips generally lasted for weeks or months. By about 1830, Newport became one of America's first playgrounds for this super-rich leisure class.

As one might expect, the earliest summer residents of Newport hailed from feverishly hot and fetid climes: the southern United States and even Cuba and the West Indies. As they had before the war, these residents took immediately to Newport's breezy location, where the air was fresh and opportunities to bathe in the ocean abundant. The very failure of the Industrial Revolution to take root in Newport, though it stunted the city's growth, helped preserve the city's mostly rural and attractive appearance. Downtown Newport during these years was, as it had been for a couple centuries, compact and tightly settled. But the greater peninsula of rolling meadows and light woodland, which extended east and south of downtown, out to Breton Point, had barely been developed. Visitors began buying their own waterfront plots of land, and almost immediately bunches of small summer cottages went up all over Newport's rural outskirts. A couple of substantial mansions were constructed at the then fairly remote intersection of Bowery Street and Bellevue Avenue.

NEWPORT "ARRIVES"

Real-estate speculators soon bought land south and east of downtown, and in 1851, Bellevue Avenue was extended south some ways, and intersecting lanes set out with plots and gracious landscaping. New summer cottages were built at a faster rate each summer, and they were built larger and larger. A mix of Boston and New York industrialists joined many Southerners in this increasingly exclusive summer colony. The value of land skyrocketed, and the boom continued through the late 1850s.

Following a short-lived recession, civic leaders decided to throw a sumptuous party for summering bigwigs as well as the many past Newport residents who had not been back for some time. The ball was a huge success, and the tradition of summer entertaining continued to grow each subsequent year. Of course, the Civil War interrupted Newport's growth as a resort, but as soon as this engagement ended, grand summer life in Newport returned stronger than ever.

This time, the ranks of summer residents included visibly fewer Southerners and many more wealthy families from Boston, New York, and Philadelphia. Local society movers and shakers included Mrs. Nicholas Beach, who hosted well-attended dance balls; Ward McAllister, who popularized the tradition of sumptuous picnics; and Mrs. August Belmont, who threw over-the-top dinner parties. For several weeks every summer, these rituals of entertaining on the grandest scale became embedded in Newport's regimen, as the very wealthiest hosts sought to outdo one another. Into the 1880s, the presence of Newport's superrich part-time residents began to pay off in the form of significant investments in infrastructure improvements. A city water system was inaugurated in 1881, and private telephone service the following year. Electric trolley service, which ran from Commercial Wharf up over Bath Street

(now Memorial Boulevard) to Easton's Beach, became a reality in 1889. Upper-class leisure activities also made inroads during these years, with the earliest national tennis matches commencing in 1881, followed by polo and then golf tournaments. The little city by the sea, virtually bereft of industry or commercial clout, became a powerhouse owing to its sterling reputation as a playground for the rich and famous.

The ostentation hit its peak beginning the following decade. As recorded in the WPA guidebook on Rhode Island, which was written in 1937, "probably America will never again see such lavish entertaining as took place at Newport during the summer seasons of the 'gilded years,' 1890–1914. Into six or seven weeks each season were crowded balls, dinners, and parties of every description. . . . Huge sums were spent in the prevailing spirit of rivalry. Mrs. Pembroke Jones set aside $300,000 at the beginning of every Newport season for entertaining, and some hostesses spent even more. Sometimes a single ball cost $100,000." Even by the outlandish standards of today, as evidenced by multimillion-dollar Hollywood weddings, the social excesses in Newport remain unmatched.

Looking back it's hard to imagine that most of these very rich Newporters even derived much pleasure from their wealth or their social standing. The jockeying for favorable social position was a blood sport, and it's supposed that many an upper-class family in America avoided Newport altogether, unwilling or unable to compete in this major league of snobbery and self-aggrandizement.

Newport year-rounders, sneeringly called "footstools" by the elite, despised the summer "cottagers" all the while, in many cases, undertaking their lowliest chores. A slightly higher class of full-time resident made out rather well, running shops or offering services, and gouging the summer-comers for all they were worth. There was absolutely no shame among Newporters in attempting to live well off these unbelievably rich visitors. And there was almost no play between the summer visitors and the full-time Newporters—even streetcars were not allowed to travel along Bellevue and Ocean Avenues.

In the Gilded Age, Harry Lehr and Mrs. William Astor became the leading society players in Newport, more or less controlling every aspect of the social season, determining who could move in the city's most desirable circles and who should be kept down. The so-called Newport 400, a social precursor of sorts to today's *Forbes* 500, comprised those individuals fortunate enough to attend the ball held each summer in the ballroom of the Astor home. The room accommodated 400, and so Harry Lehr and Mrs. Astor pored over the Social Register each year to arrive at a definitive guest list. To be on this list could easily legitimize a person's social standing; to be excluded from it could scar one's reputation irreparably.

The outrageous antics of Newport's society mavens gradually began to wear on those outside looking in, namely the press. The gossip writers of the time took great glee in reporting each and every excess, from the time that Harry Lehr and Mrs. Stuyvesant Fish held a party at which a diminutive trained monkey was booked as the guest of honor, to the infamous dog gala, when Lehr invited some 100 canines and their owners to a lavish sit-down meal where thousands of dollars were spent on food. The public backlash against these displays was finally such that the summer party-throwers began to exercise a modicum of restraint. But the over-the-top parties still continued for many years.

WORLD WAR I TO THE PRESENT

As the Civil War had altered the character of Newport's social scene, so the first World War had a great impact, and in this case a very somber one. During the war years, from about 1914 through 1918, summer entertaining was kept to a respectful minimum. The parade of summer people through the 1920s became less steady and predictable, as fortunes came and went according to the whims of the tumultuous stock market. Newport's old guard had largely passed away or moved on to other places by these years, and the great stock market crash of 1929 left the city reeling. Not only did the summer cottage scene diminish dramatically and nearly instantly, but daily wage-earners in town suffered without a busy summer season to look forward to.

Additionally, as lavish spending and conspicuous consumption fell out of favor, Newport came to be thought of during America's Depression as something of a curious and distasteful freak show, even though the outrageous parties and acts of wastefulness were now pretty much a thing of the past. City leaders realized, especially after 1929, that they would have to make an effort to appeal to solid, middle-class summer visitors if they were to rejuvenate the city during these months. Additionally, Newport worked to become a more desirable and vibrant year-round place both to live and visit, partly as a measure to accommodate the growing naval presence on the north part of town.

The naval base in Newport had grown rapidly since its expansion at the close of World War I; by the mid-1930s, the military employed nearly 4,000 civilians and played a vital role in the city's economy. Meanwhile, a more low-key sort of summer visitor, the middle-class family, began to spend time visiting Newport during the summer months.

For the last half-century, Newport has shifted gradually from being a wealthy resort colony to a major naval base to an again-fashionable vacation destination. But over time, the city's appeal has become considerably more diverse than it once was.

Sights

DOWNTOWN AND THE HARBOR

Newport has an unusually large and useful visitor information center, at 23 America's Cup Ave., 401/849-8098 or 800/326-6030, website: www.gonewport.com; it's right at the northern entrance to downtown, adjacent to the city's bus terminal and also the large and fancy Newport Marriott. It's an excellent place to begin your explorations of the city, and it has a large pay-parking lot and garage, making it a good spot to ditch your wheels. Newport's downtown and harbor area can be managed easily on foot, and you can take public transportation from the visitor center to other parts of the city, including Ocean Drive and the mansions down on Bellevue Avenue.

From the visitor center, turn down Thames Street, toward Newport Harbor. On you're right you'll come to Long Wharf, which is home to the **Thames Museum,** 77 Long Wharf, 401/849-6966 or 800/587-2872, website: www.thamesandkosmos.com. Formerly known as the Thames Science Center, until a science-kit publishing and educational services company— Thames & Kosmos—bought it in 2001, the museum continues to focus on interactive, kids-oriented exhibits with a scientific bent. It's always a good idea to phone ahead or check the website of the museum before visiting, as the daily goings-on here change regularly and usually revolve around a specific program or exhibit. The museum is especially popular with groups, but individuals are also welcome. The museum's Sea Safari excursions are one of its most popular and intriguing programs. The naturalist-led boat trips depart the docks at Perotti Park, right beside the museum, and last anywhere from an hour to several days depending on the theme; the shorter trips are generally available to the general public, while longer trips are booked more often as group outings or field trips. Some of the most popular safari excursions include whale- or shark-watching, sunset bird-watching, and stargazing trips. Fields ranging from biology to mathematics to architecture to engineering are incorporated into the exhibits and programs here. Admission is $5. Open Mon.–Wed. 10 A.M.–6 P.M., Thurs.–Sat. 10 A.M.–7 P.M., and Sun. noon–5 P.M.

Historic Hill

Cross Thames Street, and explore the many shops and eateries that make up the Brick Market Place. Anchoring this complex is the **Museum of Newport History,** at the Brick Market, Thames Street, at the bottom of Washington Square, 401/841-8770 or 401/846-0813, website: www.newporthistorical.org. This is an excellent museum to begin your explorations of Newport, as its exhibits give a nice overview of the city's and southern Rhode Island's history, and also the stately architecture that so defines Newport. The building itself is a fitting venue for an exploration of grand building traditions. The space is crammed with many artifacts that trace the city's history, from decorative pieces and artwork to vintage photos and ship models. Admire the rarified furniture of Newport's Goddard-Townsend firm, during its heyday the most acclaimed such company in New England. On a computer you can explore some of the city's most noteworthy architectural accomplishments; and in a re-created 1890s omnibus (the precursor to today's buses) you can watch a video tour of Bellevue Avenue's mansions. You can see the printing press on which James Franklin, brother of Ben, produced the city's colonial newspaper. The focus is as much on Newport's working class as on the wealthy colonial merchants and then late-19th-century industrialists with whom the region is more commonly associated. Exhibits touch a bit on the city's founding fathers, John Clarke and William Coddington, as well as on the indigenous tribes who lived here for many centuries. Exhibits shed considerable light on the diverse ethnic and religious makeup of Newport's earliest citizens, from Quakers and Jews to Portuguese and African-Americans. Admission is $5. Open Mon. and Wed.–Sat. 10 A.M.–5 P.M., and Sun. 1–5 P.M.; hours are shorter in winter.

NEWPORT

NEWPORT

DOWNTOWN NEWPORT

Middletown

AQUIDNECK AVE.
138A
211
138A

PURGATORY RD.

NEW ENGLAND AQUARIUM EXPLORATION CENTER

Easton's/First Beach

Green End Pond

Easton Pond

MEMORIAL BLVD.

Easton Bay

0   0.25 mi
0   0.25 km

OCEAN DRIVE

Cliff Walk

FORTY STEPS

CLIFF AVE.

EUSTIS AVE.

GIBBS AVE.

MERTON RD.
DRESSER ST.

ANNANDALE RD.

RHODE ISLAND AVE.

SALVE REGINA UNIVERSITY

NARRAGANSETT AVE.

PRESERVATION SOCIETY OF NEWPORT COUNTY

OLD BEACH RD.

CATHERINE ST.

KAY ST.

NEWPORT HISTORICAL SOCIETY

WANTON-LYMAN-HAZARD HOUSE
UNITED BAPTIST CHURCH
TOURO SYNAGOGUE
FRIENDS MEETING HOUSE
Washington Square

BROADWAY

REDWOOD LIBRARY

NEWPORT ART MUSEUM

NEWPORT

MEMORIAL BLVD.

INTERNATIONAL TENNIS HALL OF FAME AND MUSEUM

BELLEVUE AVE.

BERKELEY AVE.

PARKER AVE.

Historic Hill

CHURCH ST.
MILL ST.
Touro Park

NEWPORT PUBLIC LIBRARY

BOWERY ST.

KINGSCOTE MANSION

PERRY ST.

ELMS

DIXON ST.

138A

SPRING ST.

START OF OCEAN DRIVE

ISLAND CEMETERY

WHITFIELD ST.

FAREWELL ST.

TRINITY CHURCH
NEWPORT ARTILLERY CO. MUSEUM
NEWPORT CONGREGATIONAL CHURCH

ST. MARY'S CHURCH

SAMUEL WHITEHORNE HOUSE

THAMES ST.

238

THAMES ST.

NEWPORT VISITOR INFORMATION CENTER
MUSEUM OF NEWPORT HISTORY

238
138A

Point District

HUNTER HOUSE

THAMES MUSEUM

SEAMEN'S CHURCH INSTITUTE
BOWEN'S WHARF

INTERNATIONAL YACHT RESTORATION SCHOOL

Newport Harbor

King Park
Wellington

WELLINGTON AVE.

ROSENEATH AVE.

SANFORD-COVELL VILLA MARINA

WASHINGTON ST.

138

To Goat Island

IDA LEWIS YACHT CLUB

© AVALON TRAVEL PUBLISHING, INC.

From May through September, guided walking tours that focus on the city's history leave from the museum Thursday through Sunday at 10 A.M. The Thursday and Friday tours are of the Historic Hill neighborhood; the Saturday tour is of the Point District. Tour admission is $8; a combination ticket allows discounted admission to the museum, the society's nearby Wanton-Lyman-Hazard House, and the guided Historic Hill tour. Also on Saturday mornings at 10 A.M., the society leads Cliff Walk tours, which depart from Salve Regina University's Ochre Court (parking is available at Miley Hall). Other tours offered occasionally throughout the year by the society include African-American Heritage and Religious Heritage walks; check with the society (401/846-0813) for details.

From Washington Square, walk east along Touro Street, the southern border of this park. Note the grand three-story redbrick building, crowned by a long balustrade, overlooking the square; here stands the **Old Colony House,** 401/846-2980, website: www.newporthistorical.com, which dates to 1739. It was here on May 4, 1776, that the state assembly foreswore its allegiance to the British crown, thus establishing Rhode Island as the young nation's first independent state. It is the fourth-oldest standing building in the United States to have served as a state capitol. Inside you'll find one of Rhode Islander Gilbert Stuart's famous portraits of George Washington. Architect Richard Munday, who's also responsible for the nearby Seventh Day Baptist Meeting House and Trinity Church, designed this Georgian-style building, which has been the site of several other important events, including the inquisition into the burning of the *Gaspee* in 1772 and the joyous announcement of the repeal of the Stamp Act. In 1776, British forces occupied the city and used the building as military barracks; three years later, after the British had abandoned the city, French forces turned the building into a hospital. But for these interruptions, the building served as the one of the two Rhode Island State House until 1901, when the new facility in Providence opened. It then served as county courthouse. The house is now administered by the

Newport Historical Society, through which tours are available by appointment.

Just south off the square, down Clarke Street, is the Newport Artillery Co. Museum, 23 Clarke St., 401/846-8488, which is housed in a cut-granite Greek Revival building. The Newport Artillery dates to 1741, when it was commissioned by King George II. Military objects and artifacts from more than 100 nations fill these rooms. A donation is recommended, and hours are mid-May–mid-Oct., daily 10 A.M.–5 P.M.

Continue down Clarke Street to the intersection with Mary, and on the northeast corner you'll see the **Vernon House,** headquarters for Rochambeau during the Revolutionary War—it's here that he met with George Washington. It's a fine colonial house with a hipped roof; parts of it have been attributed to Peter Harrison; but research shows that the original structure probably dates to quite a while before his time. Rochambeau, the Commander of French expeditionary forces during the American Revolution, assumed control of the house in 1780, after British forces ceded control of the city. He entertained George Washington in this house for a week in early March 1781, during which time the two reportedly planned the Continental Army's coup de grâce against the British at the Battle of Yorktown. The Marquis de Lafayette also visited Vernon House on several occasions.

Retrace your steps to Touro Street, turn right, and walk east to Spring Street, where a left turn leads to the 1846 **United Baptist Church,** John Clarke Memorial, 30 Spring St., 401/847-3210. This congregation was established in Portsmouth in 1638, established by pastor Dr. John Clarke, the very one who obtained Rhode Island's Royal Charter in 1663 from King Charles II. This handsome church is open to the public on weekdays 9 A.M.–1 P.M.

Continue north on Spring Street, make the first left onto Stone, and then make a quick left on Broadway back toward Washington Square. Here is the Newport Historical Society's **Wanton-Lyman-Hazard House,** 17 Broadway, 401/846-0813, website: www.newporthistorical.org, which dates to 1675—it's one of the oldest restored houses in the state. The imposing house was

DORIS DUKE AND ROUGH POINT

The Newport Restoration Foundation has been an amazingly successful force in preserving the city's tremendous stock of 18th-century architecture, much of which had begun to deteriorate by the mid-1960s—at that time, the Point and to a lesser extent the Hill Districts had become urban slums. From the foundation's origins in 1968 through about the mid-1980s, it helped to fully restore more than 80 threatened structures, employing the skills of top architects and craftsmen in the painstaking process. Heiress Doris Duke was the main backer of this foundation; her efforts are a big reason that we have this "wooden" city, of sorts, today. The foundation owns three houses, including the Samuel Whitehorne House, the Prescott Farm, and Rough Point, the former estate of Doris Duke.

Rough Point is a grand mansion, built in 1889 for Frederick W. Vanderbilt, that occupies a rocky point overlooking the ocean. James B. Duke, Doris's father, purchased the estate in 1922 but lived in it for just three years before his death. Duke, whom the esteemed North Carolina university is named for, made his fortunes in tobacco and electrical power plants—he was one of Newport's wealthiest residents during his time here.

Inside Rough Point, which only opened to the public following the death of Doris Duke in 1993, you'll find a collection of rare Ming vases and ceramics, plus original paintings by Renoir, Van Dyck, and portraitist Joshua Reynolds. There is also a phenomenal collection of furniture and antiquities. Although some of Newport's mansions contain the furnishings of the original occupants, many more do not—the houses weren't preserved with the expectation that they'd someday become museums, and as wealthy families passed on or divided their estates, a good many personal items were sent to other places or auctioned off to total strangers.

Rough Point can only be visited as part of a group tour—these are offered regularly at the Gateway Visitors Center, or you can book an visit online at www.newportrestoration.com/roughpoint/tickets/month.html; only these online tickets can be obtained in advance, whereas the tours given at the center are available on a first-come, first-served basis; from the visitors center they're offered throughout the day, Tues.–Sat., beginning around 10 A.M.. Tours are available June through November and cost $25 per person, a rather steep admission. But keep in mind that the proceeds go toward the very worthy cause of continuing to preserve the city's best architecture, and the tour is also quite extensive.

built as the residence of wealthy sea captain Stephen Mumford. The most famous owner was the former governor of Rhode Island (in 1741), Richard Ward, and the house takes its name for members of the family that occupied the house from 1782 through 1911. Several additions were made to the house during its first 100 years, including the fine interior crown molding and wood paneling. By the time the Newport Historical Society bought the house in 1927, the place was a shambles; architect Norman Isham restored the house in several colonial styles—a bedroom on the second floor looks as it would have when the house was built, and the kitchen retains the style of the 1720s. The society is working with the Newport Garden Club to restore its gardens. Admission $4 (or $7 for a combi-

nation ticket for here, the Museum of Newport History, and the guided Historic Hill walking tours that leave from the museum on Thursday and Friday mornings). Open late spring–early fall, Thurs.–Sat. 11 A.M.–3 P.M.

Just around the corner, near the junction of Farewell and Marlborough Streets, stands another of the Newport Historical Society's buildings, the **Friends Meeting House,** 401/846-0813, website: www.newporthistorical.org, parts of which date to 1699—when it was built, this was the largest and most prominent building in Newport, visible to ships arriving in Newport Harbor from some ways out. The structure has been expanded several times. The Quakers used this as the setting for the New England Yearly Meetings for 205 years. Inside this, the oldest surviving house of worship in Newport, you'll discover a re-markably well-preserved example of post-medieval architecture. The Society of Friends was an important influence on Newport society during the 18th century, a time when this then-radical religion was harshly persecuted in other parts of the New World. The Society of Friends formed in the 1630s; the first group of them sailed to Newport in 1657, where their message of "inner light" caught on rapidly. Many outsiders believed them to be witches or satanic practitioners. In fact, the Quakers were—and remain—a group that exalted pacifism, virtue, and individualism. Newport Quaker Nicholas Easton was elected the Governor of Rhode Island in 1672; he helped move forth young America's earliest known conscientious objector law, which allowed any citizen to turn down military enlistment if his religion forbids him from fighting. Quaker buildings have stood on the site of the Meeting House since 1639, when Nicholas Easton built a house here.

Nearby, note **St. Paul's United Methodist Church,** 12 Marlborough St., whose congregation dates to 1800. The church was built six years later, becoming the first Methodist church in the world with a steeple, bell, and fixed pews. At 26 Marlborough St., the **White Horse Tavern** is said to be the oldest extant tavern in the United States, having opened in the 1687. During the state's early history, when Newport was the capital, members of the Rhode Island Assembly often convened in the tavern.

Touro Synagogue

From St. Paul's, follow Farewell Street back a few blocks to Touro, and make a right, continuing past Spring Street. You'll soon come to the **Touro Synagogue,** 60 Touro St., 401/847-4794, website: www.tourosynagogue.org, the oldest such house of worship in the United States—it's also one of the most impressive 18th-century buildings in New England. Like so many historic buildings on the Eastern Seaboard, the Synagogue's brochure brags that George Washington spent time here—if that helps draw visitors who might not otherwise venture into a synagogue, okay then. But Touro Synagogue should be on every visitor's short list of Newport attractions. The historic footnote about

George Washington is more than a gimmick: Washington did visit, and he declared to the congregation that the newly formed nation's position on religious freedom would be one of tolerance and protection of civil liberties. Specifically, he pledged that he would "give to bigotry no sanction, to persecution no assistance."

In the mid-17th century, it was Sephardic Jews from Portugal and Spain who caught wind of Roger Williams' Rhode Island colony and its unyielding tolerance of all religious persuasions. A small group of Jews arrived on Newport soil in the 1650s and formed a small congregation that met for decades in private homes and other temporary spaces. In 1677 the congregation bought land for a cemetery, and over the next several years, their numbers increased manifold, drawing, in addition to hundreds more Sephardim, Jews from Eastern and Central Europe. Eventually, the Newport Jews made plans to construct a synagogue. The few congregations already in the New World, including the earliest one in the colonies, Shearith Israel in New York City, donated funds. And one of the young nation's most prominent architects, Peter Harrison, volunteered to design the facility, which broke ground roughly a century after the earliest Sephardim had arrived, in 1759. Four years later, on December 2, 1763, the Rev. Isaac Touro led the first service in the synagogue that today bears his name. Interestingly, many non-Jews attended this first service—amazing considering the complete intolerance of not only Jews but all non-Congregationalists in most of the neighboring New England colonies. The new congregation chose the name Yeshuat Israel ("Salvation of Israel").

The architect Peter Harrison had come to Newport from England in 1740 and immediately prospered as an area merchant. But Harrison was really a Renaissance man, proficient in everything from wood-carving to architectural design. He generally built structures in the Georgian English tradition, and by the mid-1700s he had become New England's most famous architect. In Newport alone he also built the Brick Market and the Redwood Library; in Boston he built the famous King's Chapel, and across the Charles River in Cambridge he designed Christ Church.

His designs for Touro Synagogue presented some unusual challenges. He had to adapt his typically Georgian ideals to accommodate the Sephardic traditions. The Jews, as custom dictated, wanted the synagogue to be located on an inconspicuous side street, a far cry from the Protestant tendency to place houses of worship at a community's most prominent crossroads. The building stands diagonally on its plot, thus allowing its worshipers to face eastward when in prayer before the Holy Ark, toward Jerusalem. Off one side of the building a small wing was designed for the religious instruction of children.

Harrison's exterior design was elegant but austere, a simple brick facade. But inside there's an almost sumptuous chamber supported by 12 Ionic columns, which represent the ancient tribes of Israel. These columns support an upper gallery, from which 12 Corinthian columns reach skyward to support a domed ceiling. As is called for in the Orthodox Jewish tradition, women sit in the gallery, and men sit beneath them in on the main floor of the chamber. One of the most notable features of the interior is the five huge brass candle chandeliers—these were gifts from prominent Newport merchants during the 1760s. On the east side of the room stands the Holy Ark, which contains the Torah—the scrolls are hand-printed and set on wood rollers. Above this, the Ten Commandments are painted in Hebrew.

Newport's Jewish community enjoyed something of a heyday from this period through the American Revolution, and several area locals become quite prominent in shipping, notably Aaron Lopez, who became known as the "Merchant Prince of New England." Unfortunately, during America's bid for independence, the British occupation of Newport resulted in a near-abandonment of the city by most of its Jews. The synagogue actually closed for a time.

Following the war, quite a few Jews returned, but as many did not. The synagogue stood as one of relatively few public buildings undamaged by the British occupation, and so in addition to serving the Jewish community, Touro also hosted the Rhode Island State Assembly from 1781 through 1784, and also the state supreme court on many occasions. It was during this nadir in Touro's history that George Washington visited, in 1790, and uttered his pledge against religious bigotry. Alas, the synagogue ceased holding religious service not long after this fateful day, as the congregation was simply too small. The final members of Congregation Yeshuat packed up and moved to New York City, and that city's Shearith Israel congregation assumed stewardship of the Newport Synagogue (it didn't bear the name of Isaac Touro for many more years).

While the building fell into a state of neglect, many in Newport rallied for its preservation, among them the sons of Isaac Touro, Abraham and Judah. The two sons had become wealthy merchants, and each left immense fortunes on their deaths in 1822 and 1854, respectively, to care for the building and cemetery, and ultimately to reopen the building to worship and hire a rabbi. Finally, in 1883, Touro Synagogue reopened, attended mostly by Jews of Eastern and Central European descent, who were by now the most prominent members of the region's community. The new congregation became Yeshuat Israel (later spelled "Jeshuat Israel"), and it has continued to operate—in the Sephardic tradition of worship—ever since.

Except on Saturdays and Jewish holidays, Touro Synagogue is open for tours daily, 10 A.M.–5 P.M. in summer, with shorter hours the rest of the year. Tours are given every half-hour, the last tour a half-hour before closing. You can easily walk from here up Touro Street to the congregation's burial ground, where lie Judah Touro, Aaron Lopez, and other prominent members of the community.

Continuing Along Historic Hill

A bit farther down the street you'll reach the headquarters of the **Newport Historical Society,** 82 Touro St., 401/846-0813, website: www.newporthistorical.org, which is also Newport's historic **Seventh Day Baptist Meeting House.** This first home of the Seventh Day Baptists dates to 1730. In addition to the other buildings and tours described in this chapter, the society is responsible for the interpretive signs set along the sidewalks of Historic Hill that detail the history of buildings along the walk. The organization produces self-guided tour brochures, available here and at the history museum. One important feature of this facility is the extensive genealogical library, where visitors can trace their family lines. The society also presents changing exhibits.

The Seventh Day Baptist Church formed in 1660 when a handful of members of the Newport Baptist Church determined that the Ten Commandments should be interpreted strictly to mean that the Sabbath should be observed on Saturdays. They formed their own congregation in 1671 and worshiped in a couple of smaller places before moving into this space in 1730. Richard Munday designed this rather simple building that looks far more like a house than a place of worship. The congregation in Newport thrived until the British occupation, when many of the members moved to Westerly, while others set out in different directions. Various conventional Baptist congregations worshiped here during the 19th century, including a mostly African-American one. The Newport Historical Society, which was founded in 1854, purchased the building in the 1880s and has used it as its headquarters ever since, although the actual offices and exhibit areas are in an addition behind the church itself. Admission free. Open Tues.–Fri. 9:30 A.M.–4:30 P.M. and Saturday 9:30 A.M.–noon.

From here, you can take a right and cut down School Street a couple of blocks, turning left and walking back down toward Thames Street and the harbor along graceful Church Street. On your left, at the intersection with Spring Street, you'll come to **Trinity Church,** 401/846-0660, which overlooks leafy Queen Anne Square. The elegant building dates to 1726 and is modeled after the London churches designed by famed British architect Christopher Wren—with its lofty white spire, this dignified building is one of Newport's most recognizable and impressive structures. Definitely try to peek inside to see the nation's only three-tiered, center-aisle, glass pulpit. Note pew No. 81, in which George Washington once worshiped. The building is open Sundays for worship and also on weekdays, usually from about 10 A.M. to 4 P.M.

Two blocks south on Spring Street is another of Newport's elegant places of worship, the **New-port Congregational Church,** Spring and Pelham Streets, 401/849-2238. The fine interior of this 1880 structure is one of only two churches left standing in the United States with an interior designed entirely by noted architect John LaFarge, who also perfected the technique for creating the opalescent glass that's used in the windows. On the interior walls are elaborate and colorful murals. Open Mon.–Sat. 9 A.M.–noon and on Sunday mornings at 10 A.M. for worship.

The Waterfront

Down the hill, more shops and restaurants line the east side of Thames Street, while wharves jut into Newport Harbor across the street. These wharves now contain a mix of businesses, including several hotels. You might stop at the **Seamen's Church Institute,** 18 Market Square, just off Thames Street, 401/847-4260, to catch your breath and to admire this handsome building that has served the needs of seafarers for nearly a century. The building is open daily 6 A.M.–6 P.M. and contains a small nondenominational chapel, a café, public restrooms with a coin laundry and showers, and a library. At this stretch, Thames Street is known as America's Cup Avenue and is a broad and busy road with fast-moving traffic—you'll only want to chance crossing it at a traffic signal.

But at Commercial Wharf, Thames changes into a narrow, one-way street with an easy and quaint pace. Auto traffic is mostly funneled up the hill via Memorial Boulevard toward Bellevue Avenue, another part of the city that bears exploring. Just a block up Memorial from Thames Street, a quick right on Spring Street leads to **St. Mary's Church,** Spring Street at Memorial Boulevard, which houses the oldest Catholic parish in the state, established in 1828. Catholics were as ill-received as the other non-Protestants in early America, and it took some time before this parish formed. The present church dates to 1852 and is considered one of the finest examples of Gothic Revival architecture on the Eastern Seaboard. But the building's real claim to fame is having served as the setting for the wedding John F. Kennedy and Jacqueline Bouvier, on September 12, 1953. The building is open to the public on weekday mornings.

© BILLY BLACK

Newport Harbor

Just south of here a couple of blocks you'll come to leafy Aquidneck Park, bounded by Spring, Golden Hill, King, and Bowery Streets. Adjoining the park is the imposing **Newport Public Library,** 300 Spring Street, 401/847-8720, a general-purpose facility that also has some impressive special collections, the focus of which include Newport history, U.S. history, cookbooks, African-American studies, and Chinese culture and Chinese-language books. Also facing the park is the handsome **Edward King House,** 401/846-7426, now a senior citizen community center. Visitors are welcome to look inside and tour this Italian villa–inspired house built by noted architect Richard Upjohn in 1846.

Walk back down to Thames, start strolling south, and you can enjoy yet more window-shopping and people-watching; you'll also find many spots for a full sit-down meal or a quick snack. A few blocks down, note the **Samuel Whitehorne House,** 416 Thames St., 401/847-2448, which is overseen by the Newport Restoration Foundation, 51 Touro St., 401/849-7300, website: www.newportrestoration.com. This Federal-style house, which dates to 1811, belonged to one of Newport's most successful shipping merchants, Samuel Whitehorne, who earned his for-

tune in rum-distilling, shipping, and—although it's not documented conclusively—the slave trade. Interestingly, Whitehorne never lived in the home he commissioned; he went bankrupt following the loss of two of his ships at sea. Shops and apartments occupied the house for most of its existence, before the Newport Restoration Foundation came along in 1969. The house has all the classic elements of Federal architecture: a symmetrical hipped roof, a lavish formal garden, and a circular entryway. The house is filled with fine furnishings that show the restraint and grace of the age—it's a very interesting contrast with the garish museums of Bellevue Avenue. The late heiress Doris Duke, who took a great interest in the furniture crafted by Newport's top cabinet-makers, assembled an incomparable collection of Federal and colonial pieces. As the founder of the Newport Restoration Foundation, Duke placed much of this collection in the Whitehorne house, as this is the only Federal house-museum in the city. Admission is $8. Open Monday and Thurs.–Fri. 11 A.M.–4 P.M., weekends 10 A.M.–4 P.M., and by appointment.

The stroll down the rest of Thames is engaging for the several interesting businesses you'll pass along here, as well as the sampling of colonial,

Victorian, and early-20th-century architecture. But the **International Yacht Restoration School,** 449 Thames St., 401/848-5777, website: www.iyrs.org, pretty much ends the sightseeing aspect of this walk. The IYRS is a nonprofit organization whose mission is to teach the "skills, history, and science needed to construct, restore, and maintain classic watercraft." Regardless of your own knowledge of and experience with classic boats, you might just stop in to check out the school's impressive collection of fine old boats, from Chris Crafts to vintage rowboats and canoes. There's no admission fee, and IYRS is open to the public year-round. You can also watch students at work building and restoring different vessels, tour the IYRS flagship, the *Coronet,* or stroll through the property's harborfront yard. The 167-foot *Coronet,* one of the most impressive vintage yachts in the world, was built in Brooklyn in 1885 and carries an astounding 8,500 square feet of sail. The ship has sailed around the world and hosted such luminaries as Alexander Graham Bell and the King of Hawaii. The IYRS obtained the ship through donation in 1995, and it continues to work toward a complete restoration of the vessel; the ship still contains original mahogany paneling and cut-glass mirrors. Hours at IYRS vary, and it's best to call ahead—a trip here makes a great prelude to checking out the Museum of Yachting at Fort Adams.

THE POINT DISTRICT AND GOAT ISLAND

The Point District, which contains one of New England's finest concentrations of colonial architecture, extends from just north of the Newport Visitors Center north to the Newport bridge. Just to the west of the southern end of the neighborhood lies Goat Island. In 1723 about two dozen pirates were convicted and hanged by Long Wharf and their bodies carted to Goat Island, where they were buried on the shore between the high- and low-tide marks.

Note the Historic Newport Depot, 19 America's Cup Ave., just as you head north from the visitors center. From here, before you venture into the heart of this small city, you might want to walk west a couple of blocks from the visitors center toward Goat Island, turning left onto the Goat Island Connector Road. It's a pretty stroll across the causeway to Goat Island, which itself isn't all that thrilling for exploration. But you can always shoot a couple of pictures of Narragansett Bay and then, on a warm day, drop by the Hyatt Regency, which has a hip little patio restaurant that serves light food and tropical drinks all summer long.

Back on the mainland, the blocks north along shore clear up to the Goat Island causeway constitute the historic Point District, one of the city's oldest neighborhoods. It's also one of the best-preserved colonial residential districts of any seaport in the nation. It's a thoroughly engaging neighborhood for a stroll, its narrow streets packed with colonial and more recently constructed Victorian homes, most of them painted in traditional Newport blues, slates, brick reds, mustards, and creams.

A highlight of the neighborhood is **Hunter House,** 54 Washington St., 401/847-1000, website: www.newportmansions.org, which sits at the southwest edge of the Point District, very near Goat Island. This slate-gray Georgian mansion contains a priceless collection of 18th-century furnishings, ceramics, silver, and pewter—it was built in 1748, financed with the considerable spoils of a prominent sea merchant. Note the ornately carved woodwork, one of the house's highlights. The furnishings inside include a priceless collection of wooden pieces created by Newport's famous Townsend and Goddard families in the second half of the 1700s. Open mid-May–mid-Oct., 10 A.M.–5 P.M. daily; admission is $10.

It's worth the time just to stroll the dozen or so blocks from Hunter House up Washington along the waterfront about as far as the Newport Bridge, and then back down 2nd Street, which runs parallel to Washington a block east. You'll pass dozens of wonderfully preserved homes along these two narrow streets, and also on the cross streets that intersect them. Hunter House is the only one open to the public, except during holiday or other tours sponsored by the Point Association, but there are several notable houses worth admiring from the street.

Just a block east of Hunter House, at 77 Bridge Str., note the **Pitt's Head Tavern,** which is actually

NEWPORT

not original to the neighborhood. This 1724 gambrel-roof building was built on Washington Square but moved here in the mid-1960s. This end-chimney house once operated as one of colonial Newport's most popular coffeehouses—places where locals convened to discuss politics, commerce, and the events of the day. Back on Washington, walk north past Hunter House and you'll come to a pair of distinctive buildings, the **Capt. John Warren House,** 62 Washington St., and the **Thomas Robinson House,** 64 Washington St. The capacious Warren House was built in 1736 and is notable for its elegant central fanlight front door and fine wrought-iron railings. Several generations of the same family have owned the Robinson House for the past two centuries.

Just a bit farther north is the **Sanfred-Covell Villa Marina,** 72 Washington St., now a bed-and-breakfast. Designed by William Ralph Emerson, a leading 19th-century architect in New England, this towering Victorian mansion stands out considerably among its many colonial neighbors.

BROADWAY

An untouristy but increasingly hip neighborhood that begins on the eastern edge of downtown and extends northeast into Middletown, Broadway is everything that the rest of Newport is not: slightly countercultural, highly quirky, untouristy, and offbeat. You can understand why some locals refer to it as the East Village of Newport. Broadway is a repository of thrift shops, cheap eateries, pubs, and piercing parlors—it's the city's nod to Wickenden Street in Providence. Just walk along to get a sense of it all; it's refreshing if you're a bit tired of seeing hordes of tourists and neatly preened yachtsmen.

OCEAN DRIVE

One of the most famous scenic drives on the East Coast, 9.5-mile Ocean Drive is a roughly C-shaped route that begins at the lower end of downtown, on Wellington Avenue at the intersection with Thames Street. Ocean Drive isn't any one road but rather the name of the route that connects several of them; it's very well marked

with signs and it's easy to follow. At least half the fun of this journey, which can take from an hour to half a day depending on how often you stop, is simply peering out the window at the stunning homes, sandy beaches, and ocean vistas.

Still right in town, on Newport Harbor, you'll pass little **King Park** on your right as you drive west along Wellington; this is the city's small but pleasant in-town beach. Also off Wellington, a bit farther down, you'll see the entrance to the **Ida Lewis Yacht Club,** a private facility that's named for a keeper of the lighthouse here, which was used during the 19th century and still stands, along with its keeper's cottage, at the end of a long pier. Ida Lewis was the daughter of the original keeper; on his death, she took over the job. At the end of Wellington, a hard left (your only option) takes you up Halidon Avenue, by some attractive old mansions, where you'll hit Harrison Avenue; turn right and follow this about a mile until you reach the entrance to **Fort Adams State Park.**

A National Historic Landmark and one of the most formidable coastal forts ever built in the United States, **Fort Adams,** Eisenhower House, Fort Adams State Park, 401/841-0707—which served the region from the 1820s through World War II—occupies a grassy point opposite downtown Newport, about a mile across Newport Harbor. The site of the U.S. Naval Academy at the onset of the Civil War, the fort served originally as protector of Narragansett Bay but grew in significance to become the command headquarters for a series of important coastal fortifications throughout the Northeast United States. Today at the fort you can tour the structure, including bastions, officer's quarters, the enclosed 6.25-acre parade, and the exterior dry moat that helped prevent the fort ever from being compromised by the enemy.

Supposedly, a fort of some kind has occupied this site since 1683, when settler William Brenton had two cannons sent over from England and placed on the point to protect his estate, nearby Hammersmith Farm. Colonists built a more substantial earthwork fort and observation post here in 1740, to answer to the widespread threats in that period of an invasion by France. In 1799 Major Anne-Louis Toussard dedicated the first permanent fortifications to U.S. President—and early champion of the U.S. Navy—John Adams. By the War of 1812, however, the fort had already fallen to disuse, and it played virtually no role in this debacle, prompting—by 1824—the federal government to commission construction of a more substantial fort. The structure was completed, at a cost of $3 million, in 1857.

Fort Adams was designed to withstand attacks from sea and from land. Three ranks of cannons guarded the eastern passage of Narragansett Bay, and a complex series of ditches and ramparts made attack from land extremely difficult. Granite walls surround the entire structure. Entrance to the main fortification is by guided tour only, 10 A.M.–4 P.M.

Newport's legacy as one of the world's great centers for boating is well documented at the **Museum of Yachting,** Fort Adams State Park, 401/847-1018. The museum's mission, to preserve traditional skills, documents, vessels, and artifacts relevant to yachting throughout the world, manifests itself here in several exhibits. One section illuminates the impact Newport's Gilded Age had in developing the city's reputation as a yachting center, when Astors, Vanderbilts, and Morgans spent untold hundreds of thousands of dollars outdoing one another to create the biggest and fanciest steam yachts. The on-site restoration school displays several full-size yachts that have been reworked here, and a small-craft gallery shows a mix of relatively diminutive boats. You can see a bit of Newport's legacy in racing in the America's Cup Gallery, where photos and records document the races since the 1930s. Different events are held throughout the year, including the Classic Yacht Regatta (Labor Day Weekend), and several smaller regattas and events. The Classic Yacht Regatta includes races, high-profile balls and parties, and a classic yacht parade. Admission fee is $3, and it's open mid-May–Oct. 31 daily 10 A.M.–5 P.M., other times by appointment.

On leaving the park, continue back onto Harrison Avenue. Although it's no longer open to the public, **Hammersmith Farm,** off Harrison Avenue, next to Fort Adams State Park, is one of Newport's most fabled properties. It's a working farm, the only one within Newport city limits, and it's anchored by a stunning 1887 mansion,

but Hammersmith is best-known for having been the site of Jacqueline Bouvier and John F. Kennedy's wedding reception in 1953. When Kennedy became president, it came to serve as the "summer White House" for the First Family. The house was open for tours until rather recently, but it's not clear when or if Hammersmith will ever reopen in this capacity.

A short way farther along Harrison, make a right run onto Ridge Road and follow this around, passing the elegant Ocean Cliff Hotel. This road meets with Castle Hill Avenue, off of which a small lane leads to the **Castle Hill Coast Guard Station,** 401/846-3676 (tours by appointment). Back on the main route, you'll finally reach Ocean Avenue, which runs right along the water with mostly contemporary and colonial-style beach homes on the inland side of the street.

Where Ocean Drive turns nearly 90 degrees around Brenton Point, you'll find a parking area for **Brenton Point State Park,** a rugged, rocky promontory overlooking the ocean. You can picnic here or stroll along the beach. The facilities are few, but this is one of the most charming ocean vantage points in Rhode Island.

From here, continue along Ocean Drive along the waterfront back toward Newport, passing the Newport Country Club, some private beaches, and several gorgeous homes, ranging from century-plus-old Victorian castles to rather recently built compounds with lavish decking and many-gabled roofs. Officially, Ocean Drive ends at Coggeshall Avenue, where a left turn will bring you back into lower downtown, about two miles away. Or make a right turn, follow the road a short way, and then make a left onto Bellevue Avenue, and you can begin a tour of the Newport mansions of the Gilded Age—just keep in mind that you'll be going in the opposite direction of the tour described below, which starts from town, as the majority of visitors to the mansion approach it that way.

BELLEVUE AVENUE

Bellevue Avenue runs parallel to Thames Street a few blocks east and up the hill from Newport Harbor, along a comparatively high stretch of

TIPS ON TOURING NEWPORT'S MANSIONS

With its history of wealthy summer residents constructing massive "cottages" throughout the late 19th and early 20th centuries, Newport has enough magnificent mansion-museums to keep even a diehard visitor busy for days. All told, if you also count the handful of colonial and other historic houses, the city has more than a dozen homes open for tours. People who attempt to visit even a handful of these over the course of one weekend often end up feeling burnt out and overwhelmed. Here are a few ways to help maximize your enjoyment of Newport's famous mansions.

First, think about how much time you truly want to spend on indoor activities. Although many of Newport's homes have beautiful grounds, house-touring is largely an interior activity. And tours of various homes can range from one to a few hours. If you have just a weekend, try focusing on one or two mansions per day. If you're touring homes with children, you might want to limit your ambitions even further. Some tour guides do an excellent job with kids, but traipsing through these lavish buildings—where much of the focus is on antiques, art, and construction—can be taxing on young ones. The Astors' Beechwood, whose guides consist of costumed actors playing the parts of various family members and household staff, is a great choice for kids. Another engaging choice is Green

Animals Topiary Garden in Middletown.

If you're planning to tour more than one mansion, keep in mind that the Preservation Society of Newport County operates most of the top house-museums in town, including Chateau-sur-Mer, the Elms, the Breakers, Marble House, Rosecliff, Kingscote, Chepstow, the Hunter House, Green Animals, and the Isaac Bell House. They are a terrific central source of information on all of the above houses; you can call them, 401/847-1000, or visit their website, www.newportmansions.org, for detailed information on specific house hours and times of tours. And you can also purchase tickets on the website.

The most famous Preservation Society property, the Breakers, is open daily for tours nearly all year (excluding major holidays), and several others—including Chateau-sur-Mer, the Elms, Marble House, and Rosecliff—are open daily most of the year from mid-April through December. The Elms and Chateau-sur-Mer also stay open on weekends from January through mid-April. The remaining Preservation Society properties tend to be open daily from mid-May through mid-October.

Hours vary greatly from house to house, and from season to season (but are given in detail and regularly updated on the Preservation Society website). In general, most houses are open from 10 A.M.

land. The whole neighborhood is much more recently developed than downtown—the northern part of Bellevue, from Touro Street to Memorial Boulevard, was laid out fairly early. The extension, which runs south from Memorial Boulevard about two miles to the southern end of a narrow peninsula, was added in the 1850s. In those years, the area south from Memorial Boulevard (then called Bath Street) and east toward the ocean was almost entirely rural. Gradually, beginning about the 1840s, a few wealthy families from other parts of the country began building summer cottages in this area.

By the time of the Civil War, Bellevue Avenue and its environs had become a wealthy, exclusive retreat, and those summer cottages were built larger and larger each new season. De-

velopment continued following the Civil War and peaked from about 1890 to 1914, generally referred to as Newport's Gilded Age. During these 25 years, unbelievably wealthy industrialists and high-society types built massive, fortresslike homes and threw parties that sometimes cost more than $250,000. Many of the grandest of these houses still stand today, but now most of these properties are operated as house-museums and open to the public—a legacy that Newport's self-important summer bigwigs would have deemed unacceptable. The **Preservation Society of Newport County** 401/847-1000, www.newportmansions.org, operates tours of most of the houses. Several different tour possibilities are available, including combination tickets that provide a dis-

through 6 P.M., with the last guided tours typically departing at 5 P.M.; hours are a bit shorter in winter, and the Breakers opens at 9 A.M. during the busiest times of year.

You can buy a single ticket to tour the Breakers for $15, or to tour the Breakers and any one other Preservation Society property for $22. The admission to any one house other than the Breakers is $10. Special tours, such as the Rooftop and Behind-the-Scenes tours at the Elms, cost $15; it's wise to book these ahead at least 24 hours. However, you can save a great deal of money by purchasing a combination ticket, which is good throughout the entire calendar year. The Gilded Age Experience ticket costs $31 and includes admission to five houses: the Breakers, Chateau-Sur-Mer, The Elms, Marble House, and Rosecliff. The Connoisseur's Newport ticket is good for the five properties open only from mid-May through mid-October (Chepstow, Green Animals, the Isaac Bell House, Hunter House, and Kingscote) and also costs $31. Keep in mind that all prices quoted above are subject to change, and that these are prices for adult tickets; the ticket costs for kids (ages 6 to 17) are usually just 25 to 40 percent of the adult prices.

Finally, if you purchase a membership to the Preservation Society, you'll be entitled to unlimited admission to all of the aforementioned properties, and you'll receive a number of additional benefits, including the society's publication and discounts at museum gift shops. Membership for the year costs $50 for an individual and $75 for a household (good for two adults and all children under age 17 and living at same address). Even if you're just planning to spend a week in Newport, the annual membership makes the most economic sense and will afford you the greatest freedom in mansion touring.

Keep in mind, however, that some of Newport's most distinguished mansions are not operated by the Preservation Society. The Astors' Beechwood and Belcourt Castle are individually owned and operated (hours and admission are given in the descriptions of these properties within the chapter). The National Museum of American Illustration occupies Vernon Court, and Salve Regina University uses a number of Newport's most famous mansions as school buildings but does sometimes offer tours of at least a few of these buildings. Lastly, the Newport Restoration Foundation, 401/849-7300, www.newportrestoration.com, administers three noted Newport County homes, Whitehorne, Prescott Farm, and Rough Point—all of these are described in detail elsewhere in the chapter.

count. See "Tips on Touring Newport's Mansions" for specific details about pricing.

Begin the tour of Bellevue Avenue at its intersection with both Mill and Redwood Streets, which is a couple of blocks north of where Memorial Boulevard cuts across it. Here, on the east side of the avenue, is the **Redwood Library,** 50 Bellevue Ave., 401/847-0292, website: www.redwood1747.org. Tours of the library are given weekday mornings at 10:30 A.M., but the public is welcome to visit the facility anytime during regular library hours. The neoclassical structure was built in 1750 by one of the nation's earliest architects, Peter Harrison. Gilbert Stuart, an early Newport resident later to become the nation's most famous presidential portraitist, spent a good bit of time within the library's hallowed confines. Brothers William and Henry James, along with their friend Edith Wharton, also studied and read here.

Just a block south, nearly across the street, is the **Newport Art Museum,** 76 Bellevue Ave., 401/848-8200, website: www.newportartmuseum.com, which shows the works of regional artists. The exhibits here change quite often, but the museum has recently undergone a major expansion and renovation, thus allowing more extensive shows. Most often the exhibits here show a mix of contemporary regional works and earlier Newport art, much of it depicting the city's rich maritime history. Also at the museum is the quirky little **Croquet Hall of Fame Gallery,** which displays memorabilia related to this sport that was so popular in Newport during the city's Gilded Age.

NEWPORT

Interactive computer exhibits explain the game, its history, and its rules. The museum is housed within the 1864 John N. A. Griswold Mansion, the Beaux Arts 1919 Cushing Memorial Gallery, and the much newer Gilbert S. Kahn Building. The Griswold House is a fine example of stick Victorian architecture. Admission is $4. Open Mon.–Sat. 10 A.M.–5 P.M. and Sun. noon–5 P.M.; the museum closes an hour earlier in winter.

Across Bellevue, down Mill Street, is the Old Stone Mill, which anchors Touro Park. Much controversy surrounds this structure, which many locals had believed was built by Vikings a thousand years ago until improved forensic research cast doubt on this explanation. Another story is that one of the city's earliest residents, and Rhode Island's first governor, Benedict Arnold, built the structure some time in 18th century.

Continue south down Bellevue. It's possible to walk this tour, ideal to bike it, and also practical either to bus (during the summer months) or drive it. But keep in mind that the entire length, from Redwood Library down to the southernmost mansions, is about two miles.

As you cross Memorial Boulevard, the first major attraction you'll come to is the **International Tennis Hall of Fame and Museum,** 194 Bellevue Ave., 401/849-3990 or 800/457-1144, website: www.tennisfame.org, which encompasses the Newport Casino and its 6 acres of manicured grounds and grass-lawn tennis courts. Tournament tennis in America has its roots in Newport: the U.S. National Lawn Tennis Championship (which went on to become the U.S. Open) was first played at this facility in 1881. The museum contains about a dozen exhibit rooms displaying memorabilia of the game, including an Andy Warhol portrait of Chris Evert, a timeline display that traces the game's history, the original 1874 tennis patent granted by the Queen of England to Major Walter Clopton Wingfield, and a gallery celebrating tennis champions of the early 20th century. The WTA Tour Women's Gallery pays homage to the many great women of the game, from Billie Jean King to Pam Shriver to Martina Navratilova. The Peggy Woolard Library occupies what had been the Newport Casino Reading Room—it has been

fully restored and decorated as it looked a century ago. The museum is unusual in that it remains a working tennis facility, and one that's open to the public for play (this is the only lawn tennis facility in the country that's not a private club). There's also a quite extensive gift shop, as well as a restaurant overlooking the courts. Admission is $8, which includes court access. Open daily 9:30 A.M.–5 P.M.

From this point southward, the sights along here consist of Newport's many lavish mansions. The northernmost of these is **Kingscote Mansion,** at the corner of Bowery and Bellevue Avenues, 401/847-1000, website: www.newportmansions.org, on the west side of the street. This Gothic Revival mansion dates to 1839. A favorite feature here is the elaborate dining room, which was added in 1881 according to the design of Stanford White and contains what is believed to be the earliest ever installation of Tiffany glass. A wealthy planter from Georgia built this dramatic "cottage" before selling it to China Trade merchant William Henry King—today the house contains the fine artwork and furniture amassed by five generations of Kings. Open mid-May–mid-Oct., 10 A.M.–5 P.M. daily; admission is $10.

The **Preservation Society of Newport County,** 424 Bellevue Ave., 401/847-1000, website: www.newportmansions.org, oversees the upkeep, staffing, and visitation of several Bellevue Avenue mansions along with several other historic houses in Newport County. The society also offers a series of garden tours of historic homes during the summer months; call for details and prices.

The next attraction to the south is the **Isaac Bell House,** Bellevue Ave., 401/847-1000, website: www.newportmansions.org, which ranks among the nation's most impressive examples of shingle-style architecture. One of the earliest commissions of the acclaimed architectural firm of McKim, Mead, and White, the house was completed in 1883. Currently undergoing a full restoration, this is a quirky house even by Newport standards, with bamboo-style porch columns and an open floor plan inspired by the grand houses of Japan. Three narrow brick chimneys rise from the many-gabled roofline. Even as it's being worked on,

the Elms mansion

© THE PRESERVATION SOCIETY OF NEWPORT COUNTY/JOHN CORBETT

NEWPORT

you can tour the house. Open mid-May–mid-Oct., 10 A.M.–5 P.M. daily; admission is $10.

A block farther leads to one of the most appealing of Newport's mansions, the **Elms**, 424 Bellevue Ave., 401/847-1000, website: www.newportmansions.org. For a lot of visitors, the big advantage to visiting this 1901 mansion modeled after an 18th-century French château is that tours are self-guided by digital audio player, a format that allows you to walk through the house in anywhere from 30 to 90 minutes, depending on how many specific topics you choose to hear about. House curators and various experts on etiquette, art, and furnishings narrate enriching portraits on many aspects of the Elms' interior, grounds, and history. Some commentaries talk about a particular piece of furniture or painting, while others might describe how a certain room was used during the mansion's heyday. The house itself is a manageable size, not as mammoth or even as grandiose as the Breakers or Marble Hall. Open 10 a.m.–5 p.m. daily (closes one hour earlier Jan.–mid-Apr.); admission is $10.

The grounds consist of 10 acres of landscaped parkland containing about 40 species of tree, plus dignified marble statuary and perfectly groomed shrubs. The interior, though almost cozy when compared with some mansions, reveals owner Edward J. Berwind's penchant for early technology. Gadgets abound, as the Elms was among the very earliest Newport homes to be lighted and run by electricity. As sumptuous and stunning as are the Venetian-style dining room, the grand ballroom, and the airy conservatory, the Elms' most fascinating rooms are the service quarters and working areas. You'll have the chance to tour the incredibly well-organized kitchen and pantry, the laundry room, and a coal tunnel and boiler room that heated every square foot of this imposing mansion. If this aspect of mansion life really interests you, consider taking one of the Elms' Behind-the-Scenes guided tours, which give a particularly detailed sense of the inner workings of this mansion, told from the perspective of the 40 women and men who groomed the grounds, cleaned the quarters, and prepared the meals. It's recommend that you book these Behind-the-Scenes tours at least 24 hours in advance, as space is limited; the cost is $15 per person.

Just a bit south is the new **National Museum of American Illustration (NMAI)**, 492 Bellevue Ave., 401/851-8949, website: www.americanillustration.org. This museum is housed in one of the grand mansions along Bellevue, the 1898 Vernon Court, which is modeled after a 17th-century château. John Merven Carrere and Thomas Hastings, who were also responsible for the New York Public Library and the Frick Collection, designed the mansion that's noted for its marble Great Hall and its steep roof punctuated by nine tall chimneys. The museum was formed with a mission to preserve and present America's finest illustrated art—works commissioned to appear in magazines, books, advertisements, and other print products. The collection displays work by dozens of famous illustrators, among them Maxfield Parrish, Norman Rockwell, N. C. Wyeth, Charles Dana Gibson, Howard Chandler Christy, and many others. As you tour the mansion you'll also see a vast array of decorative arts and period furnishings. Visitation is by reservation only, or when the green flag is flying outside the building; admission is $15 for a self-guided tour, and $25 for a guided tour.

A BRIEF HISTORY OF TENNIS

The game of tennis is at once an extremely ancient game, with roots in 11th-century France, and also a rather modern game that—in its present and most celebrated form—dates to around the 1870s. Various forms of tennis have been documented to the beginning of the second millennium A.D., when monks batted a ball about with their hands on the grounds of French monasteries. This activity, called *jeu de paume* ("game of the palm") evolved gradually over the years into a sport of royals, played in French castles during the Middle Ages. First played barehanded, tennis gradually took on new and improved technological innovations, from gloves to crude rackets.

English's King Charles I installed a tennis court at Hampton Court palace in 1625; that venue hosts tournaments to this day—though it has been modified slightly. A court at the French palace of Versailles was installed in 1686 and is now a museum. The popularity of tennis peaked in 17th-century England and France, and in the latter country, as it had been a game of the nobility, it declined almost overnight following the French Revolution. For a variety of reasons, the game's popularity declined in England as well for a time.

It was around the 1870s that tennis as a leisure sport in England enjoyed a revival, with many wealthy Brits installing the courts on the properties of their country manors. Similarly, as a wealthy leisure class was emerging in the United States, especially in New England, an interest in tennis began there.

In 1874, the British Major Walter Clopton Wingfield devised a new form of tennis that combined the century-old game described above, which is now generally referred to as "court tennis" or "real tennis," with some characteristics of badminton, which has Native American origins. This variation on the game, called lawn tennis, is the true ancestor of the game we now popularly and professionally play today, while real tennis is a comparatively obscure game played in few places.

Wingfield's game, which was first actually played at a gala he was attending in Wales, was set on an hourglass-shaped grass court. A year later, the game was being played at many homes in Britain and even on its colonies; in Bermuda, a New Yorker named Mary Ewing Outerbridge happened to learn the game from a friend of Wingfield, and she immediately introduced the sport back home. Quickly there were changes to equipment, and a rectangular court replaced the hourglass one; by 1877, the All England Croquet Club at Wimbledon had hosted the very first world championship match of tennis.

Just a few years after its introduction to the high society of New York, America's first tennis championship was held at the Newport Casino; a women's championship was added in 1887. International competitions began in 1900 with the

---

Just off the east side of Bellevue is the attractive campus of **Salve Regina University**, Ochre Point Avenue, 401/847-6650, website: www.salve.edu. There are 18 historically significant buildings on this property a few blocks east of Bellevue Cliff Walk. The school is highly involved in preservation programs, sponsoring lectures and preservation events and working hard to preserve its many prominent structures. Probably the most famous building on campus is Ochre Court, one of the city's earliest grand summer cottages, completed in 1892 with a design by Richard Morris Hunt. Ochre Court was donated in 1947 to serve as the foundation of Salve Regina, and over the past few decades,

several other summer cottages in the adjoining neighborhood have been donated to the school. Noted architects whose works are now part of the campus include H. H. Richardson (the father of Richardsonian Romanesque), Charles Eamer Kempe, and the firm of McKim, Mead, and White. Designers who have worked on these homes and grounds range from Louis Comfort Tiffany to Frederick Law Olmsted. You can walk through the main floor of Ochre Court, which serves as the school's main administration offices, on weekdays 9 a.m.–4 p.m.; there's no charge for this, but keep in mind that this isn't a formal house-museum with tour guides. The Newport Historical Society, 401/846-0813, does

commencement of the Davis Cup, which started solely as a men's tourney between the United States and England (tennis had already developed a strong following in Australia, France, Holland, and many other nations).

Although tennis was something of a blue-blooded country-club activity during its first half-century, its popularity spread to the general public during, ironically, the Depression, when a number of federally funded New Deal programs led to the construction of tennis courts at public parks and schools.

Professional tennis, of course, has enjoyed an almost meteoric rise in popularity over the past three decades. Players began entering tournaments professionally, for money, as early as the beginning of the 20th century, but when Wimbledon finally began inviting both amateurs and professionals to participate in its tourney in 1968, the men's tennis tour really caught on. Wimbledon is now one of the four majors, along with the Australian Open, the French Open, and the U.S. Open—this last championship is the modern-day descendant of that first championship held in Newport in 1881. The women's professional tour was begun in 1971 and is now just as popular, even more so. In 1988, tennis became an official sport of the Olympic games.

Today, of course, you might not necessarily associate Newport with tennis—certainly not if your main sources of information on the game are the televised major tournaments. The Newport Casino's fortunes have waxed and waned since it hosted the first U.S. tennis tournament in 1881, which marked the formation of the United States National Lawn Tennis Association—now simply the United States Tennis Association (USTA).

For about 35 years, the Newport Casino and its illustrious tournament served as the U.S. equivalent of Wimbledon, and it might still today but for Newport's relative isolation from the Northeast's major population centers. In 1915, the U.S. Open was shifted from Newport to Forest Hills, Long Island—on the fringes of New York City—where vastly greater numbers of people could enjoy the event. In 1978, yet again the tourney venue shifted, this time across town, to a brand-new and massive tennis stadium at Flushing Meadow, where the U.S. Open is played to this day.

Nevertheless, from 1915 onward an invitational tournament continued to be staged on Newport's grass court, and in 1954 the Newport Casino was converted into the home of the National Tennis Hall of Fame. In 1977, the National Tennis Foundation merged with the Hall of Fame, which helped its owner restored the by-then decaying casino building. And since 1976, the Newport Casino has hosted the Miller Lite Hall of Fame Tennis Championship, the only pro tournament in the nation still played only on grass courts.

lead tours of the neighboring Cliff Walk on Saturday mornings at 10 a.m.; these depart from Ochre Court and cost $7 per person.

Just north of the campus on Narragansett Avenue, **Chepstow,** 401/847-1000, website: www.newportmansions.org, is an Italianate villa designed by George Champlin Mason and completed in 1860. The esteemed collection of Hudson River School paintings is worth the price of admission alone. A descendant of Lewis Morris, a signatory of the Declaration of Independence, owned this cottage. Open mid-May–mid-Oct., 10 A.M.–5 P.M. daily; admission is $10.

Back on Bellevue, a left turn south leads to **Château-sur-Mer,** Bellevue Ave., 401/847-1000,

website: www.newportmansions.org, which was built in 1852 by merchant and Far East importer William S. Wetmore, whose son George Peabody Wetmore later served Rhode Island in the U.S. Senate. Before those pesky Vanderbilts moved to Newport in the 1890s, this massive home was the largest residence in Newport. Details throughout the house include fine Victorian wallpapering and stencilwork, and rather florid Victorian furniture and ceramics. Behind the house you can stroll through a colonial revival garden pavilion and on to the Victorian-inspired park with century-old copper beech trees and weeping willows. Open mid-Apr.–Oct., 10 A.M.–5 P.M. daily; admission is $10.

At the southeast end of Salve Regina's campus, a couple of blocks east of Bellevue, you'll reach **the Breakers,** Ochre Point Ave., 401/847-1000, website: www.newportmansions.org, a 70-room Italian Renaissance mansion filled with priceless objects. It was built in 1895 by Cornelius Vanderbilt. One of the highlights here is the extensive 13-acre grounds, which overlook Cliff Walk and the Atlantic Ocean—it was the sound of the waves smashing against the rocks below that earned the Breakers its name. Cornelius was president of the New York Central Railroad, and his vast fortune allowed him to spare absolutely no expense in creating this grandiose home. Semiprecious stones and rare marble were used in the construction of many rooms and walls, and in the bathrooms, faucets provide both running fresh and salt water. Two rooms were actually constructed and furnished in France and shipped to Rhode Island. The 45-foot-high Great Hall was the site of countless soirées during the Breakers' heyday. Open 9 A.M.–5 P.M. daily (closes one hour earlier Jan.–mid-Apr.); admission is $15. Also be sure to check out the **Breakers Stable,** Coggeshall and Bateman Avenues, which was designed by Richard Morris Hunt and contains a collection of road coaches and other memorabilia from the Vanderbilt clan. It's a block west of Bellevue, by way of Ruggles Avenue.

A bit south of Salve Regina's campus lies **Rosecliff,** Bellevue Ave., 401/847-1000, website: www.newportmansions.org. A silver heiress from Nevada, Tessie Fair Oelrichs hired Stanford White to create this beauty in 1902, modeled after the garden retreat of French royalty at Versailles, Grand Trianon. Oelrichs knew how to throw a fete, and the house is remembered for having hosted a magic-themed party at which Harry Houdini entertained the guests, and many other outlandish events. A tour highlight is walking through the largest ballroom in Newport (and that's saying a lot in this city). You may recognize the house from *The Great Gatsby,* parts of which were filmed here in 1974. Open mid-Apr.–Oct., 10 A.M.–5 P.M. daily; admission is $10.

The **Astors' Beechwood Mansion,** 580 Bellevue Ave., 401/846-3772, website: www.astorsbeechwood.com, has long been a favorite on the "cottage" circuit. Here costumed actors in character bring to life the world of John Jacob Astor IV and his distinguished family, as though it were still the year 1891. Beechwood is a refreshing change of pace in that none of the rooms are roped off, and the mood is light and humorous, rather than formal and forbidding as at some house-museums. As a visitor, you'll be taken through the house and treated as though you're one of the distinguished early guests. Open year-round, but daily in summer and on limited days during the off-season. Hours vary seasonally. Admission is $15.

Marble House, Bellevue Ave., 401/847-1000, website: www.newportmansions.org, contains some 500,000 cubic feet of marble. The house was built in 1892 by Richard Morris Hunt for William K. Vanderbilt, heir to the family's railroad dynasty. He commissioned the house as a gift for his wife, Alva, for her 39th birthday (kind of makes you wonder what he gave her on her 40th). After the Breakers, this is one of Newport's most-visited house-museums—visitors can't seem to get enough of the stairwells, columns, and floors of Italian, American, and African marble. Open 10 A.M.–5 P.M. daily (closes one hour earlier Jan.–mid-Apr.); admission is $10.

You'll find some 2,000 works of art—from paintings to sculptures to antiquities—at **Belcourt Castle,** 657 Bellevue Ave., 401/846-0669, website: www.belcourtcastle.com. This Louis XIII–style castle hosts afternoon teas and many special events. The home was built by the rather idiosyncratic Oliver Hazard Perry Belmont, who inherited untold millions of dollars as the heir to the Rothschild fortune. Built in 1894 by Richard Morris Hunt, the 60-room cottage cost $3 million. Belmont kept a staff of about 40 servants and owned an ornate collection of carriages—using each different one to taxi him about Newport, depending on the time of day. Rare armor, manuscripts, and art from more than 30 Asian and European nations fill the house; on the grounds were exotic trees and plants, as well as a small menagerie. (The grounds are still beautiful, if not quite so exotic, and the menagerie is long gone.) The present owners of the house, the Tinneys, still live in a portion of the castle.

In a bit of local intrigue, Alva Vanderbilt divorced her husband, William K. Vanderbilt, in 1895 and then promptly married the wealthy bachelor of Belcourt Castle, O.H.P. Belmont. The Indomitable Alva, born of a wealthy cotton-planting family, championed women's rights throughout her later years and entertained often at Belcourt. After the owners' passing in the early 1930s, the house stood virtually dormant for some years before it was restored and brought back to life in the 1950s.

Tours are given three times daily. On these walks you can examine the mansion's superb collection of French antiquities and art, most pieces dating from Louis XI through the Napoleonic periods. Tours touch on not only the history of Belcourt, but also that of several European royal castles, some of whose treasures now adorn this grand mansion. Belcourt also has its inevitable ghosts, and you can learn more of this during the Thursday ghost tours held at 5 P.M. from late May through mid-November. General admission is $10. Ghost and French history tours cost extra. Regular summer hours (Memorial Day–mid-October) are daily 9 A.M.–5 P.M.; the house is also open daily from February through Memorial Day and from mid-October through November with shorter hours, and several days a week through most of December and early January for candlelit holiday tours.

CLIFF WALK

You can gain a very interesting perspective on the mansions along eastern Bellevue by embarking on one of the most famous oceanfront strolls in all of America, Cliff Walk. This 3.5-mile jaunt begins from the north at Memorial Boulevard and twists and turns along the craggy shore. It seems to end at the southern end of Bellevue Avenue, down the shorter Ledge Road, but in fact if you're comfortable scrambling over sharp rocks, you can actually follow the path to the very east end of exclusive Bailey's Beach, near which the walk finally terminates once and for all at the corner of Bellevue and Coggeshall Avenues. For a detailed sense of the walk's history and highlights, log onto the official website, www.cliffwalk.com, which is an exceptionally well-done

site with hundreds of great pictures of vantage points and mansions along the walk.

For many who walk it, the Cliff Walk is an opportunity to gaze at fancy estates and experience the same ocean views that mesmerized Newport's wealthy turn-of-the-20th-century summer visitors, but this is also a wonderful nature trail, abundant with opportunities for bird-watching, and for admiring fields of wildflowers. The cliffs along the walk rise to some 75 feet in places, and it's a good idea to keep your eye on the ground beneath when in motion, lifting your head to look elsewhere only when you're stopped, and sure of your footing. Especially after a rain, the rocks along the trail can be quite slippery. There is fencing along some of the especially precipitous spots, but at other points one could easily amble off the path a bit and enter a hazardous area. This is a public right-of-way, and the trail cuts over a considerable amount of private property—be respectful of the grounds.

Historically, people have been walking along portions of Cliff Walk for as long as anybody can remember, but since about the 1850s, a more formal effort to maintain a trail here has been under way, and not always to the delight of property owners affected by the path. Even today, sections of Cliff Walk are under a certain degree of dispute, but legally, the rights of persons to walk along the cliff's edge is guaranteed. In fairness, most of the owners along here are extremely gracious, and many have taken great efforts to keep the spans of Cliff Walk nearest them attractive and well-kept. Major improvements have been made to the walk during the past three decades, by the U.S. Army Corps of Engineers in the 1970s, and by the Department of the Interior in the 1990s.

To access Cliff Walk, you have several options. First, there's no rule that says you must start from the beginning—there are a number of access points along the trail, but none of these are near ample public parking, so really only pedestrians and cyclists can access it at these points. (Sheppard Avenue, Webster Street, and Wetmore Avenue intersect the walk about midway and have some limited street parking.) During the summer a bus runs up and down Bellevue Avenue, the main paved road that parallels the walk, and you can take the bus to any of the cross streets that access the walk. To start at the beginning, you can drive and park at Easton's Beach, or you can try to find a metered space on Memorial Boulevard. From downtown, along Thames Street, it's just under a mile to reach the beginning of the trail, but the walk involves a bit of a steep trek up Memorial Boulevard. You can access the trail from right off Memorial Boulevard, just below the Cliff Walk Manor hotel and restaurant, or from just a bit south off either Cliff Terrace or Seaview Avenue, which run east from Cliff Avenue.

There are several highlights along Cliff Walk. Less than a mile into it, at the end of Narragansett Avenue, you'll come to the **Forty Steps,** a sharply descending stone stairway that climbs down nearly to the see below; from a small promontory at the base of the steps you can watch the waves smashing against the rocks. Soon after Forty Steps, the path meanders by some of Newport's most famous homes, including several fine mansions that are now part of the campus of Salve Regina University. After passing Sheppard Avenue, you'll see the grandiose Breakers "cottage" on your right—the back lawn runs right to the edge of Cliff Walk. You can stroll up Ruggles Avenue from the Cliff Walk to tour the Breakers, if you wish.

Continuing south after Ruggles, the path curves along the now twisting shore, past Ochre Point and down around Rosecliff, another of the very famous mansions along the walk. You'll then come to Marine Avenue, the last access point to the trail before it reaches Ledge Road, at the very southern tip of this peninsula—that's about two miles farther. As you stroll along this lower half of the walk, keep in mind that only portions are paved, and others are dirt or gravel—it's a bit more slippery along this span, and it requires a good bit more care. Past Rosecliff you'll come to a small artists' studio along the cliff's edge, and shortly thereafter you'll pass by Astors' Beechwood and then, set a bit farther back from the actual trail, Marble House. Soon after, on your right and just above the path, you'll see the ornate, red Chinese Tea House commissioned by Marble House's owner, Mrs. William Vanderbilt—at this

juncture the Cliff Walk cuts through a short tunnel before emerging again for another fairly well-maintained stretch and then a second tunnel.

Once you emerge from this final tunnel, Cliff Walk becomes a scramble on the wild side, as it hugs the rocky shoreline by a series of large, private homes. This span is aptly nicknamed **Rough Point,** and rather crude and ugly chain-link fences separate the path from private properties along this rugged stretch. Nor'easters and hurricanes have taken their toll on Cliff Walk's southern reaches, and in some places the seawall has been ripped out. It's all entirely passable, and it's generally not so steep or high up along here, but you do want to be wearing sturdy hiking shoes. In a few spots, you must walk along the top of a fairly narrow sea wall, with a 10-foot drop beneath you; needless to say, it's best to walk this span with a buddy. As you cut around the southeastern tip of the peninsula, you'll be able to see the Doris Duke estate, Rough Point, which is just off Bellevue where it bends from south to west.

As Cliff Walk turns west around the southeastern tip of Newport, you'll come to Ledge Road, a short dead end that shoots south off Bellevue Avenue. At this point you might think that Cliff Walk comes to an end—indeed, a short walk up Ledge does lead you back to where buses pass along Bellevue Avenue, if you'd like to end your walk here. But the more intrepid among you might want to continue forth—just keep in mind that beach erosion over many decades has cut away the official trail just as you pass Ledge Road. What you can do is climb a bit along the jagged rocks, treading carefully, for a short way around the southwestern tip of this small peninsula. After a little more than a quarter mile of cutting your own trail, the official Cliff Walk resumes, now in a northerly direction along the western end of the peninsula. To your left, looking northwest, you'll see **Bailey's Beach**, and before too long you'll actually reach the eastern edge of this fabled stretch of sand. Efforts are under way to get the Department of Transportation to make the final improvements on this southern end of Cliff Walk, but for now it's a rather rough stretch.

Until relatively recently, public access to the beach was very limited. In the late 19th century,

Bailey's Beach became the ultra-exclusive playground for Newport's wealthiest summer residents—interlopers were unceremoniously shooed away by paid security guards, while high-society sorts waded in these waters, often clad in absurdly formal swimming attire. In the mid-1960s, the Spouting Rock Beach Association (SRBA), which owns Bailey's Beach, erected fences to keep strollers along Cliff Walk from entering the association's private and restricted playground. Up until this point, the far east end of Bailey's Beach had been quite accessible to the public,—it was well away from the secure private section. This span of beach came to be known as Rejects Beach, for the fact that its bathers were unwelcome on the private section of Bailey's Beach. Still, once people made it as far as the east end of the beach, a good many of them managed to sneak all the way to the restricted section, and thus the actions of SRBA to discourage any access whatsoever. The fence, however, restricted access along the very end of Cliff Walk, and quite a few local Newporters protested. Eventually the city council intervened on their behalf.

Much to the horror of the SRBA, research into the original layout of Bellevue Avenue revealed that in fact a good chunk of Bailey's Beach was not legally private at all. Bellevue, which runs in an east-west direction at the southern tip of Newport, had been laid out with a 50-foot-wide, public right-of-way that extended to the waterfront. Rather than fight this matter to the death, the SRBA and the city of Newport reached a compromise. The city would waive its right of way if the SRBA removed its fences and granted a permanent easement on the eastern end of Bailey's Beach, where the general public could enter freely.

As you reach this east end of Bailey's Beach from the Cliff Walk, the path skirts inland slightly to the corner of Coggeshall Avenue and Bellevue Avenue. This marks the official end of both Cliff Walk and Bellevue Avenue.

From here you can grab a bus back to Memorial Boulevard or hoof it back. about two miles. You can also walk north along Coggeshall back into town; Coggeshall eventually becomes Spring Street, which runs just a block east of Lower Thames Street; from this point to the corner of Wellington and Lower Thames Street, it's just under a two-mile stroll.

COASTERS ISLAND

The U.S. Navy has its earliest traditions in Narragansett Bay, and Newport contains the site of the first Naval recruit training center, which opened in 1883.

You can glean a strong sense of Newport's impressive military history at the **Naval War College Museum,** Gate 1 of the Naval Education and Training Center, Coasters Harbor Island, 401/841-4052 or 401/841-1317. With a distinguished roster of graduates that includes Admirals Chester W. Nimitz, William F. Halsey, and H. Kent Hewitt, Newport's Naval War College is the world's senior such facility, and the most elevated educational institution in the Navy. The U.S. Navy established the college in 1884 and it grew to great prominence throughout the 20th century. The museum, through highly detailed if rather dry exhibits, details the general history of U.S. naval warfare, paying especially close attention to theories and strategies of sea power, and maritime war and diplomacy. With a more regional focus, additional exhibits discuss the role of the U.S. Navy in and around Newport; the very first naval mission dates to 1775, when the Continental Congress sloop *Katy* successfully neutralized the British sloop *Diana*. Much is also made of the esteemed naval careers of Newport sons Oliver Hazard Perry and Matthew Calbraith Perry, who served in the War of 1812 and the Mexican-American War. Free, open weekdays 10 A.M.–4 P.M., weekends noon–4 P.M.

Middletown and Portsmouth

Middletown is mostly a bedroom community of about 17,000 people (down by more than 10 percent since 1990, in part because quite a few military jobs in the area have been eliminated) north of Newport, but here, too, are some of the region's top beaches and a number of lesser-known but intriguing neighborhoods with beautiful architecture. The community, formerly part of Newport, cut off the mother city and incorporated in 1743, naming itself for its position as the central-most of Aquidneck Island's three towns. Even when it was part of Newport, this more rural and wooded area enjoyed a very distinct personality from the more cramped city. And still today, Middletown feels somewhat agrarian. Like Newport, Middletown suffered at the hands of the Brits during the American Revolution. A fleet of 11 British ships landed in Middletown in December 1776 to begin their occupation of lower Aquidneck Island. They are said to have looted many private homes in Middletown, and more than a quarter of the community's residents fled to the mainland.

A good place to begin your explorations is at the Newport/Middletown border, where Memorial Boulevard crosses by Easton's Beach (on the right) and Easton Pond (on the left) and, at the border, becomes Purgatory Road.

There aren't a whole lot of cultural attractions and things to see and do out by Easton's Beach, but you can tour the **New England Aquarium Exploration Center,** 175 Memorial Blvd., Middletown, at the Rotunda at Easton's Beach, 401/849-8430, website: www.neaq.org/visit/newport.html. This small facility that's especially popular with kids contains a menagerie of marine life, from sea urchins to hermit crabs to periwinkles. And, of course, you can get a close-up look at Rhode Island's famed quahog clam. Many of these creatures are kept in a touch tank, thus allowing youngsters a chance to hold some of them. Most of the creatures here are native to Narragansett Bay. This is an affiliate of the esteemed New England Aquarium in Boston; members of the main branch get free admission to the Newport one. Among the programs are summer-camp

sessions for kids ages 8 through 10—a fun and engaging activity if you're vacationing with kids for a week or so in the summer. Open in summer daily, 10 A.M.–4 P.M. Admission is $4.

From Easton's Beach, follow Purgatory Road east. Note the campus of **St. George's School,** off Purgatory Road, a private seminary for boys that was founded in 1896. The imposing English Tudor chapel, with its crenellated turret, rises high over the 12-acre campus and can be seen from the beaches and several other parts of town. Most of the other campus buildings are in the Georgian colonial style. After passing St. George's, bear left onto Paradise Road and then quickly right onto Sachuest Point Road—you'll see parking for Second Beach on the right. Next, bear left onto Hanging Rocks Road, and then make your first left onto Third Beach Road.

A short distance up the hill you'll come to the **Norman Bird Sanctuary,** 583 Third Beach Rd., 401/846-2577, website: www.normanbirdsanctuary.org, which occupies a small hill overlooking Second and Third Beaches, Sachuest Point, and the ocean. It's undergoing major renovations at present and offers a peaceful break from the sometimes intense beach crowds. Of course, bring a camera or binoculars. The refuge encompasses some 450 acres of farm fields, meadows, woodlands, and rocky ridges. It's a great spot for hiking, as from some trails you can take in a wonderful view out over Second Beach; look for a particularly scenic promontory called Hanging Rock. Many educational walks and programs are offered throughout the year, geared toward experts and novices, adults and families. During the spring and fall migrations bird walks are given on Sunday mornings, 8 A.M. Admission is $4. Open daily in summer 9 A.M.–5 P.M. (till 9 P.M. on Wednesdays), with shorter hours the rest of the year.

From the sanctuary, retrace your way back down the hill to the intersection with Hanging Rock Road, but this time make a left turn onto Indian Avenue (note that if you continue straight you'll reach Third Beach). This rolling road is lined with handsome, mostly early-20th-century homes and fringes the Sakonnet River—it's a beautiful stretch that's less fancy but also much less pretentious than Ocean Drive and Bellevue Avenue. Indian Avenue runs for about 2.5 miles before dead-ending; shortly before it ends, make a left turn onto Old Mill Lane, and follow this a short way to Wapping Road. This is the main north-south route on the southeastern side of Aquidneck Island, and you can take it for a ways north by some bucolic farmsteads and marvelous scenery—this is ideal bike-touring country. Alas, at least some parcels of this rolling land are being subdivided for residential development; one imagines that the rural character of Middletown will not last for much longer.

From where Old Mill intersects with Wapping, it's roughly a mile until you reach the right-hand turnoff for **Greenvale Vineyards,** 582 Wapping Rd., 401/847-3777, website: www.greenvale.com. Tastings at this attractive winery are held in a distinctive old gray building with a mansard roof. The breezes from the Sakonnet River keep things here pretty cool even on hot summer days, making it a nice excursion in July and August. Open daily in summer 10 A.M.–5 P.M., with more limited hours the rest of the year.

Back on Wapping, head north another mile or so until the road runs into Sandy Point Avenue; here a right turn leads down the hill to **Sandy Point Beach,** along the western shores of the Sakonnet River. This scenic beach is broad and flat and ideal for a picnic.

In the other direction, Sandy Point Avenue runs west for about a half-mile until hitting East Main Road (Route 138); at this point you're now in Aquidneck Island's northernmost town, Portsmouth. You have a couple of options at this point—just keep in mind that Route 138 is a busy road and not as appealing for bike rides as the roads leading up to this point. The tour as described below leads up into Portsmouth and eventually works its way down to some attractions in the southern end of Middletown—if you'd rather keep this tour on the short side, just cut down to the part of the tour that follows from the Whitehall Museum House.

Plenty of visitors to Newport miss out on Portsmouth, one of New England's earliest settlements, and a town steeped in history. Newport's founders, John Clarke and William Coddington, first settled Portsmouth in 1638, having fled the Massachusetts Bay Colony with a band of about 20 fellow colonists. Another Massachusetts dissident, Anne Hutchinson, came to Portsmouth with another group soon after, and Portsmouth grew rapidly. Coddington, Clarke, and Nicholas Easton moved on to form Newport in 1639, while Hutchinson led the group that remained behind—despite some philosophical differences, Newport and Portsmouth operated under a joint government during these earliest years.

Portsmouth endured the same fate as Middletown and the rest of Aquidneck Island during the Revolutionary War—the British occupation left many homes damaged and citizens harassed, and many locals moved out to parts of the state that supported the revolution. British General Prescott occupied a house here during the war, and here he was captured by a band of American soldiers. Another important event during the war was the Battle of Rhode Island, which took place in August 1778 as a group of American troops led by General John Sullivan ventured by boat from Tiverton to Portsmouth, where they drove British forces back nearly to Newport with the plan of reclaiming that city in a joint attack with French naval commander Count D'Estaing. After a couple of weeks of holding their position, Sullivan was forced to abandon the mission and retreat because French commander D'Estaing decided not to attack Newport by sea after all, and instead sailed out to sea. About midway up Route 138, at the corner of Union Street, a granite memorial stone marks the site of the Battle of Rhode Island.

This potentially catastrophic turn of events actually ended up working generally in the Americans' favor. During their retreat, British forces took the opportunity to attack them, but while the Americans gained no ground, they did at least make it back to Tiverton having lost not a soldier. According to most reports, they caused several British casualties.

Portsmouth's early economy combined two things that Aquidneck Island has long excelled in: farming and shipbuilding. Although you might not expect it, the town also did quite well with coal-mining for a time—a large coal field on the western side of town produced large quantities of combustible coal. Portsmouth today has its own rather modest summer colony, mostly along or just off Route 138, which runs down the eastern side of the town overlooking the Sakonnet River. The population hovers around 17,000.

If you head just north from Sandy Point Avenue, about a half-mile north you'll come to the **Portsmouth Historical Society,** East Main Road (Route 138) at Union St., 401/683-9178, which occupies the town's former Christian Union Church (ca. 1865). Also on the grounds are the 1845 Portsmouth Town Hall and the Southernmost School, Rhode Island's oldest one-room schoolhouse, which dates to 1725. The church contains exhibits documenting the town's early history. You can visit either by phoning ahead to schedule an appointment or coming during the limited regular hours: Sundays Memorial Day–Columbus Day, 2–4 P.M.

From here it's a rather long but pleasant journey north on Route 138, which passes its share of modern shopping centers along the way but is generally an appealing thoroughfare with several good vantage points out over the Sakonnet River and toward the Sakonnet Peninsula. After about 4.5 miles, Route 138 bears right (becoming Park Avenue), which leads to an interesting, rather modest beach community called Island Park. Where Route 138 abruptly shifts to the left, stay on Park Avenue and continue straight for another mile or to the Stonebridge Marina, on your right. You'll pass some fun little seafood eateries along this stretch, the most famous being Flo's Clam Shack.

The marina marks the spot where a stone bridge across the Sakonnet River once connected Portsmouth to Tiverton, but the bridge was removed in 1956 and is now a fishing pier on both shores—it's less than 200 yards between the two ends of the piers. There's also a nice sandy beach by the marina. To the north, in the immediate distance, you'll see the massive new highway bridge, over which Route 138/24 now runs between Portsmouth and Tiverton.

From Stonebridge Marina, drive about a half-mile north and under the Route 138 overpass,

making a left turn onto Hummocks Avenue, following this a short ways south until it becomes Anthony Road (you're paralleling Route 138/24, which is on your left). When you reach Boyds Lane, turn right and head into the small village of Bristol Ferry, where the ferry boat used to carry passengers across Narragansett Bay to the southern tip of Bristol. In 1927, the Mt. Hope Bridge was constructed, carrying traffic along Route 114 across the bay—it's a narrow, graceful bridge, and from the top of its arch you'll enjoy great views out over the bay and Aquidneck Island.

Whether or not you make a trip over the bridge, resume your journey back at Bristol Ferry by turning south down Route 114—stay on this road for nearly three miles, turning right when you get to Cory's Lane. After passing the campus of prestigious Portsmouth Abbey prep school, you'll come to Green Animals Topiary Garden.

Especially if you have kids in tow, the **Green Animals Topiary Garden,** Cory's Ln., 401/847-1000, website: www.newportmansions.org, is a must-see. At this fanciful farmstead overlooking Narragansett Bay, 7 acres of shrubs and plants have been trimmed to resemble all different kinds of animals. The estate was purchased in 1872 by Thomas E. Brayton, treasurer of the Union Cotton Manufacturing Company in Fall River, Mass. Eventually the estate passed on to Brayton's children, the last of whom, Alice, passed away at age 94 in 1972; she coined the estate's name for the dozens of animal-shaped topiaries set about the property. Today there are some 80 topiary pieces throughout the beautifully kept gardens, including nearly two dozen that take the form of birds and mammals; others are geometric or ornamental. California privet and yew trees are used for the animals, which include camels, lions, and bears, and traditional English boxwood and California privet are used for the others. There are acres of flowers gardens and other trees and plantings. Also on the grounds is a small museum of Victorian toys and, as you might guess, there's a quite extensive gift shop of toys, garden items, and the like. Open late April–October, daily 10 A.M.–5 P.M.; holiday tours are given on weekends from late November through late December, and daily for the five days following Christmas. Admission is $6 during the regular season and $7 during the holiday season. Green Animals admission is also included with the combination ticket for Hunter House and several Bellevue Avenue mansions.

Backtrack to Route 114 and drive south about 3.3 miles, turning into the driveway for **Prescott Farm,** 2009 W. Main Rd., Middletown, 401/847-6230, website: www.newportrestoration.com, which is run by the Newport Restoration Foundation and has an original 1812 windmill, still used today to grind grains. This 40-acre farmstead, which Restoration Foundation doyenne Doris Duke purchased, makes an engaging alternative to the crowded mansions of Newport, and it offers a fascinating look at Aquidneck Island during colonial times. The island had many farms of this kind up until even a century ago, as the salt air, fertile soil, relatively long growing season (by New England standards), and terrain of mostly low woodland and scrub made it ideal for this end.

Here you can explore the four-story windmill, 1815 country store, and a 1730s guardhouse that contains notable Early American furnishings from the 17th century. In this guardhouse, the farm's owner, General Richard Prescott, commander of England's 4,000-strong forces on Rhode Island, was captured and held during the Revolutionary War. Prescott was not well-liked by either the enemy or his own troops, and this coup was a tremendous morale booster for the Continental Army. It began the night of July 11, 1777, when Revolutionary War Colonel William Barton led a party of about three dozen infantrymen in boats from Tiverton around the northeastern tip of Portsmouth and down through the East Passage of Narragansett Bay, landing at the mouth of a brook that flowed from the farm—all this in the darkness of night. Somehow a group of them managed to elude British guards as they snuck up along the banks of the brook. They made their way to Prescott's bedchamber, captured Prescott and an aide, and snuck back to the boats with them at gunpoint, then rowed back to Tiverton with their bounty in hand. The British didn't discover the kidnapping until many hours after Barton's troops had returned safely to Tiverton.

The windmill has spent time on several prop- erties in the area since it was first built and installed on a farm in Warren. The history of the country store is less certain, but it was moved to this site in 1970 from a position near where the Mt. Hope Bridge now carries traffic between Bristol and Aquidneck Island—it's believed that it was operated by the owners of the ferry that once transported passengers to Bristol. Assorted bric-a-brac and household items from the colonial period now fill the small interior. There are also three restored colonial homes—including the 1730 Overing House in which Prescott was captured— but these are rented to private tenants on a long-term basis and not open to the public. The grounds include medicinal- and culinary-herb gardens, and an edible-flower garden. It's recommended that you take one of the guided tours, which are free with the $3 admission. Open May–Oct., weekdays 10 A.M.–4 P.M.; the grounds themselves are open daily, sunrise–sunset, free.

From here continue south along Route 114 for about a mile, then make a left onto Oliphant Lane. About a half-mile later you'll come to Rhode Island's only microbrewery (apart from a few brewpubs that serve food and ale on the premises), **Coastal Extreme Brewing Co.,** 307 Oliphant La., Middletown, 401/849-5232, website: www.newportstorm.com, which opened in summer 1999 and produces a nice range of ales and beers, including Hurricane Amber Ale, Regenschauer Oktoberfest (available only in the fall), Blizzard Porter, Thunderhead Irish Red, and Maelstrom IPA. Many restaurants in Newport and the surrounding area serve Coastal Extreme brews on tap, and it's available at a number of local liquor stores. Free tours and tastings are given every Friday evening at 6 P.M.; call ahead or visit the web page for directions and to confirm that the tour is running.

Continue heading east along Oliphant Lane, and then turn south onto Route 138. Almost immediately you'll come to the second of the area's wineries, **Newport Vineyards,** 909 E. Main Rd. (Route 138), Middletown, 401/848-5161, website: www.newportvineyards.com, which offers tours and tastings daily (coming directly from Newport, by the way, it's just a 10-minute drive north from downtown). On the property you'll also find a toy store, garden center, art gallery, and small restaurant; and a farmers market is held on the grounds Wednesday afternoons and Saturday morning from June through October. Tours are at 1 and 3 P.M., and the wine shop is open daily 10 A.M.–5 P.M. (from noon on Sundays).

Continue south down Route 138, bearing left after about .4 miles onto Turner Road; a short way later, by Middletown Cemetery, make a left turn onto Wyatt Road, and then a right (south) onto Berkeley Avenue. Noted Irish philosopher George Berkeley—for whom the city in California is named—lived in Middletown from 1729 through 1731, and his home, the **Whitehall Museum House,** 311 Berkeley Ave., 401/846-3116 or 401/847-7951, website: www.georgeberkeley.org.uk, is open to the public in summer. Since 1900, the Rhode Island chapter of the National Society of the Colonial Dames has managed this stately red saltbox, which is furnished with period pieces, although none that belonged to Berkeley himself. The interior is austere but elegant; the enormous kitchen fireplace is among the more impressive interior highlights.

In case you thought grant-writing was a thing of recent times, Berkeley drafted this sort of proposal in 1725, with plans to found a college in Bermuda and then to educate the sons of colonists and Indians in the New World. The distinguished scholar was granted 20,000 pounds from English Parliament, and in 1729 he sailed to Aquidneck Island with his wife and some colleagues and purchased a tract of land here. Berkeley had considerable expertise in architecture, and he greatly influenced the construction of Whitehall, designing the hipped roof and rear lean-to construction, and other rather formal elements that were little known in New England at that time. A literary and ecclesiastical salon of sorts was begun here during Berkeley's time in Rhode Island; from this group came the impetus for creating the Rosewood Library in Newport. Berkeley also helped influence the founding of both Brown University and King's College in New York City (which we now know as Columbia University). As fate would have it, the 20,000-pound grant he was promised never came to be, so after three years of Rhode Island living, Berkeley packed up and returned to Ireland, where he was appointed Bishop of County Cloyne. Berkeley left his entire estate to Connecticut's Yale College. It housed British officers during the Revolutionary War. Admission is $3. Open July–Aug., Tues.–Sun. 10 A.M.–5 P.M. You can also visit the house by appointment other times of the year.

From here you're just a four-mile and 10-minute drive south down to the heart of Newport.

Jamestown

Jamestown, population 5,600 (up more than 12 percent since 1990), is the name of the town that occupies all of Conanicut Island, which actually consists of one main cigar-shaped swath of land and then a smaller one off the southwestern tip. It's exactly between Aquidneck Island and the mainland of western Narragansett Bay—two long and tall bridges connect it to each respective piece of land. The island is not at all densely populated, although as improved and faster bridges have been built in recent decades, and southern Rhode Island has expanded in general, Jamestown has become a full-time home for a greater number of people.

It's a lovely island for exploring, and Jamestown's tiny but picturesque downtown has several cute shops and a handful of notable eateries and accommodations. Best of all, it's very easy to get here from Newport without a car—ferry service between Newport Harbor and the island's downtown runs frequently during the warmer months. Most of Jamestown's businesses are right by the ferry landing. Like Newport, Jamestown—which was named for King James II of England—was occupied by the British from about 1776 through 1779, during which more than half of the population fled to the mainland.

Jamestown's leading attraction is, as you might expect from this island's charmed location, one of tremendous scenic beauty. **Beavertail State Park,** Beavertail Road, 401/423-9941 or 401/884-

2010, covers about 150 acres of pristine scrub and low woodland across a rocky point at the southern end of Conanicut Island. A loop road runs through much of the park and accesses several scenic overlooks, including one that takes in Beavertail Lighthouse. The park is laced with hiking trails, and throughout the summer park naturalists lead many walks. This is also an excellent spot for surfcasting into the ocean. Just keep in mind that the waters in these parts can be treacherous, as can be the rocky shoreline—swimming can be extremely dangerous.

Shopping

Newport can keep even the most dedicated shoppers quite content for days. Especially in the downtown area, along Thames Street and the lanes and wharves just off it, you'll find dozens of mostly independent clothiers, jewelry shops, art galleries, and gift shops. Chain businesses have made some inroads here, but for the most part you'll find a nice mix of stores that you won't find back home, or even in other parts of Rhode Island.

Most of the mansion-museums along Bellevue Road have outstanding gift shops, and the proceeds help to keep these houses up and running. Books on local and regional architecture and decorative arts, prints, and housewares are among the most common items you'll find in these shops.

Another Newport retail specialty is decorative and practical wares with a nautical bent, from the requisite ship's wheel and scrimshaw kitsch to high-quality maritime paintings and prints, sailing clothing and gear, and antique barometers, ships' clocks, and such. Quite a few local artists live in or near Newport and have their creations represented at galleries all over town.

SHOPPING AREAS

Several of the wharves in Newport function today as mini-malls, many of them on the wharves jutting into the harbor. **Bannister's Wharf,** off Thames Street, website: www.bannisterswharf.com, has several fine shops. The **Golden Dog,** 1 Bannister's Wharf, 401/849-1444, carries Maurice Lacroix watches and custom-made jewelry; and **Mark, Fore & Strike,** 33 Bannister's Wharf, 401/848-9817, carries smart men's and women's sportswear. Pick up fine leather handbags and accessories at the **Brahmin Factory Store,** 22 Bannister's Wharf, 401/849-5990. There's been a wharf here since 1742, when John Bannister built this structure. **The Narragansett,** 1 Bannister's Wharf, 401/849-4381, has a wide selection of classic women's and men's sportswear, from Polo Ralph Lauren to Austin Reed.

Bowen's Wharf, Thames Street at America's Cup Avenue, 401/849-2120, website: www.bowenswharf.com, is a bit smaller than Bannister's Wharf but contains an engaging mix of businesses. **Thames Glass,** 8 Bowen's Wharf, 401/842-0579; also 688 Thames St., 401/846-0576, carries the hand-blown glasswork of Newport artist Matthew Buechner. The **Brick Marketplace,** Thames Street at America's Cup Avenue, 401/846-4733, contains 32 varied and eclectic shops, plus several good restaurants.

ARTS AND CRAFTS

There are many very good sources of nautical and marine art in town. One of the most extensive, **Arnold Art Store and Gallery,** 210 Thames St., 401/848-8200, website: www.arnoldart.com, fills three floors with original paintings and prints. Also highly acclaimed is **William Vareika Fine Arts,** 212 Bellevue Ave., 401/849-6149, website: www.vareikafinearts.com, which carries exceptional American paintings, drawings, and watercolors from the past three centuries. **North Star Galleries,** 105 Spring St., 401/846-7200, website: www.northstargalleries.com, carries fine watercolors, paintings, ship models, vintage photos, sailing instruments, and marine antiques. **Priscilla Malone,** Elm Tree Cottage, 336 Gibbs Ave., 401/849-1610, website: www.priscillamalone.com, is noted for her still life and landscape watercolors, pastels, and prints of Newport.

Sheldon Fine Art, 59 America's Cup Ave., 401/849-0030, carries the works of several prominent artists, including John Mecray and John Philip Hagen. **Spring Bull Studio and Gallery,** 55 Bellevue Ave., 401/849-9166, is a cooperative gallery of 17 area artists. Contemporary jewelry and decorative arts are the specialty at **Suydam + Diepenbrock,** 9 Bridge St., 401/848-9090. At **Cadeaux du Monde,** 140 Bellevue Ave., 401/848-0550, you can browse folk art, textiles, clothing, and decorative arts from around the world, especially Latin America and South America. **Roger King Fine Arts,** 21 Bowen's Wharf, 401/847-4359, carries an impressive selection of 19th- and 20th-century paintings, especially nautical ones.

ANTIQUES, GIFTS, AND HOME FURNISHINGS

With two locations, **Watercolours,** Brick Market Place, Newport, 401/845-0041; 102 W. Main Rd., Middletown, 401/845-0000, sells an impressive range of gifts and home furnishings meant for just about every occasion. The **Griffon Shop,** 76 Bellevue Ave., 401/848-8200, carries a wide range of antiques and odds and ends, plus original artwork by several local artists and craftspeople. The **Doll Museum,** 520 Thames St., 401/849-0405, displays a tremendous range of antique and modern dolls of all kinds, as well as stuffed animals and miniatures. It's the shop in Rhode Island for this pursuit.

Another bric-a-brac emporium of solid repute is the **Eagle's Nest Antique Center,** 3101 E. Main Rd. (Rte. 138), Portsmouth, 401/683-3500, a multi-dealer space with more than 100 stalls representing every possible kind of antique, collectible, jewelry, and toy. Also in Portsmouth,

Emerald Acre Antiques, 1050 E. Main Rd. (Rte. 138), 401/683-9353, specializes in primitives, Oriental pieces, nautical collectibles, and estate jewelry. **MacDowell Pottery,** 138 Spring St., 401/846-6313, proffers an interesting selection of hand-thrown pottery and glassworks, plus lamps, clocks, cards, and whimsical gifts.

Karen Vaughan, 148 Bellevue Ave., 401/848-2121, carries a natty array of hip home furnishings and decorative arts. Furniture-maker Jeffrey Greene crafts fine 18th-century-inspired designs at **The Ball & Claw,** 55 America's Cup Ave., 401/848-5600, which also carries porcelain, quilts, chandeliers, and lamps. **Rue de France,** 78 Thames St., 401/846-3636, website: www.ruedefrance.com, stocks a stunning display of lace, linens, pottery, and other Parisian-style finery. For nearly a century, **J. T.'s Chandlery,** 128 Spring St., 401/846-7256, website: www.jtschandlery.com, has been a leading supplier of all things nautical; it's still a must-do for yachting and boating aficionados. It's a great source of gifts, too.

You can pick up authentic reproduction home furnishings, gifts, and jewelry of Newport's Gilded Age at the **Museum Store,** Preservation Society of Newport, 1 Bannister's Wharf, 401/849-9900, website: www.newportmansions.org.

PICK-YOUR-OWN FARMS

Pick-your-own farms are more popular in other parts of the state, but **Sweet Berry Farm,** 19 Third Beach Rd., Middletown, 401/847-3912, is a great spot for this activity within a short drive of downtown Newport. In summer go for strawberries and raspberries, move on to cut flowers and vegetables as the months progress, before heading here for pumpkins in the fall and Christmas trees in early winter.

Sports and Recreation

Outdoor activities in Newport revolve almost exclusively around the water, whether it be jogging on the beach, biking around Ocean Drive, or sailing on the water. Opportunities for these adventures are everywhere. Elsewhere on Aquidneck Island—in Portsmouth and Middletown—you'll find a few golf courses and plenty of wide open space, including exceptional biking terrain.

Newporters spend a lot of time out of doors, even during the winter months. Aquidneck Island is famous for fishing, boating, sailing, and other water-borne activities, but you'll also find that the island's gentle slopes are ideal for long bike rides and short walks and hikes.

BEACHES AND WATER SPORTS

The city of Newport itself actually doesn't have the best or the most accessible public beaches on Aquidneck Island, but sunbathers do regularly head to **Brenton Point State Park,** on Ocean Drive. Here you'll find a medium-sized parking area and a small pavilion with changing rooms. This is too rocky and rough a beach for swimming, but it can be ideal for beachcombing and lying in the sun. The one in-town possibility is little **King Park,** on Wellington Avenue (just off Lower Thames Street, on the south end of the harbor). Here you'll find a relatively small patch of sand and a swimming area that's presided over in summer by a lifeguard (daily 9:30 A.M.–4 P.M.). There's also free parking along Wellington. Across the harbor, **Fort Adams State Park** has a designated swimming area, plus a picnic area and a fishing pier.

Perhaps the most intriguing beach in Newport is **Bailey's Beach,** which can really only be accessed on foot, by bicycle, or by way of the Bellevue Avenue bus, as there is no public parking anywhere near it.

There are several wonderful beaches beginning in eastern Newport by the Middletown border, and then farther into Middletown itself. These stretches of golden sand are largely undeveloped and pristine, some of the most beautiful on the Atlantic seaboard—there are few concessions and amusements. It's fantastic territory for biking and jogging, although roads are narrow and can be clogged with traffic in high season.

As you leave Newport on Memorial Avenue (Route 138A), you'll immediately come to **First Beach,** aka **Easton's Beach.** This is a classic family beach, with cabanas for rent, a historic beach carousel (50 cents a ride; open Memorial Day–Labor Day, daily 10 A.M.–6 P.M.), and lots of activities going on at all times, from sandcastle-building contests to live music (on Tuesdays) to water sports—you can rent windsurfing equipment, surfboards, and other aquatic toys from a couple of surf shops located just steps from the beach. During the city's snobbish Gilded Age, Easton's Beach was looked upon as the commoner's bathing venue, where anybody without the name or the connections to sunbathe at exclusive Bailey's Beach could enjoy themselves. It remains Newport's most accessible beach, although it is no longer considered the turf of the elite's "footstools," as unworthy local residents were nicknamed by the summertime elitists. Children's programs are conducted early on Thursday evenings. And facilities include outdoor showers, a gift shop, a snack bar, and lockers and changing rooms, plus the New England Aquarium Exploration Center. The beach officially begins in Newport at the northern tip of Cliff Walk and extends north to just past the Middletown town line. Several restaurants edge the beach, and a number more are within walking distance, making this the most social but also least secluded and pristine of the city's beaches—it's perfect if you're with a group of friends or seeking diversions beyond simply the natural beauty of the beach. That being said, the sand along here is lovely. Parking for nonresidents costs $10 on weekends and holidays and $8 on weekdays (just $6 on weekdays if you arrive before 9:30 A.M.). The parking lot holds about 600 cars and fills up fast in summer. If you're staying

NEWPORT

for longer than a week, it's worth buying a non-resident parking sticker good for the entire season (Memorial Day through Labor Day) for $45.

From here follow Purgatory Road a short way east to Paradise Avenue, onto which you turn left and then go down the hill until you reach the parking area for **Second Beach,** also known as **Sachuest Beach,** which quite a few locals consider the best beach for sunning in all of Newport. Second Beach lies directly facing the Atlantic, sheltered by Eastern and Sachuest Points. It's a long, three-mile crescent, ideal for walks and with great exposure for sun bunnies; parking costs $10 on weekdays, and $15 on weekends—prices that clearly reflect the beach's immense popularity (nonresidents can also buy a season parking pass for $90); there's plenty of parking over several lots. The parking lot nearest Newport at Second Beach is a short walk from **Purgatory Chasm,** a 160-foot fissure in the cliffs that ranges in width from 8–15 feet at the top to 2–20 feet at the bottom. There's a small parking area (30-minutes maximum) at the short trail to the chasm itself. This narrow and perhaps overhyped geological feature, with a nice little wooden bridge over it, has been a curiosity for as long as anybody can remember. Still, it's fun to sit on the rocky promontory and admire the view down over Second Beach. Second Beach also has a small campground that occupies an enviable spot between Sachuest Point and Gardiners Pond; camping facilities include RV hookups and restrooms.

From here, continue east along Sachuest Road to reach **Sachuest Wildlife Refuge,** Sachuest Point Road, which has a visitors center that's good for trail maps and local information. The center sits on a small bluff that affords nice views back toward Newport. Looking up the hill to the north of Newport, you'll also see the Gothic towers of St. George's prep school. Fishermen appreciate the miles of rocky shoreline; the preserve also has some good hiking.

Backtrack along Sachuest Road past Gardiners Pond, make a right onto Indian Avenue, and follow this to Third Beach Road, which leads to—you guessed it—**Third Beach,** a somewhat

isolated crescent facing northeast toward the Sakonnet River, which opens to the ocean just south. It's well sheltered and popular among those who don't like wind, and a boat ramp allows access for seafarers into a fairly calm stretch of the river. You'll often see surfcasters here in the off months. A narrow lane leads to the beach through marshlands. Parking here is $10 on weekdays, $15 on weekends.

As you drive north along the eastern shore of Aquidneck Island you'll come to a couple of other good beaches. **Sandy Point Beach** is a wide, peaceful expanse of sand along the Sakonnet River, about midway up the east side of Aquidneck Island. It's off the beaten path and less intensely crowded than many Newport beaches, and it's a favorite for surf-casting, boating, and swimming; there are picnic facilities, grills, and restrooms here, too. Parking costs $5 on weekdays, $10 on weekends, and $25 for nonresidents for the season. This sheltered beach is a bit less touristy than the others closer to or in Newport. **Teddy's State Beach,** by Stonebridge Marina, off Point Road, in the Island Park section of Portsmouth, offers a quiet crescent of pebbly sand alongside the preserved portion of Old Stone Bridge, a narrow two-lane structure that once connected Aquidneck Island to Tiverton. There are picnic tables. You'll often see fishermen on both sides of the old bridge, casting lines as though it's a jetty. To one side is Stone Bridge marina.

Water sporting enthusiasts will find plenty of like-minded souls at Newport's beaches, especially those into surfing or windsurfing. The premier areas for surfing are Easton's and Second Beaches, both of which have designated areas for this activity—you'll find a cluster of surf shops near Easton's Beach, just over the Middletown border. Windsurfers also enjoy the consistently good breezes off both of these beaches, but they also favor Fort Adams State Park and Sandy Point Beach.

BICYCLING AND JOGGING

Newport and the rest of Aquidneck Island is prime territory for bicycling enthusiasts. Any of the walking or driving routes described earlier in the chapter are excellent for two-wheeling, as is all of Conanicut Island (Jamestown), especially down around Beavertail State Park. Stores in Newport that rent bicycles include **Ten Speed Spokes,** 18 Elm St., 401/847-5609, and **Adventure Sports,** 142 Long Wharf, 401/849-4820.

Jogging is popular all over Newport, especially up Washington Street and back down Second Street, out to Goat Island, along the narrowest stretch of Thames Street, and along Bellevue Avenue. For a more challenging run, you might consider a portion of Ocean Drive—park at Fort Adams or at Brenton Point, and run from there. The area of Middletown just over the border from Newport also makes for excellent jogging and bicycling. Just follow the route described above in the Beaches section, from Newport out to Sachuest Wildlife Refuge, or perhaps all the way to Third Beach.

BOATING, CANOEING, AND KAYAKING

Newport is one of North America's great sailing and yachting hubs. There are several full-service marinas in town, including **Bannister's Wharf,**

off Thames Street in Newport Harbor, 401/846-4500, website: www.bannisterswharf.net/bann-mrna.htm, a relatively small facility in the heart of downtown Newport with gas, diesel, ice, electricity, showers, laundry, and phone. The marina has been home to several America's Cup winners, including Dennis Connor's *Stars & Stripes.*

Look to **Adventure Watersports,** 142 Long Wharf, 401/849-4820, website: www.adventurenewport.com, for rentals of Jet Skis, outboard motorboats, kayaks, sailboats, and dinghies. The company also customizes boat tours, fishing trips, and charters. At Fort Adams State Park, **Sail Newport,** 60 Fort Adams Dr., 401/846-1983, website: www.sailnewport.org, rents 19- to 22-foot sailboats and provides professional instruction for all ages.

A great all-around resource for boat charters of all kinds is the **Newport Yacht Charter Association,** 28 Church St., website: www.newportcharters.com, a member-based organization of brokers who can help you choose the right vessel for you or your group to charter. These brokers work with about two dozen vessels, which specialize in everything from sailing to motor yachting to sportfishing. These boats range from 155-foot schooners

© BILLY BLACK

sailing on Narragansett Bay

that can accommodate 80 passengers to 36-foot sailboats that can handle up to 15. Rates vary, from about $25 to $65 per person for a two-hour sunset sail to several thousand dollars for a week-long charter. Newport Yacht Charter's brokers can also help you decide what kind of charter is right for you, or whether you're qualified to charter a bareboat overnight ship, where there's no crew and you sail the boat yourself.

Sea-kayaking is a very popular activity along Newport's winding shoreline, and up and down the Sakonnet River—there are hundreds of inlets and quite a few islands to explore within reasonable paddling distance of Newport and the surrounding towns. Best sources for rentals include downtown Newport's **Adventure Sports Rentals,** Inn on Long Wharf, off Thames Street, 401/849-4820, and the **Sakonnet Boat House,** 401/624-1440, which is just across from Portsmouth in Tiverton. Both outfitters can also provide lessons. The **Newport Kayak Company,** 18 Elm St., 401/849-7404, is another source of kayak rentals.

FISHING

From spring through fall, Newport is one of the Eastern Seaboard's premier destinations for saltwater fishing—you'll see surfcasters up and down the beaches from Newport north along the Sakonnet River and all the way around Aquidneck Island, vying for Narragansett Bay's stripers, bluefish, and bonito. Fishing from a boat in greater Newport's waters provides the opportunity for many more species, among them mahimahi, tarpon, trigger fish, Atlantic mackerel, flounder, swordfish, and many others. There are about eight freshwater ponds on the island that are stocked with bass and trout, including Easton's Pond, which is just beyond the beach of the same name, on the Newport/Middletown border.

If you're trying to find out the best approach to fishing in these waters, first consider whether you simply want to cast a line into the surf or into one of the island's freshwater ponds, or if you and possibly a group of friends are more interested in a full boating trip. You can rent equipment and buy bait at a number of locations, including **Beachfront Bait and Tackle,** Welling-ton Avenue, 401/849-4665, **Sam's Bait and Tackle,** Aquidneck Avenue, Middletown, 401/858-5909, or **Zeek's Bait & Tackle,** North Road, Jamestown, 401/423-1170. The **Saltwater Edge Fly-Fishing Company,** 561 Thames St., 401/842-0062, is your one-stop shop for information and tackle for surfcasting or boat-fishing in saltwater; you can also hire guides here.

Fishin' Off Charters, 88 McIntosh Dr., Portsmouth, 401/683-5557, website: www.visitnewport.com/fishingoff, arranges sportfishing charters—both full- and half-day—on a 36-foot cabin cruiser. The trips leave from Goat Island and can accommodate from one to six passengers. There are no deep-sea fishing charters available from Newport; you'd have to head over to South County's Port of Galilee to find the nearest of these.

JAI ALAI

One of very few jai alai frontons remaining in the United States, the once-popular Basque gaming sport is still played in Rhode Island at **Newport Grand Jai Alai,** 150 Admiral Kalbfus Rd., 401/849-5000, website: www.newportgrand.com. You can watch live jai alai here, play the slot machines, and bet on simulcast greyhound and thoroughbred racing.

GOLF

There are three public golf courses on Aquidneck Island, the most popular of which is **Montaup Country Club,** Anthony Road, Portsmouth, 401/683-9882. Another option is **Green Valley,** 371 Union St., Portsmouth, 401/847-9543; both are 18 holes. A nine-hole course in Portsmouth is **Pocasset Country Club,** 807 Bristol Ferry Rd., 401/682-1760. Across Newport Bridge, there's **Jamestown Country Club,** 245 Conanicus Ave., Jamestown, 401/423-9930, another nine-holer.

ICE-SKATING

At the **Born Family Skating Center,** Newport Yachting Center, 401/846-3018, website:

www.skatenewport.com, a spacious outdoor rink on the city's waterfront, you can glide across the ice for $5 per three-hour session (adults); rentals are available, as are lessons for all abilities. A zamboni grooms the ice hourly.

POLO

Polo has been an important rite during Newport's summer social season since the 1880s. At the **Newport Polo Club,** Glen Farm, Rte. 138, Middletown (6 miles north of downtown Newport, between Union St. and Sandy Point Ave.), 401/847-7090, www.newportinternationalpolo.com, visitors can watch matches on Saturdays from June through September. These contests pit international teams from the United States, England, Ireland, France, Italy, Chile, and Argentina against one another. Matches commence at 5 P.M., admission is $8. Part of the tradition is setting up "tailgating" picnics on the grounds—this is one of Newport's, and even New England's, most unusual weekly summer events.

SCUBA DIVING

For the very reason that the waters around Newport and Aquidneck Island have proven treacherous to ship's captains for many centuries, scuba divers love this part of Rhode Island. Lurking beneath the ocean surface are countless coral reefs, ledges, and interesting—though potentially dangerous—formations; and there are plenty of sunken ships in these parts. For information on rentals, local laws and restrictions, and advice, contact **Newport Diving Center,** 550 Thames St., 401/847-9293, website: www.newportdiving.com, which also offers dive charter excursions.

TENNIS

The **International Tennis Hall of Fame,** 194 Bellevue Ave., 401/849-3990 or 800/457-1144, website: www.tennisfame.org, is the only place in America where any two travelers can drop by and play lawn tennis. Access to the "Royal" court is included with admission to the museum ($8). There are 13 grass courts, open May through October.

In mid-July, the Hall of Fame hosts the **Miller Lite Hall of Fame Tennis Championship,** 401/849-3990, website: www.tennisfame.org, which draws 32 top players from the ATP tour for the only grass-court professional tennis tourney in the nation.

Accommodations

Newport's summer population booms, and it's always a good idea to plan as early as possible when thinking of a visit here. Especially during key summer events—the folk festival, the jazz festival, the Newport Music Festival, and so on—rooms sell out fast. Other times, you can almost always find a spot at one of the motels or hotels in Middletown or Portsmouth, or you can even base your operations in South County, a 20- to 30-minute drive from Newport over a pair of long bridges that span the Narragansett.

That being said, Newport has the greatest variety of hotel accommodations in the state, including dozens of inns and B&Bs. There are relatively few larger hotels in Newport, and those here are very expensive, especially during the summer months. If you're looking for mid- to low-end chain properties, try Middletown, a short drive away. Just over the Newport border along Route 138A in Middletown, you'll also find a variety of oceanside inns, motels, and hotels, offering a wide range of rates. Newport proper has relatively few oceanfront accommodations, although several properties downtown overlook the harbor. If you want to be within walking distance of hotels, shops, and nightlife, downtown Newport is your best option. But keep in mind that you'll pay for this privilege.

There are a few reservations services in Newport, which make good sense if you're having trouble finding a room on your own. These companies can sometimes work out better rates

NEWPORT

DOWNTOWN NEWPORT LODGING

Easton Bay

OCEAN DRIVE

SEAVIEW INN
SEA BREEZE INN
RHEA'S INN BY THE SEA
AQUIDNECK AVE. (214) (138A)
(138A)
SEA WHALE
Middletown
BEST WESTERN ATLANTIC BEACH HOTEL
INN AT NEWPORT BEACH
PURGATORY RD.

Green End Pond

Easton Pond

MEMORIAL BLVD.

Easton's/First Beach

THE CHARLES
CLIFF VIEW COTTAGE
CLIFFSIDE INN
CLIFF AVE.
Cliff Walk

EUSTIS AVE.
ELM TREE COTTAGE
GIBBS AVE.
MERTON RD.
DRESSER ST.
ANNANDALE RD.

RHODE ISLAND AVE.

CATHERINE ST.
OLD BEACH RD.
OLD BEACH INN
ATTWATER VILLA
NEWPORT
MEMORIAL BLVD.
SALVE REGINA UNIVERSITY

KAY ST.
LA FARGE PERRY HOUSE
BROADWAY
ABIGAIL STONEMAN INN
HYDRANGEA HOUSE INN
INN ON BELLEVUE
HOTEL VIKING
Touro Park
BELLEVUE AVE.
BERKELEY AVE.
PARKER AVE.
NARRAGANSETT AVE.

Washington Square
CLARKESTON
SHEPLEY
CLARENDON KITT
Historic Hill
MILL ST.
CHURCH ST.
ADELE TURNER INN
WYNSTONE
(138A)
BOWERY ST.
SAMUEL DURFEE HOUSE
PERRY ST.
DIXON ST.

WARNER ST.
FAREWELL ST.
PILGRIM HOUSE
VANDERBILT HALL
MILL STREET INN
BLACK DUCK INN
BALDWIN PLACE
FRANCIS MALBONE HOUSE
SPRING ST.
START OF OCEAN DRIVE

ISLAND CEMETERY
THAMES ST.
(238)
THAMES ST.
WELLINGTON AVE.

CLEVELAND HOUSE/ ADMIRAL FARRAGUT INN
INNTOWNE INN
NEWPORT BAY CLUB AND HOTEL
HARBORSIDE INN

WILLOWS OF NEWPORT
Point District
(238) (138A)
ELM STREET INN
NEWPORT MARRIOTT

SARAH KENDALL HOUSE
WASHINGTON ST.
(138)
To Goat Island

Newport Harbor

King Park Wellington
ROSENEATH AVE.

0   0.25 mi
0   0.25 km

with area inns and hotels than are available to the general public. **Bed & Breakfast Newport,** 401/846-5408 or 800/800-8765, website: www.bbnewport.com, is a reservation service with more than 350 options. Another possibility is **Anna's Victorian Connection,** 401/849-2489 or 800/884-4288, website: www.lodging-in-newport.com. And there's **Bed & Breakfast of Rhode Island,** 401/849-1298 or 800/828-0000, website: www.visitnewport.com/bedandbreakfast. Also try **America's #1 Reservation of Newport,** 401/848-5888 or 800/804-5336, website: www.americasreservation.com.

DOWNTOWN

$100–150

The Old Beach Inn, 19 Old Beach Rd., 401/849-3479 or 888/303-5033, website: www.oldbeachinn.com, is a thoroughly renovated Victorian home with exquisitely decorated rooms. A wealthy doctor built this elegant house in 1879. Guest rooms are named for garden plants and flowers, and are contained within both the main house and a mansard-roof carriage house that dates to the 1850s. The decor is over-the-top Victorian—the Rose Room has a lavish four-poster bed with a floral canopy, for instance. Guests have use of a pantry stocked with tea-and coffee-making supplies, plus snacks and bottled water. There's a gazebo out back, surrounded by gardens, a brick patio, and wrought-iron patio furniture and Adirondack chairs. Continental breakfast is included. The inn is just a couple of blocks east of Bellevue Avenue at Touro Park, an easy walk to Easton's Beach. The mansard-roof **Pilgrim House,** 123 Spring St., 401/847-7077 or 800/525-8373, website: www.pilgrimhouseinn.com, is an informal spot along a charming stretch of upper Spring Street. This 1809 inn with gingerbread trim has 10 guest rooms with a smattering of antiques. Overall the mood is very casual and low-key; rooms have rose carpeting, and some have sleigh beds. There are no TVs or phones in the rooms; it's more a place to get a good night's sleep than to hang out. The best feature is the third-floor sundeck, which offers terrific harbor and downtown views. Continental

breakfast is included. Another of the best deals in town, **Cliff View Cottage,** 4 Cliff Terrace, 401/846-0885, is a charming house with a mansard roof that lies down a tranquil lane close to the city's famous Cliff Walk. There are just four rooms, two with an ocean view that share a bath, and two others with private bathrooms but no glimpse of the ocean.

Attwater Villa, 22 Liberty St., 401/846-7444 or 800/392-3717, website: www.attwatervilla.com, just off Bellevue Avenue, is one of the more distinctive-looking B&Bs in Newport—it was built in 1910 as a Bavarian restaurant called the Hof-Brau, which became a hoity-toity tearoom during Prohibition. The building was restored and converted into a European-style guest house in the 1980s; until 2001 it was called Villa Liberte. Rooms vary a great deal in size and layout, from standard units with queen-size beds to suites and apartments. The common areas are lovely, including an airy sunroom done in country French style and a very private sundeck. There's air-conditioning and a phone in every room. And an expansive Continental breakfast buffet is included, served in an attractive room with hunter-green walls and floral draperies. A real gem with decent rates considering the location near Aquidneck Park on a lovely stretch of Spring Street, the **Samuel Durfee House,** 352 Spring St., 401/847-1652 or 877/696-2374, website: www.samueldurfeehouse.com, has five spacious and neatly decorated rooms done with mostly Federal antiques that match the home's 1803 construction. One room has a beautiful Robert Adam–carved mantel, another Chinese Chippendale twin beds and Asian rugs. An impressive full breakfast—a specialty is Portuguese sweet bread French toast—is served in the stately parlor or, when weather permits, on the shaded back patio. The setting is marvelous, quietly set away from the noise of Thames Street yet an extremely easy walk to several good restaurants. **Inn on Bellevue,** 30 Bellevue Ave., 401/848-6242 or 800/718-1446, website: www.innonbellevue.com, is one of Newport's great bargains, with a terrific location and small but funky rooms with a smattering of antiques. The least expensive rooms, which are

NEWPORT

TIME-SHARING IN NEWPORT

One option worth considering before you decide among the many hotels and inns in the area is a luxury time-share company called Equivest, a vast timeshare company based in Connecticut and publicly traded under its parent company Cendant; Equivest owns 28 resorts in more than 16 parts of the Eastern United States. One branch of the company is **Eastern Resorts Corporation,** 800/225-3522, www.eastern-resorts.com, which is based in Newport. The company operates four resorts right in the city of Newport, and two more across the bay in Jamestown, the **Bay Voyage Inn,** 150 Conanicus Ave., 401/423-2100 and **Newport Overlook,** 150 Bayview Dr., 401/423-1886. If you're seeking seclusion and a stunning setting with great views back toward Newport, Bay Voyage and Newport Overlook are great picks. In Newport, **Long Wharf Resort,** 115 Long Wharf, 401/847-7800, is one of the nicest luxury condo resorts in the Northeast, and its location on the harbor, just a block off Thames Street, makes it a highly sought-

after destination. A smaller property nearly next door, the **Inn on Long Wharf,** 142 Long Wharf, 401/847-7800, is also home to the very nice Long Wharf Steakhouse. **Inn on the Harbor** and **Newport Onshore,** 405 Thames St., 401/849-1500, are additional options farther down Thames.

There are big advantages to choosing any of these six properties over a conventional hotel or inn, especially if you visit Newport often or are traveling with a family or group of friends. First, the locations and settings of all of them are top-notch. The units themselves are contained within large rambling shingle buildings—in Newport they're mostly four- or five-story apartment buildings, while the Jamestown structures spread out more and feel a bit more house-like. There are studio, one-bedroom, two-bedroom, and three-bedroom properties available, and each property has a full slate of amenities, including pools, spas, exercise rooms, children's playgrounds, and the like. The units themselves are furnished with

---

tiny and share a bath, start at just $50 on summer weekdays. Other units have Jacuzzi tubs. This creaky old inn is right at the upper end of Bellevue, near where it meets Touro Street—you just can't find rooms this cheap in Newport at this location. As you might expect, the staff and the clientele tend to be young and outgoing, somewhat artsy and very laid-back. The colonial revival **Kitt Shepley House 1932,** 23 Division St., 401/848-0607 or 877/362-8664; website: www.kittshepleyhouse.com, is a reasonably priced 1930s B&B in the Historic Hill section of downtown. There are just two guest rooms in this cozy, easygoing inn, one of them a full suite with French Provincial decor and an tile bathroom with a whirlpool tub, and the other a standard room with a brass bed and hand-painted furniture.

$150–250

The **Cliffside Inn,** 2 Seaview Ave., 401/847-1811 or 800/845-1811, website: www.cliffsideinn.com, not to be confused with the more conspicuous Cliff Walk Manor nearby on Memo-

rial Boulevard, is one of the city's most distinctive inns. The Second Empire mansion was built in 1880 as the summer retreat of Maryland's governor Thomas Swann; it briefly served as the campus for St. George's School at the turn of the 20th century before the Turner family of Philadelphia bought it in 1907. Daughter Beatrice Turner lived here for some 40 years, becoming, posthumously, one of Newport's best-known artists—her works are famous in part because they were mostly only discovered following her death in 1948, when executors of her estate found the house crammed with some 3,000 paintings, about a third of them self-portraits—alas, all but about 100 of these were set on fire by her executors. The inn has 13 guest rooms, as well as three rooms in a more contemporary cottage across from the inn's front lawn and gardens—the latter building has *three* fireplaces in each of its three suites (there are a total of 17 fireplaces in the main mansion). Of the 100 surviving Turner works, virtually every one can be viewed in this inn—some are originals and others high-quality reproductions; you'll find them in guest rooms

tasteful, rather upscale contemporary resort furniture, and all have kitchens; the majority of them have water views, depending on the property, of course. These are not historic buildings, and some critics complain that they lack character. But they do make a lot of sense for the right traveler.

Eastern Resorts is in the business of selling shares of ownership in vacation resorts, not merely renting out hotel rooms. This is something you need to keep in mind before you consider staying at one of these properties. Time-share schemes came under a lot of criticism in the 1980s and 1990s because they often proved highly inflexible or impractical, and in some cases their owners were shady at best. Eastern Resorts is a legitimate and reputable company, but you will be hit with sales pitches if you stay at one of these properties, and that can be a turnoff for persons uninterested in actually buying into the time-share premise.

If you simply want to vacation in one of the six condos described below, you can expect to find

rates of about $135 to $300 per night in high season (May–October) for a one-bedroom unit to $425 to $600 per night for a three-bedroom unit. Off-season, the rates drop by as much as 50 percent. However, if you're willing to attend a 90-minute open-house presentation on buying a time-share condo, you can work out a very nice two-night vacation at one of the condo properties, plus a $30 dinner certificate, for about $30 total. This, of course, is pending availability and by advance reservation. If you actually buy a share in Newport, you're eligible to swap a week of your time there for a week at one of the other Equivest properties in New Orleans, St. Thomas (Virgin Islands), San Antonio, Branson (Missouri), Ocean City (Maryland), Williamsburg, the Berkshires, Myrtle Beach, St. Augustine, Atlantic Beach (North Carolina), or the Wisconsin Dells. Read the terms and program descriptions carefully, and you may just find that Equivest works for you; either way, it's worth considering as a vacation alternative.

and common areas. The antiques that fill this property are far more characterful than your usual hotel pieces; the Cliffside is noted for its estimable collection of Victorian beds, as well as many other fine collectibles. The guest rooms are also notable for their elaborate, and often huge, bathrooms; most of them have whirlpool baths, and four even have working fireplaces—the ultimate romantic touch. Afternoon tea and a quite stunning formal breakfast complete the experience of staying at this wonderful, luxurious small hotel. On a quiet residential street just off Bellevue Avenue, an easy walk either from the beginning of Cliff Walk or Easton's Beach, you'll find **Elm Tree Cottage,** 336 Gibbs Ave., 401/849-1610 or 888/ELM-TREE, website: www.elm-tree.com. This romantic property was an opulent summer home during Newport's Gilded Age. In 1882, William Ralph Emerson, a cousin of that famous Massachusetts Emerson, designed this mansion that incorporates both colonial revival and Queen Anne design elements. The present owners, Thomas and Priscilla Malone, are both professional artists—you

can see the stained glass of Thomas and watercolors by Priscilla in many parts of the house, and you can visit their artists' workshop in the basement. The six guest rooms contain a mix of family treasures and antiques culled mostly from estates in Newport, England, and France; one room has a working fireplace. Common areas include a 1930s pub with portholes whose interior is inspired by a classic yacht; the inn has no liquor license, but you're welcome to BYOB and mix drinks with the set-ups provided by the Malones. The full breakfasts here are among the best in town, served on fine china at individual tables in the large dining room.

Inns of Newport, 401/848-5300 or 800/524-1386, website: www.innsofnewport.com, is a consortium of five lavish inns: At the **Wynstone,** 232 Spring St., each of the five rooms has a TV and VCR, stereo-CD player, featherbed, fireplace, and two-person whirlpool tub. The decorating is exquisite and evocative of the city's Gilded Age: museum-quality antiques fill the rooms, as do custom-made fabrics and window treatments and elegant paintings and tapestries.

Bathrooms have marble tubs and vanities, separate marble showers, terrycloth robes, and high-quality sound systems. A full breakfast is served fireside in your guest room each morning. These inns define luxury in Newport. The convenient and prestigious location is another huge draw—the inn is along Spring Street, just a block from the harbor, on a quiet street just in from busy Memorial Boulevard. Dozens of restaurants and shops are within an easy stroll. The similarly luxurious **Clarkeston,** 28 Clarke St., is two blocks from the water—this exquisitely preserved 1705 colonial captures the charm of early Newport, with wide-plank floorboards and vintage antiques, but the house was restored top-to-bottom in 1993 and now contains guest rooms with such modern touches as whirlpool tubs and air-conditioning. The sleigh and canopy beds are supremely romantic. Across the street, the 12-room **Cleveland House,** 27 Clarke St., has a Victorian ambience that's more appropriate to its late-19th-century construction. The 300-year-old **Admiral Farragut Inn,** 31 Clarke St., carries on the elegant standards of this fine hotel group; its rooms contain Shaker-style four-poster beds and brightly painted and stenciled chests and armoires. In the authentic colonial keeping room, full breakfast is served. Lastly, the **Elm Street Inn,** 36 Elm St., is a favorite with families, because several of its suites sleep four. A stunning boutique property in the heart of downtown, the **Mill Street Inn,** 75 Mill St., 401/849-9500 or 800/392-1316, website: www.millstreetinn.com, occupies a 19th-century mill whose high ceilings, exposed brick walls and wood beams, and warm character have been nicely preserved. There are 23 suites, some with private decks that look out over downtown and the harbor; the upper-level townhouse suites have two floors. Continental breakfast, afternoon tea, and parking are included.

The recently christened **Adele Turner Inn,** 93 Pelham St., 401/847-1811 or 800/845-1811, website: www.adeleturnerinn.com, formerly known as the Admiral Benbow Inn, has received a top-to-bottom makeover since its reincarnation in 2001. The 13 rooms in this stately 1855 sea captain's mansion are filled with Victorian antiques and working fireplaces along with such modern amenities as TVs with VCRs (there's a large selection of videos and books on loan in the library), private phones, and in some cases two-person whirlpool tubs. Fabulous views of the harbor, just two blocks away, are had from the expansive rooftop sundeck. It's especially romantic to sit up here at night, looking down over quaint First Street, the nation's first gaslighted street. Full breakfast is served buffet-style; afternoon tea is also served daily. One of the most conveniently located small downtown properties, the **Black Duck Inn,** 29 Pelham St., 401/841-5548 or 800/206-5212, website: www.blackduckinn.com, looks across Thames Street toward Bowen's Wharf's myriad shops and restaurants—within a 15-minute walk are countless more opportunities to browse and nosh. The inn takes its name for an infamous rum-running ship that smuggled bootleg liquor into Newport Harbor during the late 1920s. The interior is on the frilly side, with floral fabrics and wallpaper borders. Most rooms have queen-size beds; there's also a two-bedroom suite that's nice for families or friends traveling together. Some units have hot tubs. With so many Newport inns looking and feeling roughly the same—nautical bric-a-brac, frilly fabrics—**Baldwin Place,** 41 Pelham St., 401/847-3801 or 888/860-3764, website: www.baldwinplaceinn.com, offers a nice change of pace. The inn is highly luxurious—the rooms in this decadent Second Empire Victorian have TV/VCRs and phones with voicemail, but the furnishings are Victorian through and through. Each room is named and themed for one of Newport's famous mansions. Leafy, ebullient gardens surround the house and make for a soothing respite on a warm day. There's a hot tub in one garden.

An elaborate, almost decadent Edwardian mansion oozing with character and run by friendly innkeepers Dennis Blair and Grant Edmondson, the **Hydrangea House Inn,** 16 Bellevue Ave., 800/945-4667, website: www.hydrangeahouse.com, sits near the beginning of Bellevue Avenue, just up the hill from the harborfront. The state house was built in 1876, and the lavish details of that period have been colorfully preserved. Among the more enticing units among the six guest rooms, the Hydrangea Suite has a king-size canopy bed, marble bath, double whirlpool tub with its own fireplace, Oriental rugs, steam bath, and cable TV with VCR—it's hard to think of a good reason ever to leave your room when you're surrounded by such plush amenities. Guests are treated to afternoon tea, chocolate-chip cookies before bed, and a Continental breakfast that's superior to most: eggs, raspberry pancakes, and home-baked breads are among the offerings. There's a sundeck on the third floor, and an enclosed balcony on the second. The inn offers a great Sunday-through-Wednesday special during the winter months, where you get your second night free. The young and enthusiastic innkeepers who run **La Farge Perry House,** 24 Kay St., 401/847-2223 or 877/736-1100, website: www.lafargeperry.com, have done a great job balancing a homey ambience with striking decor and furnishings. There are five spacious suites—the John La Farge contains convincing reproductions of paintings by the distinguished artist for whom it is named. The house is named for La Farge, who bought this capacious Victorian home in 1861 with his wife, Margaret Perry La Farge (granddaughter of the noted naval commander Oliver Hazard Perry). Bathed in whites and pale blues, the Honeymoon Suite has a bathroom with a double whirlpool tub. The dining-room walls are painted with a mural of Newport from the turn of the 20th-century, and deep armchairs and comfy seating fills the common areas. Depending on the season, iced tea or sherry is served during the afternoons in the formal parlor. The bright, sunny house is especially impressive when decked out with holiday decorations in December.

A pale blue four-story gambrel-roof inn just off Thames and near the Brick Market, **Inntowne Inn,** 6 Mary St., 401/846-9200 or 800/457-7803, website: www.inntowneinn.com, has a great, central location. Decor throughout the public areas and guest rooms is traditional, if a bit frilly—note the ample use of Oriental rugs, floral-upholstered armchairs and settees, canopied four-poster beds, and wicker chairs and bureaus. The condo suites in a nearby building are a favorite of families, as studios, one-bedroom, and two-bedroom units are available, and all have

cooking facilities. Amenities include a sundeck with great harbor views, plus a pool and health club. Included is Continental breakfast and afternoon tea.

For an opportunity to stay in one of the Point District's most delightful waterfront homes, consider the **Sarah Kendall House,** 47 Washington St., 401/846-7976 or 800/758-9578, website: www.sarahkendallhouse.com, an 1871 Second Empire house with a high, green turret and a porch full of comfy wicker chairs and lounges overlooking the harbor and Newport Bridge. Historic Hunter House is just a couple of doors down, and the location so near the southern end of the Point District puts many shops and eateries within a very easy stroll. Rooms—with polished hardwood floors and four-poster beds—are furnished with a tasteful restraint that's not always so apparent in Victorian mansions; many units have working fireplaces. From the sitting room lodged in the third-floor turret, terrific views are had of the water and Goat Island. Afternoon tea and full breakfast are provided. Another of the few lodgings in Newport's distinctive and historic Point District, the **Willows of Newport,** 8 Willow St., 401/846-5486, website: www.thewillowsofnewport.com, is perhaps most famous for its spectacular gardens, which have won several prestigious awards. The inn actually comprises a pair of historic townhouses, one a gambrel-roof colonial dating to 1740 and the other a Greek Revival dating to about 1840, their differing, adjacent rooflines creating a quirky effect. The six romantic rooms include hand-crafted canopy beds, fresh-cut flowers, and breakfast served in bed on bone china with silver service. Other details among the six rooms include fine Charisma bedding, some nonworking fireplaces, skylights, Oriental teak furniture in one room, and a stunning crystal chandelier in another. As you might guess, the Willows is a favorite of honeymooners.

Over $250

A sister property of the famed Cliffside Inn, the **Abigail Stoneman Inn,** 102 Touro St., 401/845-1811, website: www.abigailstonemaninn.com, occupies a grand Renaissance-style 1866 mansion on one of the city's most prominent streets.

Named for the woman who is credited with being Newport's first female entrepreneur and innkeeper, this inn is—like Cliffside and the company's other property, the Adele Turner—a slightly kooky and completely sumptuous hostelry. Among the unusual draws here: Original drawings by Victorian *Vanity Fair* author William Makepeace Thackeray; a bath menu of some 20 soaps, salts, and oils from 11 different nations; a pillow menu of some 17 types, from UltraFoam Deluxe to magnetic buckwheat hull to tri-down; and a complimentary water "pub" that features 15 kinds of bottled H2O, ranging from good old Perrier to Fiji Island artesian well water. The location is steps from Touro Synagogue and an easy walk from the harbor and Bellevue Avenue. As to the rooms, there are just five ornate bedchambers, all with high ceilings, TV/VCR/CD players, huge whirlpool tubs or steam showers, and decor from different eras. In the Vanity Fair suite, the furnishings are from 1865 through 1900, while the hip Above and Beyond contains pieces from the post–World War II period, from about 1947 to 1975. This last room is truly a showstopper—a six-room, third-floor suite with a magnificent paneled library, a media center with its own fireplace, a kitchen-dining room, and many other breathtaking features—there may not be a more memorable and romantic accommodation in Rhode Island than this suite, which rents for $525 per night, a hefty sum but really not much more than what you'd pay for a fairly ordinary room in an upscale hotel in Boston or New York City.

Carved out of a classic mansion, Newport's most elegant new property, **The Chanler,** 117 Memorial Blvd., 401/847-1300, www.thechanler.com, is set on a dramatic five-acre bluff with stunning ocean views. It's an easy walk down the hill to the beaches. Rooms are decorated individually in either Early American, French Provincial, Tudor, or Mediterranean designs. All units have fireplaces; many have in-room whirlpools and private outdoor hot tubs. Other amenities include two outdoor terraces and a top-notch restaurant.

Vanderbilt Hall, 41 Mary St., 401/846-6200 or 888/VAN-HALL, website: www.vanderbilthall .com, was built by the Vanderbilt family in 1909 as a gift to the citizens of Newport. After being used as the Newport Men's Social Club and later as headquarters for Doris Duke's Newport Restoration Foundation, it was turned into a luxury hotel in 1997. Today it ranks among the most regal accommodations in Rhode Island, and even if you don't stay here, consider attending one of the famously decadent afternoon teas (tea is complimentary for hotel guests). There are just 50 guest rooms, all of them decorated individually, and many with unusual touches like romantic sleeping lofts reached by spiral staircases. The old-world billiards room is a favorite spot to sip brandy and smoke a cigar, or play hearts with a few friends in the card room. There's also a clubby, white-glove Alva Restaurant, which is open to the public—you'll want to dress nicely here. There's nothing hip or trendy about this hotel, but if you want to feel like one of Newport's elite summer visitors of a century ago, Vanderbilt Hall is an excellent place to stay. The top suites cost more than $500 nightly.

A favorite of families or groups of friends seeking a luxurious, harborside accommodation that has full kitchens and plenty of legroom, the **Newport Bay Club and Hotel,** 337 Thames St., 401/849-8600, website: www.newportbayclub.com, may lack the history of some of the city's colonial and Victorian inns—on the other hand, it outshines the majority of them in terms of both amenities and water views. All things considered, the rates aren't bad either—starting at $349 on summer weekends, but with deep discounting for midweek stays, and staggered rates that drop to just $129 on some winter weekends. For this you get a unit that sleeps at least four (the one-bedroom suites have pull-out sofas) and as many as six, a marble bathroom with a Jacuzzi tub, a kitchenette with microwave (a few have stovetops), and a nice-size living room with a dining area. Many units overlook the water, and city-side rooms have great views of the activity along Thames Street. The bilevel two-bedroom townhouses have private decks on each floor. Furnishings are contemporary and attractive, if not all that more memorable than what you'd find at a typical, upscale chain property. Continental breakfast is included. One of Newport's undisputed class acts, the **Francis Malbone House,** 392 Thames St., 401/846-0392 or 800/846-0392, website: www.malbone.com, occupies a ravishing 1760 shipping merchant's mansion across the street from the harbor. This grand house, built by Peter Harrison (who also built the Rosewood Library and Touro Synagogue), contains 18 exquisitely furnished rooms with fine crown molding, period window treatments and fabrics, four-poster beds, Oriental rugs, and delicate colonial furniture. The walls are painted in bold colors. Many rooms have hot tubs and fireplaces. Afternoon tea and full breakfast are included in the rates. The staff is highly personable and well-trained, and yet the inn retains a surprisingly informal air. The owners also run the adjacent Benjamin Mason House, a 1750 stunner with a guest suite and guest room. Although its name suggests a doddering old seaside hotel with rickety floors and warped-glass windows, the **Harborside Inn,** Christie's Landing, Thames Street, 401/846-6600, website: www.historicinnsofnewport.com, is actually a rather new construction at Christie's Landing, smack in the heart of the city's festive waterfront. This deluxe all-suites property has spacious units with refrigerators, wet bars, sleeping lofts, and balconies. The same management company has several other inns in Newport, including the Yankee Peddler Inn on Touro Street, the Jailhouse Inn on Marlborough Street, and the Newport Gateway Hotel on West Main Road in Middletown. It's a disparate group of properties with a wide range of rates.

The **Hotel Viking,** 1 Bellevue Ave., 401/847-3300 or 800/556-7126, website: www.hotelviking.com, has undergone a major renovation, but it's hard to see where all the money went—it still feels dark, unimaginatively decorated, and a little too formal for an increasingly more casual town. Nevertheless, the massive top-to-bottom restoration in 2000 greatly improved the general appearance of this hulking historic hotel, which has a neat location equidistant from Broadway's hip eateries, Bellevue Avenue's mansions, and Spring Street's antiques shops. The 237 guest rooms, while nicely maintained, are rather dull, and a kitschy early-1960s addition to the hotel spoils its overall appearance. Public areas retain the glamour of yore, but somehow the Viking's overall effect is unintentionally retro. The hotel was built in 1926 and was one of New England's premier addresses for many years— it was commissioned by the owners of Bellevue Avenue's summer "cottages" as a place to put up guests and visitors. Furnishings are reproduction Queen Anne and Chippendale, but the rooms have all the modern trappings you'd expect of a luxury full-service hotel: TVs with in-room movies, climate control, hair dryers, irons and ironing boards, and phones with data ports. There's also a pool, health club, and sauna. The hotel's Bellevue Bar & Grille serves steaks, seafood, and other favorites. The rooftop bar is great fun, affording terrific views of downtown and the harbor—it's a fine place to meet up with friends or take a date. The **Hyatt Regency Newport,** 1 Goat Island, 401/851-1234 or 800/233-1234, website: www.newport.hyatt.com, is a pricey but nicely maintained option that occupies a terrific spot on Goat Island, with outstanding views back toward downtown and of the Point District in one direction and the Newport Bridge and Jamestown in the other. While there's nothing wrong with this luxury hotel and spa, rooms are disappointingly unexceptional given rates that start at $250 on weekends in summer. The staff is well-trained and professional, and the facilities are top-notch, but make sure you're going to use all these features before you spend the money to stay here. These facilities include a full-service spa with massage, facials, and treatments, plus an impressive fitness center, a tennis court, indoor and outdoor pools, two restaurants, and lots of meeting space—it's a popular site for conventions. The **Newport Marriott,** 25 America's Cup Ave., 401/849-1000 or 888/634-4498, website: www.newportmarriott.com, is a grand luxury hotel on the edge of downtown that's relatively new. Some rooms open onto a bright atrium and others face downtown or the harbor. It's very attractively furnished, but this is still a large (317-room) chain hotel, and it doesn't exactly ooze with character. Amenities abound, including an indoor pool, outdoor deck, and a full health club. There are also scads of meeting rooms; indeed, the Marriott is often packed with conventioneers.

ELSEWHERE IN NEWPORT

$100–150

The **Inn at Newport Beach,** Memorial Boulevard, 401/846-0310 or 800/786-0310, website: www.innatnb.com, is the best of the First Beach area properties—it's just across the street from the water and sand, and the staff is polite and well trained, the rooms decorated with attractive, upscale colonial-style furnishings, satiny-striped wallpaper, and the usual amenities: cable TV, phones, air-conditioning. Rooms are generally smaller than at newer properties in town, but they're no less attractive—and the rates are fair. There are 50 units, some of them suites with elegant sitting areas and others with two bedrooms. Rates vary considerably depending on room size and availability, but even in summer—during weekdays—you can sometimes find accommodations here for as little as $89 nightly. Included in the price is a substantial Continental breakfast. There's also a decent restaurant on premises.

$150–250

The extraordinarily sumptuous **Castle Hill Inn,** 590 Ocean Dr., 401/849-3800 or 888/466-1355, website: www.castlehillinn.com, enjoys one of Newport's most enchanting settings, perched on a grassy promontory jutting into the ocean, with outstanding views of Narragansett Bay. The small Castle Hill Lighthouse (ca. 1890) warns ships from the rocks nearby. Accommodations are in the main Agassiz Mansion, as well as three distinguished outbuildings. In the main building, the 1874 summer home of Harvard marine biologist Alexander Agassiz, there are 10 rooms, most of them quite large and all with well-chosen antiques—the sorts of pieces you might expect to find decorating one of the summer cottages along Bellevue Avenue. Typical features include bay views, CD players, custom marble whirlpool tubs, Oriental rugs, gas fireplaces, pitched ceilings, and stately beds with goosedown comforters and imported damask linens. It's easy to understand why these are some of the priciest rooms in Rhode Island, and yet the Castle Hill measures up where some other luxury properties don't quite. A small Gothic chalet-style building, once Agissiz's laboratory, now contains two handsome suites; about 100 yards from the mansion, down directly facing the water, are Castle Hill's eight more contemporary beach-house rooms; these lack the historic ambience of other units but are no less plush. Additionally, they contain galley kitchens, French doors opening onto water-view decks, full entertainment centers with VCRs, and double whirlpool cast-iron tubs. If it's seclusion by the sea rather than old-world style that you're seeking, these units make a superb choice. Lastly, just to the side of the mansion, a row of similarly contemporary harbor cottages sit on a short cliff over the water, and also measure up to the rest of the property's very high standards. An interesting bit of literary history: Thornton Wilder was a frequent guest of the Agassiz family and based portions of his book *Theophilus North* here.

JAMESTOWN, MIDDLETOWN, AND PORTSMOUTH

$50–100

Middletown isn't so agrarian these days, but the **Country Goose,** 563 Green End Ave., Middletown, 401/849-5384 or 877/25-GOOSE, website: www.countrygoosebnb.com, feels and looks like it could be a farmhouse in the sticks, save for its location on a slightly busy road. It's just a short ways east of Shadow Lawn, also an easy drive or even bike ride into downtown Newport or to the beaches. This striking white 1898 house with gingerbread trim sits on a large lawn with mature shade trees and colorful gardens. Rooms have high ceilings and contain a mix of family heirlooms and newer pieces; some have shared baths, others private. The 155-room **Howard Johnson Inn,** 351 W. Main Rd., Middletown, 401/849-2000 or 800/IGO-HOJO, website: www.hojo.com/middletown00467, has an indoor pool, sauna, and hot tub, refrigerators and microwaves in some units, and tennis courts; there's an Applebee's restaurant next door. The property is not as new or updated as some of the others in town, but rates are correspondingly a bit lower. Some pets are welcome.

The **Sea Whale,** 150 Aquidneck Ave., 401/846-7071 or 888/257-4096, website: www.sea-

© ANDREW COLLINS

beach cottages in Middletown

whale.com, looks a bit dreary from the exterior, but this 16-unit motel faces directly onto Easton Pond (white chaise longues sit out back on the lawn overlooking the water). Rooms are basic but well kept and those on upper level have balconies; all of them face the pond. All have cable TV, refrigerators, hairdryers, phones (with free local calls), and plenty of parking. It's a 10-minute walk to Easton's Beach, and you really can't beat the price for this location. With among the lowest rates of any chain motel in the area, the **Travelodge Middletown,** 1185 W. Main Rd., Middletown, 401/849-4700, website: www.travelodge.com, is a basic, no-frills property with simple rooms—perfect if you're not going to spend much time back at the hotel.

An outstanding value and a big hit with families, the **Seaview Inn,** 240 Aquidneck Ave., 401/846-5000 or 800/495-2046, website: www.seaviewnewport.com, is set on a hill a short way from the ocean—it's a long walk to the beach but a short drive, and bikes are available free to guests (along with kites and board games). All of the 40 rooms, especially on the upper floors, have unobstructed views out over Easton Pond, the Route 138A causeway, and the ocean beyond that; each has two double beds or a king, cable TV, a phone, and air-conditioning. The management takes exceptionally good care of this property—all units are fully modernized and meticulously kept. Adiron-

dack chairs dot the large lawn; the views of the Abbey at St. George's are a reminder how popular this place can be with parents of those prep school kids. Rates begin at an amazingly low $69 on weekdays in season. Continental breakfast is included (served in a light-filled coffeeshop rather than the usual lobby that's common in many motels), and guests have free use of a pool and health club next door. You really won't find a better deal in this area, which means that the hotel books up fast in high season, so reserve early.

$100–150

The **Holiday Inn Express,** 855 W. Main Rd., 401/848-7128 or 800/333-4121, website: www.hiexpress.com/middletownri, behind Chili's, is one of the better chain properties in Middletown. This 98-room low-rise has an indoor heated pool, exercise room, sundeck, guest laundry, and a small business center. A Continental breakfast buffet is included in the rate. Rates usually start a bit lower than those at the **Ramada Inn Newport,** 936 W. Main Rd., Middletown, 401/846-7600 or 800/846-8322, website: www.newenglandramadas.com. Though it occupies a busy and charmless stretch of road, this property has well-maintained rooms, all with refrigerators, microwaves, irons and boards, coffeemakers, hairdryers, voicemail, and other helpful touches; there's also a guest laundry. You'll find a casual full-service restaurant on-site with darts and pool tables, a game room with Ping-Pong and video games, and a very nice gym and indoor pool. All the extra amenities and common areas make it a popular choice for families. The **Newport Courtyard Marriott,** 9 Commerce Dr., Middletown, 401/849-8000 or 888/686-5067, website: www.courtyard.com, is another reliable chain property a few miles north of downtown Newport. There are 130 rooms and 10 suites, plus an indoor/outdoor pool, hot tub, a small gym, and a laundry room; Continental breakfast is included.

Rhea's Inn by the Sea, 42 Aquidneck Ave., Middletown, 401/849-3548, website: www.rheasinn.com, occupies a three-story cedar-shake building that's just a five-minute stroll from Easton's Beach. Although it's in the style of the old beach houses of yore, Rhea's is contemporary through and through, and all the motel-style furnishings feel new. There are nine rooms with private baths, air-conditioning, cable TV, and phones—all the basics. Two of the rooms have separate living areas, and some have whirlpool tubs. There's a common area on each floor. This is a reliable, economical option. Most of Middletown is dominated by hotels and fairly traditional, if unspectacular properties, but the stately **Inn at Shadow Lawn,** 120 Miantonomi Ave., Middletown, 401/847-0902 or 800/352-3750, website: www.shadowlawn, is a notable exception. Because it's not right in the heart of Newport, the rates here are a little lower than what you'd pay for comparable accommodations down near Thames Street; in fact, Shadow Lawn isn't far from either the beaches or downtown, located in an attractive residential neighborhood near the northern end of Easton Pond. Guests at this hybrid Italianate-stick Victorian can choose from among eight rooms and suites, each named for a noted woman of Victorian letters, such as George Eliot or Charlotte Brontë. Four-poster beds, working fireplaces, hardwood floors, and elegant but not frilly antiques are typical of these rooms, which also have modern touches like TVs and VCRs, refrigerators, hairdryers, and irons with ironing boards. The amenities and

ambience strike a nice balance between luxury hotel and atmospheric B&B. Architect Richard Upjohn, who also built Bellevue Avenue's Kingscote, designed this masterful house in 1853.

$150–250

The three-story, clapboard **Best Western Atlantic Beach Hotel,** 34 Wave Ave., Middletown, 401/847-5330 or 800/528-1234, website: www.bestwestern.com, is an attractive hotel with an inviting, warm color scheme and an appealingly beachy look. The ocean is practically across the street, and many rooms have views. Although it's technically outside of Newport, this attractive and recently built Best Western is just steps from the town line, and it's extremely close to area beaches. Among the units, there are 43 mini-suites with two phones, large work desks, microwaves, refrigerators, and coffeemakers, plus separate sitting areas. The staff can be a little rushed and cursory. Rates are not cheap here, and often rise to above $150 in the heart of tourist season, but cheaper deals can be had depending on availability.

The **Sea Breeze Inn,** 147 Aquidneck Ave., Middletown, 401/849-1211 or 877/227-8400, website: www.theseabreezeinn.com, is a small Mediterranean-style hotel with a small restaurant on premises. The six rooms have floral-upholstered bedding, marble-floor bathrooms, the usual amenities (cable TV, air-conditioning, free local calls), plus decks, some of which overlook the ocean and others Easton Pond. A full breakfast is included. The owners also rent two apartments (a one-bedroom and a two-bedroom), as well as a three-bedroom house—rates range from $1,200 to $2,400 per week in season. It's an attractive place, not fancy, but the decor is cheerier than some of the more prosaic motels along this stretch (of course, the rates are also quite a bit higher). On a busy stretch of Route 138, the tan-brick **Royal Plaza Hotel,** 425 E. Main Rd. (Rte. 138), 401/846-3555 or 800/825-7072, website: www.royalplazahotel.com, looks vaguely like a condo complex. Rooms are well kept, reasonably large, and clean and comfortable, but there no views and it's a (fairly short) drive from the beaches.

Food

For many years, really until quite recently, it was difficult to find innovative cuisine in Newport. That's not to say that there weren't plenty of terrific restaurants, but that fairly traditional seafooders, steak and chops houses, and natty old dining rooms serving haute Continental and French cuisine were the rule. In the early 1990s, a few restaurants started experimenting with more interesting fare, and over the past few years several places serving highly creative regional American and globally influenced cooking have opened. Of course, it's still extremely easy to get a traditional fried clam dinner or a juicy steak in Newport. It's just that now you have quite a few creative alternatives, too. What's still lacking is a decent selection of ethnic restaurants, especially Asian ones—with so many good ones in Providence, it's hard to see why these kinds of places have so far resisted Newport. Fortunately, a great sushi restaurant opened on Thames Street in 2000, and an innovative, organic Pan-Asian eatery opened on Broadway soon after.

The island has pretty much the usual gamut of chain restaurants, both regional and national, although few of these are found right in downtown Newport itself. If you want to go this avenue, venture out along Route 138 just north of town to where it intersects with Route 114; in these parts you'll find IHOP, Newport Creamery (which, because it's local, is reviewed farther down in this section), Burger King, Taco Bell, KFC, and the usual standbys.

Keep in mind that the vast majority of Newport's high-end, formal restaurants have taverns or pubs attached that serve less-pricey food and demand much less fancy attire.

NEWPORT

Upscale

The **White Horse Tavern,** 26 Marlborough St., 401/849-3600 ($28–38), is said to be the oldest still-running tavern in the United States, having opened in the 1687. In its early years, representa-tives from the nearby Rhode Island Assembly often met here for food and conversation. The building itself dates to 1673 but was a private residence early on. It was a boardinghouse during the first half of the 20th century, but preservationists took over in 1954 and restored it to its present appearance. The red, gambrel-roofed building is one of the city's most dramatic-looking historic buildings. The kitchen turns out superb, lavish fare—specialties include an appetizer of Maine lobster and gulf shrimp stacked high with crispy wontons, roasted corn salsa, and a citrus-thyme vinaigrette. Mainstays from the entrée list include seared yellowfin tuna and Hudson Valley foie gras, with crispy-potato and caramelized-onion rosti, finished with a red wine and wild-mushroom sauce; and Angus-beef filet mignon char-grilled with a caraway potato cake, sautéed Swiss chard, and cranberry marmalade, with a rosemary-wine sauce. Sunday brunch here is a local tradition. The poached eggs over lobster crab cakes are to die for—they're served with a roasted-garlic gazpacho sauce. **La Petite Auberge,** 19 Charles St., 401/849-6669 ($23–35; $11–18 in the bistro), occupies a 1714 house that's warmly lighted and wonderfully atmospheric. A lighter menu is offered in a more laid-back side café. This little restaurant has chugged along rather quietly since it opened in the mid-1970s, presenting first-rate classic French fare in a formal setting (men are asked to wear jackets but not required to wear ties). In winter the dining rooms are warmed by the roar of a fireplace, during the warmer months there's dining on an enchanting patio, and any time of year it's a supremely romantic setting for a special meal. The kitchen here does not stray at all from tradition—try frogs' legs in garlic butter, country pâté, or rack of lamb in a heavenly tarragon sauce. Presentation here is of the utmost importance, as servers bring food to your table in copper pots and pans and serve everything with great fanfare. A great find here is the small bistro-and-bar off in a side room, where you can sample the same high-quality cooking in smaller portions,

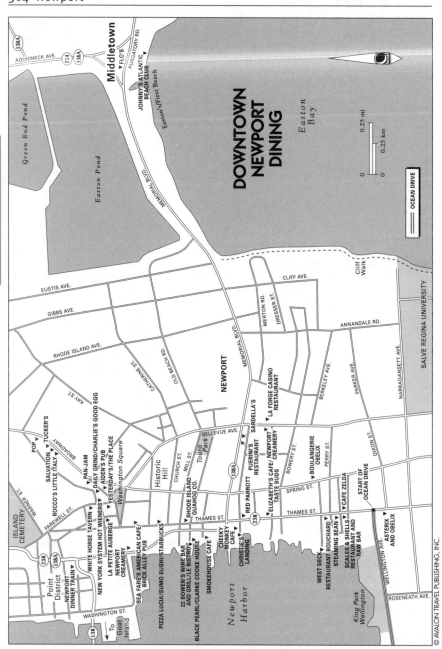

NEWPORT

DOWNTOWN
NEWPORT
DINING

OCEAN DRIVE

© AVALON TRAVEL PUBLISHING, INC.

with informal dress, and at a fraction of the cost. One of the city's definitive dress-up spots, **Le Bistro,** 41 Historic Bowen's Wharf, 401/849-7778 ($18–30), specializes in rich seafood, choice Angus steaks, and other rather elaborate Continental grills. It's won countless culinary and wine awards, and the views of Newport Harbor make it a favorite place for special occasions. Service is superb, refined, and always right on the nose. Refined, traditional French food is served at the slightly formal and inviting **Restaurant Bouchard,** 505 Thames St., 401/846-0123 ($18–26), which occupies the ground floor of a small B&B. Fine china and crystal and deft service set the tone for such rarefied French fare as sliced tender lamb with red wine and a hint of curry sauce, roasted duck with currants, sautéed chicken breast with a creamy morel-mushroom sauce, and wild mushroom ravioli with a balsamic–walnut oil vinaigrette.

The **Castle Hill Inn,** 590 Ocean Ave., 401/849-3800 ($25–38), apart from owning one of the most dramatic locations in the city, serves stellar regional American fare. Consider a starter of pulled-pork tamales with aged cheddar, smoked papaya salsa, and New Mexico red chile purée, followed by skillet-roasted spiced pork medallions with fried-potato wedges, braised summer greens, gorgonzola aioli, and sweet-and-sour peach glaze. A favorite finisher is the Godiva chocolate soufflé with caramel crème anglaise, sugared berries, and biscotti. There are several dining rooms, all with large windows, and from many tables you'll enjoy a view over Narragansett Bay. For this reason, a number of people prefer dining here during the day, either for lunch or for the decadent Sunday brunch buffet. In the evening, when water views aren't such a draw, you might opt to dine in the main Castle Hill Room, which once served as the formal drawing room of this magnificent mansion by the sea. Flash back to the 1950s and you'll appreciate the appeal of **La Forge Casino Restaurant,** 186 Bellevue Ave.,

> *Flash back to the 1950s and you'll appreciate the appeal of La Forge Casino Restaurant, a supper club known for classic Continental fare—appropriate for the restaurant at the vaunted Newport Casino, one of McKim, Mead, and White's most distinguished works.*

401/847-0418 ($17–29; $7–14 in the pub), a supper club kind of spot known for its classic Continental fare. To really live it up, order the chateaubriand for two with wine, a complete meal for $53 that includes flame-grilled center-cut beef tenderloin carved tableside with baked stuffed potato, stuffed tomato Florentine, fresh vegetables, and béarnaise sauce (plus a half-liter of house wine). With all the new eateries cropping up throughout the state, serving trendy and sometimes bizarre fusions of this and that, it's refreshing to see a restaurant that refuses to depart from ancient (by culinary standards) traditions. And this is an appropriate style of cuisine for the restaurant at the vaunted Newport Casino, one of McKim, Mead, and White's most distinguished works of architecture. The casino also has a much less formal Irish pub, where you can sample oysters Kinsale (baked in the half shell with blue cheese and potato stuffing), club sandwiches, fish and chips, and the like.

The **Black Pearl,** Bannister's Wharf, Pelham Street off Thames Street, 401/846-5264 ($16–26, $6–19 in the tavern), has been a Newport institution since the 1960s, only back then it was little more than a pub serving the most casual seafood food to a fairly rowdy crowd. Now it's two restaurants in one, as are so many along the wharves off Thames Street—in one, the Commodore's Room, you'll find a menu of pricey, rather unimaginative American food, and in the tavern there's a fairly simple seafood menu that's remarkably true to the restaurant's roots. The ambience in both spaces is wonderfully festive and warm, although a jacket is requested at dinner in the Commodore's Room. Wherever you dine at the Black Pearl, consider ordering the clam chowder if you're a fan of this dish—nobody in Newport does it better. In the main dining room, starters like pear-and-Roquefort salad and oysters on the half shell effectively tempt the palate. Salmon with mustard-dill hollandaise sauce and filet mignon are longtime entrée favorites. **Clarke Cooke House,** Bannister's Wharf, 401/849-2900, website: www.bannisterswharf.com, consists of two restaurants; the Porch ($23–30) is the more formal of the two, set high overlooking Newport Harbor. Down at wharf level, the Candy Store ($9–23) is much more casual both in cuisine and style. Some locals have grumbled in recent years that the Porch is resting on its laurels, but the kitchen seems to have responded to these complaints and heavily revamped its menu. Today's French-inspired menu might offer pan-seared breast of squab with a roasted-corn pancake, foie gras, and black mission figs in a phyllo pastry, followed by roast rack of lamb with caramelized onion, potato-turnip gratin, and a minted tarragon glaze. Down in the Candy Store, which is open for lunch, Sunday brunch, and dinner, signature dishes include steak au poivre with a brandy-madeira brown sauce and Mediterranean fish stew, but you can also order simpler burgers, light pastas, and creative salads. **22 Bowen's Wine Bar and Grille,** 22 Bowen's Wharf, 401/841-8884 ($18–36), is a hot spot that offers a new take on the old seafood-and-chops theme. You can also order fresh seafood from the excellent raw bar. This is a pricey option, but the city's many young movers and shakers seem all too willing to pay for 24-ounce Porterhouse steaks, grilled tuna steaks, and broiled lobster. Each entrée comes with a choice of sauce, which could include green-peppercorn mustard, Maytag blue cheese butter, shallot-and-dill butter, horseradish cream, and several others. Additional house specialties include broiled scallops with shallots, lemon, parsley, sherry, and seasoned bread crumbs; and grilled pork tenderloin with apricot-sausage stuffing and rosemary-garlic jus. The dining room, with its pitched ceiling and timber beams, has rows of tall windows overlooking the harbor.

The **Newport Dinner Train** departs from 19 America's Cup Ave., 401/841-8700 or 800/398-7427, website: www.newportdinnertrain.com. The line presents a number of theme excursions, including wine-tasting and murder mysteries. On Saturday mornings, kids are invited for a tour on the Musical Magical Train, a 90-minute journey with sing-alongs, games, and entertainment by a musician. Dinner rides last 2.5 hours and run along 22 miles of track, looking out at Narragansett Bay most of the way. Both lunch and dinner rides are available, and the food is better than you might expect, given the logistics of preparing high-quality cuisine onboard a train. The menu is limited to just three or four entrée choices: hickory-smoked baby back ribs, baked stuffed fillet of sole, and chicken Vanderbilt (boneless breast of chicken layered with prosciutto, sundried tomatoes, spinach, and provolone, and then finished with a tomato-basil cream). A vegetarian option is also offered, but only by advance reservation. These meals come with a salad, fresh vegetable side, dinner rolls, potatoes or rice, a dessert, and coffee or tea. But you really don't make one of these journeys for the culinary experience so much as to relax and take in the phenomenal views. The costs vary according to the theme, but a typical dinner ride runs about $45 to $55 per person; package deals that include overnight accommodations at Middletown's Ramada Inn are also available.

Creative but Casual

It's touristy, and it can take a little effort to score a table, but **Christie's Landing,** off Thames Street, 401/847-5400 ($18–25), is the quintessential Newport harborfront restaurant, especially in summer when tables are arranged along a huge wharf jutting into the water, surrounded by yachts and sailboats. At this very dock a number of America's Cup celebrations have taken place, and on any given night in summer, you'll see scads of seafaring types dining here. The restaurant has been a city fixture since 1945—the food is traditional, but the preparations consistently good. Consider fried clam roll, lobster salad, Narragansett seafood pie (shrimp, sole, scallops, and lobster smothered with a rich seafood dill sauce in a pie crust), broiled salmon, chateaubriand for two, or maple-roasted duck. Inexpensive, lighter fare is served in Christie's pub. Less well-known, and therefore less touristy, than some of the other eateries facing Newport Harbor, the **West Deck,** 1 Waites Wharf, 401/847-3610 ($18–28), prepares some of the best and most creative fare in town. Broiled cod marinated in miso sauce over soba noodles with mustard oil shows some of the Pacific Rim influences on this kitchen helmed ably by chefs James Mitchell and Michael Cheney; chef's cut chicken grilled and simmered in a banana-mango curry reveal some Latin American kick. There are also several nouvelle takes on steak, chops, and lobster, plus a long and creative list of appetizers and salads. The ambience is easygoing here, and the staff friendly and knowledgeable.

Always-bustling **Yesterday's/The Place,** 28 Washington Square, 401/847-0116 ($20–30 in dining room, $6–9 in pub), sounds, smells, and looks like a festive tavern—the main room is filled with revelers, has a long bar and a tile floor, and is usually noisy to nearly a fault. But off to one side you'll find a smaller wine bar and dining room called The Place that turns out pricey but first-rate globally inspired fare like Thai lobster "martini" with a vermicelli-noodle stir, seafood Napoleon with coconut/lemongrass broth, and rack of lamb with a pecan-mustard crust with fennel and apples. Refined though the fancier part is, nowhere at Yesterday's will you encounter attitude or stuffiness—and plenty of folks dine in the more formal section and guzzle in the other. The food in the pub, though simple, is commendable also: try the house salad with apple, walnuts, and feta over seasonal greens, or the grilled yellowfin sandwich with wasabi mayo and sliced fresh tomatoes. **Sea Fare's American Cafe,** Brick Market Place, 401/849-9188 ($13–19), presents an eclectic and surprisingly affordable menu of creative American cooking. Several small plates are offered, such as a chorizo-and-goat-cheese quesadilla with tomatillo sauce, and roasted lobster with a corn-and-red-pepper salsa and cornmeal pancakes. Top entrée picks include roast cod over stewed white beans, and rack of lamb with mint risotto. The same chef-owner runs the Sea Fare Inn in Middletown.

The **Cheeky Monkey Cafe,** 14 Perry Mill Wharf, 401/845-9494 ($18–31), is one of the more innovative restaurants in Newport, with humorous monkey paintings on the walls and a clever, whimsical menu of world-beat cooking. Fave dishes include Thai-style codfish cakes with a curry-lobster cream and Asian-style cole slaw, followed by braised-beef short ribs served with shiitake-mushroom bread pudding and smothered savoy cabbage. The kitchen has been accused of being a bit gimmicky and flashy—but not many people leave here unhappy with the quality and quantity of cooking. Desserts are simply stunning, from the butterscotch crème brulée to the rich bananas Foster. The dining room—with high ceilings, tall windows, and hard-wood floors—is slick and contemporary; it can get pretty noisy in here, but the high level of festivity is part of the draw. The bar is hugely popular, and plenty of patrons come just to clink martini glasses and check out the stylish crowd. The same owners run the acclaimed Gatehouse in Providence. **Cafe Zelda,** 528 Thames St., 401/849-4002 ($15–22), has two identities—on one side it's an informal and always-packed pub; on the other side you'll find a dark, romantic, and festive space that's more appropriate for a full meal. You can order from the same menu on either side. The food tends toward hearty and robust, with specialties including balsamic-roasted half chicken with herb gnocchi, and filet mignon with port wine gorgonzola. Either space can get loud, which makes it a pretty fun spot to hang out with friends. There's a significant wine cellar here. Step off busy Thames Street into **Elizabeth's Cafe,** 404 Thames St., 401/846-6862 ($18–24), a fascinating little nest of fresh flower arrangements, bric-a-brac, dark floral tapestries, and chatty diners smiling over the remarkably tasty food and no-attitude service. Elizabeth's doesn't conform to many restaurant rules in Newport: it's BYOB, the menu and decor borrows heavily from Wales, the hours tend to change according to the whim of the owners (and market demand), and entrées are served on massive serving plates for two. Owner Elizabeth Burley, a film producer and top-notch chef, presides over the kitchen and is responsible for such signature dishes as bouillabaisse with scallops, shrimp, mussels, and steamers sautéed in a lobster-sherry cream, browned with mozzarella cheese, and served inside a bowl of fresh sourdough bread accompanied by sausage, peppers, onions, mushrooms and such. When it's in season, lobster paella is another must-try experience.

NEWPORT

A trendy yet understated seafooder on Lower Thames, **Scales & Shells Restaurant and Raw Bar,** 527 Thames St., 401/846-FISH ($12–21), prepares simple, fresh fish and shellfish in an austere yet handsome dining room—just a few mounted fish on the walls decorate this airy room with hardwood floors. The simply prepared, outstanding fish can be ordered mesquite-grilled, broiled, or with a couple of other straightforward treatments—monkfish, bluefish, and tuna are among the possibilities. Also consider the clam pizza. The lobster fra diavolo for two is a signature dish and a real favorite. One of Newport's true stand-out dining experiences, **Asterix & Obelix,** 599 Thames St., 401/841-8833 ($20–28), occupies an old service station on Lower Thames—the pair of glass garage doors now act as enormous windows for the front of the dining room. Exposed air ducts, an unfinished floor, and an open kitchen create the feel of a little food theater, where the entertainment lies as much in watching the chefs at work as it does in dining on their always delicious creations. The food here is not overly complicated or stylized, just good, and the menu always offers plenty of specials. House specialties include a lobster salad starter that can easily work as a meal, rare tuna with a green peppercorn sauce, bouillabaisse, and classic moules et frites (mussels steamed and served with fries, Belgian style). There's a long bar on the left where you can dine or sip cocktails or wines by the glass (the wine list is extensive). Asterix & Obelix is self-assured without being stuffy, handsome without feeling formal. The crowd is good-looking and chatty, and you'll feel at ease here whether dressed to the nines or clad in jeans and a tucked-in shirt.

Puerini's Restaurant, 24 Memorial Blvd. W., 401/847-5506 ($11–19), is a great local spot for outstanding Italian food, in both classic and innovative preparations. This attractive space is set up a little from busy Thames Street, away from the madding crowds. Reservations are not accepted, which can translate to a wait on weekends. Another locals' favorite for Italian, **Sardella's,** 30 Memorial Blvd. W., 401/849-6312 ($14–20), is right next to Puerini's and favors a more Southern Italian menu. Chicken marsala, eggplant parmigiana, grilled New York steak with roasted-garlic butter, pasta Bolognese, and gnocchi with sweet Italian sausage, cherry peppers, and plum tomatoes are recommended dishes. In warm weather there's dining on the patio overlooking the garden.

With a stylish young chef who describes herself as a "Gen-X Martha Stewart," **Salvation,** 140 Broadway, 401/847-2620 ($8–14), the eclectic (verging on pan-Asian) fare sometimes dazzles, sometimes comforts, but always piques one's curiosity, and appetizers are especially fun. Consider the sweet-potato shrimp cakes with a coconut-lime dipping sauce, the pumpkin ravioli tossed in cinnamon sage butter and freshly shaved asiago, or the Kama Sutra Platter of pork vindaloo, chickpea masala, cucumber riata, and garlic naan. Cocktails are a big to-do at this spot, which stays open to 11 most evenings and draws a young, hip crowd. This is truly Newport's oddest, hippest, and happiest little bistro—a Pan-Asian–eclectic fun house decked in feather boas, a giant retro Gulf gas station sign, lime walls, a gilt-framed painting of a pink flamingo, and all sorts of other curiosities. Another of Broadway's wonderfully offbeat restaurants, **Tucker's,** 150 Broadway, 401/846-3449 ($15–22), contains a pair of narrow dining rooms with ruby red walls, elaborate chandeliers of several shapes and sizes, gilt mirrors, and—from the tableware to the water glasses—mismatched everything. It feels like a Victorian salon—oil paintings, which are for sale, line the walls, and soft music ranging from Billie Holiday to Verdi operas plays in the background. The decadent, flavorful food matches the ambience—you might sample orange-ancho-glazed pork chops or shepherd's pie layered with sweet corn and mashed potatoes; Thai shrimp nachos are an arresting appetizer. Or knock back a stein of Newport Storm beer while noshing on steamed mussels on a cold winter evening. Homemade Bailey's is another specialty of the bar. For dessert consider white chocolate, dried cherry, and pecan bread pudding.

Broadway's latest hot spot is **Pop,** 162 Broadway, 401/846-8456 ($4-15), a swank lounge with mod furnishings and a terrific menu of small plates and tapas. Baked shrimp with roasted garlic aioli and wood-grilled sausage with four-cheese polenta are stand-outs. Plenty of devotees come simply for the ambience, glowing fireplace, and sophisticated cocktails.

Pizzas, Pastas, Seafood, and Pub Grub

If you're craving barbecue, head to the **Smokehouse Cafe,** at the Mooring, Sayer's Wharf, 401/846-2260 ($7–17), which serves a delicious smoked Cajun catfish sandwich, and another piled high with jerk calamari steak. Other specialties include St. Louis–style pork ribs, jumbo gulf shrimp with a chile marinade, and grilled salmon with sesame-ginger sauce. The smoked corn and crab chowder is another favorite. The dining rooms overlook the harbor, and there's an expansive waterfront patio, too. **Rhode Island Quahog Co.,** 250 Thames St., 401/848-2520 ($10–20), operates with a sort of gimmicky theme, serving just about anything you can imagine with clams in it—if you stick to these dishes you'll probably come away with a pretty decent meal. Portions are enormous, too, so you won't leave hungry. Steamers, clam cakes, chowder, baked cod, and all the usual seafood standards are offered, plus some inventive specials like pan-seared red snapper with lobster and gauva sauces. The cavernous dining room with cream walls and royal blue napery is also the site of live music many nights; in warm weather, grab a seat on the attractive, tiled terrace overlooking the activity on Thames Street.

A favorite hangout all summer of college students as well as quite a few tourists, the **Red Parrot,** 348 Thames St., 401/847-3800 ($7–14), is a rambling restaurant with large open windows that face out over Thames Street and across the way to Perry Mill Market— ceiling fans whir overhead, as friends fill up here on booze and comfort food. Specialties include Jamaican jerk chicken, Oreo mud pie, lobster pizzas, mussels, fajitas, and big colorful frozen drinks that fall on the brash side. There's nothing especially subtle about this place, but

there's no denying that it's good fun. It looks, feels, and actually smells like one of those old-world Italian restaurants on Federal Hill, and sure enough, **Pizza Lucia,** 190B Thames St., 401/847-6355 ($6–10 for small pies), turns out some of the best pies you'll ever taste. This simple BYOB space that's as popular for take-out as for dining in prepares a superb white pizza with mascarpone, mozzarella, fontina, provolone, onion, and roasted sweet peppers, plus a memorable eggplant parmigiana version. The real house specialty, however, is the artery-clogging *crescentina,* a stuffed and fried pizza with Northern Italian lineage. Order it stuffed with pepperoni and provolone, or perhaps with romano beans, a spicy tomato sauce, and herbs. Antipasto salads and a few vegetable sides are also available.

Aidan's Pub, 1 Broadway, 401/845-9311 ($5–11) (also in Bristol) is a highly authentic rendering of an Irish pub, with wide-plank floors, candles glowing on every table, a wood-burning stove, and elegant wood paneling. On quirky Broadway, the pub draws some tourists but many more regulars who appreciate the friendly service and reliable food. Hefty burgers (the Limerick serves Irish bacon and cheese), fish and chips, pot pies, and bangers and mash round out the menu. **Brick Alley Pub & Restaurant,** 140 Thames St., 401/849-6334 ($6–16), has long been a reliable, if usually quite crowded, standby for tasty comfort fare. The long menu includes Cajun catfish, broiled chicken and artichoke sandwiches, bacon burgers, spinach fettuccine, and sole Veracruz. The staff is friendly and fun, the crowd lively and loud. This is not a place for a quiet evening. A long-time Broadway fave, **Rocco's Little Italy,** 124 Broadway, 401/848-4556 ($5–15, large pies $9–15), is a modest BYOB hangout that offers a nice range of grinders, pastas, a few grills, stuffed pizzas, calzones, and traditional New York pies. The buffalo chicken and shrimp-and-clams versions are both well regarded.

Ethnic Fare

Good Asian and other ethnic fare has been slow to come to this decidedly traditional New

England town, but in fall 2001, the funky Broadway neighborhood became home to **Pan-Jam,** 22 Broadway, 401/841-0700 ($12–22), a cutting-edge source of delicious Pan-Asian, mostly organic, and extremely healthful cooking. The menu borrows from cultures all over the planet, but there's an emphasis on ingredients from Japan, Thailand, and China. You might kick things off with mussels in a coconut curry broth with lemongrass, ginger, and cilantro. Several hefty and fresh salads are offered, including wasabi salmon over mixed greens. More substantial fare includes the Sichuan tofu bowl with veggies and brown rice, lobster braised in a chili-lime broth with steamed bok choy, and grilled lemongrass chicken with a sweet-and-sour dipping sauce. The colorful, sleek restaurant shares a space with the Area 22 nightclub. Sushi fanatics converge on **Sumo Sushi,** 198 Thames St., 401/848-2307 ($10–25), for exquisite Japanese food, plus several Korean dishes and stews. Korean barbecue is one classic dish, as is spicy kimchee stew with beef, pork, vegetables, and tofu. Several Japanese teriyaki grills are also offered. From the sushi side of the menu, maki rolls include spicy scallop, salmon skin and cucumber, pickled radish, and more than a dozen others. The sedate, warmly furnished dining room is a calm alternative to some of Thames Street's busier restaurants.

Quick Bites

The local chain **Newport Creamery,** 181 Bellevue Ave., 401/846-6332; also 49 Long Wharf Mall, 401/849-8469; and in Middletown at 208 W. Main Rd., 401/846-2767 ($4–8), is often compared with the larger Massachusetts-based Friendly's Ice Cream chain. It's a cheap and cheerful option for light diner-style food, including seasoned French fries, club sandwiches, turkey-and-Swiss melts, burgers, chicken fajita wraps, fried clam dinners, and an extensive selection of breakfast foods. Of course, the big draw is ice cream—there's a long dessert menu of sundaes and Awful Awfuls, those thick shakes that Rhode Islanders seem completely addicted to. The owners of Asterix & Obelix

have opened **Boulangerie Obelix,** 382 Spring St., 401/846-3377, a wonderful option for light sandwiches, chocolate croissants and heavenly French pastries, and other snacks. You can dine in this cozy space with exposed beams and a few café tables, or grab a meal to go with you to the beach or on a bike ride. Dozens of artesan breads are offered, and the Belgian chocolate–chip cookies are to die for. If you're a fan of the main restaurant down on Thames Street, you shouldn't miss this.

Down-home **Charlie's Good Egg,** 12 Broadway, 401/849-7817 (under $8), is a downright downcast diner that serves excellent breakfast food all day along, including about 10 kinds of pancakes (chocolate chip, banana, raisin, etc.). Omelets are the specialty, as well as several kinds of French toast. Sandwiches and pastas are served later in the day. The no-frills space is packed with old photos and mismatched furnishings that seem culled from garage sales. Newport has its own famous hot dog purveyor, just like virtually every other town in Rhode Island. **New York System Hot Wieners,** 1 Farewell St., 401/846-9501 (under $5), keeps late hours (it's open to 2 A.M. on weekends), making it a popular choice after barhopping. The dogs here are made of blended and seasoned beef, veal, and pork, topped with a Greek-style sauce, onions, and celery salt. Sausage-and-pepper subs, meatloaf sandwiches, fried chicken dinners, shepherd's pie, fries-and-mushrooms in gravy, and plenty of other artery-clogging favorites round out the menu.

You might not expect one of Newport's best-kept secrets to be a restaurant at the Hyatt Regency, but **Pineapples on the Bay,** Hyatt Regency Newport, Goat Island, 401/851-1234 ($7–13), has a terrific setting, by the pool and looking out over the Newport Bridge and Narragansett Bay. It's a great spot at sunset. Hotel guests often eat here, of course, but not a lot of nonguests know about it. The food is fresh and interesting—mostly creative seafood, sandwiches, and the like; it's only open from late May through mid-September. Dining is at teak patio tables. It's the perfect spot to sip a fruity drink and enjoy the breezes off the water. **Taste Buds,** 406 Thames St., 401/846-1577 (under $5), is a simple storefront café on Thames offering a wide and varied selection of coffees and teas, plus Italian ices, pastries, cookies. More substantial fare includes spicy tuna sandwiches, hummus platters, and brie and sundried tomatoe sandwiches. There are just a few tables but this is also a good take-out option.

Java Joints

A cool coffeehouse on hip Broadway, **Daily Grind,** 2 Broadway, 401/848-5558, occupies a ramshackle old blue-clapboard house with a sun-filled dining room and ample seating. In addition to various hot and iced elixirs, the kitchen serves light food, ranging from spinach-salad wraps to assorted cakes and cookies. An elegant storefront space on Lower Thames, the **Steaming Bean,** 515 Thames St., 401/849-5255, is hung with framed artwork and has a dining room of pretty blond-wood tables and chairs, plus a wide selection of magazines to peruse. It's Newport's favorite yuppie haunt for coffees and snacks. Say what you will about the franchising of America, the **Starbucks,** 212 Thames St., 401/841-5899, on Thames Street is a lovely, inviting space with a particularly comfy seating loft overlooking the action down below.

Gourmet Goods and Picnic Supplies

Here's an option that's great fun if you're staying someplace with a kitchen, dining area, or patio, or you're planning an outing on a boat or to a nearby park or beach. **McGrath Clambakes,** 401/847-7743, www.riclambake.com, delivers lavish summer meals to your location hot and ready to serve. Included in each meal is a 1-pound lobster, steamed clams, corn on the cob, butter and broth, mussels, baked potatoes, and Portuguese sausages ($25 per person; minimum of 10 people per meal, 24-hour reservations required). **Portabella,** 136 Broadway, 401/847-8200, sells delicious prepared Italian foods, octopus salad, lasagna, homemade sauces, gourmet groceries, artisan breads, and dozens of cheeses. There are plenty of tables and chairs inside, and seasonal outdoor seating, too.

Another terrific source of delectable gourmet prepared foods and groceries is the **Market Newport Gourmet,** 43 Memorial Blvd., 401/848-2600. Just a short sampling of goodies regularly available here includes white-bean salad, bay scallops wrapped in bacon, designer sandwiches, and many kinds of casserole and grill. Chocolates, vinegars, jams, cheese, exotic produce, and smoked meats are also sold.

MIDDLETOWN, PORTSMOUTH, AND JAMESTOWN

Upscale

Offering among the best views of any restaurant in the area, the **Bay Voyage Inn,** 150 Conanicus Ave., Jamestown, 401/423-2100 ($22–32), is worth the drive or ferry ride from Newport, chiefly so you can sit in the elegant dining room and gaze back across Narragansett Bay toward the city. Sunday brunch is an especially popular occasion at this historic old inn that's part of the ubiquitous Eastern Resorts time-share company. Creative, world-beat cooking is the hallmark of the kitchen—you might start with pan-seared ostrich fillet served with a potato–and–goat cheese gallette and finished with a dried-cranberry demi-glace, before sampling an entrée of seared monkfish sautéed with a citrus risotto, wild mushrooms, and asparagus. Everything on the menu is wonderfully fresh. A jacket is requested. Little Jamestown also claims one of the best regional Italian restaurants around with **Trattoria Simpatico,** 13 Narragansett Ave., Jamestown, 401/423-3731 ($18–25). Among the stellar starters is a velvety lobster bisque with fresh blue crab, sweet corn, and a goat cheese crostini. Jumbo pan-seared sea scallops with a pineapple–soy miso broth, steamed black rice, and sautéed julienne vegetables shows the chef's skill with both healthful and globally inspired dishes. In fact, the Italian menu borrows heavily from the American Southwest, Asian, and Latin America. Corn-crusted halibut with double-corn polenta, black bean salsa, and grilled jalapeño and tomato jam is another terrific dish. Traditionalists can still find a delicious linguine with shrimp in white wine. There's live jazz many nights, and in summer you can dine alfresco. The **Sea Fare Inn,** 3352 E. Main Rd. (Rte. 138), Portsmouth, 401/683-0577 ($18–27), is a bit off the beaten path for Newport visitors, but it's worth the trip for what many consider to be the best seafood on Aquidneck Island. Inside this stately 1880s white house fronted by elaborate gardens and a neatly trimmed lawn, dining rooms abound with Oriental rugs, white-linen table-cloths, fine crystal, and fireplaces.

Creative but Casual

It's worth trekking up to Middletown from New-port for some of the finest Italian food on the is-land at **Buon Appetito,** 823 W. Main Rd. (Rte. 114), 401/848-2252 ($14–24), a 1999 sister to the Canton, Connecticut, mainstay opened by Vietnamese chef Hoa Nguyen in 1992. The restaurant is stuck unceremoniously by a muf-fler shop and a Dunkin' Donuts, but inside you'll find a dapper dining room with pale-pink walls and simple, unadorned tables. Nguyen's fare is generally light and always utilizes fresh ingredi-ents—chilled buffalo mozzarella with fresh basil, sliced plum tomatoes, and a balsamic dressing makes a great appetizer. The seafood risotto comes simmering with calamari, salmon, sea scallops, mussels, littleneck clams, and shrimp in a clam-saffron-tomato broth, finished with asiago cheese. In addition to pastas, a number of grilled fish and meat dishes are offered, from basic veal marsala and lemon chicken to a first-rate shrimp tarragon. Beer and wine are served. The **15 Point Road Restaurant,** 15 Point Rd., Portsmouth, 401/683-3138 ($14–22), is a dapper cottage right by the beach at Stonebridge Marina, in the Is-land Park section of Portsmouth. Popular with northern Aquidneck Island locals and folks on the Sakonnet Peninsula, 15 Point Road is also a great option for Newporters seeking creative, deft-ly prepared cooking without the crowds and high prices of Thames Street. First and foremost this handsome little dining room is a neighborhood restaurant, and the staff is easygoing and friendly, always willing to explain a particular preparation or ingredient. Seafood is a major player here—the Block Island scallops over a nest of angel hair pasta in a light garlic-white wine sauce is terrific. The kitchen also turns out a tender and delicious beef Wellington and a rich lobster casserole baked in sherry and cream and topped with puff pastry.

A family favorite in Middletown, **Gold's,** 21B Valley Rd., 401/849-3377 ($7–19), serves three meals daily, with an emphasis on pizzas, pastas, and mostly Mediterranean-inspired grills. The space is bright and casual, and the staff low-key and friendly—this is a much less touristy option than you'll find in Newport. Breakfast faves in-clude apple-cinnamon pancakes, and also ham, apple, and Swiss cheese frittatas. At lunch, con-sider the chorizo, onion, and pepper sandwich on toasted French bread, or the duck fettuccine with a Triple Sec butter sauce. Dinner offers wide-ranging fare, from seared scallops with sweet pota-to pancakes and avocado as a starter to pecan-seared salmon with summer squash and coconut milk to pizzas topped with portobello and shiitake mushrooms. Valley Road runs be-tween Routes 138 and 114.

Steaks, Seafood, Pizzas, and Pub Grub

A casual, longtime favorite in Jamestown, **Chopmist Charlie's,** 40 Narragansett Ave., 401/423-1020 ($11–17), serves lunch and din-ner, specializing in local seafood. Fairly straight-forward and always fresh stuffies, calamari, shrimp steamed in beer, shrimp scampi, and seafood au gratin are doled out in generous portions. Right on the Newport/Middletown border, **Johnny's Atlantic Beach Club,** 55 Purgatory Rd., 401/847-2750 ($14–19), is a spacious eatery whose greatest attribute is its fine views over Easton's Beach and the ocean, enjoyed from an enormous patio or a similarly large dining room. The menu presents a fairly standard variety of somewhat upscale seafood dishes, including grilled yellowfin tuna, baked scrod, and lobster salad; rack of lamb Grand Marnier is popular among the nonfishy fare. A reasonably priced and dependable option in Middletown, the **Glass Onion,** 909 E. Main Rd. (Rte. 138), 401/848-5153 ($10–16), serves a nice range of American food, much of it with oniony themes: French onion soup, onion omelettes, and the ubiquitous (if dreaded) fried onion blossom. Pastas and grills round out this menu that's especially strong on seafood. The dining room is rustic and warmly decorated, with two large fireplaces, hanging greenery, and tall ceilings.

Pete & Flo's, Island Park Beach, Portsmouth, 401/847-8141; also Aquidneck Avenue (Route 138A), Middletown/Newport line, 401/847-8141 ($4–11), is an Island Park institution, known to many folks simply as Flo's. You dine on painted blue picnic tables, which look across Park Avenue toward an especially broad expanse of the Sakonnet River. Long lines can be expected all summer, but most devotees agree that the wait is worth it for some of the freshest seafood around. Flo's opened in 1936, just a couple of decades after the first clams met with the crackle of frying oil in Ipswich, Massachusetts. In additional to fried clams, Flo's serves clam cakes, chowder, fish and chips, calamari, burgers, hot dogs, and the usual array of summertime seaside foods. On weekdays you can get oysters and littlenecks from the raw bar for just 50 cents a pop at happy hour—there are some 90 sauces available to dress your shellfish. A couple of hurricanes have destroyed Flo's buildings over the years (the most recent in 1991), but the restaurant always comes back stronger than ever. Flo's closes from mid-October through about April. There are a handful of additional casual seafood eateries in Island Park, some of them seasonal. **501 Park Avenue,** 501 Park Ave., 401/683-0750, and **Tremlays,** 514 Park Ave., 401/683-9899, are particular popular.

Ethnic Fare

Sea Shai, 747 Aquidneck Ave., Middletown, 401/849-5180 ($10–17), is the only Korean restaurant in Rhode Island; here you can sample fine Korean and Japanese fare. The sushi here is first-rate. **Ching Tao,** 268 W. Main Rd. (Rte. 114), 401/849-2112 ($6–13), serves good if somewhat predictable Chinese food. Specialties include asparagus with pork ginger sauce, hot and spicy crispy bean curd and seafood in a sizzling red wine sauce, and mango chicken in a white-wine reduction. A reliable option for fairly standard Mexican fare, **Tito's Cantina,** 651 W. Main Rd., Middletown, 401/849-4222 ($7–15), is known for fiery and fattening jalapeño poppers, plus the usual fajitas, tamales, chimichangas, and taco salads. The chips and salsa have enough of a following that the restaurant sells them to go.

Quick Bites

In Jamestown, **Slice of Heaven,** 32 Narragansett Ave., 401/423-9866 (under $8), a dapper bakery-café, packs them in for weekend brunch: the breakfast burrito with black beans, eggs, and salsa serves up plenty of kick. A cute diner with a couple of U-shaped counters, plus red vinyl booths and nautical photos on walls, **Reidy's,** 3351 E. Main Rd., Portsmouth, 401/683-9802 (under $8), is a local gathering spot, especially at breakfast. The kitchen serves fairly typical diner fare, plus some Greek and Portuguese specialties. Breakfast is served all day. Consider excellent kale soup, veal parmigiana, tapioca pudding, clam cakes, stuffies, and homemade muffins.

Gourmet Goods and Picnic Supplies

Foodies should not miss the **Aquidneck Growers' Market,** 909 E. Main St., Middletown, 401/848-0099, held twice a week from mid-June through late September on the grounds of the Newport Vineyards and Winery. The Saturday markets are held from 9 A.M. till 1 P.M.; the Wednesday version is 2–6 P.M. Here you can find both organic and conventional produce, fruits, flowers, wine, baked goods, breads, jams and jellies, sauces, cheeses, and other delicious foods.

Entertainment

ARTS AND CULTURE

Considering Newport's glittering legacy of sophisticated and wealthy summer visitors, and its well-endowed visual arts scene, the city is relatively lacking when it comes to the performing arts.

One of the most popular entertainment venues is the **Newport Playhouse & Cabaret Restaurant,** 102 Connell Hwy., near the foot of Newport Bridge, 401/848-PLAY, website: www.newportplayhouse.com, which presents several generally light theatrical performances each year, from April through December. The show comes with a substantial buffet dinner, and the theater has a full liquor license. Different kinds of music concerts are sometimes held at the city's house-museums, churches, and at Salve Regina University's **Cecilia Hall,** in the Carey Mansion, Ruggles Avenue, 401/341-2945. It's best to check with the Newport County Convention & Visitors Bureau, 23 America's Cup Ave. (adjacent to the bus terminal), Newport, 401/849-8098 or 800/326-6030, website: www.gonewport.com, for details on what's happening where. And during the summer and fall months, Newport comes alive with some of New England's leading music festivals. The city also has a popular film festival (June) and a comedy series (July). For more on these, see Festivals and Events, below.

NIGHTLIFE

For a city of just 26,000, Newport does pack quite a punch when it comes to nightlife. There are dozens of bars and many live-music venues. Many, if not most, of the restaurants described in the Food section are also popular as drinking hangouts. Among the trendiest with locals are **Aidan's Pub, Cafe Zelda,** the **Cheeky Monkey, Tucker's Bistro, Salvation Cafe, Asterix & Obelix, Pop** and **West Deck.** The latter serves the best cosmo in the state. Other hot spots that pull in a more touristy crowd include **Rhode Is-**land **Quahog Co., Yesterday's,** the **Red Parrott,** the **White Horse Tavern,** the **Black Pearl,** and many others. Of course, there's no hard rule about any of this, and you're likely to see some mixing of visitors and locals at all these places.

Here are some other spots not covered in Food that bear checking out. There's often live music at **Christie's Landing,** off Thames Street, 401/847-5400, a fun gathering spot any time for schmoozing; the crowd tends to be fresh-scrubbed and good-looking, fresh out of a J. Crew catalog. Beneath the Candy Store at Bannister's Wharf, the **Boom Boom Room,** 401/849-2900, draws a fairly mainstream and somewhat touristy crowd for dancing to DJ-spun Top 40 and disco hits. Upstairs in the bar at **Candy Store,** yachting enthusiasts and Newport socialites trade gossip and cruise over wines by the glass and fancy cocktails. **J. J. Phelan's,** 162 Broadway, 401/848-5555, is a convivial and often crowded pub on Broadway. **Sabina Doyle's,** 359 Thames St., 401/849-4466, is a more centrally located Irish pub that's also quite fun. Over near the beaches, summer vacationers often congregate at **K. J.'s Pub,** 59 Aquidneck Ave., 401/848-9991, which serves decent seafood and burgers and often books live acoustic, blues, and other tunes.

Sing-alongs are a favorite pastime at the piano bar at **La Forge Casino Restaurant,** 186 Bellevue Ave., 401/847-0418, which gets going on Friday and Saturday evenings. This tends to be a nice and less chaotic alternative to the sometimes rowdy collegiate bars down along Thames Street. Another option that's also more of a hit with the over-35 set is the bar at the **Long Wharf Steakhouse,** Long Wharf and Washington Street, 401/847-7800. The views over the water are stupendous, and there's live music on Friday and Saturday evenings. **Vincent's on the Pier,** 10 W. Howard's Wharf, 401/847-3645, presents very nice piano music, and nearly every table in this restaurant-bar overlooks Newport Harbor. The kitchen turns out first-rate, upscale Mediterranean and New American cuisine.

Live Music and Clubbing

Since it opened in summer 2001, the **Rhino Bar and Grille,** 337 Thames St., 401/846-0707, has become a mainstay for listening to live bands and dancing to DJ-spun techno, hip-hop, and dance tunes. The crowd is young and cruisy, generally on the make and looking to have a good time. The grille serves better-than-average American food, pizzas, burgers, and grills, and presents a surprisingly sophisticated wine list. **Canfield House,** 5 Memorial Blvd., 401/847-0416, is a snazzy supper club that also books torchy live-music acts of all kinds. **Newport Blues,** 286 Thames St., 401/841-5510, apart from serving pretty decent American fare, presents some terrific live blues and jazz bands. It's set in a distinctive old bank building. Entertainment is pretty much nightly, from 10 P.M. on, so if you're just here to dine or drink with buddies, consider arriving a bit earlier—it's pretty loud when the music starts. **One Pelham East,** 270 Thames St., 401/846-5652, is a favorite haunt for live music, from R&B to alternative rock. It's a favorite hangout with Newport's preppy collegiate set, who enjoy the tunes and the warm, dark-wood interior and nautical memorabilia. There's pub food also.

Festivals and Events

SUMMER

In early June, the **Great Chowder Cook-off,** 401/846-1600, website: www.newportfestivals.com, is great fun. This is one of the city's top food-related festivals. You can get a neat behind-the-fence look at many Newport properties at the **Secret Garden Tour,** 401/847-0514, website: www.secretgardentour.com, which is held about the same time. Shortly after that, there's the **Sunset Music Festival,** 401/846-1600, website: www.newportfestivals.com, and just after that the **Newport Maritime Arts Festival,** website: www.bowenswharf.com.

Also in early June, look for the **Newport International Film Festival,** 401/848-9443, website: www.newportfilmfestival.com, a prestigious six-day festival of dozens of films, from features, special screenings, and documentaries to numerous shorts; there's usually a retrospective each year, too (in 2002 it was George Harrison's movies). Many lectures, parties, and other events coincide with the film festival.

Newport's Portuguese Cultural Festival, 401/848-0841, is held in early July. A variety of venues hosts the **Newport Music Festival,** 401/846-1133, website: www.newportmusic.org, which has been going strong since the late 1960s. This festival runs for roughly the last two weeks in July and presents about 60 chamber-music and other classical concerts at some of the city's most famous mansions, including the Elms, the Breakers, Marble House, Salve Regina's Ochre Court, Rosecliff, and Belcourt Castle. Some of the concerts are held in ballrooms and indoor spaces, while others are presented under tent cover on the lush grounds. The **Newport Summer Comedy Series,** Newport Yachting Center, America's Cup Avenue, 401/846-3018, website: www.newportcomedy.com, runs from mid-July through the end of August and consists of a series of comedy shows held every Sunday night. The sponsors book mostly New England–based comedians, including several who have performed on late-night talk shows and taken awards at the prestigious Boston Comedy Festival.

Also in early July, there's the **Newport Kite Festival,** 401/846-3262, website: www.buyakite.com. At Rosecliff, the **Newport Flower Show** is held around the same time, 401/847-1000, website: www.newportmansions.org. Toward the end of the month, there's the **Black Ships Festival,** 401/847-7666, website: www.newportevents.com.

More music enjoyment is had at the **Newport Folk Festival,** 401/847-3700, website: www.newportfolk.com. This three-day event held at Fort Adams is one of the nation's top such festivals and has drawn dozens of major performers over the years; recent performers have included Bob Dylan, Shawn Colvin, Arlo Guthrie, Dar

Williams, and Bruce Cockburn. The following weekend there's the similarly prestigious **JVC Jazz Festival,** 401/847-3700, website: www.festival-productions.net/jvc/jvcindex02.html. Recent performers at the jazz fest have included Tony Bennett, the Dave Holland Quintet, the Preservation Hall Jazz Band, Isaac Hayes, Arturo Sandoval, and many others.

FALL

Over Labor Day, the **Classic Yacht Regatta and Parade Day,** 401/847-1018, website: www.moy.org, features about 100 vintage sailing vessels racing on Narragansett Bay; there's also a parade of ships. About the same time you might enjoy the **Annual Newport Waterfront Irish Festival,** 401/846-1600, website: www.newportfestivals.com. The city's many avid yachters make a big point of visiting the **Annual Newport International Boat Show,** 401/846-1115, website: www.newportexhibition.com. Later in the month you can attend the **Guinness Stout/Bass Ale Taste of Rhode Island Festival,** 401/846-1600, website: www.newportfestivals.com. **Haunted Newport,** 401/845-9123, website: www.hauntednewport.com, is held throughout October and includes tours of area houses set up for the ghoulish holidays.

The city's **Fiesta Italiana,** 401/845-9123, website: www.gonewport.com, celebrates Newport's Italian heritage with food, music, storytelling, and other family-oriented events. The same weekend is **Oktoberfest,** 401/846-1600, website: www.newportfestivals.com. Mid-Octo-

ber is the **Bowen's Wharf Seafood Festival,** 401/849-2120, website: www.bowenswharf.com. The same weekend is the **Norman Bird Sanctuary Harvest Fair,** 401/846-2577, website: www.normanbirdsanctuary.org.

WINTER AND SPRING

All through mid-November till Christmas, there are **Victorian Christmas Tours** at the Astors' Beechwood, 401/846-3772, website: www.astors-beechwood.com; and also **Christmas at the Newport Mansions,** 401/847-1000, website: www.newportmansions.org. And then all through December is the **Annual Christmas in Newport Celebration,** 401/849-6454, website: www.christmasinnewport.org.

Newport tries hard to keep things lively throughout the colder months by throwing **12 Weeks of Winter,** held from January through March; call 401/845-9123, website: www.gonewport.com, for details. Each week has a different theme—popular ones include Cultural Arts Week, Mystery Week, Antiques and Collectibles Week, Black Heritage Week, the Kinsale, Ireland, Festival of Fine Food (Kinsale is Newport's sister city), and the Newport Winter Festival.

In mid-May you can attend the **Sail Newport Family Sailing Festival,** 401/846-1983, website: www.sailnewport.org. The same day is often **Fort Adams Day,** 401/847-1018 or 401/841-0707, website: www.may.org. Later in the month, the **Bank of Newport Memorial Day Regatta,** 401/846-1983, website: www.sailnewport.org.

Information and Services

VISITOR INFORMATION

Pamphlets, brochures, and tourism information are available from the **Newport County Convention & Visitors Bureau,** 23 America's Cup Ave. (adjacent to the bus terminal), Newport, 401/849-8098 or 800/326-6030, website: www.gonewport.com. The convention and visitors bureau offers a great winter package (call 800/976-5122) from November through March, which includes significantly reduced rates at more than 40 properties, breakfast for two at your hotel each day, admission for two into one of the city's mansions, admission for two on a narrated city bus tour, a coupon book for many area businesses and restaurants, and a couple of other knickknacks.

GETTING AROUND

Buses

From T.F. Green airport, **Cozy Cab,** 401/846-2500 or 800/846-1502, runs a shuttle-bus service to Newport; the cost is $17 each way.

Bonanza Bus Lines, 401/751-8800, website: www.bonanzabus.com, offers service from Logan Airport (via Boston) several times daily; the cost from Boston is $16.75 one-way, $30.25 round-trip. The ride takes about 90 minutes, not counting the short trip from Logan to Boston's South Station. Bonanza also has a run from Newport to New York City, with one stop in Narragansett, Fridays through Mondays only, twice per day; it takes about four hours. The fare is $35 one-way, $53 same-day round-trip.

RIPTA, 401/781-9400, website: www.ripta.com, has service from T. F. Green, but it involves a change. From the airport, take Bus 66 (Providence-URI) to the stop at U.S. 1/Route 138 (about 30 minutes); from the U.S. 1/Route 138 stop, take Bus 64 (URI-Newport) to Newport (also about 30 minutes). Buses arrives in Newport at the station attached to the Newport Visitors Center on America's Cup Avenue, right in the center of downtown and within walking distance of many hotels and businesses. RIPTA also has di-

rect bus service between downtown Providence and Newport, by way of the East Bay; Bus 60 runs several times daily and takes about an hour and 15 minutes.

Within Newport, RIPTA operates local bus/trolley service that runs among downtown, the outlying shopping centers, the mansions on Bellevue, and Cliff Walk and Easton's Beach. The fare is $1.25 one-way, or $5 for an individual day pass and $10 for a one-day family pass. You can park at the garage adjacent to the Gateway Information Center for just $1 for the entire day if you present the cashier with a parking ticket validated by RIPTA.

Driving and Parking

All major car-rental companies have representation at T. F. Green Airport, which is only a 45-minute drive from Newport (without major traffic—allow more time at rush hour or during holidays, especially in summer). There's also an **Enterprise** car-rental agency, 800/736-8222, website: www.enterprise.com, fairly close to Kingston train station, which has Amtrak service, and also at the Amtrak station in Providence. There are also several agencies right in or near Newport, including **Avis,** 401/846-1843, website: www.avis.com; **Enterprise,** Middletown, 401/849-3939 or 800/325-8007, website: www.enterprise.com; **Hertz,** 401/846-1645 or 800/654-3131, website: www.hertz.com; and **Thrifty,** Middletown, 401/846-3200 or 800/367-2277, website: www.thrifty.com.

Driving times from major cities to Newport are: from Providence, 45 minutes to an hour; from Boston, 90 minutes to two hours; from Cape Cod's Bourne Bridge, an hour to 75 minutes; from Hartford, about two hours; from New York City, about three hours. Add at least a half-hour to these times during busy periods, including most summer weekends.

Parking in Newport is not terribly difficult from after Columbus Day through about Memorial Day, but those three to four months of summer can be a nightmare. Much of the

© PROVIDENCE WARWICK CONVENTION & VISITORS BUREAU

Newport-Providence Ferry

angst, though, seems to come from locals and regulars who are so accustomed to finding ample parking in the off-season that they kick and scream when they can't find a free or metered spots on the street during the warmer months. In truth, if you can stomach paying a bit for a parking space in summer, you won't have much trouble finding one. There are several large municipal and private garages set around town—see Buses, above, for information on how to park cheaply at the Gateway Information Center and use RIPTA transportation around town.

Taxis

You can definitely get by in Newport without a car, using a cab for the few longer trips that might come up and relying on sightseeing tour buses or companies for trips out around Ocean Drive and to various outlying attractions. Local cab companies include **Cozy Cab,** 401/846-2500; **Rainbow Cab,** 401/849-1333; and **Yellow Cab,** 401/846-1500 or 800/846-1502.

Ferry Service

To Providence: RIPTA's **Newport-Providence Ferry,** 401/781-9400, website: www.ripta.com, runs from Providence to Newport several times daily, May through October. The fare is $4 one-way. In Providence the boats dock at Point Street Landing, and in Newport at Perrotti Park, by Long Wharf and very close to the bus station. This is a nice alternative to driving, mostly for the scenery, and perfect if you're staying in either Newport or Providence and would simply like to spend a day in the other.

To Block Island: This service is provided by **Interstate Navigation,** 401/783-4613, website: www.blockislandferry.com. Ferries leave from Newport daily at 10:15 A.M. and return daily from Block Island at 4:45 P.M.—the sail time is about two hours. The fare is $8.25 for adults one-way ($11.85 round-trip, but only for same-day passage), and $2.30 one-way for bicycles. Children's and seniors discounts are available.

The terminal is at Fort Adams State Park, on

Harrison Avenue; inexpensive water taxis run passengers back and forth between Fort Adams and downtown Newport (where there are plenty of lots and garages with long-term parking).

To Jamestown: Even if you have a car, it's quite practical and pleasant to travel between Newport and Jamestown via the **Jamestown-Newport Ferry,** 401/423-9900, website: www.jamestown-ri.com/meetings/ferry.html-ssi. This can be a very interesting trip, in part because the ferry stops not only in downtown Newport and Jamestown, but also at some intriguing points between them. From Jamestown, the boat leaves several times a day for Newport's Bowen's Wharf, which is right off Thames Street; it crosses over to Goat Island, then back to Bowen's Wharf, and then returns to Jamestown, where it is based. The earliest boat leaves Jamestown at about 8:15 A.M., and the last one returns about 11:30 P.M.

However, during the morning and afternoon runs, the ferry from Jamestown makes a couple of added stops. First, the boat calls on little Rose Island, a small 16-acre wildlife refuge in the middle of Narragansett Bay, just south of Newport Bridge; most people know it from the Rose Island Light Station, which you can see from many points in the area. Both the light station and an old military outpost called Fort Hamilton can be toured from July through Labor Day. You could easily enjoy a full day of exploration on Rose Island—it's ideal for beachcombing, fishing, swimming (keep in mind that there's no lifeguard). There's a picnic grove and public toilets but no concessions or camping. The landing fee at Rose Island is $3 per person (less $1 if you present your ferry ticket).

From Rose Island, the boat continues to Fort Adams, where you're also free to get out and wander around, and then continues on to Bowen's Wharf and Goat Island.

The ferry itself is a small, handsome boat with a friendly staff; it has a full liquor license, a snack bar, and soft drinks available. Daily service is from late June through Labor Day weekend; weekend service is also offered beginning around Memorial Day weekend and ending in mid-September. The fare varies according to the itinerary,

but ranges from $2, from Bowen's Wharf to Goat Island or Fort Adams, to $7 for a one-way trip from Jamestown to Bowen's Wharf or from Jamestown or Fort Adams to Rose Island, to $12 for a round-trip complete circuit—you can also buy a one-day pass for $12, which is the best deal if you're planning to explore multiple sites.

Around Newport and Aquidneck Island: There are also a handful of launch services, including **Conanicut Marine Service,** 401/423-1556; **Goat Island Marina,** 401/849-5655; and **Oldport Marine Services,** 401/847-9109. These leave from Newport Harbor and can be chartered to a variety of destinations, including Fort Adams and Goat Island.

MEDIA

Most locals read the ***Providence Journal*** or ***Boston Globe*** as their daily news source. Newport's local newspaper is *Newport This Week,* website: www.newportthisweek.com, which is mainly an arts and entertainment weekly.

TOURS
By Boat
From the Blount Shipyard in Warren, **Bay Queen Cruises,** 461 Water St., Gate 4, 401/245-1350 or 800/439-1350, website: www.bayqueen.com, set sail around Narragansett Bay and to both Newport and Providence. These runs, held aboard the double-deck, all-season *Vista Jubilee,* typically revolve around a meal and often a special event (a concert, lecture, or festival), which may occur onboard or at a venue along the ferry route. See the Tours section of the East Bay chapter for information on specific tours that pass through Newport's waters.

Oldport Marine Services, Sayer's Wharf, 401/847-9109, offers cruises along Narragansett Bay and through Newport Harbor on the M/V *Amazing Grace.* These hour-long narrated tours are offered daily from mid-May through mid-October. The fare is $8.50 per person. **Sightsailing of Newport,** 32 Bowen's Wharf, 401/849-3333 or 800/709-SAIL, website:

www.sightsailing.com, gives daily narrated tours aboard the 50-foot *Sightsailer* sloop.

Classic Cruises of Newport, Christies Landing, 401/849-3033 or 800/395-1343, website: www.cruisenewport.com, has daily cruises from Bannister's Wharf. These include the 72-foot schooner *Madeleine,* the high-speed Prohibition-era *Rumrunner II,* and the *Arabella,* a 155-foot sailing cruise yacht that makes three-night excursions out to Martha's Vineyard, Nantucket, and elsewhere in the Northeast. Narrated tours of Newport Harbor are given aboard the *Flyer,* 401/848-2100 or 800/TO-FLYER, website: www.flyercatamaran.com, a 57-foot catamaran with a large sundeck and room for more than 60 passengers; amenities include a full cocktail bar and a shaded seating area. This is a beautiful ship and a great way to experience Newport's glorious waters. The boat departs regularly from Newport, May through October, four times daily. Rates are $30 per person for most sails, $35 for the sunset runs.

Viking Boat Tours, Goat Island, 401/847-6921, website: www.captain-cook.net/viking_tours.htm, presents one-hour narrated tours of Newport's waters aboard the 140-passenger *Viking Queen,* from mid-May to mid-October. There are several sailing charters in town. **America's Cup Charters,** 401/846-5868, website: www.americascupcharters.com, offers daily sunset cruises from aboard actual America's Cup–winning yachts. These tours sail around Narragansett Bay and cost $75 per person, for a two-hour tour.

On Foot

Newport Historical Society Walking Tours, 401/846-0813, website: www.newporthistorical.org, offers extremely interesting walks through the city; these leave from the Museum of Newport History at Brick Market on Fridays and Saturdays, May through October. The tours cost $7 per person and take in parts of Cliff Walk, the historic Point District, and several other intriguing sections of town.

By Bus

Viking Bus Tours, Gateway Visitors Center, 401/847-6921, website: www.captain-cook.net/viking_tours.htm, provides narrated bus tours of the city, including Ocean Drive and the mansions area along Bellevue.

By Train

People sometimes get confused about the sightseeing trains that depart from Newport's vintage rail depot. The **Newport Dinner Train,** see Food, is a separately owned company from the other excursion train that uses these tracks, the **Old Colony Railroad,** 401/849-0546, website: www.ocnrr.com. On either train you'll enjoy a breathtaking journey over tracks used for passenger service from the 1860s for roughly a century; they wends for five miles along the shore of Narragansett Bay, well beyond the Newport Naval Base, and then five miles back. The Old Colony tours are given in vintage rail cars about a century old. Tours last about 80 minutes and cost $6 for adults.

The East Bay and Sakonnet Peninsula

The peninsular towns of Barrington, Warren, and Bristol dangle jaggedly off the mainland like stalactites, fringed on various sides by Narragansett and Mt. Hope Bays and the Seekonk, Warren, and Barrington Rivers. All told the three towns share about 20 miles of shoreline throughout Bristol County, meaning that strollers, in-line skaters, cyclists, and joggers find ample and alluring scenery for roaming about, and boaters and windsurfers consider this part of the state ideal. Best of all, the entire region lies sheltered from—but completely accessible to—the Atlantic Ocean. Among the major draws,

the 14.5-mile East Bay Bike Path runs along an ancient railroad right-of-way past breathtaking seaside vistas and grand colonial homesteads. One of New England's great centers for boatbuilding and yachting, the region is home to the Herreshoff Marine Museum, as well as museums on agriculture and anthropology. There's relatively little to see and do in mostly residential Barrington, an attractive but fairly quiet bedroom community just 10 miles from Providence, but bustling Warren and courtly Bristol have a considerable number of attractions, restaurants,

skiffs at the Sakonnet Yacht Club

and shops—easily enough to keep visitors busy for a long weekend or more.

A short drive southeast, the Sakonnet Peninsula hugs the Massachusetts mainland on one side and the Sakonnet River, an extension of Narragansett Bay, on the other. Close to Newport and the towns of Bristol County, as well as busy Massachusetts cities like Fall River and New Bedford, the Sakonnet Peninsula nevertheless enjoys an easygoing, if downright sleepy, pace. It encompasses two small towns, Tiverton up north along the river and Little Compton fronting the ocean.

The East Bay

Barrington

Approaching the East Bay from downtown Providence, take I-195 east into East Providence, and for the quickest access follow it a few miles to the exit for Route 114 South, which will first take you into the small bedroom community of Barrington, a town that still identifies heavily with the state of which it was long a part, Massachusetts.

In 1632, Baptists led by the Welsh Rev. John Miles were banished from Plymouth, whose righteous Puritans despised this heretical form of Christianity. Miles and his group settled in the far western reaches of the Plymouth Colony and named the new settlement Swansea for the town in Wales whence he came. The Barrington section (named for a British lord and theologian who espoused religious tolerance) of Swansea splintered into its own municipality in 1717, but border disputes between Rhode Island and Massachusetts cast doubt as to the future of the little town. It seems that Plymouth's banishment of the Miles clan to present-day Swansea actually trampled on boundary limits set by a King Charles II charter for Rhode Island, which granted the tiny new colony all land three miles east of the shore of Narragansett Bay; indeed, this roughly defines Barrington's town limits to this day. Back then, however, and for well more than a century, the border dispute festered on and on.

Finally, in 1747 Barrington (along with Warren, Bristol, Tiverton, and Little Compton) was awarded to Rhode Island by royal decree, at which time it became merely the northwestern end of the town of Warren. In 1770 Barrington became incorporated as its own town within Rhode Island—and so it remains. It's a checkered history for what is basically a pleasant if nondescript suburb today. The town did play a significant role in King Philip's War, the thrust of which occurred throughout the East Bay. John Miles' own house was used as a rude garrison by the terrified settlers of the region.

Like Warren and Bristol to the south, Barrington has made a name for itself over the years in shipbuilding and fishing, although it was perhaps best known for many years as a major producer of bricks. Many of Barrington's oldest and most attractive homes lie in the Nayatt Point section of town, which you reach by following Route 114 about six miles south from I-195, and then turning right onto Route 103 North. A little more than a mile later, at Washington Road, Route 103 curves right to the north—this would lead you slowly back to East Providence were you to continue along it, but instead you should make a left onto Washington and follow it south a couple miles to Nayatt Road. At this intersection you'll find yourself in the heart of Nayatt Point. Many of the houses in this section face out over this relatively narrow span of Narragansett Bay, where it closes like a bottleneck during its final reach toward Providence and Pawtucket; it's quite easy to see the shores of Warwick and planes taking off from and landing at nearby T. F. Green Airport, just across the water. During the early part of the 20th century, Barrington became popular as a summer destination among wealthy urbanites—much more low-keyed than Newport but with some of the same panache. Indeed, you'll see some enormous "summer cottages" around Nayatt Point and the other neighborhoods along the water.

To continue on to Warren, follow Nayatt Road east by the Rhode Island Country Club, away from Nayatt Point, and make a left onto Rumstick Road, which takes you to Route 103/114. For a short but interesting detour through another exclusive residential neighborhood with several fine homes, you could turn right instead of left onto Rumstick Road and follow it south a short way onto Rumstick Point, once known as Chachapacasset. The tiny piece of land jutting into Narragansett Bay took its current name from the description of its shape, which resembled that of the stirrer sea captains used with their rum toddies. Continue back north up Rumstick Road to reach Route 103/114, onto which a left turn leads a short way to the **Barrington Preservation Society Museum,** lower floor of Barrington Public Library, 281 County Rd. (Rte. 103/114), 401/246-0999, which contains exhibits and documents that trace the town's history. Free. Open Tues. and Sat., 10 A.M.–2 P.M.

Barrington is without major attractions, although **Tyler Point Cemetery,** Tyler Point Road (off Route 114), makes for an interesting excursion, especially if you're a fan of Revolutionary War history. On this site a local patriot killed a Hessian soldier on his way from the burning of Warren. The graveyard is on the small spit of land between the Barrington and Warren Rivers, easily visited on your way down Route 103/114 to Warren.

WARREN

At 6.2 square miles, making it the smallest town in the smallest county in the smallest state, Warren has continued to grow in popularity in recent years among professionals, educators, and artists. A mix of great historic buildings and comparatively affordable homes (compared with Newport or Boston) have helped encourage an emerging arts scene. Proximity to Providence, Newport, and New Bedford make it a practical base for commuting. The population stands at about 11,500.

Settled by Pokanot Indians, the village called Sowams, which would eventually become Warren, was ruled by the chieftain Massasoit. Loyal to the Pilgrims virtually from their first meeting

with him in 1621 to his death in 1653, the respected leader went well out of his way to accommodate and assist the English—even to help them thwart the efforts of neighboring unfriendly tribes that were bent on war. It's sadly ironic that one of Massasoit's sons, King Philip, would come to be known as one of the Pilgrims' greatest enemies, largely in response to the betrayal by the English of Massasoit's eldest son, Alexander. In any event, Massasoit deeded Sowams "and lands adjacent" shortly before his death in a treaty with the Plymouth Colony—at that time, it and neighboring Barrington and Bristol were simply southern fringes of Swansea, Massachusetts. By the time of King Philip's War, a short while later, there were said to be 18 houses in the new settlement—named for British fleet commander, Admiral Peter Warren. All of these buildings were destroyed during the skirmish, the residents driven south to Aquidneck Island (now the site of Portsmouth, Middletown, and Newport).

Warren, which officially became part of Rhode Island in 1747, developed rapidly into a productive shipbuilding and commercial center. During the American Revolution, the Redcoats targeted the community and its similarly productive neighbor Bristol, knowing that an attack here would hamstring the seafaring capabilities of the Continental Army. May of 1778 saw a particularly brutal assault, during which the raiding troops burnt some 75 American boats, plus the local grist mill, Baptist church and manse, a munitions store, and a number of civic buildings. The British (and with them many Hessian mercenaries) sacked local homes and took several residents prisoner. One of the town's earliest histories does relate a tale of valiant resistance: a small posse of women sought refuge in the local bakery on Warren's bustling Main Street throughout the ordeal. Out a window they watched the enemy marauders moving hurriedly to Bristol, but one straggler—weighted down by a massive drum—fell far behind his fellow soldiers. Seizing the moment with great bravado, the women shot out of the shop and surrounded the weary fellow menacingly, demanding his surrender. Whether his response proved the formidable

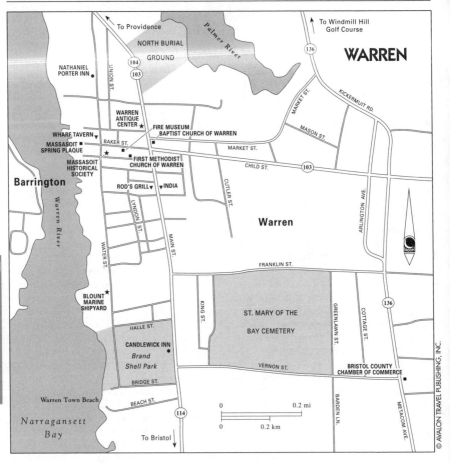

EAST BAY AND SAKONNET

fury of these women or the utter exhaustion of their captive, the man set down his drum and surrendered immediately.

Warren lost more than a dozen large ships during the Revolution, in addition to many smaller vessels. It did bask in the spotlight for a time, however, as the headquarters for Lafayette when he took command of the American forces in summer 1778. It took many years for the town to recover fully from the war, but eventually Warren returned to its shipbuilding prominence and produced some of the 19th century's finest vessels, while also pursuing trade, manufacture, and whaling (by the 1820s its fleet of 30 whalers

made the town one of the Northeast's greatest concentrations of this endeavor). Most residents made a living working at least indirectly with boats or the water, many hauling cod and tuna out at sea or loading ships with bales of cotton and cases of rum.

The town turned to textile manufacturing in the mid-1800s; the mills lured workers from different parts of the world, and so Warren's—and the East Bay's—blue-blood personality changed with the significant immigration of Italians, Portuguese, and Irish. A history written in the 1880s notes that "the commerce of Warren has now entirely vanished. All the energies of the town are devoted to manufactures. In its three great cotton mills more than a thousand operatives are employed."

Although not as stately in appearance as Bristol, Warren does contain a princely stock of fine colonial houses—dating mostly from the 1750s to 1820s—quite a few of them built by the exceptionally skilled ships' carpenters who worked in the town. The historic downtown, less than two miles southwest of the Massachusetts border, is compact. As you drive into town along Route 114, grab a parking spot anywhere once you begin detecting commercial activity, and for the next couple hours (or more if you're an ardent shopper) plan to amble about this warren of teensy crooked blocks lined with vintage houses, shops, and eateries.

While it shares some history with Bristol, Warren is not as gentrified and quaint. Nor is it as heavily developed as East Providence, but it is still fairly industrialized—you'll pass the odd factory here and there. At the north end of town, for instance, as you enter from Barrington, notice the old mill that was begun as the Warren Manufacturing Company, which later became the factory for Samsonite/American Tourister luggage (the luggage-making has moved elsewhere, but the company is still based here). Quite a few homes and commercial structures in town have yet to be touched by the magic wand of restoration. It's without the influence of precious chain shops and high-profile eateries, but there's a good bit to keep you busy here, especially if you're into shopping for antiques.

In the center of town, the old Lyric Theatre was renovated in 1993 and turned into the 200-stall multi-dealer **Warren Antique Center,** a move that put the town squarely on the bargain-hunting map. Across from the center, note the 1844 **Baptist Church of Warren,** 407 Main St., 401/245-3669, on which site Hessian and British soldiers burned the original church in 1776. The church had been presided over by pastor James Manning, who established Rhode Island College here in 1764. The college's first commencement was held in Warren five years later. Six years later, Rhode Island College moved to Providence and changed its name to Brown University. Open by appointment.

The center of town has several interesting buildings of historic note, including the 1844 **First Methodist Church of Warren,** 25 Church St., 401/245-8474, whose 160-foot spire and clock tower defines the town's skyline. From the churchyard extends Warren's simple but appealing town common, which is fronted by several of the community's most striking old homes. You can easily intersperse your antiques browsing with a tour of prominent sites, or just wander without a specific plan around the streets emanating from the intersection of Main (Route 114) and Child (Route 103) Streets.

Just off Child Street, at Railroad Avenue, you can pick up brochures and information at an information kiosk, which is right by a municipal parking lot that has a large bike rack. Baker Street has a couple of noteworthy buildings, including the former headquarters of the Federal Blues, which served during the American Revolution as the town's militia. Across the street the hulking building at 39 Baker St. is the oldest continuously operated Masonic Temple; it was built in 1799 with timbers from sunken British ships of war. It's open by appointment; call 401/245-7652. Other notable structures nearby include the 1890 copper-domed **Warren Town Hall,** on Main Street, and the Romanesque **George Hail Library,** 520 Main St., which was built in 1889 and completely restored in the early 1980s. This structure also contains the Charles W. Greene Museum, 401/245-7686, where you can examine a fascinating collection of artifacts from South and North American indigenous tribes, including beads, farming implements, and currency. Open Wed. 2–4 P.M.

Across from the Masonic Temple, the **Fire Museum,** 42 Baker St., 401/245-7600, contains the documents and ephemera of the Narragansett Steam Co. #3. The building, a mid-19th-century fire barn, also contains the company's earliest fire engine, the hand-pumping, wooden-axle *Little Hero,* which dates to 1802. The ancient hose is made of leather and strung together with copper rivets. Open by appointment.

From this part of Main Street, you can take any intersecting street west a few blocks down toward the water to see Warren's bustling little dock, where oyster houses and boatyards thrive as they have for centuries. Views are especially good from the outdoor decks of the Wharf Tavern restaurant. These blocks cover what was once woodland and swamp settled by the Wampanoags under Massasoit and, later, his son King Philip. A bronze plaque at the foot of Baker Street marks the spot of **Massasoit Spring,** where King Philip presided over his tribe. You can learn more about the Wampanoags' history at the **Massasoit Historical Society,** 59 Church St., 401/245-0392, a 1750s central-chimney Georgian colonial built by the prominent Maxwell family, which made its fortunes in local shipbuilding and trading. Inside, in addition to a multitude of documents and exhibits concerning Warren's past, there are two beehive ovens and a mix of colonial and Victorian furnishings. Open mid-August–mid-July, Sat. 10 A.M.–2 P.M.

Warren's shipbuilding tradition continues today at the **Blount Marine Shipyards,** Gate 4, 461 Water St., 401/245-1350 or 800/439-1350, which is now the home of the regional **Bay Queen Cruises** and **American Canadian Caribbean Line,** a fleet of small ships that offers cruises throughout North America and the Caribbean. Owner Luther Blount made headlines in 2001 when he pledged $1 million to help the town of Warren buy and preserve its downtown waterfront as open space. (Blount also owns a big chunk of land on Prudence Island, which is protected from housing development.)

BRISTOL

From Warren, both Route 114 and Route 136 lead directly through Bristol, although Route 114 is without question the more scenic and historic of these routes. (Route 136 suffers a surfeit of modern shopping centers and fast-food outlets.) Few communities in Rhode Island so balance the aesthetic of colonial Americana with the unprepossessing charm of a small and friendly village.

Like the other towns in the area, Bristol figured significantly in King Philip's War. Historical records often locate the crux of this engagement in Swansea, Massachusetts, the town just over the state border from Bristol. But the primary encampments of the Wampanoags, of which Philip was a leader, actually stood on the western fringes of Swansea, an area that today comprises Bristol, Warren, and Barrington: Rhode Island's East Bay County.

Philip was born to the Chief Massasoit, one of the most stable and reliable allies among the indigenous inhabitants of the Pilgrims. His tribe had lived on the very Mount Hope lands that would later become colonial Bristol's most desirable neighborhood. (It should be noted, by the way, that there are no mountains—or even hills of note—in Bristol. Mount Hope is simply the anglicized version of Montaup, the name given to this area by the Wampanoags.)

The building momentum of colonial settlement threatened Massasoit from the very start, but the chief never wavered in his loyalty to the Europeans. On Massasoit's death, tribal leadership fell into the hands of his eldest son, Alexander. There was little reason to doubt Alexander's loyalties, but suddenly the Plymouth Pilgrims began to question whether the younger chieftain would carry out his father's wishes and honor the treaties long established with the Europeans. Alexander, accused of treachery, defended the trumped-up charges before a colonial magistrate in Plymouth; he was treated badly and without respect, and no charges were ever proven. Within a year of having succeeded his father, Alexander became sick and died, his illness—according to some—brought on by the awful treatment he received at the hands of his accusers.

His younger brother, Philip, succeeded him and for a time maintained ostensibly friendly relations with the Plymouth colonists. But this wise and now embittered chieftain saw the handwriting on the wall. It had become apparent to him that Indian and white settlements could not, ultimately, manage to live harmoniously side by side, and that the escalation of European colonization throughout the New World spelled one thing: the demise of all indigenous tribes.

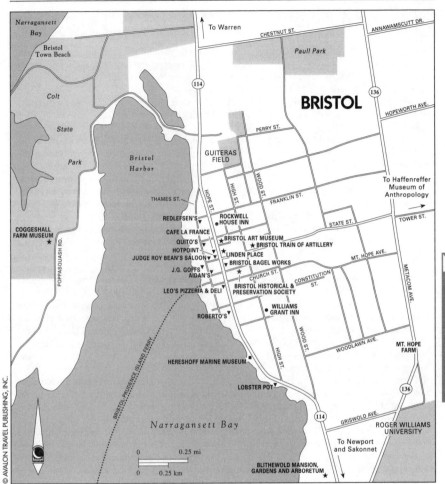

EAST BAY AND SAKONNET

History has, of course, proven Philip's prophecy correct. In his lifetime, backed into a corner, he decided to challenge this fate with a brilliantly executed though still doomed plan to unite the various Indian factions throughout the Northeast in a warlike front against their aggressors.

A major problem with Philip's goals, of course, lay in the fact that numerous rivalries—some of them virulent—caused friction among tribes throughout North America. Though loosely united in their mistrust, if not outright hatred, of the white settlers, tribes often despised one an-

other just as strongly. And still other Indians sought actively to align themselves with the settlers. In fact, ultimately, Philip would lose his grip on the war because Indians secretly loyal to the colonists leaked information about his plans and whereabouts.

Nevertheless, King Philip made a noble—and brutal—stand against the Europeans. Since roughly the Pequot wars of the 1630s, there had been general peace between the Indians and the Pilgrims—long enough for a certain degree of ease and complacency to overcome the latter. When

A BRIEF HISTORY OF THE AMERICA'S CUP

In yachting circles, perhaps no competitive event carries more weight and prestige for its victor than the America's Cup race, which has been won a number of times by Rhode Island boats. Halsey C. Herreshoff of the America's Cup Hall of Fame in Bristol calls it the Holy Grail of yacht racing. The event was begun in 1851, as a companion to the Great London Exhibition, which sought to promote the world's many great technological successes to that point, including those of transportation.

Held that year off the shores of the Isle of Wight, the competition of 1851 was called the All Nation's Race. In that event, a schooner called the *America* and helmed by John Cox Stevens, of the New York Yacht Club, defeated a field of more than a dozen British ships to claim the prize. The long-shot victory, in which America pretty well embarrassed its royal hosts, set the stage for this fierce competition. Making the loss all the more stunning was that the Royal Navy of those years was considered a world leader on the seas, and that Great Britain was the de facto birthplace of leisure yachting.

Several years later, the owner of the *America* ship, and thus the prize—then called the 100 Guinea Cup—from the 1851 race, bequeathed the trophy to the New York Yacht Club, which boldly invited yachting crews from around the world to challenge the *America* in a race—the winner would receive the 100 Guinea Cup, which beginning with this proclamation came to be called the America's Cup.

For the next 80 years, a series of challenges were made on the trophy. The first true America's Cup race didn't occur until 1870, some 13 years after the New York Yacht Club invited another crew to challenge it. The race was set off Long Island and consisted of a 39-mile run; 19 American yachts gunned for the prize along with just one British entrant, the *Cambria,* a schooner representing the Royal Thames Yacht Club. A rather modest sloop sponsored by the New York Yacht Club took the prize and became the first defender of the America's Cup.

Over the course of all those years, from 1870 through 1983, the United States defended the America's Cup race continuously, disappointing challengers on no fewer than 25 occasions. Irish tea magnate Sir Thomas Lipton proved to be perhaps the most formidable threat to the Americans, challenging on no fewer than five occasions from 1899 through 1930.

Rhode Island became famous for its ties with the America's Cup races starting in 1893, when the *Vigilant,* designed by Nathanael Green Herreshoff of the Herreshoff Manufacturing Company in Bristol, won the event. The next four competitions were won again by Herreshoff boats, in 1895, 1899, 1901, and 1903—the most famous of these ships was the *Reliance,* which today serves as the logo for the Herreshoff Marine Museum. Following a long break in the competition, Herreshoff produced the next America's Cup winner, in 1920, the *Resolute,* and then two more ships that won in the 1930s and were helmed by magnate Harold S. Vanderbilt. Finally, in 1937, with a victory by the *Ranger,* for the first time in almost a half-century America won the Cup with a ship that was not built at the Herreshoff boatyard. The 1930 America's Cup event was the first of many that would be held off Newport, thus helping to ensure that city's reputation as the yachting capital of the world.

In 1983, the race was held off Newport again. Of special interest that year was the Australian ship owned by three-time challenger Alan Bond; the *Australia II* became instantly infamous for its non-

---

King Philip executed his first surprise attack on June 20, 1675, his victims, settlers at Pokanoket Neck, were caught largely off-guard. He and his Wampanoags attacked and obliterated many colonial villages in southeastern Massachusetts and what is now Rhode Island's East Bay—and a number of fellow Indian tribes throughout the Northeast burned and pillaged settlements, too.

Historians now question the degree to which Philip actually orchestrated the similar Indian rebellions of this period staged elsewhere. His legend grew so quickly that settlers automatically associated any aggression by indigenous tribes with King Philip, and so the broad but violent string of battles came to be known, collectively, as King Philip's War. Over the next year or so, more

traditional design, which incorporated a so-called winged keel. Bond and the Aussies first had to win the right to compete using such a design. Finally, the courts paved the way for the *Australia II* to challenge the U.S. defender, captained by perhaps the most famous yachtsman in the States, Dennis Conner.

First, however, Bond and his team had to clear another racing hurdle. In 1983, an elimination race, the Louis Vuitton Cup, was instituted as a preliminary race prior to the America's Cup. This event was used to thin out the competition so that there would be just one official challenger competing against one defender in the America's Cup race itself. The Bond-owned *Australia II* won that event handily, defeating the other six entrants. In the actual America's Cup Race, which had by then evolved into a series of challenges, Dennis Conner's team at one point held a three-to-one advantage over the Aussies, needing just one final win to assure a best-of-seven victory. But against all odds, just as the Americans had been an unlikely winner in the 1851 race against the Brits, the Aussies fired off three consecutive come-from-behind wins to hand the United States their first America's Cup loss in the history of the event.

Perhaps it was the dramatic loss of the Cup by the Americans four years earlier that so fascinated the general public, but for whatever reason, 1987 proved to be one of the most publicized and televised America's Cup Races. Off the Australian coast, America's *Stars and Stripes,* helmed by Dennis Conner, first took the Louis Vuitton Cup, defeating Team New Zealand, before shutting out the Australians to reclaim the America's Cup for the United States—this time the trophy was brought to the San Diego Yacht Club, which sponsored Conner's yacht.

Since '87, the course of America's Cup events has hit some interesting bumps. Just after Conner's Aussie victory, a team from New Zealand challenged the Americans to a race for the cup—again the legal system was put to the test, as questions about the race's rules and regulations, and about ship dimensions and size, came to the fore. The New Zealanders won the right to challenge, Conner and his Americans defeated them using a never-before-seen catamaran, the New Zealanders successfully sued to have the Americans' catamaran disqualified, and the Americans successfully countersued to have the Cup returned to them.

This debacle, which tarnished the Cup's reputation almost as quickly as it had risen during the 1980s, was followed by a tight rewriting of the America's Cup rules. In 1992, order was restored, and the rules were changed to allow larger, more technologically advanced yachts to compete (over the years, the size of America's Cup boats and their crews had gradually become smaller). The Italians and New Zealanders ultimately competed for the Louis Vuitton Cup, the former taking the prize and then competing off San Diego's waters against the defender *America3,* helmed by Buddy Melges. The United States won four to one.

The next race occurred in 1995, and this time around the United States could not defend—the New Zealand team took the prize that year. In the 2000 event, the Americans were nowhere to be seen, and for the first time in the Cup's illustrious history, no U.S. ship either challenged or defended the title. None of the five U.S. yachts that entered the Louis Vuitton elimination race won. In the America's Cup that year, Team New Zealand held off an attempt by that year's final challenger, Team Luna Rossa of Italy, sponsored by the fashion powerhouse Prada. It was the first time a non-U.S. yacht defended the America's Cup title.

EAST BAY AND SAKONNET

than a dozen towns were completely burned, many of their residents killed, and just as many or more Indians lost in counterattacks. The colonists quickly rallied and formed an immense army to respond to Philip's raids, and in time contained the warring Indian faction. The English also captured Philip's wife and son. By now the warrior had moved his operations from Bristol down to the Sakonnet Peninsula, where he oversaw his war for more than a year. With his family taken from him and his efforts losing strength, he retreated to a swampland in Mount Hope.

Alderman, one of the Little Compton Indians still loyal to the crown, found Philip in Bristol and shot him dead. The English beheaded and quartered Philip's corpse, displaying it both in a celebration of victory and as a warning to similarly inclined Indians. In New England, King Philip's War marked the final time that Indians would prove a significant threat to the onward march of English colonization. The war, even though the settlers won it only with the help of friendly tribes, also furthered growing sentiment among the settlers that Indians could never be trusted or allowed to exist in this part of the world—that the removal, and even extermination, of Indians was justified.

Immediately following the war, the border disputes concerning the Mount Hope lands began in earnest among the three neighboring colonies: Rhode Island, Massachusetts Bay, and Plymouth (at this time the two Massachusetts colonies were rivals, having not yet united as one political entity). The court of King Charles II settled the matter by awarding the lands to the Plymouth Colony, and in the fall of 1680 the town of Bristol was formally settled and laid out, its name borrowed from the British seaport. The decision was reversed by a royal decree in 1747, when the East Bay towns were returned to Rhode Island.

Depending on what you read and who you talk to, Bristol's recorded history may predate the Wampanoags by a considerable degree. Several local histories present the theory that Icelandic and old-Norse fishing and exploratory expeditions long convened in these parts. As the story goes among them, Leif Ericson spent at least a few moments here—this fact is backed up by references to ancient Viking records that purport to describe a bay and land similar to southeastern Rhode Island. For a time, locals bolstered this claim by suggesting that vague inscriptions on Northmen's Rock, a jagged boulder in Narragansett Bay off the Mount Hope section of town that's visible during low tide, were made by Vikings. In fact, scholars have proven that the words trace to Portuguese explorers who landed here during the 1500s. In the end, there's really no hard evidence that the Vikings ever landed here, much less settled, but as is often the case, the mythology concerning these events makes a much better stories than the reality.

Unlike many New England towns, Bristol was founded not as a religious settlement or with

goals merely of self-sustaining agriculture and local commerce. Rather, the town's early fathers saw Bristol as the heir to its British namesake—as someday one of the New World's greatest seaports. With this goal in mind, the town derived a good bit of its commercial success in the infamous slave trade, a legacy that started around 1700. Ironically, although it was governed until the 1740s by the strictly Puritan colonists of Massachusetts and it engaged in slave trade, Bristol was a relatively liberal community that practiced the same brand of religious and social tolerance espoused by Roger Williams and his fellow freethinkers in nearby Providence and Newport. It was also a forward-thinking town in its own right, establishing provisions for public schooling before any other town in Rhode Island.

Throughout the colonial age, ships from all over the state, especially in Newport and Providence, trafficked heavily in human misery and injustice, a highly profitable endeavor that involved shipping rum (produced locally in distilleries set up near Bristol's wharves) to Africa, where it were traded for slaves; the ships then continued back across the Atlantic to the West Indies (and later to Charleston, South Carolina), where the Africans were unloaded in exchange for a variety of goods, including the molasses used to manufacture more rum. The terms of each cargo proved extremely favorable to the Rhode Islanders, and throughout the 18th century fancy mansions went up all around the better neighborhoods of Providence, Newport, and Bristol.

To give an idea of the state's and the town's contribution to this ignominious period in U.S. history, consider that between 1804 and 1808 approximately 8,500 of the 40,000 slaves brought through Charleston, South Carolina were delivered on Rhode Island–registered ships; of these about 4,000 of them came through specifically on boats registered in Bristol (with 3,500 on Newport boats, 600 on Providence boats, and about 300 on Warren vessels). Also, while 59 of the 202 slave ships that docked in Charleston during this period were registered officially in Rhode Island, it's believed that a great many more were manned by Rhode Islanders but registered, for various reasons, elsewhere—so in fact the numbers reported above don't even fully reflect the tremendous degree to which the Ocean State profited in the slave trade. In total, historians believe that about half the number of slaves who were brought to North America came over on Rhode Island ships. In 1808, slave importation was banned in the United States. (Slave-trading had already been banned in Rhode Island in 1774 and owning slaves had already been declared illegal in Rhode Island in 1784).

In contrast with Newport, which lay just 10 miles southwest as the crow flies, Bristol harbored relatively few British sympathizers during the American Revolution, and even furnished one of the boats that attacked the armed English schooner, the *Gaspee,* on June 9, 1772 (more than a year before the Boston Tea Party). The British clearly remembered the biases of the residents of Bristol when, on October 7, 1775, they sailed several war ships to the town harbor and began an intense bombing campaign that damaged many buildings but hurt no one—except an elderly local clergyman who was found dead in a field the following morning; apparently his heart had failed from the fright of the attack. The British fleet left after collecting a "levy" of 40 head of sheep. A far worse attack occurred three years later, in the heat of the Revolutionary War, when about 600 British soldiers and Hessian mercenaries marched through town and burned virtually every structure (even the local Anglican church, an oddity given that its parishioners were no doubt loyal to both the church and the government of England).

Further drama ensued during the War of 1812—U.S. ships commonly set out up and down the nearby coast to attack British brigs. Bristol's fleet provided one of the most impressive such vessels, the *Yankee,* which over the course of six voyages captured dozens of British ships, netting its crew roughly 1 million pounds in property.

Following the outlawing of slavery, Bristol continued to rake in steep revenues on shipping and trade well into the mid-19th century, with ships sailing in and out of Bristol Harbor to China, the Mediterranean, northern Europe, the northwest coast of Africa, and the Caribbean. Later exports from Bristol, in addition to rum, in-

cluded horses, sheep, pickled fish, and vegetables, while imports ranged from sugar and coffee to tropical fruits and spices. And from China came furs, lacquered furniture, and other exotic goods.

Merchants made a collective error, however, during the mid-1820s—a mistake made throughout much of New England—when it began focusing much of its commercial boating industry on what has come to be considered yet another shameful pursuit: the whale fishery. There were more than 25 Bristol-based whale ships sailing about New England by the 1840s, but the industry burned out quickly, partly because the gold rush out West drew untold thousands of eastern ship-workers to the other side of the continent, and even more because the supply of whales in North Atlantic waters was depleted and better sources of fuel, soap, and other whale derivatives were developed. By the end of the U.S. Civil War, Bristol's commercial sailing fleet lay tattered and comparatively insignificant.

As shipping declined, several industries picked up here during the 19th century, including wool- and cotton-milling, sugar refining, and the Burnside Rifle Company, which was established in 1849 by none other than Colonel Ambrose E. Burnside (whose famous facial hair gave him the nickname "Sideburns," the now common term for this style). Burnside had invented a breech-loading rifle during his time in Mexico. The company's success in Bristol was short-lived.

Burnside, who was born in 1824 in Liberty, Indiana, left Rhode Island for Illinois following the closure of his company. He became treasurer of the Illinois Central Railroad in 1858, and upon the outbreak of the Civil War entered the fray as colonel of the First Regiment of Rhode Island Volunteer Infantry. He led a brigade at the famous Battle of Bull Run, and as major-general he oversaw a major portion of the Union Army at Antietam. He's most remembered, however, for his failure to take General Lee at Fredericksburg; at this point in December 1862, he had replaced General George B. McClellan as commander of the Army of the Potomac, but his bold advance across the Rappahannock River in northern Virginia was handily struck down. Returning to

Rhode Island following the war, he became state governor from 1866 to 1869, and U.S. Senator from 1875 until his death in 1881.

For many years the town has been famous for the international yachts built at Herreshoff Manufacturing Company, which opened in 1863 and took over the factory space of the old Burnside Rifle Company. Industry led to an influx of Portuguese and Italian immigrants, many of whose descendants still influence Bristol's character—you'll find ample evidence of this heritage on local menus (from linguica sausage to puttanesca seafood dishes). Throughout much of the 20th century, fish and shellfishing operations have also contributed heavily to Bristol's economy, but today the majority of residents are commuters from Providence and even Newport. The town is not really suburban in character or appearance, however, as it retains an organic, small-town spirit.

Hope Street, the name for Route 114, is one of those slice-of-Americana thoroughfares that looks nearly flawless enough to be a movie set. Shops and eateries line the west side of the street, grand colonial and Victorian mansions the other, and mature shade trees run along both. Restaurants range from upscale bistros to wiener joints and pizza parlors. Many of the businesses along Hope sell antiques, making it and Warren together one of New England's top districts for such shopping. It's a family town, a place where kids ride their bikes downtown, and locals push strollers, and teens loiter harmlessly around park benches—not menacingly but in a way that you can't help but envy, wishing you had so few cares that you could laze about all day yourself.

There are few New England towns with a better clutch of finely crafted and restored colonial homes. You'll see carved lintels, tooth-like dentil molding, glazed sidelights and fanlights, and pedimented windows and dormers, on buildings up and down Hope Street. The brownstone Rogers Free Library, for instance, is a comparatively small and unheralded building whose elegant detailing and inviting entryway merit a look. It looks older than it is, having been built in 1959 largely in the style of the 1877 original, which burned in a fire two years

before. Some of the other fine houses along here contain B&Bs and shops.

The name Samuel Colt is better associated these days with Connecticut—in Hartford you'll find the Colt factory village and former estate. However, the more famous Colt's nephew, Samuel P. Colt, has roots in Bristol, tied to the grand, if garish, 1810 classical revival mansion (with major Victorian and Greek revival alterations) now called **Linden Place,** 500 Hope St., 401/253-0390, website: www.lindenplace.org, in which his magnate grandfather, General George DeWolf, resided. The mansion eventually passed on to Colt, who founded the U.S. Rubber Company (now Uniroyal) and the Industrial Trust Company (now Fleet Bank). Hollywood has had its brushes with this structure as well. The matriarch of the (in)famous acting dynasty, Ethel Barrymore lived here at one time, and parts of it played a role in the 1974 film adaptation of *The Great Gatsby.* Washington, D.C., has also paid its respects in the way of visits by Presidents James Monroe, Andrew Jackson, Ulysses S. Grant, and Chester Arthur. The mansion, now a museum, contains decadent furnishings from the period, outbuildings that go as far back as the 1750s, an elaborate ballroom from 1902, an 1820s carriage house, and neatly manicured grounds set with dramatic sculptures. Open May–Columbus Day, Thurs.–Sat. 10 A.M.–4 P.M., Sun. noon–4 P.M.

Occupying the ballroom, the small **Bristol Art Museum,** enter from Wardwell Street, off Hope Street, hosts local and national art exhibits throughout the year, with hours changing depending on the exhibition. Call or visit the web page of Linden Place for more information.

Just off Hope Street, the **Bristol Historical & Preservation Society,** 48 Court St., 401/253-7223, overflows with photographs, letters, deeds, reports, and other bits of historical artifact spanning the town's several centuries. The displays are set in the town's 1828 jail, which was constructed with the granite ballast of incoming Bristol ships. You'll find about 2,000 books and documents in the society's research library. Library open Wednesday afternoons, museum open June–Sept. afternoons, or by appointment. Donations are encouraged.

Nearby, by appointment or at special times, you can visit the **Bristol Train of Artillery,** 135 State St., 401/521-9136, which has been running strong since its formation in February 12, 1776. Today the B.T.A. houses a small museum filled with vintage—and often rare—military weapons and memorabilia, sabers, shoulder arms, and such. Some of these materials date back to the B.T.A.'s inception.

Visitors to Rhode Island typically flock to Newport to tour the greatest homes of the Gilded Age, but make a point of seeing Bristol's spectacular—and somewhat underrated—**Blithewold Mansion, Gardens & Arboretum,** 101 Ferry Rd., 401/253-2707, website: www.blithewold.org. It's as famous for its lush 33-acre grounds as for the 17th-century-style English manor house, which was built in 1908. Noted New York landscape architect John De-Wolf laid out the grounds, which include some 200 varieties of tree, plus more than 2,000 woody plants. A prize among these is a towering 90-foot giant sequoia, said to be the largest of its kind east of the Rocky Mountains. In spring the flower-power of 50,000 daffodils draws garden enthusiasts from all over, and the property's own bamboo grove offers a chance to see exotic flora rarely found in the United States. Fragrant rose gardens are another favorite feature. The property was bequeathed to the Heritage Trust of Rhode Island upon the death of Marjorie Van Wickle Lyon, who summered here until her death in 1976 at the age of 93; her parents, Augustus and Bessie, built the property. Inside the house's stone-and-stucco walls you can tour 45 rooms decorated mostly with pieces from the original family's impressive collection. Grounds are open daily 10 A.M.–5 P.M.; mansion open April–Oct., Wed.–Sun. 11 A.M.–3:30 P.M.; gift shop open April–Dec., Tues.–Sun. 10 A.M.–5 P.M.

> *The Bristol Train of Artillery has been running strong since its formation in February 12, 1776. The B.T.A.'s small museum is filled with vintage and rare military weapons and memorabilia,— sabers, shoulder arms, and such— some dating back to the group's inception.*

For now Bristol is the home of Brown University's **Haffenreffer Museum of Anthropology,** 300 Tower St., Mount Hope Grant, 401/253-8388, website: www.brown.edu/facilities/haffenreffer, which overflows with exhibits and some 80,000 artifacts that discuss the indigenous cultures of the world's farthest reaches. These include intricate carved masks from Zaire, kachina dolls from the Hopi tribal lands of the American Southwest, ancient Peruvian wool tapestries, and reproduction teepees. You reach the museum from Route 136—it's about 1.5 miles east on Tower Street. It makes perfect sense that such a museum would sit here, on the very land where Chief Metacom (referred to more commonly these days as King Philip) held tribal council meetings. The verdant 500-acre grounds, overlooking the eastern fringes of Narragansett Bay, make for a delightful stroll or even a picnic. There are also lectures and performances held throughout the year. Brown does plan at some point to move the Haffenreffer to its campus in Providence. The museum is on the east side of town, off Route 136. Admission is $3. Open Sept.–May, weekends 11 A.M.–5 P.M., June–Aug., Tues.–Sun. 11 A.M.–5 P.M.

Few U.S. states enjoy closer links to the ocean, in terms of both recreation and livelihood, than Rhode Island. You can get an intimate sense of this at one of the state's best attractions, the **Herreshoff Marine Museum,** 7 Burnside St., 401/253-5000, website: www.herreshoff.org. Herreshoff has long been famous as one of the world's most respected and longest-running manufacturers of ships. Brothers John Brown Herreshoff and Nathanael Greene Herreshoff, both of them named for legendary figures in Rhode Island history, founded the boat maker in 1863. John, an avid boatsman, became blind from an illness at the age of 18 but still managed to design and build a yacht for a local client. John—famous for his photographic memory and keen

PRUDENCE ISLAND

One of the state's strangest little places, Prudence Island—which is about six miles long by a mile wide—lies just a few miles southwest of Bristol in the middle of Narragansett Bay. It technically falls within the town limits of Portsmouth, from which it lies just west. It was entirely wooded until the American Revolution, when the British used it as a source for lumber. The island is largely undeveloped today but does have several summer homes and a small convenience store. It's a ideal spot for beachcombing, hikes, and taking advantage of nature lectures and strolls, which are sponsored by the **Audubon Society of Rhode Island,** 401/949-5454, website: www.asri.org.

Near the boat docks at the southern end of the island and a four-mile bike ride or hike from the ferry landing, the **Narragansett Bay National Estuarine Research Reserve,** South Reserve Drive, 401/683-6780, encompasses many acres of salt marsh, tidal flats and pools, forest, and even a historic farm site. Birding is a favorite activity at the reserve, where you'll also find a butterfly garden and several nature trails. While this is a great place for exploring, keep in mind that deer ticks are a major problem on the island—take necessary precautions when exploring, especially the wooded areas. Open Fri.–Mon., 11 A.M.–3 P.M., and by appointment.

You can reach it by ferry from the Thames Street dock in Bristol; call for times, 401/253-9808. You can also dock your own vessel at the southern tip of Prudence Island.

sense of detail—laid out the plans for the craft, and his brother Nathanael handled the execution. Together the team formed what became one of the world's leading and longest-running shipbuilders. In its first year, Herreshoff produced nine sailboats, and it wasn't long before the company had taken over the old Burnside Rifle plant and begun making steamers. In 1885, the boatyard produced the first-ever torpedo ship, the wood, 94-foot *Stiletto,* constructed originally as a yacht but refitted for the government for military purposes.

Since that time the company has produced several successful defenders of the America's Cup (beginning with the *Vigilant* in 1893), plus powerful steamers, sumptuous but sleek yachts, and other fine craft. Inside the museum's extensive exhibit hall you can admire some 45 Herreshoff-made boats, including the 1859 *Sprite,* built by the brothers before they formally started up the company, plus eight vintage America's Cup defenders. Additionally, there are dozens of fine ship models and other historic memorabilia. A film, which includes early 1900s film footage of early boat-making, tells the company story and discusses some of the sporting feats that have made Herreshoff boats famous. Cruises are given regularly aboard the 56-foot *Belisarius,* a vintage yawl that was Nathanael Herreshoff's final de-

sign—you'll usually see the boat tied up in the bay outside the museum. There's a Discovery Center geared for kids and families, where staff conduct workshops on sailing and boat construction. Parents or guardians can bring kids (the reasonable $5 admission covers an entire family) to read and participate in hands-on marine science and technology Open May–Oct., weekdays 1–4 P.M. and weekends 11 A.M.– 4 P.M. Admission is $5 per family.

Similarly relevant to Bristol's heritage is the **Audubon Society of Rhode Island's Environmental Education Center,** 1401 Hope St. (Rte. 114), 401/245-7500, website: www.asri.org. Set on a 28-acre wildlife refuge on Narragansett Bay, this kid-popular facility contains the largest aquarium in the state, plus well-executed 3-D natural history dioramas, marine-life touch tanks, and other provocative hands-on exhibits. This is an excellent resource for conservation education, but more important—to kids at least—the center is great fun. Nowhere else in Rhode Island can you walk inside 33-foot-tall life-size right whale. Open May–Sept., Mon.–Sat. 9 A.M.–6 P.M., Sun. 10 A.M.–6 P.M.; Oct.–April, Mon.–Sat. 9 A.M.–5 P.M., and Sun. noon–5 P.M. Admission is $5.

On the northeastern edge of downtown, you can learn about the East Bay's esteemed industrial history at the **Mosaico Community Development Corp.,** Elder Car One Community Room, 150 Franklin St., enter though Wood Street tunnel, 401/253-4627, which is set inside the old Kaiser industrial complex, the home over the years of Kaiser Aluminum, National India Rubber Co., Bristol Lace Works, Bristol Manufacturing, and U.S. Rubber Co. Open early July–late Aug., Sun afternoons. Admission is free.

To get a full sense of the agrarian life that also characterized this part of the state during much of the past few centuries, pay a visit to the **Coggeshall Farm Museum,** Poppasquash Road, off Route 114, 401/253-9062, which sits on 35 rolling acres overlooking Mill Gut inlet, a sheltered expanse of Narragansett Bay. Whether or not you're here to partake of the exhibits, it's a princely property for a stroll, especially if you've got kids along with you—they tend to get a kick out of the vintage and reproduction-antique farming tools and the yards of livestock. Seasonal gardens bloom with herbs, flowers, vegetables, and fruits, and the main 1790s house is currently being restored. Throughout the year, docents conduct tours, lectures, and demonstrations, often in the farm's outbuildings (which include a blacksmith shop and a fieldstone spring house). Also note the many special events, such as sheep-shearing days in May, the late-September Harvest Fair, and maple-sugaring demonstrations in early March. Open Oct.–Feb., daily 10 A.M.–5 P.M., March–Sept., daily 10 A.M.–6 P.M. Admission $1.

Rhode Island College may have left Warren for Providence (where it became Brown University), but the East Bay still has one very well respected academic institution, **Roger Williams University,** 1 Old Ferry Rd., 401/254-3500 or 800/458-7144, which sits along 125 beautiful acres at the southern tip of Bristol. Views of Narragansett Bay and Mount Hope Bay are had from many spots. This co-ed liberal arts school, founded in 1956, is particularly noted for its business, law, engineering, and architecture programs. Undergrad enrollment is 2,500. Just north of campus, **Mt. Hope Farm,** 250 Metacom Ave., 401/254-5059, dates to 1745 and is open to

pedestrians and bicyclists only. The 127-acre plot overlooks Mt. Hope Bay.

At the southern tip of Bristol, the narrow Mount Hope Bridge arches steeply and gracefully over Narragansett Bay, connecting the mainland with Aquidneck Island (a left turn onto Route 24/138 leads to the Sakonnet Peninsula towns of Tiverton and Little Compton, while a right turn onto Route 114 leads to Newport). When it was built in 1929, this $4 million structure with a main span of 1,200 feet was the 13th-longest-spanned suspension bridge in the world (and the longest in New England). The apex of the road rises to 135 feet over the water below, and the two bridge towers climb to 284 feet. The toll is less today (at 50 cents) than in the 1930s, when one-way passage cost 60 cents. A ferry ran where the bridge now stands beginning way back in 1680.

SHOPPING
Barrington
In Barrington, the **Stock Exchange,** 57 Maple Ave., 401/245-4170, has three floors of vintage housewares and furniture. And **Ross-Simons,** 308 County Rd. (Rte. 114), 401/245-5350, presents a fine selection of locally crafted jewelry, plus fine china and silver—it's one of the best such shops in a state famous for its history of manufacturing jewelry. Browse the whimsical selection of gifts, bed-and-bath items, gourmet goodies, and furniture at **Teapots and Tassels,** 280 County Rd. (Rte. 114), 401/247-0980.

Bristol
Quite a bit more than a general-interest indie bookstore, **Good Books of Bristol,** 495 Hope St., 401/254-0390, is also the place for crafts and artwork from Mexico, South America, Africa, and other far-off corners of the globe. In a striking yellow colonial house on Hope Street, **Alfred's Gifts and Antiques,** 331 Hope St., 401/253-3465 (also Alfred's Annex, at 297 Hope St.), is one of Bristol's shopping highlights. There are several showrooms with an extensive selection of high- and low-ticket items, including many Christmas decorations and home accessories. Nearby **Kate & Co.,** 301 Hope St.,

WARREN'S ANTIQUE SHOPS

Warren's antiques scene is concentrated in a tight area, mostly around Main (Route 114) and Market Streets, and then a couple blocks west along Water Street, which runs parallel to Main. It's generally not hard to find a parking spot on or just off Main, and from there you can walk to most of the key shops in town, including the **Warren Antique Center,** 5 Miller St., 401/245-4571, where you'll find some three floors of highly varied antique dealers. A funky departure from some of the more traditional shops here, **Acktiques,** Main Street, 401/247-5994, specializes in what owner Ted Ackley describes as "yard/garage/rec room haute couture," plus locally made pottery and artworks. At **Alanjays,** 438 Main St., 401/247-1336, you can search for vintage LPs, CDs, instruments, sheet music, and music memorabilia; there's also an eclectic assortment of furniture and glassware.

Appropriate given Rhode Island's history of manufacture in these fields, **Hall's Antiques** 139 Water St., Warren, 401/245-0305, specialize in fine textiles, jewelry, rugs, and linens. At **India Antiques,** 520 Main St., 401/245-4500, admire the fascinating collection of furnishings and decorate arts from India and the Far East. **The Square Peg,** 51 Miller St., no phone, concentrates on the little things: brassware, pottery, housewares, tools, bottles, toys—plus a great range of furniture. Search for precious Staffordshire, Limoges, and other fine porcelain, crystal, and sterling at **Wren & Thistle Antiques,** 19 Market St., 401/247-0631.

401/253-3117, is similarly inviting boutique—gourmet foods, gifts, accessories, and clothing. A nice mix of goods with a country bent.

Robin Jenkins Antiques, 278 Hope St., 401/254-8958, specializes in country pieces, painted tables and chairs, garden and architectural elements, and estate items—the selection is quite impressive. Browse both period and custom-made mahogany furniture at the **Center Chimney,** 39 State St., 401/253-8010. There are several other excellent shops in town.

SPORTS AND RECREATION

Beaches

The East Bay makes for an excellent beach outing, and while none of these towns front the ocean they all have lovely spots for sunbathing, swimming, and playing in the summer sun. You'll find the most popular of the region's expanses at **Bristol Town Beach,** Colt Drive (off Route 114), a sprawling complex that includes athletic fields and tennis and basketball courts. The beach is long and attractive. From Memorial Day to Labor Day there's a parking fee of $4 for non-residents on weekdays and $5 on weekends. The **Warren Town Beach,** South Water Street, has parking for residents only; however, it's fairly easy to reach on foot from downtown, where there's meter parking and some public lots. It's also just off the East Bay Bike Path.

Bicycling

The 14.5-mile **East Bay Bike Path** is a flat, 10-foot-wide, and wonderfully scenic asphalt trail that hugs many portions of eastern Narragansett Bay, from India Point Park in Providence to Colt State Park in Bristol. The path also welcomes joggers, strollers, bladers, and just about anybody with a yen for scenic rambles (provided they're not using a motorized vehicle). The path, which follows the former Penn Central rail bed, encounters a tremendously varied landscape, from undeveloped waterfront to the lively commercial districts of Warren and Bristol. You can picnic at several spots along the way, and at several points on or just off the path, you'll encounter places to stock up on snacks, deli sandwiches, and drinks. Bicyclists should keep to the right, others to the left. Dogs are permitted but must be on a leash (and you must pick up after them).

You can rent or buy bikes and equipment at **Your Bike Shop,** 51 Cole St., Warren, 401/245-9755, as well as at shops in Providence.

Fishing

There's great saltwater fishing throughout the waters of Mt. Hope and Narragansett Bays, and along the banks of the Warren and Sakonnet

© ANDREW COLLINS

park at Bristol Harbor

Rivers. Bluefish, snappers, scup, tautog, and flounder are among the most common catches. No license is required for saltwater fishing.

Golf

There are two short golf courses in the East Bay. The **Windmill Hill Golf Course,** 35 Schoolhouse Rd., Warren, 401/245-1463 or 401/245-8979, has nine par-three holes ranging from 118 to 220 yards. There's also a nice little restaurant open daily for breakfast, lunch, and early dinner (to 9 P.M.). The **Bristol Golf Club,** 95 Tupelo St., 401/253-9844, is also just nine holes but plays a bit longer with a par of 36 (including one par five) and a yardage of 2,273.

Hiking and the Outdoors

Bird-watchers, hikers, and outdoors enthusiasts take to the nature trails at the **Osamequin Wildlife Sanctuary,** Route 114, Barrington.

Sailing and Boating

As one of the world's great sailing hubs, it's not surprising that Bristol has an excellent school for this leisurely summer activity. The **East Bay Sailing**

Foundation, 401/253-0775, offers adult and youth sailing training on several kinds of sailboat.

There are public boat launches throughout the East Bay, including the Town Beach, off Bay Road, in Barrington; Haines Memorial Park, off Narragansett Avenue, in Barrington; by the commercial fishermen's pier off Water Street, in Warren; at Bristol Narrows in Mount Hope Bay, off Narrows Road, which is off Route 136, in Bristol; at Colt State Park, in Bristol; and at the foot of State Street, off Route 114, in downtown Bristol. The latter two launches are the most popular and scenic among visitors, and they put right into Bristol Harbor, from which you have good access to Narragansett Bay, the Sakonnet River, and the ocean.

You'll also find public marine facilities, with water, electricity, and other amenities, at the following marinas: **Ginalski's Boat Yard,** 6 Johnson St., Warren, 401/245-1940; **Stanley's Boat Yard,** 17 Barton Ave., Barrington, 401/245-5090; and **Striper Marina,** 26 Tyler Point Rd., Barrington, 401/245-6121. Striper Marina also offers full- and half-day sport-fishing charters on seven vessels.

ACCOMMODATIONS

There are a smattering of B&Bs in Bristol and Warren, but it's also easy to explore the East Bay as a day trip from Providence or Newport, where there are many more lodging options. Also, just across the border in Seekonk, Swansea, and Fall River, you'll find a full range of chain hotels and motels.

$50–100

In Warren, the fortunes of the **Nathaniel Porter Inn,** 125 Water St., 401/245-6622, website: www.nathanielporterinn.com, have waxed and waned but the place has certainly peaked in recent years. This is a lovely full-service inn with a reliable restaurant and attractive rooms with private baths, antiques, and canopy beds. One of Warren's many wealthy sea captains built the Federal-style colonial in 1795. Around the corner, the **Candlewick Inn,** 775 Main St., Warren, 401/247-2425, website: www.candlewickinn.net, is, architecturally at least, something of a newcomer. This homey clapboard bungalow was built in the early 1900s and retains the feel of that period, with its polished wood floors, high ceilings, and scads of antiques and country quilts, many of them from previous generations of the innkeepers' families. There are just two rooms, one with twin beds that can be converted to a king, and the other with one queen-size bed. Breakfast is a big to-do here. Well-tended gardens surround the house and are visible through several windows.

$100–150

In Bristol, the **Williams Grant Inn,** 154 High St., 401/253-4222 or 800/596-4222, website: www.wmgrantinn.com, occupies a twin-chimney, Federal-style colonial from 1808 that's right along Bristol's famous Fourth of July Parade route. The inn contains many original features, including seven fireplaces (three of them in guest rooms) and two beehive ovens. Antiques and folk art fill the rooms. Accommodations are in five rooms, decorated with a mix of Victorian and colonial pieces, from blue-and-white porcelain lamps to dark-wood four-poster beds with floral quilts and throws. A full breakfast is served,

with specialties ranging from blueberry-and-apple-cinnamon pancakes to bacon-and-egg pie. There's a peaceful fenced-in yard and patio out back. Along Hope Street, steps from shopping and dining, is the **Rockwell House Inn,** 610 Hope St., 401/253-0040, website: www.rockwellhouseinn.com. The exquisitely restored Federal-style house dates to 1809, but various architectural elements and decorative details reflect the Greek revival and Italianate influences of the subsequent decades. Rooms in this pink palace have high ceilings, high-quality period antiques, plush beds with soft linens, working fireplaces, and polished wood floors. Rockwell House is upscale and romantic but without the quaint-factor overkill prevalent in so many historic inns, and the rates are quite reasonable compared with similarly lavish B&Bs 20 minutes south in Newport. A full breakfast is included.

The East Bay's newest property, the 40-room **Bristol Harbor Inn,** 259 Thames St., 401/254-1444 or 866/254-1444, www.bristolharborinn.com, was reconstructed from circa-1800 buildings along the scenic waterfront. Rooms are large and smartly furnished. Many excellent restaurants are within walking distance.

FOOD

Considering the East Bay's small size and proximity to culinary powerhouses Providence and Newport, the peninsula has a surprisingly varied and polished dining scene. You'll find the best and brightest eateries in Bristol, most of them downtown along or just off Hope Street. Less refined perhaps than Bristol, Warren's dining scene is extremely eclectic—and it's very easy to find a great meal here without spending a bundle of cash. Barrington has but a handful of casual eateries. If you're in the mood for fast-food or chain dining, cruise up and down Route 136.

Upscale

A local favorite for special occasions and romantic tête-à-têtes, the dining rooms at the **Nathaniel Porter Inn,** 125 Water St., Warren, 401/245-6622 ($14–26), abound with colonial antiques and nautical artwork. The more formal areas are lighted by candles and decked with fine linens, while in the wood-beamed tavern you can sip imported ales before the glow of a roaring fireplace. There's also dining in a courtyard out back. The food tends toward Continental and arrives at the table in lavish portions and presentations; specialties include grilled French rack of lamb with a bing cherry sauce over a bed of field greens, and scallops flambéed with whiskey, finished with a Dijon-cream sauce, and served in a puff pastry. Desserts are predictably rich—note the Belgian white chocolate mousse served in a cup fashioned out of dark chocolate with a raspberry coulis. A fixture overlooking Bristol Harbor since 1929, the **Lobster Pot,** 119–121 Hope St. (Rte. 114), Bristol, 401/253-9100 ($8–26), really must be experienced during daylight hours to be appreciated: window-side tables put you directly on the water, and at dusk you can watch the sun slowly fall over the islands of Narragansett Bay. This is a spacious and somewhat dressy spot, though still casual, and service is excellent, especially for one of the East Bay's more touristy venues. The menu ranges from fairly simple and light bites (lobster salad sandwiches, Welsh rarebit with bacon served with a Caesar salad) to considerably more formal dinners—the usual surf-and-turf options, a decadently rich and delicious seafood casserole baked with butter and bread crumbs, blackened swordfish, and scallops Nantucket (baked with sherry and cheddar cheese). But the real pull here are the fresh-caught lobsters, which are available in several sizes either boiled, broiled, grilled, or baked-stuffed "fisherman style" (that is with claws removed and filled with choice lobster meat and scallops). For a mere $56 you can delve into the largest serving of the restaurant's eponymous crustacean—it's three pounds of pure joy, unless of course you're the lobster.

Creative but Casual

A cozy hole-in-the-wall on State Street, **HotPoint,** 31 State St., 401/254-7474 ($8–21), looks from the outside like a diner but is in fact a sophisticated bistro with a carefully planned wine list. Tables are tightly packed into the diminutive dining space (and out on the sidewalk in warm weather), where the menu lists veal chop, burgers, sand-

wiches (try the crab cake sandwich with roasted corn, chipotle-dill mayo, and sliced red onion), salads, penne pasta, and the like—all with quite creative ingredients. An entrée of sea scallops pan-seared with butter and served with Maytag blue cheese polenta and a green peppercorn sauce really shows off this kitchen's imaginative execution. Bristol foodies celebrated the opening of a terrific new contemporary Italian restaurant in 2001, **Roberto's,** 301 Hope St., 401/254-9732 ($13–20). The preparation of the soft and silky polenta starter changes daily, and entrées like cheese tortellini with prosciutto, snow peas, and yellow squash with a light pink cream sauce wow diners with superb execution and market-fresh ingredients. Beef eaters can savor the black Angus New York steak with a mushroom Madeira demi-glaze. Roberto's is intimate, relaxed, unprepossessing yet casually self-assured—the small dining room is staffed by a low-keyed, friendly bunch. **Redlefsen's,** 444 Thames St., Bristol, 401/254-1188 ($13–22), begun as a German restaurant, now offers a varied American and Continental menu and is particularly noteworthy for its crab cakes and rotisserie chicken. A very nice weekend brunch is served. Other favorites from the kitchen include Wiener schnitzel lightly breaded, sautéed and garnished with anchovy, lemons, and capers; and breast of chicken simmered in a sundried tomato and garlic cream sauce and finished with gorgonzola cheese. On the menu, two wines are suggested with each entrée, a nice touch whether you're a seasoned veteran of wine-tasting or a novice curious to try new things.

Pizzas and Pub Grub

With the most dramatic setting of any eatery in Bristol (even better than the Lobster Pot, although the latter has a more refined dining room), **J. G. Goffs,** 251 Thames St., 401/253-4523 $5–12), sits out on a dock at the end of State Street, an area that has undergone a complete redevelopment in recent years. The entire second floor is a beautiful open-air deck with views of Prudence Island and clear down to Aquidneck. On the main level, you can dine or rub shoulders with local college students, professionals, and tourists in a nautically themed pub-type room with ample seating (although it's tough to get a table in here on weekends). Happy hour draws a youngish, cruisy crowd and there's live music many evenings. Casual American chow with an emphasis on seafood keeps everybody happy, but it's the ambience that makes this a big winner. A very true rendering of a genuine Irish pub, **Aidan's**, 5 John St., 401/254-1375 ($5–11), makes a lovely diversion, whether killing time before boarding the ferry to Prudence Island, catching live music on a weekend evening, or hanging out with buddies over pints of stout and plates of hearty cooking. Friendly waiters and waitresses haul out heaping platters of burgers, fish and chips, bangers and mash, and pot pies. Across the street from Rockwell Waterfront Park, Aidan's has a handsome outdoor deck overlooking the bay. There's a branch on Broadway in Newport, too. **Judge Roy Bean's Saloon**, 1 State St., Bristol, 401/253-7526, is another atmospheric tavern with decent pub fare and a broad selection of imported ales, stouts, and porters. It's in the 1884 Holmes Block Building, a decadent three-story redbrick Victorian with a distinctive turret. Inside is a warmly furnished, old-fashioned saloon.

In Warren, dine on decent American and Continental fare—lobster Thermidor, broiled lamb chops—at the **Wharf Tavern**, 215 Water St., 401/245-5043 ($10–20), which is most famous for its wonderful views of the town's busy dock area and Narragansett Bay—it's especially memorable at sunset. The pubby dining area has varnished woods, maritime memorabilia aplenty, and oil lamps on each table. There's live entertainment on weekend evenings.

Ethnic Fare

The acclaimed Providence restaurant **India**, 520 Main St., Warren, 401/245-4500 ($11–18), serves excellent Indian fare at its East Bay branch in downtown Warren. In addition to the usual standbys, India offers some unusual options like mussels steamed in garlic, lemon juice, and chat masala (tomato, cream, cardamom, fenugreek, and fresh cilantro); chicken in sweet-and-sour mango sauce; and fiery green-pea and chickpea pulao (with jalapeños, onions, cilantro, and mustard seed). One of the best eateries of this genre in

New England—both for the food and the imaginative and bold decor.

Quick Bites

Just a block from the ferry to Prudence Island, **Leo's Pizzeria & Deli**, 365 Hope St., Bristol, 401/253-9300 (regular-size pies $7.25–10.75, sandwiches $4–6), opened in 1948, albeit at a different location, and ranks among one of Bristol's most memorable dining traditions. The handsome, old-fashioned storefront shop has high pressed-tin ceilings and ample sidewalk seating during the warmer months; it's a great spot for a light bite or a full meal after biking or strolling along Hope Street. The pizzas here are exceptional and come with a variety of fine toppings, from broccoli rabe to chopped Portuguese sausage to caramelized onions. A nice range of sandwiches is offered, too, including a mouthwatering meatball sub. Beer and wine are served. **Bristol Bagel Works**, 420 Hope St., Bristol, 401/254-1390, is another appealing little spot for lunch or a snack break. In this sunny little café with blond-wood tables and Windsor chairs, you can nosh from a nice selection of bagels (about 15 kinds) and spreads; traditional sandwiches are offered, too.

Always mentioned when locals start debating about who serves the best New York System Wieners in the state, **Rod's Grill**, 6 Washington St., Warren, 401/245-9405 ($2–7), serves not only these juicy dogs with all the fixins but also a tantalizing array of short-order soups, sandwiches, and snackables. Open breakfast and lunch only. **Quito's**, 411 Thames St., Bristol, 401/695-3918 ($6–18), little more than a seafood shanty just steps from the waterfront, is the perfect spot to sample littleneck clams scampi, any of several fried-seafood platters, lobster casserole with a lemon-butter crumb topping, scrod oregano, and all your usual local favorites (stuffies, Rhode Island chowder). The cooking here is consistently fabulous. Closed Jan.–Feb.

Java Joints

Break up an afternoon of strolling with refreshments at **Cafe La France**, 483 Hope St., 401/253-0360, an attractive café and coffeehouse with delicious hot and iced drinks (the vanilla chai is a favorite), ice cream, French pastries, and gourmet sandwiches like Tuscan-style roasted chicken breast with roasted red peppers. The menu changes often. There are several tables along the sidewalk, putting you in the heart of downtown Bristol's people-watching action, and also ample seating inside, including a few cushy couches.

ENTERTAINMENT AND NIGHTLIFE

While the East Bay isn't a major center of nightlife, Bristol does have several lively pubs, most of them near the waterfront and popular with a mix of students from nearby Roger Williams University, yuppies, blue-collar factory workers and fishermen, and tourists—especially on weekends, it's quite a mix in these spots. Favorites include J. G. Goff's and **Gillary's,** 198 Thames St., 401/253-2012, another pub by the waterfront. This one has live music quite often (plus open mike on Wednesdays and karaoke on Thursdays). Barbecue is served on the outdoor patio on summer weekends. Above the lively Judge Roy Bean's Saloon, **Jersey Lillie's,** 1 State St., 401/253-7526), is a happening, collegiate nightspot on weekend evenings. The saloon is good for a laugh any night and serves a great selection of imported ales and cordials. The high-style Victorian bar has been masterfully preserved.

FESTIVALS AND EVENTS

No town in America has been celebrating the **Fourth of July** longer than Bristol, a community that ushers in this patriotic holiday with nearly fanatical fervor—notice as you stroll up Hope Street that even the fire hydrants are painted red, white, and blue. Nobody takes the parade through town lightly, and true devotees have been known to pitch mini-camps along the route

as early as 4 A.M. the morning of the big event. In mid-August, the Prudence Island Community Center hosts an annual **Firemen's Fair,** with food, an auction, and other festivities.

Off Route 114 in Warren, Burr's Hill Park hosts an annual **Bandshell Concert Series** throughout the summer; it's free and features live music and dramatic performances. A similar series, **Concerts on the Common,** is held in Bristol. In mid-September, the annual **Harvest Fair,** Coggeshall Farm Museum, Poppasquash Road, off Route 114, Bristol, offers a weekend of pony rides, live music, hay-bale tosses and other farming fun, a jonnycake and sausage breakfast, children's games, and crafts demonstrations. Earlier in the month, similarly family-oriented festivities mark Warren's annual **Mum Festival,** Frerich's Farms, 43 Kinnicutt Ave., which is also a great place to buy the flower of the same name.

INFORMATION AND SERVICES
Visitor Information
Pamphlets, brochures, and tourism information are available from the **Bristol County Chamber of Commerce,** 654 Metacom Ave., P.O. Box 250, Warren, 02885, 401/245-0750 or 800/556-2484, website: www.eastbaychamberri.org; and the **East Bay Tourism Council,** 888/278-9948, website: www.eastbayritourism.com.

Getting Around
This is one part of the state where public transportation isn't practical, although these towns are small enough that you can see many of the key attractions and businesses either on foot or by bicycle. You'll want to use a car, however, both to get here and to travel among the three towns of Barrington, Warren, and Bristol. There's ample sidewalk parking in all three towns, as well as in municipal lots in Warren and Bristol. These towns are also served by RIPTA bus service.

The Sakonnet Peninsula

Originally named Pocasset by the Seaconnet Indians who resided here before selling the land to the Plymouth Colony in 1680, Tiverton—and Little Compton to the south—make up the Sakonnet Peninsula. It forms a land border with Massachusetts to the east, but otherwise the entire peninsula is cut off from the rest of Rhode Island except by way of the Sakonnet (Route 24/138) bridge, which carries traffic to Portsmouth, on Aquidneck Island.

Both Tiverton and Little Compton are small and pastoral, with rolling hills, still quite a few working farms, and few attractions. It's amazing, after exploring them both, to consider that these two towns encompass an area considerably larger than either Aquidneck Island (home to Newport, Portsmouth, and Middletown) or the East Bay towns of Barrington, Bristol, and Warren. Suburbia has crept slowly but surely into both towns, especially the northern reaches of Tiverton, in recent years, but it's amazing just how bucolic these communities remain, despite being relatively close to both Boston and Providence. Little Compton has a large and close-knit summer community, many of the families having been regulars here for generations. There are no mini-golf courses or amusements, however; just a handful of informal eateries, a yacht club, and a smattering of beach houses, most of them set down quiet dirt lanes out of the public eye. It would be a gross understatement to call the summer resort scene here low-key. Tourism isn't discouraged on the Sakonnet Peninsula, but neither will you find many places to stay or things to do.

Here are a few passing conversations recorded at the Commons Restaurant in Little Compton on a Thursday afternoon just after Labor Day one recent autumn:

As each new customer enters this modest, almost shabby diner, a young waitress in her early 20s shouts back to the kitchen: "a black coffee for Chester, an order of fritters for Anita," and so on. None of the regulars receives, much less looks at, a menu. Invariably, each arriving patron comments aloud, to no one in particular, "gee, it's quiet in here today," to which everybody seems to reply, nearly in unison, "it's quiet everywhere. The summer folks have all gone home."

Eventually, a stout, bespectacled man in his mid-50s offers this assessment of the summer crowds: "They're very nice if you're nice to them. They have all the big houses down by the water—they form the town's tax base. They've given us the good schools and the good roads—they keep the town strong."

"They say it's coming in warmer," laments one elderly woman to her similarly frail but cheerful dining companion, considering the hot-and-humid spell predicted for the weekend. There's a slight sadness about the way people greet each other this quiet first week of September. It's nice if you're a visitor—peaceful, understated—but the locals seem oddly dejected by the absence of tourists.

On his way out the front door, another man, one of the few nonlocals, is delayed slightly by the deliberate hobble of a heavyset woman with salt-and-pepper hair tied up into a bun. Just as she's nearly made it out into the hazy fall afternoon sunshine, the woman turns back to the man and says sheepishly, "I'm sorry to keep you waiting there, hon."

The man offers back cheerfully, "Oh, that's no problem at all—I'm in absolutely no rush."

"Neither am I," she says, grinning, her eyes cast out across the street toward Little Compton's peaceful cemetery common, "and isn't that the loveliest way to be?"

Welcome to the Sakonnet Peninsula.

TIVERTON

Although Plymouth settlers bought the land that is now Tiverton in 1680, the town wasn't incorporated until 1694, the name replacing the old Indian one of Pocasset. Little happened here during its early years, however, and in fact no provisions for a church or school were made until 1746, shortly before it—with its East Bay neighbors to the north—were transferred to the Rhode Island colony. Just to make things a little more

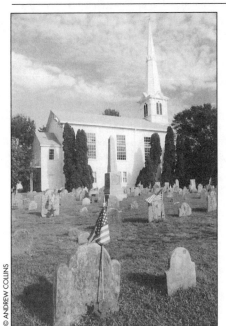

© ANDREW COLLINS

Congregational Church in Little Compton

Attractions are few in this pretty little town today. Shoppers will want to congregate around **Historic Tiverton Four Corners,** a historic village of mostly 18th-century houses full of boutiques, galleries, and cafés. It's at the junction of Routes 77 and 179, a few miles south of Route 24, the main connecting route through the peninsula. Beachcombers should wander along **Grinnell's Beach,** Route 77, a narrow spit of sand where the old stone bridge used to cross the Sakonnet River, before the towering Sakonnet Bridge replaced it. It's a scenic place to admire the river.

LITTLE COMPTON

Once the land of Seaconnet Indians, which were ruled in the late 1680s by a female chieftain named Awashonks, Little Compton is one of the most enchanting towns in Rhode Island for bicycling and country driving. You can reach it most easily and scenically by driving south from Tiverton either on Route 77 down the west side of town or down Route 81 on the east side.

During King's Philip's War, the town—like the rest of what is now southeastern Rhode Island—sat squarely in the midst of battle. It's also where Awashonks and the earliest white settler on these lands, Captain Benjamin Church, made a pact that would ultimately hasten the demise of King Philip. Prior to the onset of the war, in a tense meeting, Church met with Awashonks, who was escorted by hundreds of somewhat hostile or at least skeptical tribal followers, and agreed to sign a treaty that Church would then deliver to Plymouth to be ratified. Per the terms of this accord, Awashonks and her followers would, in the event of any aggressions on the part of neighboring Indian tribes, side with the English. As it happened, Philip launched his attacks before the pact could be ratified, and so for a time it remained unknown whether Awashonks and the Seaconnets could be counted on as allies. But a year into King Philip's War, Church again had the chance to speak with Awashonks. In this meeting, after much negotiation, Awashonk pledged to side with the English and work against Philip.

Word soon got back to Philip that Awashonks had officially defected from the Indian cause,

confusing, keep in mind that yet another chunk of Tiverton was transferred back to Massachusetts (to the city of Fall River) in 1862.

During the American Revolution, however, the town's high bluffs overlooking the Sakonnet River and Aquidneck Island made it of tremendous strategic importance. From the town's shores the Continental Army launched several raids on the British, who had settled comfortably in Newport and elsewhere on Aquidneck Island. Beyond this shining moment, Tiverton for its first 300 years maintained a mostly agricultural existence, and a lesser but still significant fishing industry. A report from the late 19th century predicted that Fall River's industrial gloom would eventually envelope Tiverton: "It may be that the next generation will see tall chimneys rising from its valley, and its breezy hillsides covered with a monotonous array of factory tenement-houses." Fortunately, for the most part, Tiverton avoided this fate.

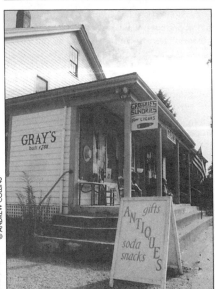

Gray's Gristmill in Adamsville

and it's said he was devastated by this, knowing full well that it meant a price had now been placed on his head not only by English militia, but by fellow Indian warriors. In the end, it was one of Awashonks' followers, Alderman, who shot King Phillip to death in a swamp in Bristol.

The town of Little Compton incorporated soon after in 1682, borrowing its name from an English village in Oxfordshire. By 1790 there were 1,500 inhabitants, a figure that has remained fairly constant, if high at times, since then. The town's history as a summer resort predates even the Civil War, making it one of New England's oldest such retreats. Like Tiverton, it has also drawn heavily on fishing and agriculture to support itself.

As you explore Little Compton along the west side of town, you can enjoy great views of the Sakonnet River and the many historic homes in this part of the community from along Route 77, whether by car or by bike. On your left, not too long after crossing from Tiverton into Little Compton, you'll reach the **Wilbur House,** Route 77, 401/635-4035, which comprises a lovely old clapboard farmhouse and several restored outbuildings. Portions of the house date to the 1690s, but it has been added onto several times over the centuries. You can also picnic on the alluring grounds. Tours are given mid-June–mid-Sept., Wed.–Sun. 2–5 P.M.

Still farther south, note the sign on the left for **Sakonnet Vineyards,** 162 W. Main St. (Rte. 77), Little Compton, 800/91-WINES, website: www.sakonnetwine.com. Down a half-mile winding lane off Route 77, this is a gracious spread that's quite substantial. The winery occupies a rustic U-shaped barnlike structure, and a seating area out front is the fitting spot to gaze out over the acres of vineyards. The winery's unusual vidal blanc has garnered numerous awards; you'll also find a very nice chardonnay, pinot noir, gewürztraminer, merlot, port, and cabernet franc. Owners Susan and Earl Samson began the winery in 1975, basing their predictions for success on careful research that suggested similarities between southeastern New England's climate and soil with those in northern France. Sakonnet produces some 50,000 cases of wine each year, proving that it's far more than a boutique winery these days. Tours Memorial Day–September, daily 10 A.M.–6 P.M.; October–Memorial Day, daily 11 A.M.–5 P.M.

At the southern end of Route 77, you'll come to a little clapboard cottage on stilts called the Sakonnet Yacht Club. Here at **Sakonnet Point** a small harbor fills each summer with sailboats and yachts, and sunbathers crowd the local beach. But this vacation community remains sleepy and laid-back, looking much as it probably did a century ago. There are no businesses in Sakonnet Point, just homes and the town beach, as well as a lighthouse at the very southern tip of the point.

From here backtrack up Route 77 a short distance north and make a right turn onto Meeting House Lane; at the end of this short road you'll come to **The Common,** perhaps the most enchanting little town green in Rhode Island. Almost entirely absent of commercial enterprise, the grassy plot stretches out beneath the towering spire of the United Congregational Church, most of it covered with gravestones (some dating to the 1600s). Across from the church you'll find the legendary town commissary, the Commons Restaurant.

Adamsville

Continue east of The Common along Simmons Road, make a left onto East Main Street, and follow this north as it jogs up to Peckham Road. Make a fast right and then a left again onto Long Highway, make another quick right onto Cold Brook Road, and follow this into the lovely old village of Adamsville (part of the incorporated town of Little Compton). There's little more to see here than in Sakonnet Point or around The Common, but this historic neighborhood is similarly beguiling. A brass plaque erected in 1925 sits in the center of the village, set into a stone wall, directly behind home plate of a Little League baseball field. It commemorates the Rhode Island red, a type of fowl that was raised right here in Adamsville and revolutionized chicken farming, as it was the first both to lay eggs and provided meat.

A little farther east along Main Street (Route 179), just before you hit the state border marker for Westport, Massachusetts, you'll pass a quirky old shop on your right called **Gray's Gristmill.** This ramshackle place abounds with gifts, homemade jams, a few odd furnishings, and inexpensive bric-a-brac ranging from junk to some neat little finds. Just beyond the property, Adamsville Brook empties into the West Branch of the Westport River.

SHOPPING

In Tiverton, you'll find several fine shops at **Historic Tiverton Four Corners,** Route 77 and Route 179, most of them set inside the restored 18th- and 19th-century houses in which this village's residents once resided. Among the highlights is the **Metalworks,** 401/624-4400, which specializes in antique lanterns but can also custom-create all kinds of home furnishings and arts. In the arresting 1750s gambrel-roof **Arnold Smith House,** 401/624-8791, you'll find an excellent survey of fine country and colonial antiques. **Little Purls,** 401/625-5990, carries a colorful and clever assortment of children's clothing and gifts, while **Sakonnet Purls,** 888/624-9902, offers one of the greatest assortments of

yarn and needlework in southern New England. At the **Toy Mill,** 401/624-6188, browse for unusual, often hand-crafted, dolls, toys, and games for kids of every age. Check out the fabulous array of hand-hooked rugs, throws and pillows, imported Italian and French pottery and ceramics, pine furniture, and stylish home accents at **Lou Lou's Decor,** 401/624-8231.

In Little Compton, the **Sakonnet Painters Cooperative Gallery on the Common,** 401/625-5415, has wonderful changing art exhibits. There's also a branch at Historic Tiverton Four Corners. Just southwest of Adamsville Center, the **Old Stone Orchard,** 33 Cold Brook Rd., Little Compton, 401/635-2663, has pumpkins, apples, and such.

RECREATION

There aren't many formal venues for recreation in this region, but it's nevertheless a wonderful place for many kinds of activities, especially bicycling (just follow any of the roads described above in the tours through Tiverton and Little Compton). The terrain is relatively flat, and excellent views of the sea and rolling meadows are had from throughout both towns, especially Little Compton. There's excellent birding and hiking, as well as beachcombing, down at the southeastern tip of Little Compton, at **Goosewing Beach Preserve,** off South Shore Road, 401/331-7110. There's a beach parking fee of $5 from Memorial Day to Labor Day; other times it's free. The Nature Conservancy oversees this pristine barrier beach and neighboring Quicksand Pond; guided nature walks are given throughout the summer.

Fishing enthusiasts will find great opportunities for saltwater fishing from Grinnell's Beach, by the old Stone Bridge site off Route 77 in Tiverton, and also a bit farther south at Sapowet Point. Grinnell's Beach also has swimming, with lifeguards, changing rooms, and restrooms.

Hiking

Northwest of the Common in Little Compton, between it and Adamsville, you'll pass the turn-off for **Simmons Park,** a 400-acre plot laced with trails, shrub wetlands, a red maple swamp, and oak and American beech woodland. Through here you can spot cottontail rabbit, foxes, mink, wood and mallard ducks, osprey, and owls. Wild turkeys were released here a few years back and are somewhat common. However, this is also the town hunting grounds; all visitors must wear Day-Glo fluorescent orange when walking through the preserve during hunting season (October through February).

Horseback

Sakonnet is gorgeous country for riding, and **Roseland Acres Equestrian Center,** 594 East Rd., 401/624-8866, offers English-style and Western-style rides through some of the most appealing terrain. Hour-, two-hour, and sunset trail rides are available, and no prior experience is necessary—the excursions traverse the property's extensive wooded grounds. Summer children's and school-vacation camps are also offered. This is a full-service, family-run equestrian facility, where virtually every type of lesson is available, to both groups and individuals. At various times of year, the center holds sleigh rides and horse-drawn hayrides, which are followed by clambakes, barbecues, or similar festivities.

ACCOMMODATIONS

Your options for spending the night, short of befriending a resident, are highly limited in Tiverton and Little Compton. You'll find just two inns, both in the latter community. Still, it's a short and easy drive to the Sakonnet Peninsula from Newport, Bristol, and Fall River, Massachusetts, all of which have ample lodging choices.

Country Inns and B&Bs

One of the more unusual lodging options in Rhode Island (and one of only two in Little Compton), **Stone House Club,** 122 Sakonnet Point Rd., 401/635-2222, website: www .stonehouseclub.com, is technically a private club. The policy is that the accommodations and restaurant are intended for "members and their guests, primarily residents and folks who summer here, who find us to their liking." Most of the guests came to know the club through

friends or associates who live in the area, but an introduction is not required. If you call and ask about staying, and you're comfortable with the terms, the Stone Club will book you a room (but you first must agree to pay the $25 one-year membership fee). It's a great deal, considering the rooms here have rates beginning at just $60 or so for shared bath and about $90 for one with a private bath (Continental breakfast is included). The building dates to 1836, when the builder of Little Compton's first breakwater, at Sakonnet Point, constructed this stone house for his wife and family (numbering 13 children!). A narrow spiral staircase winds up to the guest rooms—those in the rear face out over a broad, neatly groomed lawn and then over an estuary out toward the ocean. Furnishings are charmingly simple and even a little scruffy, as rooms have wood paneling, wood floors or rather dated carpeting, and cozy beds that in some cases take up two-thirds of the living space. Rooms range greatly in size, and include a large suite that accommodates a family of five and has a kitchen, as well as several modest units with tight quarters. Because this is a private club, the hotel has a particularly friendly, low-key feel—not one of exclusivity, but rather common interest and appreciation of Little Compton and its anti-growth, preservation-minded ethic. Sakonnet Light is a short bike ride away, and this place has considerably more charm than the hundreds of comparably priced motels throughout much of coastal Rhode Island. There's a full-service restaurant here, too (again, members only), which is useful if you're staying at the hotel. Dining is in a tap room and formal dining room, and food ranges from simple country tavern cooking to quite elaborate French and Pan-Asian specialties.

Intimate and romantic, **The Roost,** Route 77, Little Compton, 401/635-8407, website: www.sakonnetwine.com, offers a peaceful, easygoing vibe. You'll feel miles and miles removed from the touristy fray of Newport and urban bustle of Providence at this three-room B&B that occupies an old shingle farmhouse at Sakonnet Vineyards. Of course, oenophiles adore The Roost, as it puts them just steps from Sakonnet's tasting room—accommodations also face out over the 45 rolling acres of neatly planted grape vines and beautifully manicured gardens. Rooms, all with private bath, have been recently updated with a neat mix of colonial and country furnishings; it's not fancy, but for the setting, The Roost represents a terrific deal.

FOOD

Though not as limited in dining possibilities as with places to stay, the Sakonnet Peninsula has but a limited number of eateries. However, quality and quirky ambience are hallmarks of dining in these parts—what restaurants you'll find are generally quite good and in some cases worth a trip from anywhere in the state. The Stone House Club also has a restaurant, but you need to join before planning to dine here.

Creative but Casual

The top pick in this area when it comes to special occasions, **Four Corners Grille,** 3841 Main Rd., 401/624-1510 ($5–15), is, on the outside, nothing fancy. This neighborhood spot with cozy wooden booths, warm lighting, down-to-earth service, and often-challenging parking (or lack thereof) excels in the food department, however, presenting a consistently excellent menu of regional American and Italian dishes at extremely fair prices. In season, try the soft-shell crab scampi. Other treats include hickory-smoked pork chops with grilled sweet-potato pancakes and apple sauce, shrimp Mozambique (a house specialty, in which shrimp is served over pasta with hot peppers and a piquant sauce popular in Portuguese restaurants), shellfish marinara, and herb-crusted grilled scrod with Maryland-style Creole crab cakes. Several kinds of burger, scallop rolls, tuna-steak sandwiches (with a lime-cilantro dressing), and seafood bisques round out the lighter and less expensive menu items. The **Stone Bridge Restaurant,** 1848 Main Rd., Tiverton, 401/625-5780 ($6–17), overlooks the boating activity along the Sakonnet River, sitting just across the street from the former bridge after which it's named. This is a locals' favorite, a good bet for unfussy yet surprisingly sophisti-

cated Greek and Italian fare—the starter of mussels steamed in white wine with feta sits well on a chilly winter day. You can get traditional standbys here, the usual mix of pastas, meatballs, steaks, and clam platters, but it's the more interesting Greek sausage with fresh Greek salad or roast duck with a tangy-sweet black cherry sauce that deserve the greatest acclaim. If you're more in the mood for something light, keep in mind the many lighter options and sandwiches, available even at dinner. Whatever you're seeking, it's all remarkably tasty here.

Quick Bites

Gray's Ice Cream, 16 East Rd., 401/624-4500, occupies a low-slung shingle building at Tiverton Four Corners; since 1923 it's been making fans of frozen sweets happy all year long with such homemade flavors of ice cream as blueberry, pumpkin, maple walnut, peach brandy, and ginger. Swarms of devotees check in regularly to order their favorites and check on the new flavors added each season. In the pedestrian section of eastern Tiverton, just over the Massachusetts border, you'll find a modest-looking snack bar called Macray's Seafood II, 115 Stafford Rd., 401/625-1347 ($2–6), which serves immodest and inexpensive portions of delicious short-order seafood (takeout only, but there are plenty of picnic benches). Macray's is known for its clam cakes, but sample a platter of whole-bellied fried clams and you'll really come to understand the mystique. Great fish and chips, too. Nearer the Sakonnet River, and overlooking Nanaquaket Pond, **Evelyn's Drive-In,** 2335 Main Rd. (Rte. 77), 401/624-3100 ($2–9), delivers a somewhat more substantial variety of short-order goodies, from grilled tuna and swordfish to the usual lobster rolls, fried oysters, and chowders. It's perfect before an outing at the beach.

One of the Ocean State's great culinary institutions, the **Commons Restaurant,** on The Common, 401/635-4388 ($2–9), boasts an epic menu of diner-esque favorites, include massive but thin—almost crèpe-like—jonnycakes. The enormously popular gathering spot of locals and tourists, year-rounders and summer folks, has wine-colored linoleum floors, mauve-vinyl booths, and wood-paneled walls that could very well date to the restaurant's opening in 1966. At least half the patrons in here on any given day, especially in the morning, are on a first-name basis with the staff. Breakfast is served all day—the jonnycake (spelled "johnnycake" here) special comes with two eggs, two cakes, and bacon. Stuffed seafood rolls are a favorite, the quahog chowder good but not quite worthy of its legendary status. Old-timers sure seem to like the liverwurst sandwiches. And few desserts hit the spot better than the Commons' strawberry ice cream with fresh-made strawberry sauce. This endearing little restaurant is named for the town common, which it faces. **The Barn,** 16 Main Rd., Adamsville, 401/635-2985 ($3–8), occupies an elegantly weathered, clapboard, 200-year-old barn. It's all about breakfast here—the places closes at 11:30 A.M. on weekdays and 12:30 P.M. on weekends. More than a few foodies claim The Barn serves the best breakfasts in Rhode Island. A specialty is eggs on the Bayou, poached eggs on English muffins with crab cakes and Creole hollandaise sauce. Sweet tooths can dig into raspberry-filled French toast with crème anglaise, toasted almonds, and fresh berries. And be sure to order a side of ostrich sausage. Is it any wonder the lines here on summer weekends can be so maddeningly long?

Java Joints

In a tiny little cottage adjoining Walker's fruit stand and nursery, **Olga's Cup and Saucer,** 261 W. Main Rd. (Rte. 77), Little Compton, 401/635-8650, sits right on the main road between Little Compton and Tiverton. From the arrangement of colorful mismatched chairs out front you can watch customers at Walker's squeeze produce and examine the flowers. On a breezy summer afternoon, Olga's feels like a little slice of country paradise. In addition to coffees, the tiny kitchen serves up tasty sandwiches, soups, and other noteworthy snacks.

Gourmet Goods and Picnic Supplies

In Tiverton Four Corners, you'll find a pair of shops stocked with fine foods, picnic supplies, and enchanted edibles. **HomeGrown Marketplace,** 3838 Main Rd., 401/625-2400, in a cheerful cottage just north of the intersection, proffers freshly made gourmet breads, salsas, pastries, plus chai teas, espressos, and lattes; there are several outdoor tables. You can also stock up here on fresh produce. The salsa—available roasted, fresca, or verde—is downright famous and is sold through mail-order or over the web (www.homegrownsalsa.com). They also make a wicked Szechwan peanut sauce and a piquant Moroccan herb marinade. **The Provender,** Tiverton Four Corners, 401/624-8084, occupies the ground floor of a magnificent three-story Second Empire house crowned with a tall square cupola. There are long wooden benches on the wraparound porch, which is a lovely place to watch the world go by. In addition to selling imaginative, high-quality sandwiches and sweets, the Provender has fresh picnic supplies and a fine choice for goods before a bike ride. Olive oil, fancy mayonnaises, and sauces are sold. The Virginia Lynch Gallery is attached.

ENTERTAINMENT AND NIGHTLIFE

On Sakonnet Peninsula, folks head either across the border to Massachusetts or across the bridge to Newport or Bristol for nighttime diversions. A few of the restaurants in these parts have a bar scene, and in Little Compton, **Sneekers,** 186 E. Main Rd., 401/635-8444, is a popular spot with the collegiate set for cocktails.

INFORMATION AND SERVICES

Visitor Information

Pamphlets, brochures, and tourism information are available from the Newport County Convention & Visitor's Bureau, 23 America's Cup Ave., Newport, RI 02840, 800/976-5122, website: www.gonewport.com.

Getting There

Most visitors to the East Bay and Sakonnet Peninsula use a car to get around. It's a short drive from Providence and Newport. However, you can also manage—at least through the East Bay towns—by relying on **RIPTA (Rhode Island Transportation Authority) buses,** 401/781-9400 or

800/244-0444, website: www.ripta.com, which pass through the busy town centers of both Bristol and Warren and connect with Newport, Providence, and other large towns in the region.

Getting Around

As in the East Bay towns, a car is your only viable way to get around the Sakonnet Peninsula. These are quiet little towns where parking is easy to find, usually off-street, excepting in summer by the beach in Little Compton.

Media

The *East Bay Window,* 401/253-6000, website: www.eastbayri.com, is a useful paper with tidal charts, features, and local tips—while it's geared toward locals, visitors will find it filled with useful information. The same publishers also produce the *Sakonnet Times, Warren Times Gazette, Bristol Phoenix,* and *Barrington Times.*

Tours

From the Blount Shipyard in Warren, **Bay Queen Cruises,** 461 Water St., Gate 4, 401/245-1350 or 800/439-1350, website: www.bayqueen.com, set sail around Narragansett Bay and to Newport or Providence. These runs, held aboard the double-deck, all-season *Vista Jubilee,* typically revolve around a meal and often a special event (a concert, lecture, or festival), which may occur onboard or at a venue along the ferry route. Particularly popular during the day, especially among photo and history buffs, are the lighthouse cruises, which

include lunch and last five hours, passing by various beacons around Narragansett Bay (call for details on when these are given). Six-hour brunch cruises include a two-hour stop in downtown Newport, where passengers are free to sightsee, shop, and wander as they please; these are given weekends, Tuesdays, and holiday Mondays April–Oct. Wednesday through Friday, shorter four-hour luncheon cruises take to the water and include live music and historical narration—these do not make any stops. In the evenings, from May through December, dinner and dinner-dance cruises include a tour of Mount Hope Bay, a lavish, even excessive, dinner buffet, and dancing to live big-band music. Views of Newport at night can be stunning, but because it's dark these evening excursions give a less impressive sense of Narragansett Bay than the daytime runs. Special-event cruises are also given year-round. These include a cruise to the Wickford Art Festival in July, the six-day Fall River tall ships and fireworks festival in August, the guffaw-inducing *Angie & Aidan's Italian-Irish Wedding* cruises held June–Sept., murder mystery cruises June–Sept., and Christmas/holiday and New Year's Eve runs from late November through December. Cruises are offered May through December, with times varying according to the theme. For instance, brunch, luncheon, and lighthouse cruises depart at 11 A.M. and return to Warren at 5 P.M., 3 P.M., and 4 P.M., respectively. The three- or four-hour sunset dinner and dinner-dance cruises leave at 7 or 7:30 P.M.

Resources

Suggested Reading

Rhode Island hasn't exactly been written about to death, but there are a number of useful and colorful books out there on the Ocean State. Most of those listed below focus exclusively on Rhode Island or at the very least Southern New England, but bear in mind that a number of additional titles—general guidebooks, B&B guides, historical reviews—discuss the state as a component of its greater identity, New England.

For further information on other states in the northeast, including Rhode Island's neighboring states, check out the following cousins of *Moon Handbooks Rhode Island: Moon Handbooks Connecticut,* also by Andrew Collins; *Moon Handbooks Coastal Maine,* by Kathy Brandes; *Moon Handbooks Massachusetts,* by Jeff Perk; *Moon Handbooks New Hampshire,* by Steve Lantos; and *Moon Handbooks New York State,* by Christiane Bird.

You may recognize "Images of America" series, by Arcadia Publishing, 888/313-BOOK, www.arcadiaimages.com, from the trademark sepia covers of its hundreds of small soft-cover historic-photo essays on more than 1,000 communities across the country. These fascinating books are produced by a small firm in Charleston, South Carolina, and each title typically contains from 200 to 250 early black-and-white of a particular region, along with running commentary that is usually authored by a local historian, librarian, or archivist from that area. The books cost from $15 to $25 and presently there are 62 titles on Rhode Island. These cover nearly every township in the state, several smaller villages (Peace Dale, Wakefield, Watch Hill, etc.), and then an amazing variety of special topics, including *The History of Mass Transportation in Rhode Island, America's Cup, Italian-Americans In Rhode Island, Naval War College, Providence College Basketball,* and *Rhode Island's Mill Villages.*

Description and Travel

Bodah, Paula M. *Rhode Island: The Spirit of America.* Harry N. Abrams, 2000. Handsome,

illustrated book detailing the state's cultural, natural, and architectural highlights.

Cheek, Richard, and Gannon, Tom. *Newport Mansions: The Gilded Age.* Foremost Publishing, 1982. A photo-filled discussion of Newport during its grand heyday.

Curley, Robert. *Rhode Island: Off the Beaten Path.* Globe Pequot Press, 2002. A guide that sheds light on some of the region's more unusual and out-of-the-way attractions.

Digital Destinations. *Historic Newport Mansions.* Digital Destinations, 2000. If you're a fan of interactive visuals, check out this CD-ROM produced by Digital Destinations; it gives an amazingly informative and exhaustively researched tour of that city's many stunning homes, including a full audio narration and hundreds of digital photos.

Gannon, Tom, and Meras, Phyllis. *Rhode Island: An Explorer's Guide.* Countryman Press, 2000. A general-interest guidebook on the state.

Grosvenor, Richard. *Newport: A Painter's Impressions of Its History and Architecture.* Commonwealth Editions, 2002. Beautiful, art- and photo-filled book on Newport.

McElholm, Jim. *The Rhode Island Coast: A Photographic Portrait.* Twin Lights Publishers, Inc., 2000. Grand coffeetable-style photography book with stunning images.

Petro, Pamela. *Great Destinations: Newport and Narragansett Bay Book.* Berkshire House, 1998 (out of print). This useful guidebook focuses on the state's coastal regions.

Rocheleau, Paul; Wiencek, Henry; and Young, Donald. *Southern New England.* Stewart Tabori & Chang, 1998 (part of the Smithsonian Guides to Historic America series). Beautiful book with excellent writing and vibrant photography; this edition covers Rhode Island, Connecticut, and Massachusetts.

Rogers, Barbara Radcliffe, and Rogers, Juliette. *Secret Providence and Newport.* ECW Press, 2002. Here's a look at some of the more unusual and lesser-known sites in the state's two most famous cities.

Rogers, Barbara Radcliffe, and Rogers, Stillman D. *The Rhode Island Guide.* Fulcrum, 1998. Another general-interest guidebook on the state.

Works Progress Administration, *Rhode Island— A Guide to the Smallest State.* Houghton Mifflin Company, 1937 (out of print). Arguably the best treatment of the state ever written is this dense and fascinating work compiled by the Works Progress Administration (WPA) Workers of the Federal Writers' Project. Part of the amazingly well-executed and thoroughly researched American Guide Series, the book is long-since out of print (many titles within this series have been picked up in recent years and reprinted by current publishing houses, but not yet Rhode Island, alas). Your best hope of finding a copy of this wonderful tome is by scouring the racks of used bookstores or websites such as e-Bay. Depending on its condition and age (and whether it has its original cover and map), this guide should sell for anywhere from $15 to $75.

Maps and Orientation

There are a number decent folding maps on Connecticut, and if you call the state tourism office, 401/222-2601 or 800/556-2484, you'll be sent the free annual *Rhode Island Travel Guide,* which contains a very good general state map.

Arrow Map. *Rhode Island Street Atlas* (Arrow Map, 1999) and *Street Atlas Greater Providence.* (Arrow Map, 2001). These excellent Arrow Maps are greatly detailed; the Providence map is the best and most thorough map of the state capital.

DeLorme. *Connecticut/Rhode Island Atlas and Gazetteer.* DeLorme Publishing, 2002. DeLorme publishes a state atlas that includes both Rhode Island and neighboring Connecticut as part of its Gazetteer series. While this series shows much greater detail than your run-of-the-mill atlas, it's not very trustworthy as a serious navigational aid. A disturbing number of errors appear on these pages—in particular, the DeLorme atlas has a tendency to show dirt roads and even trails as primary paved thoroughfares, creating the potential for all sorts of frustrating wild goose chases.

Microsoft. *Microsoft Streets and Trips.* Microsoft, 2003. A very useful digital tool, Microsoft Expedia Streets covers the entire United States (and Canada). With this disc, you can type in virtually any street address in Rhode Island (or any other state for that matter) and instantly have it pinpointed on a full-color detailed map on your computer screen.

Rand McNally. *Rand McNally StreetFinder: Rhode Island.* Rand McNally & Co., 2000. Very precise maps on the state are published by Rand McNally. The easy-to-read and well-labeled Rand McNally StreetFinder: Rhode Island is an excellent atlas with great detail, including city coverage.

History

Beade, Lisa Roseman. *Wealth of Nations: A People's History of Rhode Island.* Community Communications Corp, 1999. Traces the state's history by examining different groups that have lived here, from Native Americans to Europeans to French Canadian immigrants.

Douglas-Lithgow, R.A. *Native American Place Names of Rhode Island.* Applewood Books, 2000. Provides the lore behind countless Rhode

Island rivers, villages, lakes, and other features from the state's Native American history.

Fuoco, Joe. *Rhode Island's Mill Villages.* Arcadia Tempus Publishing Group, Inc., 1997. A short but useful primer on the state's industrial history.

Gaustad, Edwin S. *Liberty of Conscience: Roger Williams in America.* Judson Press, 1999. For a closer look at the man who founded Providence, check out this engaging biography.

Hawes, Alexander Boyd. *Off Soundings: Aspects of the Maritime History of Rhode Island.* Posterity Press, 1999. A colorful and well-written chronicle of the state's fascinating nautical past, this makes a great read and details everything from the state's infamously profitable slave trade to piracy.

McLoughlin, William G. *Rhode Island, a History.* W.W. Norton & Company, 1986. Provides a nice general overview of the state's past.

Special Interest

Freeman, Lisa, and Sloan, Susan, editors. *Sloan's Green Guide to Antiquing in New England.* Globe Pequot Press, 1997. The perfect companion for fans of bargain-hunting.

Hamilton, Harlan. *Lights & Legends: A Historical Guide to Lighthouses of Long Island Sound, Fishers Island Sound and Block Island Sound.* Wescott Cove Publishing Co., 1987. This is an interesting read about the many striking lighthouses off the shores of Rhode Island.

Stetson, Barbara Sherman. *It's Rhode Island Cookbook.* Barbara Sherman Stetson, 1999. A must for anybody interested in the state's distinctive cuisine.

Hiking and Recreation

Alden, Peter. *National Audubon Society Field Guide to New England (National Audubon Society Field Guide to New England).* Knopf, 1998. A great field guide on New England.

Bourque, Gene. *Fishing New England: A Rhode Island Shore Guide.* On The Water, LLC, 2001. The best guide in the state for anglers.

Kricher, John C., and Morrison, Gordon. *A Field Guide to Eastern Forests North America* (Peterson Field Guide Series). Houghton Mifflin Co., 1998. The best all-around guide on New England's geology, flora, and fauna.

Stone, Howard. *Short Bike Rides in Rhode Island.* Globe Pequot Press, 1999. The perfect source for plotting a good bike trip through this scenic and mostly flat state.

Vanover, Cliff. *The North South Trail: A Guide for Traveling Across Rhode Island for Hikers, Equestrians, and Mountain Bikers.* Great Swamp Press, 2002. An indispensable resource for the state's hikers, this guide traces the state's great hiking path from start to finish, with plenty of advice and information about what you'll see along the way.

Weber, Ken. *Walks and Rambles in Rhode Island: A Guide to the Natural and Historic Wonders of the Ocean State.* Countryman Press, 1999. A good reading companion for avid strollers.

Boating and Sailing

Childress, Lynda Morris; Childress, Patrick; and Martin, Tink. *A Cruising Guide to Narragansett Bay and the South Coast of Massachusetts: Including Buzzard's Bay, Nantucket, Martha's Vineyard, and Block Island.* International Marine/Ragged Mountain Press, 1995. One of several books that are handy for visitors taking to the waters that so dominate the Rhode Island landscape. It details technical points (tides, currents, weather, harbor facilities) along with detailing the region's boating highlights, both on and off shore.

Tuckerman, Steve. *AMC River Guide: Massachusetts—Connecticut—Rhode Island.* Appalachian Mountain Club, 1991. The Appalachian Mountain Club publishes a favorite book of kayakers, rafters, canoeists, and fishing enthusiasts.

Wilson, Alex. *Quiet Water Canoe Guide: Massachusetts, Connecticut, Rhode Island.* Appalachian Mountain Club, 1993. If it's advice on freshwater boating that interests you, check out this well-written volume.

Literature: Biography, Memoir, and Fiction,

Briody, Thomas Gately. *Rogue's Wager.* St. Martin's Press, 1997. Set in Rhode Island; this book's main character, Mitty Navel, is a quahog fisherman caught in a plot of intrigue and deceit. The book was very well-received by critics.

Clark, Mary Higgins. *Moonlight Becomes You.* Pocket Books, 1997. A tale of intrigue by the famous mystery writer, set amid the wealth and high society of Newport.

Delinsky, Barbara. *The Vineyard.* Simon & Schuster, 2000. Set at a long-running fictitious Rhode Island vineyard, Delinsky's novel is a fun, slightly soap-operatic tale about the vineyard's well-to-do matriarch falling in love with the vineyard manager, whose of a much lower social standing. The book offers a nice glimpse of coastal Rhode Island society, and would be especially fun if you're planning a visit to Sakonnet Vineyard.

Dershowitz, Alan. *Reversal of Fortune.* Random House Inc., 1986. Even better than fiction is this gripping account of the controversial trial of Claus von Bulow (accused of trying to murder his diabetic wife, Sunny). It was written by the famous trial lawyer Alan Dershowitz and later made into a movie starring Jeremy Irons and Glenn Close.

Gardner, Lisa. *The Survivors Club* Bantam Doubleday Dell Publishers, 2002. This gripping book by best-selling suspense writer Gardner recounts the plight of three Providence women who were raped by the same man on College Hill and their attempt to see justice carried out against him.

Macauley, David. *Mill.* Houghton Mifflin Co., 1989. A critically acclaimed book that came out in the late '80s, *Mill* details the development of a fictional New England textile mill town, called Wicksbridge, that could be just about anywhere in the region but bears a strong resemblance to the massive facilities that thrived in Pawtucket, Woonsocket, Slatersville, and Peace Dale. It's a well-researched and skillful bit of historical fiction that makes great reading for anybody touring the Blackstone River Valley.

Updike, John. *The Witches of Eastwick.* Random House Inc., 1986. A novel that's perhaps more famous as a movie, this comic tale set in the small (fictitious) fishing village of Eastwick; the movie—starring Cher, Susan Sarandon, Michelle Pfeiffer, and Jack Nicholson—was filmed partly in Wickford.

Weldon, Fay. *Rhode Island Blues.* Grove Press, 2002. Known for such socially sharp and bitingly funny novels as *Big Girls Don't Cry* and *The Life and Loves of a She-Devil,* Fay Weldon set this clever novel in the Ocean State.

Internet Resources

Because Rhode Island is so small, it has relatively few regional websites but several statewide ones that go into great detail on every corner of the state. Furthermore, a number of national sites covering everything from transportation to the outdoors have specific webpages on just Rhode Island.

Tourism and General Information
Ocean State Online
www.oso.com

One of the best general online resources is this catch-all compendium of Rhode Island news, job listings and other classifieds, entertainment, real estate, and other information. It's geared toward residents of the state but provides a good bit of information that's useful to travelers, such as dining reviews and listings of upcoming events.

The Providence Journal
www.projo.com

This website produced the state's most widely read paper may be the most comprehensive and informative online resource in Rhode Island. This site also contains stories, reviews, and information from the state's glossy lifestyle magazine, *Rhode Island Monthly*, which makes it even more useful. On this site you'll find the same in-depth news coverage you will in the daily *Journal* newspaper, and you can search for older stories. There are direct links to separate subsites such as www.tasteri.com (dining reviews), Theater (a directory of performing arts events), other areas. There's also a specific section just for "Travel & Visitors" that includes information on attractions, business travel, family travel, reservations, transportation, and so on.

Citysearch
www.providence.citysearch.com

Excellent for scoping out the latest info on hot new restaurants, museum exhibitions, which movies are playing where, and where to find a great hotel. While the coverage is chiefly about Providence, you'll also find listings for the metro area, including Warwick, Cranston, Pawtucket, some of the Blackstone River Valley towns, and even towns just over the border in Massachusetts.

Digital City
www.digitalcity.com/providence

The competing web company of Citysearch, Digital City also has a Providence page—it covers more of Rhode Island and specifically has a number of listings on Newport. Overall, the coverage on Digital City sometimes falls a bit short when compared with that of Citysearch, but both sites are useful. Both sites also include ratings by site users, which can be very useful and extremely entertaining.

The Official State of Rhode Island Home Page
www.state.ri.us

The official state website comes in handy when you're looking for detailed information on state and local politics, regional demographics, the state library, and local laws.

The Official State of Rhode Island Tourism Home Page
www.visitrhodelands.com

The mother of all Rhode Island travel and tourism websites, with links to the state's six regional tourism sites: Blackstone River Valley, as well as northern and northwestern Rhode Island (www.tourblackstone.com), Block Island (www.blockislandinfo.com), East Bay (www.eastbaytourism.com), Newport, Aquidneck Island, and Sakonnet (www.gonewport.com), Providence (www.goprovidence.com), South County (www.southcountyri.com), and Warwick (www.warwickri.com). Within each site you'll find a trove of links to regional attractions, dining, lodging, events, transportation, and other valuable information.

Transportation

Several sites are very useful for exploring the different transportation options in Rhode Island, from flying to training to catching the ferry.

T.F. Green Airport
www.pvd-ri.com
Find out about parking, airlines, check-in information, and arrivals and departures the state's main airport.

Amtrak
www.amtrak.com
Home page for the national rail service with several stops in Rhode Island.

Bonanza Bus Lines
www.bonanzabus.com
Has details on interstate bus service to and from Rhode Island.

Rhode Island Public Transit Authority (RIPTA)
www.ripta.com
The site for Rhode Island's in-state bus line; it's an excellent, easy-to-use site with maps and schedules that show all of the bus routes throughout the state.

Block Island Ferry
www.blockislandferry.com
Find out about rates and scheduling for the ferry that serves Block Island.

Rhode Island Department of Transportation
www.dot.state.ri.us
Provides extensive information on numerous publications, traveler resources and road conditions, licenses and permits, upcoming roadwork and projects, legal notice, and construction bid notices.

Sports and Outdoors

Rhode Island Department of Environmental Management (DEM)
www.state.ri.us/dem
Among Rhode Island's top internet resources for outdoors enthusiasts, the DEM home page provides information and policies pertaining to boating, hiking, beach-going, and many other activities.

State of Rhode Island Division of Parks and Recreation
www.riparks.com
This site provides links to every property in the state park system. Also has information on primitive camping at state parks.

Rhode Island chapter of the Nature Conservancy
www.tnc.org/states/rhodeisland
Hikers might want to visit this site, which contains information about the Conservancy's many Ocean State refuges and preserves.

Audubon Society
www.asri.org
Great site for birding, with specifics on the society's Rhode Island chapter.

Ocean State Campground Owners Association, Inc.
www.ricampgrounds.com
Great for ideas about where to find a desirable commercial campground.

Rhode Island Division of Fish & Wildlife
www.state.ri.us/dem/programs/bnatres/fish wild/index.htm
Covers rules, licenses, boat launches, and tidal charts.

Rhode Island Golf Association
www.rigalinks.org
Here golfers can learn all about the state's many public courses.

Rhode Island's Online Golf Source
www.rigolf.com

Another great home page for Ocean State golfing enthusiasts.

Rhode Island Party and
Charter Boat Association
www.rifishing.com/charter.htm

Lists private fishing, sightseeing, and sailing charter boats throughout the state.

Index

Beaches

Wildlife Refuges

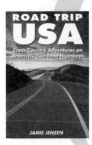

U.S.~Metric Conversion

1 inch	=	2.54 centimeters (cm)
1 foot	=	.304 meters (m)
1 yard	=	0.914 meters
1 mile	=	1.6093 kilometers (km)
1 km	=	.6214 miles
1 fathom	=	1.8288 m
1 chain	=	20.1168 m
1 furlong	=	201.168 m
1 acre	=	.4047 hectares
1 sq km	=	100 hectares
1 sq mile	=	2.59 square km
1 ounce	=	28.35 grams
1 pound	=	.4536 kilograms
1 short ton	=	.90718 metric ton
1 short ton	=	2000 pounds
1 long ton	=	1.016 metric tons
1 long ton	=	2240 pounds
1 metric ton	=	1000 kilograms
1 quart	=	.94635 liters
1 US gallon	=	3.7854 liters
1 Imperial gallon	=	4.5459 liters
1 nautical mile	=	1.852 km

To compute celsius temperatures, subtract 32 from Fahrenheit and divide by 1.8. To go the other way, multiply celsius by 1.8 and add 32.

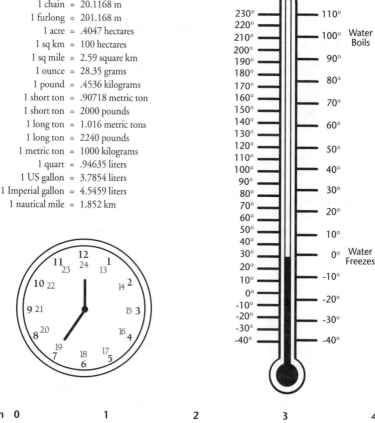

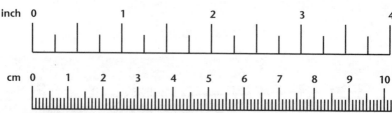